Natural Disasters

Natural Disasters

Volume III
Icebergs and Glaciers — Wind Gusts
Index

Editors

Marlene Bradford, Ph.D.
Texas A&M University

Robert S. Carmichael, Ph.D.
University of Iowa

Project Editor
Tracy Irons-Georges

SALEM PRESS, INC.
Pasadena, California   Hackensack, New Jersey

Editor in Chief: Dawn P. Dawson   *Project Editor:* Tracy Irons-Georges
Copy Editor: Lauren Mitchell   *Assistant Editor:* Andrea E. Miller
Research Supervisor: Jeffry Jensen   *Research Assistant:* Jeff Stephens
Acquisitions Editor: Mark Rehn   *Photograph Editor:* Philip Bader
Production Editor: Joyce I. Buchea   *Layout:* William Zimmerman

Library of Congress Cataloging-in-Publication Data

Natural disasters / editors, Marlene Bradford, Robert S. Carmichael.
    p. cm.
Includes bibliographical references.
    ISBN 0-89356-071-5 (set : alk. paper) — ISBN 0-89356-072-3 (vol. 1 : alk. paper) — ISBN 0-89356-073-1 (vol. 2 : alk. paper) — ISBN 0-89356-082-0 (vol. 3 : alk. paper)
    1. Natural disasters.   I. Bradford, Marlene.   II. Carmichael, Robert S.
    GB5014 .N373 2000
    363.34—dc21

                                               00-058763

First Printing

Contents

CONTENTS

Natural Disasters

Icebergs and Glaciers

(AP/Wide World Photos)

Glaciers are gigantic ice masses flowing down and over land, whereas icebergs, which originate from glaciers, are ice masses that typically float in oceans. Over the centuries, glaciers and especially icebergs have caused much destruction of human property and lives.

FACTORS INVOLVED: Geography, geological forces, gravitational forces, ice, snow, temperature, weather conditions, wind

REGIONS AFFECTED: Coasts, forests, lakes, mountains, oceans, rivers, towns, valleys

SCIENCE

Glaciers, which cover about 10 percent of the earth's surface, are large masses of freshwater ice formed by the compacting and recrystallization of snow in polar regions and in other regions' high mountains. When the aggregated ice is large and thick enough, it generally starts flowing downhill by gravity and spreading outward because of its increasing volume. Moving glaciers may terminate on land, where their melting ice turns into a river of water, or they may end in a lake or ocean. Various scientists estimate the number of glaciers at 70,000 to 200,000, depending on how their sizes are defined. Glaciers can vary from an area of about one-third of a square mile to nearly 5 million square miles (12.5 million square kilometers), the size of the great Antarctic ice sheet. About three-quarters of the world's freshwater exists as glacial ice.

Climate and topography cause differences in a glacier's size, shape, and physical characteristics. When an ice mass grows so large that it covers an area of about 19,300 square miles (50,000 square kilometers), glaciologists call it an ice sheet, and it usually spreads over vast plateaus, flowing from its center outward. The Antarctic and Greenland ice sheets are the only ones now existing, but during the ice ages of the Pleistocene epoch (1.8 million to 10,000 years ago) ice sheets covered the northern parts of Europe and North America.

If the area covered is less than 19,300 square miles, the glacier is called an ice cap, a flattened, dome-shaped glacier covering both mountains and valleys. In Arctic regions ice caps occur at fairly low altitudes, whereas in such temperate regions as Iceland they occur on high plateaus. In valley glaciers, the flow of ice is confined between a valley's hillsides or mountainsides. These glaciers may originate from ice sheets or ice caps, but they may also flow out of cirque glaciers nestled in the steep-walled hollows of mountain flanks.

Because a glacier is essentially a flowing ice river, it has a tendency to move from its initial high altitude toward sea level. When glaciers are unconfined by geological barriers, they are able to flow to the sea, where, because of erosive action of changing tides and winds, large chunks of ice split from glacial tongues and ice shelves. These floating masses of freshwater ice are called icebergs, and calving is the process of making them by fracture from a glacier's seaward end. Icebergs can be white, blue, green, or even black (from the rock materials they contain).

Scientists have categorized icebergs by their sizes and shapes. Tabular (table-shaped) icebergs, also called "ice islands," are large blocks of ice that protrude several feet above sea level and average 1,640 feet (500 meters) in diameter. Tabular icebergs are rare in the Arctic but common in the Antarctic. Pinnacled icebergs, also called castellated after their castlelike shape, are characteristic of northern polar oceans. Whether tabular or pinnacled, an iceberg has only one-ninth of its mass projecting above the the water's surface, though the ratio of an iceberg's vertical height above water to its height below varies because of icebergs' irregular shapes.

Icebergs form mostly during the spring and summer, when warm weather increases the rate of calving. In the Northern Hemisphere glaciers in west Greenland produce about ten thousand icebergs. An average Greenland-born iceberg weighs approximately 2 billion pounds (1 million metric tons) and lasts from two to five years. The West Greenland Current carries these icebergs northward and westward, until eventually many of them are captured by the cold Labrador Current as it moves south to encounter the warm Gulf Stream. They then drift into the region of the Grand Banks, a submarine plateau extending from the Newfoundland coast. Canadian scientists have found a nearly linear decrease in the numbers of icebergs as they wander from northern to southern latitudes. Nevertheless, sufficient numbers survive to populate the North Atlantic shipping lanes with potential hazards to navigation.

GEOGRAPHY

Glaciers develop in geographical regions of the earth where such precipitation as snow and hail exceeds the aggregated frozen precipitation that melts during the summer. This growing glacial accumulation occurs in polar regions where summers are cool and short, but glaciers are also found in temperate zones on high mountains, such as the Alps in Switzerland, and even in the tropics on very high mountains, such as Mount Kilimanjaro in Tanzania. Glaciers occur on all the earth's continents, except Australia, and on all the world's great mountain ranges. Whether a glacier develops in a certain geographical region depends on both its latitude and its altitude. Approximately 91 percent of the volume of the earth's glacial ice (85 percent of its area) is concentrated in Antarctica, whereas 8 percent of its volume (12 percent of its area) is in Greenland. This means that only 1 percent of the total volume of the earth's glacial ice exists in the world's mountain ranges.

Arctic icebergs are the products of glaciers in Greenland, Canada, Alaska, and Russia, but western Greenland is by far the major source of icebergs in the Northern Hemisphere. Icebergs are rare in the north Pacific Ocean because those that are calved from Alaskan glaciers generally drift northward, whereas in the north Atlantic Ocean icebergs generally drift southward (icebergs have been reported as far south as Bermuda).

Another geographical source of icebergs is the Antarctic. Because the immense weight of the Antarctic's ice sheet has depressed its underlying landmass, most Antarctic ice tends to remain inland rather than flow to the coast. Nevertheless, the sloping coastal edges of the Antarctic ice sheet constantly calve icebergs. For example, in 1927 a section about eight times the size of the state of Rhode Island broke from the Antarctic shore and floated north along the coast of Argentina.

The Bering Glacier in Alaska, which shrank 6-7 miles in length during the twentieth century. Scientists think global warming may be the reason. (AP/Wide World Photos)

PREVENTION AND PREPARATIONS

Because glaciers move slowly and because they are located in sparsely populated regions, they do not pose the same threat to human life and property that icebergs do, but they are not devoid of hazard. Glaciers are capable of overrunning buildings or small settlements, as they did in seventeenth century Switzerland during the start of what came to be called the "Little Ice Age." Glacial movements can block streams, and when these ice dams fail, human structures and lives are at risk. Today, remote-sensing mapping techniques are able to identify glacial areas of potential dangers to human communities.

Throughout the period of sailing ships and even during the period of steamships, icebergs caused massive loss of life and property. Because of the tragedy precipitated by *Titanic*'s collision with an iceberg in 1912, an international conference was held in London in 1913 to determine what needed to be done to prevent such disasters in the future. The International Ice Patrol (IIP) began its service in 1914,

and through aerial surveillance of icebergs supplemented by observations from commercial ships, the IIP tracked dangerous icebergs, alerted ships to their presence, and prevented collisions. After World War II, radar and sonar techniques were developed to precisely monitor iceberg movements. Canadians were particularly successful in developing airborne ice-mapping sensors, including side-looking airborne radar (SLAR). Scientists from the United States and Canada have also used satellite images to study the loss of glacier mass by calving, and these quantitative data have proved more accurate than estimates based on iceberg reports from ships. A measure of the success of the IIP's efforts is the fact that, since its inception, not a single reported loss of life or property has occurred from a cooperating vessel's collision with an iceberg.

RESCUE AND RELIEF EFFORTS

Glacier-related disasters are generally neither as dramatic nor as catastrophic as major earthquakes, but their cumulative costs in property loss and human fatalities mean that survival and rescue become important after such disasters occur. When the lobe of a glacier blocks a stream or an iceberg threatens a seabed oil installation off Labrador, sufficient time exists to evacuate people from a potential glacial surge or to lift workers by helicopter from an oil rig.

During the days of sailing ships, rescues were

largely matters of chance. When *John Rutledge*, traveling from Liverpool to New York, collided with an iceberg off the Newfoundland banks on February 20, 1856, its 120 passengers and 16 crew members tried to survive in five lifeboats (with one compass among them), but by the time *Germania* picked up one of the lifeboats eight days later, only one young boy remained alive. During the time of the great steamships, the most dramatic rescue of passengers and crew from an iceberg-sunk ship was *Titanic*. Its 705 survivors owed their lives to the wireless telegraph, for the Cunard liner *Carpathia* heard *Titanic*'s SOS messages and sped to the disaster site.

Modern technology has improved survival rates and rescues at sea. Training and drills on ships, emergency alarms, and detailed evacuation systems, as well as superior lifeboats, life rafts, life jackets, and immersion suits, have all facilitated rescues and lessened the loss of life. Because of hypothermia, only 14 people who went down with *Titanic* were pulled alive out of the water, and only half of those survived. Thermal protective suits now enhance the chances that rescue ships will pull survivors rather than corpses out of cold ocean waters.

Impact

In the early twenty-first century, only a small number of glaciers existed near inhabited areas, minimizing their impact on humans. Icebergs cause disasters on a short time scale, such as collisions with ships, but glacier-related hazards can also be serious when considered on a long-term basis. Variations in the amount of glacial ice are crucial to human populations. Throughout geological history, particularly during the ice ages, glaciers have had a powerful effect on humans and their environment, as they forced our species to adapt or migrate. At the height of the last ice age, about twenty thousand years ago, much more ice existed on continents than exists today, preventing humans from using much valuable land in North America and northern Europe. Some scientists predict that the earth will eventually experience another

ice age that might last 50,000 years and that this would have devastating effects on human beings.

On the other hand, many scientists are worried about the effects of future global warming on the earth's glacial ice. If all this ice were to melt, the resulting rise in sea level of about 200 feet (60 meters) would submerge every major coastal city. Glaciers are sensitive indicators of climate change, expanding and contracting in response to temperature fluctuations. During the lifetime of our species, humans have adapted to immense expansions and contractions of gigantic polar ice sheets, and if the present understanding of glaciologists about the periodic nature of these fluctuations is correct, humans will need to continue their adaptations well into the future.

Robert J. Paradowski

Bibliography

Benn, Douglas I., and David J. A. Evans. *Glaciers and Glaciation*. London: Arnold, 1998. The authors create a contemporary synthesis of "all important aspects of glaciers and their effects." Particularly valuable is an extensive set of references.

Hoyle, Fred. *Ice: The Ultimate Human Catastrophe*. New York: Continuum, 1981. In this popular account Hoyle presents the arguments of those scientists who believe that an ice age is imminent, while offering practical suggestions about what needs to be done to avoid its catastrophic consequences.

McCall, G. J. H., D. J. C. Laming, and S. C. Scott. *Geohazards: Natural and Man-made*. London: Chapman and Hall, 1992. This book, written by geoscientists experienced in the practical problems of natural disasters, enlightens readers through descriptions of geohazards (including glaciers and icebergs), their assessment and prediction, and the mitigation of their effects.

Tufnell, L. *Glacier Hazards*. London: Longman, 1984. The dangers to human life and property posed by ice sheets in glacierized regions can be significant, and the author shows how to identify such high-risk areas and to reduce their dangers.

Notable Events

1912: The Sinking of *Titanic*

SHIP COLLISION
DATE: April 14-15, 1912
PLACE: North Atlantic Ocean
RESULT: 1,513 dead, entire ship and contents lost at sea

On its maiden voyage from Southampton, England, to New York City, the British luxury passenger liner *Titanic*, the largest vessel then afloat, struck a massive iceberg just before midnight on April 14, 1912. The sumptuous *Titanic*, which was more than halfway across a heavily traveled route in the North Atlantic, collided with the iceberg about 400 miles south of Newfoundland (41 degrees, 16 minutes north latitude; longitude 50 degrees, 14 minutes west).

Although the sea was unusually calm and the night was clear, the lookouts failed to see the iceberg until it was too late, and the ship, cruising at nearly full speed, suffered a glancing blow on the starboard side below the water line, which ruptured five of the

The *Titanic as it leaves from Southampton, England, on April 10, 1912. It would sink five days later after hitting an iceberg.* (AP/Wide World Photos)

ship's compartments. Until *Titanic* was actually explored at the bottom of the sea in 1985, it was thought that the iceberg had torn one long enormous gash in the ship, but the iceberg in fact cracked and buckled the plates and rivets along the ship's side and created a series of thin gashes long the hull. As water poured into compartment after compartment, *Titanic* began to go down at the head, sinking into the sea at 2:20 A.M. Of the passengers originally on board, little more than a third were rescued by a passing ship. Among those lost in the dark and freezing waters were the ship's captain, the ship's designer, and members of wealthy and influential American, British, and European families, including John Jacob Astor IV, Benjamin Guggenheim, and Isador Straus.

Because the great ship had a double-bottomed hull that was divided into sixteen compartments that were thought to be watertight, it had been considered unsinkable. This misplaced confidence in the ship's buoyancy may have led the captain to minimize the five separate warnings he received of an ice field up ahead. The captain and the crew's faulty decisions before and after the collision, as well as the dubious and sometimes grandiose executive decisions of the businessmen and engineers of the White Star Line, together led to the conclusion that it was human failure as much as the iceberg itself that caused this tragic and best-known maritime disaster.

Margaret Boe Birns

FOR FURTHER INFORMATION:
Eaton, John P., and Charles A. Haas. *Titanic: Destination Disaster.* New York: W. W. Norton, 1996.
Lynch, Donald, and Ken Marschall. *Titanic: An Illustrated History.* New York: Hyperion, 1998.

1959: North Sea

SHIP COLLISION
DATE: January 30, 1959
PLACE: Kap Farvel, Greenland
RESULT: 95 dead

Although the ship *Hans Hedtoft* was christened after a recent prime minister of Denmark, the disaster that overtook the newly built passenger-cargo freighter meant that, outside Denmark at least, *Hans Hedtoft*

the ship would be more widely remembered than its namesake. On January 30, 1959, *Hans Hedtoft* was cruising off Kap Farvel (Cape Farewell), the southern tip of Greenland, when it collided with an iceberg, which was largely submerged and barely visible from the ship. As with *Titanic,* this collision occurred on the ship's maiden voyage.

Hans Hedtoft radioed a report of the collision and urgently requested help, reporting that it was sinking. The United States Coast Guard joined the rescue effort along with Danish relief services. All 95 on board (40 crew and 55 passengers) were presumed dead. At first, Danish authorities believed they had detected a very weak radio signal coming from what they hypothesized was a lifeboat, but none was discovered. Because of dangerous icy weather, by February 7 both the Danes and the U.S. Coast Guard abandoned the search.

The disaster made headlines in Denmark for many days and was viewed as a national tragedy. When a life buoy from *Hans Hedtoft* washed up on the beach in Iceland, it was put on public exhibit in a church in Qaqortoq, Greenland. The Greenland Foundation 1959 was rapidly set up to raise funds through extra charges on coins and stamps to compensate the families of the victims. An investigation concluded that structural defects were to blame for the loss of the ship. In addition to the loss of lives, 13 boxes of irreplaceable archives were lost.

Margaret Boe Birns

FOR FURTHER INFORMATION:
Facts on File, January 29-February 4, 1959.
The New York Times, January 31-February 17, 1959.

1996: Iceland

FLOODING
DATE: October 1-November 5, 1996
PLACE: Vatnajökull glacier, eastern Iceland
RESULT: $17 million in damage

Most glaciers are anonymous outside the world of scientists and mountain-climbers. The Vatnajökull glacier in eastern Iceland is an exception to this rule, as it covers one-tenth of the country (approximately 3,000 square miles). Though uninhabited, the glacier area attracts the more courageous of tourists, who enjoy snowmobiling around the contours of the glacier in the subarctic climate. These tourists did not notice the underground tremors that shook through the glacier in the early autumn of 1996, the prelude to the events of September 30, when a volcano in Vatnajökull erupted.

On the 29th, a flyby glimpsed a subsidence bowl, which meant there had been a one-hour, 5.0 magnitude earthquake near the volcano Bárdarbunga. On October 5 the subterranean volcano beneath Vatnajökull began to destabilize the glacier. Although the glacier is 3,200 feet thick, melting was visible from the surface. Underground lakes beneath Vatnajökull began to flood outward. Scientists predicted severe floods, but because the volcano subsided this did not occur during October.

It was not until November 5 that the real disaster occurred: the *jökulhlaup* (water outflow). That day, the volcano spewed forth again, causing the subterranean Grimsvotn Lake to burst its boundaries and flood all around Vatnajökull. Iceland's sparse population, combined with advance warning, ensured that no human lives were ever seriously at risk. However, many roads and railways essential to Iceland's ground transportation were disrupted by the destruction of bridges. Offshore fishing was also hampered as the torrents of fresh water liberated from the burst glacier spilled over to disturb the saltwater sea bed. Scientists were intrigued by this glacier-volcano combination, in which a seemingly fixed feature of the landscape changed dramatically in a matter of days.

Margaret Boe Birns

FOR FURTHER INFORMATION:

"Iceland: Volcanic Eruption Causes Flooding," *Facts on File*, December 31, 1996, p. 995.

Young, John Edward. "The Landscape? Wait Till Tomorrow," *Christian Science Monitor*, November 27, 1996, p. 12.

Landslides, Mudslides, and Rockslides

(AP/Wide World Photos)

"Landslide" is a general term referring to any perceptible mass movement of earth materials downslope in response to gravity. The deadly forms of landslides, such as debris avalanches and mudflows, can move at speeds in excess of 249 miles (400 kilometers) per hour and can bury entire cities. The death toll from a single event can be greater than 100,000. Landslides cause more deaths and cost more money each year than all other natural disasters combined.

FACTORS INVOLVED: Geography, geological forces, gravitational forces, human activity, ice, plants, rain, snow, temperature, weather conditions

REGIONS AFFECTED: All

SCIENCE

Mass movement is the proper term for any form of detachment and transport of soil and rock materials downslope. Some forms of mass movement have extremely slow velocities, less than 0.4 inch (1 centimeter) a year. Landslides include all forms of mass movement having speeds of greater than 0.04 inch (1 millimeter) a day.

Landslides can be divided into as many as fifteen different classes. The basis for the classification is the type of material that moves (for example, mud) and the general nature of the movement (for example, flow). The names of most of the individual classes are merely a combination of the two terms used in making the classification. For example, when very small particles called mud are saturated with water and flow down a slope like a liquid, the landslide is classified as a "mudflow."

The types of materials that are involved in a mass-movement event are called debris, mud, rock, sand, and soil. These terms refer to the size of the particles that are moving. The word "soil" is used by earth scientists for particles that are less than 0.08 inch (2 millimeters) across. The word "mud" refers to the smaller pieces of soil, whereas "sand" indicates the larger-sized soil fragments. The term "rock" is used for particles that are greater than 0.08 inch (2 millimeters) across. The term "debris" is used when there is a mixture of soil and rock; however the rock sizes usually predominate in most debris.

Civil engineers, who build highways, bridges, dams, and other construction projects, have slightly modified the classification of materials. They consider "soil" any unconsolidated material, which they divide further into two classes, called "earth" when the particle size is small and "debris" when the particle size is large. The term "rock" is reserved for material that started as distinct, rigid, rock layers within the earth. Rock will usually break up into gravel-size particles during a mass movement.

The nature of the movement can be a "slide," "flow," "fall," or one of a number of special terms in which a mixture of different movements occurs. There are several key characteristic movements associated with a slide, which physically resembles a child's slide in a playground. The material usually moves as a single mass. The moving material is coherent; it does not break apart, nor do the individual fragments take differing contoured paths down the slope. Also, the base of the sliding material is usually a single, well-defined surface. A "translational slide" occurs when the surface at the base of the moving material is a flat plane having a uniform slope, which roughly corresponds to the slope on the land surface prior to the mass movement. A "rotational slide" occurs on a curved basal surface, where the upper part of the surface is steeper and the lower part is gentler, giving the surface a spoon shape.

The mass movement called a "flow" has a motion similar to that of a shallow mountain stream: The entire mass behaves as a fluid. The individual particles of moving material take contoured paths that diverge, converge, and collide with one another as they proceed down the slope. The basal surface beneath the flowing material is more undulating, having higher and lower elevations in different areas of the flow. In most cases flows have higher water content than slides; however, the fluid nature of a flow can also be generated by internally trapped air.

A "fall" occurs when material either free-falls down a cliff face or bounces down a very steep slope. A special movement called a "topple" happens when the material rotates around a fixed pivot axis near the base of the column before the fall occurs. The rotation may proceed slowly over a period of years, but this fall is the fastest of all types of movement.

Two special categories of motion are often associated with natural disasters. An "avalanche" is a special category of flow, in which a highly disaggregated material is fluidized by entrapped air and moves at very fast speeds. A "spread" is a vertical combination of a coherent upper layer that slides downslope on a lower, more fluid layer that flows. Spreads commonly occur during an earthquake, when the dry coherent material above the groundwater table laterally spreads out and sinks into the water-saturated flowing material below the water table.

Often, people are not present at the location of a landslide, and the nature of movement must be deduced from the deposits formed. The standard technique to distinguish a slide from a flow is to make a ratio of the depth (thickness) of the moving material divided by the length (or distance) the material moves down the slope. This ratio is called the depth-length ratio. Flows move greater distances down the slope even though they generally involve lesss thickness of flowing material. Flows, thus, have small values for the depth/length ratio, compared to slides, which are thick and move a short distance downslope.

Parts of a Slump

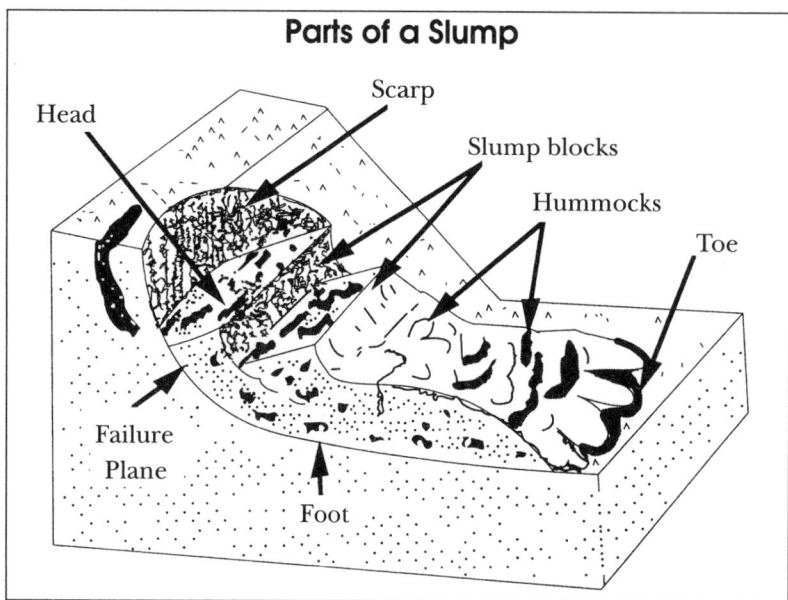

Of the fifteen classes of landslides, which are defined by the type of material and the nature of movement, all can be disasters in terms of property loss, but less than half are life-threatening. The most common disaster is when debris moves by a rotational slide; this class is called a "slump." A slump generally moves slowly, taking hours, days, months, or even years to complete its travel down the slope. The main block of material in a slump often breaks into a series of smaller blocks that appear as backward-tilted steps. A small, slow-moving earthflow typically develops at the toe of the slump. Few lives have been lost because of slumps, but when a slump develops in a city or town, every home in a section of several square blocks will have broken foundations and loss of vertical orientation of their walls and will probably need to be razed.

Mudflows and debris flows are the landslides that have generated the greatest death tolls. These events involve thick masses of mud or debris saturated with water and flowing with the consistency of wet cement. They can move at speeds of 31 miles (50 kilometers) per hour and faster. Normally, they develop after a long period of rainfall, which saturates slope materials and causes them to move. These flows also occur after sudden melting of frozen soils, often brought on by spring snowmelt. They are particularly numerous in years with heavy snowfalls and deep snowpack. As the snow melts, the water seeps into the subsurface of the slope, saturating the soil or rock mass and

beginning the landslide. Mudflows are usually unexpected, and the slurry of mud and debris rushing down the slope can destroy homes, wash out roads and bridges, fell trees, sweep away cars, and obstruct roads and streams with a thick deposit of mud.

A special class of mudflow or debris flow called a "lahar" is produced when material from a volcanic eruption is ejected onto snowfields, glaciers, or crater lakes at the summit of a stratovolcano. An eruption of Nevado del Ruiz, an ice-capped Andean volcano in Colombia, in 1985 killed no one. However, the lahar produced by the melting glacier rushed 37 miles (60 kilometers) down the valley and killed 25,000 people in the city of Armero. Lahars can travel at speeds of 93 miles (150 kilometers) per hour, and when these thick deposits of mud come to rest they become as firm as concrete in a matter of a few hours.

Mudslides can be distinguished from mudflows by the coherence of the moving mass. One eyewitness in a mudslide reported that the ground became soft and he sank to his ankles, making walking difficult while he moved several hundred yards downslope on top of a mudslide. People unfortunate enough to be atop a mudflow would immediately sink into it and become part of the churning fluid.

The landslide categories of rockslides, rockfalls, and rock avalanches are also usually lethal. A vivid example is the Vaiont Dam disaster, where a slab 1.2 miles (2 kilometers) wide by 1 mile (1.6 kilometers) long and 820 feet (250 meters) thick slid into the Vaiont Reservoir in Italy in 1963. The drop into the reservoir took less than one minute. The rockslide splashed a wave over the dam, producing a downstream flood that killed almost 3,000 people in a town 1.5 miles (2.5 kilometers) from the dam. The dam itself survived. A rock avalanche in 1962 in Peru moved 3.9 million cubic yards (3 million cubic meters) of mountain 12.4 miles (20 kilometers) down a valley in seven minutes. Observers said the landslide bounced from one side of the valley to the other at least five times before it spread out over a populated valley at the base of the mountain, killing 60 people. The same valley experienced another rock avalanche in 1970, exacting a death toll of 70,000.

The material of a rockslide differs from that of a rock avalanche in the amount of fracturing found in the rock. Rockslides involve crack development at a specific horizon where there is expansion within the rock mass. Cracks form within the rock over a relatively narrow zone; the fracturing does not penetrate the whole rock mass. Rock avalanches develop when the fracturing is continuous all the way down to the sliding surface. An avalanche involves independent movement of fragments in the entire mass above the sliding surface, as opposed to the rockslide, which involves a single direction of movement for the material above the layer of continuous cracks.

Rockfalls in mountainous regions are often controlled by an increase in temperature, causing a thaw. Rockfalls can be so continuous in mountains that spring climbing on some European peaks must be completed by 10 A.M. Several people are killed each year in the Rocky Mountain region of the United States because of rockfalls, usually motorists struck by bouncing rocks clearing the retaining wall.

All landslides are a form of slope failure. They happen when the shear stress within a slope exceeds the strength of the slope material. Then the slope fails, and millions of cubic feet of rock and soil materials can shear away from the slope and move hundreds or thousands of feet down the hill. There are a half dozen or more factors that can cause shear stresses to exceed the forces that hold the slope in place. The most significant factor promoting landslides is an increase in the angle of the slope: The steeper the slope, the more prone it is to landslides. The angle of the slope always increases directly above any region where construction has cut a relatively flat region into the hillside, such as a road, the leveling for a house foundation, or a quarry site. Fills for roads and waste from mines and quarries are often placed on slopes, making them steeper than the normal angle of rest. Slides will begin until the angle of rest (usually about 35 degrees for coarse material) is attained. The naturally steep walls of river gorges and glaciated valleys are therefore common sites for landslides.

Another common factor contributing to landslides is the addition of water to the area. Water lifts or pushes the grains apart in the soil or rock, reducing the internal friction of the soil and counteracting the gravitational forces that hold the slope in place. Much in the same way air pressure in a car's tires lifts the car, high water pressure in the pores of rock or soil will lower the stability of the slope. This added water can come from heavy rains, melting snow, or even ponds and reservoirs. The area of Southern California is like a desert most of the year; however, it can receive heavy rains in later winter and early spring, which corresponds to the landslide season. Human influence has added water to the ground by construction of septic tanks, ponds, reservoirs, or irrigation canals. In one case in Los Angeles, a man went on vacation leaving his lawn sprinklers running, which caused an earthflow.

Landslides can also be caused by earth tremors. Earthquakes, volcanic eruptions, and even heavy machinery or trains passing on nearby roads or railroads have been known to induce tremors that start landslides. Most of the victims of the 1998 earthquake in Afghanistan were killed not by the earthquake itself but by landslides caused by the quake. In January, 1994, an earthquake in Northridge, California, triggered more than 11,000 landslides over an area of approximately 3,861 square miles (10,000 square kilometers). The largest measured rockslide had a volume in excess of 130,790 cubic yards (100,000 cubic meters). Dozens of homes were destroyed or damaged, roads were blocked, and an oil-field infrastructure sustained damage from the slide.

Another factor that promotes landslides is the removal of lateral or basal support from a slope. In nature, this occurs because of erosion by either meandering rivers or wave action on ocean cliffs. Every year numerous million-dollar homes are lost to earthfalls from wave erosion along the Pacific coastline.

Vegetation changes contribute to landslides in a variety of ways. In high mountain valleys the bedrock is wedged apart by roots of trees. In regions of rockslides the depressions created where small-scale movements have occurred are often the very sites where trees will take root and grow. On gentler slopes vegetation helps to anchor loose soil materials and prevent landslides. Wildfires have been responsible for promoting landslides by destroying tree cover; areas freshly clear-cut by the logging industry or cleared for housing developments have also been reported as sites of increased landslide activity.

The repeated freezing and thawing of water in cracks can be responsible for rockfalls. The process is called frost wedging, in which the expansion during freezing widens the crack and allows the water to penetrate deeper into the rock when the thaw occurs. Individual blocks can be wedged out of the cliff face, falling independently or causing such a loss of cohesion that larger portions of the cliff face can collapse.

GEOGRAPHY

Mass movement occurs in varying degrees almost everywhere. Huge landslides have been identified on the Moon, on Mars, and beneath the Atlantic Ocean on continental margins. A landslide discovered on Mars in 1978, was about 37 miles (60 kilometers) long and 31 miles (50 kilometers) wide.

Mudflows often result from extended rainfall, which saturates slope materials and causes them to move. (Courtesy of R. Carmichael)

The number of landslides increases in regions that have steep slopes, high precipitation, sizable fluctuations in seasonal temperatures, much clay in the soils, and frequent earthquakes and volcanic eruptions. Some countries that are among the hardest hit by landslides are Switzerland, Italy, Japan, China, Peru, and Colombia.

Landslides occur in every state of the United States. California, West Virginia, Utah, Kentucky, Tennessee, Ohio, and Washington have the most severe landslides. Many of the disastrous landslides in the United States have occurred in the West; these states are among the most arid, and the occurrence of landslides is strongly correlated with unusually heavy rainfalls or the melting of winter snowpack.

Once a landslide has occurred in a given area the chances of a repeat occurrence are very high. Governments spend a considerable amount of time and money attempting to identify geographic regions where landslides have occurred. Satellite images are used to identify large landslides by noting changes in soil and vegetation cover. Photographs taken from planes are used to record the extent of sliding land.

PREVENTION AND PREPARATIONS

The standard method used to evaluate the potential of a landslide is the determination of the "factor of safety." A numerical value is determined for every factor related to the occurrence of a landslide. The factor of safety is a ratio in which all the values that resist landsliding are divided by the sum of all the values that favor a landslide. The slope is considered stable when the factor of safety has a value that is greater than 1. Landslides are considered imminent when the value is less than 1.

Myriad techniques and equipment are used to assess the instability of a slope. Conventional surveying methods measure and record the development of cracks, subsidence, and uplift on slopes. Tiltmeters are used to record changes in the slope inclination near cracks and areas of weakness. Inclinometers and rock noise instruments are installed to record movements near cracks and ground deformations. Dating cracks and subsidence and upheavals of slope areas can help scientists assess the past changes in climate and denudation, along with rainfall and earthquake and volcanic activities, which can act as triggers for future slope failures.

Recording air-temperature thresholds forecasts the onset of landslides brought on by snowmelt. Research is demonstrating that 85 percent of landslide events occurs within two weeks after the first yearly occurrence of a six-day average temperature of 58 degrees Fahrenheit. This sort of forecasting can allow ample time to prepare persons in the area to evacuate. One of the safety problems of landslides is that they normally happen within seconds, pouring tons of material on homes and buildings in their path, not allowing the populace enough time to evacuate the area.

Trends from past measurement coupled with current monitoring of slopes increase the ability to predict future landslides. Monitoring rainfall and pore water pressure are other ways to try to predict potential landslides. However, predicting landslides is a very inexact science because some cracks can form on slopes and cause landslides within minutes of their formation. Other slopes have been known to sustain cracks, subsidence, or buckling for years and then fail suddenly, with little or no warning.

Local officials are turning more to the development of landslide hazard mapping. Each area is rated as to the potential for movement and assigned to one of six designations. Areas of similar designation are grouped together as regions on a map. Local legislation places restrictions on and develops greater monitoring of the areas having the highest hazard rankings. In San Mateo County in California the hazard maps are used to restrict the number of homes that may be built there. The normal density allowed is one home per 5 acres, whereas high-hazard areas are restricted to one home per 40 acres.

People living in landslide areas need to note common warning signs of potential slope failure. Some signs of landslides are doors or windows sticking or jamming for the first time on a home. New cracks appearing in plaster, tile, brick, or the foundation of houses can be a precursor of earth movement. Widening cracks on paved streets or driveways also indicate movements in landslide areas. Sometimes underground utility lines will begin to break as result of earth movement. Water will sometimes break through the ground in new locations, and fences, retaining walls, utility poles, and trees will tilt more. A faint rumbling sound, increasing in volume, can be heard as the landslide nears. If any of these warning signs are experienced, evacuation plans should be made. It is recommended that there be at least two planned evacuation routes, because roads may become inaccessible from deposit of slide materials.

Japan spends approximately $4 billion annually to try to control mud- and debris flows. The Japanese government has built *sabo* dams along the river systems in urban areas to trap mud and rock that slide down the mountains. In the United States an American version of these dams is found in Los Angeles County, where there is a system of temporary fortifications to protect areas such as Pasadena and Glendale from debris flows that originate in the San Gabriel Mountains and canyons after hard rains.

The best form of landslide prevention is to not build on areas where landslides have occurred, at the base of slopes, at the base of minor drainage hollows, at the base or top of old fill slopes, or on hillside developments where leach-field septic systems are used. Unfortunately, landslide, rockslide, and mudslide areas are very scenic and are known to entice people to build houses. The West Coast, one of the most slide-prone areas in the world, is a prime example of an area that attracts building in spite of the dangers of landslides.

RESCUE AND RELIEF EFFORTS

A variety of agencies are usually dispatched to the scenes of disastrous landslides. Search and rescue teams are trained in recovery techniques that are appropriate for landslides, such as rescue dogs and proper digging methods. The dangers that are associated with disease, hunger, and lack of water and shelter are handled by entities such as state governments, the Federal Emergency Management Agency (FEMA), and the American Red Cross. The National Landslide Hazards Program, within the United States Geological Survey, responds to emergencies and disasters to provide information on the continuing potential for movement while rescue efforts are taking place.

The National Flood Insurance Program was amended in 1969 to include payment for damage incurred by mudslides caused by flooding. Most home-owners' insurance policies do not cover damage caused by landslides. Federal assistance is available for areas declared a national emergency.

IMPACT

The United States Geological Survey reported that more people died from landslides in the last three months of 1985 than were killed during the previous twenty years by all other geological hazards (such as earthquakes and volcanic eruptions). In terms of property damage, landslides have cost Americans three times the combined costs from all other natural disasters, including hurricanes, tornadoes, and floods. The average annual statistics for the United States report 25 people killed and $1.5 billion in damage.

Landslides are a major worldwide hazard. Thousands of people are killed each year across the world in landslides. A region of southern Italy experienced a series of landslides in 1973, causing 100 villages to be abandoned and 200,000 people to be displaced. A single mudflow event in the Kansu Province of China in 1920 is thought to have been the deadliest land-slide, with an estimated 200,000 people killed. Property damage from landslides worldwide is estimated to be in the tens of billions of dollars.

Dion C. Stewart and Toby R. Stewart

BIBLIOGRAPHY

Bloom, Arthur L. *Geomorphology: A Systematic Analysis of Late Cenozoic Landforms*. 3d ed. Upper Saddle River, N.J.: Prentice Hall, 1998. Chapter 9, entitled "Mass Wasting and Hillslopes," provides a low-level technical discussion of factors contributing to landslides.

Bryant, Edward A. *Natural Hazards*. New York: Cambridge University Press, 1991. A nontechnical book that cites nearly twenty additional readable references on land instability.

Cooke, R. U., and J. C. Doornkamp. *Geomorphology in Environmental Management*. Oxford, England: Clarendon Press, 1990. This book provides details on hazard assessment and risk calculations. It gives detailed examples from foreign countries as well as the United States.

Easterbrook, Don J. *Surface Processes and Landforms*. 2d ed. Upper Saddle River, N.J.: Prentice Hall, 1999. This college textbook is quite good for a general audience. It provides excellent descriptions, pictures, and accounts of over ten classes of landslides.

Erickson, Jon. *Quakes, Eruptions, and Other Geological Cataclysms*. New York: Facts on File, 1994. One of the books in the series entitled The Changing Earth. Chapter 4 is devoted to earth movements, and it provides a descriptive treatment of landslides.

Plummer, Charles C., David McGeary, and Diane H. Carlson. *Physical Geology*. 8th ed. New York: McGraw-Hill/Wm. C. Brown, 1999. A superb introductory textbook. Chapter 9 is devoted to mass wasting and landslides, including descriptions of common forms of landslides and a section on prevention.

Ritter, Dale F., R. Craig Kochel, and Jerry R. Miller. *Process Geomorphology*. 3d ed. Dubuque, Iowa: Wm. C. Brown, 1995. This book provides the technical details of how to evaluate all factors involved in the calculation of the factor of safety. Requires a good background in mathematics, including trigonometry and vectors.

Notable Events

Historical Overview

Historically, the most deadly landslides have occurred in the mountainous regions of Asia, Europe, and the Americas. While landslides are also frequently experienced in Africa and Australia, the quantity of slides and the resultant loss of life in those regions do not compare to those in other parts of the world. Most landslides occur in hilly or mountainous regions where sloping conditions make such activity more likely, but they can happen almost anywhere.

In the United States, landslides and rockslides have occurred most frequently in the Rocky Mountain region and along the Pacific coast. Utah, Colorado, California, and Washington have been the most susceptible to landslide disasters. West Virginia holds that distinction on the U.S. East Coast, primarily as a result of slope instability caused by mining and the debris and waste that it creates. Alberta, British Columbia, and Quebec are considered the most landslide-prone provinces of Canada.

The largest and most devastating landslides have been caused by earthquakes. Most landslides occur with little or no warning, often in tandem with seismic activity. In one of the worst slides in recorded history, a 1920 earthquake in Gansu Province, China, sheared off unstable cliffs, destroying 10 cities and killing 200,000.

Milestones

1512:	A landslide causes a lake to overflow, killing more than 600 in Biasco, the Alps.
September, 1618:	Two villages are destroyed by landslides, and 2,427 are reported dead in Chiavenna Valley, Italy.
September, 1806:	Portions of Rossberg Peak collapse, destroying 4 villages and killing 800 people in Goldau Valley, Switzerland.
April, 1903:	A 0.5-mile section of Turtle Mountain near Frank, Alberta, slides down the mountain, killing 70 people in the town.
December, 1920:	An earthquake shears off unstable cliffs in Gansu Province, China, destroying 10 cities and killing 200,000.
1959:	Hurricane rains and an earthquake combined with a series of massive landslides bury the 800 residents of Minatitlan, Mexico, and kill another 4,200 in surrounding communities.
October, 1963:	A landslide caused by an earthquake destroys the Vaiont Dam, drowning almost 3,000 residents of Belluno, Italy.
November, 1963:	Grand Rivière du Nord, Haiti, is devastated by landslides brought about by tropical downpours; an estimated 500 tourists and residents are killed.
1964:	Earthquakes and rains cause landslides near Niigata, Japan, killing 108, injuring 223, and leaving more than 40,000 homeless.
1966:	A slag heap near Aberfan, Wales, collapses and kills 147—116 of them children.
1968:	More than 1,000 are killed in Bihar and Assam, West Bengal, by floods and landslides.
January, 1969:	Torrential rains lasting more than a week trigger mudslides that kill 95 and cause more than $138 million in damage in Southern California.
July, 1972:	Landslides caused by torrential rains kill 370 persons and cause $472 million in property damage throughout Japan.
1974:	A landslide in Huancavelica, Peru, creates a natural dam on the Mantaro River, forcing the evacuation of 9,000 living in the area and killing an estimated 300.
September, 1987:	Mudslides wipe out entire sections of the Villa Tina area of Medellín, Colombia, killing 183 residents and leaving 500 missing.
July, 1998:	Waves created by an undersea landslide caused by an earthquake kill 2,000 in Papua New Guinea.
August, 1998:	The village of Malpa, India, is destroyed by boulders and mud, leaving 202 dead; only 18 survive.

Human activity has also been a major contributor to the death toll caused by landslides. Ground that is normally stable may slide after human activity alters its natural state. Many deadly landslides have occurred when development altered slope and groundwater conditions. In Virginia, a state not considered a prime site for landslide activity, 8 people were killed in 1942 when a coal waste heap slid into a river valley near the city of Oakwood. The worst landslide in the history of Wales occurred when a human-made slag heap outside of Aberfan shifted, sending 2 million tons of rock, coal, and mud downhill into the city and killing 147 people, most of them children.

Scientists were long unaware of the potential for destruction from underwater landslides. A scientific team that visited the site of a 1998 tsunami in Papua New Guinea later concluded that the deadly waves were probably caused by an underwater landslide set in motion by a small earthquake. This theory forced many scientists to seriously consider the possibility of a connection between landslides and tsunamis.

Unlike many other natural disasters, landslides often have a long-lasting effect on the physical environment. Landslides have collapsed mountains, sent rivers on new and destructive courses, and created huge lakes that inundated populated fertile valleys. A 1925 landslide sent some 50,000 cubic yards of debris into the Gros Ventre River of Wyoming, creating a natural dam 350 feet high. A 3-mile-long lake formed behind the dam. It is not unusual for a landslide to permanently displace animals and humans.

Property damage from landslides is a common occurrence throughout the world, resulting annually in billions of dollars in property damage. A variety of methods are now employed throughout the world to prevent landslides. One way of avoiding catastrophe is diversion and drainage of water before it reaches potential problem areas. Building contractors consider the potential for landslide damage to buildings and other structures prior to excavation and construction. The disposal of construction, logging, and mining waste is closely monitored by many governments in efforts to avoid potential slide disasters.

Donald C. Simmons, Jr.

1903: Canada

ROCKSLIDE
DATE: April 29, 1903
PLACE: Turtle Mountain, Alberta, Canada
RESULT: 70 dead

An undated rockslide in Frank, Alberta, Canada. (National Oceanic and Atmospheric Administration)

In the village of Frank, coal miners' houses and the Canadian Pacific Railroad station lay beneath a cliff-like face of the 3,500-foot-tall Turtle Mountain. The rock rose so abruptly that on the summer solstice the village was cast into shadow by 3 P.M. Before sunrise on April 29, 1903, either an earthquake or an underground explosion caused the mountain to fall upon the town, burying houses beneath 150 feet of rock. The shattered cliff spread boulders across the mile-wide valley and to an elevation higher than the village on the other side. Some of the rock fell vertically, which is known as subsidence. The disaster encompassed 10 square miles of Crow's Nest Pass and dammed Old Man Creek, which ran through the valley. On the northern side of Turtle Mountain, behind the rockslide, lunar cracks or fissures, which were many feet wide, extended for three-quarters of a mile.

The landslide crushed 17 houses and the plant of the French Canadian Coal Company and covered 2 miles of railroad track. Many of the 70 who died remained buried under deep deposits of rock, and of the 19 bodies recovered, some were unrecognizable. The transformed mountain remained unstable, and clusters of rock weighing hundreds of tons crashed into the valley below, making the futile rescue effort very dangerous. All but 2 of the remaining houses were abandoned by the next evening. Mounted police and workers were sent to the region to repair telegraph lines, build a wagon road, and unblock Old Man Creek. The railroad, which took months to rebuild, suffered worse monetary damages than the mine.

Approximately five months later, on the afternoon of September 23, a second mass of rock fell down Turtle Mountain. Although no lives were lost, the slide did considerable damage to the mine and caused a general exodus from the village of Frank. At the time of the slide, a passenger train was approaching the town. Witnessing the falling rock, the conductor stopped the train and reversed for a few miles. An hour later, when the train came into the station, most of the town's population boarded and were shuttled to Blairmore and other neighboring towns.

Theodore Weaver

FOR FURTHER INFORMATION:

"Destruction at Frank." *The New York Times*, May 1, 1903.

"Second Landslide at Frank." *The New York Times*, September 24, 1903.

1926: Colombia

LANDSLIDE
DATE: November 5, 1926
PLACE: Pereira, Colombia
RESULT: 100 dead, 60 injured

On November 5, 1926, near Pereira, Colombia, a landslide crashed down on numerous houses and buried their inhabitants alive. The landslide originated from the right of way of the Caldas Railroad. Part of the earth and rocks was deposited in the Otun River, redirecting its flow and causing floods in the partially buried village. The disaster injured 60 people and killed more than 100. The bodies of the dead could not be immediately located beneath the wreckage.

Theodore Weaver

FOR FURTHER INFORMATION:

"Landslide Kills 100." *The New York Times*, November 6, 1926.

1931: Ecuador

LANDSLIDE
DATE: January 10, 1931
PLACE: Huigra, Ecuador
RESULT: 165 railroad workers dead

After two days of rain, a small landslide covered about 200 yards of the Quito-Guayaquil Railroad on January 9, 1931. Early the next morning, 170 workers began clearing the debris from the tracks in the narrow Cleanchan River Valley. The almost-vertical walls rise 2,000 feet above the 300-foot-wide passageway below. Just after 5 A.M. a second slide, descending from the opposite wall, buried all but 4 of the workers. The massive deposit of earth and stone dammed the Cleanchan River, creating a 50-yard-deep reservoir behind the landslide.

Residents and rescuers from Huigra, which is located just downstream, hurried to the scene when the river went dry. Finding no signs of life in the deposited earth, the townspeople soon fled to the hills fearing that the dam would break and a wall of water would wash away their town. Instead, upon reaching the upper lip of the dam, the river slowly washed a new bed in the dirt.

The four surviving workers, who had been sent to get water when the accident occurred, observed the mountainside come crashing down. Two victims were eventually recovered from the slide that day, one injured, the other dead. President Ayora, for whom the track was being cleared, came to the scene that afternoon on horseback. Weeks and months later, as the river slowly eroded the dam, bodies of the railroad workers occasionally washed into Huigra, where mothers, sisters, and spouses tried to identify the men.

Theodore Weaver

FOR FURTHER INFORMATION:

"Ecuador Landslide Buries 170 Workers." *The New York Times*, January 11, 1931.

Henriquez, V. E. "Ecuador Landslide Gave No Warning." *The New York Times*, February 15, 1931.

"164 Workmen Killed." *The Times* (London), January 13, 1931.

"Toll in Ecuador Near 200." *The New York Times*, January 12, 1931.

1932: France

MUDSLIDES
DATE: May 8, 1932
PLACE: Lyons, France
RESULT: 27 dead

A retaining wall stood 100 feet tall between the slope of the Croix Rousse Hill and apartment houses in the Cours d'Herbouville quarter of Lyons, France. Just before 8:30 A.M., a few stones fell onto the buildings' roofs, causing 5 people to rush into the street. Dr. Joly, who was picking up his mail, also fled to the street just moments before the wall toppled under pressure from the rain-soaked mountainside. The mudslide completely buried one building and tore down half of another. The mayor of Lyons witnessed the disaster and quickly made contact with ambulances and firemen. Nine people climbed down from the partially demolished building on ladders. Two and a half hours passed before the first survivor was dug from the rubble. About that time, broken gas pipes erupted into fire.

To the dismay of the rescuers, a second avalanche of mud slipped down the mountain. In an attempt to make a third precarious mound come down, fire-

men, policemen, soldiers, and volunteers shot more than two hundred bullets into the mud. Later a rock broke the chief of the fire brigade's leg. By the end of the day, 8 wounded survivors had been removed from the debris, but no bodies had been found. A total of 27 died in the incident.

The next day in the Chambéry Valley, 2 houses sank and another 10 were damaged in an 18-acre landslide caused by rain-saturated soils. All the houses had been evacuated. At St. Génix-sur-Guiers, 30 miles east of Lyons, there were several small landslides, inciting 1,600 farmers to abandon their homes and cattle, fearing that 7.5 million square feet of soil was going to bury their town.

Theodore Weaver

FOR FURTHER INFORMATION:

"French Homes Sink in Mountain of Mud." *The New York Times*, May 10, 1932.

"Landslip at Lyons." *The Times* (London), May 9, 1932.

1941: Peru

MUDSLIDE
DATE: December 13, 1941
PLACE: Huaraz, Peru
RESULT: 2,000 dead

At 7:30 A.M. on December 13, 1941, the incredibly swollen Santa River destroyed half of Huaraz, which is the capital of its Peruvian department. The mudflow, reportedly containing lava, mud, rock, and water, killed over a quarter of the town's population and was followed by an earthquake. The 150-foot-deep and 0.5-mile-wide liquid mass left no survivors in the city's residential section and obliterated small American Indian communities in the outskirts.

At 5:50 A.M. on December 14, a minor earthquake shook the region, adding panic to the already chaotic rescue effort. The tremor and badly damaged highways delayed the Peruvian president, Manuel Prado y Ugarteche, who had planned to visit the disaster area. Some 500 bodies were trucked to the hospital that day, and many bodies found in the mudslide's 6-mile path were immediately buried by survivors. A week after the catastrophe, the official death count was 650, but a total of 2,000 were believed to have perished, accounting for those missing and the anonymously buried. Further down the Santa River, whose path was permanently altered by deposited debris, a suspension bridge and a railroad bridge were swept away. The nearby volcano Rataquehua showed no signs of having erupted despite the sightings of lava.

Theodore Weaver

FOR FURTHER INFORMATION:

"53 Perish in Peru as River Floods City." *The New York Times*, December 14, 1941.

"Flood Toll Rises in Peru." *The New York Times*, December 19, 1941.

"Waterslide Takes 500 Lives in Peru." *The New York Times*, December 15, 1941.

1954: Haiti

LANDSLIDE
DATE: October 22, 1954
PLACE: Berly, Haiti
RESULT: 262 dead

In the second week of October, 1954, Hurricane Hazel blew into southwestern Haiti, which is located directly to the east of Cuba. Torrential rains and winds wreaked havoc on the country, flattening the town of Jérémie and rendering most roads impassable. Relief and rescue crews came to coastal towns by ship. On Tuesday night, October 19, rain-drenched soils in a mountainous region 20 miles south of Port-au-Prince gave way and buried the entire town of Berly, killing over 260 people, according to rural police. A woman who was visiting friends in the outskirts, and a child who allegedly escaped ahead of the landslide were the only 2 survivors. Military helicopters flew to the scene, but little could be done but assess the damage.

Theodore Weaver

FOR FURTHER INFORMATION:

"85 Hurricane Deaths in Canada." *The Times* (London), October 19, 1954.

"Hurricane Damage in South Haiti." *The Times* (London), October 14, 1954.

"Hurricane Deaths in Haiti." *The Times* (London), October 13, 1954.

"Landslide Buries Village; 260 Feared Lost in Haiti." *The New York Times*, October 23, 1954.

1955: Mexico

LANDSLIDE
DATE: October 18, 1955
PLACE: Atenguigue, Mexico
RESULT: 100 confirmed dead

About a week after flooding along the Gulf of Mexico, and two weeks after a landslide killed 12 near Mexico City, torrential rains and strong winds moved into western Mexico, causing more flooding and numerous landslides, one of which killed 100 people in the village of Atenguigue. The slide, which reportedly carried trees along with the usual mud and rock, buried much of the town and did considerable damage to one of the country's only paper mills.

Communication was downed, adding to the chaos in the flooded states of Jalisco, Colima, and Michoacán. Impassable and buried roads hampered relief efforts by the Mexican and U.S. Armed Forces. The Zamora and Jiquilpan Rivers swelled over their banks. In the city of Jiquilpan, some 2,500 people lost their homes. Another 200 people were reported missing in the towns of Madrid and Tecomán.

Theodore Weaver

FOR FURTHER INFORMATION:

"Floods Endanger Western Mexico." *The New York Times*, October 19, 1955.

"Mexico City." *The Times* (London), October 3, 1955.

"Mexico City." *The Times* (London), October 19, 1955.

1958: Nova Scotia

ROCKSLIDE
DATE: October 23, 1958
PLACE: Near Spring Hill, Nova Scotia, Canada
RESULT: 84 dead

The most interesting aspect of the Cumberland Number 2 Pit disaster that trapped 174 miners and killed 84 was that it resulted not from a rockfall but from a rock upheaval. In higher levels of the mine, an upward pressure pushed the floor into the roof; then coal and sandstone tumbled down to the deeper expanses. The mine collapse caused the earth to tremble in the nearby community of Spring Hill. In lieu of an explanation, the mine inspector simply stated that the area was "susceptible to bumps," meaning any sort of subterranean disturbance.

Draegermen, or professional mine rescuers, came to the aid of the trapped miners by tunneling through shafts blocked with debris, but they were hampered at the lower recesses by dangerous levels of gas. The concentration of methane gas, which exists naturally in coal mines, was very high, and ventilation efforts failed. Of the dead, only 8 bodies were discovered in the first twenty-four hours, and gas poisoning affected many who came out alive. Six supervisors who had coincidently entered the mine that day to study its dangers numbered among the dead.

The mines, operated by the Cumberland Rail and Coal Company, were significantly more hazardous than other mines, due in part to their high gas content. Two years earlier, 39 miners died in Cumberland Number 4 Pit. The Number 2 Pit extended 2.7 miles to a depth of 4,400 feet, making it the longest coal mine in North America.

Following the disaster, miners' wives and children waited in a building near the entrance, and a few hundred people who came out of curiosity were kept at a distance with ropes. The government investigated the mine and donated $50,000 to a nationwide relief fund for the miners' families.

Theodore Weaver

FOR FURTHER INFORMATION:

"Hope Fading for 85 in Nova Scotia Mine." *The New York Times*, October 25, 1958.

"Hunt for 84 in Pit Is Moving Slowly." *The New York Times*, October 26, 1958.

"96 Miners Missing, 69 Safe in Nova Scotia Rock Shift." *The New York Times*, October 24, 1958.

1960: South Africa

ROCKSLIDE
DATE: January 22, 1960
PLACE: Near Johannesburg, South Africa
RESULT: 550 dead

When a mile-long shaft in a coal mine collapsed in Coalbrook, South Africa, 440 coal miners perished—crushed by falling rock, poisoned by methane and carbon monoxide gas, or drowned in water. At 4:30 P.M. on January 22, 1960, a ventilating fan exploded, and the roofs of at least two tunnels dropped out. Hundreds of men were rescued or managed to escape, but many remained inside. Families of the miners, who lived in nearby shantytowns, congregated at the mine opening. At 7:30 P.M. two more explosions of gas were followed by an audible cave-in, shutting off a mile of tunnel and causing the earth's surface to drop 3 feet in places. Twelve-inch cracks split apart area roads. That night the South African General Investment Trust, which owned the mine, issued this statement: "It is feared that 6 whites and approximately 500 Africans are trapped in the mine and rescue operations are proceeding uninterruptedly."

Measures were taken to ventilate the mine, and many who lived through the first collapse reentered with gas masks in an attempt to rescue their coworkers. Two days later, after more rumbling collapses, rescuers, who had been working in chest-deep water, were withdrawn. Due to the amount of fallen debris, officials estimated that it would take at least a week to reach the trapped men. No communication, such as knocking sounds, had been made with the lost miners since the original rockfall. Carbon monoxide gas, which is poisonous, and methane gas which is poisonous and volatile, naturally exist in coal mines, so chances of survival were slim. Two funeral services were held by the Salvation Army at the main pit entrance, one for 6 white men and the other for 334 black men.

Theodore Weaver

FOR FURTHER INFORMATION:

"Efforts to Save 440 Miners Halt." *The New York Times*, January 24, 1960.

"500 Miners Trapped in South African Pit." *The New York Times*, January 22, 1960.

"Hope Dim for 350 in African Mine." *The New York Times*, January 23, 1960.

1960: Philippines

ROCKSLIDE
DATE: January 22, 1960
PLACE: Mindanao, Philippines
RESULT: 40 schoolchildren dead

A massive downward movement of rock and dirt on January 22, 1960, reduced a small school to rubble; it had been located at the base of a mountain on the island of Mindanao. The slide occurred during afternoon classes. In the next twenty-four hours, a rescue crew recovered only 10 bodies of the 40 missing children from the wreckage. Little hope remained for any survivors. State officials sent soldiers from Zamboanga to dig through the debris in an attempt to locate the remaining 30 corpses.

Theodore Weaver

FOR FURTHER INFORMATION:

"40 Philippine Children Buried by a Landslide." *The New York Times,* January 24, 1960.

1961: Ukraine

MUDSLIDE
DATE: March 13, 1961
PLACE: Kiev, Ukraine, Soviet Union
RESULT: 145 dead

In the outskirts of Kiev, an earthen dam held silt and water in the Babi Yar Ravine, which engineers were making into a park. Winds blowing at 66 feet per second caused water to pour over the dam's lip and erode the mound at 8:30 A.M. on March 13, 1961. Thousands of tons of mud then washed into a Kiev suburb, destroying 22 houses, a tram station, shops, and 2 factories; 145 people died.

Two weeks after the catastrophe, the official Ukranian Communist Party newspaper first reported the incident, and a correspondent in Moscow read the information by telephone to journalists in the United States. By that time, more than 80 of the 143 injured had left the hospital, and all the homeless had been relocated. Soviet courts charged the responsible engineers with "mistakes in design and violations of technology."

Theodore Weaver

FOR FURTHER INFORMATION:

"145 Killed in Kiev Dyke Disaster." *The Times* (London), April 1, 1961.

"Soviet Bears Death of 145 in Mud Slide." *The New York Times,* April 1, 1961.

1961: Japan

LANDSLIDES AND MUDSLIDES
DATE: June 27-July 1, 1961
PLACE: Central Japan
RESULT: 244 dead, 972 injured, $70 million in damage

Poor city planning and housing developments were a major factor in the widespread destruction and death that resulted from seven days of heavy rain in Central Japan in 1961. Real-estate developers, who had cut down hillside forests above towns and cities, were blamed for landslides, particularly in the city of Kōbe. Where tree and plant roots had stabilized topsoil for centuries, rivers of mud and full-scale landslides crashed through insubstantial rock walls, destroying hundreds of houses and flooding some 300,000 more. Even in Tokyo, where storms were less severe, running and stagnant rainwater filled the streets because natural and artificial drainage systems had been filled to create space for construction. The Central Meteorological Agency was also criticized for not giving more advance warning.

The downpour began on June 23, in southwestern Japan, then moved to the central and eastern parts of the country. Telephone lines were downed and 51 people were confirmed dead on June 27. The next day, more landslides elevated the death count to 90; another 89 were considered missing, as were 30 fishermen off the coast of the Philippines. On July 1, as the storm subsided, 244 were counted dead, 168 were missing, 972 were injured, and thousands of acres of crops were destroyed. A month and six days later, landslides and floods killed another 115 people in western Japan.

Theodore Weaver

FOR FURTHER INFORMATION:

"Japan Floods Subside." *The New York Times*, July 1, 1961.

"115 Dead in Japanese Floods." *The Times* (London), August 7, 1961.

"Rain Toll up in Japan." *The New York Times*, June 28, 1961.

Rosenthal, A. M. "Japanese Say Builders' Greed Contributed to High Flood Toll." *The New York Times*, June 30, 1961.

"Toll in Japan 90 Dead from 4 Days of Storm." *The New York Times*, June 29, 1961.

1962: Peru

MUDSLIDE
DATE: February 28, 1962
PLACE: Conchucos, Peru
RESULT: 60 dead

After days of heavy rain in late February, 1962, a massive chunk of a glacier slipped into a lake and sent ice, water, and mud cascading down onto the Peruvian town of Conchucos. Sixty people died in the partially buried farming community. The storms also downed telegraph lines, making communication with the disaster-stricken area difficult. On March 1, the Peruvian government sent doctors, rescue crews, medicine, and supplies to the town, located 250 miles northeast of Lima. The nearest road to Conchucos, which had a population of about 5,000 including the surrounding area, was reportedly 13 miles away.

Theodore Weaver

FOR FURTHER INFORMATION:

"Peru Valley Gets Aid in Wake of Avalanche." *The New York Times*, March 2, 1962.

"Slide Hits Peru Town." *The New York Times*, March 1, 1962.

1963: The Vaiont Dam Disaster

LANDSLIDE
DATE: October 9, 1963
PLACE: Belluno, Italy
RESULT: Almost 3,000 dead

During the early 1960's a magnificent concrete dam (*Diga del Vajont*) was constructed about 10 miles (16.2 kilometers) northeast of Belluno, an Italian town along the Piave River. The dam spans the Vaiont gorge, an old glacial trough in the heart of the spectacular Italian Alps. The area is within the southern part of the majestic Dolomites of the northern Italian region. This region is characterized by near-vertical cliffs composed mostly of massive carbonate rocks. The dam, which cost approximately $100 million to build, is 11 feet (3.4 meters) wide at the top and 74 feet (22.7 meters) wide at the base and stands 875 feet (265 meters) high at the highest point. It was designed to create a large lake for the generation of hy-droelectric power. The dam impounded a reservoir of 316,000 cubic feet (8,943 cubic meters) of water. The curved, thin-arch dam still stands as an engineering marvel and a testament to humanity's ingenuity.

Downstream from the dam, the gorge intersects the Piave River Valley near the mountain villages of Pirago and Longarone. Casso, a small highland village, is along the northern edge of the valley on Mount Pul. This farming community overlooks the Vaiont dam and reservoir. Upstream from the dam, the village of Erto is situated along the highland area of the Vaiont Valley.

Local Geology. The stratigraphic sequence in the area consists mostly of Mesozoic rocks. The Jurassic Dogger epoch formation creates steep cliffs along the valley. These rugged rock walls consist mostly of dolostone, a rock composed of the mineral dolomite, calcium magnesium carbonate. The Dogger stratus is underlain by Triassic rocks; the subjacent Cretaceous and Tertiary strata are composed mostly of limestone but contain some argillaceous units. These clay-bearing layers represent potential zones of weakness in the rock column. Limestone near the dam site has been weakened by solution features, such as joint fissures, sinkholes, and underground caverns.

Structurally, the dam is situated along an east-west-trending asymmetrical syncline designated the "Erto Syncline." This fold plunges to the east, or upstream. The limbs of the syncline dip from 25 degrees to 45 degrees toward the Vaiont Valley. The steep dips and fractured strata, as well as the weak layers within the stratal packet, render the area landslide-prone. There is evidence of earlier slope failure at some places, and in 1960 a large slide block composed of 916,000 cubic yards (700,000 cubic meters) of debris moved downslope from Mount Toc into the reservoir. Although the slide did no significant damage because of the low water level, it did alert local citizens and scientists associated with the project to a potential problem. Geologists investigated the slide area and determined that it was part of a much larger landslide block. The slide block was about 1.1 miles (1.8 kilometers) long and 1 mile (1.6 kilometers) wide. The total volume of the block was estimated to be more than 787 million cubic feet (240 million cubic meters), much larger than originally suspected by engineers.

A landslide results from the movement of a mass of rock and soil downslope in response to gravity. This movement can be either slow or rapid. If infini-

and 1963. This excessive rainfall was probably the trigger that led to the major disaster in the area.

The Vaiont Disaster. On October 9, 1963, instruments within the slide mass recorded as much as 32 inches (80 centimeters) of movement per day. The creep rate had become dangerously high, and people in local villages were warned of possible flooding. Animals grazing south of the reservoir probably sensed the movement and abandoned the area a few days before the disaster. Late on the evening of October 9, at 10:41 P.M., disaster struck. During a heavy downpour, about 350 million cubic yards (270 million cubic meters) of rock and soil slid off the flank of Mount Toc and moved at a rate of 68 miles per hour (30 meters per second) into the reservoir.

Initially, there was a loud noise and rush of air that caused damage to some homes in Casso; water from the reservoir was lifted 792 feet (240 meters) up the north slope of the gorge and more than 325 feet (100 meters) vertically above the top of the dam. The displaced water rushed down the valley and entered the Piave River, where it moved both upstream and downstream. The wave that flowed upstream engulfed most of the town of Longarone. A photograph taken after the flood shows almost total destruction of the southeast part of the village. The strip along the river was swept clean of buildings and trees. In less than five minutes the raging waters destroyed most of the village and left more than 2,000 people dead. Some water was diverted downstream along the Piave more than 1.4 miles (2 kilometers). In the uppermost part of the reservoir the wave bypassed the town of Erto but hit with full force the village of San Martino at the northeast end. In all, nearly 3,000 lives were lost, including engineers, technicians, and workers living in barracks along the crest of the dam.

tesimally slow, the movement may not be evident to the casual observer but can be recorded by sensitive instruments placed within the unstable mass. During 1960 and 1961 monitoring stations within the slide at times recorded 10 to 12 inches (up to 25 to 30 centimeters) of creep per week; the rate of creep slowed to 0.5 inch (about 1 centimeter) per week during 1962 and 1963. This reduced level of creep led most scientists to the conclusion that the imminent danger of mass movement was probably over.

However, heavy rains occurred at times during the late summer and early fall of 1963. This precipitation soaked into the slide area, adding weight to the mass and hydrating some of the clay layers. Data recorded at Erto indicated that more than 90 inches of rain fell in the area from February to early October in 1962

Aftermath. According to author Patrick L. Abbott, the event has been called the world's worst dam disaster. The final tragedy was played out when the chief engineer of the dam project, Mario Pancini, packed his bags for a trip to court at L'Aquila in southern Italy and "taped the cracks around the doors of his Venetian room and turned on the jets of his gas range." The dam stands today not only as a stark monument to man's engineering expertise but also as a grim reminder of his ineptness in selecting a geologically safe site for construction.

Donald F. Reaser

FOR FURTHER INFORMATION:

Abbott, Patrick L. *Natural Hazards.* Dubuque, Iowa: Wm. C. Brown, 1996. Pages 209 to 211 describe the large debris slide that resulted in the Vaiont Dam disaster. Abbott lists five geological factors that contributed to the massive landslide and catastrophic flood.

Coch, Nicholas K. *Geohazards.* New York: Prentice Hall, 1995. Pages 242 to 245 describe and illustrate with color figures the Vaiont Dam site. Coch includes a detailed map and cross section of the area with the text.

Henderson, A. J. Army Corps of Engineers publication (DACW 39-79-C-0063), 1985. Provides technical information about the Vaiont slide. This is the best reference to acquire geological and meteorological data concerning the disaster.

Kiersch, G. A. "The Vaiont Reservoir Disaster." In *Civil Engineering,* Vol. 34. New York: American Society of Civil Engineers, 1964. Pages 32 to 39 show surface features in the vicinity of the dam site as well as the pathway of water in the reservoir that was displaced by the landslide.

Montgomery, Carla W. *Environmental Geology.* Dubuque, Iowa: Wm. C. Brown, 1989. Pages 452 to 454 describe the factors leading up to the Vaiont reservoir disaster.

1966: Rio de Janeiro

LANDSLIDES, ROCKSLIDES, AND MUDSLIDES
DATE: January 11-13, 1966
PLACE: Rio de Janeiro, Brazil
RESULT: 239 dead

On January 11, 1966, the heaviest rains in Rio de Janeiro since 1883 wreaked havoc on the city, with the slum dwellers bearing the brunt. By sundown, 114 corpses had been recovered from the rubble in shantytowns across the city. An enormous rock loosened by the rains rolled down the Euclides da Rocha Hill in Copacabana Beach, demolishing 5 houses and killing 27 people. A mud avalanche near the city's commercial center in Santa Teresa washed away another 5 dwellings, leaving 8 dead and 16 missing, including a family of 6.

The water-saturated ground beneath 8 shacks in the Ipanema section gave way to the downward pull of gravity, burying and crushing another 14 people. In other parts of the city a baby in its crib was dug from the mud and debris, as was the body of a twenty-two-year-old woman. She was entangled in a wedding dress that she had been sewing. Authorities evacuated 20 patients from a mental hospital with sagging pillars. When the power went out, commuters were stuck in electric trains for hours. Twenty-four more people perished in a midnight landslide in Corcorado.

Another 9 inches of rain fell in the next twenty-four hours. On a residential street in Santa Teresa, a midday landslide engulfed a truck carrying 6 workers, buried 3 stone houses, then crumpled the first four floors of a modern seven-story apartment building. A 150-ton boulder careened down a hill and crashed into the Guanda Aqueduct, depriving 40 percent of the city of potable water. Mud-caked rescue workers and 20,000 homeless people swarmed the flooded streets.

The relief effort included transforming a sports stadium, schools, universities, and a shopping center into shelters for the homeless. Announcements on the radio asked for food, medicine, and blood donations. Emergency inoculation programs were set up—the sea was believed to be contaminated with typhoid 2 miles out from shore. By January 22, a $2.7 million loan for reconstruction had been arranged by the United States. Because of mourning in Rio de Janeiro, it was suggested that Carnival be postponed until the end of March.

Theodore Weaver

FOR FURTHER INFORMATION:

"Brazil Gets U.S. Food Aid." *The New York Times,* January 22, 1966.

"Carnival Facing Delay Because of Rio Floods." *The New York Times,* January 17, 1966.

De Onis, Juan. "Landslides Set off by Downpour Kill 114 in Rio." *The New York Times,* January 12, 1966.

"Landslide Crushes Apartments in Rio; Storm Toll Tops 300." *The New York Times,* January 14, 1966.

"Many Killed in Brazilian Floods." *The Times* (London), January 12, 1966.

"Rio de Janeiro Bathers Face Typhoid Risk." *The Times* (London), January 19, 1966.

"Rio Flood Havoc Still Mounts." *The Times* (London), January 14, 1966.

"Storm Disaster in Rio Causing Major Relief Problem." *The New York Times,* January 13, 1966.

"Sun Shines on Rio Flood Havoc." *The Times* (London), January 15, 1966.

1966: The Aberfan Disaster

LANDSLIDE
DATE: October 21, 1966
PLACE: Aberfan, Wales, United Kingdom
RESULT: 147 dead (116 children, 31 adults), 32 injured, a school and 8 houses destroyed

The tightly knit mining village of Aberfan lies in the valley of the Taff River, one of many steep-sided valleys that cut through the mountains of Wales. The area had been the site of coal mining for two hundred years. During that time, huge tips (dumps or stockpiles) of mining waste, debris, and ashes piled up on the mountain slopes. The coal mine that was served by the miners of Aberfan had produced such tips, one of which was 700 feet high by 1966, after thirty years of continuous use, and which was being added to by some 36 tons each day.

The coal mine in question, the Merthyr Vale Colliery, had been in private hands until 1947, when, with the nationalization of the British coal industry, it passed into the hands of the National Coal Board, which then assumed responsibility for its working safety. The miners came largely from the village of Aberfan and surrounding villages. The younger children of the village attended Pant Glas Primary (Elementary) school, which was sited on Moy Road and lay directly under the 700-foot tip. On the other side of Moy Road were houses. Between the foot of the tip and the back of the school lay a small farm and the schoolyard.

Heavy rain had fallen in October of 1966, with almost continuous rain on October 19 and 20. Tip workers had noticed some cracks at the top of the tip, caused, it was believed, by the crane or derrick that upended the waste trucks as they were hauled up from the colliery on the valley floor. The crane was ordered moved back, which it was.

The Slide. The morning of Friday, October 21, was a dark, foggy, damp morning. It was the last day for Pant Glas school before the usual midterm break. The 7:30 A.M. shift at the colliery began as normal, with the tip workers setting out for the top. By the time they had reached it, around 9 A.M., and peered through the fog, they saw only a crater in front of them. The whole side of the tip had slipped down onto the school, the farm, and the houses opposite on Moy Road.

In fact, a solid wall of mud and sludge, made up of water, ash, and coal waste, had crashed down on the school and other buildings and, like an avalanche, engulfed and filled them, as well as demolished parts of their structures. The resulting deaths were therefore as likely to have been caused by suffocation as by the impact of falling debris and collapsing buildings. At the same time, a black dust engulfed the village. Ironically, the fog began to clear from the mountain slopes above.

The school itself was a solid Victorian brick edifice, two classrooms in depth, consisting of an assembly hall, some six juniors' classrooms, and two infants' classrooms. The landslide hit those juniors' classrooms facing toward the tip, largely demolishing them. Those facing Moy Road were less severely affected. The two infants' classrooms, being at one end of the school, were largely undamaged. Opposite the school, 7 houses had also been demolished. At one point, it was estimated that the sludge lay 45 feet deep in the schoolyard.

The Children's Experience. For the children attending the school, at 9:15 A.M. assembly had just finished and classes had just begun. One of the surviving children in one of the worst-affected classrooms described her experiences: They first heard a tremendous rumbling sound; the whole school seemed to go dead, and everyone was terrified. The sound grew louder and louder until they could see the blackness descending outside the window. After that she was knocked unconscious, waking to find her leg trapped and broken under a huge radiator that had been ripped from the wall but which had saved her from suffocation. Most of her classmates were not so fortunate.

Another student described the landslide like water pouring down the hillside. She saw two boys run right into it and be sucked away. It hit the school like a huge wave, splattering everywhere, crushing the buildings. Another child, the last one to be brought out alive, had been completely buried but had managed to stick her fingers through a gap and to call out.

Some surviving children suffered horrific injuries. One boy lost three fingers and suffered a fractured pelvis and an injured leg. He would have bled to death because of his internal injuries, but the mud caked around him. As it was, his ear was ripped off and had to be sewn back on. A few children were more fortunate. One fourteen-year-old boy was late for school. He arrived just as the head teacher was letting all the unscathed children go home.

The first rescuers, who included many of the mothers, climbed through the windows and began to pass children back out. Hearing so many cries, they worked frantically, deep in mud, which was up to 5 feet deep in some classrooms, trying to find those buried. Some of the children managed to escape on their own. The rescuers did not dare move anything, however, in case there was further collapse. Some of the rescuers were themselves injured and needed hospital treatment.

As soon as the colliery was informed, the shift was halted and the miners rushed to the scene, to be joined by other miners from a nearby colliery. The slide was still moving, the fog on the valley floor still persisted, and the road was narrow and a dead-end, so rescue conditions were very difficult, though, in a community used to mining disasters, never chaotic. The dead and injured had to be evacuated, and the sludge had to be dug through and cleared to allow access and to find bodies. Some 25 houses were evacuated by the police.

Engineers with heavy bulldozers were brought in to try to halt the flow of the slag, a move made more urgent by the fear of further rain. However, by the time they arrived the chances of finding anyone else alive were slim. In fact, the last person to be rescued alive was at 11 A.M., less than two hours after the initial

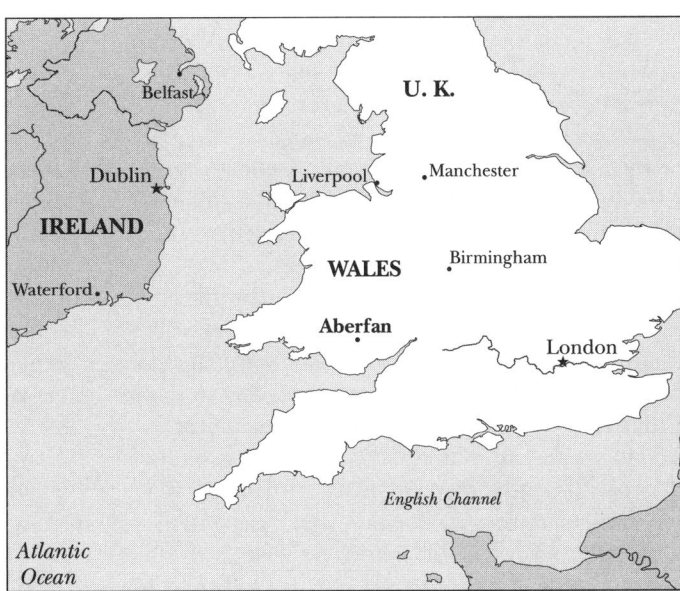

impact. Nevertheless, it took a further six days to recover all the bodies. Many of the truck drivers worked up to six hours at a time clearing the debris; some miners worked for ten hours at a time. The police also joined in the initial digging.

Of 254 children on the school roll, 74 had been declared dead by the end of the first day. Another 2 children had been killed in the farm, together with their grandmother. Eight other adults had been identified as dead, including 3 teachers. About 36 people were in the hospital, and some 80 people were still missing. The deputy head teacher, Mr. D. Beynon, was found clutching 5 children in his arms, dying as he tried to protect them. All of the 38 children in his class appeared to have died. As badly affected was the senior class, those studying for the examinations to gain entrance into high school, where Mrs. M. Bates and 37 children had been killed. In the other senior class, the teacher had been brought out safely, but some 27 children were unaccounted for.

Immediate Aftermath. The engineers had been unable to halt the flow of slide on the first day. On the next day, Saturday, military rescue units arrived. By the end of the day, the torrential flow of water finally ceased its ferocity. At its height, the tip had been discharging 100,000 gallons of water per hour.

By the end of the day 137 bodies had been recovered—106 children and 16 adults being identified, and a further 15 still unidentified. At least 32 people were still in the hospital. Most of the school had been cleared, but it was feared that up to 60 people could be buried in the surrounding rubble. In fact, there were 8 bodies recovered the next day, Sunday, and 1 body a week later, bringing the final toll to 147, plus 1 of the injured, who died in hospital. Twenty-six rescuers were injured. Almost the entire age range of nine- to eleven-year-old children of the village had been wiped out.

The whole nation was deeply shocked by the disaster. The same day as the accident, the British prime minister, Harold Wilson, promised a high-level independent inquiry, and he himself traveled to Merthyr Tydfil, the nearest town, to meet with local officials. The next day, Saturday, the duke of Edinburgh, the queen's husband, visited the disaster. An appeal fund was immediately set up that day, which grew later to tremendous proportions. Princess Margaret, the queen's sister, appealed for toys for the injured and bereaved children. Also on that day, the public inquiry, which was to become one of the biggest ever

held in the United Kingdom, was set up under the Tribunals of Enquiry Act of 1921, to be conducted by Lord Justice Edmund Davies, a respected lord justice of appeal, who had been born only 2 miles from Aberfan and who had known the area all his life. The speed of such moves was unparalleled. The necessary legislation for the tribunal was put before Parliament and cleared by October 25.

One unfortunate repercussion of this was that all comment on the tragedy was banned by the attorney general, as the affair was now in the hands of the law. Many felt uneasy about this, believing that fair comment was being censored. However, legal aid was granted to all who had been affected, so that they could be legally represented at the inquiry.

An inquest was opened on Monday, October 24, in a small chapel vestry. Over 60 relatives crowded in, and feelings ran high. "Our children have been murdered," was a common cry. The coroner gave the causes of death as asphyxia and multiple injuries but

The city of Aberfan after the 1966 landslide, the effects of which are visible in the rear center of the photo. (AP/Wide World Photos)

had to explain it was not his job to apportion blame; that was for the tribunal of inquiry.

The first funerals were held on Thursday, October 27. At the Baptist Church, the minister performing the service had lost his own son. A mass burial was arranged for the Friday, to which an estimated 10,000 people came. Two 8-foot trenches were dug for the coffins, and a 100-foot-tall cross was made from the wreaths sent. It was said that there was little weeping. Some years later, the appeal fund constructed a memorial garden and cemetery for the victims on the site of the demolished school. On Saturday, October 29, the queen and the duke of Edinburgh visited the village, and flags were flown at half-staff throughout the nation.

Long-Term Aftermath. The psychological scars on the surviving children and their parents remained for a generation; many needed medical and psychological rehabilitation. The survivors had to be moved to other schools; finally, a new school was built nearby. The village remained in deep shock for many years but never lost its cohesiveness. The nation as a whole was also deeply affected for months, even years. For some, it became a crisis of faith.

The inquiry lasted five months and took statements from 136 witnesses. The National Coal Board was held legally liable for not maintaining their property, the disaster being the result of waste materials being allowed to block an original water course. The water, instead of escaping out at the bottom of the tip, as was normal, soaked into the tip and built up enormous pressure within it. The rains of the preceding few days finally rendered the whole tip unstable, and it had therefore collapsed with considerable force.

As a result of the tribunal report, the Mines and Quarries Act of 1989 was passed by the British Parliament, giving the government wide-ranging powers to supervise the safety of mines, quarries, and tips. An earlier act, the Industrial Development Act of 1966, which was designed to help reclaim derelict land but whose implementation had been hampered by lack of funds, was reenergized, especially in Wales. By 1967, the secretary of state for Wales had published a policy document that in future years lead to large-scale reclamation of mining sites in South Wales.

In July, 1968, it was decided to remove all the tips of the Merthyr Vale Colliery, though the colliery itself did not cease working until 1989, as part of the overall decline of the Welsh coal-mining industry. The forestry commission replanted much of the waste-land, and the area became a recreation site, which attracts visitors from around the world. The appeal fund was used not only to relieve the suffering of the families affected but also to build new facilities for the village, as well as fund educational research.

David Barratt

FOR FURTHER INFORMATION:

David, Gerald. *Report of the Management Committee of the Aberfan Disaster Fund.* Aberfan, Wales: October, 1966-August, 1968.

Life International, February 6, 1967.

Madgwick, Gaynor. *Aberfan: Struggling out of the Darkness—A Survivor's Story.* Blaengarw, Wales: Valleys and Vales Autobiography Project, 1996.

Thomson, G. McKecknie, and S. Rodin. *Colliery Spoil Tips: After Aberfan.* London: Institute of Civil Engineers, 1972.

The Times (London), October 22-29, 1966.

1967: Rio de Janeiro

LANDSLIDES, ROCKSLIDES, AND MUDSLIDES
DATE: February 17-20, 1967
PLACE: Rio de Janeiro, Brazil
RESULT: 224 dead

After thirty hours of rain, and about a year after the catastrophic 1966 landslides in Rio de Janeiro, disaster struck again. Late at night on February 19, 1967, in the suburb of Laranjeiras, rainwater washed the stabilizing earth from beneath a mammoth boulder. The rock rolled down a gully, crashed through a house, then tore out the foundation of an eight-story apartment building. This building collapsed in turn, falling onto a neighboring four-story building and leaving nothing but a pile of crumbled and shattered debris in which few large pieces could be seen. After rescuers recovered 22 bodies the next day, deep sections of the rubble still remained untouched. Other landslides toppled shanties, and 4,000 were made homeless. The death toll had risen to 119 people by February 21, and over 100 more were feared dead. Rescue workers sifted through the wreckage, occasionally setting aside something of value.

In lower parts of the city, 3 feet of water ran in the streets, carrying thick, brown mud from the higher elevations. In southern Brazil, where flooding caused the Paraíba and the Paria Rivers to swell, an estimated 30,000 people were homeless.

Theodore Weaver

FOR FURTHER INFORMATION:
"Death Toll from Rio Flood at 119 and Expected to Rise." *The New York Times*, February 22, 1967.
"100 Dead as Rio Storm Makes Buildings Collapse." *The New York Times*, February 21, 1967.
"Rain Causes 49 Deaths in Rio." *The Times* (London), February 21, 1967.
"2 Rio Apartment Houses Collapse in Heavy Rains." *The New York Times*, February 20, 1967.

1968: Democratic Republic of Congo

MUDSLIDE
DATE: March 8, 1968
PLACE: Luhonga, Congo
RESULT: 150 dead

Approximately 150 people disappeared when a mudslide swept away the small African village of Luhonga in 1968. The almost-mile-long flow of mud was 15 feet deep when it engulfed the village and washed over its fields. None of the village structures survived the muddy inundation. After several days of heavy rain, one side of the 1,600-foot Mandwe Mountain gave way to the force of gravity. The mountaintop divided, and tons of muddy earth poured into the Ruzizi Valley below. After rescuers located 7 people who survived the catastrophe, the local press put the death toll at 150.

Theodore Weaver

FOR FURTHER INFORMATION:
"Landslide Buries Hamlet in Congo." *The New York Times*, March 13, 1968.

A mudslide blocks the Pacific Coast Highway in Los Angeles in 1969. (AP/Wide World Photos)

1969: Southern California

MUDSLIDES
DATE: January 18-26, 1969
PLACE: Several communities in Southern California, from Santa Barbara to Los Angeles
RESULT: 95 dead

Nine days of heavy rain in California resulted in a plethora of floods, mudslides, collapsed homes, and traffic accidents. On January 27, 1969, Governor Ronald Reagan estimated the property damage at $35 million.

Two children were buried alive when a mudslide

pushed their Highland Park home across its yard and into the street. Rescuers dug through 5 feet of mud in the children's room before removing their mother from beneath a water heater and other rubble. Two playing Los Angeles boys were swept into an underground flood control channel. Rescuers found the ten-year-old brother alive 4 miles away, but his eleven-year-old brother remained missing. In a similar incident in Santa Barbara, floodwaters washed sixteen-year-old Mark Williams into a culvert under U.S. Highway 101. The boy drowned, along with 2 men trying to save him. A 3-man rescue team came to the aid of a teacher and 6 boys camping in the Los Padres National Forest. A large bulldozer they were riding down the Sespe River stalled and the water rose; when the numbed men and children could no longer hold on, the current swept them away. A helicopter later picked up Mr. Eckersley, the twenty-eight-year-old teacher, from the riverbank. The others drowned.

Mudslides hit the Los Angeles suburb of Glendora particularly hard because a fire had swept across 77,000 acres in the area the summer before, burning plants and trees that stabilize the soil. Slides as deep as 12 feet damaged and destroyed more than 200 houses, despite sandbag barricades built by firefighters. After the first series of inundations, workers bulldozed the residual silt into protective walls, but to little avail. Mud filled one home to the ceiling days after the owner had cleared it of mud 2 feet deep from a previous slide.

In other areas, a sixty-one-year-old woman drowned in the muddy water after it rushed in through her window; a couple met a similar fate when the mud flowed through their sliding doors. Mud from two slides buried forty-one-year-old Michael Riordan in his Brentwood home, and 6 firemen seriously injured themselves trying to rescue him. Mudslides carried away houses in Topanga Canyon, and 500 people were momentarily trapped while evacuating. By the ninth day of the storm, raw sewage had polluted 7 miles of Pismo Beach, four times the normal number of traffic accidents had occurred, and 9,000 people were temporarily homeless. President Richard Nixon declared the entire state a disaster area.

Theodore Weaver

FOR FURTHER INFORMATION:

Dye, Lee, and Leonard Greenwood. "Storm Lashes Southland." *Los Angeles Times,* January 20, 1969.

Dye, Lee, and Robert Rawitch. "Southland Reels Under Series of Storms." *Los Angeles Times,* January 21, 1969.

"11 Die in Coast Mudslide." *The New York Times,* January 26, 1969.

"Rainstorm Lashes a Forest Coast." *The New York Times,* January 22, 1969.

Shuit, Doug. "Six Youths, Four Adults Swept Away." *Los Angeles Times,* January 22, 1969.

————. "Water Sweeps 2 Boys Through Underground Flood Channel." *Los Angeles Times,* January 25, 1969.

"Storm Destroys Homes in California." *The New York Times,* January 23, 1969.

Thackrey, Ted, Jr. "600 Evacuated in Worst Southland Storm Since 1938." *Los Angeles Times,* January 25, 1969.

Thackrey, Ted, Jr., and Dial Torgerson. "Rescue Crews Press Work." *Los Angeles Times,* January 27, 1969.

Torgerson, Dial. "Sudden Last Blow of Storm Destroys 15 Homes." *Los Angeles Times,* January 23, 1969.

Townsend, Dorothy. "2 Children Die as Mudslide Crushes Highland Park Home." *Los Angeles Times,* January 26, 1969.

1971: Afghanistan

LANDSLIDE
DATE: July 30, 1971
PLACE: Khinjan Pass, Afghanistan
RESULT: 100 dead

Inundations in northern Afghanistan caused a lake in the Hindu Kush mountains to overflow its shores, sending floodwaters, then mud and rocks onto a village at Khinjan Pass. Initial reports of the landslide estimated the death toll to be 1,000, but the number was soon reduced to 100. Some of the victims in the town were buried under the flow of earth, whereas others died by drowning. As rescue teams dug through the wreckage for bodies, the American and British Red Cross came to the aid of the homeless.

Theodore Weaver

FOR FURTHER INFORMATION:

"Afghanistan Flood Toll Put at 1,000." *The New York Times,* July 30, 1971.

"More than 1,000 Killed in Afghan Floods." *The Times* (London), July 30, 1971.

"Toll in Afghanistan Revised Downward to 100." *The New York Times*, August 1, 1971.

1972: Hong Kong

LANDSLIDES
DATE: June 18, 1972

Landslides destroyed buildings in Hong Kong in 1972 after 26 inches of rain fell in three days. (Courtesy of R. Carmichael)

PLACE: Hong Kong
RESULT: 100 dead

After three days of heavy rain, landslides buried squatters' huts in a "resettlement estate" north of the Kai Tak international airport and toppled 2 houses and an apartment building above Victoria City Center on Hong Kong Island. Six days after the catastrophe, over 100 were confirmed dead and many were still missing. Of the thousands left homeless by the landslides, 83 on the official missing list reappeared when the government began dispensing aid money.

On Hong Kong Island, after 26 inches of rain had fallen, a deep section of the mountainside tumbled down on 2 houses, then slammed their remains into a twelve-story apartment building where approximately 100 people lived. Henry Litton, a barrister, was among the 19 rescued with injuries. Another man talked casually with rescue workers as they carefully removed massive chunks of debris that had trapped him for eight hours.

As the rain continued to fall, another section of the mountain threatened to slip at the second disaster area in the Kwun Tong suburb. The landslide here killed more than 50 and left hundreds missing when it buried 78 primitive shelters. Displaced earth blocked roads and caused a power outage in Victoria and Kowloon. Hong Kong's governor received a message of sympathy from the queen of England.

Theodore Weaver

FOR FURTHER INFORMATION:

"50 Reported Dead near Dacca." *The Times* (London), June 22, 1972.

"Hong Kong Toll Reduced." *The New York Times*, June 24, 1972.

"More Deaths Feared in Landslips." *The Times* (London), June 20, 1972.

"300 Feared Dead in Hong Kong After Landslips." *The Times* (London), June 19, 1972.

Tons of mud rushed onto this home in Pacifica, just south of San Francisco, in January, 1982. (AP/Wide World Photos)

1982: San Francisco

LANDSLIDES AND MUDSLIDES

DATE: January 5, 1982
PLACE: Near San Francisco, California
RESULT: 21 dead

In January of 1982 a tropical storm originating near Hawaii brought heavy rains and disaster to the San Francisco area. Much of the soil in the region contains clay, which absorbs water and is prone to slipping. Vast property damage and 21 deaths resulted from separate incidents of mudslides, landslides, and flooding. Because of water-damaged tracks, the California Zephyr train derailed near Richmond, although with no deaths and few injuries. In Santa Cruz, a falling tree killed 1, and 4 more died in 3 houses that slipped and collapsed. In Sausalito, a duplex crashed down onto a house, killing 1. One

neighborhood evacuated all of its 500 residents. A boy died when a mudslide washed him from his backyard. The Golden Gate Bridge was closed for several periods when blocked by mud, and a 100-foot wide, 60-foot deep portion of earth dislodged itself from beneath U.S. Highway 101. Governor Edmund G. "Jerry" Brown, Jr., declared a state of emergency.

At 11 P.M. January 5, mud poured from 400 feet above into the Velez household in Pacifica. Mr. Velez ran first to his son's bedroom but was stopped by a wave of mud. Unable to reach the room of their two daughters, the Velez parents fled outside, where neighbors restrained Mr. Velez from reentering. A Mr. Patel's house then slipped downhill and crashed into the Velez house. Flowing mud swept the sleeping thirty-six-year-old engineer from his bedroom into the garage, where he reportedly heard the Velez girls screaming below him. Patel's father was unable to pull him from the mire, and neighbors aided in the rescue. Working through the night, more than 36 firemen and policemen were unable to locate the children. Trained rescue dogs found their bodies the next day beneath tons of wet earth and wreckage.

In the La Honda region, a helicopter was used to search for a missing Bengal tiger. The 175-pound cat and its cage, in which it may have remained trapped, disappeared when a mudslide struck a farm.

Theodore Weaver

FOR FURTHER INFORMATION:

Goode, Erica, and Michael Harris. "Slide Peril in Sausalito." *San Francisco Chronicle*, January 6, 1982.

Turner, Wallace. "Floods and Mudslides Kill at Least 12 in California." *The New York Times*, January 6, 1982.

Wegars, Dan, and Michael Grieg. "3 Children Buried in House." *San Francisco Chronicle*, January 6, 1982.

1996: Yosemite National Park

ROCKSLIDE
DATE: July 10, 1996
PLACE: Yosemite National Park, California
RESULT: 1 dead, 14 injured

Just before dusk during the height of tourist season in 1996, a 200-foot section of a granite cliff shattered in Yosemite National Park. Boulders tumbled for 2,400 feet into the valley below and churned dust hundreds of feet into the air. The rockslide—and the powerful gust of wind it created—uprooted and snapped hundreds of pine trees, leaving a barren patch stretching for a quarter of a mile near the John Muir Trailhead. Falling trees killed a twenty-year-old Southern California man and seriously injured 2 young women who were celebrating their high-school graduation. The dozen others injured suffered from breathing in the granite dust, which settled an inch thick on the valley floor. A part-time employee recounted the event: "I was about a mile away when I heard this rumble. . . . it was like an earthquake and all of a sudden I saw this smoke." The dust was described as being ash-colored and so thick that one could not see a hand in front of one's face.

Throughout the night, rescue crews wearing surgical masks used trained dogs and fiber-optic devices to search for victims. Geologists explained the

rockslide as an example of exfoliation—when layers of rock separate from each other—and attributed the occurrence to the significant amount of precipitation in previous winters.

Theodore Weaver

FOR FURTHER INFORMATION:

Arax, Mark. "Yosemite's Fearsome Wonders." *Los Angeles Times*, July 12, 1996.

Corwin, Miles, and Carla Hall. "At Least 1 Dead in Huge Slide at Yosemite." *Los Angeles Times*, July 11, 1996.

1996: Oregon

MUDSLIDES
DATE: November 18-22, 1996
PLACE: Primarily Oregon, also Washington State
RESULT: 12 dead

Heavy precipitation in late November, 1996, caused flooding, mudslides, sinkholes, and collapsed buildings in Oregon and Washington. The results were numerous traffic accidents, 12 house fires, and 80,000 to 100,000 homes and offices without electricity. A hunter died when a tree fell on his mobile home, and an eighty-five-year-old man died when the roof of his garage collapsed under heavy snow. Road crews found an Oregon woman buried in her car after a mudslide washed over a road. People walked knee-high in water in Portland streets.

Rick and Susan Moon and 2 visitors, Sharon Marvin and Ann Maxwell, died when a mudslide ripped the Moons' house to splinters. "There was just a roar when it came," recounted Jeffrey Orr, who witnessed the event. The Moons' possessions, including jackets, running shoes, credit cards, and children's toys, littered the muddy area 300 yards above Hubbard Creek Road. The Moons' two children escaped before the house was struck.

A party of elk hunters rescued a logger, Jack Gillem, who was trapped in his truck, which had been tumbled off the road by a landslide. The rescue effort included sawing off the man's steering wheel. Stranded in the Umpqua River area, the hunters and logger broke into an empty house to take shelter for the night. Because roads were impassable, a professional rescue crew took Gillem and a man with a broken leg down the Umpqua River the next day on inflatable rafts.

At 1:15 A.M. on November 22, a voluminous sinkhole opened up on Interstate 5. The two back trailers of a three-trailer semi-truck fell into the 100-foot-long, 30-foot-wide, and 20- to 30-foot-deep hole after the cab and first trailer miraculously made it over. All the truck's wheels were ripped from underneath it. William Gress was at the scene waving his arms to warn an oncoming semi. Turning to avoid the hole, the truck ran over Gress's foot, which surgeons later amputated. The driver of a pickup that proceeded to crash into the sinkhole was able to walk away from his flipped vehicle.

Swift waters carried away a woman who was evacuating her rural house at 3 A.M. on November 20. The fifty-seven-year-old managed to grasp onto a tree branch and began yodeling to call attention to herself. She continued to yodel for over half an hour before rescuers with a searchlight discovered her.

Theodore Weaver

FOR FURTHER INFORMATION:

Mapes, Jeff, and Dana Tims. "Storm Claims Five Lives." *The Oregonian*, November 20, 1996.

"Severe Storms in Northwest Leave 12 Dead." *The New York Times*, November 22, 1996.

"Snow and Rain Bring Havoc to the Pacific Northwest." *The New York Times*, November 20, 1996.

Tims, Dana, Mark Larrabee, and Jonathon Brinkman. "I-5 Sinkhole Swallows 2 Trucks." *The Oregonian*, November 22, 1996.

Tomlinson, Stuart. "Snowfall Surprises Portland." *The Oregonian*, November 19, 1996.

"Woman Yodels as Flood Waters Rage." *The Oregonian*, November 20, 1996.

1997: Australia

LANDSLIDE
DATE: July 30, 1997
PLACE: Thredbo, Australia
RESULT: 18 dead

Just before midnight at Australia's Thredbo ski resort, a landslide, which may have been caused by an underground spring, crashed down upon 2 lodges, then stopped abruptly before demolishing others. A smell of sulphur accompanied the ground movement, which was described by one eyewitness as sounding like a fighter airplane taking off. The body of a woman who had been taking a walk with her husband was recovered fairly quickly. Occupants of neighboring lodges could hear the wailing of other victims, coming primarily from beneath the wreckage of the second lodge, which housed 18 resort staff members. However, nothing could be done to help those trapped beneath tons of debris and collapsed walls. "We could hear three voices. We tried to form a human chain and pull the rubble out, but as we did the cars teetering on the edge were in danger of coming down on top of us," recounted Glenn Milne, who was on vacation at the resort.

Danger of a second slide delayed 200 rescuers by over eleven hours, by which time the cries of the buried had ceased. Employing heat-seeking devices, workers picked with their hands through the precarious piles of wood, cement blocks, and dirt. Only 1 man was rescued: After sixty-four hours, Stuart Diver was lifted from where he lay between two slabs of concrete.

Environmentalists initially attributed the catastrophe to overdevelopment, but Professor Ian Plimer from Melbourne University and Russel Blong from the Natural Hazard Research Centre claimed the slide was natural and inevitable. Landslides are relatively common in the Kosciusko National Park, with notable examples occurring in 1992 and 1978, when rocks and dirt blocked and washed away roads in the area.

Theodore Weaver

FOR FURTHER INFORMATION:

"Landslide Kills 19 in Australia." *The New York Times*, August 1, 1997.

"Man Rescued from Landslide in Australia." *The New York Times*, August 3, 1997.

"Nature Blamed for Landslide." *The Times* (London), August 1, 1997.

"Ski Lodge Rescue Hopes Fade." *The Times* (London), August 1, 1997.

Lightning Strikes

(Weather Stock)

Lightning strikes fatally wound between 50 and 100 persons each year in the United States, mostly within the thunderstorm season that occurs during the spring and summer months. Lightning also causes tens of millions of dollars of damage each year by sparking large forest fires and destroying buildings and various forms of electrical and communication systems.

FACTORS INVOLVED: Chemical reactions, rain, temperature, weather conditions
REGIONS AFFECTED: Cities, coasts, forests, lakes, mountains, plains, towns, valleys

SCIENCE

A lightning bolt is a high-voltage electrical spark which occurs most often when a cloud attempts to balance the differences between positive and negative charges within itself. Lightning bolts can also be generated between two clouds, or between a cloud and the ground, although these conditions occur much less often. A lightning bolt is generally composed of a series of flashes, with an average of four flashes. The length and duration of each flash will vary greatly.

Thunder is caused by the heating of air surrounding a lightning bolt to temperatures as high as 72,032 degrees Fahrenheit (40,000 degrees Celsius), which is approximately five times hotter than the Sun, causing a very rapid expansion of air. This heated air then moves at supersonic speeds under a force ten to one hundred times normal atmospheric pressure, thus forming shock waves that travel out from the lightning at speeds of approximately 1,083 feet (330 meters) per second.

Thunderstorms are local rainstorms that feature lightning and resultant thunder claps; they sometimes produce hailstones. Much less often, lightning is created by snowstorms, dust storms, or clouds produced by volcanic eruptions or thermonuclear explosions. The explosive release of electrical energy within a thunderstorm cloud creates a lightning bolt, which is most often produced by accumulations of electrical charge within the same cumulonimbus cloud. Cloud-to-cloud lightning involves one cloud which is seeking an oppositely charged cloud to neutralize itself. Cloud-to-ground lightning involves a lightning bolt which is seeking the best conducting route to the ground, thus hitting lightning rods, tall buildings, and trees.

Thunderstorms occur when the atmosphere is unstable and moist air at the ground surface rises, creating several small cumulus clouds that initially dissipate while producing rain or electrical charges. As the clouds increase in size and combine, they surge upward and generate rain and lightning. The average storm produces five to ten flashes per minute, whereas larger clouds can produce electrical discharges of over a thousand flashes per minute. A single thunderstorm cloud has the potential to build up an electrical charge of approximately 1 million volts per meter, produced by the action of the rising and falling of air currents. This electrical charge is transferred through the cloud as raindrops, hailstones, and ice pellets collide with smaller water droplets and possibly ice. A falling stream of electrons creates a negative charge, which generally accumulates in the lower part of the cloud, with the positive electrons simultaneously creating a positive charge in the upper part of the cloud. Lightning is essentially the reaction that neutralizes these positive and negative charges.

Other functions of lightning are to enhance rain and snow formation, supply energy to tornadoes, and assist in the fixation of atmospheric nitrogen. Other forms of lightning include ball lightning, also called *kugelblitz*, a rare phenomenon in which round balls of fire appear, often near telephone lines or buildings. Heat lightning involves lightning seen from a distant thunderstorm which is too far away for the thunder to be heard.

American scientist Benjamin Franklin performed the first systematic study of lightning in the late eighteenth century, working from his hypothesis that sparks observed in his laboratory experiments and lightning were both forms of the same type of electrical energy. During a Pennsylvania thunderstorm in 1752, he flew the most famous kite in history, with sparks jumping from a key tied to the bottom of the damp kite string to an insulating silk ribbon tied to Franklin's knuckles. The kite took the place of a lightning rod, and Franklin's grounded body provided the conducting path for electrical currents originating from the storm clouds. Franklin's experiments proved that lightning strikes do contain electricity and determined that the lower parts of the clouds were negatively charged, with Earth providing the positive charge. Franklin's research also laid the groundwork for the implementation of lightning rods as a means of protecting buildings.

GEOGRAPHY

An estimated fifteen hundred to two thousand thunderstorms occur somewhere on the Earth's surface at any given moment. These thunderstorms are estimated to trigger approximately one hundred or more lightning flashes every second, which corresponds to approximately 8.6 million strikes every day and more than 3 billion every year. Lightning has also been known to occur within atmospheric storms on other planets within Earth's solar system, such as Jupiter and Venus.

Lightning occurs most commonly in warm and moist climates, with the hot and humid climate of Central Florida experiencing the highest occurrence of lightning strikes and the Pacific Northwest seeing the lowest occurrence.

PREVENTION AND PREPARATIONS

The National Lightning Detection Network was set up in the 1970's to assist meteorologists in locating and tracking thunderstorms and lightning strikes. This intricate computer network utilizes lightning detection images from orbiting satellites and other equipment which reveal precisely where severe storm activity is located, in addition to the exact locations where lightning has occurred and has possibly hit the ground.

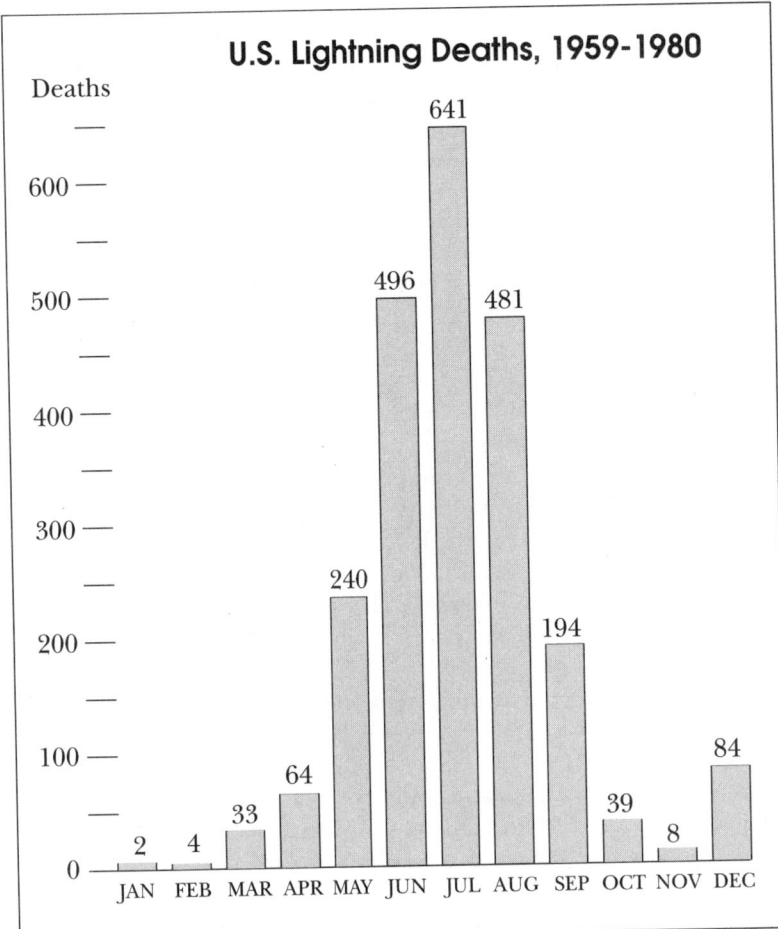

U.S. Lightning Deaths, 1959-1980

Deaths

Month	Deaths
JAN	2
FEB	4
MAR	33
APR	64
MAY	240
JUN	496
JUL	641
AUG	481
SEP	194
OCT	39
NOV	8
DEC	84

This graph represents the deaths caused by lightning in the United States by month from 1959 to 1980. Lightning strikes most often during spring and summer, when the air is warm and moist.

Thunder is an important warning signal by nature which reveals that a lightning bolt has just fired within approximately a 10-mile radius. The commonly used "flash-to-bang" method is effective in estimating how far away this most dangerous part of a storm is occurring. Once a flash of lightning is visibly observed, the number of seconds until thunder is heard is counted. The speed of light is 186,300 miles per second, thus enabling lightning to be seen immediately after it flashes. By contrast, sound waves travel about a million times slower at approximately 1 mile every five seconds. To estimate the approximate distance from the location of an individual to the lightning strike, one should divide the number of seconds between the "flash" and the "bang" by 5 to obtain the distance away that the lightning occurred in miles. If the lightning and thunder are extremely close together, one should divide the difference between the lightning and thunder by 360 to obtain the estimated distance away that the lightning occurred in yards.

Common sense dictates that an individual caught near a thunderstorm should seek safe shelter immediately, particularly if the "flash-to-bang" time is only ten to fifteen seconds, as this means that the lightning is only 2 to 3 miles away. Successive lightning strikes within the same storm can be used to determine if the thunderstorm is approaching one's location or moving away. If the time interval between the lightning and the thunder is getting progressively shorter, the storm is getting closer. If time between the lightning and the thunder is getting progressively longer, the storm is moving away from one's location.

The best defense against getting struck by lightning is prevention, in the form of examining the weather forecast before participating in any outdoor activities. Continually being on the lookout for clouds that appear to be forming into thunderstorms is critical, as is heading for shelter at the first sight of lightning or the first sound of thunder. The occurrence of thunder means that lightning must be present somewhere even if it is not directly visible, with the flash often hidden within thick clouds.

The best shelter from lightning is a large, permanently fixed, and electrically conductive building, staying away from windows and other breakable objects. Sheds and small buildings, particularly those constructed with wood and masonry and that do not contain a lightning rod, do not provide nearly as much protection. In the event that a building is not available, taking refuge in a motor vehicle with a metal roof can provide some protection, as the lightning current has a chance to pass harmlessly down through the vehicle and dissipate into the ground. Regardless of the structure in which a person seeks cover, it is important to refrain from touching any metal surfaces. Locations that contain flammable fuels, such as gasoline, should be avoided during a thunderstorm.

Persons are advised to avoid being exposed in open areas, high places, or near isolated trees during lightning danger periods. Those caught in the water during a storm, such as while swimming, have a much greater chance of experiencing electrical shocks in the event that lightning strikes an area nearby. Saltwater, a better conductor of electricity, is less dangerous than freshwater as the electrical current tends to flow around, rather than through, an individual or boat in the water.

Lightning rods are important protection devices required to be placed within all modern structures. They are made from metal strips that conduct lightning discharges through the building and into the ground. Arresters are often used in locations where power, telephone, and antenna wires enter buildings. Ground wires involve cables that are strung above other wires in an electrical transmission line, in the hope that they will become the preferred target for a lightning surge.

RESCUE AND RELIEF EFFORTS

The heavy currents of large lightning bolts have been known to shatter masonry and timber, and they often start fires. Lightning has been documented injuring critically or even killing persons talking on the telephone, taking a bath, or sitting near electrical units such as a computer. Cadaver studies on victims of fatal lightning strikes reveal that death can occur from heart damage, inflated lungs, brain damage, and burns.

For those who survive a lightning strike, immediate medical attention is necessary. If the victim is not breathing, artificial respiration can provide adequate short-term life support, though the victim may become stiff or rigid in reaction to the shock. Survivors of electric shock, from lightning or other sources, may suffer from severe burns and permanent aftereffects, including cataracts, angina, or nervous-system disorders. Amnesia and paralysis can also occur.

IMPACT

Lightning thunderbolts have long been feared by societies with beliefs in the supernatural, such as the Greeks, Vikings, Buddhists, and Native Americans. Science has confirmed that lightning is one of the strongest forces in nature, with larger bolts generating an average potential difference of 100 million volts of energy, approximately equivalent to the power contained in a middle-sized nuclear reactor.

Data collected by the National Lightning Detection Network reveal that lightning strikes kill an average of 75 people each year in the United States and injure hundreds more, mostly during the spring and summer months. Most fatalities occur from a direct hit, but electrical activity occurring along the ground following a severe strike has also proved fatal.

Lightning is also to blame for over 10,000 forest fires each year in the United States alone, with the total property replacement cost in the tens of millions of dollars. Lightning research greatly increased in the 1960's, motivated by the danger of lightning to both aerospace vehicles and the solid-state electronics used in computers and other technical devices. Commercial airliners performing a normal number of service runs are subjected to an average of one lightning strike per year, and in many cases the lightning is triggered by the airplane itself.

Daniel G. Graetzer

BIBLIOGRAPHY

Dennis, Jerry. *It's Raining Frogs and Fishes: Four Seasons of Natural Phenomenon and Oddities of the Sky.* New York: HarperCollins, 1992. Very readable manuscript highlighting lightning strikes and other natural phenomena within the atmosphere.

Gardner, Robert L., ed. *Lightning Electromagnetics.* New York: Hemisphere, 1990. Text applying examples from physics and electronics to the natural events occurring during a thunderstorm.

Salanave, Leon E. *Lightning and Its Spectrum: An Atlas of Photographs.* Tucson: University of Arizona Press, 1980. Document relating the physics principles behind lightning formation and its spectrum.

Uman, Martin A. *The Lightning Discharge.* Orlando, Fla.: Academic Press, 1987. Excellent description of the intricate process of lightning discharge in various environments.

Williams, Jack. *The Weather Book.* 2d rev. ed. New York: Vintage Books, 1997. An often-referenced text giving excellent descriptions of various weather patterns such as thunderstorms and catastrophic events such as lightning strikes.

Notable Events

Historical Overview

Lightning predicted a victory by Gilgamesh, Sumerian hero of an epic dating to the third millennium B.C.E. Zeus, chief god of the Greeks, hurled thunderbolts, and Thor, the thunderer, was the strongest of the Norse gods. Thunderstorms occur throughout the globe, even in Africa's Sahara Desert, and many societies have produced myths that associate lightning, a frightening and long-misunderstood phenomenon, with supernatural power. Thunder and lightning on Mount Sinai preceded presentation of the Ten Commandments to Moses. The Romans considered the location of lightning to be an omen favoring or discouraging personal and governmental business. Many cultures believed that objects struck by lightning held magical powers, but people's primary concern has been protection from the unpredictability of lightning, with its associated fire and destruction. Romans wore laurel leaves for protection, and, in the Middle Ages, European fire festivals sought protection for communities.

Simultaneously, rational explanations for lightning have encountered superstition. Greek philosopher Socrates described a storm as "a vortex of air." Aristotle theorized that a cooling and condensing cloud forcibly ejects wind which, striking against other clouds, creates thunder. He wrote, "As a rule, the ejected wind burns with a fine and gentle fire, and it is then what we call lightning." Greek historian Herodotus observed that lightning strikes tall objects, and Mongol law recognized the fatal association between lightning and water, forbidding washing of clothes or bathing during thunderstorms. Italian artist and scientist Leonardo da Vinci theorized that clouds forced together by opposing winds could only rise, and he thus connected storm clouds with updrafts.

Not until the eighteenth century was lightning associated with electricity, itself a little-understood phenomenon named in the late 1500's by Elizabethan court physician William Gilbert after the Greek philosopher-scientist Thales of Miletus's experiments with amber, or, in Greek, *electra*. During the seventeenth and eighteenth centuries, electricity and magnetism attracted experimentation and showmanship. Only when knowledge of European experiments and gifts of apparatus, including glass Leyden jars capable of holding and storing electrical charges, came to American Benjamin Franklin in 1746, did a theory of electricity emerge. Franklin determined that there was a single type of electricity, confirmed speculation that lightning was electricity and, in 1749, first proposed that metal rods could protect buildings and ships from strikes. His suggestions for construction, placement, and grounding appeared in the 1753 *Poor Richard's Almanac*.

Practical applications of electricity, beginning with American inventor Thomas Alva Edison's 1879 invention of a durable light bulb, and the subsequent problems of distribution along power lines vulnerable to lightning, encouraged lightning research. De-

Milestones

1769:	1,000 tons of gunpowder stored in the state arsenal at Brescia, Italy, explode when struck by lightning. One-sixth of the city is destroyed, and 3,000 people are killed.
1786:	The people of Paris make bell-ringing during thunderstorms illegal. The ringing of church bells was believed to prevent lightning strikes but often proved fatal to ringers.
April 3, 1856:	4,000 are killed on the Greek island of Rhodes when lightning strikes a church where gunpowder is stored.
1900:	The first quantitative measurements of peak current in lightning strikes are conducted.
1917:	The first photographic record of the spectrum from lightning using a spectroscope is made.
1918:	In Nasatch National Forest, Utah, 504 sheep are killed by a lightning strike.
1925:	The U.S. Weather Bureau applies sensors to airplane wings to record atmospheric conditions.
July 10, 1926:	Explosions triggered by lightning at an ammunition dump in New Jersey kill 21 people, blasting debris 5 miles.
1927:	French scientists produce the radiosonde, an instrument package designed to measure pressure, temperature, and humidity during balloon ascents and radio the information back to earth.
1929:	American scientist Robert H. Goddard launches a rocket carrying an instrument package that includes a barometer, a thermometer, and a camera.
1959:	The first meteorological experiment is conducted on a satellite platform.
1963:	The first quantitative temperature estimates are made for individual lightning strikes.
1963:	Lightning strikes a Boeing 707 over Elkton, Maryland, killing all 81 persons on board. This is the first verified instance of a lightning-induced airplane crash.
December 23, 1975:	A single lightning strike in Umtrali, Rhodesia (now Zimbabwe), kills 21 people.
1990's:	National Oceanographic and Atmospheric Administration (NOAA) polar-orbiting and geostationary satellites employ advanced microwave sounding units for improved storm intensity estimates. Weather satellites view entire storm systems, sense conditions of the ocean, measure temperatures at different altitudes, and provide humidity profiles of the atmosphere, as well as surface winds.

spite lightning rods on poles, lightning struck power lines and disrupted service. Solutions required accurate measurements of lightning voltage and speed of discharge, studies led by Westinghouse and General Electric engineers. German immigrant Charles Steinmetz built high-voltage generators to simulate lightning. Generators produced 50-foot bolts of lightning for New York World's Fair visitors in 1939, but laboratory apparatus could not equal the energy of natural lightning.

In 1925, Sweden's Harold Norinder, using the European-developed cathode-ray oscilloscope, measured a lightning-induced electrical surge of about a ten-thousandth of a second, and Americans measured lightning strikes on power-transmission lines of 5 million volts in under two-millionths of a second. Understanding the magnitude of the problem led to improved protection, reducing power failures.

Research leading to recognition of weather conditions likely to produce lightning, and knowledge of the location of lightning strikes serves military, commercial, and public interest and furthers technological advances. Practical applications of scientist Robert H. Goddard's 1929 Massachusetts launch of a rocket carrying a barometer, thermometer, and camera improved both World War II rocket design and television cameras. In 1959, scientists conducted the first meteorological experiment on a satellite platform. On April 1, 1960, the launch of the polar-orbiting Television Infrared Operational Satellite, TIROS-1, inaugurated the era of satellite meteorology. Capability expanded December 6, 1966, with the launch of the first geostationary meteorological satellite. Research begun at the University of Arizona in the 1970's evolved into the U.S. National Lightning Detection Network under Global Atmospherics Incorporated, the product of a 1995 merger, which supplies data to local forecasters.

As of 1995, lightning caused more deaths than tornadoes or hurricanes in the United States but far fewer injuries and less property damage. Despite advances in radar and satellite remote sensing and increasing reliability of forecasts, weather predictions warn only of the potential for lightning, and technology locates lightning only as it occurs. Public and private agencies stress public awareness and education in safety procedures to minimize exposure to strikes and fatalities.

Mary Catherine Wilheit

1769: Italy

DATE: 1769
PLACE: Brescia, Italy
RESULT: More than 3,000 dead

Designated the second-worst unplanned explosion in history (as opposed to intentional explosions set during wars or demolition activities), the Brescia lightning strike decimated surrounding communities. The modern capital of Brescia Province in northern Italy's Lombardy region, the city is traditionally known for its munitions factories, industries, and crafts. Brescia originally attracted pious residents who built churches. In addition to serving as places of worship and administrative centers for Catholic church leaders, these churches were used to store ammunition in the 1700's.

Most accounts state that the St. Nazaire Church held 100 tons of gunpowder in its vault. When lightning struck the building, the ammunition exploded, killing 3,000 people in Brescia. Approximately one-sixth of Brescia was razed by the blast. Some sources say that the state arsenal was the building that exploded, although this might have actually referred to the church's role as an armory. Eighteenth century people, instead of recognizing their conductive possibilities, believed that church bells could repel lightning, and thus used religious buildings to store valued goods. Scientists believe that floating dust inside the vault probably was ignited by lightning and landed on the gunpowder.

Elizabeth D. Schafer

FOR FURTHER INFORMATION:

Cornell, James. *The Great International Disaster Book.* 3d ed. New York: Charles Scribner's Sons, 1982.
Hewitt, Ronald. *From Earthquake, Fire, and Flood.* New York: Charles Scribner's Sons, 1957.

1807: Luxembourg

DATE: June 25, 1807
PLACE: A mountain in southern Luxembourg
RESULT: 18 dead, 40 injured

In 1807 a lightning bolt hit a gunpowder magazine in Luxembourg that exploded, causing damage in the area around the arsenal. Produced by a severe thunderstorm, the lightning caused the ammunition to ignite upon contact. The armory was located on a mountain in the southern part of Luxembourg. In 1807, Luxembourg was occupied by France, which dominated Europe as a result of Napoleon's conquests. Strategically important because of its position between France and eastern Europe, areas throughout Luxembourg maintained large stores of gunpowder and weapons in both buildings and underground passages. The fortress in the city of Luxembourg was especially strongly fortified and popularly known as the Gibraltar of the north.

The fortress section built in 1732 in the city quarter of Kirchberg was formally named for an Austrian commander in chief, Baron von Thüngen. A moat there may have attracted lightning strikes. Near the 1807 explosion site, two adjacent streets were razed by the impact. Several buildings were affected by shockwaves and fire resulting from the explosion. Approximately 18 people were killed, and another 40 individuals were injured. Three circular towers survived. The London *Times* reported the explosion one month after it occurred as a news item from Tonnigen that stated: "This city has been plunged into the greatest consternation and distress."

Elizabeth D. Schafer

FOR FURTHER INFORMATION:
"Tonnigen Mail." *The Times* (London), July 20, 1807, p. 2.

1856: Greece

DATE: April 3, 1856
PLACE: Rhodes, Greece
RESULT: 4,000 dead

Considered to have been historically the most damaging accidental explosion, the lightning strike on the island of Rhodes in 1856 caused extensive casualties and damage. Greek mythology includes numerous legends about weather, particularly about the god Zeus using lightning bolts to punish people. Controlled by the Ottoman Turks in 1856, Rhodes served as a strategic storehouse for weapons and ammunition during the Ottoman Empire's efforts to dominate the Balkans. Churches were appropriated

to keep gunpowder dry. Ironically, many piles of ammunition were never used militarily.

A lightning bolt ignited the combustible powder in the church of Agios Ioannis's vaults, resulting in 4,000 people dying in the ensuing explosion. This accounted for the largest number of casualties related to a lightning-derived explosion. Prior to the atomic bombs being detonated over Nagasaki and Hiroshima in 1945, the Rhodes explosion had caused the most deaths. Medieval sites such as Helion de Villeneuve's fourteenth century Palace of the Grand Magistrates, also called the Knights' Palace and Castello, located on the northwestern side of a Rhodes fortress, had survived invaders' sieges but were razed by the blast. Ancient sites such as temples to gods and goddesses were also affected. The palace and chapel were not rebuilt until 1939.

Elizabeth D. Schafer

FOR FURTHER INFORMATION:
Cornell, James. *The Great International Disaster Book.* 3d ed. New York: Charles Scribner's Sons, 1982.
Hewitt, Ronald. *From Earthquake, Fire, and Flood.* New York: Charles Scribner's Sons, 1957.

1926: New Jersey

DATE: July 10, 1926
PLACE: Lake Denmark, New Jersey
RESULT: 21 dead, dozens injured, $100 million in damage

A summer thunderstorm was the catalyst for an explosive nightmare at the United States Naval Ammunition Depot and Picatinny Army Arsenal in 1926. The naval reservation consisted of approximately two hundred magazines containing high explosives, such as dynamite. Around 4:30 in the afternoon, a lightning bolt hit one of the buildings. Smoke rose from the roof, a fire alarm sounded, and officers and enlisted men gathered to fight the blaze when the magazine exploded. The fire quickly spread to other buildings and to the adjacent Army site. A total of three explosions occurred, followed by showers of burning debris as far as 5 miles from the depot.

Commanders in New York and Washington, D.C., received reports and dispatched emergency crews, who were unable to access the area because of the thick smoke and exploding shells. Fortunately, several hundred civilian employees at the ammunition plant had gone home at noon. Search teams decided to scour the adjoining woods but did not find any victims. For forty-eight hours, the ammunition continued to explode. In nearby communities, houses were ripped from foundations. People were ordered to evacuate, including children at nearby camps.

As the haze subsided, shell-shocked soldiers began reporting back to duty. Some had been blown out of their boots. Shattered, crushed, and burned bodies were recovered and identified when possible by fingerprints. Survivors had shrapnel and concussion injuries. The blackened reservation with craters 30 feet deep reminded veterans of World War I French battlefields. This disaster resulted in Americans expressing concerns about local arsenals. Civilian and military damage claims skyrocketed to almost $100 million.

Elizabeth D. Schafer

FOR FURTHER INFORMATION:

"Explosions Ended; Two More Victims, One a Woman, Found." *The New York Times,* July 14, 1926, p. 1.

"Lightning Bolt Blows up Navy Munitions Near Dover, N.J." *The New York Times,* July 11, 1926, p. 1.

1957: Finland

DATE: July 13-28, 1957
PLACE: Helsinki, Finland
RESULT: At least 25 people killed

Although storms raged through Finland during a two-week period in July, 1957, minimal information about their impact was reported in international newspapers. *The New York Times* noted that approximately 25 casualties blamed on lightning strikes had been verified. The incessant storms devastated the Finnish countryside. On Saturday, July 27, a tornado produced by this storm system killed 3 people in the town of Imatra, near the border with the Soviet Union. Another 10 individuals were listed as missing.

Rural residents suffered extreme damage during the lightning storms, and many houses and crops were destroyed by lightning-sparked fires. Helsinki, Finland's capital, which had been rebuilt several times after historic fires, withstood the lightning storms. Forty years later, the Finnish Meteorological Institute was concerned with bizarre weather patterns similar to those experienced in 1957, such as an extended summer, premature snows, erratic rainfall, and tornadoes.

Elizabeth D. Schafer

FOR FURTHER INFORMATION:

"Lightning Kills 25 Finns." *The New York Times,* July 30, 1957, p. A4.

1963: Maryland

DATE: December 8, 1963
PLACE: Over Elkton, Maryland
RESULT: 81 dead

In 1963 the deadliest lightning strike to spark an airplane crash occurred. Pan American Clipper flight 214, a Boeing 707, was en route from San Juan, Puerto Rico, to Philadelphia, Pennsylvania, after a brief layover at Baltimore, Maryland, where seventy-one people disembarked. Gusty storm winds as high as 50 miles per hour from a cold front whipped the aircraft, and lightning illuminated the sky. Because of the weather and heavy aviation traffic, the Federal Aviation Administration (FAA) ordered flight 214's pilot to follow a holding pattern near New Castle, Delaware. While waiting for permission to land the airplane was struck by a lightning bolt. Air controllers heard the pilot radio a distress call before they lost contact with the aircraft.

Eyewitnesses heard, felt, and saw the airplane explode and plummet to the ground northeast of Elkton, Maryland. At the Merryland Roller Rink in Glasgow, Delaware, Helen Warner said, "We thought it was an atomic bomb." Others believed that the "orange glow" they were watching was a meteorite, then realized that it was a burning airplane. "There was a big flash and a few seconds later you could see the wing torn off," skater Jerry Greenwald explained. "You could actually see people falling out. The plane came down slowly, and when it hit ground it looked like it exploded again." Burning fragments fell in a field, setting corn stubble on fire and creating a large crater in the ground.

Large cities, with their tall buildings, often attract lightning. Because many airports are located in or near cities, lightning poses much danger to airplanes. (PhotoDisc)

Everyone on board, including 2 babies, was killed. The Civil Aeronautics Board conducted an investigation, determining that a lightning strike had hit the left wing near a vent that released flammable vapors. The lightning ignited the left wing's reserve fuel tank, then the other fuel tanks exploded, and the left wing was blown off. As a result of the first lightning-caused American air disaster, the FAA established a lightning-protection committee and developed requirements for lightning-repelling devices on aircraft.

Elizabeth D. Schafer

FOR FURTHER INFORMATION:
"81 on Jet Killed in Flaming Crash Near Elkton, MD."
   The New York Times, December 9, 1963, pp. 1, 40.
Witkin, Richard. "Bolt of Lightning May Have Hit Jet:
   Vapor-Filled Wind Panels Indicate Explosion."
   The New York Times, December 13, 1963, p. 69.

1975: Rhodesia

DATE: December 23, 1975
PLACE: Umtali, Rhodesia (now Zimbabwe)
RESULT: 21 dead

A lightning storm struck this gold-mining, agricultural, and commercial community on December 23, 1975. Residents rushed inside a hut for protection and to keep dry from the torrential rain. Several lightning bolts hit the hut, killing 21 people immediately. The casualties included 14 children. The Rhodesian police released information about the extreme nature of weather during late 1975 in that country: Between October 1 and the December 23 strike, approximately 53 people died as a result of lightning. Commentators noted that people living in southern Africa were more likely to be killed by lightning than by snakebite or attacks by other dangerous indigenous creatures. Rhodesia became the independent country of Zimbabwe in 1980, and Umtali was renamed Mutare.

Elizabeth D. Schafer

FOR FURTHER INFORMATION:

"Lightning Kills 21 in Africa." *The New York Times*, December 25, 1975, p. 43.

1995: Honduras

DATE: June 3, 1995
PLACE: Puerto Lempira, Honduras
RESULT: 18 dead, 35 injured

As Tropical Storm Allison moved through the Gulf of Mexico in 1995, thunderstorms produced by that system loomed over a Honduran athletic field during a Saturday soccer match. Fans gathered underneath a zinc-roofed shelter adjacent to the playing field in order to keep dry from the pouring rain. A lightning bolt struck the shelter, instantaneously killing 11 people, including 2 boys and 9 men who were Mizkito Indians. Dozens of people were injured, and 7 individuals later died from wounds and burns. Survivors said they initially believed that the strike was a bomb detonating. An eyewitness described his experience: "I felt like the ground opened up. My whole body was paralyzed, and I heard a loud noise in my ears."

A primitive, isolated fishing village, Puerto Lempira was difficult to access by land, and canoes and planes were used to evacuate victims to clinics. Cultural explanations for the disaster varied. The local police chief thought that witchcraft had created the lightning, and a priest claimed that the storm was God's retribution for people choosing to watch the soccer game instead of attending a community religious meeting. The Puerto Lempira tragedy was an example of how most victims are struck by lightning while participating in or observing outdoor sports.

Elizabeth D. Schafer

FOR FURTHER INFORMATION:

Chwialkowska, Luiza, Tamala M. Edwards, Sinting Lai, and Megan Rutherford. "Chronicles: The Week June 4-10." *Time International*, June 19, 1995, 9.

King, Jeanne. "Lightning Kills 16, Injures 22 in Honduras." *Reuters* press release, June 3, 1995, online at Electric Library, http://www.library.wisc.edu/.

1998: Democratic Republic of Congo

DATE: October 25, 1998
PLACE: Kinshasa, Democratic Republic of Congo
RESULT: 11 dead, dozens injured

During a soccer game in Kinshasa, a lightning bolt struck the field, killing an entire team simultaneously. Representing the village of Bena Tshadi from the province of Eastern Kasai, 11 players died. Approximately 30 observers were hurt and burned on the sidelines. The stricken team's opponents were from the village of Basangana; because no one on that team was injured, local investigators blamed the lightning bolt on witchcraft. The Congolese culture encouraged belief in sorcery. People often performed magical rites in attempts to sway soccer games. Most Congolese thought that witchcraft caused sickness and other calamities.

The Kinshasa newspaper, *L'Avenir*, reported that when the lightning struck, the score was tied at 1-1. Lightning also hit another soccer field in South Africa, where 6 players were wounded. The storm system triggered flash flooding that killed 1 child and swept away houses throughout the capital city of Kinshasa. The Nyamuragira Volcano was also erupting during this time, and political unrest intensified natural chaos; a rebellion against Congo president Laurent Kabila caused strife. A week after the lightning strike, soldiers shot spectators at another Kinshasa soccer match, and other African soccer matches were halted by violent fans.

Elizabeth D. Schafer

FOR FURTHER INFORMATION:

"Lightning Deaths." *Los Angeles Times*, November 5, 1998, p. B2.

"Lightning Kills Team." *The Times* (London), October 29, 1998, p. 20.

Meteorites and Comets

(NASA)

The effects of meteorite and comet impacts on Earth range from the insignificant to the greatest natural disaster humankind may ever face—the extinction of most of the life on Earth.

FACTORS INVOLVED: Chemical reactions, geography, gravitational forces, temperature, weather conditions
REGIONS AFFECTED: All

SCIENCE

The Moon viewed through even a small telescope is a spectacular sight. It is covered with craters. Samples brought back from the Moon prove that they are impact craters, not volcanic craters. Because Earth and the Moon are in the same part of the solar system, it follows that Earth has been subjected to the same bombardment from space that produced craters on the Moon. Having been largely erased by erosion, Earth's own cratering record is not so obvious. Earth's atmosphere protects it from the rain of smaller meteoroids, a protection the Moon lacks, but the fact remains that Earth has been hit countless times in the past, and no doubt it will be hit countless times in the future.

Objects that are out in space that might hit Earth include dust, meteoroids, asteroids, and comets. In modern terminology, a meteoroid is a natural, solid object in interplanetary space. A meteor is the flash of light produced by frictional heating when a meteoroid enters a planetary atmosphere. Particularly bright meteors are called fireballs or bolides (especially if they explode). Meteorites are meteoroids that survive their passage through the atmosphere and reach the ground.

Photographs of three meteorites during their meteor phase—from Pribram, Czechoslovakia, 1959; Lost City, Oklahoma, 1970; and Innisfree, Alberta, 1977—have allowed pre-impact orbits to be calculated. The orbits of all three were traced back to the asteroid belt. Beginning in 1969, various workers were able to match the spectra of meteorites with those of asteroids, and it is now widely accepted that most meteorites are chips from asteroids. A few have been identified as having come from the Moon or from Mars.

Rocky or metallic objects larger than about 328 feet (100 meters) across are called asteroids. They are so named because they look like stars—like points of light—in a telescope, but they have more in common with planets than with stars. It is believed that when the Sun first formed it was surrounded by a platter-shaped cloud of gases and dust grains. These grains accreted to form ever-larger objects, and the largest ones became the planets. Asteroids and comets are leftover objects that were never incorporated into planets. Asteroids larger than about 18.6 miles (30 kilometers) in diameter contained enough radioactive elements to melt their insides, allowing nickel and iron to sink to the center and stony material to float to the top. Over the eons, collisions among the asteroids have produced the collection present today. Nickel-iron asteroids are the remnant cores of asteroids whose outer, stony material has been chipped away. To penetrate deeply enough into Earth's atmosphere to cause severe damage, objects must be more than about 131, 164, and 328 feet (40, 50, and 100 meters) in diameter for metallic, stony, or icy bodies, respectively.

The main asteroid belt lies between the orbits of Mars and Jupiter. Further out in the solar system, beyond the orbit of Neptune, ice was the most abundant solid building material. (Here, ice means mostly frozen water, but it also includes frozen carbon dioxide, methane, and ammonia.) The solid part of a comet, the nucleus, forms from these ices mixed with silicate and hydrocarbon dust grains. An inactive comet looks much like an asteroid, but as a comet nears the Sun, vapor streams from the nucleus as the ices evaporate. Inactive comets are difficult to detect, but a large, active comet is a spectacular sight. The nucleus is surrounded by a vapor cloud 621,400 miles (1 million kilometers) across and has a gas tail up to 62,140,000 miles (100 million kilometers) long.

Asteroids or comets that may hit Earth are of obvious interest. Richard P. Binzel, a professor at the Massachusetts Institute of Technology, developed a scale to help scientists communicate with the media and the public about the perceived risks associated with these objects. This scale is named the Torino Impact Hazard Scale and was adopted by the International Astronomical Union (IAU) in 1999. A Torino scale 0 object is either too small to cause damage or will not hit Earth. Torino scale 1 objects will probably not hit Earth, but they merit careful watching. Torino scale 2, 3, and 4 objects merit concern, and scale 5, 6, and 7 objects are progressively threatening. Torino scale 8, 9, and 10 objects will hit Earth and are expected to cause local, regional, or global damage, respectively.

GEOGRAPHY

Any place on Earth may be hit by a meteorite; no location is particularly safe, but seacoasts are the most vulnerable. The 1908 Tunguska impact was a Torino scale 8 event with localized destruction. Had the Tunguska meteorite been just large enough to reach the ground intact, the destruction still would have been largely local. However, if such an object struck the ocean it would generate tsunamis that would cause widespread coastal destruction.

The impact of a Tunguska-scale object on the gla-

The Torino Impact Hazard Scale

Assessing asteroid and comet impact hazard predictions in the 21st century.

Events Having No Likely Consequences (White Zone)	0	The likelihood of a collision is zero, or well below the chance that a random object of the same size will strike Earth within the next few decades.
Events Meriting Careful Monitoring (Green Zone)	1	The chance of collision is extremely unlikely, about the same as a random object of the same size striking Earth within the next few decades.
Events Meriting Concern (Yellow Zone)	2	A somewhat close, but not unusual encounter. Collision is very unlikely.
	3	A close encounter, with 1 percent or greater chance of a collision capable of causing localized destruction.
	4	A close encounter, with 1 percent or greater chance of a collision capable of causing regional devastation.
Threatening Events (Orange Zone)	5	A close encounter, with a significant threat of a collision capable of causing regional devastation.
	6	A close encounter, with a significant threat of a collision capable of causing a global catastrophe.
	7	A close encounter, with an extremely significant threat of a collision capable of causing a global catastrophe.
Certain Collisions (Red Zone)	8	A collision capable of causing localized destruction. Such events occur somewhere on Earth between once per 50 years and once per 1,000 years.
	9	A collision capable of causing regional devastation. Such events occur between once per 1,000 years and once per 100,000 years.
	10	A collision capable of causing a global climatic catastrophe. Such events occur once per 100,000 years, or less often.

ciers of Greenland or Antarctica might melt 35,315 cubic feet (1 cubic kilometer) of ice, but that would produce only an imperceptible rise in the ocean level. However, the impact on Antarctica of a 6-mile-diameter asteroid, such as is thought to have killed the dinosaurs, could melt enough ice to raise sea level more than 230 feet (70 meters). Another environmentally sensitive site for a giant impact is a thick limestone deposit such as exists on the Yucatán Peninsula. It seems likely that the copious amounts of carbon dioxide released from the Yucatán limestone contributed to a warmer climate for thousands of years after the impact.

PREVENTION AND PREPARATIONS

The first step in meteorite prevention and preparation is to make a survey of objects that come close to Earth. These are called near-earth objects (NEOs). Under the auspices of the International Astronomical Union, the Spaceguard Foundation was established on March 27, 1996, in Rome. The foundation coordinates international efforts to discover NEOs. As of July 29, 1999, 760 NEOs had been discovered and their orbits calculated. The most dangerous of these are 184 potentially hazardous asteroids (PHAs). PHAs are larger than 492 feet (150 meters) in diameter and will come within 4.7 million miles

(7.5 million kilometers) of Earth. More refined orbital information should eventually tell whether or not they will actually hit Earth. As of July, 1999, there were no known PHAs with more than a minute probability of hitting Earth.

If it is discovered that an asteroid is about to hit Earth, can anything be done about it? The answer depends upon three key factors: the amount of warning time, the size of the asteroid, and the state of readiness of the space program. Taking the third factor first, there are normally no spacecraft on standby that are capable of reaching an asteroid. That means that if the warning time is only a few months, the only thing to be done is to evacuate the probable impact site, or to evacuate coastal areas if an ocean impact is predicted. Such an evacuation will be difficult and disruptive for a Torino scale 8 (local damage) object and will approach the impossible for a Torino scale 9 (regional damage) object. It would be incredibly difficult to evacuate the eastern United States, for example. For a Torino scale 10 object (global catastrophe), preparation efforts will be to provide food, shelter, and energy stores to maximize the number of survivors.

Once an asteroid is discovered and observed for a period of time, its orbit can be predicted accurately for fifty to one hundred years into the future. Deflecting the asteroid into a slightly different orbit becomes an option if there is a ten- to twenty-year warning time. Deflection is probably superior to attempting to destroy the object. Objects small enough to be vaporized with nuclear weapons are small enough to be destroyed by Earth's atmosphere. If an asteroid were not vaporized, but rather only shattered, by a nuclear explosion, the cloud of fragments would continue in the asteroid's orbit and still strike Earth. If there were enough fragments, or if there were large fragments, Earth would still be devastated.

Another solution is to explode a nuclear weapon above the surface of the asteroid. Prior experimentation and manned exploration may be necessary to determine how best to do this. Heat and radiation from the blast will vaporize asteroidal surface material, causing it to push against the asteroid like a rocket engine and thereby change the asteroid's orbit. Only a small change in orbit would be necessary if done far enough in advance. A neutron bomb would be the weapon of choice since neutrons would penetrate deeper beneath the surface and therefore launch more material into space than would the gamma rays and X rays of a conventional thermonuclear weapon.

If humankind were to develop sufficient spacefaring capacity, workers might land on the asteroid. Given enough time and an energy source such as a nuclear reactor, the orbit of the asteroid could be changed by launching rocks from a catapult device (mass driver) acting as a rocket engine. If there were sufficient water available, as ice in a comet nucleus, or combined in minerals as in some carbonaceous asteroids, steam rockets mounted on the object might be used to change its orbit. Three properties of comets make them more difficult to deal with: The vast majority can be discovered only months before their closest approach to Earth, and they are fragile and may break apart if one tries to maneuver them. They also travel faster than asteroids. Typical approach speeds relative to Earth are 9.3 miles (15 kilometers) per second for asteroids, but are 15.5 to 31 miles (25 to 50 kilometers) per second for comets.

RESCUE AND RELIEF EFFORTS AND IMPACT

If the damage from a meteorite were local, the aftermath would resemble that of other large-scale disasters, such as massive flooding, large earthquakes, destructive hurricanes, volcanic eruptions, or massive bombings. Rescue and aid workers would come from outside the area, but if a large city were destroyed, it would probably take days to bring sufficient resources to bear. As with the Tunguska event, most impacts occur in sparsely inhabited areas, but such events are expected to occur between once every fifty years to once every thousand years.

If the destruction were regional, it might take many weeks to bring in sufficient aid. During that time the tragedy would be greatly compounded. Such regional events are expected to occur between once every thousand years and once every hundred thousand years. If the destruction were worldwide, sufficient aid would not exist. People in steel and stone buildings might survive the sky becoming baking hot (because of the fiery reentry of debris) unless the air became too hot to breathe or too oxygen-depleted by conflagrations. Both Switzerland and China have large systems of underground shelters built for nuclear war, and many other nations have some shelters. Those who survive the initial impact, earthquakes, tsunamis, hot sky, secondary fires, possibly toxic vapors and gases, and rising sea level (from melting ice) will need food and energy to keep warm for a few months to a year until the worldwide dust cloud settles from the air and the Sun shines again. Then they will need crops that will grow in the new, warmer climate. They will also need to deal with greatly increased ultraviolet radiation from the Sun, plagues, and the breakdown of civilization. Yet, except in an extreme worst case, some people should survive. Global climatic catastrophe due to asteroid or comet impact is expected to occur once every hundred thousand years or less often.

Charles W. Rogers

BIBLIOGRAPHY

Burke, John G. *Cosmic Debris: Meteorites in History.* Berkeley: University of California Press, 1986. An engaging treatment of how science discovered the truth about meteorites.

Chapman, Clark R., and David Morrison. *Cosmic Catastrophes.* New York: Plenum Press, 1989. This book treats the K/T impact, in which a meteorite hit the earth 65 million years ago, and other disasters.

Cox, Donald W., and James H. Chestek. *Doomsday Asteroid.* Amherst, N.Y.: Prometheus Books, 1996. A good treatment of the efforts needed to locate and deflect potentially dangerous asteroids and comets.

Lewis, John S. *Rain of Iron and Ice: The Very Real Threat of Comet and Asteroid Bombardment.* Reading, Mass.: Addison-Wesley Publishing Co.: 1996. A good account of various impacts, including interesting, but less well-known, ones.

Sagan, Carl, and Ann Druyan. *Comet.* New York: Random House, 1985. An excellent book by this very successful husband-wife writing team. It explains what we know about comets and how we learned this. The book is easily read and profusely illustrated.

Steel, Duncan. *Rogue Asteroids and Doomsday Comets: The Search for the Million Megaton Menace That Threatens Life on Earth.* New York: John Wiley & Sons, 1995. A good book for the general reader on mass extinctions and the K/T impact, the Tunguska object, and early detection efforts.

Verschuur, Gerrit L. *Impact! The Threat of Comets and Asteroids.* New York: Oxford University Press, 1996. An excellent and authoritative popular work written by an active astronomer.

Notable Events

Historical Overview

Humankind's observations of meteorites and comets surely extend back to the times before recorded history. Some suggest that the ancient Greek myth of Phaethon's ride is based upon a close brush with an active comet. According the legend, Phaethon, son of the sun god, Helios, receives reluctant permission to drive the sun chariot across the sky. The inexperienced Phaethon drives too close to Earth and scorches it. To curtail further harm to Earth, Jupiter slays Phaethon with a lightning bolt. Helios reclaims the sun chariot, but in his grief, he refuses to bring light to Earth. All of this makes a fairly good description of a small comet rising in the east just before the Sun, a comet fragment producing a Tunguska-like fireball, and dust from an impact blocking sunlight. There is evidence for a destructive blast wave and for wildfires sweeping the Middle East four thousand years ago.

The Greek word *meteoros* means "high in the air." Some ancient Greeks considered comets to be meteors, that is, fiery gases high in the atmosphere. Others thought them to be "long-haired" stars (*astēr komētēs*), properly belonging to the heavens beyond the orbit of the Moon. Because comets often look like swords in the heavens poised to strike Earth, they were usually regarded as ill omens portending drought, famine, or war. Long ago, the term "meteors" also included rainbows, clouds, rain, snow, the aurora borealis, hailstones, and thunderstones. Thunderstones were unusual stones that were imagined to have been formed by lightning fusing dust in the air or by lightning striking the ground and launching stones into the air. Discovered thunderstones actually included some fossils, certain minerals, ancient stone tools, and meteorites.

Throughout history some people claimed to have seen stones fall from the sky, or they have found things they believed to have come from the sky. Certainly, an iron meteorite is different enough from normal rocks that its finder would seek a special explanation. The Assyrian term for iron meant "metal from heaven." The earliest-known iron objects were made from meteoric iron, and it is quite possible that working with this "sky metal" aided the Hittites in ushering in the iron age by smelting iron ore around 1400 B.C.E.

Several meteorites became objects of veneration because they were considered gifts from the gods in the heavens. The temple of Artemis at Ephesus housed a meteorite, and the stone of Emesa in Syria was regarded as an incarnation of the sun god, Heliogebalus. The most famous is the black stone mounted in the corner of the Kaaba in the court of the Great Mosque at Mecca. The black stone of the Kaaba is said to have fallen from the sky as a sign of the divine calling of the prophet Abraham.

By 1790 scientists had shown that most thunderstones did not come from the sky, and they supposed that none did. That supposition changed over a period of only ten years. In 1794 the physicist Ernst Florens Friedrich Chladni published a treatise exploring the evidence for a dozen falls—cases where the meteorite was seen falling and was then recovered. In 1802 the chemist Edward Charles Howard announced that the minerals and chemical constituents of several meteorites were similar to each other but different from terrestrial rocks. In 1803 the physicist Jean-Baptiste Biot reported on a fireball that dropped many stones at L'Aigle in Normandy, proving that meteorites did fall from the sky.

In the 1500's several astronomers noted that because comet tails always pointed away from the Sun, comets must be in heavenly realms and cannot be luminous gases in Earth's atmosphere. Tycho Brahe attempted to measure the distance to the comet of

Milestones

2.02 billion B.C.E.: An asteroid impact at Vredefort, South Africa, produces a 186-mile-diameter crater, the largest known on Earth as of 1999.

1.85 billion B.C.E.: An asteroid impact at Sudbury, Ontario, Canada, produces a 155-mile-diameter crater. Groundwater, upwelling through fractured rocks, eventually produces one of the world's richest nickel deposits.

65 million B.C.E.: A 6.2-mile-diameter asteroid produces a 112-mile-diameter crater on the Yucatán Peninsula. The associated environmental disaster causes most of the species then living, including the dinosaurs, to become extinct.

49,000 B.C.E.: The impact of a huge nickel-iron boulder forms the Barringer meteorite crater in Arizona.

1680: Scientist Isaac Newton notes that the comet of 1860 passes less than 621,400 miles (1 million kilometers) from the Sun and deduces that its nucleus must be solid in order to survive.

December 25, 1758: The first predicted return of Comet Halley is observed.

1794-1803: Scientists prove that meteorites do fall from the sky.

1861: Earth passes through the tail of the Great Comet of 1861 with no measurable effects.

c. 1920: The Barringer Crater is the first crater recognized to have been caused by a meteorite impact.

June 30, 1908: A huge boulder or a small comet explodes over Tunguska, Siberia, causing widespread destruction.

January 3, 1970: The fall of the Lost City, Oklahoma, meteorite is photographed, and its orbit is later traced back to the asteroids.

August 10, 1972: A house-sized rock forms a brilliant fireball as it hurtles through Earth's atmosphere and back into space.

June, 1980: Luis Alvarez and others at the University of California at Berkeley publish an article in *Science* presenting the hypothesis that an asteroid impact caused the extinction of the dinosaurs.

March, 1986: The nucleus of Comet Halley is photographed.

October 9, 1992: A meteorite smashes the rear end of a 1980 Chevy Malibu automobile in Peekskill, New York.

July, 1994: The impact of the fragmented Comet Shoemaker-Levy 9 on Jupiter is widely observed.

1577 and showed that it was far beyond the Moon, thereby settling that question. Sir Isaac Newton maintained a lifelong fascination with comets. He eventually proved that the comet of 1680-1681 followed the same laws of motion and gravitation that planets did. It was Edmond Halley who fired the public's imagination with his successful prediction of the return of the comet that carries his name. Noting that the comets of 1531, 1607, and 1682 had very similar orbits, Halley supposed that they were the same comet and predicted that it would return near the end of 1758— it did, on Christmas night.

Charles W. Rogers

Scientist Luis Alvarez, who theorized that a large meteorite destroyed most life on Earth in 65,000,000 B.C.E. (©The Nobel Foundation)

c. 65,000,000 B.C.E.: Atlantic Ocean

METEORITE
DATE: About 65 million years ago
PLACE: Yucatán Peninsula
CLASSIFICATION: 10 on the Torino Impact Scale; energy equivalent to at least 100 million megatons of TNT released
RESULT: Instantly destroyed most life within 621-mile radius and caused worldwide climate changes resulting in the extinction of up to 85 percent of species then living

A team of scientists led by Luis and Walter Alvarez, father and son, were studying the thin clay layer that lies between the rocks of the Cretaceous geological period and the rocks of the following Tertiary period. This boundary is designated the K/T boundary. (By convention, Cretaceous is abbreviated *K*. The letter *C* is used for the earlier Cambrian period.) Knowing that the element iridium is more abundant in meteorites than in earth rocks, and supposing that small meteorites fall at a more or less constant rate, they supposed that the amount of iridium in the clay would be a clue to how long it took to form the clay layer. To their great surprise, they discovered that the iridium concentration in the clay was three hundred times that of the rocks above and below it. In 1980, they startled the world with this result and with their theory of what had ended the reign of the dinosaurs 65 million years ago.

According to their theory, now widely accepted, a rocky asteroid 6.2 miles (10 kilometers) or more in diameter hurtled toward Earth at tens of miles per second. Plunging through the atmosphere in a few seconds, its energy of motion was converted into heat as it struck the ground, vaporizing itself along with a great deal of the target rock. The resulting explosion lofted 100 million megatons of dust and rock vapor into the air, much of it out into space. It also produced an earthquake 30,000 times more energetic than the San Francisco earthquake of 1906.

There is a huge crater about 112 miles (180 kilometers) across at Chicxulub, Yucatán. It is 65 million years old and is thought to be the impact site of the Alvarez asteroid. Fittingly, Chicxulub (pronounced CHEEK-shoe-lube) means "tail of the devil." Today, the crater is completely covered with surface rock. Further evidence of an impact is that all around the Gulf of Mexico there is a 65-million-year-old layer of tsunami-wave rubble 33 feet (10 meters) thick, including large boulders washed far inland. Shock-fractured crystals found in the K/T boundary layer are another key piece of evidence. While a large impact can form these crystals, volcanic activity cannot.

Shock and heat from the impact killed nearly everything above ground within 621 miles (1,000 kilometers). The vapor that was lofted into space cooled and condensed into rocky globules that reheated as they plunged back into the atmosphere all around the world. Their heat started forest fires worldwide. The amount of soot found in the worldwide K/T boundary layer shows that much of Earth's total biomass burned. Smoke from these fires combined with dust lofted into the stratosphere by the impact formed a worldwide pall that blocked sunlight for months, causing Earth to cool about 40 degrees Fahrenheit and photosynthesis to cease. This has been called "impact winter."

Heat from the fireball caused nitrogen and oxygen in the atmosphere to combine to form nitric oxide, which was lofted into the stratosphere, where it destroyed the ozone layer. Less than 2 percent of Earth's surface is covered with layers of limestone and evaporite 1.2 to 1.9 miles (2 to 3 kilometers) thick, but the Yucatán Peninsula is such a place. Vaporizing these deposits released huge amounts of sulfur dioxide and carbon dioxide. Nitric oxide and sulfur dioxide combined with water vapor in the air to form acid rain. There may not have been enough acid rain worldwide to be a serious problem by itself, but it did add to the environmental insult. As the dust cleared, "impact winter" turned to "impact summer," and the climate warmed about 40 degrees Fahrenheit above normal for thousands of years. These elevated temperatures were possibly due to a greenhouse effect caused by the extra carbon dioxide and water vapor in the atmosphere.

Which species became extinct and exactly when that happened remains somewhat controversial; however, the most complete studies support the hypothesis that the dinosaurs died because of the climate-

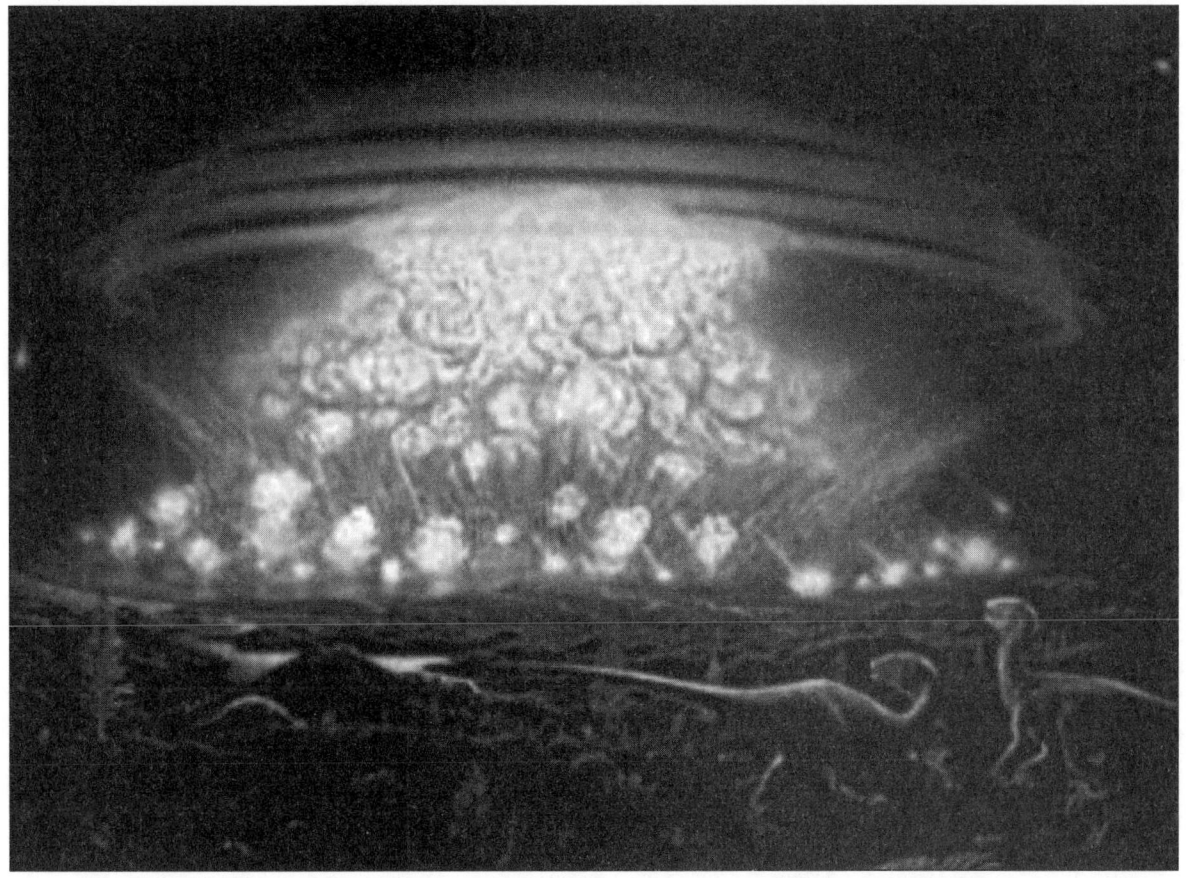

An artist's rendering of the meteorite that struck Earth 65 million years ago, wiping out the dinosaurs. (NASA CORE/Lorain Valley JVS)

changing effects of an asteroid impact. The general pattern is that species such as dinosaurs, whose food chain depended upon living plant material, became extinct. Species whose food chain depended upon organic detritus left in logs, soil, or water survived and eventually expanded into niches previously dominated by extinct species. Apparently, mammals survived on insects, arthropods, and worms until the sun began to shine again and plants to grow again.

Charles W. Rogers

FOR FURTHER INFORMATION:
Alvarez, Luis W. "Mass Extinctions Caused by Large Bolide Impacts." *Physics Today,* July, 1987, 24-33.

Beatty, J. Kelly. "Killer Crater in the Yucatán?" *Sky and Telescope,* July, 1991, 38-40.

Raup, David M. *The Nemesis Affair: A Story of the Death of Dinosaurs and the Ways of Science.* New York: W. W. Norton, 1986.

Verschuur, Gerrit L. *Impact! The Threat of Comets and Asteroids.* New York: Oxford University Press, 1996.

c. 48,000-13,000 B.C.E.: Arizona

METEORITE
DATE: About 50,000 years ago
PLACE: Meteor Crater, near Winslow, Arizona
CLASSIFICATION: 8 on the Torino Impact Scale; energy equivalent to about 20 megatons of TNT released
RESULT: At least 695 square miles (1,800 square kilometers) devastated

While most sources place the meteorite event about fifty thousand years ago, some place it as recent as fifteen thousand years ago. In what must have been a terrifying sight, a huge nickel-iron boulder about 151 feet (46 meters) in diameter (half the size of a football field) slammed into the ground at 11 miles (18 kilometers) per second (more than fifty times the speed of sound). Upon impact, the energy of motion turned into heat, vaporizing the huge boulder along with a good deal of the target rock. Within seconds,

Meteor Crater in Arizona. (NASA CORE/Lorain Valley JVS)

the explosively expanding vapor carved out a crater 591 feet (180 meters) deep and 4,003 feet (1,220 meters) in diameter. Bedrock was overturned to form the crater's rim. Globules of stone and iron formed as the vapor condensed. Such globules, along with nickel-iron fragments, were strewn throughout the debris. Numerous iron fragments, perhaps stripped from the main body before it struck the ground, were thrown into nearby Canyon Diablo—the "canyon of the devil."

The recognition that the crater was produced by meteorite impact was a pivotal event in science. Previously recognized craters, such as Crater Lake in Oregon, were clearly volcanic in origin, and it was assumed that the craters on the Moon were also volcanic. Grove Karl Gilbert, a leading geologist, supposed that it had been formed by an underground steam explosion. Meteor Crater was first known as Coon Butte or Coon Mountain, but it is most properly called the Barringer Meteorite Crater.

In 1902, a wealthy mining engineer named Daniel Moreau Barringer formed a company to mine the crater. The iron meteorites found in the area also contained nickel, small amounts of platinum, and some tiny diamonds. Barringer calculated that it took a 10-million-ton meteorite to make such a crater, and that such a ball of metal would be worth more than $250 million. While his company sank several shafts in various parts of the crater, looking for the buried meteorite, Barringer collected evidence.

Barringer noted that the rock beds beneath the debris of the crater floor were undisturbed and that there were no volcanic rocks in the area, so a steam explosion seemed unlikely. Iron meteorites were mixed with crater debris in a fashion suggesting they fell at the same time. He found millions of tons of finely pulverized silica, which could only be produced with the intense pressure of an impact. To answer critics who thought it more likely that a meteorite would make an elliptically shaped crater, Barringer showed that a high-speed rifle bullet made a round hole in mud even when fired at an oblique angle.

By about 1920, scientific opinion favored Barringer. In 1924, the astronomer Algernon Charles Gifford explained that the lunar craters were caused by impacts. The craters were round because large meteorites vaporize explosively upon impact. The mathematician and astronomer Forest Ray Moulton confirmed this for Barringer's crater in 1928.

Barringer was both vindicated and devastated. The crater had been caused by a meteorite, but the meteorite had vaporized—there was no mining bonanza. Barringer died later that year.

Charles W. Rogers

FOR FURTHER INFORMATION:

Burke, John G. "New Directions: 1900-1950." In *Cosmic Debris: Meteorites in History.* Los Angeles: University of California Press, 1986.

1908: Siberia

COMET OR METEORITE
DATE: June 30, 1908
PLACE: Tunguska, Siberia
CLASSIFICATION: 8 on the Torino Impact Scale; energy equivalent to at least 10 to 20 megatons of TNT released
RESULT: 2 dead, several nomad camps destroyed, more than 1,000 reindeer killed, 811 square miles (2,100 square kilometers) of forest flattened

Early on the morning of June 30, 1908, witnesses along a 621-mile (1,000-kilometer) path saw a fireball streak across the sky from the east-southeast. It was as bright as the Sun and cast its own set of shadows in the early morning light. The object exploded at 7:14 A.M., local time. Based upon seismic and barographic records, and upon the destruction caused, the explosion released energy equivalent to that of ten to twenty megatons of TNT, making it the most devastating cosmic event on Earth during historical times. Depending upon the altitude of the explosion and the composition of the object, the energy released may have been as high as 50 megatons.

Had the explosion occurred over New York City, fatalities would have been in the millions. As it was, the object exploded over a sparsely inhabited forest in Siberia, roughly 43.5 miles (70 kilometers) north of Vanavara, a small village on the Stony Tunguska River. The region is one of primeval forests and bogs inhabited by nomads who tend large herds of reindeer. Near the epicenter (ground zero), trees burst into flame. Farther out, a great shock wave felled trees over an 811-square-mile area, pointing them radially outward, bottoms toward, and tops away from the epicenter. Right at the epicenter where the force of the blast wave was directly downward, a bizarre grove remained. Trees were left standing upright, but they were stripped of all their branches, like telephone poles.

An eyewitness in Vanavara said the sky was split apart by fire and that it was briefly hotter than he could endure. Because it was just after the summer solstice, the Sun remained above the horizon twenty-four hours a day north of the Arctic Circle. Dust, lofted high into the stratosphere, scatted so much sunlight back to the ground that even south of the Arctic Circle, in northern Europe and Asia, nights were not really dark for three days. People were amazed that they could read, or even take photographs, in the middle of the night. At least 1,000 reindeer were killed, and several nomad camps were blown away or incinerated. Some nomads were knocked unconscious, but remarkably, there are only 2 known human fatalities. An old man named Vasiliy was thrown 39 feet (12 meters) through the air into a tree. He soon died of his injuries. An elderly hunter named Lyuburman died of shock.

Scientists supposed that the seismic waves had been caused by an earthquake, but no scientists went immediately to investigate because of the remoteness of the site. It was not until 1927 that Leonid Kulik, the founder of meteorite science in Russia, reached the site after spending many days plunging through trackless bogs on horseback. Expecting to find a huge crater and a valuable nickel-iron mountain, Kulik and his assistant were amazed to find only a shattered forest stretching from horizon to horizon.

Careful research has since shown that the Tunguska object shattered about 5.3 miles (8.5 kilometers) above the ground. If it were a small comet, it must have been inactive, for there is no credible evidence of a tail. It must have been at least 328 feet (100 meters) in diameter and had an asteroidal core, because microscopic metallic particles were recovered that are more closely associated with asteroids than with comets. Russian scientists favor this hypothesis. The object's trajectory and timing are consistent with it being a fragment of Comet Encke. Western scientists favor the possibility that it was a small, dark, rocky asteroid, perhaps 197 feet (60 meters) in diameter.

When a solid object of this size plunges into the atmosphere, it piles up air in front of it until the air acts like a solid wall. The object shatters, its kinetic energy is converted to heat, and the object vaporizes explosively. Microscopic globules form as the vapor condenses. Such globules have been recovered from peat bogs and tree resin at the site, as well as from ice layers in remote Antarctica. The cosmic dust cloud truly spread worldwide. These globules have more of the elements nickel and iridium than normal Earth rocks do—clear signatures of their cosmic origins.

Charles W. Rogers

FOR FURTHER INFORMATION:

Chaikin, Andrew. "Target: Tunguska." *Sky and Telescope*, January, 1984, 18-21.

Fernie, J. Donald. "The Tunguska Event." *American Scientist*, September-October, 1993, 412-415.

Gallant, Roy A. "Journey to Tunguska." *Sky and Telescope*, June, 1994, 38-43.

Smog

(AP/Wide World Photos)

Smog is a common component of urban life in many parts of the world. It was responsible for thousands of deaths after the widespread use of fossil fuels led to damaging emissions in local urban areas. Governments have responded by setting emissions standards in many countries.

FACTORS INVOLVED: Geography, human activity, temperature, weather conditions
REGIONS AFFECTED: Cities, towns, valleys

SCIENCE

Smog is one of the major atmospheric problems of modern urban life and is found in two varieties. Until the middle part of the twentieth century, smog was formed by the mixture of particulate matter and sulfurous compounds combined in the atmosphere in regions where coal burning was common. This type of sulfurous smog is commonly called gray air or "London-type" smog. With the increased use of automobiles and trucks, a second type of smog, generated by the impact of sunlight on pollutants, became prevalent in many urban areas. This second type is called photochemical smog and results primarily from exhausts of vehicles in urban areas that have certain meteorological and topographical characteristics. The general term "smog" is a combination of the words "smoke" and "fog" and covers both types of air pollution.

Air pollution formed by the burning of coal is not just a modern phenomenon. As far back as the thirteenth century, laws controlling the burning of coal were enacted to reduce the amount of smoke and haze that formed in London. However, the increased reliance on that common energy source produced more and more episodes of this type of air pollution in Europe and in other areas where coal was burned in quantity.

When coal is burned, large quantities of particulate matter are released into the atmosphere, and these particles can cause health problems when inhaled in sufficient quantity. These small particles also act as nucleation sites for water vapor to condense and form water droplets, leading to the formation of a fog. In addition, most coals contain a significant amount of sulfur, and, when burned, this sulfur is combined with oxygen and released into the atmosphere as sulfur dioxide. The sulfur dioxide may then combine with the water droplets formed on the particulate matter to create sulfuric acid.

Major episodes of sulfurous smog generally occur when certain topographical and meteorological features coincide. If the urban area is located in a basin, then the pollutants can be easily trapped if an atmospheric inversion develops in the region. An atmospheric inversion forms when winter anticyclonic conditions and low temperatures occur and little low-level atmospheric circulation is produced.

As a result, the pollutants are pumped into a basin sealed by a meteorologic "lid," and there is little to no dispersion of the particulate matter and sulfuric acid droplets. These meteorologic conditions may continue for days, during which time the resultant air pollution will worsen. The smog will be dispersed only if meteorologic conditions change such that breezes can move the pollution over the surrounding hillsides and out of the basin. In some areas, there is no topographic basin that retains the pollutants; rather, the input of pollutants is so great that horizontal flow is not fast enough to remove the smog. The classic examples of this type of smog were the London smogs of the 1950's.

Photochemical smog is formed in very different ways. This type of smog has been recognized since the 1940's in Southern California and is now common in many large urban areas. Once again, the major culprit in the formation of this type of air pollution is the burning of fossil fuels, particularly oil. The combustion of gasoline in motor vehicles and industrial plants produces a wide variety of exhaust particles and compounds. Particularly important in the formation of photochemical smog are hydrocarbons and nitrogen oxides. Through a series of complex chemical reactions, these compounds and others lead to the formation of photochemical oxidants such as ozone and peroxyacetyl nitrate (PAN).

The chemical reactions begin when nitrogen dioxide (NO_2) is split by the ultraviolet radiation of sunlight and the oxygen atom released by the reaction, then combines with oxygen (O_2) in the air to produce ozone (O_3). Ozone is a major component of photochemical smog, causing numerous respiratory health effects. In the absence of other compounds the ozone will decompose, releasing an oxygen atom that will combine with nitrogen oxide (NO), which was produced when nitrogen dioxide was split by sunlight. Thus, the concentration of ozone will generally not rise to high levels unless the latter reaction is not allowed to proceed.

Automobiles and trucks release large quantities of hydrocarbons during operation, and these hydrocarbons are degraded in the atmosphere by oxygen, creating volatile organic compounds. These volatile organic compounds then enter into a number of complex reactions with the NO and thus short-circuit the reaction of NO and ozone that keeps the level of ozone quite low. The reactions of the volatile organic compounds and the nitric oxide may produce numerous compounds, including PAN.

Whereas natural levels of ozone, produced in the absence of volatile organic compounds, may reach background levels of 0.04 parts per million, ozone levels in urban areas may reach over 0.2 parts per million, and levels over 0.6 were recorded in the Los Angeles area during the 1950's. These higher levels of ozone and other pollutants of photochemical smog are usually developed in topographic basins where an atmospheric inversion occurs. In the Los Angeles basin, the effect of descending warm air produced by regional weather patterns tends to seal the air mass into the basin and not allow even coastal breezes to push the pollutants over the mountains to the east and north. These conditions may last for several days and keep the polluted air mass within the region. Pollution will lessen only when the inversion disappears and the smog can be dispersed into the areas east of the basin.

GEOGRAPHY

Smog has been a significant air-pollution problem in Western countries for centuries because of the development of coal and, later, oil resources as major energy sources that fuel economic development. As a result, the most significant smog episodes have been reported in Europe and the United States. Smog has killed thousands of people in London, Belgium, New York, Pennsylvania, and other industrialized areas in the Western world.

However, photochemical and sulfurous smogs are not confined to the United States and Europe. The industrialization of many other countries and the increase in automobile usage worldwide have created the unwanted side effect of atmospheric pollution. Many of the most severe smog events now occur in Eastern Europe, Mexico, Japan, and China. The number of automobiles operating at the end of the twentieth century was about 700 million, and because the number was expected to climb to over 1 billion in the early part of the twenty-first century, it is apparent that the occurrence of photochemical smog in urban areas will continue to be a significant problem for many years.

PREVENTION AND PREPARATIONS

Governments have approached the prevention of smog in a number of ways. One approach has been to attempt to control emissions by establishing laws limiting the quantity of emitted pollutants. The United States, France, Japan, Canada, Italy, Germany, Yugoslavia, Norway, and Russia have established air-quality standards. The air-quality standards vary within these countries. In the United States, the Clean Air Act, enacted in 1970 and emended in later years, established national ambient air-quality standards, which set the permissible levels of six pollutants in the air. The six original pollutants were carbon monoxide, lead, ozone, particulate matter, sulfur oxides, and nitrogen oxides.

In many cases the Environmental Protection Agency (EPA) authorized states to monitor and enforce the regulations, which have been aimed at controlling emissions from large point sources, such as coal and oil-fired factories and utilities, in an attempt to reduce the emission of gaseous and particulate pollutants. The localized nature of these point sources makes the control of emissions manageable but often expensive.

However, the formation of photochemical smog is the result of emissions from millions of automobiles, trucks, and buses. Four approaches have been tried to reduce the emission of tailpipe pollutants. One approach has been to set emissions standards that all automobiles must meet in order to be licensed for

Mexico City in 1996. The bottom photo shows a clear day, and the top photo, of the same view, is of a smoggy day. (AP/Wide World Photos)

U.S. Air Pollution Trends, 1970-1997

In Thousands of Tons

Year	PM-10	PM-10, fugitive dust	Sulfur dioxide	Nitrogen dioxides	Volatile organic compounds	Carbon monoxide	Lead
1970	13,190	(NA)	31,161	21,639	30,817	128,761	220,869
1975	7,803	(NA)	28,011	23,151	25,895	115,968	159,659
1980	7,287	(NA)	25,905	24,875	26,167	116,702	74,153
1985	4,695	40,889	23,230	23,488	24,227	115,644	22,890
1990	5,425	24,419	23,678	23,436	20,935	95,794	4,975
1995	4,306	22,454	19,189	23,768	20,558	89,151	3,924
1997	8,428	25,153	20,369	23,582	19,214	87,451	3,915

Source: U.S. Department of Commerce, *Statistical Abstract of the United States, 1999*, 1999.
Note: PM-10 emissions consist of particulate matter smaller than 10 microns in size.

the road. Smog tests are required for cars, and those not passing the test must be repaired before use. Second, since the total emission is related to total gasoline usage, an increase in car efficiency would reduce pollutants. Miles-per-gallon standards have been established for automobile manufacturers, although these standards have been modified at times.

The third method of reducing emissions has been alteration of the fuel itself. Gasoline additives such as methyl butyl ether (MTBE) have reduced tailpipe pollutants by helping to burn the fuel more completely. Unfortunately, MTBE has been shown to be a groundwater pollutant and will be phased out of use; alternative compounds will be substituted to reduce emissions. Finally, general conservation methods such as carpooling and mass transit can reduce total fuel use and result in fewer emissions. These regulations have resulted in a great reduction in some of the pollutants—lead and particulate matter—but reducing the levels of the other air pollutants has been more difficult.

IMPACT

The health impacts of smog are various but are generally associated with respiratory effects. People most affected by sulfurous smogs are children, the elderly, and those with chronic obstructive pulmonary disease. Also affected are people with heart disease. It has been estimated that the London smog event of December, 1952, resulted in an excess of over 4,000 deaths above the average. Most of these deaths were attributed to pulmonary problems, with those having chronic bronchitis resulting in the highest number of deaths. In addition, a significant number died because of heart failure.

Photochemical smogs also affect the young, elderly, and the sick most severely. Epidemiological studies have not shown that photochemical smogs alone cause death, but the combination of smog and high temperatures has resulted in increased mortality. Because ozone is a gas, it most frequently affects respiratory function, and short-term exposure may lead to coughing, wheezing, shortness of breath, chest tightness, headaches, nausea, and throat dryness. The long-term effects of ozone exposure are not well understood, but there is some indication of scarring in lung tissue and the development of lung fibrosis. The primary eye irritants found in photochemical smog are PAN, peroxybenzol nitrate, and acrolein.

In the case of both types of smog the advice is the same. All people, particularly those most at risk, should restrict exposure to smog during these air-pollution events by remaining indoors and restricting exercise. Children are particularly at risk to smog because their air intake is higher per unit of body weight than that of adults, and they should be supervised appropriately during a smog event to reduce exposure.

Smog also has significant impacts on agriculture and forests. Ozone, a significant component of photochemical smog, causes an estimated annual economic loss of over $3 billion in the United States because of a reduction in productivity of crops. Particularly susceptible plants include tomatoes, spinach, pinto beans, and tobacco. Ozone and other oxidants also cause damage to forests. Significant tree loss or damage because of ozone has been reported in Southern California, Mexico, Israel, and Europe.

Smog can also cause damage to many consumer products. Stretched rubber exposed to ozone will rapidly degrade and crack, but damage is controlled by adding ozone inhibitors during the production of automobile tires and insulation. Other consumer products affected by ozone include textiles, dyes, and some fabrics.

Jay R. Yett

BIBLIOGRAPHY

Benarde, Melvin A. *Our Precarious Habitat.* New York: John Wiley & Sons, 1989. The author presents information on a wide variety of environmental problems, including smog. Good data are given on specific instances of air pollution and its effects.

Elsom, Derek M. *Atmospheric Pollution: A Global Problem.* Oxford, England: Blackwell Scientific Publishers, 1992. This is an excellent text on all types of atmospheric pollution and includes very informative chapters on smog and its effects. The book covers scientific, economic, political, and social aspects of air pollution.

Graedel, T. E., and Paul J. Crutzen. *Atmospheric Change.* New York: W. H. Freeman, 1993. The authors are primarily concerned with long-term climate change, but their book is a good introduction to physical and chemical processes of the atmosphere. Also contains an important chapter on urban air quality.

Keller, Edward A. *Environmental Geology.* New York: Macmillan, 1992. A well-written text that covers atmospheric pollution as well as other geologically important environmental problems.

Soroos, Marvin S. *The Endangered Atmosphere.* Columbia: University of South Carolina Press, 1997. All aspects of air pollution are treated in this book, which includes an informative section on gaseous pollutants.

Notable Events

Historical Overview

Air pollution has been a problem in some parts of the world since the use of coal and oil became important and common. As early as the twelfth and thirteenth centuries in London, the air became so polluted with smoke from coal fires that complaints were frequent, and in 1273 a law was enacted to reduce the amount of soft coal burned. This was followed in 1306 by a proclamation issued by Parliament requiring citizens to burn wood instead of coal in an attempt to rid London of the dreaded gray fogs that periodically caused illnesses and deaths in the city. However, the meteorologic conditions in southern England and the continued use of coal by industries and residents led to numerous smog episodes throughout the years. In the latter part of the nineteenth century, major smog events in London occurred in 1873, 1880, 1881, 1882, 1891, and 1892. An additional major air-pollution episode occurred in 1901.

Smog generated by the industrial use of coal and, later, oil continued to be a significant environmental problem in the twentieth century. In December, 1930, a very heavy fog developed in Belgium along the Meuse River. The fog mixed with the emissions from blast furnaces, fertilizer plants, glass factories, and other industries and created a deadly smog, which caused thousands to become ill and resulted in at least 60 deaths.

In 1948, Donora, Pennsylvania, experienced one of the most deadly air-pollution events in the United States. This area in the Monongahela River Valley was engulfed in a dense polluted fog for four days. The air was polluted with the emissions from coal burning as well as those from a zinc smelter and a steel mill. This stew of air pollutants was responsible for approximately one-half of Donora's population becoming ill and about 20 deaths.

Beginning in the early 1940's in Southern California a new type of smog was recognized. Photochemical reactions produced a type of air pollution that consisted of ozone and other irritants. Initially, it was thought that this smog was produced in much the same manner as those smogs of London or New York. In Los Angeles, politicians thought that the smog could be eliminated within just a few months by restricting the emissions of a number of industries in the city. However, these controls were not successful. In 1949 the role of automobiles in the production of photochemical smog became evident, when such a smog developed in Berkeley, California, where there were no major industrial plants. Fans attempting to reach a football game at the University of California there were stalled in a massive traffic jam, and the idling cars released emissions that were converted into smog.

During the 1950's and 1960's London and New York City continued to suffer very severe, deadly air pollution episodes. Over 4,000 people died in London in December, 1952, and another 1,000 people were killed by smog in the same city in 1956. Killing smogs occurred in New York City in 1953, 1963, and 1966. At least 500 people died from these smog events.

The widespread nature of smog became more evident beginning the 1970's and continuing throughout the remainder of the century. China revealed the heavy toll air pollution had on its population in large cities. It was reported that about 3,500 people died per year in the city of Wuhan alone and that many other Chinese cities suffered severely from the smogs created by the burning of coal.

Milestones

12th and 13th centuries:	Air pollution in London is caused by extensive burning of coal.
1273:	A law passes in London to restrict the burning of soft coal in an attempt to improve air quality in the area.
1306:	England's Parliament issues a proclamation requiring citizens to burn wood instead of coal in order to improve local air quality.
December, 1873:	An air-pollution event in London kills between 270 and 700 people.
February, 1880:	Approximately 1,000 people die in London from an air-pollution event.
December, 1892:	A smog episode kills 1,000 people in London.
December, 1930:	A thick fog settles in the industrialized area along the Meuse River in Belgium and is trapped for three days; thousands of people become ill and 60 die.
1943:	A major smog episode in Los Angeles leads local officials to begin to look at regulations to reduce air pollution.
December, 1948:	Smog accumulates over Donora, Pennsylvania, and is trapped in the valley of the Monongahela River for four days, resulting in 18 deaths above the expected number.
November, 1949:	A smog forms in Berkeley, California, from the exhaust of automobiles being driven into the area for a football game.
December, 1952:	A dense fog develops over London and remains stagnant for five days, leading to 4,000 deaths above the expected number for that time interval.
1953:	Smog accumulates in New York City, causing at least 200 deaths.
1956:	A severe smog episode in London leads to the deaths of 1,000 people.
November, 1956:	At least 46 people die in a smog episode in New York City.
1962:	Over 700 people die in a smog event in London.
December, 1962:	60 people die from smog in Osaka, Japan.
January-February, 1963:	Smog kills up to 400 people in New York City.
1966:	A four-day smog event in New York City results in the death of 80 people; Governor Nelson A. Rockefeller declares a state of emergency.
1970's:	Severe smog conditions are recognized in many Chinese cities; death rates as high as 3,500 people per year are reported in some areas in 1979.
1980's-1990's:	Reports of increase of deadly air pollution conditions in Eastern Europe, Mexico, and China.

Air pollution has been extremely damaging in Eastern Europe, although the exact nature of all the damage is not yet known. In addition, Mexico, particularly Mexico City, suffered extreme air pollution in the latter part of the twentieth century. The increasing development of Third World countries will, in all probability, lead to more frequent damaging smog episodes.

Jay R. Yett

1943: Black Wednesday

DATE: September 8, 1943
PLACE: Los Angeles, California
RESULT: Hundreds hospitalized

The city of Los Angeles had been largely free of significant air pollution prior to the 1930's. Two factors contributed to the change: the significant increase in the population of the region beginning in the 1930's and the burgeoning war industry, as defense plants were established in the Los Angeles area.

Between 1940 and 1943, manufacturing employment increased from 150,000 to nearly 450,000 persons. In 1942, in response to the need for synthetic rubber, the Rubber Reserve Corporation converted a facility of the gas company near downtown Los Angeles for the production of butadiene, a petroleum derivative essential to production of a synthetic rubber. No pollution controls of significance were included in the conversion.

The gentle southerly winds that had previously contributed to the ideal climate of Los Angeles now served to blow smoke both from the plant and from automotive emissions into the region between the San Gabriel Mountains on the east and the Pacific Ocean to the west. A blanket of hot air began to lie over the city, preventing the smog from moving.

By July, 1943, the atmosphere over the Los Angeles area had absorbed all the pollutants it could hold. On July 26, and again on September 8, a pall of smoke and fumes settled over the region. Unlike the pollution later observed in London, the problem was not due to the burning of coal. Rather, it was a large quantity of oxidants produced from automobiles and from the rubber plant. The smog consisted of acrid fumes that burned the eyes and made it difficult to breathe. It was also unusual in that the smog formed during the day. Eventually it was established that the immediate cause of oxidant production resulted from sunlight reacting with various automotive emissions, creating ozone.

In response to the smog problem, the rubber plant installed, at considerable expense, a number of pollution controls. The effect was minimal, as some 45 smog alerts were reported in the next two years alone. The problem was exacerbated by local laws that allowed industry immunity from government controls if their activities were considered "reasonable and necessary." Eventually, other pollution-control measures were passed. While the problem of smog would remain in Los Angeles, the city and the state represent prototypes of both the air-pollution problem and attempts to bring it under control.

Richard Adler

FOR FURTHER INFORMATION:
Brienes, Marvin. "Smog Comes to Los Angeles." *Historical Society of Southern California* 58, no. 4 (1976): 515-531.
Lewis, Howard. *With Every Breath You Take.* New York: Crown, 1965.

1948: Pennsylvania

DATE: October 26-31, 1948
PLACE: Donora, Pennsylvania
RESULT: 20 dead, more than 5,900 injured

Donora, Pennsylvania, is situated in the west-central portion of the state about 30 miles south of Pittsburgh, in a horseshoe-shaped valley created by the path of the Monongahela River. In the period surrounding World War II, the major employment was heavy industry. Numerous plants produced products such as steel, wire, zinc, and sulfuric acid. The riverfront contained a continuous string of steel-, zinc-, and acid-producing mills along a 3-mile stretch of the river. Rows of smokestacks continually belched smoke of varied colors.

During the late summer and fall of 1948, a stagnant high-pressure system of air settled over much of the eastern portion of the United States, including most of Pennsylvania. The result was an inversion in the atmosphere, preventing the movement of air currents and the accumulation of pollutants in the lower atmosphere. The physical character of Donora contributed to the problem. The town is situated beneath bluffs and hills on all sides, contributing to the stagnation of air.

The disaster in Donora began early in the day of Tuesday, October 26, as accumulation of moisture in the air created extensive fog. The upper layer of the fog absorbed enough sunlight to warm significantly and trap any pollutants near the ground. The smog began to deposit itself as a greasy black coating on the surface of the soil. Within two days, the smog was so thick that it was impossible to see across the street. Cars and trucks had to use headlights even during the day. Despite a strong odor of sulfur dioxide, most citizens of the town were unaware of the danger. The pervasiveness of the smell was so common that its significance was overlooked. Crowds watching a Halloween parade on Friday, October 29, had to breathe through handkerchiefs; parade marchers themselves appeared as if in a fog. It was only on Saturday, the 30th, when high school football players during a game in front of a large crowd began to become ill, that people recognized the significance of the pollution. That evening, health officials began to organize emergency services.

Seventeen persons died that Saturday from illnesses related to the pollution. The Red Cross and the local chapter of the American Legion established aid stations in the community center. Volunteers from the community and the local fire department administered oxygen to those who came to the center. Nevertheless, during the following week another 13 citizens died from the effects of the smog. Approximately 45 percent of the town's population eventually became ill.

On Sunday, heavy rains washed the air, cleansing the atmosphere of pollutants. The tragedy in Donora represented the first known air-pollution disaster in the United States. As a result, the Pennsylvania health department, after an extensive investigation lasting over a year, began to establish air standards in the hope of averting similar disasters.

Richard Adler

FOR FURTHER INFORMATION:

Lewis, Howard. *With Every Breath You Take.* New York: Crown, 1965.

1952: The Great London Fog

DATE: December 4-8, 1952
PLACE: London, England
RESULT: More than 4,000 dead

The city of London is situated along the valley created by the Thames River. On the afternoon of Thursday, December 4, 1952, a high-pressure air mass encompassed the Thames Valley in which the city is located. Cold air moving westward from the European continent displaced a warm air mass that had settled over much of London, creating an inversion in the atmosphere and trapping the gases created both by industry and by coal-burning heaters in homes.

That evening the chill resulted in many Londoners piling extra soft coal in their furnaces. The result was an increased buildup of smoke, soot, and sulfur dioxide in the air. By the morning of the 5th, a dense pall had settled over most of the city. As the day progressed, the fog became so thick that public transportation was suspended, even in the suburbs. Traffic backed up, and motorists began to abandon their cars. All river traffic came to a halt.

Because of the cold temperatures, coal fires continued to burn in the homes, creating even more smoke and pollutants in the now completely still air. By Sunday the 7th, the cover had become so dense that sunlight could not even penetrate most areas. The smog was situated over an area covering hundreds of square miles; all traffic remained at a halt as visibility was reported to be less than 5 yards on most roads. In addition to the difficulties in breathing for many individuals, the heavy smog contributed to numerous accidents. A commuter train ran over a gang of workmen, killing 2. On Monday the 8th, two commuter trains collided near London Bridge.

The first evidence for the deadliness of the fog came on Friday, December 5. At the London livestock exhibition, it became necessary to slaughter a prize heifer that began to suffocate from the soot-laden air. Other cattle were saved only when their owners placed over their faces improvised gas masks made from whiskey-soaked grain sacks. By that evening, physicians began to observe a sharp rise in patients suffering respiratory distress, usually presenting as an irritating cough, but sometimes including vomiting and black phlegm expelled while coughing.

Hospital admissions rose to four times the normal level by the third day of the smog. Coroners began to report a significant increase in the number of deaths they were called to investigate; an unusual number involved persons who were either sleeping or sitting quietly while reading or sewing. On both Sunday and Monday, the reported number of deaths in the city was triple the normal average.

By Tuesday the 9th, the fog began to lift as fresher air entered the city. Nevertheless, delayed effects from the smog continued to result in an increase in the number of deaths. A conservative estimate as to the total number of deaths directly attributable to the smog was approximately 4,000. However, excess deaths continued for some twelve weeks after the "Great London Fog," and the total number of dead may have reached as high as 8,000.

In response to the tragedy, London began to set in place a smog-control program. The Clean Air Act, passed in 1956, allowed local governments to take emergency measures in quickly dealing with potential disasters. Coal as a source of heat was gradually replaced. Although heavy buildup of smog would continue to occur at intervals, the number of deaths that occurred in the 1952 disaster was never approached again.

Richard Adler

FOR FURTHER INFORMATION:

Lewis, Howard. *With Every Breath You Take*. New York: Crown, 1965.

Wise, William. *Killer Smog: The World's Worst Air Pollution Disaster*. Chicago: Rand McNally, 1968.

1962: London

DATE: December 3-7, 1962
PLACE: London, England
RESULT: 106 dead, more than 1,000 hospitalized

Beginning Monday night, December 3, 1962, the worst London fog in ten years began to envelope the area. As with the deadly fog of 1952, a thermal inversion and lack of wind combined to concentrate pollutants in the atmosphere at close to ground level.

The 1962 tragedy began when two giant concentrations of fog descended simultaneously on the London area. The first, some 60 miles in width, passed over the Hampshire coast south of the city, moving northward toward the Essex marshes. The second fog bank, approximately 70 miles wide, came from west of London, through the industrial regions, into Yorkshire. Additional areas of fog appeared as far north as Scotland.

The pollutants consisted of a combination of smoke and sulfur dioxide. Much industry was concentrated within the city of London; also, many of the homes in the city were still being heated through the burning of coal. According to calculations released by the Department of Scientific and Industrial Research, in the twenty-four hours following the convergence of the two fog belts the level of smoke in the atmosphere was twelve times higher than average, and the levels of sulfur dioxide were nearly nine times higher than average. Such levels approached those found during the "killer" fog of 1952.

The sulfurous smog created a pall over the city, which made it nearly impossible to see anything more than a short distance away. London's airports were closed, and even trains were delayed hours in leaving the yards. Highways were littered with abandoned cars. In the first three days, over 60 people were reported to have died from the pollution in the air.

In response to the fog, homeowners were asked to burn coke instead of coal and to refrain from burning rubbish or making other fires. Industrial plants were temporarily closed. Hospitals worked under emergency conditions.

By December 7, the fog began to lift as a weather front passed over the island, dissipating the fog. The number of deaths ultimately credited to the fog was reported at 106, with approximately 1,000 more hospitalized. While the death toll was higher than average, the passage of the Clean Air Act of 1956, which reduced the number of coal fires, was credited with keeping the number of victims far below that of 1952.

Richard Adler

FOR FURTHER INFORMATION:

Lewis, Howard. *With Every Breath You Take*. New York: Crown, 1965.

Middleton, Drew. "At Least 55 Die as Fume-Laden Fog Cripples Britain." *The New York Times*, December 6, 1962, p. A1.

The New York Times, December 8, 1962, p. C3.

Tornadoes

(National Oceanic and Atmospheric Administration)

Tornadoes are violent, funnel-shaped whirlwinds that extend downward from thunderstorm clouds. Each year, hundreds of tornadoes touch down worldwide, causing billions of dollars in damage and claiming many lives.

FACTORS INVOLVED: Geography, temperature, weather conditions, wind
REGIONS AFFECTED: Cities, coasts, forests, mountains, plains, towns, valleys

SCIENCE

A tornado is a violently rotating column of air in contact with the ground and extending from the base of a thunderstorm or a towering cumulus cloud. A condensation funnel does not need to reach the ground or even be visible for a tornado to be present. A waterspout is a tornado occurring over water. The word "tornado," a hybrid of the Spanish *tronada* (thunderstorm) and *tornar* (to turn), appeared in sixteenth and seventeenth century English writings but referred to a tropical Atlantic thunderstorm, often with torrential rain and sudden violent gusts (probably a hurricane). Eighteenth and nineteenth century Americans called tornadoes "whirlwinds" or "cyclones." Not until the twentieth century did the word "tornado" define a vortex over land.

A tornado is usually a white, gray, black, or invisible funnel-shaped cloud, but some tornadoes may resemble a wall of smoke rolling across the landscape. Path widths vary from a few yards to more than a mile; path lengths, averaging 4.5 miles, range from 0.25 mile to more than 200 miles. In the United States, the storms move most often from southwest to northeast or west to east at ground speeds from nearly stationary to 70 miles per hour. A tornado may last from a few minutes to more than an hour. Winds in tornadoes generally whirl in a counterclockwise (cyclonic) direction in the Northern Hemisphere and a clockwise (anticyclonic) direction in the Southern Hemisphere, although about one in one thousand whirls in the opposite direction. Scientists do not know the minimum pressure within a tornado but estimate that it may be as low as 60 percent of normal air pressure, or about 600 millibars of mercury. Witnesses have variously described the sound of a tornado as like a freight train, a jet airplane, or a high-pitched squeal.

Wind speeds range from below hurricane strength (75 miles per hour) to more than 300 miles per hour, but about 70 percent of tornadoes produce winds of less than 110 miles per hour. The appearance of a tornado is not an indication of its intensity. No instrument to measure wind speed has ever survived a strong tornado. Theodore Fujita at the University of Chicago devised a tornado rating scale, called the Fujita scale or F-scale, which examines structural damage to assess the wind speed of a tornado. Meteorologists and engineers assign each U.S. tornado a rating, from F0 to F5, based on the single most intense example of damage in its path. Only 2 percent of tornadoes have received an F4 or F5 rating, but they have caused 70 percent of deaths. An F5 tornado is extremely rare; only twenty of the more than twenty-seven thousand tornadoes from 1970 through 1998 received that rating.

The Fujita Scale

Rating	Strength	Wind Speeds	Damage Levels
F0	weak	40-72 mph	light damage
F1	weak	73-112 mph	moderate damage
F2	strong	113-157 mph	considerable damage
F3	strong	158-206 mph	severe damage
F4	violent	207-260 mph	devastating damage
F5	violent	261-318 mph	incredible damage

Although tornadoes can appear at any hour of the day, most form between noon and 9 P.M., peaking between 5 and 6 P.M. The majority of tornadoes occur in spring and summer, but they have occurred during every month of the year. A tornado has a distinct life cycle. It is usually born as a thin funnel descending from a parent thunderstorm cloud. As it matures and expands, the rotating column of air picks up material in its path and acquires the color of the circulating debris. In its dying stage the funnel may appear as a long, thin rope. A tornado is capable of massive destruction during all stages. Some tornadoes have multiple vortices, or several small funnels rotating around a central axis. Occasionally, a tornado "outbreak" occurs, when a single weather system produces numerous tornadoes in one day.

Annually, the United States is home to about 100,000 individual thunderstorms; about 1,000 of them produce a tornado. Conditions for formation of a tornadic thunderstorm exist when a layer of warm, moist air becomes trapped beneath a layer of cold, dry air by an intervening layer of warm, dry air. If a cold front or disturbance in the upper levels of the atmosphere disturbs the delicate layering, the warm, moist air pushes upward through the cold air. As the thunderstorm develops, winds of different speeds and directions at varying heights in the atmosphere create an invisible, horizontal spinning effect near the earth's surface, much like a rolling pin moving across a table. The rising warm air tilts the rotating air from horizontal to vertical (stands the rolling pin on end while it is still turning), producing an area of rotation about 2 to 6 miles in diameter within the storm.

Tornadoes appear from this rotating area, called a mesocyclone, but not all mesocyclones produce tornadoes. A majority of tornadoes form in conjunction with cold fronts, but in the central plains many tornadoes develop along a dryline, the dividing line between very moist warm air to the east and hot dry air to the west. Both cold fronts and drylines can produce supercell thunderstorms with clouds towering to 50,000 feet or higher. Supercells produce most of the violent tornadoes. Tornadoes also form when tropical storms or hurricanes move over land, but these tornadoes are usually weak. Scientists have not found the last piece of the puzzle, the exact mechanism that triggers the formation of a tornado.

The capricious nature of tornadoes is well documented. Tornadoes have completely destroyed a house but left food on a table untouched or leveled one house and left the neighboring one intact. The howling winds have carried people and objects great distances and deposited them back to earth unhurt.

They commonly drive blades of grass or splinters of wood into trees or houses.

Tornado myths abound. One says that areas near lakes, rivers, and mountains are safe from tornadoes, but in reality these barriers have no effect on tornadoes. They have traveled across lakes and up and down mountains; more than thirty tornadoes have crossed the Mississippi River. Other myths include that tornadoes are always preceded by hail, mobile homes attract tornadoes, and opening windows will keep a building from exploding.

Geography

More than one-half of the world's tornadoes occur annually in the United States, where the conditions for their formation are ideal: a moisture source to the

Theodore Fujita, who developed the Fujita scale for determining tornado intensity, shown here with his tornado simulator. (AP/Wide World Photos)

south, a cold source to the north, mountain ranges to the west, deserts to the southwest, and an active jet stream. These meteorological conditions converge most often in an area designated "Tornado Alley," which extends from Texas northward to Nebraska.

From 1880 to 1998, more than 35,000 killer tornadoes brought death to virtually every state of the union. The Great Plains, Midwest, and Southeast experienced the greatest loss of life. Only seven states—Alaska, Hawaii, California, Nevada, Utah, Rhode Island, and Vermont—reported no fatalities. Texas led the nation in the number of tornadoes and total deaths. Oklahoma had the greatest tornado concentration per square mile. Mississippi led in deaths per million people.

About twenty other countries, including Canada, Russia, Australia, India, China, Bangladesh, England, Italy, France, and Japan, have conditions favorable for tornadoes. In most of these countries, tornadoes are weak and take few lives. Fujita studied tornado damage reports from throughout the world and concluded that tornadoes rated F4 or greater occur only in the United States, Canada, Bangladesh, and India. Statistics for countries outside the United States may be misleading, however. No standards for identifying and rating tornadoes exist, and no organization compiles international tornado statistics. Countries with large, sparsely populated areas, such as Australia, Canada, and Russia, may experience many more tornadoes than are reported.

Second to the United States in the number of tornadoes is Canada, which averages 80 tornadoes and 1 or 2 deaths annually. Most Canadian tornadoes occur in areas near the U.S. border and in western New Brunswick and interior British Columbia. The United Kingdom, which experiences 33 weak tornadoes in an average year, has the highest frequency of tornadoes per unit area in the world. The most susceptible areas are the Midlands and eastern England; tornadoes are rare in Northern Ireland and Scotland. About 15 tornadoes occur annually in Australia in the summer and winter, particularly in the eastern, southeastern, and western coastal areas.

PREVENTION AND PREPARATIONS

Humans cannot prevent tornadoes or lessen their destruction, but they can take several steps to lessen loss of life. A successful preparation program includes four integral parts: the issuance of a tornado forecast or watch, the spotting of a tornado, the dissemination of warnings to the public, and the response of an educated public to the warnings.

The United States is the only country to have a national office responsible for issuing severe weather forecasts. The Storm Prediction Center in Norman, Oklahoma, issues a tornado watch (forecast) when atmospheric conditions that could produce a tornado arise. A watch, which usually covers an area of 20,000 to 30,000 square miles, activates spotter networks within the watch area. These volunteers are amateur radio operators, law enforcement officials, or ordinary citizens who receive training in recognizing and reporting tornadoes within their county. A tornado watch also activates emergency procedures at the local National Weather Service (NWS) offices, law enforcement agencies, and emergency management offices. If spotters see a tornado, or if Doppler radar indicates that one may be forming, the local NWS office issues a tornado warning for the affected county. Local television and radio stations break into programming to warn citizens of impending danger, and many communities sound a warning siren. The media, especially television, relay information on the path of the tornado and the safety precautions to take.

In Canada and Australia, provincial and regional weather offices are responsible for tornado forecasts and warnings. Canada has a weather alert system that scrolls severe weather information across television screens, and completion of a Doppler weather radar network was projected for 2003. Most other countries where tornadoes occur have no organized method of forecasting or warning of tornadoes.

Because tornadoes occur so rapidly, all the potential victim has time to do is seek shelter. Doppler radar has increased the average warning time for tornadoes that strike in the United States to about fifteen minutes, but many occur with much less notice. To educate the public about the actions to take when a tornado threatens, the NWS and the Federal Emergency Management Agency (FEMA) distribute millions of tornado-safety brochures to schools and the general public, and states susceptible to twisters have a severe weather safety week each spring. Among the other countries that produce tornado-safety materials are Canada and Australia.

The key to survival in a tornado is to avoid flying and falling debris. The best place to take shelter is in a storm cellar or basement. In homes without basements, the safest place is on the lowest level in an interior room. The idea is to put as many walls as possible between oneself and the tornado and to stay away from windows. People in public buildings should go to an inside hallway on the lowest level and avoid wide-span roofs such as those found in auditoriums, gymnasiums, and shopping malls.

Mobile homes and vehicles are especially vulnerable in a tornado and should be abandoned. In the United States 50 percent of the tornado fatalities from 1985 to 1997 occurred in mobile homes and vehicles. Those caught outdoors should seek shelter inside a building, and if nothing is available they should lie in a ditch. In all cases, arms or pillows should be used to protect the head and neck. Texas Tech University's Wind Engineering Research Center studied building construction for many years in an effort to design homes that could withstand tornado and hurricane winds. In 1998 FEMA made plans for inexpensive home shelters that the Tech Center had designed available to the public and encouraged their construction.

RESCUE AND RELIEF EFFORTS

Because tornadoes occur with so little warning, and the odds of their striking one particular locale are so minute, few communities have specific tornado rescue plans. Often the streets are blocked by debris after a tornado, so much of the initial search for victims and rescue of trapped people comes from the survivors themselves. The greatest hazard in a tornado is being buried by falling debris. Frequently, those who seek shelter in a basement have the house fall in on them. When a tornado struck downtown Waco, Texas, in 1953, brick buildings crumbled, burying victims under 20 to 30 feet of rubble. In Saragosa, Texas, in 1987, 22 of the 30 fatalities occurred when the concrete block community center collapsed.

Local law enforcement agencies are usually in charge of search and rescue. When the tornado is of great proportions, the governor may call in the National Guard for assistance, and if a large number of people are unaccounted for, FEMA may send search dogs to sniff through the rubble.

A very strong tornado may hurl victims about like pieces of paper, sometimes many yards from their places of shelter. In the most violent tornadoes, victims may be found in trees or wrapped in telephone or electric lines. Those who remain in mobile homes or cars are often found entangled in twisted metal.

Tornado victims tend to have specific types of inju-

ries. Most fatalities are from crushing injuries and head traumas. Broken bones, gashes, cuts, puncture wounds, and embedded glass are among the most common nonfatal injuries. In nearly all tornadoes, a majority of the victims are the elderly and children.

An immediate concern is to turn off the gas and electricity to prevent fires and electrocutions. The National Guard may be mobilized to restore order and patrol against looting. If many fatalities are involved, law-enforcement officials will order everyone out of the devastated area until the bodies are recovered. When the victims are allowed to return to what remains of their homes and businesses, they usually find very little that is salvageable. What the wind does not destroy, the rain that frequently follows does.

Simultaneously with rescue efforts, national relief organizations, such as the Red Cross and the Salvation Army, begin feeding the victims and rescue workers and setting up shelters for the homeless. A designated agency, often the Red Cross or a local government entity, compiles lists of survivors and fatalities. Within hours of the disaster, religious and civic organizations as well as individuals provide food, clothing, household items, and money for the victims. Many also help in the cleanup and rebuilding process.

If the tornado has left behind substantial property damage, the governor may request a national disaster declaration. This designation, which the president must sign, provides federal assistance to individuals and communities for rebuilding.

IMPACT

Tornadoes rarely have a long-lasting effect on the physical environment. Unlike many natural disasters, such as floods or volcanic eruptions, "twisters" do not alter the topography of the area that they strike. The greatest environmental impact of a tornado is on trees, animals, humans, and the artificial environment. Violent tornadoes snap off trees, leaving only stubs, while most smaller tornadoes only break off branches. Occasionally, a twister downs thousands of trees in a forest. More commonly, the greatest damage to vegetation is to agricultural crops, which are readily replanted.

Tornadoes often kill wildlife. Frequently, frogs, fish, and various types of birds "rain" from the sky when they are caught in the rotating winds and dropped some distance away. During a 1978 tornado in Norfolk, England, 136 geese fell from the sky along a 25-mile track. Few reports of tornadoes killing larger wild animals exist, but it is probable that tornadoes killed many bison that once roamed the American Great Plains. Deaths of farm animals are common in tornadoes. Tens of thousands of cows, horses, pigs, and chickens have died through the years when winds carried them distances before dropping them or when barns or chicken houses collapsed. Dogs and cats are also frequent casualties of tornadoes.

Tornadoes cause incredible damage to human-made objects. Stronger storms can reduce brick and wooden buildings to piles of rubble in seconds, and even weak ones can demolish mobile homes. Tornadoes have dumped bridges into rivers and lakes, leaving behind only twisted iron or steel and concrete pillars. A violent tornado can scour pavement from roads, toss cars and trucks like matchsticks, and derail trains. The annual price tag for tornado damage is unknown, but single tornadoes have been known to cause more than $1 billion in damage. The tornado that struck Omaha, Nebraska, on May 6, 1975, left behind $1.135 billion in damage (in 1995 dollars), and the tornadoes that ripped through the Oklahoma City area on May 3, 1999, cost more than $1 billion.

Tornadoes leave their greatest impact on humans. During the twentieth century, these storms killed almost 15,000 and injured approximately 125,000 in the United States. In 1998, a record 1,426 tornadoes touched down in the United States and took 130 lives, the most in twenty-five years. Although they do not keep tornado statistics, India and Bangladesh combined may lead the world in tornado fatalities. A single tornado north of Dhaka, Bangladesh, killed 1,300 and injured 12,000 in 1989, and one in 1996 took more than 1,000 lives in the same area. The number of homeless and bereaved left in the path of tornadoes is uncountable.

Marlene Bradford

BIBLIOGRAPHY

Bluestein, Howard. *Tornado Alley: Monster Storms of the Great Plains.* New York: Oxford University Press, 1999. This book by a leading meteorologist and tornado chaser is a history of tornado research interspersed with magnificent photographs.

Church, Christopher, Donald Burgess, Charles Doswell, and Robert Davies-Jones, eds. *The Tornado: Its Structure, Dynamics, Prediction, and Hazards.* Washington, D.C.: American Geophysical Union, 1993. This collection of articles by meteorologists, statisticians, and members of the broadcast media addresses the topics noted in the title.

Eagleman, Joe R. "The Strongest Storm on Earth." In *Severe and Unusual Weather.* Lenexa, Kans.: Trimedia, 1990. The author describes the basic science of tornadoes in terminology that general readers can understand.

Flora, Snowden D. *Tornadoes of the United States.* Norman: University of Oklahoma Press, 1953. This book served as the standard reference work on tornadoes for years. Although outdated in many respects, it offers excellent historical accounts of many destructive tornadoes.

Grazulis, Thomas P. *Significant Tornadoes: 1680-1991.* St. Johnsbury, Vt.: Environmental Films, 1993. This massive book contains basic tornado information, maps, statistics, and a description of every tornado rated F2 or higher that occurred in the United States from 1680 to 1991.

Lane, Frank. *The Violent Earth.* Topsfield, Mass.: Salem House, 1986. This book by an Englishman devotes one chapter to the science of tornadoes and historical anecdotes and includes some information on tornadoes in England.

Ludlum, David. *Early American Tornadoes: 1586-1870.* Boston: American Meteorological Society, 1970. The author describes every reported tornado that occurred within the present United States until 1870 and discusses early American scientific thought on these storms.

Whipple, A. B. "Thunderstorms and Their Progeny." In *Storm.* Alexandria, Va.: Time-Life Books, 1982. This chapter mixes the science behind tornadoes with excellent meteorological drawings, magnificent photographs, and historical accounts of tornadoes.

Notable Events

Historical Overview

Although Greek philosopher Aristotle, the founder of meteorology, described tornadoes (or what he called "whirlwinds") around 340 B.C.E, few accounts of nature's most violent storms exist before 1600 except in the legends of several American Indian tribes. Tornadoes occurred infrequently in Europe and, except in England, received little notice until settlement began in North America, the prime natural habitat of these storms. Even then, tornadoes were not common occurrences. Only twenty such storms were recorded in pre-Revolutionary War times, including the July 8, 1680, storm in Cambridge, Massachusetts, which claimed the life of John Robbins. This was the first written account of a tornado and a victim within the future United States.

A Jesuit priest's narrative of the tornado that struck Rome in 1749 is one of the few published accounts of a European tornado outside England to appear before the nineteenth century, and after 1800 most of the interest in tornadoes centered in the

United States. A twister that struck New Brunswick, New Jersey, on June 19, 1835, stirred an ongoing scientific debate between U.S. meteorologists James Pollard Espy and William Redfield over the origin and nature of the storms. During the 1850's and 1860's, the Smithsonian Institution collected weather data from volunteer observers and military posts, and in 1862 it distributed circulars to the public warning about tornado dangers and asking for reports on these storms. The first weather forecast in the United States, which meteorologist Cleveland Abbe issued on September 2, 1869, raised the possibility of forecasting severe storms and tornadoes in the future.

On February 2, 1870, the federal government created a national weather service and placed it under the jurisdiction of the Army Signal Corps. One corpsman, John Park Finley, began a systematic study of tornadoes in 1877. Based on personal observations of the storms in the Great Plains and historical tornado data, Finley devised a set of rules for forecasting tornadoes. The corps allowed Finley to issue trial tornado predictions in 1884, and he claimed a 95-98 percent success rate. These forecasts never reached the public because the prevailing thought of the time was that people would panic if they thought a tornado might appear. This fear, along with a lack of interest in tornadoes among the scientific community, led to a prohibition on the use of the word "tornado" in any weather forecast until 1938.

During the nineteenth century, four tornadoes in the United States claimed more than 100 lives each: May 7, 1840, in Natchez, Mississippi, 317 deaths; June 3, 1860, in rural Iowa and Illinois, 112 deaths; May 27, 1896, in St. Louis, Missouri, 306 deaths; and June 12, 1899, in New Richmond, Wisconsin, 117 deaths.

The large population increase in the sections of the United States most prone to tornadoes led to greater tornado disasters during the first half of the twentieth century. The worst tornado disaster in U.S. history (as of 1999) occurred on March 18, 1925, when a boiling mass of black clouds rolled 219 miles through parts of Missouri, Illinois, and Indiana, killing 689 and injuring more than 2,000 in its path. This "Great Tri-State Tornado," also the holder of the record for the longest path, helped make 1925 the deadliest year (794 deaths) and the 1920's the deadliest decade on record for the United States (3,169 deaths).

Annual deaths during the first half of the century averaged 210, and in addition to the Great Tri-State

Tornado, eight tornadoes claimed 100 or more lives each: May 18, 1902, in Goliad, Texas, 114 deaths; April 24-25, 1908, in Louisiana and Mississippi, 143 deaths; March 23, 1913, in Omaha, Nebraska, 115 deaths; May 25-26, 1917, in Mattoon, Illinois, 103 deaths; April 2, 1936, in Tupelo, Mississippi, 216 deaths; April 6, 1936, in Gainesville, Georgia, 206 deaths; June 23, 1944, in Shinnston, West Virginia, 151 deaths; and April 9, 1947, in Woodward, Oklahoma, 181 deaths.

The Weather Bureau lifted the ban on the use of the word "tornado" in forecasts in 1938 and gave its local offices responsibility for issuing severe storm and tornado forecasts, but local offices rarely mentioned the word. World War II brought a change in attitude toward these deadly storms. Many munitions plants and Army Air Corps fields were located in the tornado-susceptible Great Plains and South. To lessen the possibility of many deaths should lightning strike a munitions plant and to decrease the potential loss of airplanes, the bureau organized storm-spotting networks around the crucial facilities. A few of these remained after the war and became the nucleus of a nationwide spotter network organized in the 1950's.

On March 20, 1948, a tornado raked Tinker Field in Oklahoma City. Air Force meteorologists Ernest Fawbush and Robert Miller studied the atmospheric conditions that existed before the storm occurred. Five days later, when they recognized nearly identical conditions, the officers issued a tornado forecast for Tinker Field, the first such forecast in modern history. They were correct—a tornado touched down on the base. Fawbush and Miller continued to issue forecasts for the military, but the civilian population did not receive the same type of advanced notification until 1952. The Weather Bureau issued the first tornado forecast to the American public on March 17 of that year, but no tornadoes occurred within the watch area. Four days later, the bureau issued another tornado watch, and this time it was a "success"—one tornado occurred within the designated area and time—but there was no cause for rejoicing on March 21. The 17 tornadoes that struck Arkansas, Tennessee, and Mississippi that day took 202 lives and injured over 1,200. In May, the Weather Bureau formed a Severe Weather Unit, the ancestor of the Storm Prediction Center, to issue both tornado and severe thunderstorm forecasts for the United States.

In 1953, tornadoes hit three U.S. cities, with terrible consequences. On May 11, a twister plowed

Milestones

500-600 B.C.E.: Perhaps the first recorded tornado is the "whirlwind" mentioned in Ezekiel 2:4 and 2 Kings 2:11 of the Old Testament.

October 17, 1091: The earliest British tornado for which there is an authentic record hits London, killing 2 and demolishing 600 houses.

June 30, 1916: Canada's most lethal twister to date kills 28 in Regina, Saskatchewan.

March 18, 1925: The United States' worst tornado disaster to date occurs when a 219-mile-long twister destroys entire towns along its path through Missouri, Illinois, and Indiana, causing 689 deaths, more than 2,000 injuries, and $16-18 million in damage.

March 25, 1948: Air Force officers Ernest Fawbush and Robert Miller issue the first tornado watch in the United States, but it is for military use only.

March 17, 1952: The U.S. Weather Bureau issues the first tornado watch to the American public.

May 11, 1953: A tornado destroys much of downtown Waco, Texas, leaving 114 dead and 1,097 injured.

June 8, 1953: The last U.S. tornado to date to claim 100 lives devastates parts of Flint, Michigan, killing 120 and injuring 847.

June 9, 1953: The worst tornado to date to strike the northeastern United States plows a path greater than a half-mile wide through Worcester, Massachusetts; 94 people are killed, 1,288 are injured, and more than 4,000 buildings are damaged or destroyed.

April 11, 1965: The "Palm Sunday outbreak" of around fifty tornadoes kills 271, injures more than 3,100, and causes more than $200 million in damages in Illinois, Indiana, Iowa, Michigan, Ohio, and Wisconsin.

June 8, 1966: The first $100 million tornado in the United States cuts a path through Topeka, Kansas, killing 16 and destroying more than 800 homes and much of the Washburn University campus.

May 11, 1970: A powerful tornado twists the frame of a twenty-story office building as it plows through downtown Lubbock, Texas, killing 26 and injuring more than 1,500. This tornado initiates a new interest in tornado studies, including Theodore Fujita's development of a tornado rating scale.

January 10, 1973: South America's worst tornado to date destroys parts of San Justo, Argentina; 50 people are killed.

April 3-4, 1974: In the largest U.S. tornado outbreak to date, 148 tornadoes, including six rated F5, kill 308 and injure almost 5,500 in eleven midwestern and southern states; an additional 8 deaths occur in Canada. Hardest hit communities include Xenia, Ohio (35 deaths and 1,150 injured), and Brandenburg, Kentucky (31 deaths and 250 injured).

June 9, 1984: Europe's worst tornado to date kills over 400 and injures 213 in Belyanitsky, Ivanovo, and Balino, Russia.

(Continued)

April 26, 1989:	The world's deadliest tornado to date occurs in Bangladesh when a twister slashes a 50-mile-wide path north of Dhaka; about 1,300 people are killed, more than 12,000 are injured, and almost 80,000 are left homeless.
May 13, 1996:	A large tornado levels several towns near Tangail, Bangladesh; more than 1,000 are dead and 34,000 are injured, with 100,000 left homeless.
May 3, 1999:	One of the most expensive tornadoes in U.S. history destroys nearly 2,500 homes and kills 49 in Oklahoma City and its suburbs; damage estimates approach $1.5 billion.

through downtown Waco, Texas, taking 114 lives; on June 8, a tornado struck Flint, Michigan, killing 120; and the following day, nature's fury struck Worcester, Massachusetts, leaving 94 dead. These deadly storms ushered in a decade of vast improvements in tornado forecasting and warning, primarily the result of radar and an expanded communications system.

After the Waco tornado, Texas A&M University converted surplus navy radar to weather radar and installed it at various Weather Bureau offices around the state to create the country's first comprehensive tornado warning system. Meteorologists noticed that frequently a tornado formed a distinctive radar pattern, called a hook echo, and they began issuing tornado warnings based solely on radar. During the 1950's, their partner in spreading the warning of approaching danger to the public was radio (95 percent of U.S. households had a radio in 1950), but by the next decade, television had replaced radio as the primary warning medium.

The weather establishment began to realize that one of the best ways to save lives was to educate the public. The Weather Bureau (which became the National Weather Service in 1970), state disaster offices, newspapers, television stations, and schools began a campaign in the late 1950's to teach the public the difference between a tornado watch (meaning a tornado is possible) and a tornado warning (meaning a tornado has been sighted) and the precautions to take to save lives. Most communities in tornado-prone areas organized volunteer spotter networks. Television stations began to acquire radar and to hire professional meteorologists. The White House designated the National Oceanic and Atmospheric Administration (NOAA) Weather Radio as the sole government system to provide direct warnings of natural

or nuclear disasters to private homes in 1975, and many Americans bought a special radio that sends out a warning when severe weather threatens their area. In the 1990's, the National Weather Service installed a vastly improved tornado detector, Doppler radar, at all its offices throughout the United States, Puerto Rico, and Guam, and many television stations bought their own Dopplers.

All these advances, along with improved building construction, contributed to a substantial reduction in the U.S. tornado death rate after the 1950's, the last decade to register more than 1,000 tornado deaths. As of 1999, no individual tornado had claimed more than 100 lives since 1953, and the last single tornado to kill more than 50 Americans occurred in 1971. These statistics are remarkable considering that the population in the southeastern and southern plains states, the areas most susceptible to tornadoes, increased more than 60 percent in the second half of the twentieth century.

In spite of all the technological and educational advances that the United States has made, nature's most vicious storm occasionally triumphs. An outbreak (several tornadoes in the same day) of 148 tornadoes on April 3-4, 1974, claimed 316 lives and injured more than 5,000 in eleven states. Other deadly outbreaks occurred on April 11, 1965, when 271 died in six midwestern states and on February 21, 1971, when 110 died in Louisiana and Mississippi.

During 1994 and 1995, scientists from many U.S. universities and U.S. and Canadian weather agencies employed an armada of specially equipped vehicles, including aircraft, to gather data from thunderstorms in an effort to unlock the secret of tornado formation. A smaller version of the project continued through 1999.

Marlene Bradford

1638: England

DATE: October 21, 1638
PLACE: Widecombe-in-the-Moor, England
RESULT: 60 dead and injured

One of the most famous of all English tornadoes struck the village of Widecombe-in-the-Moor on the southern edge of Dartmoor in Devonshire, England, on a Sunday morning. The vicar had just stepped into the pulpit to address the congregation gathered at the village church when the sky became intensely dark and violent wind and lightning struck the building. Deafening thunder followed, and smoke, dust, and the smell of sulfur filled the structure. The sound of falling stones from the tower and the roof mixed with the cries of the injured, who believed the end of the world had come.

Some of the injured suffered burns from the lightning ball that rolled through the building, but most injuries and deaths were the result of the victims being crushed by the falling debris or battered against walls and pillars. Reportedly, the twister moved some members of the congregation from one pew to another without mishap, but a dog carried aloft was not so fortunate. The violent winds carried heavy stones from the tower more than 100 yards. Several tracts about the event appeared, and numerous visitors to the village have read from painted boards a poem that the local schoolmaster composed about the tragedy.

Marlene Bradford

FOR FURTHER INFORMATION:
Lane, Frank W. *The Violent Earth*. Topsfield, Mass.: Salem House, 1986.

1840: Mississippi

DATE: May 7, 1840
PLACE: Natchez, Mississippi
RESULT: 317 dead, 109 injured, $1.26 million in damage

A tornado, more than 0.5 mile wide at times, touched down about 20 miles southwest of Natchez around 1:45 P.M. on May 7, 1840, and moved toward the riverport. About 7 miles from the city, the twister began moving up the Mississippi River, sinking flatboats and steamers. A piece of a steamboat window was carried 30 miles. According to reports, many itinerant boatmen and transients were on the river that day, making an accurate death toll difficult. The most reliable count listed 269 fatalities on the river.

By the time the tornado struck the north and central parts of Natchez, it was a mile wide. The storm indiscriminately destroyed everything from antebellum mansions to slave quarters. The Planter's Hotel, with several guests inside, tumbled down the bluff, and searchers recovered 11 bodies from the Steam-Boat Hotel. Several others died in the Natchez Theater; 48 deaths occurred within the city itself. Reports that hundreds of people died on plantations in Louisiana just across the river were not confirmed, but it is possible that many deaths, especially of slaves, occurred. As of 1999, this was the second deadliest tornado ever recorded in the United States.

Marlene Bradford

FOR FURTHER INFORMATION:
Ludlum, David. *Early American Tornadoes: 1586-1870.* Boston: American Meteorological Society, 1970.

1860: Iowa

DATE: June 3, 1860
PLACE: Camanche, Iowa
RESULT: 112 dead, about 200 injured, almost $300,000 in damage

Six killer tornadoes struck Iowa and Illinois on June 3, 1860, claiming 141 lives in total. The deadliest of these storms, known as the Great Tornado of the Northwest or the Camanche tornado, roared into the town of 1,200 people located on the west bank of the Mississippi River about 7 P.M. In the western section of Clinton County two tornadoes that had individually claimed many lives merged into one monster. As the tumbling black mass of clouds swept eastward across the countryside from DeWitt to Camanche, it killed 28, seriously injured 51, and left a strip of utter devastation between 0.25 and 0.5 mile wide. The tornado struck the unsuspecting town of Camanche with full force. With the exception of a few houses on the north side of town, every building, including the well-built, three-story Millard House and 3 churches, was destroyed or suffered severe damage.

On the river the tornado sank rafts, including one that carried 20 men; all drowned. In Camanche, 41 died instantly. The tornado continued across the river and struck the town of Albany, Illinois, where it killed 7 and injured 55. Before it dissipated, the twister claimed 16 more lives in Illinois. Although a correspondent for the *New York Herald* and Iowa historian Benjamin Gue were eyewitnesses who thoroughly documented the tragedy, one of the greatest tornadoes of the period was virtually unknown for a century. Until the 1960's, tornado chronologies and most other works on the subject failed to mention the Camanche tornado.

Marlene Bradford

FOR FURTHER INFORMATION:
Stanford, John L. *Tornado: Accounts of Tornadoes in Iowa.* Ames: Iowa State University Press, 1977.

1880: Missouri

DATE: April 18, 1880
PLACE: Marshfield, Missouri
CLASSIFICATION: F4 (estimated)
RESULT: 99 dead, almost 200 injured

At 4:30 P.M. on April 18, 1880, a tornado crossed what is now the southeast corner of Springfield, where it took 7 lives. Turning northeastward, the twister devastated Marshfield, a town of about 1,100 people; 68 died instantly, and 24 were so badly injured they died shortly thereafter. The 0.5-mile-wide storm left only 15 buildings in the town untouched. This tornado was the deadliest of seven tornadoes that claimed a total of 151 lives in Missouri on this day.

Marlene Bradford

FOR FURTHER INFORMATION:
Memphis Commercial Appeal, April 19, 1880.

1882: Iowa

DATE: June 17, 1882
PLACE: Grinnell, Iowa
CLASSIFICATION: F5 (estimated)
RESULT: 68 dead, about 300 injured

Although this tornado is known as the Grinnell tornado, 17 deaths occurred in rural areas when the 0.5-mile-wide twister leveled farm after farm in Greene, Boone, Story, and Jasper Counties, Iowa, before roaring into the town of Grinnell about 8:45 P.M. on June 17, 1882. Thirty-nine people died when the tornado, or perhaps two tornadoes, destroyed 73 homes and Grinnell College (then called Iowa College). Three students died in their dormitory rooms. Just east of the college, the twister struck a freight train, lifting the engine from the track and demolishing the cars. Farther down the track, the storm killed 2 men when it overturned a second freight train.

Moving southeastward, an uncommon occurrence, the tornado killed 10 near the town of Malcolm and 2 more just south of Brooklyn. As with many major nineteenth century tornadoes, the Grinnell tornado's death toll is only an estimate. Some sources suggest fatalities could have numbered 100. Debris from the tornado reportedly was carried as far as 100 miles. A few days after the tornado, a postal employee whose house had been destroyed opened a letter addressed to the Grinnell postmaster. Inside the envelope, she found a picture of herself and a note explaining that the writer had found the photograph 30 miles northeast.

Marlene Bradford

FOR FURTHER INFORMATION:
Stanford, John L. *Tornado: Accounts of Tornadoes in Iowa.* Ames: Iowa State University Press, 1977.

1884: U.S. South

DATE: February 19-20, 1884
PLACE: Alabama, Georgia, Kentucky, Mississippi, and the Carolinas
RESULT: 167 dead, over 1,000 injured, about $4 million in damage

In 1884, 37 tornadoes, 29 of them killers, devastated numerous rural communities across 6 southeastern states on February 19 and 20. State death tolls were as follows: 68 in Georgia, 39 in Alabama, 31 in North Carolina, 27 in South Carolina, 1 in Kentucky, and 1 in Mississippi. The early, exaggerated death toll of 2,000 is still found in books and articles. Although the tornadoes hit no sizable town, 3 communities suffered more than 20 deaths each: Goshen/Piedmont, Alabama (26 deaths); Philadelphia, North Carolina (23 deaths); and, Jasper, Georgia (22 deaths). The three tornadoes that struck these communities all were estimated as F4 level.

At Goshen the tornado blew apart the school, killed the teacher and 6 students, and injured the remaining children. Reports of bodies and cotton bales being carried great distances were common. John Finley, the United States' first tornado forecaster, mapped this outbreak and inaccurately reported more than one hundred tornadoes. The press made little effort to report the damages or deaths accurately in many of the remote communities, probably because many of the dead were sharecroppers.

Marlene Bradford

FOR FURTHER INFORMATION:
Memphis Commercial Appeal, February 21-23, 1884.

1886: Minnesota

DATE: April 14, 1886
PLACE: St. Cloud and Sauk Rapids, Minnesota
CLASSIFICATION: F5 (estimated)
RESULT: 72 dead, 213 injured, $400,000 in damage

Around 4:15 P.M. on April 14, 1886, a short-lived but devastating tornado plowed a 25-mile-long path through parts of Stearns and Benton Counties, Minnesota. What witnesses described as a "double spiral" killed 24 people and destroyed dozens of homes in the poorest section of St. Cloud. After crossing the Mississippi River, the twister then devastated the heart of Sauk Rapids, killing 37. Observers reported that the tornado had swept the river dry during its crossing. The storm continued north and killed 11 members of a wedding party, including the bride and groom, at Rice. In all, the tornado destroyed more than 200 homes and scattered tons of debris for miles. Indications of the tornado's intensity were reports that it carried a headstone for 3 miles and clothing for 62 miles.

Marlene Bradford

FOR FURTHER INFORMATION:
Minneapolis Journal, April 15-16, 1886.

1890: Kentucky

DATE: March 27, 1890
PLACE: Louisville, Kentucky
CLASSIFICATION: F4
RESULT: 106 dead, 230 injured, $3.5-4.0 million in damage

The Louisville tornado was one of several tornadoes spawned by a low-pressure system that had moved from the north Pacific coast through Colorado to center over Kansas, Missouri, and Illinois. Twenty-five

Seven people were killed at Rutgers and Seventh Streets, shown here, in Louisville, Kentucky, by the 1890 Louisville tornado. (Library of Congress)

tornadoes (16 causing a total of 146 deaths) struck Missouri, Illinois, Indiana, Kentucky, and Tennessee on March 27, 1890. At least 6 of these were F4 in force. Ten separate tracks were moving in a northeast direction. These tracks were made between 4:30 P.M. and 8:30 P.M. The destruction was so widespread that reporters traveling by train to cover the tornado began to see damage 50 miles from Louisville.

In Louisville, the light rains of the day turned to heavy rain in the hour preceding the tornado. With the heavy rain came intense lightning. At 7:50 P.M., the rain almost ceased, to be replaced by half-inch pellets of hail. A momentary lull in the wind preceded the approach of the tornado, which was accompanied by a tremendous roaring sound. Viewers described the tornado as having a balloon or turnip shape. As it left Louisville, it marked the time at 7:57 P.M. by tearing down the telegraph lines near Union Station.

The tornado that passed through Louisville first touched down on the banks of the Ohio River about 8 miles southwest of the city limits. It proceeded in a zigzag pattern through the suburb of Parkland, then moved into Louisville at Eighteenth Street and Broadway. From there it traveled in an erratic, quirky manner, with abrupt turns, including acute corners or about-faces. Its path went to Baxter Park at Thirteenth and Jefferson, St. John's Episcopal Church a block

eastward, then back to Market Street—the principal business street—to destroy Falls City Hall, north to Main Street, east down Main Street from Twelfth to Seventh, and north to Union Station and the river. After crossing the river, the storm turned north along Front Street of Jeffersonville to destroy several buildings but caused no deaths before it returned to the river for 4 miles of eastward travel to the Louisville water pumping station. The tornado finally disappeared in the southern part of Carroll County, Kentucky.

The track of this tornado almost paralleled the river for its 75-mile path. Its width averaged about 300 yards. Winds nearby were measured at 36 miles per hour. The speed of the storm system has been calculated at 36 to 40 miles per hour, but the individual Louisville tornado traveled at 80 miles per hour. A terrific electrical display accompanied the tornado. It seems that the tornado did not actually touch down in Louisville, as most of the damage was to buildings of more than one floor. However, about 1 square mile of Louisville from Eighteenth Street on the west to Seventh Street on the east and Broadway on the south to the Ohio River was left in ruins. This was the business district of the city and comprised residences for about 10,000 people.

The death toll would have been much higher if this tragedy had struck during the business day. Many businesses, including most of the tobacco warehouses, were demolished. One lifesaving quirk of the tornado was the turn at Seventh and Main: A block farther was the Louisville Hotel, which housed hundreds of tenants. The building next to the hotel was destroyed, killing several hotel employees who lived in the building. Another such case of luck was at Union Station, where there was a crowd of 40 or 50 people but only a restaurant worker was killed.

The greatest loss of life was in Falls City Hall, where several meetings were in session. Located on Market Street between Eleventh and Twelfth, this multistoried hall had about 200 people in it when the tornado struck. Fortunately, the ground floor, containing stalls of gardeners and butchers, was deserted. In upper floors were a youth dancing school, a business meeting of the executive committee of the Roman Knights, a rehearsal of a fifteen-member band, a meeting of the Jewel Lodge No. 2 of the Knights and Ladies of Honor, and decorators preparing the large hall for an upcoming occasion. In seconds the building was twisted into fragments, which fell upon the occupants. The search for survivors and victims was hampered by fires, which broke out twice. Some of the 44 victims died of asphyxiation from the gas from broken mains and the loss of oxygen to the fires.

A frantic search for trapped persons began within minutes. The main site was Falls City Hall, but digging out from the disaster was widespread. The energy and effort put forth by searchers meant that almost all the victims had been dug out within two days even though rescue efforts were slowed several times by fires. Repair and rescue efforts were also hampered on the 30th by 4 inches of snow. Most of the work done that day and the day after was to cover goods that were lying exposed to the elements. Included in these goods were much of the tobacco originally housed in warehouses near the river along Main Street.

Also, many of the residences were damaged so that the occupants' belongings were not totally protected. The cold weather caused much suffering for the people whose homes were destroyed or badly damaged. A shortage of water caused by the damage to the water pumping station added to the misery following the tornado. Aid rushed to the stricken area provided enough food so that hunger was not a problem.

The weather bureau had predicted that a violent storm could appear, but no one had an idea of the devastation that the beautiful town of 200,000 and the surrounding area would receive. The total storm was the third or fourth deadliest tornado and probably the costliest of the 1800's.

C. Alton Hassell

FOR FURTHER INFORMATION:
Grazulis, Thomas P. *Significant Tornadoes: 1680-1991.* St. Johnsbury, Vt.: Environmental Films, 1993.

1896: Texas

DATE: May 15, 1896
PLACE: Sherman, Texas
CLASSIFICATION: F5 (estimated)
RESULT: 73 dead, about 200 injured, $200,000 in damage

The narrow tornado that touched down in Denton County, Texas, about 4:30 P.M. on May 15, 1896, widened to 400 yards and intensified quickly as it moved into Grayson County. In its path across the countryside the twister left behind leveled farms and 11 fatalities, including a mother and 2 children who refused to accompany the family they were visiting to the storm cellar. Although the tornado appeared headed directly for the center of Sherman, the twister curved to the left and contracted to a width of 60 yards, just missing two women's colleges.

About 50 homes were destroyed; 20 completely disappeared. Most of the dead were found hundreds of yards from their homes. About 60 deaths occurred within the town itself, where 17 families suffered multiple deaths. In 10 families at least 3 people died, and one family lost 7 members. The steel girders of the Houston Street Bridge, which lay in a twisted mass in the town's creek, and the discovery of a trunk lid 35 miles from town attested to the storm's intensity. Relief trains brought coffins, and a sixty-man detachment prepared graves. An artist's rendering of the tornado appeared in the *Dallas Morning News* two days later—a rare occurrence in newspapers of this time.

Marlene Bradford

FOR FURTHER INFORMATION:
Lynch, Dudley. *Tornado: Texas Demon in the Wind.* Waco, Tex.: Texian Press, 1970.

1896: St. Louis

DATE: May 27, 1896
PLACE: St. Louis, Missouri
CLASSIFICATION: F4
RESULT: 306 dead, 2,500 injured, 311 buildings destroyed, 7,200 other buildings severely damaged, tremendous damage to river boats and railroad lines, $215 million in damage (in 1998 dollars)

Because the previous three weeks had witnessed violent weather across the United States, it must have come as a relief to St. Louis that the weather report for Wednesday, May 27, 1896, called for a partly cloudy day with only a chance of local thunderstorms. No one would have suspected that St. Louis could suffer the ravages of a tornado; it was considered common knowledge that tornadoes do not strike large cities. The tornado that nearly hit St. Louis on March 8, 1871, was believed to be as close as a tornado could come.

Until 3 P.M. on May 27, 1896, it was a hot, humid, and sunny day in St. Louis, just as the newspapers predicted. The city was a booming metropolis whose population already exceeded 500,000—it was the fourth-largest city in the United States. Union Station was in its second year of operation as the mid-America passenger hub of an increasingly mobile nation. Crowning its new status in industrialized America, preparations were well under way to house the Republican presidential nominating convention, scheduled for June. Across the mighty Mississippi River, East St. Louis had become a commercial railroad center with a rapidly growing population.

After 3 P.M. the sky slowly began to darken as the barometer and thermometer began to fall. By 4:30 P.M. large black and green cloud masses could be seen approaching the city. By 5 P.M. many parts of the city were enveloped in darkness, except for forked lightning illuminating the sky. Sizzling telegraph wires and burning telegraph poles cast an eerie bluish light pattern in the streets below. People scurried for the relative security of temporary shelter wherever they could find it, a fact substantiated by the location of bodies found after the storm. Shelter in cellars offered the best protection, providing that an individual was not crushed by the upper floors caving in.

At about 5:15 P.M. the tornado struck at the southwest edge of St. Louis. It widened into a 0.5-mile-wide complex of tornado and downburst wind, heading due east toward the central city area. Along its path it demolished 311 buildings and severely damaged 7,200 others. Stone and brick houses of the affluent were smashed almost as easily as the flimsy wooden houses of the poor. The tornado devastated 6 churches and damaged 15 others. Several city hospitals suffered varying degrees of destruction.

The storm cut a 10-mile path, leaving in many places a mile-wide swath of devastation. Witnesses described the tail of the storm as being like the lash of a whip, moving north to south, while the massive body of the storm slowly moved on its eastern path of destruction. Entire neighborhoods, such as the Soulard area, were left in shambles. Nearly 500 workers were building a thirteen-building complex for Liggett and Myers Tobacco Company when the storm hit. Structures collapsed, and miraculously, only 13 workers died. However, at Seventh and Rutgers Street 17 people died when a three-story brick tenement collapsed. The new Ralston Purina Mill was also destroyed. However, a bank loan would allow the new headquarters to be rebuilt.

The storm reached maximum intensity when it came to the Mississippi River. Because of a slight turn in the storm, the tall buildings of downtown St. Louis were spared the test of whether or not they could survive tornadic winds. However, poverty-stricken families living in houseboats disappeared into the river. Sixteen boats moored in St. Louis harbor were wrecked. By the time they hit the Eads Bridge, tornadic winds were strong enough to drive a 2-by-10-inch wood plank through the $\frac{5}{16}$-inch thick wrought-iron plate of the bridge.

The great tornado then tore into East St. Louis, leveling half of the city. Thirty-five people died in the Vandalia railroad freight yard in East St. Louis. It took about twenty minutes for the worst single disaster in the history of the St. Louis metropolitan area to take its deadly and destructive toll. The storm system left 306 dead, over 2,500 injured, and 600 families homeless.

Drenching rains and lightning continued in St. Louis until about 9 P.M. Because the Edison Plant was destroyed, the city was without electricity. Rescue workers worked through the night by torchlight and through the sunshine of the next morning. Survivors were still being pulled from the rubble two days later. Meanwhile, long lines of friends, relatives, and the curious waited at the city morgue as the dead wagons

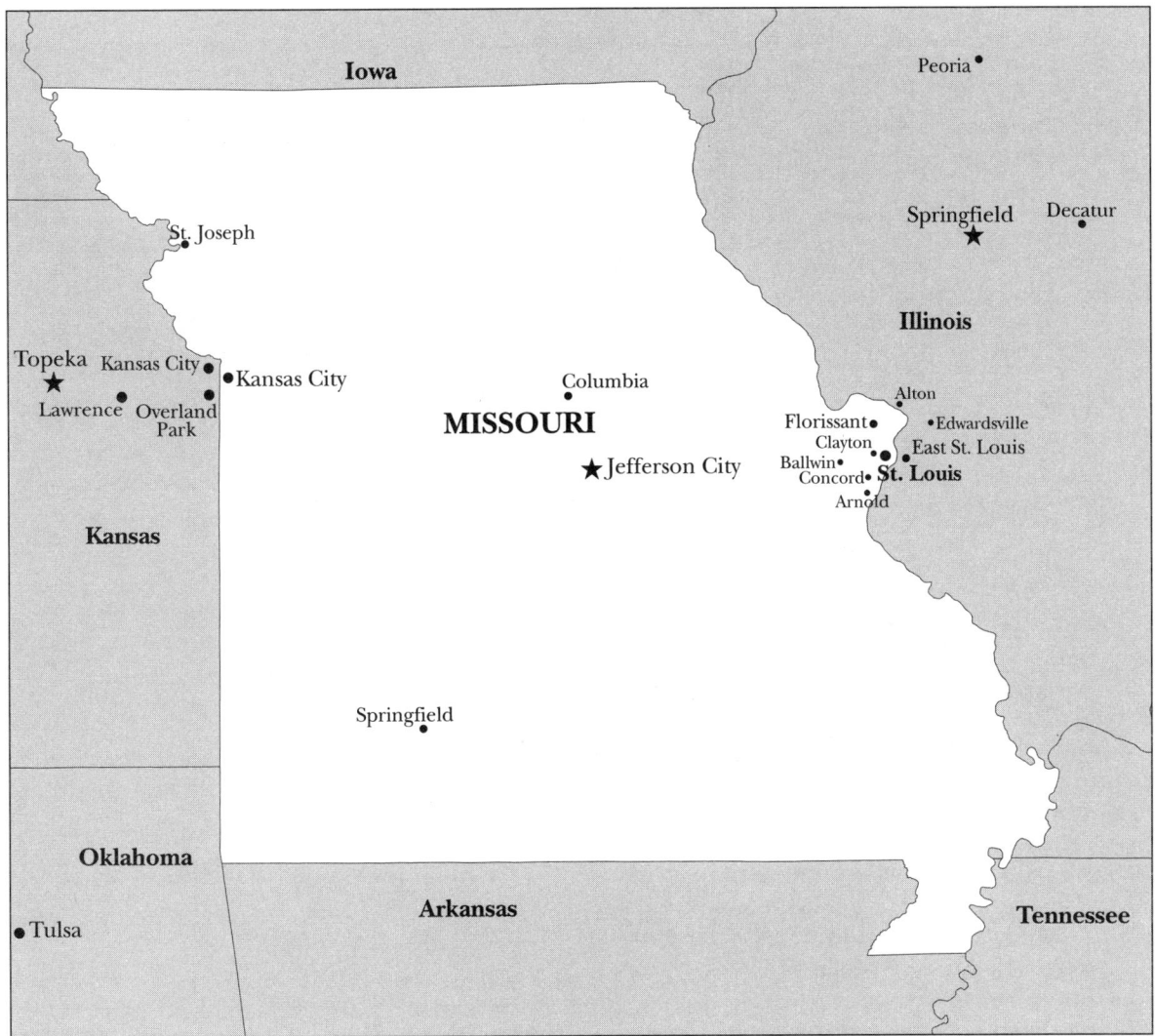

unloaded their crushed and mutilated human cargo. Many bodies were blackened and unrecognizable. Others had been turned into human pin cushions as splintered wood and other debris had been hurled at tremendous speeds into their bodies.

As news of the disaster spread, the weekend brought tens of thousands of sightseers to St. Louis, anxious to see firsthand the destruction that was wrought. Among their number were hundreds of thieves, eager to uncover valuables from demolished homes and stores. On the Sunday following the "great tornado" over 140,000 people crammed through Union Station into the streets of St. Louis. Tours had already been organized to see the destruction. For weeks after the storm St. Louis newspapers were filled with stories of miraculous escapes, tearful tragedies, and tales of heroic citizens coming to the aid of other citizens. These accounts and others were pieced together by the Cyclone Publishing Company, a group of newsmen who copyrighted their work in Washington, D.C., only nine days after the storm. An eager American public read in awe and horror about the powers of nature and the human dimensions of natural disasters.

Irwin Halfond

FOR FURTHER INFORMATION:

Curzon, Julian. *The Great Cyclone at St. Louis and East St. Louis, May 27, 1896.* Carbondale: Southern Illinois University Press, 1997.

O'Neil, Tim. "The Great Cyclone of 1896." *St. Louis Post-Dispatch,* May 26, 1996.

"St. Louis Tornado of 1896." http://www.tornadoproject.com.

1899: Wisconsin

Date: June 12, 1899
Place: New Richmond, Wisconsin
Classification: F5 (estimated)
Result: 117 dead, over 200 injured, $300,000 in damage

More than 1,000 people from out-lying communities had come to the picturesque town of 2,500 residents on Monday afternoon, June 12, 1899, to see a circus parade. At about 4 P.M. rain and small hail-stones pelted New Richmond, but the sky cleared somewhat in the southwest except for a singular darkening cloud. From the lowered base of the eastward-moving cloud several funnel clouds appeared and disappeared until a spectacular waterspout touched down on Lake St. Croix. Over land the tornado moved to the northeast and took the lives of 3 people as it leveled farms on its way to New Richmond.

At 5:40 many people were on the streets and sidewalks of the town. Those who saw the approaching tornado ran through the streets trying to warn others of its approach. Some reached storm shelters, but many were trapped in the center of town when the tornado roared through, leveling every building in a 0.5-mile-wide path. The twister blew away substantial brick buildings on Main Street, left the iron bridge spanning the Willow River a twisted heap, tossed the Methodist church building across the street, destroyed the power station and water tower, strew lumber from the town's mill for miles, and carried a 3,000-pound safe more than a block. At least 26 different families lost more than 1 family member, and 6 families lost 4 or more. Because telephone and telegraph lines were severed, help from the outside did not reach the town until the next day.

Marlene Bradford

The business section of New Richmond, Wisconsin, was destroyed by the 1899 tornado. (Library of Congress)

For Further Information:

Epley, Anna. *The New Richmond Tornado of 1899: A Modern Herculaneum.* Milwaukee: M. G. Corenthal, 1989.

1902: Texas

Date: May 18, 1902
Place: Goliad, Texas
Classification: F4 (estimated)
Result: 114 dead, about 250 injured, over $100,000 in damage

The disastrous tornado that devastated Goliad, a historic Texas town of about 1,200 people, on a Sunday afternoon in May, 1902, first touched down at the San Antonio River Bridge, south of town. The powerful storm twisted the steel bridge into a massless form and carried one of the beams for 2 miles before hurling it into the ground near the county courthouse, where it would remain. As the tornado roared through the main part of town at about 3:45 P.M., it claimed multiple victims in several locations. Unconfirmed reports of 40 or more deaths in one Methodist church and 29 victims in another house circulated.

The storm horribly mutilated many of its victims. One man received an estimated 500 puncture wounds. Most of the victims died within a few hours of the storm's passage, but at least 20 later succumbed to tetanus, or what was then called "blood poisoning." Many of the dead were buried in a mass grave because of a shortage of cemetery space or the lack of remaining family members to bury them. As of 1999, the Goliad tornado and the Waco tornado of 1953 shared the distinction of being the deadliest in Texas history.

Marlene Bradford

FOR FURTHER INFORMATION:
Lynch, Dudley. *Tornado: Texas Demon in the Wind.* Waco, Tex.: Texian Press, 1970.

1903: Georgia

DATE: June 1, 1903
PLACE: Gainesville, Georgia
CLASSIFICATION: F4 (estimated)
RESULT: 98 dead, 180 injured, about $1 million in damage

This short-lived, narrow, intense tornado cut a 4-mile-long path through the outskirts of Gainesville at about 12:45 P.M. on June 1, 1903. As the storm approached the town, many thought it was smoke from an approaching locomotive. About 1 mile southwest of Gainesville the characteristic funnel cloud touched down and struck a cotton mill filled with 750 employees. Unfortunately, 250 children worked on the fifth floor. The greatest loss of life occurred here, when the wind tore the roof and top two stories off the building, hurling blocks of marble and timber along with children's bodies into a pile in front of the building. The tornado carried an iron cupola that had covered a standpipe 50 feet high and 40 feet in diameter more than 100 feet into the air before dropping it about 100 feet in front of the building, killing 10. About 50 people died at the cotton mill.

The twister crossed the railroad tracks and seemed headed for the center of the town, but it made an eastward turn and struck New Holland, a mill village 2 miles northeast of the Gainesville depot.

The tornado spared the mill but destroyed 70 of the 120 houses where the mill employees lived. Fortunately, hundreds were at work and saved from injury, but about 40, mainly very young children and aged women, died in the destroyed homes. The fury of the storm dissipated quickly, and no damage was done to the main part of Gainesville.

Marlene Bradford

FOR FURTHER INFORMATION:
Atlanta Constitution, June 2, 1903.

1905: Oklahoma

DATE: May 10, 1905
PLACE: Snyder, Oklahoma
CLASSIFICATION: F5 (estimated)
RESULT: 97 dead, about 150 injured, $250,000 in damage1

In late afternoon on May 10, 1905, a large and violent tornado formed in Jackson County, Oklahoma, and followed an east to northeast path into Tillman County. Along the way, the twister leveled farms and small settlements and killed 10. As it crossed into Kiowa County, the tornado widened to 0.5 mile wide and reached its full intensity. Reportedly, people 12 miles away heard its roar. At Snyder, the storm destroyed more than 100 homes and damaged 150 others. Several were entirely swept away. Many residents, thinking that the huge funnel was a hailstorm, did not seek shelter underground. As a result, 87 died at Snyder.

Marlene Bradford

FOR FURTHER INFORMATION:
Oklahoma City Times, May 11-13, 1905.

1908: U.S. South

DATE: April 24-25, 1908
PLACE: Alabama, Georgia, Louisiana, Mississippi, and Tennessee
CLASSIFICATION: F4 (estimated)
RESULT: 311 dead, 1,655 injured, more than $1.65 million in damage

At least 20 tornadoes, 11 of them killers, scoured large sections of the Southeast in April of 1908, leaving behind 311 dead. State death tolls were as follows: 38 in Alabama, 30 in Georgia, 87 in Louisiana, 155 in Mississippi, 1 in Tennessee. Four of the tornadoes were estimated to have reached F4 level. By far the most devastating of these tornadoes traveled an estimated 155 miles through 4 Louisiana parishes and five Mississippi counties, taking 143 lives. The path of destruction reportedly was an incredible 2.5 miles wide at Amite, Louisiana, where the tornado claimed 29 lives. The worst destruction in Mississippi occurred in the town of Purvis, where 55 perished and 400 were injured.

Farther to the north, a tornado plowed a 105-mile-long path through the same states. This tornado left 91 dead and over 400 injured, most in plantation tenant homes. A third tornado killed 35 in Alabama, 15 of them in Albertville, where reportedly the winds carried a 9-ton oil tank for 0.5 mile. Although pre-1950 tornado statistics are frequently inaccurate, this outbreak ranked as the third (perhaps the second) deadliest in the United States at the end of the twentieth century.

Marlene Bradford

FOR FURTHER INFORMATION:
Memphis Commercial Appeal, April 26-27, 1908.

1913: Nebraska

DATE: March 23, 1913
PLACE: Omaha, Nebraska
RESULT: 115 dead, 600 homes destroyed, $5 million in damage

March, 1913, was an active weather month in the United States. There were blizzards on March 15 and 21, a hurricane in Alabama and Georgia on March 16, a freeze in Tampa, Florida, on March 17, and tornadoes in Iowa, Illinois, Indiana, Kansas, Nebraska, North Dakota, and South Dakota on March 23 and 24. Of these weather events, the most shocking to many Americans was the March 23, or Easter Sunday, tornado in Omaha, Nebraska. Many residents had believed Omaha, a city of 124,000 nestled in the hills overlooking the Missouri River, was sheltered from tornadoes and were stunned when the residential district stretching from the stockyards in South Omaha to Walnut Hill near Fontenelle Park was leveled.

A heavy rainstorm began around 5 P.M. on Easter Sunday and spawned a series of five tornadoes in Nebraska, which crossed into Iowa as well. The first formed around 5:20 P.M. in Craig, Nebraska, and continued into Monona County, Iowa. Ten minutes later, a second funnel began a 70-mile path of destruction 2 miles east of Ithaca, Nebraska. It heavily damaged Yutan, Nebraska, carried a woman for 0.25

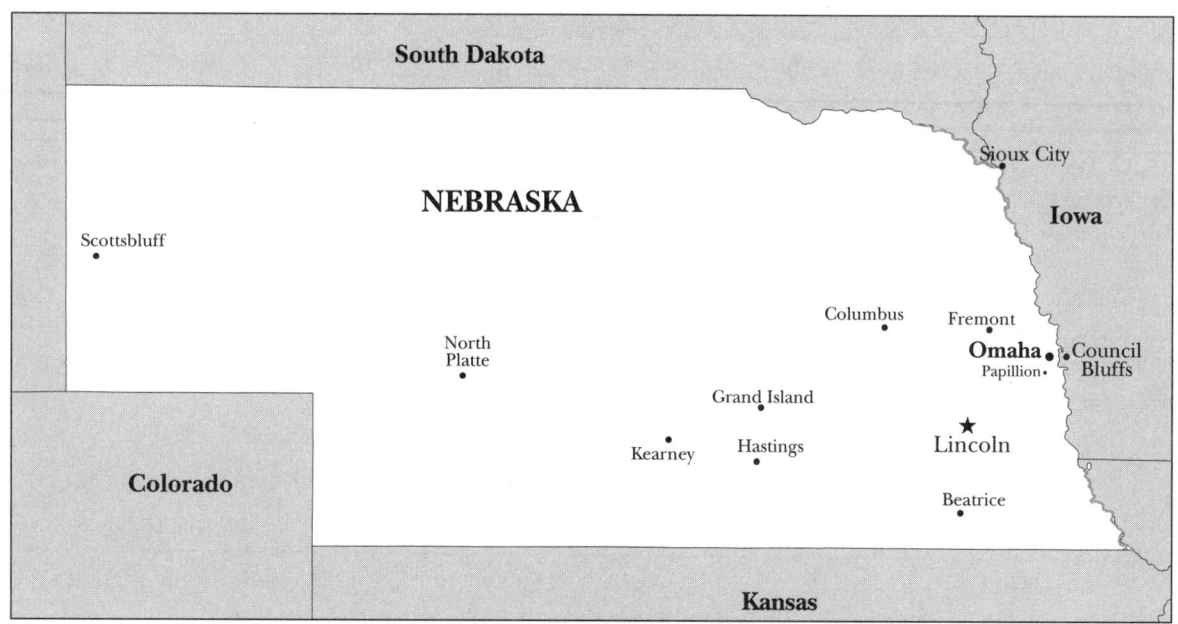

mile in the debris of her house but left her unharmed, and narrowly missed several Iowa towns. The third tornado was the Omaha tornado. Fourth, a funnel between 0.25 and 0.5 mile wide formed near Berlin, Nebraska, at 5:55 P.M., traveling on the ground continuously for 80 miles, killing 13 people in Nebraska and 8 in Iowa and narrowly avoiding Henderson, Iowa. Finally, the fifth tornado struck west of the Missouri River around 6:15 P.M., passing south of Council Bluffs, Iowa, over Mills and Pottawattamie Counties in Iowa to the town of Harlan.

The Omaha tornado formed 65 miles southwest of Omaha and destroyed an 8-mile path near Kramer, Nebraska. Then it began to alternately rise and fall. Ashland, Nebraska, 40 miles southwest of Omaha, was hit hard. William Koon, the president of a Lincoln automobile company, was taking the train to Omaha during the storm and reported watching houses collapse, a threshing machine fly straight up in the air and land 650 feet away, and a boxcar be carried for 0.25 mile, causing 6 or 7 men to fall out. The train stopped to attend to the injured and dead. Meanwhile, the tornado leveled Ralston, a recently constructed manufacturing suburb on the southwest edge of Omaha; swept over the hills; and descended upon Omaha, where it

Automobiles were upended and buildings were in ruins after the 1913 Omaha twister. (Library of Congress)

stayed on the ground for twelve minutes to clear a path 5 miles long and 0.25 mile wide. Finally, the tornado crossed Pottawattamie, Harrison, and Shelby Counties in Iowa, killing an additional 33 people and injuring 100.

Although 75 percent of the destroyed buildings were small frame cottages, more substantial structures were also devastated. The roof was torn from Joslyn Castle, while Sacred Heart Convent, a Catholic school, was destroyed, although no one was hurt since the girls were home with their families for the

holiday. The roof was blown from a motion-picture theater, and as many as 16 people were trampled in the ensuing panic. As the tornado moved across Omaha, it also struck the part of the city where many African Americans lived, killing or injuring several families in their homes and crushing 7 men with a pool table in Idlewild Pool Hall. At least 2 streetcars were knocked off their tracks, hurting the passengers.

In the immediate aftermath of the tornado, fires broke out across the city, and Omaha leaders turned off the electricity to minimize the fire risk. This forced rescuers to search by lantern. A half-hour torrential rain then fell, extinguishing the fires. It continued to rain for the next several days and even snowed 3 inches on March 25, further increasing the suffering of those who lost their homes. Telegraph communications were broken for a number of hours, and railroads were forced to use signalmen for days afterward.

Since Grand Island, nearly 140 miles to the west, was the closest city with an operating telegraph, and since Omaha mayor James C. Dahlman requested the state militia from Lincoln, most outsiders feared the worst at first. The initial newspaper accounts suggested that thousands were dead and the city was in flames. It gradually became clear, however, that although the actual numbers were still heartbreaking, Omaha would survive and rebuild. Civic leaders founded relief funds almost as soon as the funnel had crossed into Iowa. Des Moines, Iowa, sent a train of 40 doctors, and soldiers from Fort Omaha began to clear away debris. On March 24, Dahlman declined an offer of assistance from President Woodrow Wilson, stating that Omaha's citizens were responding nobly and could handle the situation themselves.

In the meantime, the storm system had moved east to Terre Haute, Indiana, where a tornado destroyed a glass factory. Rains had been falling for days in Ohio, and on March 25, Dayton flooded. Floodwaters rose from Columbus to Indianapolis and Fort Wayne, Indiana, causing the governor of Ohio to place the state under martial law. By March 29, Cincinnati was in danger, so the month ended with the severe weather unabated.

Omaha, where victims had come from all economic levels and ethnic groups, recovered reasonably well. Six years later, on April 6, 1919, another tornado struck. It also moved from southwest to northeast, but its 3- to 4-mile-long path of 200 to 600 feet in width traversed a less-populated part of the city. Only 20 were injured and $250,000 in property was damaged. What really replaced the 1913 tornado in local folklore was the only other major tornado to hit Omaha to date. This was on May 6, 1975, when 3 people died and 287 homes and 108 businesses were destroyed among $150 million of damage.

Amy Ackerberg-Hastings

FOR FURTHER INFORMATION:

Drinker, Frederick E. *Horrors of Tornado, Flood, and Fire.* Philadelphia: National, 1913.

Driscoll, Charles Benedict. *Complete Story of Omaha's Disastrous Tornado.* Omaha, Nebr.: Mogy, 1913.

Stanford, John L. *Tornado: Accounts of Tornadoes in Iowa.* 2d ed. Ames: Iowa State University Press, 1987.

1917: Illinois

DATE: May 25-26, 1917
PLACE: Mattoon and Charleston, Illinois
CLASSIFICATION: F4
RESULT: 103 dead, 669 injured, $2 million in damage

Between May 17 and June 3, 1917, 8 depression systems moved northeastward across the interior of the United States. The third of this series of depressions was over eastern Colorado on the morning of May 25. During the day the storm moved northeastward, causing tornadoes and other storms in Kansas and one tornado in Nebraska. The 5 Kansas tornadoes killed 24 people. The worst one, an F5, hit Andale and Sedgwick, killing 23 people.

The storm was over northwestern Iowa by the morning of May 26. It created two tornadoes in Illinois and Indiana. The northern tornado killed 7 people. This tornado was less than 33 miles in path length but had an intensity level of F4. The other tornado was longer and more deadly as it hit Mattoon and Charleston.

Complicating the information about these tornadoes is the fourth depression system, which caused 20 tornadoes in Missouri, Arkansas, Tennessee, Kentucky, Illinois, Mississippi, and Alabama on May 27. Three more occurred in the hour after midnight. The death total was 159 people. The most deadly one hit Tennessee and Kentucky, killing 67 people. Its path weaved through Bondurant, Clinton, and Dublin, Kentucky.

The Mattoon tornado of May 26 is also called the Central Illinois tornado or the Long Path tornado. It is often credited with having the longest path length of any tornado. The path length of 293 miles across Illinois and Indiana started at Louisiana, Missouri, and ended near Jennings, Indiana. The tornado lasted for seven hours and twenty minutes. Thomas P. Grazulis in *Significant Tornadoes: 1680-1991* (1993) claims that evidence proves that this was a series or family of tornadoes, not a single tornado, and that the path length should be listed as 155 miles, the distance from near the Missouri border to just past Charleston. At 155 miles it would still tie for the fourth-longest path.

The Weather Bureau listed 2 tornadoes on May 26, 1 in northern Illinois and 1 in Central Illinois and Indiana (the Mattoon tornado). Grazulis lists 2 northern tornadoes and 4 tornadoes in Central Illinois and Indiana. The Weather Bureau describes breaks in the path that occurred as the tornado skipped or lifted off the ground; Grazulis counted each of these breaks as a different tornado.

First sighted about noon as a tornado cloud near the Pleasant Hill-Nebo area, 7 to 10 miles east of the Mississippi River, the tornado traveled almost due east to White Hall, where it lifted houses and caused injuries. The tornado either lifted or weakened as it left White Hall to travel to Modesto, a hamlet of 500. At Modesto, 3 people were killed as 30 homes were destroyed. Palmyra, a few miles south, also reported damage.

Along the path between Modesto and Westervelt in Shelby County, 1 person was killed and much hail damage occurred. Although Virden, east of Modesto, did report damage, the damage was intermittent instead of continuous along the path. At Westervelt, 5 people were killed, and 21 were injured. Most of the injured were children who were practicing a church day program when the church collapsed. Ten homes also destroyed.

The next town to be struck was Mattoon, a city of 15,000. The tornado seemed to gain strength, and it cut a two-and-a-half-block path through Mattoon. Almost every house in the northern half of the city was

damaged or destroyed. The business district was also heavily damaged. Flying pieces of wood from the lumberyard in the tornado path caused much of the damage that occurred outside the path; pieces of wood were carried miles away. Almost 500 homes were destroyed, and another 146 were severely damaged, leaving 2,000 homeless. Extra damage was caused by a heavy hailstorm that also hampered rescue work. Fire broke out in the damaged area but was quickly contained. The rescue work had to be done by lantern at first as the electric power plant was damaged by the storm. The death toll was 53. There were about 500 injured and almost $1.25 million in damage in Mattoon.

The tornado stayed on the ground for the 11 miles between Mattoon and Charleston and damaged every farm in its way. Charleston had a population of about 6,000. The 600-yard-wide path cut right through the center of the town, destroying 220 homes, the Maple Hotel, 2 railroad stations, 3 grain elevators, a lumberyard, and 10 other businesses. It killed 38 people, caused $750,000 in damage, and left 285 families homeless.

In Charleston, it was necessary to use lights at 2 P.M. At 3 P.M. a heavy black cloud with frequent lightning was seen in the northwest. Just before 3:45 P.M. hail began to fall, then winds blew at 80 miles per hour. After the tornado came 2.5-inch hail and a deluge of rain.

After leaving Charleston, the tornado killed 2 people at Embarras, northeast of Charleston. Then the twister turned slightly southeast, destroying homes in Marshall before lifting to cross the Wabash. The turn possibly saved Terre Haute from tornado damage. In Indiana, the tornado killed 2 people about 2 miles south of Blackhawk, passed between Lewis and Clay City, then jumped to Clear Creek 3 miles south of Bloomington, where it destroyed 3 farms and 15 houses. It finally dissipated near Jennings, about 40 miles from the eastern boarder of Indiana, shortly after 7 P.M.

The tornado traveled about 40 miles per hour with a path that was usually 0.5 mile wide. The characteristic funnel cloud was seen for most of the distance that it traveled, except through and between Mattoon and Charleston. In that area it seemed to be too low for the funnel to be seen, and its path was only 0.25 mile wide. Mattoon residents reported two boiling cloud masses rolling toward each other and downward.

The storm was the third deadliest in Illinois history and the thirteenth deadliest in U.S. history to date. It had the power to move an eight-room house 41 feet, to break off elm trees 18 inches in diameter, and to overturn railcars full of bricks. Its worst damage was killing 103 people and injuring nearly 700.

C. Alton Hassell

FOR FURTHER INFORMATION:

Carey, J. P. "The Central Illinois Tornado of May 26, 1917." *Science,* June 15, 1917, 613-614.

Cornell, James. *The Great International Disaster Book.* 3d ed. New York: Charles Scribner's Sons, 1982.

Flora, Snowden D. *Tornadoes of the United States.* Norman: University of Oklahoma Press, 1954.

Grazulis, Thomas P. *Significant Tornadoes: 1680-1991.* St. Johnsburg, Vt.: Environmental Films, 1993.

Mattoon Tornado Pictures, May 26, 1917. Souvenir booklet, Mattoon, Illinois, 1991.

The New York Times, May 26-29, 1917.

"Ten Deadliest Tornadoes (in Illinois)." *The State Journal-Register,* June 5, 1999.

U.S. Department of Agriculture. *Monthly Weather Review,* June, 1917, 292-295.

1919: Minnesota

DATE: June 22, 1919
PLACE: Fergus Falls, Minnesota
CLASSIFICATION: F5 (estimated)
RESULT: 57 dead, more than 200 injured, $3.5 million in damage

At about 4:45 P.M. on Sunday, June 22, 1919, a tornado struck the town of 12,000 people situated on the Red River in northwestern Minnesota, claiming 57 lives and demolishing much of the town north of the river. Eyewitnesses reported that before the black funnel-shaped cloud appeared, there was a loud humming noise, resembling hundreds of buzzsaws running all at once.

Four children died when the storm blew a house into One Mile Lake. Other fatalities occurred at the Lake Alice Grand Hotel, but most of the deaths occurred in a three-block-wide swath through the town. About 400 buildings, including 228 homes, were destroyed. The *Minneapolis Journal* recorded several "freak" occurrences. The tornado split a huge tree, threw an automobile into the split, and closed it up. The storm removed the feathers from a flock of thirty chickens and left their corpses sitting upright in the henhouse. In one house, the tornado picked up a cut-glass vase, carried it around a corner, and set it down unbroken on the floor. One child, sitting on her father's lap, escaped injury although her shoes were torn off and her father was killed.

Marlene Bradford

FOR FURTHER INFORMATION:
Minneapolis Journal, June 23-25, 1919.

1920: Chicago

DATE: March 28, 1920
PLACE: Chicago, Illinois
CLASSIFICATION: F4
RESULT: 28 dead, 325 injured, $3.5 million in damage

The Chicago tornado of 1920 was only a small part of a storm that had begun in Alaska. In Nebraska it encountered a warm wind from the southwestern United States. The storm proceeded eastward, causing tornadoes in Illinois, Michigan, Missouri, Wisconsin, Indiana, and Ohio in the north and in Georgia and Alabama in the south. Thirty-one tornadoes were spawned by the storm system, of which 19 were killers that caused 153 deaths. The *Monthly Weather Review* indicates 163 died, while *The New York Times* counted 160. The storm finally disappeared into the Atlantic after causing tremendous damage.

March 28, 1920, was Palm Sunday. It was a warm, sunny day in Chicago. Many people were just sitting down with their families for Sunday lunch when the tornado struck with no warning. In one hour, it moved the 50 miles from 8 miles southwest of Joliet to Lake Michigan at Wilmette. It killed 20 people, injured about 300, demolished

300 houses, damaged another 300, and caused $2 million in damage. It was followed by short-lived torrential rain and hail, then warm sunshine.

The tornado first formed at about 12:15 P.M. approximately 8 miles southwest of Joliet near Channahon. The funnel shape was first seen near the Illinois and Michigan Canals. The townships of Channahon,

Plainfield, Troy, and Lockport were all damaged by the storm. Three people were killed in Plainfield, northwest of Joliet. The tornado was skipping, which meant that less damage occurred than might have.

After Lockport the tornado rose until it reached Bellewood and Maywood, about 5 miles west of the western Chicago city limits. Continuing into Melrose Park, the site of the greatest destruction and the most deaths, it reached Lake and Twenty-first streets about 12:55 P.M. It cut a 100-yard-wide path to the northeast to Division and Thirteenth Street. The 1-ton church bell of the destroyed Sacred Heart Church was carried 100 feet. From Melrose Park the tornado moved northeastward through River Grove, Leyden township, Dunning, Irving Park, Higgins Road, Norwood Park, the northwest corner of Chicago, Niles township, northwestern Evanston at Federal Street, and Wilmette, finally arriving at Lake Michigan at about 1:15 P.M. In Wilmette a 2-block-wide path was cut. Fortunately, much of the path of the tornado was open country, and although damage was done, there were fewer deaths than would have occurred in a densely populated area. At Dunning the tornado lifted just before the Chicago State Hospital for the Insane; the 3,000 inhabitants were not harmed by the storm.

The damage in Melrose Park was concentrated in the heart of the business and residential area. Although damage first occurred at Twenty-fifth Avenue and Washington Boulevard, the main damage started at Eighteenth Street (Broadway) and First Avenue and continued north for seven blocks. Three blocks on each side of Broadway were damaged; 25 houses in one block were completely destroyed. A freight car containing 1,500 pounds was carried 40 feet to smash against the depot. Near Irving Park Boulevard, just outside Melrose Park, a live baby was found lying on Nora Avenue. Later the baby was claimed by a woman from three blocks away. Even though it was raining, many fires broke out along the path. Although firefighters from neighboring towns quickly answered the call, the water system had been damaged and there was little to use against the fires. Fortunately, most fires did not spread farther than one house.

In Wilmette, practically every building in the 2-block-wide path of the tornado was damaged. Thirty business buildings and more than 100 residences were damaged. The most severe damage was in the Virginia Terrace, North Central Park Avenue, and

Central street areas. The path width of the storm was only about two blocks in Wilmette, but out in the open country houses 0.5 mile apart were damaged. It was believed that the cooling lake air destroyed the strength of the tornado and saved Evanston and Wilmette from greater damage.

Although it was reported at first that one tornado caused the damage in southern Illinois, it was determined that there were three separate tornadoes: two in Chicago and one northwest of Chicago, which damaged Elgin. The Elgin tornado first touched down about 12:05 P.M. approximately 1.5 miles southeast of Lafox and 3.5 miles southwest of Geneva. As it moved northwestward at 58 miles per hour toward Elgin, farms were damaged and 1 man was killed. The twister rose and covered the 15 miles to Elgin by 12:23 P.M., crossing the Fox River to drop into the business district of Elgin.

In addition to numerous businesses that were destroyed and damaged, the Grand Theater caved in, killing an actor and his wife; the brick tower of the Congressional Church collapsed, killing 3 ladies; and the Baptist Church was partially destroyed, killing 1 woman. More deaths might have occurred had the church services not let out a few minutes earlier. Lives were saved in the business district because it was Sunday. The tornado then left the downtown district, destroying or damaging homes along Dundee Avenue and then Dundee Road. It began to skip, passing west of Barrington, causing damage at intervals until Wauconda, where it caused its last damage. The funnel-shaped tornado covered 30 miles and caused 8 deaths and $1.5 million in damage in its 200-yard-wide path. Practically every building in Elgin was damaged to some extent.

The smaller Chicago tornado, or Clearing tornado, was a funnel-shaped cloud that destroyed several houses and caused about $150,000 in damage but no deaths. The tornado was first reported about 1 P.M., at Seventy-ninth Street and Harlem Avenue in the Bridgeview Area. It skipped to Fifty-fifth and Archer Avenue and followed Archer between Midway Airport and Cicero. Other points on its route were Ogden Avenue at about Twenty-second Street, Douglas Boulevard, Douglas Park, and Taylor Street, lifting finally at Lexington Avenue near Francisco Street, just 4 miles southwest of the Loop District of Chicago. The width varied from 100 yards to 0.5 mile.

C. Alton Hassell

FOR FURTHER INFORMATION:

American Red Cross, Chicago Chapter. *Tornado Disaster Relief.* Chicago: Author, 1920.

Chicago Tribune, March 29-31, 1920.

Flora, Snowden D. *Tornadoes of the United States.* Norman: University of Oklahoma Press, 1953.

Grazulius, Thomas P. *Significant Tornadoes: 1680-1991.* St. Johnsbury, Vt.: Environmental Films, 1993.

The New York Times, March 29-31, 1920.

U.S. Department of Agriculture. *Monthly Weather Review.* Washington, D.C.: Government Printing Office, 1920.

1920: U.S. South

DATE: April 20, 1920
PLACE: Alabama, Mississippi, and Tennessee
RESULT: 224 dead, over 1,300 injured

Seven killer tornadoes, 6 of them estimated to be F4 intensity, devastated large parts of rural Mississippi and Alabama in April of 1920. The death toll in Alabama was 92, and Mississippi suffered 131 deaths. A tornado claimed 1 life in rural Tennessee. This outbreak exemplifies the unique tornado climatology that exists in the southeastern United States. While most deadly tornadoes in the plains states and the Midwest occur during the late afternoon and early evening, they frequently occur during the night or the morning in the Southeast. This outbreak occurred between 7 A.M. and noon.

The longest and deadliest tornado of the family plowed 130 miles from Oktibbeha County, Mississippi, to Lawrence County, Alabama. In its path it left 88 dead, including 22 on the western edge of Aberdeen, Mississippi, and more than $2 million in damage. In Marion County, Alabama, the twister killed more than 500 hogs on one farm and left behind an estimated $500,000 in damage. Another tornado killed 36, including 12 on the southern edge of Meridian, Mississippi, the site of a Weather Bureau office. At Meridian the darkness became so intense about 10:30 A.M. that many fled the streets and office buildings in panic.

Marlene Bradford

FOR FURTHER INFORMATION:

Memphis Commercial Appeal, April 21, 1920.

1924: U.S. South

DATE: April 30, 1924
PLACE: Alabama, Georgia, the Carolinas, and Virginia
RESULT: 111 dead, about 1,100 injured, more than $4.2 million in damage

At least twenty-four tornadoes, sixteen of them killers, struck parts of five southeastern states throughout the day of April 30. Two of these storms were estimated to have reached F4 intensity. The state death tolls were as follows: 13 in Alabama, 16 in Georgia, 5 in North Carolina, 76 in South Carolina, and 1 in Virginia.

Nearly half the fatalities occurred in one tornado. This killer touched down 11 miles northeast of Aiken, South Carolina, and cut a path through six counties. Fifty-three deaths occurred in several small communities. Two students and a teacher died at the Steedman School, and 4 died at the Horrell Hill School. This tornado destroyed more than 300 homes and over 1,000 other buildings at a cost of more than $1 million. Another tornado tracked across the southern part of Anderson, South Carolina, and left behind at least $1.5 million in damage when it destroyed 100 small houses and 2 cotton mills. The remaining tornadoes claimed from 1 to 14 lives each.

Marlene Bradford

FOR FURTHER INFORMATION:

Atlanta Constitution, May 1-2, 1924.

1924: Ohio

DATE: June 28, 1924
PLACE: Lorain, Ohio
CLASSIFICATION: F4 (estimated)
RESULT: 85 dead, about 300 injured, $12.5 million in damage

The 400-yard-wide tornado that struck Sandusky, Ohio, at 4:35 P.M. on June 28, 1924, killed 8 people, injured about 100 others, destroyed 25 homes and 25 factories, and left behind $1.5 million in damage before it headed across Lake Erie. On the lake, the waterspout hit several boats. Several people who were on the lake at the time were still reported missing a month after the tornado and presumed dead, but they were not included in the death toll. At 5:08 the tornado roared back on shore at the Lorain Municipal Bath House, where it took 8 lives. The tornado then moved through downtown Lorain. Many of the buildings were brick structures that collapsed when the winds tore off their roofs. At least 15 of the 64 deaths in Lorain occurred at the State Theater. About 25 percent of the town's businesses but few houses were destroyed. Four more fatalities occurred just east of Lorain.

Marlene Bradford

FOR FURTHER INFORMATION:
Cleveland Plain Dealer, June 29, 1924.

1925: The Great Tri-State Tornado

DATE: March 18, 1925
PLACE: Missouri, Illinois, and Indiana
CLASSIFICATION: F5
RESULT: 689 dead, more than 2,000 injured, $16-18 million in damage

The storm that spawned the Great Tri-State and several other tornadoes on March 18, 1925, was from a northeast Pacific storm. The depression was over western Montana on March 16. On the morning of the 18th, it was over northwestern Arkansas and was moving to the northeast at about 40 miles per hour. It was over southern Illinois during the early afternoon and southeastern Indiana by 8 P.M.

The U.S. Weather Bureau described 7 distinct tornadoes in Alabama, Tennessee, Kentucky, Indiana, Missouri, and Illinois generated by the storm. Thomas P. Grazulis, in *Significant Tornadoes: 1680-1991* (1993), describes the same 7 but adds an earlier one in Kansas and a later one in Kentucky on that date. All but the Kansas tornado were killers. Fortunately, the death toll was 4 or less for all but 2 of these tornadoes. One tornado started in Summer County, Tennessee, and traveled 60 miles to Metcalfe County, Kentucky, killing 39 and injuring 95. It was of F4 force and had a path width of about 400 yards. The Great Tri-State Tornado caused 689 deaths—741 deaths for the total storm, with the death toll for the other six tornadoes 13, with 164 injuries.

The Tri-State Tornado was the most deadly and the most destructive. The Weather Bureau noted that it was different in another way. Most tornadoes occur in the southeast part of a storm system along a squall line or cold front. Seldom is a tornado formed in the center of a storm center, as the Great Tri-State Tornado was. It was especially devastating as it traveled on the ground along a ridge of mineral resources and parallel to a railroad. Thus, several mining and railroad towns were in its path.

Missouri. The tornado first touched down north of Ellington in southeast Missouri about 1 P.M. It traveled northeast to damage Leadanna, a mining town. It continued northeast to engulf Annapolis, 2 miles north of Leadanna. Annapolis was devastated, with 90 percent of the town destroyed and 2 dead. All but 7 of the 400 structures in Leadanna and Annapolis were badly damaged; the damage total was about $500,000 in the two towns. Fortunately, one schoolhouse that held 300 students was undamaged. The damage in and near Annapolis was 3 miles wide. Survivors remember that the sky became dark, and something like a smoky fog swept through the town. A funnel cloud was not seen.

The next damage occurred in and near the small towns of Lixville, Biehle, Frohna, and Altenburg. At least 32 children were injured in 2 county schools in Bollinger county. Deaths occurred in Biehle and Altenburg, 30 miles north of Cape Girardeau. In Biehle, there were 4 dead and 11 injured out of 100 villagers. For 3 miles near Biehle there were evidence and sightings of two parallel funnel clouds, which reunited later before passing into Illinois. A child was killed in a wooden schoolhouse 5 miles north of Altenburg. The toll in Missouri was 11 to 14 dead, 63 injured, and $564,000 in damage (in 1925 dollars).

Illinois. The damage in Illinois was much worse. In Gorham, it had been dark and gloomy; the drizzle increased to pouring down a flood, then the air was filled with flying debris. The town of 500 was virtually wiped out. There were 34 deaths, and over half of the town's population was killed or injured. Seven of the deaths occurred at the school. Communications were cut off such that although the tornado struck at 2:35 P.M. no aid came until 8 P.M. There was not even a healthy doctor present until aid arrived. The doctor in town was giving an injection when the tornado hit; the patient was killed, and the doctor received a broken collarbone.

Murphysboro, population 11,000, was next to be decimated. The 234 deaths were the largest number in one city in U.S. history at the time. About 800 were injured and $10 million was incurred in damage. Three schools, built of brick or stone with little reinforcement, were caved in, crushing at least 25 people. The tornado affected 152 city blocks—72 percent of the residential section and 60 percent of the city. About 1,200 homes were damaged or destroyed, leaving 8,000 people, or two-thirds of the city, homeless. Fires ravaged the destroyed area and 70 more blocks in a residential district, demolishing homes still standing and burning victims caught under collapsed buildings. Fires could be seen as far as 60 miles away. The tornado had destroyed the water plant, as well as many of the hydrants. A "rigged" system restored water pressure to fight the fires. Other casualties of the tornado were the 2,000 jobs lost due to the destruction of the Mobile and Ohio Railroad shop, the Brown's Shoe Company, the Isco-Bautz silica plant, and other industries. Businesses sustained almost $1 million in damage but had only $122,000 in insurance.

The next town hit was DeSoto, a hamlet of 600, where 33 were killed at one school, setting the record for school deaths in a tornado. A total of 69 were killed in or around DeSoto. The town itself was obliterated. Only a dozen houses were left standing, none left undamaged. An outbreak of fires caused more damage to the ravaged town.

The hamlet of Bush was next in the storm's path; there, the tornado left 7 dead and 37 injured. It also left only one building standing in Hurst, a town of 200. The rural area between DeSoto and West Frankfort suffered 24 deaths. Even the Illinois Central railroad bridge on the Zeigler branch was shifted by 6 feet. One of the rescue jobs after the tornado was to clean the debris off of farm land so that planting could be done within the next few weeks.

Between West Frankfort and Orient was a small school attended by Mavis Flota. It was a warm day, but late in the afternoon it became so dark that the students could not read by lamplight. The clouds became streaked with lightning, and thunder boomed. A roar like the sound of a train told the teacher that there was a tornado coming. It tore off one room, spilling Flota onto the ground and into the golf-ball-size hail. When she stood, she was picked up by the storm and carried 2 miles, landing scratched and bruised but otherwise unhurt, except for the soles of her new shoes being pulled off.

The tornado cut across the northwest part of West Frankfort, the largest town in its path, with 20,000 people. This part of town was composed mostly of small residences, many of them miners' homes. Sixty-four blocks of houses were damaged in the 0.25-mile-wide path, and 13 blocks were wiped out. The 925 damaged or destroyed houses left 3,000 homeless and half a million dollars in damage. There were 127 dead, 450 injured, and 117 hospitalized, with a total $800,000 in damage. Almost 800 miners were 500 feet below earth's surface when they lost electrical power. They had to climb out a narrow escarpment and then face the damage and injuries caused by the tornado; many of the dead and wounded were women and children.

A small community, called Eighteen because it was near Number 18 Mine, was devastated. Nearby Parrish contained about 40 buildings, but only 3 were left after the tornado. Although the population was only 300, there were 46 deaths and 100 injured. There, the tornado was preceded by thunder and a violent succession of lightning flashes, and the funnel cloud was seen by Parrish inhabitants. It struck Parrish at 3:15 P.M. Hailstones the size of apples came after the tornado. Parrish never rebuilt, existing only as a few older homes.

In the forty-five minutes required for the tornado to travel through Gorham to Parrish, 541 people were killed. Leaving Parrish, the path of the tornado went through rural areas in Hamilton and White Counties before reaching Carmi, near the Indiana border. The destruction and death in the rural areas was unprecedented, as many farms were completely destroyed and 65 people were killed. At least three different White County schools claimed deaths from the tornado. It was estimated that 1,500 farms needed debris cleaned off of the land so that they could be planted.

Indiana. The town of Carmi had 2 deaths and the border town of Crossville reported 1 before the tornado crossed into Indiana. In Illinois the tornado caused 606 deaths, about 1,600 injuries, and $13 million in damage.

Just beyond the Wabash River was the small town of Griffin. The tornado did not leave a habitable structure out of the 150 homes in Griffin. Two children on a bus were killed; the total death toll there was 34, with 200 injured out of 375 inhabitants. Identifying victims was difficult, as mud was embedded into their skin. Fires occurred in the ruins and added to the destruction and agony.

Leaving Griffin, the path of the tornado, 0.75 mile wide, veered north by 9 degrees. The new path would include Owensville and Princeton. At Owensville, 17 deaths occurred, including three generations of one family. In this rural area, 85 farms were totally destroyed.

Princeton, the county seat of Gibson County, was caught, like most other towns, unaware. A blackness moved over the south side of town, killing 45 and injuring 152 and causing $1.8 million in damage. One-fourth to one-half of the town was located in the devastated area, so after 200 homes were destroyed and 100 were damaged, 1,500 people were left homeless. The two largest industries, the $2 million Southern Railway shops and the H. T. Heinz factory, were demolished, as was the village of workers' homes nearby. Fortunately, only 3 people lost their lives at the industries (2 at Southern, 1 at Heinz). Luckily, the Princeton school had let out about twenty minutes earlier, and the children were out of the tornado's path; the school was caved in. An estimated 100,000 people visited Princeton to view the damage.

The deadly tornado finally lost its steam and lifted near Petersburg, 16 miles northeast of Princeton, about 4:30 P.M. East of Princeton, irregular-shaped chunks of ice as large as goose eggs were reported to fall. In Indiana, the tornado had appeared as three funnels for part of its path. Many people described it as a turbulent, boiling mass filled with debris. It often looked like a big black mass, similar to a thunderstorm. The tornado had killed 30 people in Indiana, injured 354, and caused $2,775,000 in damage.

Conclusions. The Great Tri-State Tornado is considered the single deadliest tornado in U.S. history to date. It maintained contact with the ground for the longest distance (219 miles) and for the longest time (3.5 hours). It was moving quickly for a tornado, at an average of 62 miles per hour—73 miles per hour in Indiana. The intensity did not vary as much with this tornado as with others; it simply destroyed everything in its way. Its path was wide, varying from 0.25 mile to 1 mile, with much of the path 0.75 mile in width. It traveled an exact heading of 69 degrees northeast for 183 of the 219 miles.

The killer moved so quickly that many were not able to seek shelter. Country residents indicated that only about five minutes passed after noticing the cloud before the tornado struck. However, shelter in the form of basements, which are usually places of safety, were deathtraps to several people. In some cases, the tornado caved the house into the basement, and the wood or coal stove then set the ruins on fire, burning the trapped survivors. Nine people were found around a stove in a Griffin restaurant.

C. Alton Hassell

FOR FURTHER INFORMATION:

Cornell, James. *The Great International Disaster Book.* 3d ed. New York: Charles Scribner's Sons, 1982.

"Deadly Tornadoes." *The Indianapolis News,* April 3, 1999.

Felknor, Peter E. *The Tri-State Tornado.* Ames: Iowa State University Press, 1992.

Flora, Snowden D. *Tornadoes of the United States.* Norman: University of Oklahoma Press, 1954.

Grazulis, Thomas P. *Significant Tornadoes: 1680-1991.* St. Johnsburg, Vt.: Environmental Films, 1993.

"Inside Illinois: People and Places—60 Years Ago the Most Deadly of All Tornadoes Hit Illinois." *UPI,* March 16, 1985.

"New Twist on Forgotten Storm." *St. Louis Post-Dispatch,* March 18, 1992.

The New York Times, March 19-April 19, 1925.

U.S. Department of Agriculture. *Monthly Weather Review.* Washington, D.C.: Government Printing Office, 1925.

1927: Texas

DATE: April 12, 1927
PLACE: Rock Springs, Texas (now Rocksprings)
CLASSIFICATION: F5 (estimated)
RESULT: 74 dead, 205 injured, $1.23 million in damage

At about 7:50 P.M. on April 12, 1927, a mile-wide funnel emerged from a thunderstorm on the northern edge of Rock Springs, Texas. The twister leveled the flimsy houses on the northern edge of town before moving into the business district, where it heavily damaged the high school, crumbled churches, tore the roof from the stone courthouse, toppled the town water tower, and left buildings on the town square in ruins. Few towns have suffered such complete devastation from a tornado. One-third of the population was killed or injured, and 235 of the 247 buildings were extensively damaged or destroyed.

An injured telephone operator and a lineman connected a portable telephone unit to an undamaged wire outside town and called for help. More than five hours passed before the first outside assistance arrived, much of it from the military. The U.S. Fifth Cavalry from Fort Clark set up a field hospital and kitchen, soldiers dynamited grave sites out of solid rock, and Kelly Field sent three aircraft to transport the severely injured to San Antonio. Although the number of seriously injured was large, the administration of tetanus serum reduced the fatalities. Many of those who aided the tornado victims doubted that Rock Springs (later renamed Rocksprings) would survive, but within five months the local newspaper boasted that the new fireproof buildings around the court square were ready for occupancy.

Marlene Bradford

FOR FURTHER INFORMATION:
Lynch, Dudley. *Tornado: Texas Demon in the Wind.* Waco, Tex.: Texian Press, 1970.

1927: U.S. Midwest

DATE: May 8-9, 1927
PLACE: Arkansas, Illinois, Louisiana, Missouri, and Texas
RESULT: 224 dead, about 1,120 injured

The three tornadoes that killed 12 in rural Missouri during the late evening of May 8, 1927, were only the harbingers of their more destructive cousins that roared through parts of five states the next day. A total of 17 killer tornadoes, 8 of which received an estimated F4 rating, took 224 lives during the outbreak. State death tolls were as follows: 70 in Arkansas, 8 in Illinois, 1 in Louisiana, 105 in Missouri, and 40 in Texas. In Texas one tornado formed just outside the town of Nevada at 2:25 A.M., giving the sleeping residents no time to seek shelter. Sixteen died, and 75 percent of the town was destroyed. Within an hour another tornado killed 15 in the Dallas suburb of Garland.

Throughout the remainder of the day, 6 tornadoes claimed at least 5 lives each in Arkansas. One destroyed the central part of the town of Strong and killed 24 of its citizens, and another killed 11 at Hoxie. The deadliest storm was reserved for Mis-

souri. At about 3:15 P.M. a twister that formed in Arkansas and crossed into Missouri killed 4 people in rural homes and 6 in a touring car before turning toward Poplar Bluff, a city of about 10,000. The tornado took only three minutes to pass through the town, leaving behind at least 83 dead, including 21 in the Melbourne Hotel. Less than a dozen buildings remained standing, and those were badly damaged. The estimated damage was $2.1 million. May 9, 1927, was one of the worst tornado days in United States history, with 10 separate tornadoes killing 5 or more people each.

Marlene Bradford

FOR FURTHER INFORMATION:
Memphis Commercial Appeal, May 10-12, 1927.

1927: St. Louis

DATE: September 29, 1927
PLACE: St. Louis, Missouri; also Venice, Madison, and Granite City, Illinois
CLASSIFICATION: F1
RESULT: At least 85 dead, more than 1,300 injured, 5,000 homes damaged or destroyed, $100 million in estimated damage

By September of 1927, the Midwest had already experienced exceptionally violent weather. On May 8 and 9, 36 tornadoes had struck the region, including 1 in St. Louis, causing 227 deaths throughout the Midwest and more than $7.9 million in damage. That spring, the Mississippi River had also flooded its banks. Nevertheless, St. Louis was unprepared for the devastating five-minute tornado that swept a 20-mile path through the city, across the Mississippi River, and into Illinois on September 29. Cities had no early warning systems.

At daybreak, skies were cloudy. Rain began before dawn but ended at 7:10 A.M., although winds were strong. The sun broke through the clouds briefly after 8 A.M., but clouds gathered again at 11 A.M., with the rain following at 11:26. Lightning and thunder were heard toward the west. By 12:57 P.M., clouds were low, black, and thick. Soon after, rain and wind intensified until vision from office windows was completely obscured. By 1:02 P.M., wind was estimated at 96 miles per hour.

The tornado first struck down in the southwest suburbs of the city, where it did only moderate damage. It gained force as it swept northeast across the city. The path of the storm was estimated at 20 miles in length and ranged from about 300 to 6,000 feet in width. Damage became severe as the storm approached Kingshighway and the edge of Forest Park, site of the 1904 World's Fair. Gaining in intensity, the storm transformed more than two hundred blocks of the city into a mass of wreckage, fallen poles, downed trees, electric wires (some dangerously tangled with telephone wires), damaged automobiles, and debris. While missing the downtown business section, the storm severely damaged the fashionable Central West End and a nearby boardinghouse district. It swept through one of the most prosperous African American communities in the city, damaging almost every home. Confusion was increased and rescue efforts

hampered by the interruption of telephone service, small fires caused by fallen power lines, delayed fire alarms, and major streets blocked by debris. Some observers reported seeing mysterious sheets of flame.

Considering the path of the storm, which was estimated to have destroyed 6 to 7 percent of St. Louis's 63 square miles, there were few fatalities. Most of these apparently resulted from the absence of any warning system. Authorities attributed this to the fact that, at 1 P.M., most people were in school or at work outside the residential districts.

There were, however, seven schools, housing 6,500 students, in the path of the storm. At Central High School on Grand Avenue, 5 girls, ranging in age from twelve to seventeen, were killed when the collapse of a tower, used for storing heavy equipment, buried them in the school auditorium. Others were injured. The tower ripped out walls as it descended, leaving students in laboratories and lecture halls suddenly exposed to the wind.

Elsewhere, the lack of fatalities was surprising. At Columbia School on Garrison Avenue, approximately 700 children were in their classrooms when the storm hit. Principal G. H. Green led the students to safety as the roof caved in, burying classrooms under tons of debris. At the Riddick School on Whittier Street, more than 1,000 students were at their desks when wind tore out one wall. Only a few were slightly injured by flying glass.

Fatalities in industries were also light, despite heavy damages. Again, most resulted from lack of warning. Some workmen, returning to their jobs after lunch, were trapped in vehicles, sometimes under fallen poles and trees. Three men were killed when part of the Hydraulic Press Brick Company collapsed; 3 more died under a falling wall at the Polar Wave Ice Plant. In Venice, Illinois, 6 deaths were reported when wind blew down a building of the St. Louis Coke and Iron Company, flooding workmen with the molten metal that they were preparing to pour for casting. The suddenness of the storm and lack of warning were made evident in such deaths as that of Michael A. Clifford, seventy-two-year-old Venice chief of police and vice president of the Illinois Police Chief's Association. Clifford was killed as he was eating lunch in his home; the building collapsed on him.

As the storm crossed the Mississippi River, it decreased in intensity, but it did considerable damage in the Illinois cities of Granite City, Madison, and Venice. Towns 40 to 50 miles northeast of the McKinley Bridge, where the storm crossed the river, were affected by the tornado. In Hillsboro, Mt. Olive, and Litchfield, Illinois, residents found papers that had blown there from devastated areas of St. Louis. To them, the papers seemed to drop from the sky.

Although technological limitations in the 1920's could not lower the death toll, one technological advance of that decade enhanced the relief effort after the storm. Radio was the new popular entertainment of the 1920's. While one of St. Louis's three stations had been silenced by the storm, broadcasters from two others worked together to organize relief efforts. With one man broadcasting from atop the Central West End's Chase Hotel and the other man working at street level, they were able to direct rescue units to specific sites and to organize appeals for supplies, money, and physical assistance.

Betty Richardson

FOR FURTHER INFORMATION:
East St. Louis Daily Journal, September 30-October 2, 1927.

Engineer's Club of St. Louis and American Institute of Architects, St. Louis Chapter. *Report of the St. Louis Tornado of September 29, 1927.* St. Louis: Author, 1928.

The New York Times, September 30-October 1, 1927.

St. Louis Post-Dispatch, September 30-October 3, 1927.

1932: U.S. South

DATE: March 21-22, 1932
PLACE: Alabama, Georgia, Tennessee, the Carolinas, and Kentucky
CLASSIFICATION: F4
RESULT: 359 dead, several thousand injured, thousands homeless, millions of dollars in damage

On Monday, March 21, 1932, a moist, warm air mass moved from the Gulf of Mexico across Mississippi into southwestern Alabama. By late afternoon the air mass collided with a cold front over western Alabama, spawning a storm system that produced 33 tornadoes that struck in 6 southern states. During Monday afternoon and evening, a series of tornadoes moving northeast devastated west central Alabama. After several hours, the storm front separated. Part of the front moved north to Tennessee and Kentucky, while another portion headed east through Georgia and the Carolinas early Tuesday morning.

Alabama suffered the most damage, primarily at remote farmsteads and communities in "wild and inaccessible country." The *Birmingham News* described the tornadoes as a "satanic Storm King that danced with impish fury across the South." The newspaper reviewed the storm's route through Alabama and provided details about each stricken town. The two tornadoes that hit Marion, Alabama, were the first reported. Approximately 150 people were wounded during the storm at a plantation outside Marion. Fallen trees covered roads, and people used saws and axes to cut a path to travel into town, where 18 people had died.

To the northwest, the cities of Northport and Tuscaloosa, separated by the Warrior River, were hit hard. Witnesses said they saw a stationary black funnel cloud that slowly began to move. The tornado sounded like racing cars. A stable on Northport's Main Street was the site of several deaths, and the Tuscaloosa Country Club was leveled. Townspeople, the local militia, and University of Alabama students searched rubble for people. The wounded were injected with tetanus antitoxin. Thirty-three bodies were identified. Tuscaloosa's Druid City Hospital filled quickly with victims, and the university's gymnasium served as a temporary medical facility. Physicians, nurses, and ambulances arrived from Birmingham, and the Red Cross sent cots, blankets, and supplies. National Guard troops arrived to deliver relief goods and prohibit looting. Northport was sealed off, and only people with permits could enter the city.

Tornadoes struck nearby communities as well; 29 people died at Demopolis. At Faunsdale, a chimney collapsed, killing 1 man, and 900 people were homeless after the storm. Boxcars were blown across the Southern Railway's tracks at Linden. The town of Lomax was leveled. The storm moved northeast into Chilton County, where three tornadoes killed 40 people. In Shelby County, the Columbiana courthouse was converted into a makeshift hospital and morgue. Nurses and undertakers used oil lamps because the downed power lines cut off electricity.

Resident Wilbur B. Lyon told reporters that "[h]uge timbers 200 feet in the air told me it was a twister." He remarked that the tornado "played havoc with houses as though they were match boxes." Churches and a high school were leveled along a 20-mile path that the tornadoes traveled in Cullman County. Wounded individuals were transported to Birmingham hospitals, where national personnel from the Red Cross established emergency relief headquarters.

In east central Alabama, tornadoes destroyed all the structures in Marble Valley around 7 that night and scattered wreckage so that the town resembled an empty field. No one was killed in Marble Valley, but 19 people died in nearby Sylacauga, where more than 100 houses and 3 schools were destroyed. In the countryside, farm buildings, poultry, and livestock were blown away. A howitzer company from the 167th Infantry was sent to the city to stop looting. In north Alabama, near the Tennessee line, a tornado destroyed the Paint Rock Hosiery Mill, which was "crushed like an eggshell." Four employees died.

Tornadoes in Tennessee wiped out communities near Lewisburg, Franklin, and Pulaski and resulted in 18 deaths. Chattanooga was spared because Lookout Mountain reduced the storm's strength to 60-mile-per-hour winds and downpours, which ruined some buildings. North Georgia suffered tornado damage in rural areas, and 37 deaths were reported. The storms moved into South Carolina, where 3 people died; tenant farmers were the primary storm casualties. Relief efforts were hindered by disconnected telegraph wires. At Stumptown, North Carolina, a small African American community, a tornado flattened a dozen houses and a church, but no one died. Another tornado killed 2 people in Uniontown, Kentucky. Moving along the Ohio River, the tornado tore off buildings' roofs.

Attempts to find missing people were hindered by torrential rain and a cold wave that followed the storm front. Dogs alerted rescuers to people trapped under wreckage. Segregation policies restricted how different people were assisted. Red Cross workers erected two cafeteria tents, one for whites and one for blacks, near stricken communities. First-aid stations were also segregated. Severed communications prevented casualty lists from being tallied quickly. Also, because casualties were dispersed over isolated areas, statistics changed as bodies were located or wounded people died in hospitals. A total of 359 people died, of which 299 were in Alabama. Approximately 2,500 people were injured and 7,000 became homeless. Millions of dollars of property damage was sustained.

In Alabama, county agents stockpiled relief supplies in their offices for farmers. The agents also assessed the devastation to agriculture. In addition to livestock and crop losses, 1,000 farm homes were destroyed. Resident R. C. Lett surveyed Tuscaloosa County and stated that after buildings blew away on "some farms only land [was] left." In Clay County, many trees fell, including pecan and fruit trees. Valuable farm equipment was obliterated.

Alabama governor B. M. Miller visited tornado victims and issued a proclamation asking for contributions to the Red Cross. Acknowledging that the Depression limited people financially, he donated $50 for victims and stressed "there will be great suffering unless they are aided properly." Railroads shipped relief supplies for free. Radio stations broadcast appeals, and civic groups sponsored entertainment, donating proceeds to the Red Cross.

Elizabeth D. Schafer

FOR FURTHER INFORMATION:

"More than 300 Die in Storms." *Birmingham News*, March 23, 1932, p. 1.

"95 Dead in 4 States Hit by Tornadoes; Towns Lie in Ruins." *The New York Times*, March 22, 1932, p. 1.

"Tornado Dead 329; 7,000 Are Homeless." *The New York Times*, March 24, 1932, p. 3.

"Tornado's Death Toll 275 in South; 1,000 Injured, Damage Is Millions." *The New York Times*, March 23, 1932, p. 1.

1936: U.S. South

DATE: April 2-6, 1936
PLACE: Gainesville, Georgia; Tupelo, Mississippi; Arkansas; Alabama; and Tennessee
CLASSIFICATION: F4 and F5
RESULT: 466 dead, 3,457 injured, $25 million in damage

Tornadoes are an annual occurrence in the United States. The central and southeastern states are most frequently visited by funnel clouds. For this reason this area of the United States is called "Tornado Alley." One of the most frightening traits of tornadoes is that they often strike in batches. When dozens of funnel clouds touch down at various locations across large sections of the United States within several days, the event is called an outbreak. The second deadliest outbreak in U.S. history to date took place from April 2 to April 6, 1936. A 17-funnel system tore through 5 states, killing a total of 466 people.

During 1936, the United States was slowly bringing itself out of the Great Depression with building projects to bolster the economy, create jobs, and generally improve life. The Tennessee Valley Authority (TVA) was such a project. The TVA brought electricity to many parts of the rural south. Tupelo, Mississippi, was the first city to benefit from the power generated by the TVA. The town so proud of its TVA connection was devastated by a fierce tornado.

Tupelo was one of the first—and the hardest—hit during the four-day batch of tornadoes that reached beyond the usual limits of Tornado Alley. The tornado system stretched from Mississippi to the western Carolinas. The five states hit by the tornadoes—Mississippi, Georgia, Alabama, Arkansas, and Tennessee—suffered a combined $25 million in dam-

age. At the end of the tornado strike, casualties totaled 466 dead and 3,457 injured. Tupelo's death rate alone was 216. Gainesville, Georgia, was next, with 206 dead.

The storm system is believed to have started in North Carolina on April 2, 1936. A tornado struck near Greensboro, killing 13 people and injuring 144 others. Other small tornadoes struck across the western Carolinas, Tennessee, and Arkansas. On April 5 at approximately 8:30 A.M. a tornado hit Coffeeville, Mississippi. The funnel cloud moved northeast through Yalobusha, Calhoun, and Pontotoc Counties, entering Lee County as it continued to gain mass and speed. Traveling across the central section of Lee County on an east-northeast path, it passed through residential areas in the northern half of Tupelo, leveling over 200 homes. A section of poorly constructed homes along the Gum Pond bluff, several miles west of town, was completely swept away. Many of the residents were actually blown into Gum Pond, accounting for a majority of the deaths reported. (The one-year-old Elvis Presley survived to make music history later.) The funnel cloud then moved off, appearing as lesser storms across Alabama.

The devastation lingering on the morning of April 5 would live in the memories of many survivors. According to firsthand accounts recorded years later by the Tupelo *Daily Journal*, debris was everywhere. One man recalled how many businesses—left vacant after the Great Depression—were turned into instant morgue space. At a movie theater that was turned into a hospital for the thousands of injured, the popcorn machine was used to sterilize medical instruments.

Though the Fujita scale was not yet developed, the tornado's intensity is estimated today based on reports of ground devastation. The Tupelo tornado is estimated to have been an F5 tornado, in which large and heavy objects are lifted for over 100 yards before dropping again, strong frame houses are lifted off foundations, trees are debarked, and steel-reinforced structures are badly damaged in winds ranging from 261 to 318 miles per hour. In Tupelo, pine needles were embedded in the bark of trees still left standing, and a two-by-four was driven through a cast-iron pump cylinder, according to firsthand accounts recorded by Murray Moore and other Tupelo tornado survivors in an October, 1992, *Weatherwise* article.

The tornado that roared through Gainesville, Georgia, the following morning is estimated to have been an F4 tornado. Winds ranged from 207 to 260 miles per hour. In an F4 tornado, well-constructed homes are destroyed, and buildings with weak foundations are blown over or lifted and released some distance away. Cars are also thrown, and debris of all sorts become missiles surging through the air. At approximately 8:27 A.M. on April 6, 1936, Gainesville was actually visited by three separate tornadoes. A small tornado hit north of town, and two large funnel clouds moved east-northeast through the downtown area. One funnel cloud led into the city from the southwest; the other came in from the west. Their paths merged west of Grove Street, leveling a four-block-wide area, before they separated again to wreak further damage. In the aftermath of the tornadoes, debris was 10 feet deep in some sections of town.

A multistory factory, Cooper Pants, was crowded with young workers at the start of the workday. The building collapsed and caught fire, killing 70 people. This was the largest death toll in a single building for any U.S. tornado as of 1999. Luckily, workers at the Pacelot Mill averted an even greater tragedy. The funnel cloud was sighted coming from the southwest. The 550 workers took cover in the northeast corner of the building and survived. Newman's Department Store, where many high school students sought shelter, also collapsed during the storm, killing 20 people.

So many people were injured that hospitals in three states took in victims. Some injured children were not reunited with their families for months. Despite the ruins left from the tornadoes, the cities especially devastated proved they could once again rebuild through strong cooperation and community spirit. From the wake of the Great Depression, and then again from the tornadoes of April, 1936, these cities rose like the legendary phoenix from the ashes.

Lisa A. Wroble

For Further Information:

Erickson, Jon. *Violent Storms.* Blue Ridge Summit, Pa.: TAB Books, 1988.

Harper, Phyllis. "Killer Storm Leveled 48 Blocks in Tupelo." *Daily Journal Online!* (Mississippi), http://www.djournal.com/125/wcillers.htm, 1996.

Moore, Gary. "Trapped in the Great Tupelo Tornado." *Weatherwise* 45, no. 5 (October, 1992): 16.

Tornado Project. "Top Ten U.S. Killer Tornadoes." http://www.tornadoproject.com/toptens/top tens.htm.

Watson, Benjamin A. *Acts of God: "The Old Farmer's Almanac" Unpredictable Guide to Weather and Natural Disasters.* New York: Random House, 1993.

1942: Mississippi

Date: March 16, 1942
Place: Primarily Mississippi; also Tennessee, Alabama, Kentucky, Missouri, Illinois, and Indiana
Classification: Unknown
Result: 117 dead, several hundred injured, millions of dollars in damage

The cotton-growing region of northern Mississippi was pounded by powerful tornadoes in March of 1942 that killed as many as 81 people and hurt approximately 650 others. Sweeping northwest across an area spanning 150 miles east to west and 100 miles north to south, the tornadoes struck rural regions, where flimsy housing fell apart in the wind. Jack Dale, editor of the *North Mississippi Herald* in Water Valley, a town that was hit hard, reported that the city auditorium was being used as an emergency hospital because the town's hospital capacity was overwhelmed.

Dale said he had heard rumors that 150 people had died in Grenada, Mississippi, but thought that number was inflated. Disrupted communications prevented accurate information about casualties from being secured. Other Mississippi towns hit by tornadoes included Greenwood, Belden, Oxford, Tula, Baldwin, Avalon, and Michigan City. Red Cross disaster workers established headquarters for relief in Memphis, Tennessee. The Mississippi legislature approved $30,000 for assistance to tornado victims, which was matched by federal Works Progress Administration (WPA) funds.

Deadly tornadoes struck surrounding states that same day. Fatalities and injuries were reported in Tennessee, Alabama, Kentucky, Indiana, and Illinois. Property was destroyed in Missouri, but no humans were hurt or killed. Total damage in these states was estimated to cost several million dollars.

Elizabeth D. Schafer

For Further Information:

"100 Killed, 650 Injured as Storms Sweep 5 States in South, Midwest." *Atlanta Constitution*, March 17, 1942, p. 1.

"117 Perish in Sweep of Tornadoes." *Montgomery Advertiser*, March 17, 1942, p. 1.

"Tornadoes Sweep 6 States; 115 Dead, Hundreds Injured." *The New York Times*, March 17, 1942, p. 1.

1944: West Virginia, Pennsylvania, Maryland

DATE: June 23, 1944
PLACE: Northern West Virginia, southwestern Pennsylvania, and parts of Maryland
CLASSIFICATION: F2-F4
RESULT: 123 dead, hundreds injured, thousands of structures damaged, millions of dollars in damage

A family of tornadoes devastated areas of northern West Virginia and southwestern Pennsylvania before hitting portions of Maryland in June of 1944. Intense summer heat contributed to the formation of powerful thunderstorms on the afternoon of June 23. At 5:30 P.M., an F3 tornado tore through three counties in western Pennsylvania, killing 2 people and causing $2 million in damage. This twister preceded a more menacing storm system.

By 6:11, an F4 tornado moved through Brooke County, West Virginia, and Washington, Greene, and Fayette Counties, Pennsylvania, before passing through West Virginia again and hitting Garrett County, Maryland, killing 151 people and hurting hundreds more. A YMCA camp in Washington County, Pennsylvania, was flattened while children sought shelter in a nearby knoll. Later, a camper's letter was found 100 miles away. The tornado strengthened as it passed through Greene County, demolishing coal-mining towns. Meteorologists believe that the tornado either crossed the Appalachian Mountains or reformed on the other side. Eyewitnesses reported seeing debris in the sky half an hour before the tornado hit Preston County, West Virginia.

Simultaneously, an F4 tornado traveled through Allegheny, Westmoreland, and Somerset Counties, Pennsylvania, and another moved through six adjacent West Virginia counties (Marion, Harrison, Taylor, Barbour, Tucker, and Randolph), killing 100 people. Hundreds of houses were damaged at an estimated $5.5 million loss. At 10:25 an F3 tornado

from the same system moved through Tucker County, West Virginia, contributing to another million dollars of damage.

Elizabeth D. Schafer

FOR FURTHER INFORMATION:
"86 Die in Tornado in Pittsburgh Area." *The New York Times*, June 24, 1944, p. 15.
"Hundreds Are Homeless." *The New York Times*, June 25, 1944, p. 28.

1945: U.S. Midwest

DATE: April 12, 1945
PLACE: Oklahoma, Arkansas, Missouri, and Illinois
CLASSIFICATION: F2-F5
RESULT: 123 dead, hundreds injured, millions of dollars in damage

Mostly ignored by the national and even local press because President Franklin D. Roosevelt died the same day, a family of intense tornadoes bombarded the Midwest on April 12, 1945. At 3:25 in the afternoon, an F4 tornado struck southeast Oklahoma City, killing 8 and injuring 200. Most of the million dollars of damage occurred at Tinker Air Force Base.

Less powerful tornadoes struck nearby Oklahoma and Arkansas counties within the next hour, causing 10 fatalities. Just before 5, an F4 tornado killed 13 and hurt 200 when it hit Oklahoma's Muskogee School for the Blind, damaging a dormitory and gymnasium and causing $1.5 million dollars in damage. About the same time, an F2 tornado killed 4 people in Hulbert, Oklahoma.

Forty minutes later, an F5 tornado caused 69 fatalities and injured 353 people at Antlers, Oklahoma. One-third of the town was destroyed, with 600 buildings obliterated and 700 damaged. Smaller tornadoes injured people and property, primarily tourists' cabins, in Arkansas and Missouri. By 8 P.M. an F3 tornado had ravaged the Huntsville, Arkansas, area, killing 9 and wounding 30. Thousands of forested acres worth $70,000 were ripped from the ground. A group of F2 tornadoes traveled from Palmyra, Missouri, to Quincy, Illinois, where the business district was destroyed and the courthouse dome removed. Other Missouri towns experienced tornado damage and deaths around 9 P.M., when 10 people died and 70 were injured near Booneville and Clarksville, Arkansas. Tornadoes occurring later that night inflicted structural damage in Missouri and Illinois.

Elizabeth D. Schafer

FOR FURTHER INFORMATION:

"At Least 112 Die in 3-State Tornado; 63 Are Killed in One Oklahoma Town." *The New York Times,* April 14, 1945, p. 17.

1947: Texas, Oklahoma, Kansas

DATE: April 9, 1947
PLACE: The Texas Panhandle; Woodward, Oklahoma; and parts of Kansas
CLASSIFICATION: F5 (estimated)
RESULT: 181 dead, 970 injured

The destruction wrought throughout Texas, Oklahoma, and Kansas in April, 1947, was not caused by

just one tornado but rather by a whole family of tornadoes spawned by the collision of a Siberian Express air mass and warm, moist air drifting from the Gulf of Mexico. The Siberian Express had been hurried across the country by a high-altitude jet stream. Thunderstorms were expected in the area, but there was no prediction of severe weather. The deadly storm began in the late afternoon. The first tornado came near the Texas Panhandle town of White Deer in the early evening of April 9, 1947. Six funnels eventually descended, five at the same time, from the black clouds. With a wind speed over 200 miles per hour, the tornadoes traveled over a 221-mile track with the most destructive of the tornadoes, the Woodward tornado, covering 98 miles. The storm sped along the flat land at approximately 40 miles per hour.

The storm moved northeast through the Texas Panhandle, causing damage. The tornado stayed on a path that took it by Pampa, Miami, and Canadian, Texas. The town of Glazier, near the Oklahoma border, was demolished; all that was left was a gas station. The now-1.5-mile-wide funnel continued across the Panhandle of Texas. A conductor on a railroad line near the tornado reported seeing a house rise off the ground, shake, and then explode. The tornado hit Higgins, Texas, where over 30 people were killed and only one building was reported to be still standing, before moving into Oklahoma. It passed near Shattuck, Arnett, Gage, and Fargo, Oklahoma, causing damage to the farms and ranches in the area. Then it moved through unoccupied land for over 30 miles, on a course for the largest town in the region, Woodward.

After hitting the United States Field Station on the outskirts of Woodward, Oklahoma, the nearly 2-mile-wide funnel headed toward Main Street in the town with a population of 5,500. Residents of Woodward first saw the storm through the numerous lightning strikes it caused. Rain and hail began pelting the ground, and the characteristic roaring sound was heard. At 8:43 P.M. the tornado knocked out the Oklahoma Gas and Electric plant and plunged the town into darkness. The tornado did the most damage in the northern part of Woodward. Approximately two hundred blocks, most of them in residential areas, were leveled. One woman survived by clinging to a telephone pole. Over 1,000 homes in Woodward were damaged or destroyed. At first people did not realize the destruction was so great. There were many reports of gas lines leaking after the tornado passed. Uncontrollable fires raged for several hours. Eventually a downpour helped end the fires.

The tornadic storm continued crossing the Cimarron River, damaging buildings in Woods County and in Whitehorse. The tornado moved northeastward and crossed into Kansas, sputtering out finally around 11 that evening, 40 miles from the border near St. Leo, Kansas. Small tornadoes were also reported at Fowler, Newton, Sharon, Isabel, and Harveyville, Kansas, in the early morning of April 10.

The first eyewitness report of the disaster came from a TWA pilot who flew overhead in the early hours of April 10. He reported huge clouds of smoke still over the stricken communities, boxcars flung from railway stations, and damage that seemed to have wiped out whole areas of buildings. Radio calls poured from the communities hit by the twister. The TWA pilot even received a call from the town of Gage, asking for medical ointment and tetanus antitoxin. An emergency telephone station was set up outside Woodward.

Luckily, the hospital in Woodward survived unscathed. However, the hospital was soon overwhelmed by the victims, and some of the injured were transported to Mooreland, Enid, and Oklahoma City. The local veterinarian was even pressed into service. Ambulances made shuttle trips for the injured. An Army C-54 airplane provided a similar service to transfer

A towering funnel makes its way toward Rockwall, Texas, on April 30, 1947. A massive tornado outbreak three weeks earlier brought destruction to many towns in Texas, Oklahoma, and Kansas. (AP/Wide World Photos)

patients to the distant hospital in Oklahoma City. Searching parties used bulldozers to dig through the debris to try to find additional victims. Couriers had to be used to get messages through the wrecked areas. Early reports of vandalism spurred the community to organize patrols to prevent further theft. Looting did occur until the National Guard arrived in Woodward and sealed off the stricken areas. Corpses piled up outside hospitals, and embalmers had to be brought in from hundreds of miles away because of the crisis.

Property damage in Texas totaled $1.5 million. Total damage throughout the states was $9.7 million, with $6 million of damage in the town of Woodward. The other communities struck had smaller populations of under 1,000 people. Work by a doctor, Donald Burgess, has shown that 107 people perished in

Woodward instead of the previously reported 95. The bodies of 3 girls were never identified.

The next day the sun was out, and people began trying to clear away the debris. The Red Cross also moved into action, providing medical care, food, and clothing to the victims. Field kitchens were set up to help the survivors and emergency personnel. Fresh drinking water and food had to be trucked in for the victims. The Mennonites, a religious sect, also arrived to aid the victims. Also of great assistance was phone service. Breaking a national telephone operators' strike, operators in Woodward worked nonstop during the crisis. They ultimately resigned from the National Federation of Telephone Workers. An Army barracks 6 miles from Woodward was converted into temporary housing, where approximately 70 families lived until their houses could be rebuilt.

Jennifer S. Lawrence

FOR FURTHER INFORMATION:

Bedard, Richard. *In the Shadow of the Tornado: Stories and Adventures from the Heart of Storm Country.* Norman, Okla.: Gilco, 1996.
The New York Times, April 10-12, 1947.

1949: Missouri

DATE: May 21, 1949
PLACE: Cape Girardeau, Missouri
CLASSIFICATION: F3
RESULT: 22 dead, hundreds injured, several hundred houses damaged, $3-4 million in damage

Cape Girardeau is located 90 miles south of St. Louis on the west bank of the Mississippi River. Considered Cape Girardeau's second major tornado, the 1949 storm hit the town four minutes before 7 on a Saturday night. More than a century before, on November 27, 1850, unseasonably warm weather spawned a tornado that destroyed 100 homes and boats docked at the city's wharf and littered the ground with dead ducks, which were also blown across the Mississippi River into Illinois. The 1949 tornado wreaked greater havoc.

Traveling from the western part of the city near Gordonville Road Hill toward the Mississippi River, the tornado killed 22 people, 8 of whom were located within a 150-square-yard area. At that time, Cape

Girardeau's population was 20,000. Several hundred individuals were injured by the storm, with 72 requiring hospitalization. The tornado destroyed 202 houses, 19 businesses, and a church and caused damage at another 231 homes and 14 stores, totaling between $3 and $4 million in devastation. Houses inhabited by industrial workers on the river bank were especially hard hit. Survivors emerged from underground shelters to find the remaining rubble of their houses. The storm's torrential rains saturated structures and hindered relief efforts to dig people out from battered buildings. Downed power lines also proved dangerous in the flooded streets.

Elizabeth D. Schafer

FOR FURTHER INFORMATION:

"Red Cross Marks $500,000 for Relief of Storm Victims." *Christian Science Monitor,* May 23, 1949, 10.
"Storms Hammer Midwest; 29 Die, 250 Hurt." *Birmingham News,* May 22, 1949, p. 1.
"Tornadoes Kill 46, Strike Many Areas; 229 Injured, 900 Houses Razed, Loss in Millions—21 Dead at Cape Girardeau, Mo." *The New York Times,* May 23, 1949, p. 1.

1952: U.S. South

DATE: March 21-22, 1952
PLACE: Arkansas, Missouri, Tennessee, Alabama, Mississippi, and Kentucky
CLASSIFICATION: F2-F4
RESULT: 343 dead, 1,400 injured, thousands homeless

Over a two-day period, 31 tornadoes hit 6 southern states in the Mississippi Valley. An F4 tornado killed 8 people at Wattensaw, Arkansas, after 5 in the afternoon on March 21. The tornado damaged nearby towns in Arkansas that were home to strawberry-packing plants and cotton gins. Four people were killed and 57 were injured when a family of F3 tornadoes struck Fisher, Arkansas, about 6:45 P.M. Meteorologists believed the tornadoes dissipated near Blytheville.

This storm then reformed, causing disaster in a three-state area. An F2 tornado killed 1 person in Poinsett County, Arkansas. At 8 P.M., a strong F4 twister caused 25 fatalities and 150 injuries at Yarbro,

Arkansas, moving northeast toward Cooter, Missouri, where flimsy tenant houses were particularly vulnerable and 17 people died. Moving over the Mississippi River into Tennessee, the tornado damaged 200 houses and killed 8 people. Tornadoes inflicted $1.5 million in destruction.

Just before 10 P.M., an F4 tornado caused 17 deaths and 96 injuries as it moved from Byhalia, Mississippi, to Moscow, Tennessee. Weakening to F2 status, the tornado hit several Tennessee counties and damaged the Milan Arsenal's barracks. By 10:45, the funnel regained F4 strength, and 38 people died with 157 hurt in Hardeman, Chester, Henderson, and Decatur Counties, Tennessee. After midnight, the F3 tornado hit the Hodgenville, Kentucky, fairgrounds. Around 2:45, an F4 tornado in Morgan County, Alabama, killed 4 people and hit Redstone Arsenal. In all, 343 casualties resulted from the tornadoes, with another 1,400 injured and thousands homeless.

Elizabeth D. Schafer

FOR FURTHER INFORMATION:

"Tornado Deaths Pass 200; 2,500 Injured in Six States; Towns Razed, Wind Roars On." *The New York Times*, March 23, 1952, pp. 1, 63.

"215 Killed in Tornadoes; New Storms May Hit North Alabama." *Birmingham News*, March 22, 1952, pp. 1, 2.

1953: Texas

DATE: May 11, 1953
PLACE: Waco, Texas
CLASSIFICATION: F5
RESULT: 114 dead, 1,097 injured, $50 million in damage

According to a 1951 chamber of commerce brochure, a Huaco Indian legend claimed that Waco was immune from the furies of the elements and thus would not be hit by a tornado. On May 11, 1953, a Pacific cold front became stationary over central Texas. Although records show that it spawned only two tornadoes, both hit towns, San Angelo (about 215 miles west of Waco) and Waco.

The weather in Waco was cold with blustery, heavy rain. The Weather Bureau had issued a tornado alert; however, when the news of the 2:15 P.M. San Angelo

tornado (13 deaths) came in, a local meteorologist casually mentioned that Waco was now safe. The afternoon *Times-Herald* headline was "Storms Hit West Texas; No Cause for Alarm Here." One of the radio stations announced that Waco was safe shortly before it was knocked off the air by the tornado.

The tornado first touched down at 4:20 P.M., 3 miles northwest of Lorena, a small town 10 miles southwest of Waco. It caused some damage in Hewitt, a suburb on the southwest edge of Waco. As it continued through Waco, most of the trees from Baylor Stadium to City Hall were knocked down. The path went west of Baylor Stadium and south of old Municipal Stadium, located on Dutton and Fourteenth, across Bell's Hill to Clay and Ninth, then to the business district. It devastated the blocks around city hall, then went across the Brazos River at Bridge Street to hit East Waco, traveling about 30 miles per hour. In downtown Waco, its path was four blocks wide.

Reports say that the tornado lifted 5 miles east of Axtell, a town located 8 miles northeast of Waco. Because that town is not in line with the path through Waco and the community of Billington, east of Waco, had tornado-like damage, the tornado seen lifting east of Axtell could have been a second tornado east of the Waco tornado.

Although residences diagonally across Waco were destroyed, the major damage was in the downtown area. This tornado was the first to hit the business district of a large city during business hours. The Citizen's National Bank clock on Austin Avenue downtown stopped at 4:46 P.M. The cold rain had caused the normally crowded downtown area to be less populated; thus, many lives were saved. Egg-size hail came with the tornado and was followed by torrential rain. More than 7 inches of rain fell in the next twenty-four hours. Rains that continued for several days were both a hindrance to rescuers and a boon that prevented fires, which normally erupt when gas mains are broken and electric lines are down.

All the public utilities in most of the city were disrupted; all electrical lines were down in downtown Waco, and phone communication was impossible. Two square miles were in ruins. The five-story R. T. Dennis Furniture Company collapsed, and part of the Dennis building debris fell onto the Joy Theater, which caved in. Katy Park, home of the minor league baseball team the Waco Pirates, was destroyed. East Waco and Bell's Hill elementary schools were also destroyed. Four other schools were damaged, as were 7

churches. The spire of the First Methodist Church was blown down. In all, 196 business buildings were destroyed and another 376 damaged enough to be unsafe; 150 homes were destroyed, 250 were severely damaged, and 450 had minor damage; and 2,000 automobiles were damaged or destroyed. The damage estimate was about $50 million. Besides the 114 deaths, there were 145 persons with major injuries and 952 with minor ones.

The damage could have been worse. For most of its path, the tornado was 15 to 20 feet off the ground. Most of the damage was to upper floors of buildings. Older buildings of brick on wood frames, such as the Dennis building and the Padgett warehouse behind it, often did not survive the tornado. Steel-frame buildings, such as the Amicable Building and city hall, survived. The Amicable Building bent but snapped back, throwing occupants in upper floors against the walls.

In the block between Fourth and Fifth Streets and Austin Avenue and Franklin, 56 people died, including 22 Dennis Company employees. In the area around city hall, another 38 people died. Only 3 persons died in residential areas. Seventeen pool players died in Torrance Recreation Hall, and 5 people were entombed in cars by the collapsing Dennis building. Four more were trapped in automobiles at other locations. Most victims died instantly, but the last casualty lived until May 20.

Most of the initial rescue attempts were organized by willing groups of individuals. One rescue that became national news was the fourteen-hour struggle to rescue the seventy-year-old telephone operator who had been located on the first floor of the Dennis building. By the next day, the work had been organized, and the Texas National Guard was handling crowd control and preventing looting. Men from Connally Air Force Base were detailed to help with rescue and debris removal. The Red Cross and Salvation Army helped victims, and offers of help came from all over the country. The offer of bulldozers from Oregon was turned down because they would have required four days of travel time to reach Waco; the company sent a donation instead.

Although people in downtown Waco could not see a funnel, several people to the side of the storm path did see the traditional funnel shape of the tornado. Other people watching the cloud were scientists at Texas A&M in College Station, 85 miles away. They saw the radar signature hook echo that would help meteorologists to learn to locate tornadoes in storms by using radar. The 114 deaths from the tornado rank as tied with the Goliad tornado as the tenth deadliest in U.S. history to date. In 1987, the *Dallas Times Herald* called it Texas' worst tornado.

C. Alton Hassell

FOR FURTHER INFORMATION:

Cornell, James. *The Great International Disaster Book.* 3d ed. New York: Charles Scribner's Sons, 1982.
Dallas Times Herald, March 1, 1987.
Flora, Snowden D. *Tornadoes of the United States.* Norman: University of Oklahoma Press, 1954.
Grazulis, Thomas P. *Significant Tornadoes: 1680-1991.* St. Johnsbury, Vt.: Environmental Films, 1993.
Hauptman, William. "Blown Away." *Texas Monthly,* July, 1996, 66.
Lynch, Dudley. *Tornado: Texas Demon in the Wind.* Waco, Tex.: Texian Press, 1970.
Moore, Harry E. *Tornadoes over Texas.* Austin: University of Texas Press, 1958.
National Oceanographic and Atmospheric Administration. "The Twenty-five Deadliest Tornadoes." *Almanac—Science and Technology—Weather and Climate.* http://www.images.infoplease.com.
Risinger, Donald L., et al. *Waco, Texas, Tornado, May 11, 1953: Monster from the Skies.* Waco, Tex.: McLennan County Medical Society, 1991.
Texas National Guard. *Waco Disaster Operation.* Waco, Tex.: Author, 1953.
Waco Times-Herald and News-Tribune, May 11, 15, and 17, 1953.
Waco Tribune-Herald, May 11, 1988; May 24, 1992; May 10, 1998.
Williams, Ewell R. *A Study of Letters to the Editor of the "Waco Times-Herald and News-Tribune" Following the Tornado of May, 1953.* Austin: University of Texas Press, 1956.

1953: The Flint-Beecher Tornado

DATE: June 8, 1953
PLACE: Flint, Michigan, and northern Ohio
CLASSIFICATION: F5
RESULT: 120 dead, 847 injured, $32 million in damage

After an afternoon of several small twisters spinning through sparsely populated areas along the Michigan-Ohio border, an intense F5 tornado struck the north side of Flint, Michigan, killing 113—including many children—and injuring 547. It then moved southeast into Ohio, "calming" to an F4 tornado that pelted Cleveland with golf-ball-sized hail, tore through an industrial area, wrecked a few commercial buildings, then disappeared over Lake Erie. Ohio's casualties included 7 dead and about 300 injured. Of the 25 deadliest tornadoes to hit the United States, the Flint-Beecher tornado of June 8, 1953, was ranked number nine as of 1999.

Around 8:30 P.M. on Monday, June 8, 1953, a 2-block-wide tornado turned the quiet residential neighborhood north of Flint into a pile of rubble and splinters. Michigan's worst tornado was spawned by an oppressive thunderstorm that moved through the Midwest June 8-9 creating a tornado epidemic reaching from Nebraska to Massachusetts. Throughout the day in Michigan, smaller tornadoes touched down in northern parts of Michigan and along the Michigan-Ohio border.

The devastating tornado, known as the Flint-Beecher tornado, originally touched down in a pasture near Coldwater and Linden Roads. Witnesses described it as a "50-foot wide 'dancing funnel' with spinning 'fingers.'" In the pasture it merely over-turned clumps of grass, but it grew in size and strength, soon losing its funnel shape. It took three minutes for the twister to race through Flint, described then as "a swirling, debris-filled mass of grayish-blue and black smoke."

The tornado cut a path 800 feet wide, so completely reducing cars and buildings to rubble that it was "impossible to tell where the ruins of one ended and the next began." The debris from the tornado was scattered miles away, including a 16-foot house trailer found 8 miles away, textbooks from Beecher High School—left standing—found 35 miles away, and canceled checks that arrived in Ontario, Canada, 200 miles away.

From the list of destruction it is evident this tornado was an F5 on the Fujita scale. An F5 tornado is the most damaging and devastating on the Fujita scale. It generates automobile-sized missiles, has enough force to lift large and heavy objects over 100 yards before dropping them again, causes strong-frame houses to be lifted off foundations, debarks trees, and badly damages steel-reinforced structures with winds ranging from 261 to 318 miles per hour.

In Flint, a dime was found embedded in a tree as if it had been a bullet, and a 2-by-4 was found embedded in a concrete pillar. People witnessed cars sailing past their windows, and houses were lifted off the ground to crash against trees across the street. Eyewitness accounts also include "bright balls of fire" inside the funnel—another indication of the mightiest tornado on the scale.

State troopers in Flint, Michigan, search for victims of the Flint-Beecher Tornado. (AP/Wide World Photos)

Rescue workers searched for bodies buried under the rubble by the eerie light created by gas pouring from broken lines and burning along the ground with sputtering blue flames. Half the 113 found dead were children. Casualty tolls were high because of the time the tornado hit—8:30 P.M. Many night-shift workers from Flint's industrial factories rushed home to find both their homes and families gone. The total property damage amounted to $12 million.

The tornado moved southeast, skirting around Ann Arbor, and heading into Ohio. It swirled on a curving path through Henry, Wood, Sandusky, Erie, Lorain, and Cuyohoga Counties. By then its winds had receded to between 207 and 260 miles per hour. This equates to F4 on the Fujita scale—a devastating tornado as opposed to the incredible tornado intensity of an F5. During an F4 tornado, the winds level well-constructed houses and cause structures with weak foundations to be blown some distance, cars are thrown, and large missiles are generated by the intensity of the winds.

In twenty-nine minutes the tornado moved along its path of destruction in Ohio. It created a 0.5-mile-wide swath as it dragged across suburbs, plowed through the industrial "flats" and tumbled several buildings in downtown Cleveland, while pelting rain and hail in its wake. After a 12.5-mile course, the tornado swung toward Lake Erie and dissipated. Some 1,871 houses were leveled, with 7 people killed and another 300 injured. The total damage for Ohio amounted to $20 million.

Though the tornado scattered over Lake Erie, the storm front that created it had moved into Canada. This same storm front would create yet another tornado the next day that descended on Massachusetts.

There was no warning of the sprinkling of tornadoes throughout Michigan and Ohio. The panic that ensued, especially as the tornado descended on the crowded movie theater and people tried to flee the building, together with the terrible loss of children in Flint, Michigan, led to protocol for taking cover during tornadoes. Windows should be left open a crack, and people should retreat to cellars or basements, or the northeast corner of a room, away from windows. At schools children should take cover under desks, in a crouched position with arms covering heads for protection. Tornado drills were soon conducted in schools and encouraged in homes throughout the state.

Lisa A. Wroble

FOR FURTHER INFORMATION:

Keen, Richard A. *Michigan Weather.* Helena, Mont.: American & World Geographic Publishing, 1993.

Mosier, Tim D. *Twisters in the Heartland.* New York: Rivercross, 1998.

National Oceanic and Atmospheric Administration. "F5 Tornadoes in the United States 1950-Present." http://www.spc.noaa.gov/faq/tornado/f5torns .html.

National Weather Service. Cleveland, Ohio. "Cleveland's County Warning Area." http://www.csuohio .edu/nws/history/cletornado.html.

"Storm Encyclopedia." *The Weather Channel.* http:// www.weather.com/breaking_weather/encyclope dia/tornado/sigevent.html.

"Storm Line." *Time,* June 22, 1953, 26.

"Tornado Epidemic." *Life* 34, no. 25 (June 22, 1953): 28-29.

Tornado Project. "Michigan Tornadoes." http:// www.tornadoproject.com/alltorns/mitorn.htm.

1953: Massachusetts

DATE: June 9, 1953
PLACE: Worcester, Massachusetts
CLASSIFICATION: F5 (estimated)
RESULT: 94 dead, 1,288 injured

At approximately 4:30 in the afternoon of June 9, 1953, a black funnel cloud descended outside Worcester, Massachusetts. Massachusetts had seen warm temperatures in the nineties for the day. Thundershowers were expected, but no tornadoes were predicted for any part of the state. The funnel of the Worcester tornado cut a 42-mile-long swath across Worcester County. It first touched down near Petersham near the Quabbin Reservoir. It passed through Barre, Rutland, and Holden before reaching Worcester, a city in central Massachusetts with a population of 200,000.

The funnel crossed into the city of Worcester at 5:04 P.M. and spent fourteen minutes traveling through the city. The funnel demolished automobiles as it moved across the highways in the area. The new Norton Company machine tool plant, which had been dedicated in April, had its roof ripped off. The twister passed through Boylston Street and the heavily populated Burncoat Hill. Large hail fell

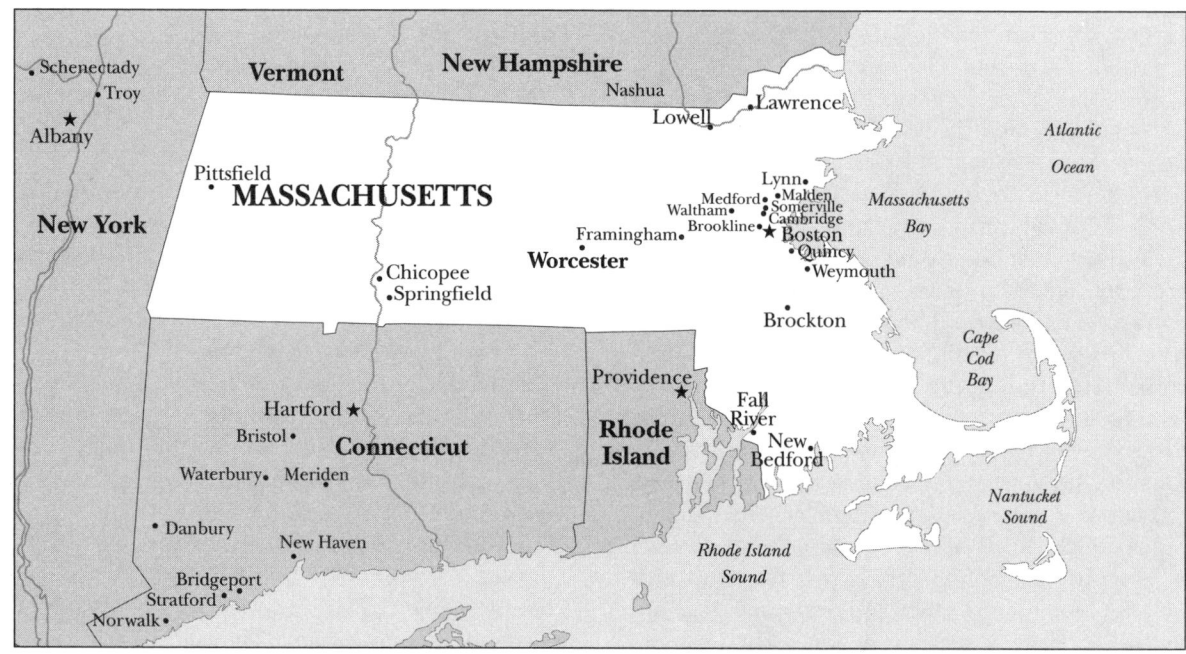

throughout the area as the tornado continued on its deadly path. The funnel barely missed the center of town. Numerous multistoried buildings were destroyed, and fires broke out among the damaged buildings. Many people were killed when their houses exploded. Roofs were sheared off and gaping holes were left in buildings. The twister caused extensive damage at Assumption College in Worcester, where a priest and 2 nuns were killed. It also destroyed the Great Brook Valley government housing project, where 1,500 residents suddenly found themselves homeless. The post office was the last building destroyed.

After leaving Worcester, the tornado's course took it to Shrewsbury, where nearly every one of the 50 homes in the Kenilworth section was destroyed. The twister then moved toward Westboro, Southboro, and Framingham. It also came near Franklin, Wrentham, and Bellingham before finally disappearing. About 10 miles to the southwest of Worcester, a smaller tornado hit, causing damage and injury to Sutton, Northbridge, and Milford.

Due to the atmospheric pressure differential between the outside air and that inside a closed building, there were numerous examples of weightlessness of small objects, such as potatoes and eggs. The winds were so powerful, they drove grass and straw into a wood-sided house on Trottier Street in Worces-

ter at the speed of several hundred miles per hour. The house appeared to be growing grass from its sides.

The nearest hospital, Hahnemann Hospital, began receiving victims approximately an hour after the tornado began. Governor Christian A. Herter declared a state of emergency in the Worcester area. Two thousand National Guardsmen arrived to give aid to the victims and stop looting; guardsmen were patrolling the streets that night. Searchlights were brought in to give light for rescue searches into the debris. The next day National Guard presence was extended to other areas of the city. A 6 P.M. curfew was enforced by the National Guard as well. The National Guard set up its own medical services in the city but ended mostly treating its own guardsmen, who were injured during their patrols. Residents had to have special passes to reach their destroyed homes to salvage what they could. Governor Herter requested an immediate $10 million in emergency aid. Bills for $25 million in aid were introduced in the House of Representatives and the Senate. Surprisingly, telephone service was restored in Worcester only four days after the tornado.

The Red Cross began its over three-month involvement in Worcester after a phone call that deadly afternoon. Emergency shelters were opened at the National Guard Armory, Worcester Polytechnic Institute, and Holy Cross College. The Red Cross set up a mobile blood donor bank for contributions and gave food vouchers to the needy. Donated clothes poured into the aid agencies working in the city. The Reconstruction Finance Corporation declared the county of Worcester a disaster area so that home and business loans to the victims could be expedited.

In all, 93 people perished in the disaster: 2 people in Barre, 2 in Rutland, 10 in Holdon, 58 in Woodward, 12 in Shrewsbury, 6 in Westboro, and 3 in Southboro. Also killed was a power-company employee who was electrocuted while trying to restore power to the city, bringing the total to 94. Over 4,000 homes were either damaged or totally destroyed by the tornado, and 15,000 people were left homeless. Injuries were so numerous that people packed the corridors, cafeterias, and basements of the nearby hospitals. Property loss was at least $53 million. Damage to Assumption College was $3 million. A new senator from Massachusetts, John F. Kennedy, visited the victims and surveyed the damage incurred by the tornado.

The massive tornado surprised nearly everyone. People were accustomed to tornadoes occurring in the Midwest, not in Massachusetts. Thousands of sightseers headed to the area to see the damage, causing clogged roadways throughout central Massachusetts.

The wind velocity of the Worcester tornado is estimated to have been between 328 and 338 miles per hour; a higher wind speed had not been observed in a tornado to date. The average width of the funnel was 140 yards, with a peak width of approximately 700 yards. A small tornado spawned from the larger one also hit 70 miles away, in the town of Exeter, New Hampshire. Debris from Worcester was spread out over a large area even into Boston (45 miles away) and the Atlantic coast. *The New York Times* reported residents near Boston seeing flying shingles and newspapers deposited by the tornado. The exact number of the injured can never be positively known because many people with minor injuries were treated in hospitals without charts being made or personal information given.

In a bizarre twist of fate, on the twentieth anniversary of the tornado in 1973, another tornado hit the city shortly after 4 that afternoon. Though smaller, with a possible F2 rating, it was a cruel and ironic reminder of nature's surprises.

Jennifer S. Lawrence

FOR FURTHER INFORMATION:
The New York Times, June 10-11, 1953.
O'Toole, John M. *Tornado! 84 Minutes, 94 Lives.* Worcester, Mass.: Databooks, 1993.

1955: Kansas, Oklahoma

DATE: May 25, 1955
PLACE: Udall, Kansas, and Blackwell, Oklahoma
CLASSIFICATION: F5
RESULT: 100 dead, 550 injured, $10.4 million in damage

F5 tornadoes are rare, but two struck small towns about 50 miles apart on May 25, 1955. At 9:30 P.M. the first tornado cut a swath eight blocks long and two blocks wide through the heart of Blackwell, Oklahoma, leaving behind 20 dead and 280 injured. The storm destroyed 400 homes and heavily damaged 500 others in the town of about 10,000. Damages exceeded $8 million. The remarkable electrical activity that accompanied this tornado caused observers to describe the funnel as "glowing" with arcs of light.

As the Blackwell tornado dissipated, a second monster tornado was forming to the east. The funnel touched down in Kay County, Oklahoma (the county in which Blackwell is located), and moved north across the Kansas border, where it killed 5 children in one home near Oxford, before taking aim at Udall, a town of 500 about 30 miles southeast of Wichita. Within minutes winds of more than 260 miles per hour virtually wiped Udall from the face of the earth. Three-fourths of the town's residents, many asleep when the storm struck, were casualties; 75 died, and 270 suffered injuries. Only 4 buildings survived; the town's new high school was not one of them.

The tornado wedged truck frames into trees and knocked over the water tower, flooding the streets. Damage estimates were $2.25 million. While Blackwell residents were able to conduct their own search and rescue operations, Udall had to rely upon help from surrounding communities and cities. Red Cross, Civil Defense, and Salvation Army workers set up headquarters in the bank and post office. Rain, mud, downed telephone and electric lines, and lack of lighting hampered efforts.

The difference in the death tolls may be partly a result of the warnings the towns received. Officials of Blackwell praised the Weather Bureau for broadcasting warnings and instructions and stated their belief that loss of life in their town would have been much greater without the advance notice. Although the Topeka Weather Bureau office released a tornado alert less than an hour before the storm hit, Udall residents complained that they had not received any warning. One resident told the *Topeka Journal* that she listened to the radio before she went to bed, but the announcer forecast only local showers. The next thing she knew, her house was tumbling down around her. To ensure that Udall would be warned in the future, the mayor of the rebuilt town patented a system that would warn residents by telephone when a tornado was spotted in the area. Through 1999, the Udall tornado has the distinction of being the deadliest tornado in Kansas history and the deadliest in the United States since the institution of a national tornado forecasting system.

Marlene Bradford

FOR FURTHER INFORMATION:
Topeka Journal, May 26-28, 1955.
Wichita Eagle, May 26-29, 1955.

1957: Missouri

DATE: May 20, 1957
PLACE: Ruskin Heights, Missouri
CLASSIFICATION: F5
RESULT: 37 dead, 531 injured, more than 850 buildings damaged or destroyed

On Monday, May 20, 1957, the Severe Local Storm Warning Center issued a tornado watch for its hometown, Kansas City. That evening, at about 6:15 P.M., a tornado that first touched down near Williamsburg, Kansas, killed 7 people as it moved northeastward through small communities. The tornado, most likely containing multiple vortices, crossed the state line into Jackson County, Missouri, and increased to F5 in strength. The nearly 0.5-mile-wide twister damaged or destroyed more than 800 homes and numerous businesses when it plowed through the southwestern Kansas City suburbs of Ruskin Heights, Martin City, and Hickman Mills.

In its wake, the storm left 37 dead, more than 500 injured, and hundreds homeless. A severe storms meteorologist who interviewed people able to take shelter as a result of the advance warning stated that without his office's forecast and the cooperation of news agencies in spreading the warnings, more than 500 people would have died. The storm was so ferocious that pilots reported debris at an altitude of 30,000 feet. A canceled check from Hickman Mills was found 165 miles away in Ottumwa, Iowa, and house keys belonging to a Ruskin Heights home were found more than 150 miles to the northeast. Among the many organizations and individuals that aided in the cleanup or raised money for the victims was former president Harry S Truman, a native of the devastated area.

Marlene Bradford

FOR FURTHER INFORMATION:
Brewer, Carolyn. *Caught in the Path*. Kansas City, Mo.: Prairie Fugue Books, 1997.
Kansas City Star, May 21-27, 1957.

1959: St. Louis

DATE: February 10, 1959
PLACE: St. Louis, Missouri
CLASSIFICATION: F2-F4
RESULT: 21 dead, 345 injured, thousands of buildings damaged, $12 million in damage

Developing after midnight on February 10, 1959, a tornado formed several miles west of St. Louis near Ellisville and moved slightly northeast into the metropolitan region. Moving through open areas and suburbs, the tornado gained strength. An F2 category twister when it hit the Warson Woods development in St. Louis around 1:40 in the morning, it damaged roofs and other property there and in the Forest Park neighborhood before proceeding along Manchester Road, a main St. Louis thoroughfare, toward McKinley Bridge. This path was similar to that traveled by tornadoes in 1871, 1896, and 1927.

The tornado reached F3 intensity by the time it struck downtown St. Louis, attaining F4 status at times. Most casualties were caused by collapsing tenement houses and apartments. Shattered gas mains resulted in fires glowing throughout St. Louis. Tall television and radio towers fell through buildings. The tornado destroyed 41 buildings and damaged at least 1,725 structures, including several hundred houses. In all, 21 people died and 345 were injured. Approximately 5,000 became homeless.

The weakened tornado also hit factories across the Mississippi River near Venice and Granite City, Illinois. President Dwight D. Eisenhower declared St. Louis a disaster area with an estimated $12 million in damage. Cold weather hindered cleanup efforts. As a result of the storm, the St. Louis Weather Bureau, which claimed it learned of the storm almost an hour afterward, installed a more efficient storm-tracking radar.

Elizabeth D. Schafer

FOR FURTHER INFORMATION:

"St. Louis Clearing Tornado Wreckage." *The New York Times,* February 12, 1959, p. 28.

"21 Die as Tornado Batters St. Louis." *The New York Times,* February 11, 1959, pp. 1, 43.

1965: U.S. Midwest

DATE: April 11, 1965 (Palm Sunday)

PLACE: Parts of Indiana, Illinois, Iowa, Michigan, Ohio, and Wisconsin across a path 350 miles long and 150 miles wide

CLASSIFICATION: 2 tornadoes—in Elkhart, Indiana, and Strongsville, Ohio—estimated as definitely F5; 17 of the other 49 tornadoes estimated as F4 or F5

RESULT: 271 dead, 3,148 injured, more than $200 million in damage

The 1965 Palm Sunday tornado outbreak of April 11, 1965, was the most devastating, until that time, in the United States. As of 2000, it was second in size and destruction to the 1974 Jumbo Outbreak. The Palm Sunday disaster resulted when a mass of cold dry air rapidly moving down from western Canada collided with a mass of warm moist air moving up from the Gulf of Mexico. The colliding air masses produced

Twin tornadoes threaten a town in Indiana during the Palm Sunday outbreak of 1965. (AP/Wide World Photos)

large storms in Texas and Oklahoma, which grew in intensity as they rapidly moved northeast. These storms followed an unusually intense jet stream that took them to the upper Midwest.

A Pleasant Sunday. In the six states that were struck in the Midwest, it was a warm and balmy Palm Sunday. It seemed like a good day for puttering with the lawn and garden or preparing for Easter celebrations. However, it was obvious to some weather experts that conditions were also ideal for the formation of tornadoes, a fact that troubled the U.S. Weather Bureau early that morning. Consequently, tornado warnings were issued throughout the morning. Yet many radio and television stations were closed for Palm Sunday or had a skeletal staff. The forecasts were not widely or adequately communicated.

Investigations after the tornado revealed that most areas had between thirty-five minutes and five hours of warning time, a situation that revealed an additional problem. The public was slow to react and dulled by the numerous tornado watches in "Tornado Alley." Also, many were outside enjoying the warm spring temperatures on a balmy Palm Sunday and were away from their radios. Lack of adequate communication and lack of response was underscored by government investigators as a major cause of the high fatality rate.

Devastation. The first small tornado struck at 1:20 P.M. south of Dubuque. An hour later six other tornadoes were reported in Iowa, Wisconsin, and Illinois. By 3:15 weather forecasters in Chicago were able to see a 100-mile-long line of thunderstorms stretching from De Kalb, Illinois, to Madison, Wisconsin, with tornadoes, and even colonies of tornadoes, spewing forth. One tornado near Crystal Lake, Illinois, leveled the Crystal Lake Shopping Center and Colby Estates housing subdivision, wreaking havoc on a path 1 mile wide and 10 miles long.

The scene was repeated throughout the day. Fifty-one tornadoes over a twelve-hour period occurred along a path 300 miles long and 150 miles wide, leaving 266 dead. More than half of the dead were in Indiana. In Russiaville, Indiana (population 1,200), every building was damaged, while in Goshen over 100 trailers were crushed into masses of torn metal. Lower Michigan also was hit hard. Two powerful tornadoes tore through Branch, Hilsdale, Lenawee, and Monroe Counties, killing 44 and causing more than $32 million in damage. Half an hour apart, the tornadoes followed a similar course. Ohio was the third

state to bear the brunt of the tornadoes. Devastation was particularly severe south of Cleveland in Strongsville, Ohio. Near Toledo, 370 homes were destroyed along a 10-mile path. Every home in Toledo's Creekside addition was destroyed.

Most tornadoes result in stories of miraculous escapes and pitiful tragedies. In the Palm Sunday tornado there were a number of fortuitous escapes. In Crystal Lake, insurance man Charles Swanson was sucked out of his shower and into the street as his house crashed in around him. Seventeen-year-old Dan Avins was asleep at home near Cleveland when the tornado hit; he awoke to find himself still in bed, 35 feet from his house. James Petro, Jr., an eight-month-old baby living in Strongsville, was hurled 175 feet from his demolished house, suffering only a black eye. Unfortunately another baby in Strongsville was ripped from his mother's hands, along with her wedding ring, and sucked out of the house. Only the mother survived.

The Aftermath. In the aftermath of the destruction, President Lyndon B. Johnson toured the devastation and walked among the twisted steel and rubble of Dunlap, Indiana, which had been torn apart by twin tornadoes. Federal disaster relief was issued rapidly, and insurance agents swarmed into the wreckage. In general, insurance companies received praise for the rapidity at which claims were paid. Among the productive activities was the work of one weather expert who traveled 7,500 miles in four days to make an aerial survey of the tornadoes' destruction. Professor Theodore Fujita of the University of Chicago noticed from the air that tornado tracks paralleled each other and seemed to move in clusters. Where one tornado destruction path would end, another would begin nearby. He also noticed cycloidal marks in open fields, providing indications of a parent tornado with rotating funnels attached to and revolving about the child tornado. These observations helped piece together the Fujita scale of tornado intensity, which has been in use since 1971 as a standard means of classifying tornadoes.

The failure of the public to respond to what seemed to be ample tornado warning was an issue seriously studied by National Weather Service investigators. In succeeding years, recommendations for improved telecommunications and siren warning systems were enacted in many localities vulnerable to one of nature's great cataclysms.

Irwin Halfond

FOR FURTHER INFORMATION:

Bluestein, Howard. *Tornado Alley: Monster Storms of the Great Plains.* New York: Oxford University Press, 1999.

"Disasters: Up the Alley." *Time*, April 23, 1965, 29.

"First the Wind, then the Waters." *Newsweek*, April 26, 1965, 25-26.

The New York Times, April 12-25, 1965.

"When 35 Tornadoes Hit 6 States 'Like Bombs.'" *U.S. News & World Report*, April 26, 1965, 50-52.

1970: Texas

DATE: May 11, 1970
PLACE: Lubbock, Texas
CLASSIFICATION: F5
RESULT: 26 dead, 1,500 injured, $135 million in damage

The 5 P.M. Weather Bureau forecast for Lubbock on May 11, 1970, only mentioned the possibility of rain, but by 7:50 P.M. atmospheric conditions had changed drastically. Thunderstorm clouds that formed at sundown towered to over 46,000 feet. The Lubbock Weather Bureau office received reports from its Amarillo counterpart, which had more sophisticated radar, that the storm clouds continued to push higher into the atmosphere, reaching an incredible 55,000 feet by 8 P.M. Forecasters in the Texas Panhandle and South Plains knew that such cloud heights signaled severe hail and often tornadoes.

At 8:05 P.M. a caller reported golf-ball-size hail 3 miles south of Lubbock, a city of 170,000 which had escaped a serious tornado threat for more than seventy years. Shortly thereafter, an off-duty policeman reported to the Weather Bureau that he had spotted a funnel 7 miles south of the airport. Based on this report and radar echoes, the bureau issued a tornado warning for Lubbock County. The city's radio and television stations broadcast the warnings, and many residents took precautionary actions.

During the next hour hook echoes, which usually signify a tornado, appeared and disappeared from the radar screen. The city and surrounding areas received a pounding from hail, but no tornado touched down. Shortly after 9 P.M. city police and the news media rushed to Lubbock's east side, where ra-

dar again indicated a tornado. While the city's attention was focused on this newest threat, around 9:35 a funnel dropped from the greenish clouds directly over the city. Touching down first just east of the Texas Tech University campus, the tornado, at times up to 1.5 miles wide, roared into the downtown area and continued northeastward through warehouse and residential areas before lifting near the Weather Bureau office at the municipal airport.

Many citizens had little notice of the impending disaster. Civil defense sirens sounded only briefly before the noise of the storm drowned them out and the ferocious winds destroyed the power lines that operated them. The city's one Spanish-language radio station had already signed off the air. Many were caught in vehicles when the storm struck.

The tornado's 8-mile-long journey through the city left behind incredible destruction. The 25-square-mile devastated area represented more than one-fourth of the city. More than 600 apartment units, 430 houses, and 250 businesses were destroyed; more than 10,000 automobiles and 119 aircraft suffered severe damage. Even worse, 26 people lost their lives, and more than 1,500 were injured. A conservative damage estimate of $135 million ($530 million in 1995 dollars) made this the third-costliest single tornado in U.S. history as of 1999. Ironically, the Lubbock storm occurred on the seventeenth anniversary of the Waco tornado, the deadliest Texas tornado to date.

One of the hardest hit areas was downtown. The tornado's winds ripped marble and concrete slabs from the sides of buildings, tossing them onto parked cars below, and shattered more than 80 percent of the windows. Upper stories of the twenty-one-story Great Plains Life Building, the tallest structure in town, swayed as windows popped. The tornado deformed the building's steel structure (the word "twist" was never used in published reports), causing it to be abandoned for several years. Emergency communications were disrupted when the tornado struck the city hall. An announcer on the city's emergency broadcast radio station, located in the *Avalanche-Journal* building, shouted into the microphone, "Take cover," as the twister struck the newspaper office.

From downtown the tornado cut a path through commercial warehouses before turning its fury on a Latino neighborhood where few structures offered any protection from the storm. Ten people died in this area as houses collapsed on them. After crossing

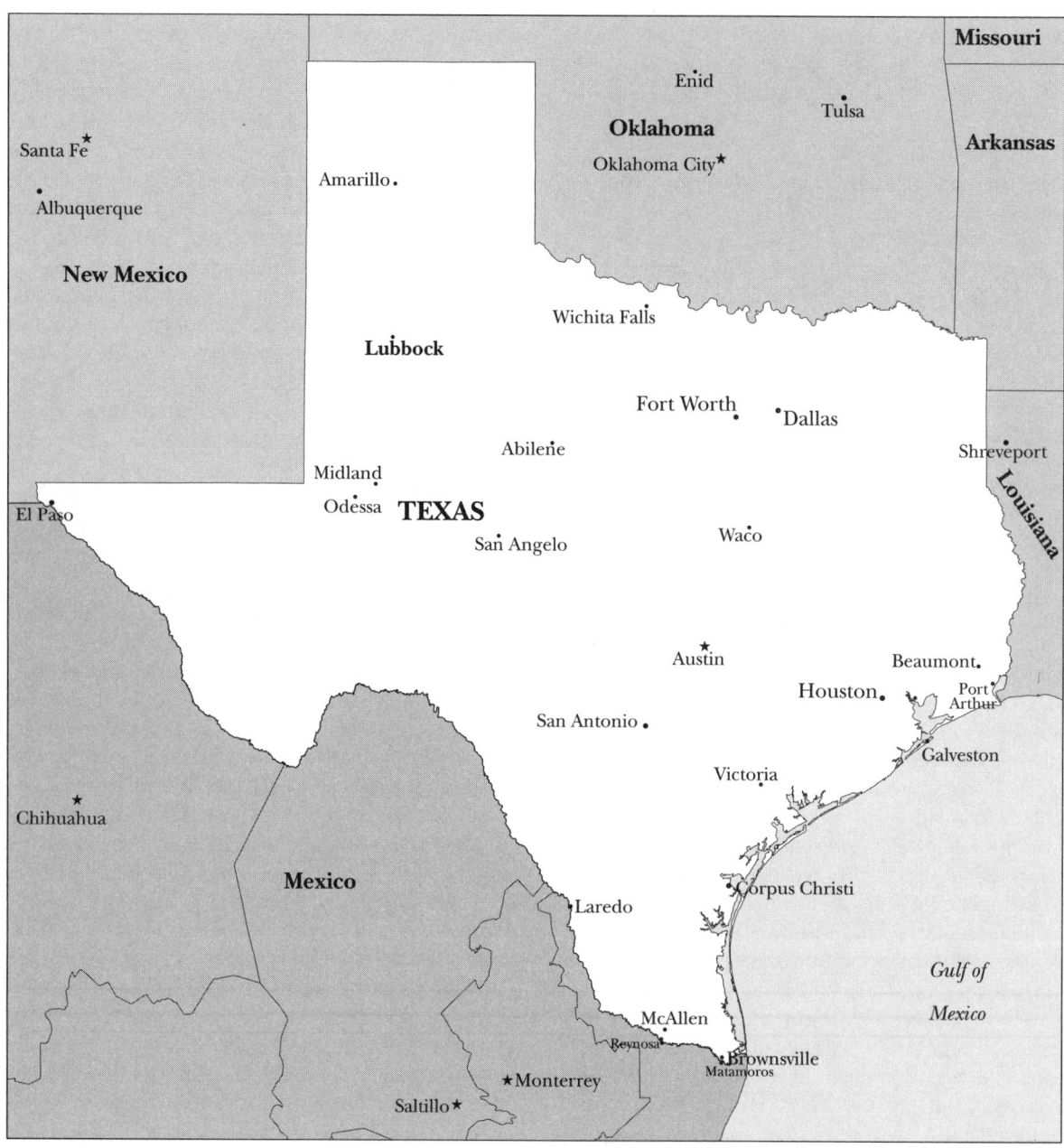

McKenzie State Park, the tornado headed for one of the city's busiest interchanges, Loop 289 and U.S. Highway 87. Three motorists died in their vehicles at this location, and the tornado destroyed several motels and other businesses that lined the highway. To the northwest of the highway, along Mesa Road, the devastation was incredible. Veteran reporters and military men described the scene as similar to that in Europe after the massive bombing raids of World War II. They did not see how anyone could have survived. Some families escaped death in storm cellars or closets, but others were not so fortunate. One entire family, a father, mother, and two preschool children, perished when the tornado flattened their new brick home, leaving behind only the concrete steps and front porch. Nearby, a father died when the tornado hurled the entire family from its house into a field.

Because a tornado of such intensity rarely strikes a large city, especially high-rise buildings, many groups studied the Lubbock tornado. Sociologists studied the rebuilding patterns of the community and the role of the media in warning the Spanish-speaking citizens. Tornado expert Theodore Fujita of the University of Chicago mapped the storm's damage patterns in great detail. His analysis showed that the tornado seemingly skipped around; some buildings were completely destroyed while those next door or across the street were virtually untouched. From this information Fujita determined that the Lubbock tornado had been a multiple vortex, one in which numerous small funnel clouds rotated around a larger central funnel. Multiple vortices help explain why tornadoes supposedly skip one house and destroy the one next door.

Fujita's studies of buildings in Lubbock that received various amounts of damage led to his development of the Fujita scale of tornado intensity, an estimation of a tornado's wind speed based on the damage it does to specific types of structures. The Weather Bureau evaluated the preparedness of the city and concluded that the death toll might have reached 500 if the citizens had not known what to do when the television and radio stations issued the warnings.

Wm. Michael Whitley

FOR FURTHER INFORMATION:

Harris, Jay. *The Lubbock Tornado.* Lubbock, Tex.: Boone, 1970.

Lubbock Avalanche-Journal, May 12-15, 1970.

Lynch, Dudley. *Tornado: Texas Demon in the Wind.* Waco, Tex.: Texian Press, 1970.

1971: Mississippi Delta

DATE: February 21, 1971
PLACE: Mississippi, Louisiana, and Tennessee
CLASSIFICATION: F2-F4
RESULT: 110 dead, thousands hurt or missing, $7.5 million in damage

Powerful tornadoes developed in the Mississippi River Delta, causing devastation in adjacent areas of Louisiana and Tennessee. At 2:50 P.M., an F4 tornado was responsible for 46 deaths and 400 injured people. Beginning in Madison Parish, Louisiana, the tor-

nado traveled northeast to the Waverly area, where 10 people in one family perished east of Delhi and were found in bayous several days later. Moving through uninhabited woods of East Carroll Parish, the tornado destroyed 7 houses and trailers at Melbourne before crossing over the Mississippi River to Issaquena County, Mississippi.

The town of Inverness, a predominantly African American community, was destroyed, with 21 casualties and 200 injuries. Over 150 buildings were ruined. At 4 P.M. an F2 tornado in Sunflower County razed tenant houses, causing 2 deaths. Another tornado, rated an F4, killed 58 people and injured 700 others.

A group of tornadoes swarmed through eight Mississippi counties. The Evanna Plantation near Cary counted 14 dead, in addition to structural destruction, and the tornado blew houses away in other communities, killing entire families. The system dissipated by the time it reached Oxford. Another F4 tornado killed 13 people and wounded 200 in Warren, Yazoo, and Holmes Counties. At 8:10, an F2 tornado caused the explosion of a brick school at Hurricane, Mississippi. President Richard M. Nixon declared the Delta a disaster area, and total damages were reported at $7.5 million, 110 deaths, and 500 injured or missing.

Elizabeth D. Schafer

FOR FURTHER INFORMATION:

Reed, Roy. "A Town's Luck Ends as Tornado Hits." *The New York Times,* February 23, 1971, p. 1.

"Tornadoes Kill 47 in the Deep South; Blizzard in Texas." *The New York Times,* February 22, 1971, p. 1.

1972: Bangladesh

DATE: April 2, 1972
PLACE: Bangladesh
CLASSIFICATION: F3
RESULT: 200 dead

Natural disasters frequently strike Bangladesh, a densely populated South Asian country, because of its geographical location, semitropical climate, and topographical conditions. Meteorologists suggest that at least one tornado occurs in that country annually. The Ganges and Brahmaputra Rivers from India and Tibet form a delta with the Meghna, an indigenous river, in Bangladesh. Northeastern Bangladesh has mountains that experience high precipitation, which often causes floods and creates warm moisture conducive to tornadoes.

The 1971 tornado struck with 150- to 160-mile-per-hour winds at Nasirabad in northern Bangladesh. Causing destruction in an 800-square-mile area in Mymensingh District, located north of Dhaka, the capital, the tornado damaged houses, trees, crops, and livestock. Initial reports counted 35 people dead, saying many others had been sent to hospitals. By the next day, accounts estimated 200 people had died when struck by blowing tin from roofs or crushed by buildings. Authorities stated that 70 bodies had been located and that relief workers were searching for others. The tornado hurt hundreds of people, and 25,000 were homeless.

The Bangladesh Red Crescent provided emergency medical teams as well as clothing, supplies, and plastic tarpaulins for temporary shelter. Relief workers included local government employees who distributed rice, wheat, and molasses. The Bangladesh Army helped clean up debris and initiate sanitary measures to prevent diarrhea epidemics. The Bangladesh government gave families tin and money for reconstruction and as reimbursement for deceased members.

Elizabeth D. Schafer

FOR FURTHER INFORMATION:

Baxter, Craig, and Syedur Rahman. *Historical Dictionary of Bangladesh.* Metuchen, N.J.: Scarecrow Press, 1989.

"35 Die in Bangladesh Storm." *The New York Times,* April 3, 1972, p. 8.

"Unofficial Toll in Storm Put at 200 in Bangladesh." *The New York Times,* April 4, 1972, p. 37.

1974: The Jumbo Outbreak

DATE: April 3-4, 1974
PLACE: 11 states in the U.S. South and Midwest, as well as Ontario, Canada
CLASSIFICATION: 6 tornadoes rated F5
RESULT: 316 dead, nearly 5,500 injured, $1 billion in damage

The largest tornado outbreak (several tornadoes in one day) to date in the United States resulted from the unusual collision of cold, dry air from the west upon warm, moist air extending east through the Ohio River Valley. The storm cell created was carried by strong, fast-moving winds common for systems in the early spring—a front moved from Colorado to Detroit in only a few hours, reaching the speed of 60 miles per hour near St. Louis. However, when the storm cell met the jet stream, events ceased to be common. Three parallel lines of squalls began to form shortly after noon on Wednesday, April 3, 1974. These squalls were more than 11 miles high and eventually a total of 2,598 miles long. They moved at an average rate of 50 miles per hour.

At 2:08 P.M. in Lincoln, Illinois, the squall line from St. Louis to Lake Michigan spawned the first of what would be 148 tornadoes in all before the activity ended at 5:20 A.M. on April 4. Meanwhile, a tornado in the second and more violent line from central Tennessee to southern Michigan touched down in Cleveland, Tennessee, at 2:10 P.M., with additional tornadoes in Jonesville and Depauw, Indiana, ten minutes later. The third line, along the Tennessee-North Carolina border, did not fully form until the early evening of April 3 but ultimately birthed just over one-third of the tornadoes in the outbreak and left 100 people dead.

The Jumbo Outbreak—or Super Outbreak, as a number of survivors have also termed it—was not only more extensive than all other known instances to date but also unusually intense, with tornado path lengths and widths one order of magnitude greater than those associated with average tornadoes. Natural barriers were thus no impediment to the powerful funnels. One of the worst storms moved continuously over 51 miles in Alabama, including across a lake. Among other damage, this tornado destroyed a mobile-home park with its winds of 260 miles per hour. Another tornado climbed the 3,300-foot peak of Rich Knob in Georgia to ravage the valley below, while another of the Alabama funnels continued on after jumping a 200-foot cliff.

Yet the tornadoes did not form in any major population centers, while many people in the tornadoes' paths survived remarkably. For example, in Branchville, Indiana, a school bus rolled 400 feet off the road, killing the driver and his wife. Another bus driver nearby, though, evacuated the children on board and had them lie in a ditch. The bus blew over them, but no one else was seriously hurt. In another tornado, the winds caused the car of a man driving home from work to somersault twice and land in his neighbor's yard. Although he was badly cut by glass, the man found his family huddled safely in the basement beneath the rubble of his home. There were also the freakish stories typically created by tornadoes, such as that of the pet rabbit in a hutch behind a home in Dawson County, Georgia, that ended up safe in the kitchen while 3 of the 5 human members of the family perished.

Overall, 11 states—Alabama, Georgia, Illinois, Indiana, Kentucky, Michigan, North Carolina, Ohio, Tennessee, Virginia, and West Virginia—and over 50,000 people experienced the outbreak in the United States. Eight people also died and more than 10 were hurt in Windsor, Ontario, Canada. The National Guard was called out in Kentucky, Tennessee, and Ohio. All three states, as well as Indiana, Georgia, and Alabama, were later named federal disaster areas. Eight hundred Red Cross workers served the stricken communities. The power system of the Tennessee Valley Authority suffered the worst damage of its forty-year history, while 90 percent of Huntsville, Alabama, was left without electricity and nine towns in Indiana and Cincinnati, Ohio, were among municipalities that lost phone service.

At the height of activity, 15 tornadoes were on the ground simultaneously. Thirteen tornadoes were rated at an intensity of F1, 22 at F2, 30 at F3, 22 at F4, and 6 at F5 through a combination of decisions by local weather offices and aerial pictures. The strongest tornadoes occurred at Xenia, Ohio; Depauw, Indiana; Sayler Park, Ohio; Brandenburg, Kentucky; First Tanner, Alabama; and Guin, Alabama. Etowa, Tennessee; Cleveland, Tennessee; Tanner, Alabama; Harvest, Alabama; Huntsville, Alabama; and Livingston, Tennessee were all struck twice by funnels. In Huntsville, one injured man went to a church to wait for an ambulance, only to be killed by the second tornado ten minutes later. There were two cases of family tornadoes, or several tornadoes spawned from one funnel: near Monticello, Indiana, where 150 homes and 100 businesses valued at $100 million were destroyed, and along the Indiana-Kentucky border near Cincinnati, Ohio. During the outbreak, a moderate earthquake centered in Springfield, Illinois, occurred coincidentally. There were no injuries or damage caused by the tremor, though. The two communities hit hardest during the Jumbo Outbreak were Xenia, Ohio, and Brandenburg, Kentucky.

Xenia, Ohio. In Xenia, near Dayton, the storm began around 4:30 P.M. Eastern time on April 3 as two small funnels twisting around each other. These funnels intensified as they approached Xenia, creating suction vortices that spun over the city of 25,000 for the next forty-five minutes. One vortex moved from west to east at speeds nearing 200 miles per hour. As a whole, the Xenia tornado was composed of a dust column between 30 and 40 feet wide, probably spinning at 100 miles per hour.

There were no weather sirens in Xenia at the time, so many people had no idea the weather was deteriorating until the tornado was on top of them. By the time the tornado moved through Xenia, 35 people had died and 1 of every 25 residents (or 1,150 total) was injured. The dead included 2 National Guardsmen fighting a fire in the aftermath of the tornado and 5 people found at the A&W drive-in restaurant.

Fortunately, the elementary and secondary schools had all finished classes for the day, and students from Wilberforce College and Central State College were out of town on spring break, since there was almost no warning when the tornado first hit. Three schools were completely ruined, and 3 more were seriously damaged. At the high school, the drama troupe took refuge in a classroom outside the auditorium shortly before the roof collapsed and 3 school buses were tossed onto the stage. One family with 5 children miraculously survived despite having to take refuge in a glass shop, which exploded around them.

Half of the city's homes were damaged or destroyed. Typically, all the houses on one side of a street collapsed while the other side suffered less damage. This was because the wind blew in the garage doors on one side of the street, and the homes collapsed once the wind blew inside. All 3 power lines into Xenia were blown down, and 5 of the 7 supermarkets were demolished. Besides the National Guard, personnel from Wright-Patterson Air Force Base lent support to tornado cleanup efforts and supplied fresh water to Xenia. Damages in Xenia were estimated to be three-fourths of the $100 million total repair costs for Ohio. It took three months of 200 trucks per day to haul away the rubble.

Brandenburg, Kentucky. At 3:40 P.M., a tornado touched down near Hardinsburg, Kentucky. Half an hour later, it had grown to 500 yards across and struck Brandenburg in the most serious of the 26 tornado touchdowns in Kentucky during the Jumbo Out-

One of the tornadoes of the Jumbo Outbreak, this funnel cloud struck Xenia, Ohio, which suffered major damage. (AP/Wide World Photos)

break. Thirty-one of Brandenburg's 1,700 residents were killed when a tornado struck there, and 250 were hurt. This was a substantial percentage of the 71 dead and 280 injured reported in all of Kentucky as of April 4. Many tornado victims were apparently children playing outside after school. Soldiers from Fort Knox provided assistance with rescue and recovery, bringing searchlights the night of April 3 to search for the dead. Brandenburg's five-block downtown area was completely demolished. Total damages were estimated at $22 million.

Learning from the Jumbo Outbreak. The spring of 1974 had already shown some penchant for storms. For example, 20 tornadoes were recorded on April 1, killing 2 and injuring 51 in ten states, while damaging or destroying 72 aircraft worth $1 million at North Metropolitan Airport in Nashville (now Nashville International Airport). Meteorologists knew that the weather patterns remained volatile, yet none of them could have predicted that within three days the United States would be on its way to suffering the most tornado deaths in one year since 1953. No one guessed that the previous record for tornadoes over a twenty-four-hour period would be smashed, either. That mark was the more than 60 funnels recorded on February 19, 1884, in Alabama, Indiana, Kentucky, Mississippi, North Carolina, South Carolina, and Tennessee. That tornado outbreak destroyed 10,000 buildings, killed 800, and injured 2,500.

However, tornado researcher Theodore Fujita was determined to use the events of April 3-4, 1974, to better understand tornadoes and to improve preparedness and safety. He flew over 10,000 miles after the outbreak in a joint survey with the University of Oklahoma and the National Severe Storms Laboratory, gathering a vast amount of useful data. In fact, nearly half of the tornadoes studied by Fujita and his assistants at the University of Chicago during his career were the ones from this outbreak.

Fujita accumulated evidence from the Jumbo Outbreak—a phrase he coined based on the 747 "jumbo jet" ("74" for 1974 and "7" from the sum of April 3 and 4)—to support two of his theories. First, in one forest, Fujita photographed a peculiar starburst pattern, where the fallen trees pointed out from one spot. This helped him argue for the existence of microbursts, phenomena that can push a tornado off its path. Second, Fujita was able to demonstrate the presence of suction vortices, small vortices within a tornado that seem to suck the debris together. Three motions coincide in the suction vortex—the motion of the tornado, the rotation of the suction spot around the tornado, and the spin of the vortex—and can result in a circular area of damage with a diameter of up to 20 feet. Because the Xenia tornado was transparent and its funnel did not extend all the way from the ground to the cloud, Fujita could show the motion of suction vortices by the movement of dust and debris in home movies from Xenia.

Fujita's research into the Jumbo Outbreak helped scientists distinguish between damage caused by tornadoes and by strong winds. They thus learned more about the conditions under which tornadoes occur so that the public can be warned earlier. In addition, the outbreak encouraged meteorologists to continue trying to improve their radar systems. By the late 1990's, tornadoes that were merely "green blobs" in 1974 could be seen clearly on Doppler screens. Meteorologists also urged towns to invest in weather sirens. For example, Xenia installed a system of ten alarms. Finally, many of the communities devastated by the outbreak took pride in rebuilding their homes and making them better than before.

Amy Ackerberg-Hastings

FOR FURTHER INFORMATION:
Fujita, T. Theodore. "Graphic Examples of Tornadoes." *Bulletin of the American Meteorological Society* 57 (1976): 401-412.
_____. "Jumbo Tornado Outbreak of 3 April 1974." *Weatherwise* 27 (1974): 116-126.
Pearson, Allen, and Frederick P. Ostby, Jr. "The Tornado Season of 1974." *Weatherwise* 28 (1975): 4-11.

Rosenfield, Jeffrey. *Eye of the Storm: Inside the World's Deadliest Hurricanes, Tornadoes, and Blizzards.* New York: Plenum Trade, 1999.

1979: Texas, Oklahoma

DATE: April 10, 1979
PLACE: A dozen counties in Texas and Oklahoma, primarily Vernon, Harrold, and Wichita Falls, Texas, and Grandfield and Lawton, Oklahoma
CLASSIFICATION: F4
RESULT: 56 dead, 1,916 injured, several thousand buildings damaged, $400 million in damage

During the morning of April 10, southwestern weather forecasters became aware that conditions were favorable for tornado formation. Satellite images showed a front moving east from Utah. By early afternoon tornado watches were issued for the Red River Valley along the border of Texas and Oklahoma.

Three tornadoes struck the area in the midafternoon and evening. At 3:30, a tornado hit the southern part of Vernon, Texas, population 11,000. Lasting ten minutes, the tornado killed 11 people, injured more than 60 individuals, and damaged hundreds of homes. Crossing the Red River, the tornado penetrated 50 miles into Oklahoma. The same thunderstorm system spawned a tornado that hit farms and the small towns of Harrold, Texas, and Grandfield, Oklahoma. After 5 the tornado struck Lawton, Oklahoma, population 75,000, killing 3 people, wounding 109 others, and damaging many houses and buildings.

Before 6 P.M., a mile-wide tornado raced across the southwestern part of Wichita Falls, Texas, home to 96,000 people at that time. Eyewitnesses described seeing several vortices. The tornado killed 40 people and injured 1,700. Authorities noted that 60 percent of the fatalities occurred in cars, which people had considered shelters. The tornado, accompanied by baseball-size hail, destroyed the city's Memorial Stadium, a school, a motel, a cafe, and a truck stop. Some survivors sought shelter in supermarket and ice cream parlor coolers.

Statistics for the tornadoes totaled 56 dead, 1,916 injured, 259 hospitalized, and 2,934 houses, 139 mobile homes, 1,132 apartments, and 112 businesses destroyed. Approximately 7,759 families were affected by the tornado in twelve Texas and Oklahoma counties, which sustained $400 million damages.

Elizabeth D. Schafer

FOR FURTHER INFORMATION:

Bluestein, Howard B. *Tornado Alley: Monster Storms of the Great Plains.* New York: Oxford University Press, 1999.

Red River Valley Tornadoes of April 10, 1979: A Report to the Administrator. Rockville, Md.: U.S. Department of Commerce, National Oceanic and Atmospheric Administration, 1980.

one-third of structures destroyed. About 3,000 people became homeless after the storms. Because of the distance traveled, the 1984 tornadoes in the Carolinas have sometimes been compared to the 1925 Great Tri-State Tornado. The Carolina storm system caused hurricane-level gusts, snow, and power outages when it reached New England.

Elizabeth D. Schafer

FOR FURTHER INFORMATION:

Davis, Lee. *Natural Disasters: From the Black Plague to the Eruption of Mt. Pinatubo.* New York: Facts on File, 1992.

1984: The Carolinas

DATE: March 28, 1984
PLACE: North Carolina and South Carolina
CLASSIFICATION: F2-F4
RESULT: 61 dead, thousands injured and homeless, $200 million in damage

Twenty-four tornadoes swept through the Carolinas during one night in March, 1984, when warm air passed over a cold front, creating a turbulent thunderstorm system. The tornadoes struck at different sites along a 260-mile path through the Carolinas. They mainly hit rural, unsettled areas, minimizing damage to people and property. One F2 tornado struck Newberry, South Carolina—38 people were injured, and the town suffered $11 million in damage. Shortly before 6 P.M., an F3 tornado headed toward Fairfield damaged 254 houses, 45 trailers, 68 farm buildings, 86 business buildings, and 7 public buildings. Residents also mourned the loss of two-hundred-year-old pecan and oak trees.

An F4 tornado uprooted a pine forest in Chesterfield County, South Carolina, worth millions of dollars. At least 100 people were injured at a shopping center. Tornadoes moved on northeastern paths through North Carolina, primarily causing the most damage to homes, trailers, and timber. Many deaths were caused by trees falling on dwellings. At 10:15 P.M., a waterspout over Albemarle Sound moved onshore as a tornado in Chowan County.

These tornadoes caused 61 deaths, and 1,000 were injured. Approximately $200 million worth of damage was reported, and mobile homes constituted

1985: Canada, Ohio, Pennsylvania

DATE: May 31, 1985
PLACE: Ontario, Canada; Atlantic and Wheatland, Pennsylvania; and Newton Falls and Youngstown, Ohio
CLASSIFICATION: F4-F5
RESULT: 93 dead, thousands injured, millions of dollars in damage

When a western cold front, cool northern air, and warm moisture from the Gulf of Mexico collided over Ohio and Pennsylvania in May of 1985, twenty-four tornadoes resulted from the turbulence. The tornadoes had winds as high as 200 miles per hour. Such intense F4 and F5 tornadoes rarely occur in those regions, and, at that time, these tornadoes were considered the worst known in local history.

The first tornado touched down north of Toronto, Ontario, where 12 people died and 150 people were injured. The tornadoes in Ohio caused $4 million in damage. At Newton Falls, 300 houses were destroyed, and fires sparked by the storm razed the downtown district. Nine people died in Youngstown, where the tornado carved a 200-foot-wide path for 3.5 miles. New York State mainly suffered property damage.

Pennsylvania received the most tornado destruction, totaling several hundred million dollars. In Atlantic, 5 people died in their homes, and the tornado destroyed a grain mill and a microwave tower. The Wheatland steel plant vanished with the storm, eliminating jobs for its 500 employees, almost half of the town's population of 1,122. Mayor Helen M. Duby retreated to a cellar with her family, emerging to find that Wheatland had been blown away.

In all, 93 people died during the storm, and 2,000 people were injured. Many of the victims were Amish who rejected medical attention. One tornado moved a wagon 1 mile, and a silo was the sole structure left standing at one farm. At least 88,000 trees were sheared from the Moshannnon State Forest. Eyewitnesses reported that three minutes before the tornadoes arrived, the green sky was filled with pink insulation, shingles, and metal.

Elizabeth D. Schafer

FOR FURTHER INFORMATION:

Davis, Lee. *Natural Disasters: From the Black Plague to the Eruption of Mt. Pinatubo.* New York: Facts on File, 1992.

1987: Texas

DATE: May 22, 1987
PLACE: Saragosa, Texas
CLASSIFICATION: F4
RESULT: 30 dead, 121 injured, 85 percent of the town destroyed, $7.1 to $8.7 million in damage

Thunderstorms precipitating rain and hail struck the southwestern Texas town of Saragosa during the afternoon of May 22, 1987. Saragosa, primarily a community of 400 Spanish-speaking Mexican Americans, had a semiarid climate that supported ranches. After a June, 1938, tornado demolished Saragosa, the town was rebuilt 2 miles away, on the site that was later hit in 1987.

The May 22 thunderstorm intensified, producing a tornado after 7 that evening. Several motorists on nearby Highway 10 reported seeing a cloud with three funnels 1 mile southwest of Saragosa. Moving northeast, the tornado strengthened and expanded to 0.5 mile wide. In town, many residents had gathered in Guadalupe Hall to watch a Head Start graduation ceremony. Just before the F4 tornado hit at 7:15 P.M., one anxious parent ran into the hall to tell about the tornado and rescue his child. Outside, motorists honked car horns to alert residents of the twister. Television and radio stations issued warnings in Spanish and English; Saragosa did not have tornado sirens.

In all, 30 people died in the tornado, including 22 at Guadalupe Hall. Parents and grandparents shielded children's bodies from debris that fatally injured the adults. Sixteen of the victims were visitors, and 28 were Hispanic. About 121 people were injured. The tornado caused $7.1 to $8.7 million in damage, destroying 85 percent of the town, especially adobe houses. Cars were strewn into fields as far as 900 feet away.

Elizabeth D. Schafer

FOR FURTHER INFORMATION:

Aguirre, Benigno E., et al. *Saragosa, Texas, Tornado, May 22, 1987: An Evaluation of the Warning System.* Washington, D.C.: National Academy Press, 1991.

1989: Alabama

DATE: November 15, 1989
PLACE: Huntsville, Alabama
CLASSIFICATION: F4
RESULT: 21 dead, 463 injured, $100 million in damage

Unusually warm November air, Gulf of Mexico moisture, and a strong, swift-moving cold front contributed to the formation of an F4-strength tornado that struck Huntsville, Alabama, at 4:34 P.M., during rush hour. The tornado moved northeast from the southern part of the city toward residential and business areas. Many of the fatalities occurred on U.S. Highway 231, a main north-south artery in Huntsville, as motorists unaware of the tornado's approach were unable to secure shelter. Eighteen people died at the intersections of Highway 231, Airport, and Whitesburg Roads.

Eyewitnesses said that a dark cloud with lightning approached at dusk; they did not see a funnel. The tornado churned along a 0.5-mile-wide path for 3 miles. Iranian refugees living in Huntsville said the tornado was worse than an Iraqi bombing raid. Four shopping centers were destroyed, and damage was done to several churches, radio towers, apartment buildings, offices, homes, and cars. The top floor of the Jones Valley Elementary School was ripped off and scattered across the city; a group of kindergarten students and teachers survived the storm by hiding underneath a stairway. A total of 21 people died, with

The remains of this Huntsville, Alabama, resident's apartment building after the 1989 tornado. (AP/Wide World Photos)

463 injured, and $100 million in damage were declared. Thousands became homeless.

Temperatures dipped into the twenties, and cold rain and snow flurries complicated rescue work. About 30,000 people did not have power because the tornado destroyed 7 steel towers that transmitted electricity from the Tennessee Valley Authority. The storm system spawned additional tornadoes in Alabama, nearby southern states, and New England, where more fatalities were reported.

Elizabeth D. Schafer

FOR FURTHER INFORMATION:

Sikora, Frank, and Kent Faulk. "Nightmarish Scene Shows Tornado's Fury." *Birmingham News*, November 16, 1989, p. 1B.

"South Shivers After Storm." *Atlanta Constitution*, November 17, 1989, pp. A1.

"Tornado Toll: 18." *Birmingham News*, November 16, 1989, pp. 1A, 12A.

1991: Kansas

DATE: April 26, 1991
PLACE: Wichita and Andover, Kansas
CLASSIFICATION: F5
RESULT: 17 dead, 225 injured, 1,728 homes damaged or destroyed, $272 million in damage

From a meteorologist's viewpoint, April 26, 1991, was a perfect day for tornadoes. Very cold air was pushing rapidly eastward into warm moist air over Kansas. Shortly after noon, the National Severe Storms Forecast Center in Kansas City issued a tornado watch for central and eastern Kansas. At about 3:30 P.M., a supercell thunderstorm capable of producing hail and tornadoes developed over northern Oklahoma and moved northeastward into south central Kansas. As the rotating storm moved into Sedgwick County, the National Weather Service office in Wichita issued a tornado warning for its home county at 5:46 P.M.

Within a minute, warning sirens throughout greater Wichita sounded. At 5:55 P.M., the supercell produced a 100-yard-wide twister that uprooted trees and damaged several homes in Hayesville, just south of Wichita, as its winds increased to more than 150 miles per hour. The Weather Service reissued the warning for eastern Sedgwick County.

The tornado moved into the southern part of Wichita, where it damaged several houses. The debris cloud turned pink from geraniums that it sucked up as it destroyed the greenhouses in a nursery. After crossing the Kansas Turnpike and damaging buildings at Boeing Aircraft, the tornado headed for McConnell Air Force Base, where it destroyed hundreds of base housing units, an elementary school, and the hospital. Fortunately, the still-narrow twister missed the flight line where 84 military aircraft, including 16 B-1 bombers, were parked. At least 2 of the $280 million bombers contained nuclear warheads. After the event, physicists stated that they could not positively predict what would have happened had a tornado struck one of the armed bombers, but a ruptured weapon could have spread radioactive plutonium at least 38 miles.

After exiting the base, the tornado widened to more than 200 yards, and its winds increased to 200 miles per hour. The then-F4 tornado devastated the Greenwich Heights subdivision in eastern Wichita and took 4 lives there before crossing into Butler County. As the multiple-vortex tornado crossed an open field toward Andover, a bedroom community of about 4,000 people, its width increased to 0.5 mile and its winds surpassed 260 miles per hour. At 6:29 P.M., the National Weather Service warned the citizens of Andover that a tornado on the ground in southeast Wichita was heading their way and that they should abandon mobile homes and cars for sturdier buildings. When the town's lone warning siren malfunctioned and failed to sound, Andover police officers drove through the Golden Spur Mobile Home Park, directly in the path of the oncoming tornado, to warn as many as possible to take shelter.

The first area the tornado, which had reached F5 status, destroyed was a subdivision of relatively new homes, many with basements, where residents took shelter. No one in the houses died, but those in mobile homes were not as fortunate. Nearly 200 of

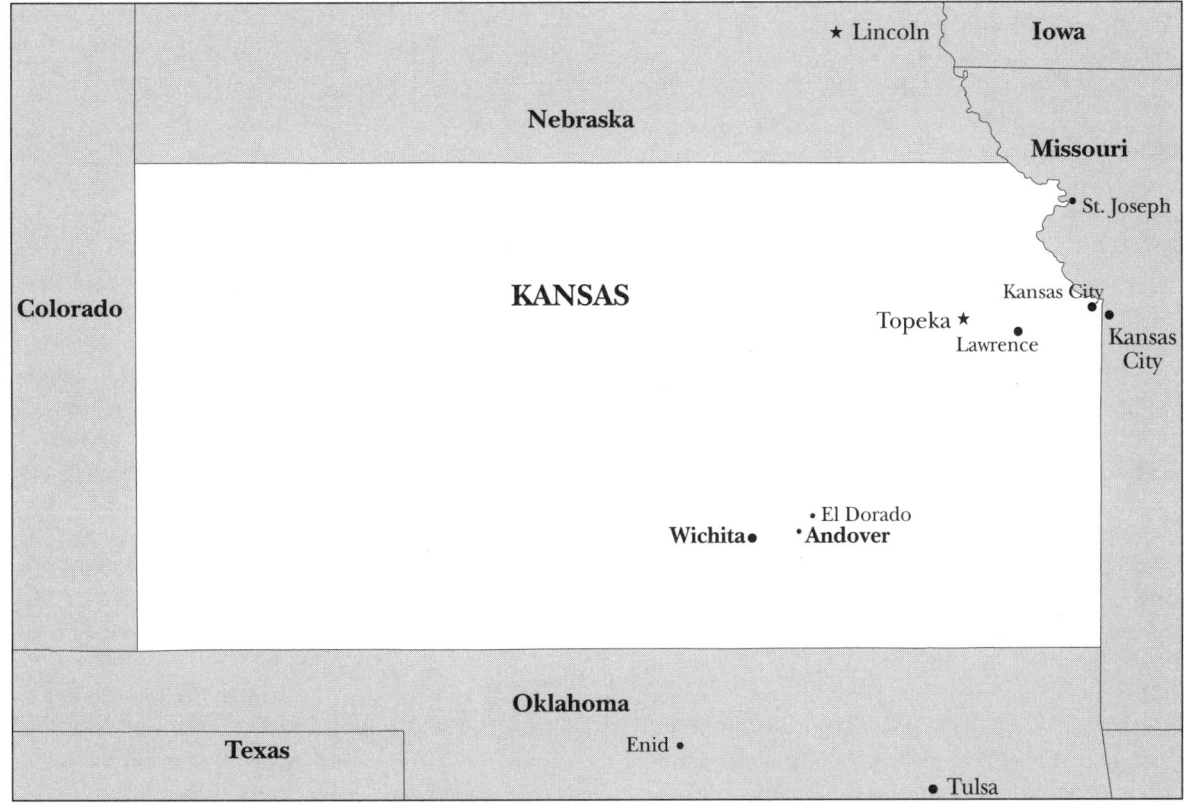

Golden Spur's 334 residents who were at home at the time of the tornado took refuge in the park's storm shelter, and many of the remainder fled to find safety elsewhere. Those who had huddled in the shelter emerged to find utter devastation. The landscape was piled knee-high with twisted metal, insulation, shards of lumber and glass, and thousands of treasures that had once graced the 231 destroyed mobile homes. Even worse, 13 Golden Spur residents perished. The weakening 0.5-mile-wide monster headed for open country, where it devoured several homes, rolled an oil storage tank a mile, and killed a number of cattle before lifting into the thunderstorm cloud about 25 miles northeast of Andover.

Immediately after the storm ended, the city began using front-end loaders to move the debris in an effort to locate victims. By midnight, law enforcement and relief agencies had tended to all the injured, sheltered the homeless, fed the hungry, turned off electricity and gas in the affected areas, and established law and order. During the next few weeks, hundreds of volunteers from around the nation moved piles of rubble; supervised the distribution of food, clothing, and household goods; found survivors places to live; counseled the bereaved; and began rebuilding homes. Countless others donated funds and goods.

Millions of Americans saw on the national news not only the devastation but also the tornado itself as it roared through McConnell Air Force Base toward Andover. As they huddled under a Kansas Turnpike bridge with some travelers, the members of a Wichita news team captured an astounding video of a companion tornado that developed from the same supercell only seconds after the Andover tornado dissipated. Most Americans have probably seen images of these two tornadoes because they appear in nearly every tornado documentary or educational video produced after 1991.

Personnel from the Weather Service and the Centers for Disease Control evaluated the effectiveness of the tornado warnings for this tornado and investigated its health-related effects. They praised the Wichita Weather Service office and the local media for providing a seven-minute warning for Andover and found that most of the Wichita area residents knew what safety measures to take. The Wichita and Andover tornado resulted in two significant pieces of legislation. The federal government appropriated more than $1 million to help Kansas communities purchase new tornado sirens (the one that malfunc-

tioned in Andover was old). Most important, this tornado motivated the Department of Commerce to expedite the installation of NEXRAD Doppler radar systems throughout the country.

Marlene Bradford

FOR FURTHER INFORMATION:

Centers for Disease Control. "Tornado Disaster: Kansas, 1991." *Journal of the American Medical Association*, April 15, 1992, 2012-2013.

Hamric, Sharon. *Like the Devil: The Kansas Tornadoes of April 26, 1991.* Wichita, Kans.: *Wichita Eagle*/Beacon, 1991.

"In the Wake of the Storm, the Nightmare Continued." *Andover Journal-Advocate*, May 2, 1991, p. 1.

Inglish, Howard, ed. *Tornado: Terror and Survival.* Andover, Kans.: Counseling Center of Butler County, 1991.

Marshall, Tim. "Countdown to Disaster: Chasing the Andover Tornado." *Weatherwise*, June, 1992, 21-23.

Wichita Eagle, April 27-30, 1991.

1994: U.S. South

DATE: March 27-28, 1994
PLACE: Alabama, Tennessee, Georgia, and the Carolinas
CLASSIFICATION: F4
RESULT: 52 dead

On Palm Sunday, 1994, high temperatures, such as Atlanta, Georgia's record 86 degrees, pushed moist, warm air into a slow-moving cold front. As the front traveled north along the Appalachian Mountains, it produced violent tornadoes from Alabama to the Carolinas. The most publicized tornado struck the Goshen United Methodist Church in Cherokee County, Alabama, at 11:35 A.M. Approximately 146 worshipers were attending a service; when the tornado struck, the children's choir was singing. The power went out just before the tornado collapsed a brick wall and the roof, trapping people in pews. Meteorologists estimated that the tornado's winds were almost 200 miles per hour.

In all, 19 people were killed, including the Reverend Kelly Clem's toddler daughter. A motorist died outside the church. Ninety people were injured. Although the National Weather Service had issued a warning thirty minutes before the tornado hit, Goshen lacked a tornado siren. Relief workers described the devastation as resembling an explosion. Ironically, another tornado was sighted later that afternoon during the cleanup effort.

Tornadoes struck seven northeastern Alabama counties, killing 2 people. Two other churches were destroyed, but no one was killed because congregations stayed in basements. The same storm system moved through 11 Georgia counties, killing 16 people and over 100,000 chickens. Rock climbers survived while scaling the face of Mount Yonah. Two people died in North Carolina, and 1 tornado-related death was reported in Tennessee. The region suffered heavy rains and flash flooding.

Elizabeth D. Schafer

FOR FURTHER INFORMATION:

"After the Storm: A County-by-County Report." *Atlanta Constitution*, March 29, 1994, p. C3.

Archibald, John, and Frank Sikora. "19 Die in Church." *Birmingham News*, March 28, 1994, p. 1A.

Faulk, Kent, and John Davis. "A Look at Alabama Counties Hit Hardest by Sunday's Storm Burst." *Birmingham News*, March 28, 1994, p. 3A.

1997: Texas

DATE: May 27, 1997
PLACE: Jarrell, Texas
CLASSIFICATION: F5
RESULT: 27 dead, 8 injured, 44 homes damaged or destroyed

During the last week of May, 1997, a cold front pushed through the central plains of Oklahoma and Kansas. The front caused severe thunderstorms and caught the attention of Dr. Charles Doswell, a research meteorologist at the National Severe Storms Laboratory (NSSL) in Norman, Oklahoma. Dr. Doswell recognized that the higher humidity near the Gulf of Mexico would add strength to the storms as the front plunged into Texas. In order to follow atmospheric developments, Doswell drove to the Fort Worth National Weather Service office on the morning of May 27.

As expected, the morning was typical of spring. It started with clear skies, high humidity, and rapidly warming temperatures. Initially, cooler temperatures aloft slowed vertical development of storm clouds. In the early afternoon, however, the sky grew darker near Waco, Texas, as a single towering cumulus erupted through the upper layers of the atmosphere to form a supercell, the strongest type of thunderstorm. Doswell's hunch of pending trouble proved correct as the cold front plowed into the rich humidity from the Gulf of Mexico. This collision of energetic air masses would sustain this individual supercell for the next six hours. However, instead of moving in the typical northeasterly direction, this supercell plunged southward, growing in strength along the intersection between the cold front and the warm moist air to the south. That uncommon southerly movement would cause one of the most devastating tornado effects ever recorded. Before the day was over, this supercell spawned 22 tornadoes, killing 30.

The first of the tornadoes formed 10 miles south of Waco at 1:37 P.M. It was followed by a continuous succession of tornadoes forming one after another. Each tornado in turn traced a southerly course, following the leisurely pace of the parent supercell. These tornadoes achieved F2-level strength, with winds approaching 150 miles per hour. One of the tornadoes in this series tracked across Lake Belton, briefly assuming the characteristics of a waterspout. A flotilla of cabin cruisers, ski boats, and party barges disappeared below the surface as this tornado sank the largest marina on the lake.

Word of the approaching tornadic thunderstorm had circulated from numerous radio and television sources during the first two hours of tornadic activity. Initially, only a small number of people were at risk. Forming just west of Interstate 35, these tornadoes spiraled through rural areas without nearing any population centers. By 3:50 P.M., a new tornado was just forming 3 miles north of Jarrell, Texas. Its forward motion was very slow, and many Jarrell residents, who had been watching the tornado for several minutes, escaped by driving south on the interstate at its approach. Unfortunately, school had let out for the day twenty minutes earlier. Many of the younger students were just reaching home either on foot or by bicycle. Aware of the danger, some of these students accompanied their friends to the new subdivision just west of town. In some instances, a few parents left work early to be with their children at home.

The Initial Touchdown. The initial touchdown point was north of Jarrell in a cotton field. Green with

maturing cotton plants, the 30-acre field was instantly defoliated. Although relatively weak, the wind force scoured away several acres of topsoil, exposing the limestone base a foot below the original surface. As a result, a great mud storm developed at the base of the tornado, plastering 4 inches of mud against fence posts, tree trunks, foundations, and farm equipment. Typical in an F2 tornado, with winds exceeding 100 miles per hour, the first farm home lost its roof.

The tornado rapidly grew in strength over the next 0.5 mile as the second home was flattened, with most of the debris strewn downwind. On this day the owner chose to drive away rather than stay in his underground storm shelter. The 4,000-pound concrete roof of the shelter was torn from its moorings, never to be found in subsequent searches. With winds now approaching 200 miles per hour, the tornado siphoned 25 vertical feet of water from the well nearby.

The track of the tornado was plainly evident in the grassland beyond the homestead. It was mostly defoliated, the few remaining blades of grass shredded and flattened to the ground. The tornado path, now 800 feet across, bore the spiraling marks characteristic of a multiple-vortex tornado. Sometimes called suction spots, these intense whirlwinds within the main funnel carved their spirals several inches into the soil.

In the field beyond, the tornado raked across a wheat field ready for harvest, sending millions of wheat shafts spiraling into the vortex. The wheat shafts, as rigid as ice picks at such high velocities, impaled the cattle in the adjoining field. Of a herd of 130 cattle, half a dozen survived, wheat stitched into their hides and underbellies. Film evidence taken at the time revealed that many of the animals were vaulted into the air and dropped to the ground repeatedly. Internal injuries were severe; most of the cattle had four broken legs. Typically, hair was removed from the hide. In extreme examples, even the hide was stripped away, exposing muscle and bone.

Double Creek Estates. For the next 2 miles, the rotational velocity and width of the tornado continued to increase. Its intensity was most apparent along the only road leading to Jarrell's newest housing addition. This is where the devastation of an F5 tornado first became apparent. Winds in excess of 300 miles per hour lifted steel, concrete, and rock as easily as a wind gust stirring a leaf pile. For example, steel posts that once supported barbed-wire fences were lashed back and forth by the strong winds, breaking them off at ground level. Many sections of roadway were destroyed by the intense pressure of wind that gripped the pavement, disintegrating the pieces as they vaulted into the air. The energy of the wind alone peeled bark from the few tree trunks still standing.

At 0.5 mile wide, the path of the tornado now curved westward, centering on Double Creek Estates. Perhaps because of its westward travel, the forward motion of the tornado had slowed to a walking speed. It would take seventeen minutes for the tornado to travel the next mile over Double Creek, pul-

A tornado that struck Jarrell, Texas, on May 27, 1997. (AP/Wide World Photos)

verizing homes, appliances, automobiles, and taking human life. One of the residents had a collection of nearly 75 vintage Chevrolets that was swept into the maelstrom. Only a handful of cars remained intact, while most were reduced to shrapnel. Even engine blocks and transmissions were shattered from the repeated blows. In the first seconds, the great wind swept entire homes from their foundations. The residents were also swept along in a torrent of wind, metal, and wood.

With the exception of shattered fragments of wood that had speared the ground, there was little debris remaining in the vicinity of Double Creek Estates. The house foundations left behind gave mute testimony to the sequence of destruction. Although most of these homes were solidly built of brick veneer construction, the force of the wind and flying debris instantly disintegrated roofs and walls. Even the bricks were launched into the air, to be shot out of the tornado in a great fusillade. Bricks were scattered across the countryside, disproportionately favoring the left side of the tornado path. Clearly, with the counterclockwise rotation of the funnel, these homes were destroyed at the first instant by the leading edge of the tornado.

In some houses, the vinyl flooring was glued to the concrete foundation in bathrooms and kitchen areas. Long slashes in the vinyl cutting from right to left also confirmed that these floors were entirely exposed in those first moments. Modern construction practices attach the lumber to the concrete slab by shooting nails through the wood into the concrete beneath. All lumber attached in this manner was removed from the slabs. Other attached objects, including door thresholds, carpet tacking strips, toilets, tubs, and brick veneer fireplaces, were also removed. Copper water lines, plastic fittings, and wires were sheared off at the surface level of each slab. Even the concrete slabs had great gashes on their surfaces, with chunks of concrete nicked away from the corners and edges. Apparently, the homes of Double Creek Estates were not simply flattened, with their debris accounted for nearby, but rather annihilated one hundred times over as the tornado ground away any object that extended above ground.

While at its maximum strength over the subdivision, even the distant surface winds plunging into the tornado created amazing effects. Round hay bales weighing 1,500 pounds were tumbled into the tornado from 0.25 mile away. About 1,000 feet south of the path, a home seemed undamaged on the side facing the tornado. However, the inbound winds shattered windows and removed shingles on the side facing away from the tornado. This homeowner also lost his tractor-trailer rig as the inflowing winds pulled it into the tornado.

The Weakening Tornado. The tornado would not lift for another 3 miles; however, the first signs of weakening began about 1 mile beyond the subdivision. Three great piles of debris spaced about 1,000 feet apart formed into a straight line near the centerline of the tornado footprint. At about 100 feet long, each streamlined hill was formed from the most massive objects available: automobile parts, appliances, trucks, and farm implements. Such objects apparently accumulated as flying debris slammed into the side of each pile. Smaller debris, perhaps transported higher in the tornado, rained down over a dozen square miles near the lift-off point. Consisting mostly of metal, plastic, and wood, these objects typically weighed just a few pounds. Finally, the lightest debris was transported by the supercell thunderstorm, later to fall to earth at great distances. Although most of this material could not be absolutely confirmed as originating from this event, a box of checks bearing the name of one of the victims was discovered 100 miles south of Jarrell.

The Aftermath. The shattering intensity of this tornado is expressed in the statistics: 27 dead and 8 injured. Other great tornadoes have claimed more lives, but no other tornado event can claim a 75 percent mortality rate. The irresistible force of 300-mile-per-hour winds sitting in place for several minutes caused more complete damage than a rapidly moving tornado of similar force.

Despite all odds, there were survivors. A woman hid in her bathtub as her home was destroyed around her. Located just outside the path under weaker wind conditions, her house was nevertheless destroyed and carried several hundred feet away. She rode along with her house while in her tub. When she stood up at the end of her ride, the bathtub fell into pieces around her.

Even more amazing is the foresight of a family that survived beneath their house in the Double Creek subdivision. Having experienced a tornado ten years earlier, this family built a storm shelter by hand-digging a hole through the slab. Taking two years to complete, this unique structure built of solid concrete and encased beneath the original foundation may have been the only shelter that could survive the intensity and duration of the Jarrell tornado.

Don M. Greene

FOR FURTHER INFORMATION:

Boyd, Deanna, and Justin Bachman. "After Storm's Fury, Residents Rage." *Fort Worth Star-Telegram,* May 30, 1997.

"FEMA Denies Jarrell Area Disaster Aid." *Waco Tribune-Herald,* June 7, 1997.

"Funnel Cloud of Death." *Newsweek,* June 9, 1997, 68.

Lindell, Chuck. "Jarrell's Healing Year." *Austin-American Statesman,* May 24, 1998.

_____. "A New Day in Jarrell." *Austin-American Statesman,* January 4, 1998.

_____. "Officer's Grim Duty Left Scars." *Austin-American Statesman,* May 24, 1998.

1997: Michigan

PLACE: Detroit, Michigan, and surrounding counties

DATE: July 2, 1997

CLASSIFICATION: F1-F3

RESULT: 12 dead, 100 injured, $135 million in damage

The Great Lakes region is not unaccustomed to storm systems arising in the summer, but the one that passed over Michigan on July 2, 1997, was unique. An intense storm system that featured a strong cold front, greater-than-normal amounts of energy at the middle levels of the atmosphere, a strong jet stream, and a very warm, humid air mass at the surface generated 16 tornadoes, a record number for a single day in Michigan. In addition, the system produced several destructive thunderstorms.

The National Weather Service office in White Lake, Michigan, determined that the conditions in Michigan that day were ripe for supercell thunderstorm production. At 5:20 A.M. the office issued a severe weather potential statement, and at 11:35 it warned residents of southeastern Michigan of the possibility of "isolated tornadoes." When a line of thunderstorms began to develop along a cold front in western Michigan, the Storm Prediction Center issued a tornado watch for much of the lower peninsula at 1:10 P.M. During the afternoon three super-

cells moved through the area, leaving behind death and destruction.

The telltale funnel clouds began to appear in the sky over southeastern Michigan in the midafternoon. The first tornado, 2 miles long and 60 yards wide, touched down in Saginaw County at 3:41 P.M.; it only reached F1 intensity. This supercell continued on its path, generating 6 more tornadoes, including one of F3 intensity that struck Thedford township, where it killed 1 person.

A second supercell generated an F2 tornado that moved through suburban Oakland County and hit the Chateau Oak Hill and Spring Grove trailer parks near the town of Holly. A forty-year-old woman died when the tornado, estimated to be 75 feet in diameter, blew another trailer on top of hers.

The last tornado-producing supercell generated an F2 tornado in Wayne County about 6 P.M. This tornado cut a 5-mile-long path across northwest Detroit, Highland Park, and Hamtramck with no loss of life. Many people in the area had heard the tornado warning on television but had done nothing because "nothing ever happened in the past." In Hamtramck several buildings had roofs removed, trees were strewn about, and a car was upside down about 50 feet from where it had been parked.

Although the tornadoes the 3 supercells produced killed 2 people, the nontornadic winds these storms generated took additional lives. The greatest loss of life was at Grosse Point Park. That afternoon a swimming meet was being held at the park, and over 400 people were in attendance. Around 6 P.M. park personnel announced over the public address system that everyone should leave the area because a storm was fast approaching. About 50 people were still in the park when the storm struck. Straight-line winds, or downbursts, with estimated wind speeds of 80 to 110 miles per hour blew down trees and tossed trash cans and loose objects about. Five people died when the winds pushed the roofed sun shelter in which they were taking cover into Lake St. Clair. Apparently, the family did not understand English very well, which may have contributed to the tragedy. Eight others at the park received injuries.

An additional 5 deaths were indirectly attributed to the storm. At Holly a seventy-nine-year-old man was electrocuted while working on his basement sump pump. Two days after the storm, a woman and her 3 grandchildren died when a generator, which had been dislocated as a result of the storm, filled their home with poisonous carbon monoxide. The storms injured approximately 100 people.

The dense population of the area meant that a large network of communication and transportation was disrupted. Detroit Edison, the local electric utility, said that over 325,000 people lost power at the height of the storms. Damage estimates were over $135 million. Officials from the Federal Emergency Management Agency (FEMA), as well as Michigan police and government agencies, began damage assessment on July 3. The American Red Cross sent teams and supplies to help with the relief efforts. In Detroit, Mayor Dennis Archer was strongly proactive, urging city workers to assist the public as expeditiously as possible.

Nicholas Birns and Marlene Bradford

FOR FURTHER INFORMATION:
Detroit Free Press, July 3, 1997.
Flint Times, July 3, 1997.
Jackson Citizen Patriot, July 3, 1997.
Saginaw News, July 3, 1997.

1998: Mississippi, Alabama, Georgia

DATE: April 9, 1998
PLACE: Mississippi; Tuscaloosa and Jefferson Counties, Alabama; and suburbs of Atlanta, Georgia
CLASSIFICATION: F5
RESULT: 39 dead, 221 injured, thousands of buildings destroyed, several hundred million dollars in damage

A swift jet stream brought cool air into north central Alabama on April 9, 1998, where it collided with warm air masses and moisture from the Gulf of Mexico to fuel a powerful tornado. Classified as an F5 tornado, the twister that struck Birmingham, Alabama, had winds estimated from 260 to 300 miles per hour. The thunderstorm system that produced this tornado began in Mississippi and moved into western Alabama. The tornado first touched down in Tuscaloosa County, then rose into the sky before striking small communities in Jefferson County at 8 P.M. and approaching within several miles of downtown Birmingham. The 0.5-mile-wide tornado also caused damage in eastern Alabama and in Atlanta, Georgia, suburbs. Casualties from the storm system totaled 1 dead in Mississippi, 33 killed in Alabama, and 5 dead in Georgia. About 5,000 acres of timber worth $3 million was destroyed.

Vice President Al Gore visited the stricken Alabama communities, which resembled war zones. Pine trees stripped of branches and bark were surrounded by bricks, twisted street signs, and clothing. Foundations were all that remained of most buildings; the community of Oak Grove was obliterated. The deadliest tornado in Birmingham's history injured 221 people and destroyed 1,023 homes, 18 apartment buildings, 5 businesses, and a school. The *Birmingham News* printed an editorial cartoon of a chimney surrounded by debris with the Bible verse Acts 24:15, promising resurrection.

Elizabeth D. Schafer

FOR FURTHER INFORMATION:
"'Awful . . . It's All Gone.'" *Birmingham News,* April 10, 1998, p. 1A.
"Night of Fury." *Birmingham News,* April 10, 1998, pp. 17A-22A.
"Special Report: Tornado Cleanup Begins." *Montgomery Advertiser,* April 11, 1998, p. 1A.

1999: Oklahoma, Kansas

DATE: May 3, 1999
PLACE: Primarily central Oklahoma, especially near Oklahoma City, and Sedgwick County, Kansas
CLASSIFICATION: Up to F5
RESULT: 49 dead, more than 900 injured, more than 17,000 buildings damaged or destroyed, about $1.5 billion in damage

Prelude. According to the weather forecast that the *Daily Oklahoman* published early in the morning of Monday, May 3, 1999, Oklahoma City was to have winds that day ranging from 10 to 20 miles an hour, but storms were possible in much of Oklahoma the following day. That forecast of storms, as events turned out, was off by a day.

At about 6:00 Monday morning in Norman, a short drive south of Oklahoma City, the Storm Prediction Center of the National Weather Service noted a

dry line extending from south to north across the panhandles of Texas and Oklahoma and said there was a low possibility of severe thunderstorms and even tornadoes in Oklahoma as a result of this meeting of hot, dry air from the west and warm, wet air from the east. By 11:15 that morning, the possibility had become moderate. By 3:49 P.M., after having received weather-balloon readings indicating layers of winds in different directions and at different speeds, the Storm Prediction Center officially revised its forecast to include a high possibility of dangerous spring storms.

When, at 4:30 P.M., radar in Norman found a tornado in a supercell, the National Weather Service sent out a tornado warning for central Oklahoma, including metropolitan Oklahoma City. Fifteen minutes later, a tornado touched the ground near Lawton, in the southwestern part of the state. An evening of death and destruction had begun for both Oklahoma and Kansas.

Storms. Of the 76 tornadoes that formed late in the afternoon and night of May 3, the worst was the 0.5-mile-wide one, which traveled about 90 miles in Oklahoma from the Lawton area northeast into the central part of the state. That long path included 19 miles through the Oklahoma City area only a little after the evening rush hour, from the unincorporated community of Bridge Creek in northeastern Grady County; through the big suburbs of Moore, Del City, and Midwest City; to the town of Choctaw in eastern Oklahoma County. According to meteorologists from the University of Oklahoma, the rotating wind in that tornado reached the very top of the F5 category of the Fujita scale—318 miles an hour—and may have set a record speed up to that date for any natural wind on earth. That monstrous tornado was one of from 3 to 5 produced along one storm path.

Among the other storm paths in Oklahoma, a second, northwest of the greatest one, reached from southern Blaine County well into Kingfisher County, where the little town of Dover endured an F4 tornado, with a wind between 207 and 260 miles an hour. A third storm path, west and north of Oklahoma City, stretched from northern Grady County into Noble County; in Logan County, that storm path generated another F4 tornado. A fourth storm path, south and east of the metropolitan area, extended from eastern Cleveland County through Pottawatomie County and into Lincoln County. That same night, in Kansas, a severe thunderstorm generated tornadoes in Sedgwick County. Most notably, an F4 tornado passed through Haysville and the adjacent southern part of Wichita.

Property. In all, tornadoes in the Great Plains on May 3 caused such damage that President Bill Clinton declared Sedgwick County, Kansas, a disaster area, along with 11 counties in Oklahoma, from Caddo and Grady Counties, southeast of Oklahoma City, to Tulsa County, in the northeastern part of the state. Property damage in the two states was about $1.5 billion, and while people in the building trades found their work in high demand after the storms, many other people worried about how they would ever make a living again.

As in all tornadoes, motor vehicles and mobile homes were especially vulnerable. Whirling winds tossed cars many yards from where they had been and flipped them upside down; even huge tractor-trailer rigs fell victim to the winds. The big tornado in Sedgwick County shredded and knocked over trailers in the Lakeshore Mobile Homes Resort and at Pacesetter Mobile Homes; earlier, the even more powerful tornado in central Oklahoma had devastated mobile homes in the Southern Hills section of Bridge Creek.

More surprising, for persons accustomed only to weak tornadoes, the most powerful of the tornadoes on May 3 virtually flattened solidly built, fairly new houses, as in the especially hard-hit Highland Park neighborhood in Moore, Oklahoma, where concrete slabs were the chief evidence after the storm of the sites of many families' homes. The devastation there and in other severely affected neighborhoods and towns resembled the devastation from wartime bombing, as one Oklahoma City survivor said. In some places, cars rested where houses had once stood, debris seemed to be everywhere, and returning citizens, deprived of landmarks, could hardly find where they had lived before the storm had struck.

Concerned neighbors in Oklahoma City aid a victim of a 1999 tornado. (AP/Wide World Photos)

Schools and businesses also sustained damage. In Moore, the F5 tornado wrecked part of Westmoore High School; not long afterward, in tiny Mulhall, Oklahoma, north of Oklahoma City, another tornado destroyed the elementary school. At Stroud, a town of 3,200 on Interstate 44, midway between Tulsa and Oklahoma City, the damage to businesses imperiled the town's economic life, because the tornado that passed through the town tore much of the roof off the Integris Stroud Municipal Hospital; devastated the headquarters of the Sygma Network, a distributor of restaurant supplies; badly damaged the Wendy's Restaurant, the Best Western Motel, and two mobile home parks; and in effect destroyed the large Tanger Outlet Mall that had for several years been a familiar sight to motorists between Oklahoma's two largest cities.

People. Even more important than the indirect effects the tornadoes of May 3 had on people through the immense destruction of property were the direct effects the tornadoes had through injuries and death. Altogether, 49 people died because of the dangerous weather, 44 in Oklahoma and 5 in Kansas. More than 900 other persons in those states suffered injuries.

The scenes of horror were many. For instance, while the F5 tornado was ravaging Bridge Creek, Oklahoma, a mother and her six-year-old son raced toward a creek to take what meager shelter they could, but the child saw his mother fly away in the wind and looked for her in vain after the storm. After the tornadoes in the Wichita area, police officers saw the body of a young, bearded man lying with his face in storm water amid the wreckage at Pacesetter Mobile Homes. On May 12, nine days after the storm, two young women were searching together on their own for the last of the Oklahoma missing, Tram Thu Bui, in the hope of finding her alive. Instead, they found her dead, her shoulder exposed amid wreckage in a ditch in Moore, 50 yards from the overpass under which she, her husband, her daughter, her son, and other persons had tried to take refuge when the tornado had approached as they were traveling on Interstate 35.

Along with the horror, however, came heroism and generosity. Official storm chasers and law enforcement officers sometimes risked their lives as they tried to warn people of oncoming tornadoes. Rescue workers, paid and unpaid, roamed through debris looking for the dead and the living. Members of the National Guard patrolled ravaged neighbor-hoods, and nurses, doctors, and other medical professionals worked hour after hour to care for the wounded. Crews from utility companies labored to ensure public safety and eventually to restore water, electricity, gas, and telephone service. Charitable organizations sent their workers and opened their buildings to help. In Moore, the First Baptist Church, just east of Interstate 35 and adjacent to the Highland Park neighborhood, became a makeshift hospital soon after the F5 tornado had done enormous damage nearby. Letting the tall, generator-lit cross at the front of the building serve as a beacon for the hurt and homeless, rescuers established a triage center in one part of the building, while the choir room became a temporary morgue.

A few of the heroes died while saving other persons. Ordinary people did extraordinary things. For example, to save her eleven-year-old son, Levi, Kathleen Walton released her grip on him as the giant tornado in metropolitan Oklahoma City sucked her out from under the overpass on Interstate 35 where they had sought shelter. Not far away, in Del City, Gustia Miller, seventy-six years old, and his wife, Dorothy, tried to use their bathtub as a tornado shelter when the same tornado approached their home. When the bathroom window broke, Mr. Miller put himself in extreme peril to hold a pillow to the opening in an effort to keep debris from hitting his wife. During the night, he died of his injuries.

Yet there were happy stories too. For days after the tornadoes, a British couple, John and Barbara Potten, were feared dead. They had been touring the United States in a motor home and had telephoned relatives in Britain around 3:00 in the afternoon of May 3 to report their arrival in south Oklahoma City. When, the next day, they failed to follow their standard practice of calling home, their relatives and Oklahoma law enforcement officers worried. In reality, however, the Pottens had quickly driven out of Oklahoma when they had learned of the possibility of tornadoes and, several days later, near the Canadian border, they called relatives in Australia. Amazingly, another person was found alive in a dramatic incident. Soon after the huge tornado had hit Bridge Creek, Oklahoma, Grady County deputy sheriff Robert Jolley, looking at rubble, spotted brown hair and realized that a silent baby was lying in the mud. When he had dug her out and started cleaning the mud from her eyes, she began crying, much to his relief; he took her to a school where emergency medical technicians were working. Thus, although her grandmother, Catherine Crago, died in the tornado, ten-month-old Aleah Crago survived without serious injury.

Lessons. Besides lessons about courage and generosity, one of the lessons Oklahomans and Kansans learned from the tornadoes of May 3, 1999, was the importance of skillfully operated, technologically sophisticated equipment for the detection both of the weather conditions that produce tornadoes and of the tornadoes themselves. The expensive Next Generation Weather Radar (NEXRAD) used by the National Weather Service meteorologists in Norman led to early and accurate tornado warnings and therefore saved many lives. Had there been no radar at all, and had there been no warnings broadcast on radio and television, the death toll would have been enormous, especially in the Oklahoma City and Wichita metropolitan areas.

Another lesson is one that President Bill Clinton mentioned while touring a devastated neighborhood in Del City, Oklahoma, on Saturday, May 8. Looking at the ruins of homes, he noted how few of them had had basements or storm cellars and urged his audience to include safe rooms when they rebuilt their houses. Designed at Texas Tech University, safe rooms are closetlike shelters on the ground floor inside houses; indeed, interest in safe rooms greatly increased in the disaster areas after May 3, as did interest in old-fashioned storm cellars and in above-ground shelters standing outside the home. Thousands of victims, along with many thousands of others, realized in the aftermath of the tornadoes of May 3 how powerful those storms can be.

Victor Lindsey

FOR FURTHER INFORMATION:
Daily Oklahoman, May 3-November 3, 1999.
"Digging out from Disaster." *Enid News and Eagle,* May 5, 1999.
Grossman, Susan M. "Storm Detection, Radar 'Flawless' May 3." *Norman Transcript,* May 30, 1999.
Kavanaugh, Lee Hill. " 'Slight' Chance of Storms, Then . . . Death Dropped from Sky." *Kansas City Star,* May 5, 1999, p. A1.
Stevens, William K. "Winds of Change." *Tulsa World,* May 16, 1999.
Wichita Eagle, May 4-5, 1999.
Zollo, Cathy. "Tornadoes Were in the Air." *Wichita Falls Times Record News,* May 5, 1999.

1999: Utah

DATE: August 11, 1999
PLACE: Salt Lake City, Utah
CLASSIFICATION: F2
RESULT: 1 dead, over 150 injured, 121 homes damaged, 34 homes destroyed, over $150 million in damage

The first fatal tornado ever recorded in Utah struck at 12:55 P.M. on August 11, 1999, in Salt Lake City, resulting in 1 death and numerous injuries. The black funnel cloud approached the city center from the southeast, coming from behind the Union Pacific building and sweeping right over the Delta Center, the basketball arena for the Utah Jazz. It cut out a diagonal swath through the downtown area, slicing through the Utah capitol grounds and the Avenues, a neighborhood just east of the capitol. The progress of the storm could be tracked by watching a series of bright flashes coming from exploding transformers on top of power poles. Along its path, the tornado ripped shingles from roofs, uprooted trees, damaged and disabled numerous power lines and transformers, overturned delivery trucks, and blew windows out of buildings.

The downtown area looked like a disaster zone, with shards of glass everywhere and police and firefighters attending to dozens of wounded people. Most of the injuries were to workers who were setting up equipment and large tents for an outdoor retailers convention to be held on August 12. Helicopters landed in the city streets to carry seriously injured victims to nearby hospitals. A Las Vegas man, Allen Crandy, a contractor for the retailer's show, was killed when he was struck in the head by a beam that fell from one of the tents.

The tornado damaged the roofs of the Delta Center and the Salt Palace Convention Center, which was hosting the outdoor retailers show. Some observers saw the roof of the Delta Center lift up when the tornado passed over. Considerable damage was done to the inside of the building and to the roof area. Numerous windows in the basketball arena were shattered on both the east and west sides. Nearby, the fifteen-story Wyndham Hotel had dozens of windows blown out, with long fragments of glass strewn on the grass below. Many victims were struck by the flying glass and needed medical attention. At the construction site of the new Mormon assembly hall north of

Temple Square, the wind snapped off the arm of a large crane, and a few workers received minor injuries.

Thirty minutes after the tornado ripped through the city, volunteers were directing traffic, clearing streets with chain saws, and handing out tarps and water. Utah governor Mike Leavitt quickly declared a state of emergency. Officials from the Federal Emergency Management Agency (FEMA) assessed the damage and were committed to providing federal cleanup assistance.

Tornadoes in Utah are very rare; the state averages 1.8 tornadoes per year. The last time that one touched down in Salt Lake City was in 1968, when heavy winds blew out hotel windows.

Alvin K. Benson

FOR FURTHER INFORMATION:
"Salt Lake Tornado Kills One." *The Salt Lake Tribune*, August 11, 1999. Also at http://www.sltrib.com/1999/aug/08111999/utah/tornado.html.

"S.L. Tornado Claims Life of Las Vegas Man." *The Deseret News*, August 11, 1999. Also at http://www.desnews.com/dn/view/0,1249,110002834,00.html.

2000: Georgia

DATE: February 14, 2000
PLACE: Southwestern Georgia
CLASSIFICATION: F3
RESULT: 18 dead, more than 200 injured, more than 350 homes damaged or destroyed, more than $25 million in damage

At least 5 tornadoes hit rural southwestern Georgia during the early morning hours of February 14, 2000, while most residents were sleeping. It was the deadliest tornado activity to hit Georgia since 1944.

An exhibition tent in downtown Salt Lake City, Utah, was destroyed by the 1999 tornado. (AP/Wide World Photos)

The tornadoes flattened many homes, turned over automobiles, and raised general havoc in Colquitt, Tift, Mitchell, and Grady Counties. Georgia governor Roy Barnes declared all four counties disaster areas. Although the initial death toll was 19, that was later revised to 18, since one of the deaths had been reported in 2 counties. The violent weather was part of a severe storm system that also hit Arkansas, Tennessee, Mississippi, Alabama, northeastern Florida, and the Carolinas.

Storm forecasters were confident that available storm-chasing technology had given emergency-management officials and people in the storm's path as much warning as possible. The National Weather Service broadcast its first tornado warnings for the area more than forty minutes prior to the first twister touching down, but the storms approached in the cloak of darkness, when most people were sleeping in southwestern Georgia and televisions and radios were turned off. Although there was a siren warning system for natural disasters in Mitchell County, the storm caused most of its damage well out of the hearing range of the sirens.

Camilla, located approximately 200 miles south of Atlanta in Mitchell County, was the worst-hit community, being ravaged when the twisters cut a 5-mile swath through a housing development. Nearly 200 mobile homes in Camilla were destroyed. The only hospital in Mitchell County, located in Camilla, was overwhelmed by the emergency. Emergency shelters were established in churches and schools in Camilla and Moultrie, the main town in neighboring Colquitt County. In Grady County, the storm moved over a 15-mile stretch, damaging or destroying dozens of homes and other buildings and flattening pine forests and pecan orchards. Throughout the disaster area, relief workers toiled many long hours searching for the missing, helping homeless survivors, clearing debris, and restoring electricity. For days, crews cut up twisted mobile home frames, brought down damaged power cables, and hauled away tons of debris. American Red Cross officials helped numerous families cope with the loss of loved ones, homes, and other property.

President Bill Clinton declared disaster areas in the four affected counties in Georgia and made federal funding available to help people and business owners get reestablished. Two days after the tornadoes struck, Vice President Al Gore visited southwestern Georgia to view the damage and report details to the federal government in order to expedite federal aid. Gore surveyed some of the long stretches of devastation from an Army helicopter, then walked the debris-littered streets of Camilla. While Georgians rallied to help the tornado victims, the federal government quickly provided financial relief and helped establish temporary housing for homeless residents.

Alvin K. Benson

FOR FURTHER INFORMATION:

"Death Toll Rises to 19 from Georgia Tornadoes." http://cnn.co.uk/2000/WEATHER/02/14/storms.05/index.html, February 14, 2000.

Duggan, Paul. "Georgia Tornadoes Kill at Least 19; More than 100 Injured, Scores Left Homeless in Southwest Part of State." *Washington Post*, February 15, 2000, p. A3.

"Gore to Tour Georgia Tornado Site." http://cnn.com/2000/WEATHER/02/16/storms.02/index.html, February 16, 2000.

"Tornadoes in Georgia Kill 22, Injure over 100." *Houston Chronicle*, February 15, 2000, p. 1.

Tsunamis

(Woodcut by K. Hokusai)

A tsunami is an ocean wave, or a series of ocean waves, of enormous energy caused most often by undersea geological disturbances, especially earthquakes. The waves can travel thousands of miles from their source to an island or coastal region, where they can cause great loss of life and massive physical damage to the natural environment and artificial structures.

FACTORS INVOLVED: Geography, geological forces, gravitational forces
REGIONS AFFECTED: Cities, coasts, islands, oceans

SCIENCE

"Tsunami" is a Japanese word that means "harbor wave." Tsunamis are also known popularly as tidal waves, although this is a misnomer because they are not caused by the tides or by Earth-Moon gravita-tional attraction, as are the tides. Tsunamis are caused by any disturbance under the ocean's surface that causes great movements in the seawater. Tsunamis can be generated by earthquakes as well as landslides or volcanic eruptions on the seafloor. Tsu-

837

namis have been called seismic sea waves because they are often caused by earthquakes. They can also be caused by the impact of a large meteorite or large volcanic debris on the surface of the ocean. A tsunami should not be confused with a tidal bore, a storm surge, or a seiche. A tidal bore is a quickly advancing frontal wave of the incoming tide when concentrated into shallow narrow estuaries. Storm surges are associated with hurricanes and cyclones, which superimpose wind-driven waves onto the normal tidal actions and the sea currents created by offshore winds. Seiches are the slow and rhythmic oscillations of water in enclosed or nearly enclosed waters, such as bays or lakes.

Tsunamis, like other waves or wave systems, are collections of energy. At a specific point in time and at a specific location, energy is transferred by a disturbance into a medium at rest, in this case the ocean, is propagated through that medium, and is ultimately dissipated, either slowly through friction with adjacent media or by the sudden transfer of the remaining energy into another medium at a moment and point of disturbance. The vast majority of tsunamis are caused by earthquakes. Earthquakes themselves are caused by the shifting of tectonic plates relative to each other at the lines, either faults or trenches, where the plates meet.

According to plate tectonics, the earth is a dynamic structure in which a dozen or more huge plates, each some 70 to 100 miles thick, float on a semimolten viscous mantle, which covers the entire surface of the earth. The energy dissipated by the circulation of the mantle causes the plates above to shift. Tectonic-plate motion is extremely slow, only an inch or two per year. If the forces that cause this motion are not completely dissipated through this slow movement they will build up and be released at once in a sudden cataclysmic shifting of the plates.

Although earthquakes are the most frequent cause of tsunamis, not all earthquakes will produce such an event. An earthquake must be located under or near the ocean, be large (tsunamis are typically caused by earthquakes measuring 6.5 and above on the Richter scale), have a focal point less than 30 miles below the seafloor, and cause movement in the seafloor. It is the movement of the ocean floor under the water above it which serves as the initial impetus for the creation of the tsunami.

Much more important than the magnitude of the earthquake are the type of earthquake and the type of motion it causes in the seafloor. Vertical shifting of the plates, especially a phenomenon known as subduction, is much more effective than transverse (side-by-side) motion in generating tsunamis. Subduction is the movement of one plate under an adjacent plate. Such subduction earthquakes are especially formative of tsunamis in the Pacific, where the thinner plates underlying the seafloor are moving downward and under the thicker adjacent continental plates. The sudden vertical movement of a subduction earthquake will displace, and thereby upset the equilibrium of, the water above.

Because water is not compressible, the movement will force upwards, or downwards, the entire column of water above the shifted area, which might measure thousands of square miles. Waves form subsequently as gravity pulls the enormous volume of disturbed water back downward to its position of equilibrium. In this type of tsunami generation the amount of vertical drop or uplift of the underlying seafloor and the area over which it occurs govern the size of the resulting tsunami. The physics of the tsunami itself render it possible for the generating energy of the earthquake or other motive disturbance to be propagated across an entire ocean and deposited on shore in powerful destructive forces. The tsunami will move outward in all directions from the point of disturbance in concentric circles, similar to the way ripples fan out in all directions when a stone is dropped into water.

Unlike the ripples on a pond, however, the tsunami waves in the deep ocean are impossible to see from the air, nor can they be felt on a ship by which they pass. It is precisely the dimensions of the tsunami that render that possible. Wave dimensions are height (the distance from the bottom of the trough to the top of the crest), length (the distance from one crest to the next), and period (the time it takes for successive wave crests to reach a fixed point). Waves caused by the wind, which are visible on a lake or at the beach, will have a period of a few seconds, a height of a few feet or less—or more in the case of storms—and a length of a few hundred feet. In such an environment an object or vessel will visibly bob up and down on the surface as successive waves pass. A tsunami wave in the middle of the ocean, however, can have a period of from ten minutes to two hours, a height of a few feet or less, but a length of 300 miles or more. The ratio of length to height is thus far greater for a tsunami than for a wind-driven wave. As a tsunami passes in the open ocean an object or vessel will only rise and fall a very short distance over a far greater length of time. The tsunami, for all the destructive power it manifests when striking a shore, is thus impossible to see or feel on the open ocean. To illustrate this irony one need only look to the example of the tsunami that destroyed the village of Sanriku, Japan, on June 15, 1896. About 90 miles offshore, an earthquake caused a tsunami that passed by the town's fishing fleet, then working only 20 miles off the coast, completely unnoticed. The fishermen returned home the next day to find their town destroyed and the bodies of some 27,000 people littering the harbor.

Tsunamis behave as shallow-water waves. Such waves are characterized by a very low ratio of water depth to wave length. Although it may be hard to imagine, given the enormous depths found in the open ocean—especially the Pacific—if one considers the dimensions it is not hard to believe. The average depth of the Pacific is between 3 and 4 miles. If a tsunami's length can be some 300 miles, then the ratio

of ocean depth to wavelength is on the order of 1 to 100. Very important for the case of a tsunami, the speed of a shallow-water wave is the square root of the product of the acceleration of gravity and the depth of the water. That means the deeper the water, the faster the tsunami.

Normal sea waves travel no faster than 60 miles per hour, even in the stormiest of weather over the deepest of seas. A tsunami can travel ten times as fast. The average depth of the Pacific Ocean is 18,480 feet. In water of such a depth a tsunami will travel 524 miles per hour. Through water 30,000 feet deep a tsunami travels at 670 miles per hour—as fast as a jet passenger plane. Furthermore, the rate of energy loss for a wave is inversely related to its length. Therefore, the longer the wave, the more slowly it loses its energy. These two factors, high velocity and slow energy loss, make it possible for a tsunami to deliver a tremendous amount of force across the entire Pacific Ocean, the largest ocean on the earth, in less than one day. A tsunami can carry so much energy that

If the trough of a tsunami reaches the shore before the crest, the water level can drop and recede, baring much of the shore bottom. This photo shows water withdrawing from the Japan coast as a tsunami approaches. (National Oceanic and Atmospheric Administration)

striking a shore will not necessarily consume all of its energy. Tsunami waves have been known to bounce back and forth across the Pacific for a week or more while their energy is slowly dissipated.

As a tsunami approaches the perimeter of the ocean or an island and begins to run into increasingly shallow water, the wave's velocity, dependent entirely upon the depth of the water, decreases. In 60 feet of water, a tsunami wave will be slowed to 30 miles per hour. However, since the wave's period will remain constant, the height of the wave will increase. Therefore, as the wave approaches land its speed decreases and its height increases. Although tsunami heights of up to 100 feet have been recorded, only very rarely will a tsunami take the form of a towering cresting wave of the sort sought after by surfers. The wave height will increase, however, and the tsunami will be noticeable, unlike on the open ocean.

A tsunami might appear as a quickly changing tide, a series of breaking waves, or even a bore—a steplike wave with a steep breaking front. It is not necessarily the case that the tsunami will cause the water first to rise. If the trough of the tsunami reaches the shore first, the water level can drop and recede to an enormous extent, baring more of the shore bottom than the lowest tide. The crest will still follow, however. It has happened that onlookers, seeing what they thought was an incredibly low tide, have ventured out onto the exposed bottom, only to be caught by the subsequent fast-moving crest and drowned.

GEOGRAPHY

Although tsunamis can occur in any ocean of the world, approximately 80 percent of tsunamis are found in the Pacific Ocean. Another 10 percent are found in the Atlantic, and the rest are found elsewhere. Most tsunamis occur in the Pacific because that ocean has far more seismic activity than the others. The perimeter of the seafloor of the Pacific, known as the "Ring of Fire," is a series of mountain chains, deep trenches, and volcanic island arcs caused by the movements of the adjoining tectonic plates that cover the surface of the earth. Major mountain ranges, such as the Andes Mountains in South America, and deep trenches, such as the Peru-Chile trench immediately off the west coast of South America, the Aleutian trench south of the Aleutian Islands of Alaska, and the Japan trench east of Japan, were created by the sudden movement of adjoining plates along fault lines.

In the Pacific Ocean at least one tsunami per year has been recorded since 1800, and there is an average of two destructive tsunamis somewhere in the Pacific per year. Hawaii, an easy target in the middle of the Pacific Ocean, suffered 37 tsunamis from 1875 to 2000, while Japan was struck by 15 major tsunamis, 8 of them especially destructive, between 1650 and 2000. Although Pacific-wide tsunamis are somewhat rare, the nations of the Pacific Ocean can expect an oceanwide tsunami on the average of once every ten or twelve years.

Tsunamis are rare in the Atlantic, but they are not unknown. In November of 1928, an earthquake off of the Grand Banks in Newfoundland, Canada, generated a tsunami that caused both loss of life and significant property damage in that region. In terms of local geography, low-lying coastal regions and islands, especially land less than 50 feet above sea level and within 1 mile of the shoreline, are at the greatest risk of damage once a tsunami strikes.

PREVENTION AND PREPARATIONS

Scientists and public officials are especially keen to lessen the damage and loss of life caused by tsunamis. Mitigation of tsunami damage depends upon three factors: prediction, warning, and preparation. Because earthquakes are the prevalent cause of tsunamis, efforts at tsunami prediction have focused on earthquakes. In spite of significant research, however, scientists remain unable to predict the incidence of earthquakes with real certitude. Tsunami researchers instead focus their efforts on distinguishing as quickly as possible tsunamigenic earthquakes from other earthquakes, thereby decreasing the amount of time necessary to issue a clear warning. The shorter the time period between tsunami generation and the issuance of a warning, the more lives that can be saved. While it remains virtually impossible to warn population centers of an oncoming locally generated tsunami—because of the great speed at which a tsunami travels—it is very possible to warn residents of areas under threat of a tsunami generated by distant seismic disturbances.

The ability to predict the arrival time of a tsunami has been in place for some time. The known physics of tsunami creation and propagation, combined with increasingly accurate mapping of the seafloor over which the tsunamis travel and precise measurements of ocean depths, make it possible to predict with reasonable, even excellent, accuracy the moment and

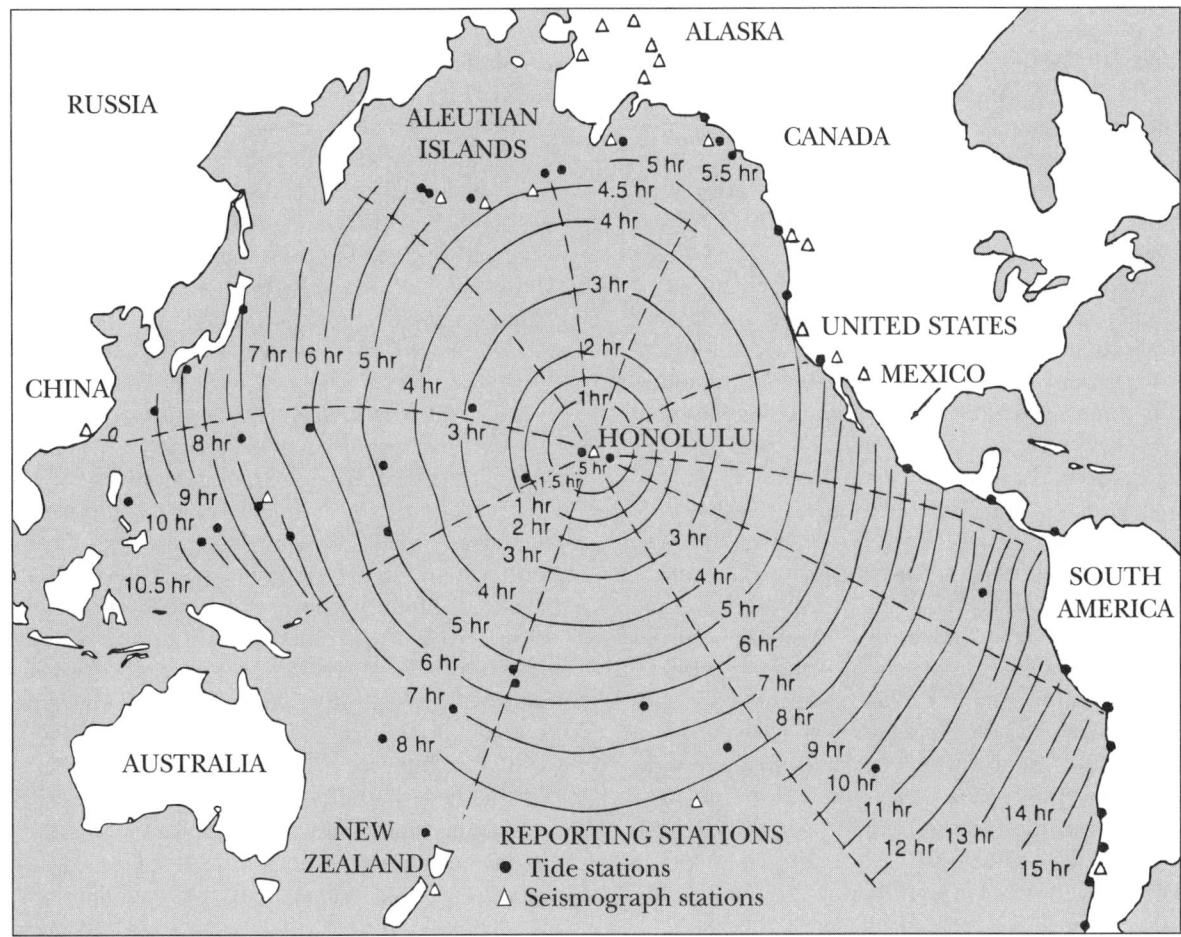

Tide and seismograph reporting stations of the Pacific Tsunami Warning System. This is a representation of the travel times for tidal waves originating at Honolulu, Hawaii. (National Oceanic and Atmospheric Administration)

point at which a tsunami will arrive ashore. An earthquake struck off the coast of Chile in 1960, causing enormous damage and loss of life to the local residents, who had been caught completely unaware. Yet once tsunami monitors were able to confirm that a tsunami had been created, they were able to predict its arrival in Hilo, Hawaii, with truly phenomenal accuracy—the tsunami arrived within one minute of its predicted time.

Later, scientists assumed a new challenge, that of ascertaining the amplitude of a tsunami once it is created. This requires a better understanding of how earthquakes create tsunamis and how they are propagated, as well as the creation of better instrumentation to detect and measure them. As part of the Pacific Tsunami Warning System, scientists and engineers have placed throughout the Pacific increas-

ingly sensitive subsurface pressure sensors that measure tsunami amplitude in the open ocean.

The study, understanding, and measurement of coastal runup and impact ashore is an equally important piece of the Tsunami Warning System. Accurate and current surveys of the local topography—both below and above the shoreline—accurate tidal measurement, numerical modeling, and historical data are combined to create worst-case impact and inundation scenarios and define evacuation zones and routes to ensure quick response when a tsunami warning must be issued. This information is also used in long-term public efforts to mitigate public and private property damage and loss of life.

Government agencies can initiate public-works projects, such as the construction and maintenance of breakwaters or floodwalls that act as physical barriers to tsunami flooding. Governments can also acquire land or regulate land usage through zoning or taxation policy to prevent, discourage, or regulate areas prone to tsunami impact or flooding. Finally, governments can foster public education and awareness of the dangers inherent in tsunami-prone areas by requiring, for instance, disclosure of such information in real-estate transactions.

The final component of efforts to mitigate loss of life from tsunami impact and flooding is the warning itself. Research, monitoring, and understanding of tsunami generation and propagation, and communication of the data relevant to them, are all essential components of any warning effort. Tsunami warnings are issued by the authorities or institutions that monitor the data coming from remote sites and sensors scattered throughout the Pacific. Once a decision to announce a warning has been made, the governmental authorities where a tsunami is expected to come ashore are alerted. The warning is then disseminated to the various appropriate regional and local civil defense organizations and other responsible agencies and broadcast to the public via radio and television.

The effectiveness of such a system, no matter how well devised and maintained, is ultimately dependent upon a well-informed and responsive public. Education and outreach are thus critical components of the work of the organizations responsible for monitoring tsunamis or issuing tsunami warnings and other agencies involved in public safety. Public awareness is essential in the case of locally generated tsunamis, where nearby coastal residents must be taught to seek refuge inland on higher ground upon feeling the tremors of a locally generated earthquake.

Education is, however, no less important in the case of tsunamis generated by distant earthquakes and for which there is thus much time to issue a warning. Residents in areas prone to tsunamis must be educated as to the complexity of the danger. People have drowned because they went out to marvel at what they thought was an incredibly low tide but which in fact was the trough of an oncoming tsunami whose crest followed.

Residents must be likewise alerted to the incidence of multiple waves. Civil defense authorities had managed to evacuate Crescent City, California, in March of 1964 when warned of a tsunami that was on the way from an earthquake that struck near the coast of Alaska. Their work paid off well; there was no loss of life after the arrival of the first two waves of this particular tsunami. Unfortunately, some residents, assuming the danger was over, decided to return to the stricken area before an all-clear signal was given and were drowned by a third wave that was much larger than the first two. It is perhaps an irony that tsunami warnings bring out sightseers interested in viewing the very danger from which they have been instructed to flee. The warnings issued in May of 1960 to Hilo, Hawaii, while instrumental in preventing large-scale loss of life, did bring out a few sightseers, all of whom were drowned.

RESCUE AND RELIEF EFFORTS

Although the areas of tsunami damage might be relatively small compared to those of other disasters, the damage is particularly thorough. Localities affected by tsunamis are usually devastated, requiring significant short-term and long-term recovery and reconstruction efforts. After a tsunami strikes, the most immediate concern for local civil defense authorities is the public health. While treatment of injured survivors is important, perhaps more critical is the condition of the water supply, typically fouled by tsunami flooding. If sewer lines are broken or the sewage system is overwhelmed, the potential public health hazard is even worse. Additionally, the bodies of the drowned must be located, recovered, and disposed of properly as quickly as possible to prevent further pollution of the water and outbreaks of communicable diseases.

Besides bringing the immediate threats to the public health under control, initial relief efforts require the recovery of the essential infrastructure, especially the water and power supply, as well as communications and transport. Without these basics it is impossible for both individuals and communities as a whole to commence the task of rebuilding. Because the tsunami will have left an enormous amount of debris in its wake, initial cleanup efforts require the removal of everything from trash and building debris to boats and motor vehicles, much of which may have been moved hundreds of yards inland. In the long term, recovery from a tsunami entails reconstruction of homes, businesses, and public spaces and even the rehabilitation of the environment, which often suffers massive damage.

IMPACT

Tsunamis cause damage in two ways: flooding and exertion of the wave's force against structures. The water that comes onto the shore and proceeds inland is called runup. Its height is the vertical distance measured from the tide level at the time the tsunami strikes the shore to the contour line of highest point on shore reached by the water. A tsunami can easily raise the water level from 20 to 30 yards above normal height and reach, especially if the stricken coastal area is particularly low, hundreds of yards inland, thereby flooding enormous tracts of land. Runup can cause enormous environmental damage, removing years of accumulated beach sand, stripping away coastal vegetation and trees, and drowning animals.

Tsunamis exert a truly powerful force against anything with which they come into contact, including human-made structures. A tsunami wave can easily flatten buildings or remove them from their foundations, wash boats and small ships hundreds of yards ashore, and toss around automobiles and even heavy construction equipment as if they were toys. The movement of such objects, as well as the debris of destroyed structures and even uprooted trees, can cause severe secondary damage when the wave carries them forward and forces them against still-standing structures, and then subsequently when the waters recede and drag the same objects back to strike against what little might still be left standing.

Besides causing severe environmental and property damage, tsunamis cause important and sometimes dangerous infrastructure damage that can threaten public health and delay post-tsunami recovery efforts. Widespread flooding almost always causes polluted water supplies. The local energy grid can be compromised or put out of service entirely if electrical or gas lines are destroyed.

A tsunami's most fearsome toll, however, is always loss of human life, attributable almost exclusively to drowning. Between 1932 and July of 1998, more people died in the United States as a result of tsunamis than as a result of earthquakes. The desire to prevent such loss of life has been the primary motivation behind the establishment of the warning system and preparatory measures now in place throughout the Pacific.

In April of 1946 an earthquake in the Aleutian trench near Alaska generated a tsunami that struck Hawaii unexpectedly, causing at least 179 fatalities and tens of millions of dollars in damage. Motivated by what is still considered to be Hawaii's worst natural disaster, the United States Coast and Geodetic Survey established in Hawaii the Seismic Sea Wave Warning System, which later became the Pacific Tsunami Warning Center (PTWC). Before the end of the twentieth century, the PTWC would be the operational center of the Pacific Tsunami Warning System, a sophisticated and coordinated international effort comprising 26 member states. These countries of the Pacific region pool their knowledge and resources to monitor the entire Pacific basin for tsunamigenic earthquakes in the hope of giving adequate warnings to population centers under threat of a tsunami and thereby lessening property damage and reducing the loss of human life.

David M. Soule

BIBLIOGRAPHY

Cornell, James. "Tsunami." In *The Great International Disaster Book*. New York: Charles Scribner's Sons, 1976. The author gives a good grounding in the basics of tsunami creation and propagation and covers major tsunamis throughout history. Those interested in learning more about the most prevalent cause of tsunamis should also refer to the chapter "Earthquakes."

Lander, James F., and Patricia A. Lockridge. *United States Tsunamis, 1690-1988*. Boulder, Colo.: National Geophysical Data Center, 1989. This is an excellent source for readers looking for more detail regarding specific tsunamis that have struck the United States and its possessions. It includes data and descriptions of individual events, their causes, and the ensuing damages. The many illustrations and tables are helpful.

Lockridge, Patricia A., and Ronald H. Smith. *Tsunamis in the Pacific Basin, 1900-1983*. Boulder, Colo.: National Geophysical Data Center and World Data Center A for Solid Earth Geophysics, 1984. Similar to the work by Lockridge mentioned above, it includes information for the 405 tsunamis that occurred in the Pacific region during the years covered. The number of tsunamis alone is a fascinating statistic.

Myles, Douglas. *The Great Waves*. New York: McGraw-Hill, 1985. This is an excellent and easy-to-read introduction, treating tsunamis throughout history and covering them from the perspectives of science, geography, and impact on people.

Petak, William J., and Arthur A. Atkisson. *Natural Hazard Risk Assessment and Public Policy: Anticipating the Unexpected*. New York: Springer-Verlag, 1982. Although addressed to specialists, the explanations of tsunamis are quite accessible to the general reader. Gives a very good idea of the problems of tsunami damage mitigation, aided by excellent tables.

Robinson, Andrew. "Floods, Dambursts, and Tsunamis." In *Earth Shock: Hurricanes, Volcanoes, Earthquakes, Tornadoes, and Other Forces of Nature.* London: Thames and Hudson, 1993. This essay gives good, but brief, coverage of the damages a tsunami can cause. Includes some excellent photographs.

Solovev, Sergei, and Chan Nam Go. *Catalogue of Tsunamis on the Eastern Shore of the Pacific Ocean.* Sidney, B.C.: Institute of Ocean Sciences, Department of Fisheries and Oceans, 1984. This catalogue provides a wealth of data on individual tsunamis.

_____. *Catalogue of Tsunamis on the Western Shore of the Pacific Ocean.* Sidney, B.C.: Institute of Ocean Sciences, Department of Fisheries and Oceans, 1984. The counterpart to the above-mentioned work. Together these two volumes provide the interested reader with great detail on the tsunamis, both real and legendary, that have occurred throughout the centuries in the Pacific Ocean, as well as on the earthquakes or volcanoes or other disturbances that may have caused them.

Whittow, John. *Disasters: An Anatomy of Environmental Hazards.* Athens: University of Georgia Press, 1979. This excellent work covers the mechanics of tsunamis and the earthquakes that cause them. The detailed explanations are superb and are aided by helpful diagrams and tables. Photos are included. This is a great source for those wishing to get a more in-depth understanding of tsunamis.

Notable Events

Historical Overview

Tsunamis occur when a sudden shock is administered to coastal waters, usually through seismic shocks. When tsunamis accompany earthquakes they are often the chief reason for the loss of life as coastal areas, frequently heavily inhabited, are inundated by sudden waves of gigantic proportions, far larger than the usual tidal surge. Unless warned, human beings can be simply swept away by the overwhelming power of such waves.

Most of the large tsunamis that resulted in major loss of life occurred in the Pacific basin and were generally the result of earthquakes caused by shifting tectonic plates along the western shore of the Pacific Ocean. Japan has frequently been the scene of tsunamis, but they have also occurred often in Indonesia, eastern Russia, and Alaska.

The earliest tsunamis of which knowledge exists—many must have happened in the more distant past but were not recorded—occurred in Japan in the seventeenth century. A tsunami appears to have occurred there as early as 1498, but two are known to have taken place in 1605 and again in 1611. As many as 4,000 to 5,000 were killed. One happened in Indonesia in 1629, though the number of lives lost was not recorded.

The eighteenth century experienced numerous tsunamis. Japan was again the scene of such catastrophes in 1707, 1741, and 1792. The Kamchatka Peninsula, in the North Pacific, experienced a tsunami in 1737, and the Ryukyu Islands witnessed one in 1771. Two took place in Peru, one in 1724 and another in 1746, and there was even one in Italy in 1783. Perhaps the most spectacular of the eighteenth century tsunamis, however, was that which struck Lisbon, Portugal, in 1755, in conjunction with an earthquake that destroyed much of the old city. The wave virtually destroyed the port. These events are famous because they play a part in Voltaire's famous novel *Candide* (1759): The hero travels to Lisbon in time to witness the catastrophe.

The earthquake and tsunami in Lisbon together claimed the lives of up to 50,000 people; the next most destructive was after the explosion of the volcano Krakatau, in Indonesia, in 1883, resulting in a wave nearly 135 feet high. About 36,000 people lost their lives in this event. More than 27,000 died in a tsunami in Japan in 1896; in 1868 tsunamis in Chile and in Hawaii cost more than 25,000 people their lives.

The twentieth century saw a number of tsunamis in the Pacific rim, although none were so costly in human lives as those of earlier centuries. Kamchatka experienced tsunamis in 1923 and again in 1952, the Aleutian Islands in 1946 and 1957. Japan was the scene of tsunamis in 1933, 1944, and 1983, and in 1964 the town of Kodiak, Alaska, simply disappeared

---

Milestones

1692:	Tsunamis spawned by an earthquake in Port Royal, Jamaica, kill 3,000.
1703:	5,000 die in tsunamis in Honshū, Japan, following a large earthquake.
1707:	A 38-foot-high tsunami kills 30,000 in Japan.
1741:	Following volcanic eruptions, 30-foot waves in Japan cause 1,400 deaths.
1755:	As many as 50,000 lose their lives in the combined earthquake and tsunami in Lisbon, Portugal.
1783:	A tsunami in Italy kills 30,000.
1868:	Tsunamis in Chile and Hawaii claim more than 25,000 lives.
1883:	The Krakatau volcanic explosion and tsunami in Indonesia result in 36,000 deaths.
1896:	As many as 27,000 die after tsunamis hit Sanriku, Japan.
1933:	3,000 are killed by tsunamis in Sanriku, Japan.
1946:	32-foot-high waves in Hilo, Hawaii, cause 159 deaths.
1946:	2,000 die in Honshū, Japan, after an earthquake spawns tsunamis.
1964:	195-foot waves engulf Kodiak, Alaska, after the Good Friday earthquake; 131 die.
1998:	A series of tsunamis in Papua New Guinea kills 2,000, mostly children.

---

as the result of an earthquake followed by a tsunami. About 5,000 people lost their lives in a tsunami in the Philippines in 1976, one of the largest death tolls from this cause in the twentieth century.

In the twentieth century scientists developed ways of avoiding the enormous death tolls of earlier centuries. The National Oceanic and Atmospheric Administration (NOAA) implemented a tsunami warning system in Hawaii, so that threatened areas could be evacuated. This system was extended to Alaska, there called the Regional Tsunami Warning System, created in the wake of the substantial losses suffered in the earthquake-tsunami of 1964. At the Pacific Tsunami Warning System headquarters in Honolulu, Hawaii, seismologists keep careful track of seismic activity throughout the Pacific basin and issue warnings whenever there is any likelihood of a tsunami. The ability to predict the likely landfall has made it possible to protect most residents of coastal areas from the dangers of tsunamis, although their coastal property remains at risk.

Nancy M. Gordon

365: Egypt

DATE: July 21, 365
PLACE: Alexandria, Egypt
RESULT: Many dead; submergence of the seacoast and of the Royal Quarter of Alexandria

Writing in the late fourth century, the Roman historian Ammianus Marcellinus reported that on July 21, 365, in the eastern Mediterranean, "shortly after sunrise . . . the stability of the entire earth was shaken and stricken, and the sea, repelled, withdrew back." The sea soon returned with devastating force, drowning multitudes who had rushed out to loot shipwrecks that had been laid bare. Ammianus continued, "Other huge ships, hurled by the wild gusts, settled on the roofs of buildings, as happened at Alexandria." In *Ekklesiastike historia* (c. 440; *The Ecclesiastical History*, 1720), the historian Sozomen, writing early in the fifth century, dwelt on the Alexandrian disaster at greater length, reporting,

A great calamity occurred near Alexandria in Egypt, when the sea receded and again passed beyond its boundaries from the reflux waves, and deluged a great deal of the land, so that on the retreat of the waters, the sea-skiffs were found lodged on the roofs of the houses. The anniversary of this inundation, which they call the birthday of an earthquake, is still commemorated at Alexandria by a yearly festival; a general illumination is made throughout the city; they offer thankful prayers to God and celebrate the day very brilliantly and piously.

One of the results of the earthquake that caused this tsunami seems to have been a settling of the Alexandrian seacoast. The harbor floor dropped some 20 feet, and the shoreline was pushed back as much as 100 yards. By the mid-fifth century C.E., many of the buildings of the "Royal Quarter" on the coast were flooded and abandoned.

Only in the mid-1990's did underwater archaeological excavations using heavy dredging equipment in the murky and greatly polluted eastern harbor of Alexandria begin to bring to light once again the monuments that had been submerged. In 1995, the site known as Fort Quit Bey was found to be the ruins of the Pharos, the great lighthouse of ancient Alexandria. In the following year, excavations on the neighboring island of Antirhodos turned up a palace built by the Ptolemaic kings of Egypt and used by Cleopatra.

Divers discovered a small temple to Isis whose existence was previously unknown. Its entrance was flanked by two dark-gray granite sphinxes, one of which bore the head of Ptolemy XII, the father of Cleopatra VII. Within the temple was found a statue of Isis. This is believed to be the area of the sanctuary called the timonium, where statesman Mark Antony fell on his sword in 30 B.C.E. after being defeated the previous year by Octavian, who later became the emperor Augustus (63 B.C.E.-14 C.E.). A black granite head belonging to a massive statue of Octavian that stood 14 feet tall was also discovered.

The earthquake that caused the Alexandria tsunami was but one of many earthquakes that Amos Nur, a Stanford University geophysicist, believes were centered on a fault line that stretched from Sicily to Cairo. Nur documented 23 earthquakes that struck the Egyptian coast between 320 and 1303.

Ralph W. Mathisen

FOR FURTHER INFORMATION:

Hellen, Nicholas, and Trushar Barot. *The Sunday Times* (London), October 25, 1998.

Schuster, Angela M. H. "Mapping Alexandria's Royal Quarters." www.archaeology.org/9903/abstracts/map.html.

The Times (London), October 29, 1998.

1596: Japan

DATE: September 4, 1596
PLACE: Uryu-Jima Island, Japan
RESULT: 700 dead

Uryu-Jima, a small island with a circumference of about 6 miles, disappeared in a tsunami following an earthquake. Uryu-Jima was located just less than a mile offshore from the coastal town of Ōita, which lies on Beppu Bay on the east end of the island of Kyūshū across the Bungo Strait from the island of Shikoku. A minor earthquake, with its epicenter probably inside Beppu Bay, struck on the morning of September 4, 1596, causing landslides and opening small fissures in the ground. The earthquake was felt strongly as far east as Kyoto and as far west as Kagoshima Prefecture, although little damage was caused in these locales. On Uryu-Jima Island itself few of the 5,000 inhabitants were alarmed by the earthquake, and a calm immediately followed. However, a tsunami was on the way, and Beppu Bay has the semicircular shape ideal for concentrating the destructive forces of a tsunami.

Estimated to be 50 feet high, the tsunami came ashore to flood half of the island instantly and drown more than 700 people. The survivors reached the safety of secure land by fishing boats while their island home of Uryu-Jima disappeared slowly into 180 feet of water. Another area, amounting to about 1,483 acres (600 hectares) on the coast of Beppu Bay, disappeared under water. In Saganoseki, the easternmost tip of Kyūshū, facing Shikoku across the Bungo Strait, some 148 acres (60 hectares) of fields were flooded, destroying 2 villages—amounting to between 70 and 80 houses.

David M. Soule

FOR FURTHER INFORMATION:

Nash, Jay Robert. *Darkest Hours.* Chicago: Nelson-Hall, 1976.

Solovev, Sergei, and Chan Nam Go. *Catalogue of Tsunamis on the Western Shore of the Pacific Ocean.* Sidney, B.C.: Institute of Ocean Sciences, Department of Fisheries and Oceans, 1984.

1640: Japan

DATE: July-August, 1640
PLACE: Hokkaidō, Japan
RESULT: 700 dead

The volcano Komagatake, located on the island of Hokkaidō, erupted with great force on the last day of July in 1640, laying ash at the foot of the volcano to a depth of more than 6 feet. There is little information regarding the eruption of Komagatake or the direct effects of the eruption, but a tsunami ensued, creating waves that were observed on both the west and east coasts of Hokkaidō and either side of the Tsugaru Strait (the strait separating Hokkaidō from the island of Honshū). It was observed as far east as the Hidaka Mountain region and even beyond in the Tokachi plain and as far west as Uchiura Bay.

Some scholars argue that volcanic rock and debris falling into the sea created the tsunami, while other researchers believe that an earthquake occurring at the same time as the volcanic eruption caused the tsunami. Regardless, the tsunami washed out to sea more than 100 seaweed-gathering ships working just off the coast of Uchiura Bay, caused over 700 deaths, and swept away more than 20 houses.

David M. Soule

FOR FURTHER INFORMATION:

Nuhfer, Edward B., et al. *The Citizen's Guide to Geologic Hazards.* Arvada, Colo.: American Institute of Professional Geologists, 1993.
Solovev, Sergei, and Chan Nam Go. *Catalogue of Tsunamis on the Western Shore of the Pacific Ocean.* Sidney, B.C.: Institute of Ocean Sciences, Department of Fisheries and Oceans, 1984.

1741: Japan

DATE: August 29-30, 1741

PLACE: The western coast of the Sea of Japan
RESULT: More than 1,400 dead

The volcano of Oshima Island, a small island that lies in the Sea of Japan, west of the island of Hokkaidō, erupted on August 23, 1741, spewing enough volcanic ash to plunge the nearby Matsumae Peninsula, the southernmost point of Hokkaidō, into darkness. The volcano erupted again on August 29, causing a tsunami with waves 30 feet in height, which brought damage along the entire coast of the Sea of Japan. This was especially true in places such as Sado Island, off the west coast of Honshū, on the Matsumae Peninsula on Hokkaidō, and in the Kumaishi region on the west coast of Hokkaidō. There, along the 75-mile-long coastline of Kumaishi, 1,467 people died, 729 homes were washed out to sea, and another 60 structures were destroyed. The tsunami also damaged 1,521 boats. In Aomori, the northernmost prefecture of Honshū, 8 people were killed, and 82 houses and 53 boats were swept away.

David M. Soule

FOR FURTHER INFORMATION:

Iida, Kumizi, Doak C. Cox, and George Pararas-Carayannis. *Preliminary Catalog of Tsunamis Occurring in the Pacific Ocean.* Honolulu: Institute of Geophysics, University of Hawaii, 1967.
Solovev, Sergei, and Chan Nam Go. *Catalogue of Tsunamis on the Western Shore of the Pacific Ocean.* Sidney, B.C.: Institute of Ocean Sciences, Department of Fisheries and Oceans, 1984.

1868: South America

DATE: August 13-15, 1868
PLACE: The western coast of South America from Colombia to Chile
RESULT: 25,000 dead, city of Arica destroyed

During mid-August, 1868, an earthquake followed by a series of tsunamis, enormous ocean waves triggered by earthquakes or volcanoes, struck the west coast of South America. The city of Arica, located in Chile near the border with Peru, was inundated by three tsunamis, leaving the city underwater and devastated.

The most vivid account of the disaster was that by Lieutenant L. G. Billings, an officer on the USS *Wateree*, which had been anchored in the harbor of the port of Arica. Billings had been observing the city at the moment the earthquake struck. He described the immediate aftermath as a "huge dust cloud which enveloped the city." In seconds Arica lay in ruins.

A large mass of survivors gathered on a long jetty along the shoreline of the city, and a rescue boat was launched from the *Wateree*. At that moment a tsunami passed under the ship and inundated the shoreline. Most of the earthquake survivors on the jetty were drowned, along with 13 of the crewmen in the rescue party.

Within minutes, the sea drew back, temporarily leaving the *Wateree* on wet sand. This was followed by a second tsunami, which rolled over the city. Hundreds of tombs on the mountain outside the city were uncovered. The dead had been buried upright, and Billings further described the surreal image of the dead "standing in ranks." At nightfall, a third tsunami struck the area, engulfing the ship and carrying it 2 miles inland. Out of the population of 15,000 in the city of Arica, there were only several hundred survivors.

The earthquake and tsunamis that it generated struck much of the coast of South America, reaching as far north as the border of Colombia. The tsunamis also rolled west across the Pacific Ocean, causing damage in Hawaii.

Richard Adler

For Further Information:

Gere, James, and Haresh Shah. *Terra Non Firma*. New York: W. H. Freeman, 1984.

Tsunami: The Wateree Horror. Chelmsford, Mass.: Tsunami Website Publishing and Design, 1994-1997.

1896: Japan

Date: June 15, 1896
Place: The Sanriku coast of northeast Japan
Result: Waves up to 115 feet (35 meters) high, 27,000 dead, 10,000 houses destroyed

One of the most destructive tsunamis of historical time struck the Pacific coast of Japan on June 15, 1896. The town of Sanriku, along with the nearby small city of Kamaishi and neighboring villages, are in Iwate Prefecture on the northeast shore of Japan's main island of Honshū. They look eastward, over the Pacific Ocean and—120 miles (200 kilometers) offshore—a long, deep seafloor depression called the Japan trench, which parallels the coast.

This is part of the huge trench system that runs from the Aleutian Islands in the north around the western Pacific to New Zealand, where the Pacific tectonic plate is moving inexorably northwestward and diving down under the adjacent plates it encounters. This is the plate-tectonics process of subduction, and it is accompanied by earthquakes and volcanism as this collision and underriding occurs. Off the Sanriku coast of northeast Japan, the Pacific Plate is approaching and then diving at a rate of about 4 inches (10 centimeters) per year, building up stress and deformation that must be relieved by periodic earthquakes.

On June 15, 1896, large crowds were celebrating a festival day at Sanriku and other communities along the coast. In the early evening on this fine summer's day they were momentarily startled by the long, undulatory roll of the ground from a distant earthquake. The tremors were not violent, as they had traveled from well offshore. Further, the Japanese frequently feel the passing ground waves from the numerous small earthquakes that occur in this tectonically active region of the globe. The unsuspecting crowds of merrymakers could not have known that this had been one of the larger earthquakes, having a magnitude on the Richter scale of about 7.6. The earthquake's epicenter was offshore to the east, at 39.60 north latitude and longitude 144.20 east. Furthermore, they did not know that the tremors were signaling their impending doom, because the earthquake had displaced the seafloor enough to generate a rapidly spreading seismic sea wave, or tsunami—to be one of the largest ever. Such a wave is now generally called a tsunami, the Japanese word for "harbor wave," because of where it is often seen to arrive and the effect it has on the shore there.

Twenty minutes after the earthquake's ground waves had passed, the sea quietly but ominously began to recede from the shore. The tsunami waves, still over the horizon, were drawing water back as they were building their height with the seafloor

This Japanese woodblock print shows the power of the tsunami that struck the Sanriku coast in 1896. (Courtesy of R. Carmichael)

shallowing toward the shore. The water receded much faster and farther than any ordinary gradual low tide. This is usually the only observable advance warning of the oncoming tsunami, preceding any sighting or hearing of it. Another half hour, and some of the celebrators heard a sound—as a sudden rainstorm—from the ocean. Then the water of the ocean returned to the shore in a growing surge, becoming higher as it rapidly approached shore. It was becoming a roiling wall of water with waves ranging as high as 82 to 115 feet (25 to 35 meters).

The surging waves engulfed the revelers, as well as whole villages, and the power of the wash and its retreat to the sea left no trace of victims or buildings. In a few brief minutes, 27,000 persons died and over 10,000 houses were swept away. While 27,000 is the death toll commonly quoted, another Japanese compilation, by K. Abe, suggests 22,000 died.

Fishermen from the coastal villages, some distance out at sea at the time, noticed nothing unusual, as the tsunami waves out there were long-length (long distances between crests) and small-amplitude (fairly flat). Their first knowledge of the catastrophe came when they returned to port and found the sea strewn for miles with corpses and the wreckage of buildings. The tsunami waves had also spread eastward from over the subsea earthquake and were recorded at Hilo, Hawaii (4,000 miles away), having an amplitude of 9.8 feet (3 meters).

A similar event happened along the Sanriku coast in the early morning of March 3, 1933, when an offshore earthquake generated a tsunami with wave heights at shore up to 75 feet (23 meters). There were about 3,000 deaths, and more than 9,000 houses were destroyed. This seafloor disturbance generated a smaller amplitude tsunami than in 1896, even though the earthquake of 1933 was much greater (magnitude about 8.9).

With its proximity to a geologically active plate boundary and a written history extending back many centuries, Japan has one of the longest and most active records of earthquake and tsunami activity. There have been more than 600 damaging earthquakes felt in Japan in the past fifteen hundred years. In that time, over 170 earthquakes in the region produced significant tsunamis. The Sanriku coastal area of northeast Japan has been an area hit particularly hard, with great earthquakes in 869, 1611, 1896, and 1933.

Robert S. Carmichael

FOR FURTHER INFORMATION:

Abe, K. "Seismicity of Japan: Earthquakes and Tsunamis." *Impact of Science on Society*, no. 145 (1986): 63-74.

Bolt, B. A. *Earthquakes*. New York: W. H. Freeman, 1988.

U.S. Geological Survey, National Earthquake Information Center. http://www.neic.cr.usgs.gov. Go to "Search earthquake database" (1999) for causative earthquakes.

Wood, R. M. *Earthquakes and Volcanoes*. London: Mitchell Beazley, 1986.

1903: South Pacific

DATE: January 13, 1903
PLACE: Society Islands, Pacific Ocean
RESULT: At least 1,000 dead

The Society Islands were struck on January 13, 1903, by what has come to be classified as a tsunami, although the ultimate cause was probably not seismic. The waves came after days of fierce hurricane weather. It was reported that on the evening of January 13, a single enormous wave estimated to be some 40 feet high swept over every single island in the chain, nearly obliterating them all and killing 1,000 people. Hundreds were listed as missing.

David M. Soule

FOR FURTHER INFORMATION:

Nash, Jay Robert. *Darkest Hours*. Chicago: Nelson-Hall, 1976.

1933: Japan

DATE: March 3, 1933
PLACE: The Sanriku coast, Honshū, Japan
RESULT: 3,000 dead, 9,000 homes destroyed

The Sanriku coast of Japan, on the northeastern shore of the island of Honshū, stretches 220 miles from the northern tip of Aomori Prefecture southward to the Oshika Peninsula in Miyagi Prefecture, forming a heavily indented shoreline famous for earthquake-born tsunamis. Directly west of and parallel to the deep Japan trench, where the Pacific Plate is being overridden and forced downward under the Eurasian Plate, the Sanriku coast has suffered two truly massive earthquakes and tsunamis, one in 1896, and another less than forty years later.

On March 3, 1933, an enormous quake, measuring 8.9 on the Richter scale, struck the western slope of the Japan trench, about 100 miles off the coast and at a depth of about 12,000 feet. Althought the quake was felt onshore, its slow, rhythmic movement failed to give the coastal inhabitants enough worry to take prompt action. The warning broadcast came too late, and the tsunami, the largest to strike Japan in the twentieth century, struck the entire coastline with waves that reached 75 feet in height in some areas.

The tsunami destroyed 8,000 boats and at least 9,000 homes and caused at least 3,000 fatalities. Not a single fatality was caused by the earthquake—every single death could be attributed to the tsunami. Unimpeded to the east, the tsunami traveled all the way to North and South America, a perfect example of how this wave energy can be propagated across an entire ocean. Abnormally high water levels were recorded in both San Francisco (5,000 miles distant) and Iquique, Chile (9,000 miles away).

David M. Soule

FOR FURTHER INFORMATION:

Cornell, James. *The Great International Disaster Book.* New York: Charles Scribner's Sons, 1976.

Myles, Douglas. *The Great Waves.* New York: McGraw-Hill, 1985.

Nash, Jay Robert. *Darkest Hours.* Chicago: Nelson-Hall, 1976.

Nuhfer, Edward B., et al. *The Citizen's Guide to Geologic Hazards.* Arvada, Colo.: American Institute of Professional Geologists, 1993.

Whittow, John. *Disasters: An Anatomy of Environmental Hazards.* Athens: University of Georgia Press, 1979.

1946: Hawaii

DATE: April 1, 1946
PLACE: Primarily Hilo, Hawaii
RESULT: 159 dead in Hawaiian Islands (179 dead total), $25 million in damage on Hawaiian Islands

It was 7 A.M. on the morning of April 1, 1946, at Hilo, on the northeast coast of the big island of Hawaii, which is at the southeast end of the Hawaiian Island chain. Locally based ship pilot and U.S. Navy Captain W. Wickland was on the bridge of a ship moored in Hilo Bay. Sea level in the port began falling and rising and repeated this pattern twice more—much faster than would happen with any normal tidal variation. Then, as he would later report, "I looked out and saw what looked like a low, long swell at sea; way out, but coming in awfully fast. Seemed like three separate waves, each behind the other, came together in one monster wave. I was on the upper bridge, some 46 feet above the waterline. That wave was just about eye-level and probably two miles long."

The Origins of the Tsunami. A tsunami was rapidly but stealthily approaching Hilo and was about to wreak destruction. It had originated with an earthquake under the seafloor, which itself was at a depth of about 13,123 feet (4,000 meters) at the Aleutian trench. Its epicenter was about 81 miles (130 kilometers) southeast of Unimak Island, the latter being at the western end of the Alaskan peninsula. At the epicenter, with location 52 degrees 80 minutes north latitude and 162 degrees 50 minutes west longitude in the North Pacific, the seafloor disturbance had generated a sea wave that was now spreading outward in all directions.

The earthquake, having a magnitude of 7.4, occurred at 1:29 A.M. local time. Within several minutes, the long-length wave had grown in height as it rapidly approached the shallowing shore of Unimak Island, and a wave 98 feet (30 meters) high crashed onto the coast. It destroyed a lighthouse at Scotch Cap that was 32 feet (10 meters) above sea level, killing the 5 inhabitants. The tsunami wave was also spreading southward. In the open, deep ocean, the distance between wave crests is typically greater than 62 miles (100 kilometers), the amplitude (wave height) about 3.3 feet (1 meter), and speed about 373 to 497 miles (600 to 800 kilometers) per hour; 497 miles (800 kilometers) per hour is about the speed of a jet airliner.

Four and a half hours after the earthquake, the waves were approaching the Hawaiian Islands, 2,400 miles (3,900 kilometers) to the southeast. As the seafloor shallows toward shore, the wave speed typically slows to perhaps 30 miles per hour and the amplitude of the wave crests builds dramatically.

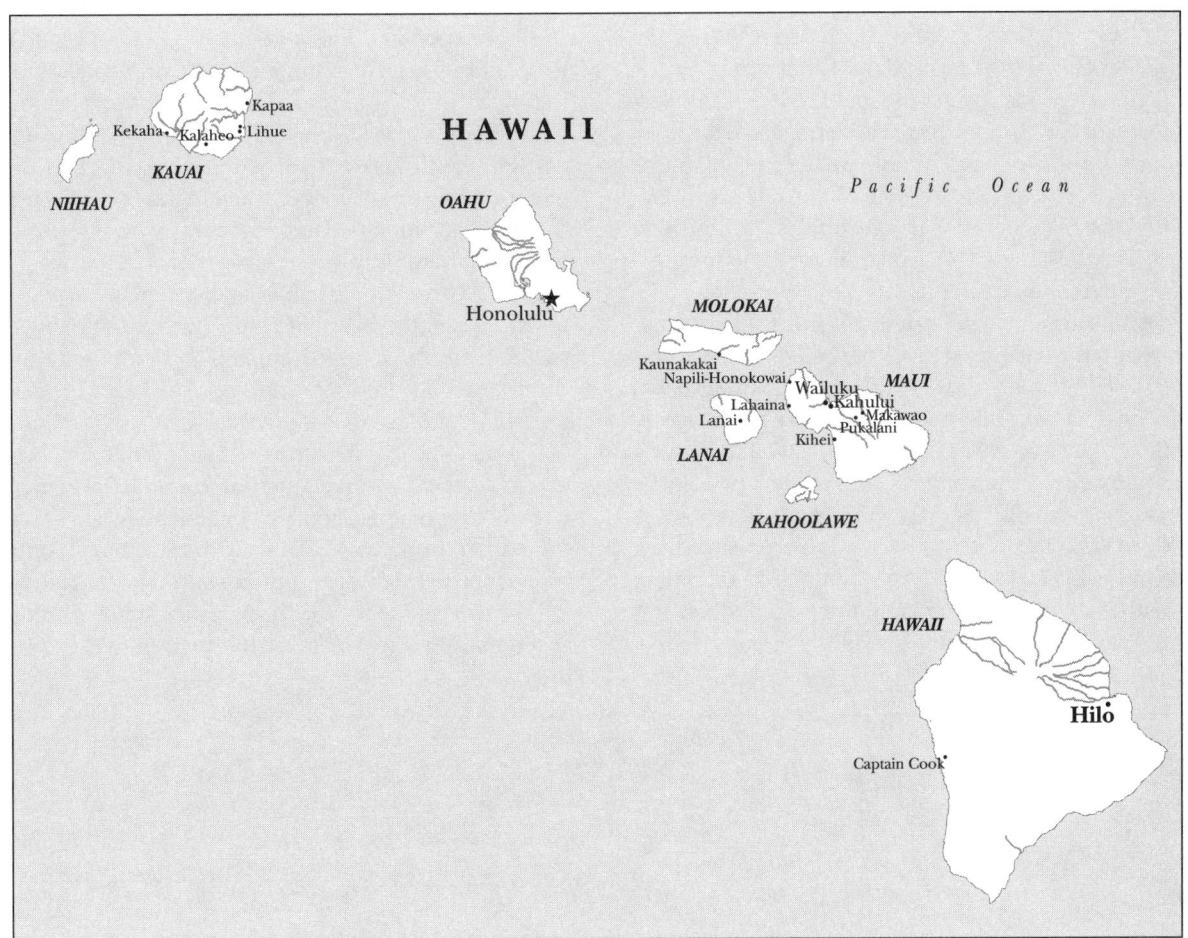

Hilo. It was now about 7 A.M. local time—Hawaii being in the adjacent time zone to the east of Unimak Island. The first wave of the sequence emptied the harbor of water at Hilo Bay, so that ships were now unexpectedly sitting on the newly exposed seafloor amid the coral reefs and some floundering fish. Then the large crest returned, uprooting and slamming the seaside buildings inland and against other buildings, taking out 7,500 feet of a 10,000-foot-long breakwater. With a great sucking sound it retreated out to sea, carrying with it much debris and several people. Twice more this process of retreat and destructive return was repeated. According to Captain Wickland, this tsunami had a crest that "broke, and tore up everything it touched. Some Coast Guard boats flew by, and a yacht was thrown up to the main highway. Every structure, building, and piece of equipment on shore seemed to take off."

The Aftereffects. One-third of the town of Hilo

vanished. The steel span of a railroad bridge across the Wailuku River was swept 328 feet (100 meters) inland. Heavy masses of coral were ripped up from the usually submerged reefs and strewn onto the beaches. The height of the tsunami waves had been from 23 to 32 feet (7 to 10 meters) at Hilo, as much as 59 feet (18 meters) locally elsewhere on the coast of the island of Hawaii, and up to 39 feet (12 meters) on the island of Oahu to the northwest. Hilo reported 96 dead, and another 63 were killed in other parts of the Hawaiian Islands—a total of 159. Twenty-six of the total died at the village of Laupahoehoe, about 25 miles (40 kilometers) up the coast northwest of Hilo, where the tsunami destroyed a schoolhouse and killed the 25 students and their teacher inside. Property damage in Hawaii was estimated to be $25 million. Twenty other persons died elsewhere from this tsunami; many of the deaths in Hawaii occurred when people—not aware that a tsunami was in progress—went down to the shore with curiosity after the first wave's water had withdrawn out to sea.

The following day in Hilo, bodies of a dozen people, recovered from the sea or from the wreckage on shore, were laid along the sidewalk under blankets. In the words of local resident Kapua Heuer, "You lifted the blanket to see if you could find those who you were looking for. The stark terror in their eyes—they died in terror."

The tsunami wave train continued spreading through the Pacific, at close to 497 miles (800 kilometers) per hour. It arrived at Valparaiso, halfway down the coastline of Chile, eighteen hours after the earthquake—and over 8,000 miles (13,000 kilometers) away from the epicenter—and resulted in a shore wave that was still 6 feet (2 meters) high. Tide gauges showed that the seismic sea waves were reflected back from Pacific coasts and hit the south side of Hawaii another eighteen hours later, then sloshed around the Pacific basin for the next couple of days.

Other Hawaiian Tsunamis. The Hawaiian Islands were hit by 7 tsunamis between 1924 and 2000, having waves at least 16 feet (5 meters) high. This includes the very early hours of May 23, 1960, when an earthquake the previous day off the coast of Chile generated a tsunami that resulted in waves at Hilo up to 23 feet (7 meters) high; 61 persons were killed, and 229 buildings were destroyed or severely damaged. On November 29, 1975, an earthquake of magnitude 7.2 on the island of Hawaii, 28 miles (45 kilometers) south of Hilo, created enough seafloor disturbance to produce waves up to 13 feet (4 meters) high at Hilo.

Tsunami-prone areas can reduce potential property damage by restricting building in low-lying coastal areas or at immediate portside. Hilo, after the destructive tsunamis of 1946 and 1960, limited commercial structures near the harbor. The area has been converted to a waterfront park that helps serve as a natural buffer for future high waves.

A tsunami bore on the Wailuku River in Hawaii in 1946. (National Oceanic and Atmospheric Administration)

Warning Systems. The best means of reducing danger and losses, particularly of life and injury, would be adequate warning of an oncoming seismic sea wave that could grow into a destructive tsunami. This shore-impacting growth into one or more walls of water depends in part on the local seafloor topography (bathymetry) and on the shoreline's shape and orientation with respect to the wave. Such a warning system is now in place for the Pacific region. In 1948, after the destructive Aleutian-generated tsunami that hit Hawaii in April, 1946, the U.S. government set up a Seismic Sea Wave Warning System. It is now known as the Pacific Tsunami Warning System and is administered by the National Oceanic and Atmospheric Administration (NOAA). With coordination and data processing at a Pacific Tsunami Warning Center in Honolulu, it quickly activates when any of its 30 participating seismic observatories, which are located around and on islands throughout the Pacific basin, detect an earthquake or other disturbance that could potentially generate a spreading tsunami. Another 78 stations have tide gauges for monitoring unusual changes in sea level, in order to detect a tsunami as it passes by. If such a wave is indeed spreading, an alert is issued, with prediction of arrival times, to Pacific nations, islands, and territories in the region.

The Warning System can typically issue a reliable Pacific-wide warning in about an hour after the occurrence of the source (such as an earthquake or volcanic eruption). This allows notice of an approaching tsunami for locations more than 466 miles (750 kilometers) from the source, because the wave train travels at about 750 miles per hour. This is adequate for trans-Pacific sites, as the tsunami travel time from, for example, Chile to Hawaii is about fifteen hours, and from the Aleutians to Northern California is about four hours.

The first use of the Warning System was on November 4, 1952, when an earthquake, detected as occurring off the Kamchatka Peninsula of eastern Russia, created a spreading sea wave. The Honolulu center predicted a time of arrival at the Hawaiian Islands about six hours from the time the earthquake occurred. People were evacuated inland, and ships or small boats were taken out to sea to ride out the subdued waves far offshore, and no lives were lost.

There are now regional systems of more localized monitoring stations and rapid data analysis, which give early cautionary warnings about ten minutes or so after an earthquake. This can be timely in reaching people and sites as close as 62 miles (100 kilometers) to a potential tsunami source. Such regional systems are in place in Hawaii, Alaska, Japan, the Kamchatka Peninsula, and French Polynesia. Before the Japanese regional system was established, there had been more than 6,000 people killed by tsunami waves in 14 events; after the system became operational, only 215 died from the next 20 tsunami events.

Robert S. Carmichael

FOR FURTHER INFORMATION:

Dvorak, J., and T. Peek. "Swept Away: The Deadly Power of Tsunamis." *Earth*, July, 1993.

Leet, L. D., S. Judson, and M. Kauffman. *Physical Geology.* 5th ed. Englewood Cliffs, N.J.: Prentice-Hall, 1978.

"On Mitigating Rapid Onset Natural Disasters: Project THRUST." *EOS/Transactions of American Geophysical Union* 69 (June 14, 1988): 649.

1946: Japan

DATE: December 21, 1946
PLACE: Honshū, Japan
RESULT: 2,000 dead, 500,000 homeless

An undersea quake, centered about 27 miles south of Honshū's Kii Peninsula and measuring 8.5 on the Richter scale, struck at 4:20 in the morning of December 21, 1946, sending a tsunami against the shores of the islands of Kyūshū, Shikoku, and Honshū. The quake itself awoke the Japanese citizens and Allied occupation troops alike, causing them to flee into the streets in the predawn subfreezing winter weather as buildings began to collapse. The earthquake caused a great deal of property damage as well as significant geographical change, with some regions rising or falling as much as 3 feet and even moving horizontally as much as 6 feet.

The subsequent tsunami consisted of three waves that caused damage at various points along the shores of the Inland Sea—the interior waterway formed by the islands of Kyūshū, Shikoku, and Honshū, and open to the Pacific in the east via the Kii Channel and in the west via the Bungo Strait—as well as on the Kii Peninsula itself and on the southern coast of Shikoku. Entering the Inland Sea at its eastern end, through the Kii Channel, the tsunami's waves went on to capsize or sink at least 2,000 vessels.

This entire region is, topographically speaking, very complex and provides striking testimony of the manner in which local geographic conditions can affect the ways in which the same tsunami will strike the shoreline differently at different places. On the east side of the Kii Channel, for example, the tsunami runup was as much as 18 feet above normal water levels. Directly across the strait, however, on the eastern shore of Shikoku, the runup was observed to be no more than 4.5 feet. Furthermore, in some places the crest of the tsunami came ashore first, while in others the trough arrived first, pulling water away from the shore and exposing the sea bottom before the tsunami's crest arrived, bringing the water back against the shore with even greater power.

In many places, the tsunami caused tremendous devastation. At least 2,000 people lost their lives. Reports accounting for property damage range from 1,451 homes to as many as 40,000. As many as 500,000 people were left homeless. The tsunami inundated a total of 60,000 square miles of land. It was registered in the Hawaiian Islands and in North and South America, far distant from Japan.

David M. Soule

FOR FURTHER INFORMATION:

Nash, Jay Robert. *Darkest Hours.* Chicago: Nelson-Hall, 1976.

Solovev, Sergei, and Chan Nam Go. *Catalogue of Tsunamis on the Eastern Shore of the Pacific Ocean.* Sidney, B.C.: Institute of Ocean Sciences, Department of Fisheries and Oceans, 1984.

Whittow, John. *Disasters: The Anatomy of Environmental Hazards,* Athens: University of Georgia Press, 1979.

1960: Hawaii

DATE: May 23, 1960
PLACE: Hilo, Hawaii
RESULT: 61 dead

The waves that struck Hilo, Hawaii, on May 23, 1960, provide instructive examples of how a tsunami can be propagated across an entire ocean only to have local geography affect the amount and the location of the damage ultimately caused. This tsunami also provides witness to the limits of complex warning and civil defense systems when faced with the mysteries of human behavior. The tsunami that caused 61 fatalities in Hilo was created by geological forces originating some 6,600 miles to the southeast. There, in the Peru-Chile trench, the longest crevasse on the face of the globe, where the Nazca Plate is sinking under the overriding American Plate, a series of at least 5 major earthquakes rocked the nation of Chile over a span of ten days.

The first quake, with a magnitude of 7.6 on the Richter scale, shook Chile at 6 A.M. on May 21, 1960. A second and stronger shock came a half-hour later. The death toll from the earthquake began to mount. The following day, just before 3 in the afternoon, another quake, still stronger, struck. Just a few minutes later, the largest of the 5 quakes, measuring 8.9 on the Richter scale, rocked the mountainous nation with a power ten times greater than the first quake. Within fifteen minutes of this fourth giant quake, a tsunami began to roar against a 300-mile-long stretch of the Chilean coast.

Shortly after this enormous quake struck Chile at 3:11 P.M. on May 22, seismographic reports began to be received at the Pacific Tsunami Warning System Control Center in Oahu, Hawaii. In less than three hours, the observers were able to use these reports to pinpoint the epicenter of the quake, recognize that a tsunami was a distinct possibility, and issue an initial warning. The tsunami was traveling westward across the eastern Pacific at a velocity of 442 miles per hour and was thus expected to reach Hawaii within fourteen hours and fifty-six minutes from the moment of its genesis in the waters of Chile. News of the tsunami damage in Chile confirmed the suspicions of the technicians in Hawaii, and they gave further warnings until they finally announced the expected arrival times for various points in the Pacific region.

As proof of the power of science and the skills of the technicians, the tsunami struck Hilo only one minute after its predicted arrival time. Unfortunately, the good intentions and work of the tsunami monitors and civil defense authorities was not enough. The citizens of Hawaii were given six hours of warning. Many residents failed to heed the call to evacuation, however, while others actually went down to the waterfront in time to witness the power of nature. Not a single sightseer survived as the tsunami crashed ashore with waves ranging from 15 to 35 feet

A tsunami in 1960 destroyed buildings, bent parking meters, and left residents of Hilo, Hawaii, homeless. (National Oceanic and Atmospheric Administration)

in height. In all, 61 deaths were recorded in Hawaii, all of them in Hilo City.

The vast majority of property damage caused in Hawaii was also caused in Hilo City, where the shape of the bay concentrated the tsunami's third wave into a bore that flooded the coastal areas around the bay up to the 18-foot level above the normal water line. Some 600 acres were inundated. Total destruction occurred in half this area; only buildings of reinforced concrete or structural steel were left standing, though they were thoroughly gutted. Frame buildings were crushed or swept away to the line of maximum floodwater level. Dozens of automobiles were destroyed, and heavy machinery and metal stocks were thrown about like flotsam. A tractor weighing 10 tons was swept out and away from the showroom in which it was on display. Boulders weighing twice that were torn from the sea wall in which they had

been placed and moved more than 500 feet inland.

Elsewhere on the island of Hawaii, damage was limited to the west and south coasts, where some dozen buildings were crushed or flooded or floated off their foundations. There was limited damage of a similar kind on the islands of Maui, Molokai, Lanai, Oahu, and Kauai. In spite of the damage it suffered, Hawaii did not absorb the entire blow of the westward-moving tsunami. Another eight hours later, after traveling some 10,600 miles from its point of origin and actually accelerating because of the increased average water depth in the western Pacific, the tsunami waves crashed ashore on the eastern shores of the Japanese islands of Honshū and Hokkaidō.

Without a history of damage from tsunamis traveling from such a great distance, the Japanese authorities were slow in issuing the necessary warning. At 6:00 in the evening of May 23, 1960, the tsunami brought against the shoreline waves ranging in height from 12 to 20 feet. After traveling across the entire Pacific, the tsunami still packed enough power to send multi-ton fishing boats over destroyed wharves and into the business districts of more than 1 town on Honshū's Sanriku coast, where they pummeled the buildings and homes. Total property losses in Japan were estimated to reach $400 million. At least 5,000 homes were destroyed, leaving some 50,000 homeless. Casualties amounted to at least 180 deaths. In the Philippines 20 people were killed, while the coastal areas of New Zealand and California suffered damage.

David M. Soule

FOR FURTHER INFORMATION:

Cornell, James. *The Great International Disaster Book.* New York: Charles Scribner's Sons, 1976.

Lander, James F., and Patricia A. Lockridge. *United States Tsunamis, 1690-1988.* Boulder, Colo.: National Geophysical Data Center, 1989.

Myles, Douglas. *The Great Waves.* New York: McGraw-Hill, 1985.

Nash, Jay Robert. *Darkest Hours.* Chicago: Nelson-Hall, 1976.

Robinson, Andrew. *Earth Shock: Hurricanes, Volcanoes, Earthquakes, Tornadoes, and Other Forces of Nature.* London: Thames and Hudson, 1993.

1998: Papua New Guinea

DATE: July 17, 1998
PLACE: Northwestern Papua New Guinea
RESULT: 2,000 dead

Michael Kaipano, a small wiry man in his sixties, sat on an iron bed in Wewak Hospital, East Sepik Province. His right leg had been amputated because of gangrene, and he was attached to an intravenous drip. The giant tidal waves that struck Papua New Guinea's remote northwestern coast wiped Kaipano's village, Arop, from the face of the earth. It also took the lives of his 6 grandchildren, 2 brothers, and a daughter.

The three giant waves that rolled toward Papua New Guinea's far northwest coast came from the horizon at extraordinary speed. An undersea earthquake about 18 miles (29 kilometers) off the northwest coast and which measured 7.0 on the Richter scale caused them. Although seismological stations in the South Pacific did measure the tremor, the earthquake erupted under the seabed so close to the Papua New Guinea coast that there was no time to send warnings to villagers to evacuate. Starting as long, silent ripples on the deep waters of the Bismarck Sea, they swept toward the shore at dusk on

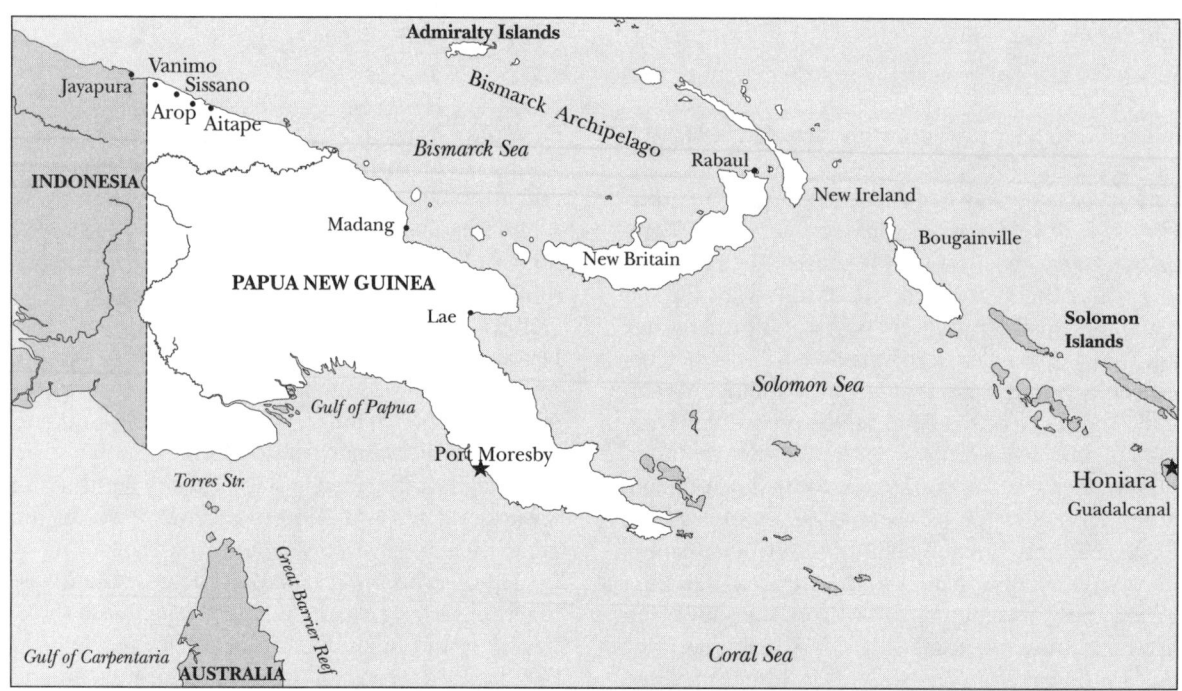

Survivors of the 1998 Papua New Guinea tsunami retrieve supplies from their destroyed home in Sissano. (AP/Wide World Photos)

July 17, 1998. The waves gathered height and power as they neared the beaches around Sissano Lagoon in West Sepik Province. At that point, they were up to 33 feet (10 meters) high and sounding, some said, like a jet plane taking off. The waves then crashed over the thatched wooden houses as villagers were preparing dinner. "We just saw the sea rise up and it came toward the village and we had to run for our lives," said a man who lost 8 members of his family.

Dead Include Many Children. The population of the affected area, a strip of land about 25 miles (40 kilometers) long and 370 miles (590 kilometers) northwest of the capital Port Moresby, was between 8,000 and 10,000. At least 6,000 people were homeless after their houses were reduced to matchwood by the tsunami. The governor of West Sepik Province said, "I am looking at a very conservative figure of 3,000 people dead, based on the number of bodies recovered so far and the number of people seen hiding in the jungle. I've had a look and all there is are bodies. The stench is overpowering." A Roman Catholic priest echoed the governor's estimate of 3,000

dead. He said that many of those killed were children who had been too small to run away and too weak to climb coconut trees to safety before the waves engulfed them. The area disaster coordinator said that the village of Warapu alone had a death toll of 500, mostly elderly people and schoolchildren. "Schools in Arop, Sissano, and Warapu will be closed because we don't have the children. They're all dead," he said.

Papua New Guinea is the eastern half of the large island of New Guinea and a former British colony. It has been a member of the British Commonwealth since 1975, when Australia, which administered the country on Britain's behalf, granted it independence. Queen Elizabeth II sent a message of sympathy to the region. "She said she was shocked at the tidal wave and that her thoughts were with the families of the bereaved and injured," a Buckingham Palace spokesperson said.

Relief Efforts. A week after the disaster, the official death toll was 1,500, but thousands remained unaccounted for. Bodies, some partly eaten by crocodiles, dogs, and pigs, were still being spotted in the lagoon and nearby mangrove and bush areas. With many of the bodies quickly deteriorating because of the tropical heat, bereaved families dug makeshift graves in the rubble of their homes. There were no coffins. The dead were simply covered with straw matting. While 700 injured were being treated in local hospitals and by doctors and nurses flown in from Australia, Japan, and New Zealand, numbed survivors gathered in makeshift aid centers. Some parents had lost all of their children. Other victims had been unable to find a single family member alive. Approximately 200 children who were visiting one of the villages for a traditional festival were feared dead, swept away in an instant.

Many of the survivors, fearing more waves, took refuge on higher ground. Some walked for four hours through dense jungle to villages that lay inland. Devastation lay behind them. Village huts, some built on the sandy shoreline shaped by a 1935 tsunami, had been ripped from the ground. The region's lack of airstrips meant that Australian Army Hercules planes ferrying in medical supplies and a mobile field hospital had to land in Vanimo, the provincial capital, about 69 miles (110 kilometers) west of the disaster zone. Their cargo was then reloaded onto small planes and helicopters to be taken to the centers where aid workers and church officials cared for survivors.

Several days after the disaster, the Adventist Development and Relief Agency (ADRA) flew into the area sixteen water tanks that had been shipped from Australia the previous year for drought victims. Helicopters were carrying another twenty of the 317-gallon (1,200-liter) tanks into accessible areas of the rugged country. The area surrounding the lagoon and the worst-hit villages of Sissano, Warapu, and Arop had been sealed off to stop the spread of disease from decaying corpses. However, some people from the vanished villages were already asking aid workers for axes and bush knives so they could rebuild their homes and vegetable plots on their traditional lands.

Dana P. McDermott

FOR FURTHER INFORMATION:

"Hundreds Dead After Tidal Wave." *Washington Post*, July 19, 1998, p. A24.

"1,000 Dead in Massive Tidal Waves." *Washington Post*, July 20, 1998, p. A13.

"Tsunami Survivors Face Disease; Many Corpses Cremated in Papua New Guinea." *Washington Post*, July 22, 1998, p. A21.

Volcanic Eruptions

(National Oceanic and Atmospheric Administration)

A volcanic eruption is the manner in which gases, liquids, and solids are expelled from the earth's interior onto its surface. Eruptions can range from calm outflows of lava to violent explosions. About fifty volcanoes erupt every year, and a truly catastrophic eruption occurs about once a century. Nearly 200,000 people have died over the last five centuries because of volcanic eruptions. Three-quarters of these deaths were caused by only 7, extremely violent, eruptions.

FACTORS INVOLVED: Chemical reactions, geography, geological forces, wind
REGIONS AFFECTED: All

SCIENCE

Volcanic eruptions are induced by and usually propelled by gas. The most common source of the gas is water, which at the high temperatures associated with volcanic activity is turned to water vapor (steam). Liquid lava is often involved in an eruption. The ratio of gas to liquid in an erupting magma (molten rock material within the earth) is extremely variable. Some eruptions are almost entirely gas with minuscule amounts of liquid, such as the Salt Lake explosion crater in Oahu, Hawaii. At the other extreme are eruptions of lava flows that have less than 1 percent gas, such as the seafloor eruptions at mid-oceanic ridges.

There are several methods to generate the water and associated gas in a magma. The gas that causes the eruption can come from the magma itself. Magmas that are deeply buried (under a high pressure) can dissolve considerable amounts of water. About 10 percent water can dissolve in a magma that resides 9.3 miles (15 kilometers) below the earth's surface. The amount of water that can stay dissolved decreases as the magma begins to rise. When the pressure drops sufficiently, the water comes out of the magma and boils to make bubbles. This process is called "vesiculation."

Vesiculation occurs in a similar manner to the opening of a champagne bottle: When the cork is removed and the pressure on the liquid is released, the dissolved gas (carbon dioxide in champagne) forms bubbles in the liquid. If an abundance of gas is produced, the bubbles can coalesce and shred the magma into droplets surrounded by turbulent jets of gas. In larger, more explosive eruptions the expanding gases can pulverize preexisting rocks in the throat of the volcano and along the walls of the magma passages. This combination of gases, ash, degasing droplets of liquid, vesiculating clots of lava, and broken fragments of hot rock can erupt as a glowing avalanche (nuée ardente), which is the most destructive and deadly of all forms of eruptions. Numerous nuées ardentes erupted in 1902 from Pelée in the Caribbean, killing 28,000 in St. Pierre within two minutes on May 8 and 2,000 in Morne Rouge on August 30.

Another source of the water needed to drive an eruption is groundwater. Water that originates as atmospheric precipitation creating lakes, rivers, and oceans is called "meteoric water." Starting at the surface, meteoric water can infiltrate into the ground to produce water-saturated rock, where it is called groundwater. Large quantities of groundwater can be raised to the boiling point as magma rises. The destructive eruption of Vesuvius in 79 C.E., which buried the city of Pompeii and killed over 13,000 people in the region, was initiated by the boiling of groundwater.

Magma reaching the surface of the solid earth can acquire a late-stage explosive nature by interacting with surface water of lakes, rivers, or oceans. The 1963 birth of the island of Surtsey in Iceland produced a pair of violent explosion plumes, a white steam cloud and a black cloud of fragmented lava. The crater region where many volcanoes have their main vent is often a circular depression that becomes filled with meteoric water to make a crater lake. The water in crater lakes is often highly acidic and filled with mud. Kelut, on the Indonesian island of Java has a deep crater lake that has repeatedly been the site of eruptions; a minor eruption in 1919 mixed the lake water and the fragmented lava to make a violent mudflow that killed 5,500 people. The deadliest eruption ever was Krakatau in 1883, which killed 36,000 people from a tsunami (tidal wave) that was generated when seawa-

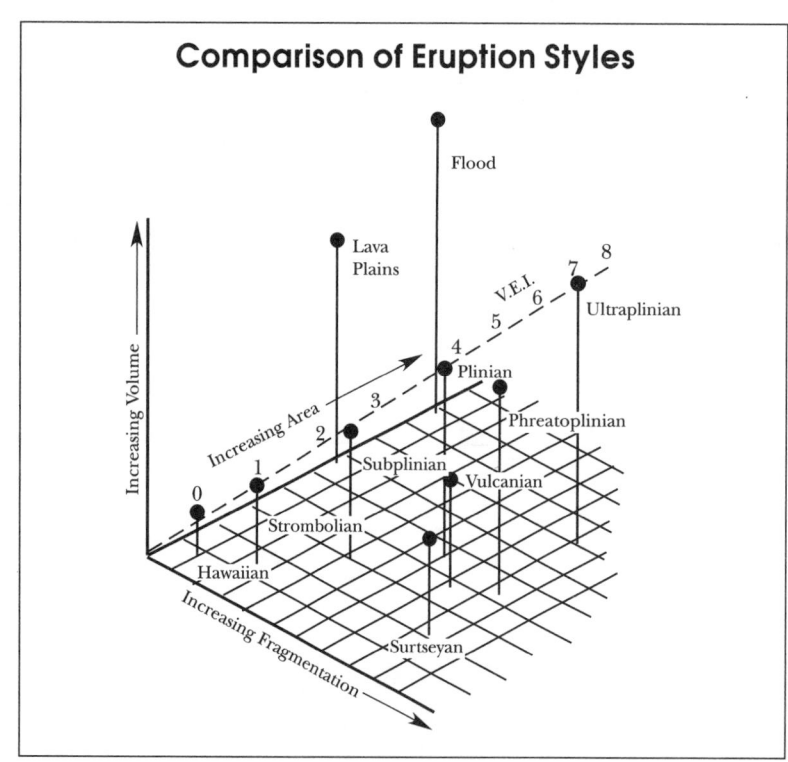

Comparison of Eruption Styles

ter entered the collapsed side of the island volcano and hit the erupting magma.

An explosion requires two components: the force (expanding gases) and a resistance to the force. To pop a balloon loudly requires that air be blown into it and that the latex rubber exert a force against the inflow of air. The explosion occurs when the pent-up force eventually overcomes the resistance. In a violent eruption the resistance comes from the very sticky nature of the liquid portion of the magma. The stickiness of a liquid is called the viscosity. Highly viscous magmas are the most explosive. The higher the amount of silicon in the magma the greater the viscosity and the more explosive the eruption when water is present.

Nuées ardentes, the most deadly form of volcanic eruptions, usually develop in magmas that have a high silicon content. About 13,000 people were evacuated in Japan in 1991 when a low-gas, high-silicon lava began erupting at Unzen, forming a thick, pasty dome of lava on top of the volcano. When the lava acquired sufficient gas it erupted as a nuée ardente, killing 42 people, mostly journalists and geologists who had stayed to study and photograph the volcano.

Volcanoes are classified into six general categories with several subgroups. The major categories are Hawaiian, Strombolian, Vulcanian, Peléan, Plinian, and Surtseyan. The classification is based upon the volcano's predominant eruptive style, which considers both the violence of the eruption (as indicated by plume height, frequency of event, and volume of material) and the type of material ejected (ranging from the effusion of liquid lava flows to a gaseous mixture that contains ash, fragments of rock, and droplets or clots of liquid). A Volcanic Explosivity Index (VEI) was developed to assist with the classification of an eruption. Calm, effusive lava eruptions are given a VEI value of 0, whereas the most violent eruptions have VEI values of 8.

The most nonexplosive class is the Hawaiian class of eruption. It involves minimal explosions (VEI values of 0 or 1) and a calm outpouring of low-viscosity, low-silicon lava. When these occur on the floor of the ocean at mid-oceanic ridges and ocean basin hot spots they are called submarine eruptions. The pressure of the overlying seawater helps to nullify the explosiveness of the eruption.

A Hawaiian eruption can emerge from a single vent that erupts almost on a daily basis for months on end. These eruptions typically form shield volcanoes with gentle slopes of 3 to 5 degrees. Shield volcanoes

may rise from the seafloor to become islands, which can continue growing for another 13,123 feet (4,000 meters) above sea level (Mauna Loa in Hawaii is 13,678 feet above sea level and still growing, as evidenced by a 1984 eruption).

When Hawaiian eruptions occur from long fissures, they can produce large volumes of liquid lava. The Great Tolbachik fissure eruption in Russia in 1975 produced over 70,629 cubic feet (2 cubic kilometers) of lava that covered more than 15.4 square miles (40 square kilometers). In Iceland the Laki fissure eruption of 1783 covered 102 square miles (265 square kilometers), destroyed four-fifths of the sheep and half the cattle, and caused 10,000 residents to starve to death during the ensuing winter.

The Strombolian class of eruptions is weakly explosive (VEI values of 1 or 2). These eruptions usually begin with the volcano tossing out molten debris to form cinders and clots of liquid that solidify in the air to fall as bombs. This high-arching, incandescent portion of the eruption resembles firework fountains. These bursts last only a few seconds, with long pauses of twenty minutes or more between the bursts. Magma can rise from 328 feet (100 meters) to 0.6 mile (1 kilometer) into the air, breaking into lava clots of all sizes. Many Strombolian eruptions are known for throwing bombs hundreds of feet into the air every few seconds. The pyroclastic display is often followed by fluid lava flows. Normally short-lived, the eruptions last a few months before pausing for a year or so. The cinder cones associated with an eruptive phase are rarely over 820 feet (250 meters) in height and the lava flow rarely exceeds 6.2 miles (10 kilometers) in length. The explosion of Etna in Italy in 1500 B.C.E. is thought to be the first historic record of any volcano recorded. Etna has over one hundred recorded eruptions of Strombolian activity, and it still erupts every few years.

The Vulcanian class of eruptions is more explosive, with VEI values ranging from 2 to 4. The magma is usually more viscous and has considerable strength. The eruption column is quite noticeable, rising from 1.9 to 9.3 miles (3 to 15 kilometers) above the volcano. There are few, if any, lava flows; rather, these eruptions are characterized by thick liquid clots being shot far into the air. Vulcanian eruptions' explosiveness is so powerful that it sometimes destroys part of the volcanic edifice.

These volcanoes can lay dormant for over one hundred years and then burst into a noisy, violent eruption. Nuées ardentes are often by-products of Vulcanian explosions, and when the nuée ardente is associated with the collapse or explosion of a volcanic dome sitting over the vent it is classed as a Peléan eruption (often considered a subclass of Vulcanian eruptions).

The dome-building phase of the Peléan eruptions can begin when the center of the crater starts to bulge upward, revealing a spine mantled with explosive debris from the floor of the crater. The dome can grow as much as 98 feet (30 meters) a day to a final height of 1,969 feet (600 meters) or more. The elevation of the crater floor can rise 328 feet (100 meters) above its normal level, changing the shape of the volcano to an almost-level platform. The explosions can shatter the dome, and its pieces can become swept up in the turbulent flow of the nuée ardente. The dome can be rebuilt in the crater again and exist in a quiet phase.

A nuée ardente has so much gas that it is a semi-frictionless fluid, and it can race down the slopes of the volcano at velocities of up to 311 miles (500 kilometers) per hour. It is an avalanche of hot, frothy clots of lava, noxious gases, fragments of molten ash, and incandescent boulders. A large cloud of ash and gas rises above the nuée ardente as it moves across the ground, and the clouds can asphyxiate animals and humans that are near the nuée ardente.

The most famous Peléan eruption is the eruption of Pelée in 1902, which became the basis for this subclass of volcanic eruptions. Lamington in New Guinea has produced both Vulcanian and Peléan eruptions. It was not thought to be a volcano until, in 1951, it erupted a nuée ardente that devastated an area of 69.5 square miles (180 square kilometers) and killed 3,000 people. Since then, several volcanic domes have grown in its summit crater and have subsequently been destroyed by later explosions.

Plinian eruptions are the most explosive and rare of the volcanic eruptions of historic record, having VEI values of 4 to 6. Although Ultra-Plinian explosive eruptions (VEI values of 7 and 8) have been deduced from the geological record of their deposits, no Ultra-Plinian eruptions have occurred in recorded history. A powerful eruption shaft develops over the vent, having speeds of several feet per second and shooting volcanic materials in a column that can reach 15.5 miles (25 kilometers) or more in height. As the volcanic fragments falls they can cover a huge area of ground (hundreds of square miles). Plinian

eruptive fragments are predominantly made of bubbly pumice and ash. Pumice falling fairly near the volcano can attain thicknesses of close to 100 feet. The Tambora eruption of 1815 in Indonesia is the largest of all historic eruptions. It killed 92,000 people, had an eruption column that was 25 miles (40 kilometers) in height, and deposited 164 feet (50 meters) of pumice in surrounding areas.

The eruption plume of a Plinian eruption will bring an abundance of ash into the stratosphere, which can circle the globe for several years before falling back to the ground. After the 1991 eruption of Pinatubo in the Philippines, the dust clouds became an aviation hazard because neither pilots nor radar could distinguish water-based clouds from dust clouds. In the months following the eruption 14 airliners developed engine problems from dust clouds, and 9 had to make emergency landings.

There is a strong correlation between large eruptions and a change in the weather conditions. The eruption of El Chichón (VEI of 4) in Mexico in 1982 was the first eruption cloud to be tracked in the atmosphere by weather satellites. The eruption injected 3.3 million tons of gaseous sulfur into the atmosphere, which converted to sulfuric acid within three months. Following the Laki eruption of 1783 the acid aerosol contaminated the pastures and animals grazing on these grasses, and they died within three days. Once dispersed, the dust and gases can reflect incoming solar radiation and reduce the earth's temperatures. Following the 1815 eruption of Tambora, the coldest summer in over 250 years of record-keeping (1738-1999) was recorded. The average summer temperature was 2 degrees colder than the second-coldest summer. The Pinatubo eruption of 1991 caused the average world temperature to drop by 0.5 degree.

GEOGRAPHY

The vast majority of the active volcanoes on Earth are associated with long, narrow belts of fractured rocks. The longest belt and the site of over 75 percent of all the volcanic activity on earth takes place underwater, along the crests of the mid-oceanic ridges. Although the ridge system is over 37,284 miles (60,000 kilometers) in length, the actual number and magnitude of the eruptions are untold. The submarine volcanic events are not counted on the list of active volcanoes until the lava deposits bring the submarine volcano to the surface as an island. Iceland, which is the largest island on the Mid-Atlantic Ridge, has twenty-two active volcanoes. Other notable volcanoes with historic eruptions from the flanks of the Mid-Atlantic Ridge are the Azores, Ascension Island, and Tristan da Cunha.

The longest belt of active volcanoes virtually circles the Pacific Ocean and is commonly called the Pacific "Ring of Fire." Two-thirds of the world's active volcanoes occur in this belt. The volcanic chains making up the Ring of Fire are the Cascades of the United States and Canada (Mount St. Helens), the Mexican Volcanic Belt (El Chichón), the Central American Belt (Santa María), the Andes of South America (Nevado del Ruiz), New Zealand (Ngauruhoe), Tonga (Niuafo'ou), New Guinea (Lamington), Indonesia (Kelut), the Philippines (Pinatubo), the Ryukyu Island arc (Kutinoerabu), the volcanic arc of the Mariana, the Izu and Bonin Islands (Miyakzima), Japan (Unzen), the Kamchatka Peninsula (Bezymianny), and the Aleutian Islands and South Alaska (Katmai).

The third major belt of active volcanoes starts at the Mid-Atlantic Ridge at the Azores and runs east through the Mediterranean Sea (Etna and Vesuvius), across the northern Arabian Peninsula, down the Malaysian Peninsula (Krakatau), and connects with the Ring of Fire in Indonesia. The smallest belt of active volcanoes that is isolated from the other longer belts is the volcanic island arc that occurs along the eastern edge of the Caribbean Sea (Pelée).

There are a number of isolated volcanic centers that occur in the interior of continents and ocean basins, usually a considerable distance from the linear belts. The island of Hawaii in the center of the Pacific basin has experienced over 100 recorded eruptions since 1700, and Nyiragongo in Zaire had a lava lake in its summit crater from the time of its discovery in 1894 until 1977, when it suddenly drained 28.8 million cubic yards (22 million cubic meters) of lava down its flanks and killed 70 people. The active volcanoes outside of the system of belts account for less than 5 percent of all historic eruptions.

PREVENTION AND PREPARATIONS

Volcanic eruptions are virtually impossible to prevent, but there have been some fairly successful ef-

Cars trapped in a lava flow in Hawaii. (National Oceanic and Atmospheric Administration)

forts made to divert or control the direction of lava flows and lahars (mudflows) once volcanoes have erupted. Lahars are flash floods, having the consistency of wet cement, which are caused when a volcanic eruption melts glacial ice or occurs in a lava lake. Less than 10 percent of the diversion barriers for lava flows have been successful. In Iceland an advancing lava flow was cooled by a spray of water from hoses, which forced the lava to spread sideways. Aerial bombing to collapse crater walls and disrupt existing magma flows has also been tried. These techniques usually at least slow down the lava flow if they do not divert it, providing for needed evacuation time.

An unusual prevention measure was used on Kelut on Java after the 1919 eruption produced a lahar that killed 5,500 people. The Dutch colonial authorities dug a series of underground tunnels through the crater wall, draining most of the lake. The volcano's next eruption, in 1951, emptied into a lake that was 164 feet (50 meters) lower. There were no lahars produced, but the tunnel system was destroyed. In 1964 the crater again acquired 52.3 million cubic yards (40 million cubic meters) of water, and scientists asked that new tunnels be dug. A 1966 eruption again caused lahars, which killed hundreds of people, and new tunnels were dug to drain the lake. In 1990 prediction techniques forewarned of another eruption, and 60,000 people were evacuated. The eruption did not produce a lahar, but 32 casualties occurred because of roofs collapsing under the heavy weight of the ash and pumice. Steps are now also made to reinforce roofs of homes and buildings in order to support the weight of falling debris.

The best prevention of a high death toll is orderly evacuation. Evacuation plans require a high degree of cooperation between civil authorities and scientists, as well as an amazing amount of preparation. In the scientific arena, the first step to being prepared for a volcanic eruption is to monitor the activity of a volcano. Most volcanoes give some warning signs of an upcoming eruption. Normally, magma will move into the area below the volcano in a reservoir called the magma chamber. The magma then travels up the chamber and begins to release gases. As the magma moves up the chamber it produces small earthquakes and ground vibrations.

There are three forms of seismic activity: short-period earthquakes, long-period earthquakes, and harmonic tremors. Short-period earthquakes are caused by the fracturing of brittle rock as the magma forces its way up the chamber; they signify that the magma is coming near the surface. Long-period earthquakes are thought to be the result of increased gas pressure in the volcano. Harmonic tremors are the result of sustained movement of magma below the surface. Scientists use seismographs to monitor the earthquakes.

As the magma moves toward the surface, a volcano will begin to swell, and the degree of slope of the volcano may change. Fumaroles, which are vents giving off gas, will often increase their sulfur content. Scientists can monitor these events with a number of tools: Tiltmeters measure the change in slope, and geodimeters measure the amount of swelling in the volcano. Gases released near the volcano can be measured by spectrometers.

Many regions have established volcano observatories to monitor ground motion for dangerously active volcanoes. The Rabaul Volcano Observatory in New Guinea recorded two swarms of 1,000 earthquakes in a two-day period in 1984. In June of that month they recorded 13,749 individual earthquakes. They also recorded an uplift of 63 inches (160 centimeters) over the nine months leading up to the earthquakes. With these techniques, scientists are becoming skilled at predicting volcanic eruptions.

Monitoring of volcanoes can save countless live. Communication with the populace is of utmost importance; restricted areas must be drawn, and certain areas must be completely or partially evacuated. In 1985, the eruption of Nevado del Ruiz in Colombia was well monitored, but due to lack of communication the town of Armero was not prepared for evacuation, and a lahar swept down the slope and killed at least 23,000 people, 90 percent of the town's population.

Before the eruption of Pinatubo in June of 1991, scientists worked closely with civil defense authorities in the Philippines to establish a four-stage plan leading to the eruption. They evacuated more than 80,000 people from the area. Each stage of the plan was implemented when the scientists measured a specific level of sulfur in the fumarolic gases, a certain number and strength of earthquakes occurred, or a specified amount of rise and tilt of the volcano came to pass. With each stage the authorities evacuated a larger area and took actions to increase their readiness. The death toll could have run in the tens of thousands, but because of advance preparations and education, only a few hundred people died.

RESCUE AND RELIEF EFFORTS

More deaths often occur in the aftermath of a violent eruption—from starvation and disease—than from the eruption itself. Survivors usually return to their homes after the eruption has waned. In the historic past, areas around Plinian eruptions were deeply buried, with complete loss of all crops and pastures and severe loss of livestock and potable water supplies. Most countries did not have disaster relief plans, nor was international aid available. This usually led to a higher death toll from starvation and disease than was attributed to the ejected materials from the volcano.

The modern world has vastly differing degrees of readiness. Mexico, with over a dozen active volcanoes, had no civil defense program or contingency plans for evacuation, shelter, or resettlement when El Chichón erupted in 1982. Italy set up its Ministry of Civil Protection in 1981. Many poor countries with active volcanoes have no volcano monitoring programs and no civil defense systems for volcanic eruptions.

Japan is at the other end of the scale in terms of readiness. That country established volcano surveillance and disaster plans in the 1950's. The On-take area is a model of preparation, with concrete volcanic shelters at intervals along all the roads in the area. Within the river systems special dams and canals have been built to impede the progress of lahars. Children wear helmets when they go to school; once a year all citizens in the area participate in a rehearsal of a full-scale evacuation. Temporary lodgings are built and maintained, and the monitoring information from the volcano is computerized and automatically transmitted to the civil authorities.

IMPACT

Volcanoes are the second most destructive natural disasters on Earth. Historically, two-thirds of all eruptions have caused fatalities. The chief causes of death from violent eruptions are suffocation and drowning. Most catastrophic eruptions occur in populated coastal regions, and tsunamis (tidal waves) generated by eruptions can exact a much greater toll than the actual erupted materials. In the past five hundred years, volcanic eruptions have killed more than 200,000 people and have cost billions of dollars in damage to homes and property. During the twentieth century, volcanic eruptions killed an average of 800 people per year.

Dion C. Stewart and Toby R. Stewart

BIBLIOGRAPHY

Bullard, Fred M. *Volcanoes of the Earth.* Austin: University of Texas Press, 1976. Still one of the best books on eruption classification, with excellent photographs, line drawings, and illustrations of volcanoes and volcanic processes.

Decker, Robert, and Barbara Decker. *Volcanoes.* 3d ed. New York: W. H. Freeman, 1997. A book for general readers that introduces all aspects of volcanology.

Fisher, Richard V. *Out of the Crater: Chronicles of a Volcanologist.* Princeton, N.J.: Princeton University Press, 1999. This is a personal narrative of visits to many of the volcanic sites mentioned in this article.

Francis, Peter. *Volcanoes: A Planetary Perspective.* Oxford, England: Oxford University Press, 1993. This book gives information on nearly five hundred volcanic eruptions. It has an interesting chapter on volcanoes and changing weather.

Macdonald, Gordon A. *Volcanoes.* Englewood Cliffs, N.J.: Prentice-Hall, 1972. This college-level textbook contains a map and tabulated data on more than five hundred active volcanoes.

Scarth, Alwyn. *Volcanoes: An Introduction.* College Station: Texas A&M University Press, 1994. This book has a large section on predictions. It also provides many interesting accounts of historic eruptions.

Williams, Howell, and Alexander R. McBirney. *Volcanology.* San Francisco: W. H. Freeman, 1979. This is a more advanced book that gives details of gas generation and mechanisms for explosive eruptions.

Notable Events

Historical Overview

A dark plume obscures the sun and the sky; acrid fumes irritate the mucous membranes as a sulfurous stench pervades the air. Intermittently, accompanied by deafening noise, lightning, and thunder, eruptions spew fire and brimstone into the air, hurling hot, sputtering chunks of rock far from the mountain. This is the experience of those who have lived near volcanic eruptions and were fortunate enough to survive. In the face of such incredible power, death and destruction, and dramatic changes in landscape, cultures throughout time have attached great religious significance to volcanoes.

Within Western European cultures, objective written descriptions of volcanic events date back to 79 C.E., when Vesuvius, a famous volcano to the northeast of the Bay of Naples in Italy, erupted. The towns of Pompeii and Herculaneum were buried beneath ash and pumice. Pliny the Elder, a well-respected admiral in the Roman navy, perished, and the historian Tacitus, reconstructing the conditions of his death, sought information from his nephew: Pliny the Younger, in two letters, described what had occurred. The volcano had not been active for several centuries, and no one considered it a threat.

Benjamin Franklin was among the first to recognize the global climatic effects of volcanoes when he speculated that the 1783 Laki fissure eruption in Iceland was responsible for the bitter winter of 1783-1784 in Paris. Temperature records for this year from the eastern United States show an average winter temperature 41 degrees Fahrenheit (4.8 degrees Celsius) lower than the 225-year average. The eruption, lasting eight months, produced the largest lava flow in historic time, but much of its deadly effect resulted from the gases that escaped.

Modern analysis of gas samples retrieved from Greenland ice cores reveals a dramatic spike in acidity corresponding to this eruption. It has been estimated that the influx of acid gases into the atmosphere from this one eruption is about equivalent to the annual global anthropogenic input. Sulfur dioxide is responsible for much of the acidity observed in the ice cores, but hydrogen fluoride from the eruption is suspected to have killed most of the cattle in the region, which caused a famine. Three-quarters of the livestock in Iceland, and 25 percent of the human population, died.

The 1815 eruption of Tambora, in Indonesia, produced much greater climatic effects. Whereas the relatively calm basaltic eruption of Laki was probably confined to the lower levels of the atmosphere, where precipitation is constantly removing dust and ash, the very explosive eruption of Tambora injected ash and gases into the stratosphere, far above these elevations. Records from astronomers show that the haze produced by this eruption persisted for at least two and a half years. During 1816, often referred to as the Year Without a Summer, New England experienced a frost every month of the summer. Crops failed, and famines struck much of Europe, Canada, and the United States.

When Krakatau erupted in 1883 it generated intense scientific interest. More than 36,000 people died, most from tsunamis that were probably generated by giant parts of the volcano sliding into the sea. The eruption was witnessed by many who survived to write about it, and it was the subject of research for the Royal Society and the Dutch government. Heard as far away as 2,990 miles (4,811 kilometers), causing atmospheric pressure fluctuations that circled the globe many times, and lowering temperatures in the Northern Hemisphere by 32.5 degrees Fahrenheit (0.25 degree Celsius) for a year or two, this eruption captured the attention of scientists in a way no earlier eruption had. Strange optical effects were observed, including blue tinges on the sun and the moon. Solar energy reaching the earth at an observatory in France decreased initially by 20 percent, then remained 10 percent below normal for many months.

By the second half of the nineteenth century the Neptunist theory, which held that all rocks had precipitated from a primitive ocean, was no longer impeding the development of the earth sciences. Many geologists went into the field to study active and ancient volcanoes. Laboratory techniques evolved rapidly, and by the early twentieth century many of the processes and reactions involved in the melting and freezing of rock had been sketched out.

Pelée erupted in 1902, and suddenly a great deal was learned about pyroclastic flows. Emanating from the volcano after a period of minor eruptive activity, these flows raced down the slopes at velocities of about 99 miles (160 kilometers) per hour, running over and totally destroying the town of St. Pierre. The force of such a blast was devastating in itself, but its temperature, estimated to have been about 1,292 degrees Fahrenheit (700 degrees Celsius), made it particularly deadly. Of the 30,000 people in the town that morning, no more than 4 survived—and they were horribly burned. These pyroclastic flows, which were given the name nuées ardentes, or "glowing avalanches," had never been witnessed before—at least not by anyone who survived.

Enough was learned, however, to be able to identify this mechanism as having been responsible for similar, but much larger, deposits displaced during the eruption of Katmai a decade later. Only distant ashfalls were directly observed from this volcano, located in a sparsely populated area of Alaska. It was not until 1916 that an expedition actually visited the site of the eruption. Still, there was enough heat left in the deposit to continue to turn water from the soil below it into steam. This region has been called the Valley of Ten Thousand Smokes ever since.

Over the next sixty years the theory of plate tectonics was developed. It explained why volcanoes occur where they do and why their rocks, shapes, and eruptive styles vary so much. The theory was able to show why some volcanoes, such as all of the Hawaiian islands—other than the big island of Hawaii—are

Milestones

5000 B.C.E.:	Crater Lake, Oregon, erupts, sending pyroclastic flows as far as 37 miles (60 kilometers) from the vent; 25 cubic miles of material are erupted as a caldera forms from the collapse of the mountaintop.
August 24, 79 C.E.:	Vesuvius erupts, burying Pompeii and Herculaneum.
June 8, 1783-February 7, 1784:	The Laki fissure eruption in Iceland produces the largest lava flow in historic time, with major climatic effects. Benjamin Franklin speculates on its connection to a cold winter in Paris the following year.
April 5, 1815:	The dramatic explosion of Tambora, 248.6 miles (400 kilometers) east of Java, the largest volcanic event in modern history, produces atmospheric and climatic effects for the next two years. Frosts occur every month in New England during 1816, the Year Without a Summer.
August 26, 1883:	A cataclysmic eruption of Krakatau, an island in Indonesia, is heard 2,968 miles away. Many die as pyroclastic flows race over pumice rafts floating on the surface of the sea; many more die from a tsunami.
May 8, 1902:	Pelée, on the northern end of the island of Martinique in the Caribbean, sends violent pyroclastic flows into the city of St. Pierre, killing all but 2 of the 30,000 inhabitants.
June 6, 1912:	Katmai erupts in Alaska with an ash flow that produces the Valley of Ten Thousand Smokes.
February 20, 1943:	Paricutín comes into existence in a cultivated field in Mexico. The eruption of this volcano continues for nine years.
March 30, 1956:	The volcano Bezymianny erupts with a violent lateral blast, stripping trees of their bark 18.6 miles (30 kilometers) away.
January, 1973:	During an eruption on Heimaey Island, Iceland, the flow of lava is controlled by cooling it with water from fire hoses.
May 18, 1980:	Mount St. Helens, in Washington State, erupts with a directed blast to the north, moving pyroclastic flows at velocities of 328 to 984 feet (100 to 300 meters) per second (nearly the speed of sound).
November 13, 1985:	Mudflows from the eruption of the Nevado del Ruiz, in Colombia, kill at least 23,000 people.
August 21, 1986:	After building up from volcanic emanations, carbon dioxide escapes from Lake Nyos, Cameroon, killing over 1,700 people.
June, 1991:	Pinatubo erupts in the Phillipines after having been dormant for four hundred years.
September-November, 1996:	Eruption of lava beneath a glacier in the Grimsvötn Caldera, Iceland, melts huge quantities of ice, producing major flooding.

truly dead and pose no risk at all, while most other volcanoes are capable of erupting centuries after their last activity.

One of those that did return to activity was a volcano of the Cascade Range in southwestern Washington, named Mount St. Helens. In 1978 scientists from the U.S. Geological Survey had predicted that this volcano would erupt again, perhaps by the end of the century. In March and April of 1980 it began to exhibit some signs of life. Seismic activity and small ash eruptions indicated that the long-sleeping giant was coming to life. Well aware of the risks it posed, government agencies began restricting access to the region and preparing evacuation plans. The media converged on the region, and there was television news coverage nearly every night.

Peculiar seismic signals, called harmonic tremors, were detected, signaling the ascent of melted rock into the upper reaches of the volcano. This magma caused the mountain to swell, increasing in size by as much as 3 feet a day. Such bulging made the slopes on the mountain steeper and thus less stable. On May 18 a moderate earthquake proved to be the last straw. A major landslide occurred, and as a huge portion of the mountain slid down, the side of the chamber of pressurized magma was exposed. A dramatic lateral blast ensued, devastating vast areas to the north in just a few minutes. This was followed by a vertical blast that transported huge quantities of ash as high as 12.4 miles (20 kilometers) into the atmosphere.

Scientists have estimated that the energy released by Mount St. Helens was the equivalent of one atomic bomb being dropped per second for nine hours. The initial blast was nearly horizontal, which had not been expected, and was far more destructive than anyone had imagined. Still, because of excellent monitoring of the developing events, cooperation between scientists and the government, and strong communication with the populace, only 60 people died.

Similar scientific work and careful monitoring were unable to avoid a calamity a few year later, in 1985, when mudflows, or lahars, from the eruption of Colombia's Nevado del Ruiz killed 23,000 people. Scientists had accurately predicted that an eruption would melt much of the glacial ice near the summit, producing huge mudflows that would flow down the river valleys toward the populated towns, including one named Armero. They also knew an eruption was imminent. As with Mount St. Helens, there had been a month of small eruptions in advance of the large one. An hour after the main eruption began authorities urged evacuation of the downstream towns, but the order to evacuate Armero was not given for another five hours. When it was given, radio communication was not established. It is likely that most of the inhabitants would have survived if effective evacuation measures had begun in a timely fashion.

No warning existed for 1,700 people in Cameroon, Africa, in 1986, when a cloud of carbon dioxide swept down on them in their sleep. Carbon dioxide enters Lake Nyos from molten rock beneath it. The lake is stratified, and most of the carbon dioxide enters the dense water near the bottom. If the water is suddenly mixed by a landslide, an earthquake, or even stiff breezes, the gas-charged water can rise to the surface, where the pressure is lower and the carbon dioxide comes out of solution. A cloud of gas, denser than air, builds up and eventually races down the valleys, killing everything in its wake by asphyxiation. Now that this hazard has been identified, efforts are underway to remove the carbon dioxide before it builds up to unstable concentrations.

The successful efforts to mitigate the effects of the eruption of Pinatubo, which occurred in the Philippines in 1991, provide hope. A series of evacuations proceeded in parallel with increasing volcanic activity. Although complicated by the arrival of Typhoon Yunya, the evacuation of more than 200,000 people undoubtedly saved a great many lives. This eruption, the third largest of the twentieth century and occurring in a densely populated area, killed only 320 people.

Otto H. Muller

---

c. 5000 B.C.E.: **Mazama**

DATE: c. 5000 B.C.E.
PLACE: Crater Lake National Park, Oregon
RESULT: 25 cubic miles of material blown out of the mountain; Crater Lake developed in 4,000-foot-deep, 5-mile-wide depression

A basic understanding of plate tectonics and the tectonic history of western North America is helpful to understand Mazama. From the surface to its center, the earth is composed of three layers: the crust, mantle, and core. The surface is subdivided into several large and small tectonic plates, each composed of

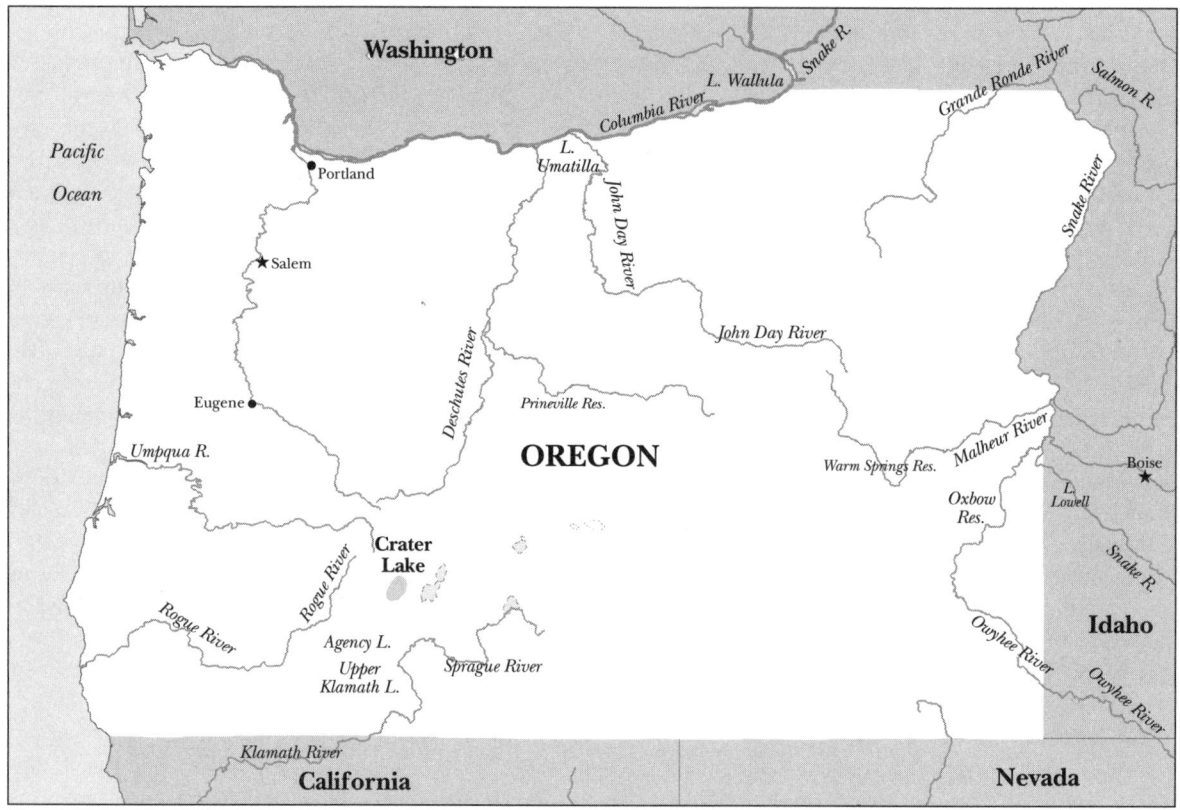

crust and the outermost layer of the mantle. Geologic forces and the plasticity of the mantle at the base of the plates result in their movement around the surface of the globe. Some plates carry continents, while others consist primarily of ocean floor. Adjacent plates either move away from one another, collide with one another, or slide past one another. Volcanic activity and earthquakes occur along all plate junctions. Collision of plates, in which one plate is forced down under the other (subducted) and is melted into the mantle, is the plate interaction most important to the creation of western North America.

The western part of North America was added to the continent as several oceanic plates subducted under its western edge. Materials scraped off the subducting plates were added to the western margin of the continent, while the leading edge of the subducting plate melted into the mantle, creating volcanic activity, sometimes miles inland from the coast.

Beginning 200 million years ago, the formations upon which Mazama was built were constructed by these processes as the Juan de Fuca oceanic plate subducted under the western edge of Oregon. At the time, the western coast of Oregon followed a diagonal line from the southwest corner to the northeast corner of the current state. The subduction created a band of volcanic mountains inland from that coastline. About 35 million years ago, the subduction zone shifted to a position parallel to the current Oregon coast. It continued to add to the continent's western boundary and eventually built the mountain range that occurs along the coast of Oregon today, the Coast Range.

At about the same time, volcanic activity farther inland buried most of eastern Oregon in layers of lava, known as the Columbian Plateau. The only surface remnants of the 200-million-year-old volcanic mountain range discussed above are the Blue Mountains in northeastern Oregon, only the tops of which protrude above the Columbian Plateau lava, and the Klamath Mountains in the southwestern corner of the state, which were west of the Columbian Plateau volcanism and escaped burial.

Before, and again at the end of, the formation of the Columbian Plateau, volcanism driven by the subducting Juan de Fuca Plate occurred along a line parallel to the coast, but well inland. The second set of volcanic mountains formed became the Western Cascades of modern Oregon. As the Coast Range was uplifted, the Willamette Valley formed between the Western Cascades and the Coast Range. All this activity was completed by about 1 million years ago, creating modern Oregon's surface geology with one dominant feature missing, the High Cascades.

A few hundred thousand years later, continued subduction of the Juan de Fuca Plate initiated development of the High Cascades, a linear range of volcanic mountains just east of the Western Cascades and just west of the Columbian Plateau. The best-known members of this mountain chain include Mounts Baker, Rainier, St. Helens, Hood, Jefferson, Shasta, and Lassen. Mount Mazama was a member of this magnificent mountain chain. Built by volcanic activity driven by the Juan de Fuca Plate and set upon older volcanic rock constructed by similar forces, Mazama was also destroyed by volcanic forces.

Mazama began forming about 75,000 years ago. It grew as lava poured out of its many conduits onto the surface and as eruptions cast materials into the atmosphere, some of which settled back on the mountain. Eventually it towered 11,000 to 12,000 feet above sea level. Then, a little more than 7,000 years ago, Mazama suffered a series of eruptions, which culminated about 6,850 years ago when so much magma (molten volcanic material from the mantle) was blown out of the mountain or drained away into some other part of the mantle that the remnant of Mazama collapsed into a great pit, or caldera. Limited volcanic activity continued for centuries, but 2,000 or 3,000 years after the climactic eruptions, water from rainfall and snowmelt began accumulating in Mazama's caldera, eventually forming Crater Lake.

Because all the events that built and destroyed Mount Mazama were prehistoric, there are no counts of the dead or reports of injuries and financial losses. Arrowheads, sandals, and other artifacts of prehistoric peoples have been found buried in the ash thrown out by Mazama's eruptions, so people were definitely affected. Presumably, animals, plants, and humans in the blast zone were killed instantaneously, and the ashfall must have had both immediate (fouling the air) and long-term (burying plants and animals and changing soil chemistry) effects on living things. The severity of those effects probably declined with distance from Mazama, but a vast area was impacted. Mazama ash fell northeast to southern British Columbia and Alberta, east to western Montana, and southeast to northern Nevada.

The historic eruption of Mount St. Helens is perhaps the best model for the effect of the Mazama blast. However, the Mazama eruption was over forty times more powerful than that of Mount St. Helens and was probably proportionally destructive. Mazama's destruction, however, also led to the creation of Crater Lake, the deepest lake in the United States (1,932 feet) and one of the most unique and scenic in the world. Because of its isolated location, the lake remains relatively pristine and absolutely charming. It is the central component of Crater Lake National Park in southern Oregon.

Carl W. Hoagstrom

FOR FURTHER INFORMATION:

Cranson, K. R. *Crater Lake: Gem of the Cascades.* Lansing, Mich.: KRC Press, 1982.

Harris, Ann G., Esther Tuttle, and Sherwood Tuttle. "Crater Lake National Park." In *Geology of National Parks.* 5th ed. Dubuque, Iowa: Kendall/Hunt, 1997.

Matz, Stephan. *The Mazama Tephra-Falls: Volcanic Hazards and Prehistoric Populations.* Anthropology Northwest 5. Corvallis: Oregon State University, Department of Anthropology, 1991.

c. 1470 B.C.E.: Thera

DATE: c. 1470 B.C.E.

PLACE: Aegean Sea

RESULT: Volcanic eruption and caldera collapse, town buried and preserved intact, possible cause of disappearance of Minoan civilization on Crete, alleged location of lost "continent" of Atlantis

The eruption of Thera (now known as Thíra) in 1470 B.C.E. has been compared in severity with the eruption in 5000 B.C.E. that formed Crater Lake, but as no written records survive, knowledge of the eruption must be deduced entirely from the geological and archaeological evidence. Judging from the pottery, archaeologists date the eruption around 1400 B.C.E. Geologists give a date of 1470 B.C.E. based on a radioactive age determination.

The volcano lies in a cluster of islands that used to be known as Santorin or Santorini. These islands form part of a convex arc of recently extinct volcanoes in the Aegean Sea, facing the Mediterranean between Turkey and Greece. Geologists describe this as a firing line where the crustal plate of Africa is plunging down beneath the crustal plate of southeastern Europe.

Prior to the 1470 B.C.E. eruption, Thera had a long and complicated volcanic history, beginning with submarine eruptions from volcanic vents lo-

cated adjacent to some bedrock islands. When ejecta from these vents reached water level, small volcanic islands appeared, which then grew together with the adjoining bedrock as eruptions continued. Ultimately this complex of overlapping volcanic cones and bedrock masses formed a circular island nearly 10 miles in diameter and with a summit that might have been as much as 1 mile high.

A period of quiescence then followed, which scientists believe lasted for many thousands of years. During this interval, fertile soils developed on the weathered volcanic rocks, lakes and marshes formed in the depressions, and vegetation appeared. Humans colonized Thera from neighboring islands, bringing with them the Bronze Age culture then prevalent in the eastern Mediterranean. The largest settlement appears to have been at ancient Akrotiri on the southern coast, a location that had a natural harbor, shelter from the strong northerly winds, and probably more rainfall than other parts of the island.

Excavations begun here in 1967 have unearthed, from beneath the mantle of volcanic debris, the most completely preserved prehistoric site in Europe. The once-thriving town of several thousand inhabitants had narrow streets; underground sewers to carry away domestic effluent; and two-, three-, and four-story homes adorned with frescoes, which are still breathtakingly fresh 3,500 years after they were first painted. In the surrounding fields, the inhabitants of the island raised sheep and goats; cultivated grapes for wine; and grew crops of lentils, split peas, and barley, from which they milled flour to make bread. Pottery discovered in the excavation indicates that the

residents maintained close trade connections with both Crete and mainland Greece.

Archaeologists have concluded that the first indication of the impending eruption was a large-scale earthquake, which caused major damage to buildings throughout the town. Then came a period of calm—perhaps several months in length—during which people began rebuilding their homes. Repairs were still in progress when the next phase of the eruption struck. This began with a fall of pellets of pumice that eventually built up a layer as much as 15 feet thick over most of the island.

By now the inhabitants of Akrotiri must have fled, taking with them whatever valuables they could carry and leaving behind the furnishings of their homes, as well as a vast assortment of pottery used for the storing, cooking, and serving of food. The absence of human or animal remains in the ruins indicates that people had time to evacuate safely. After the fall of pumice pellets came a series of minor ash and pumice falls, and then the culminating phase of the eruption: fine, white ash, with scattered basalt boulders, that blanketed the island to

An engraving from 1866 shows the eruption of Thera in the Aegean Sea, the mythic lost "continent" of Atlantis. (National Oceanic and Atmospheric Administration)

a depth of 100 feet or more. The ash is also present beneath the Mediterranean as a layer up to 7 feet thick found in core samples more than 450 miles away.

Following the ashfall—or perhaps simultaneous with it—the central part of the volcano collapsed into the underlying magma chamber, creating a huge depression in the seafloor, known as a caldera. Thera's caldera is 7 miles long and 5 miles wide and has a maximum depth of 1,575 feet. The rim of the old volcano still surrounds it in the form of three ragged islands with rocky cliffs 1,200 feet high, rising toward where the summit used to be. The volume of the collapse has been estimated at 38 cubic miles, which is about the same as the collapse at Crater Lake and more than three times the collapse at Krakatau. Tsunamis (tidal waves) were probably generated at this time, and a pumice deposit found 23 feet above sea level at Tel Aviv in Israel has been attributed to them.

About 70 miles to the south of Thera lies the island of Crete, which was the center of the highly developed Minoan civilization during the Bronze Age. Many archaeologists blame the sudden disappearance of this civilization on the eruption of Thera, citing the destructive earthquakes that accompanied the eruption, the possibility of devastating tsunamis, and the ashfalls from the volcano that could have destroyed the fertility of fields on Crete.

Thera is also cited as a possible location for Plato's famous lost "continent" of Atlantis, which he mentioned in two of his writings. He describes Atlantis as the home of a rich and powerful nation with an advanced civilization. According to him, the end of this civilization came when the island was wracked by violent earthquakes and floods and then, in the space of a single night and day, was swallowed up by the sea. This description would fit the catastrophic end of Thera perfectly.

Donald W. Lovejoy

FOR FURTHER INFORMATION:

Bullard, Fred M. *Volcanoes of the Earth.* Austin: University of Texas Press, 1992.

Doumas, Christos G. *Thera, Pompeii of the Ancient Aegean: Excavations at Akrotiri 1967-79.* London: Thames and Hudson, 1983.

Friedrich, Walter L. *Fire in the Sea: Volcanism and the Natural History of Santorini.* New York: Cambridge University Press, 2000.

79 C.E.: Vesuvius

DATE: August 24, 79 C.E.
PLACE: West coast of Italy
RESULT: More than 13,000 dead, 4 cities completely buried, 270 square miles (700 square kilometers) devastated

Vesuvius is a large stratovolcano, having a height of 4,203 feet (1,281 meters). Prior to the 79 C.E. eruption the estimated height was about 6,562 feet (2,000 meters). Mount Vesuvius is located about 93 miles south of Rome, and 4.4 miles inland from the Mediterranean coast off the Gulf of Naples. The gulf is a thriving port, being well protected by surrounding peninsulas and islands. The city of Naples was a major port of call, lying on the northern side of the gulf with the Misenum promontory making up the northern peninsula. Naples was located 7.5 miles northwest from Vesuvius. The cities of Herculaneum and Pompeii (population 20,000), which were located 4.4 and 6.2 miles, respectively, to the southwest and southeast of Vesuvius, were completely buried by the eruption. The southern side of the gulf was formed by the Sorrento Peninsula and the island of Capri, with the city of Stabiae (now known as Castellammare di Stabia) located at the tip of the southern peninsula. Stabiae, which was abandoned during the eruption, lies 9.3 miles south of Vesuvius on the coast.

The eruption of Mount Vesuvius is generally regarded as the most violent eruption in Europe during historic times. Typically, a very violent eruption of a stratovolcano only occurs after centuries of quiescence. This appears to be so for Vesuvius because the historic record of the ancient peoples in the region did not recognize Mount Vesuvius as an active volcano. The first indication of the awakening of Vesuvius was an earthquake on February 5, 63 C.E. This earthquake destroyed a portion of Pompeii and damaged the cities of Herculaneum and Naples. For the following sixteen years the area experienced intermittent earth tremors until the actual volcanic eruption began on August 24, 79 C.E.

Eyewitness Accounts. A vivid and accurate account of the eruption of Vesuvius was recorded by Pliny the Younger, who was almost eighteen years old at the time of the eruption. His account takes the form of letters to a prominent historian, and it chronicles two excursions during the eruption. The first excursion is that of his uncle, Pliny the Elder, who sailed across the bay during the early stages of the eruption. The second account chronicles Pliny the Younger's flight north from Misenum away from the eruption. Pliny the Younger and his widowed mother lived with Pliny the Elder in Misenum. Pliny the Elder was a scientist, the author of a well-known treatise on natural history, and the commander of the Roman Fleet.

At approximately 1:00 in the afternoon of August 24, Pliny the Younger's mother noticed an unusual cloud in the sky. The cloud that she observed rose in a vertical plume for several thousand feet before spreading out laterally, like a Roman pine tree spreads its branches, into the sky. The cloud was sometimes illuminated by flashes of brightness and then would turn completely dark or become lightly spotted. She brought the strange cloud to the attention of Pliny the Elder.

Pliny the Elder decided to conduct a scientific investigation of the cloud and had his crew get a light boat ready for him to sail to the source of this cloud. Just as he was ready to de-

part he received a message from a friend who lived in Resina at the foot of Vesuvius. The friend realized that Vesuvius was erupting and that her only chance of escape from the volcano was by sea. Pliny began receiving additional requests for help from other inhabitants on the coastline, and he set off to sea with a fleet of ships to rescue the frightened citizens.

As Pliny's ship drew near Resina, cinders, pieces of pumice, and fragments of burned rock from the exploding volcano fell onto the deck of the ships. Pliny observed that the shore was inaccessible, as fragments of rock and cinders were piling up on the beach, making it impossible to reach the citizens of Resina. Pliny was forced to turn southeast to the coastal town of Stabiae, where his friend Pomponianus lived. He found his friend anxious and frantic to

escape Stabiae, but the onshore winds made escape by ship impossible at that time. Pliny felt that Stabiae was far enough away from the volcano to be safe, and he assured Pomponianus of their safety and that they would have ample time to escape if danger was imminent. Pliny then decided to bathe, eat dinner, and to sleep.

As night came the citizens of Stabiae could see tall, broad flames glare out from several locations near the top of Vesuvius. During the night, conditions on Stabiae worsened, with a heavy fall of ash and pumice. When the building began to sway and shake from the eruption tremors, Pomponianus and his companions felt that the time had come to abandon the city. They decided to flee to the beach and attempt to escape by sea. They woke Pliny and tied pillows on their heads with napkins in order to protect themselves from falling volcanic debris as they made their way to the shore. They arrived at the shore, having found their way in the blackness with lit torches. Even though it was well after sunrise, the dark ash clouds continued to block all light from the sun. When they reached the shore they found that the wind was still blowing from the north, continuing to make leaving by sea impossible.

Pliny the Elder, who was overweight, began to feel ill. He lay down on a sheet that had been spread on the beach. Shortly thereafter, strong winds and flames appeared nearby, accompanied by a strong odor of sulfur. Pliny's companion began to flee in panic southward down the beach, and as Pliny the Elder struggled to get up he collapsed and died. It is clear in his letters that Pliny the Younger assumed the sulfurous fumes from the volcano overcame his uncle.

Pliny the Younger also chronicled the encounter that he and his mother went though at Misenum.

Misenum was located on the opposite side of the Bay of Naples from Stabiae, making it upwind from the volcano and thereby less affected by it. Earthquakes shook the city of Misenum all night, and by 6 in the morning the volcanic ash was so thick that it partially obstructed the sun.

Pliny and his mother decided to flee the city in chariots. They were joined by chaotic mobs of frightened people. Pliny the Younger and his mother took solace in the open country, feeling that they were safe from the falling buildings in the city. However, around 8:30 A.M. the land was ravaged by a series of strong earthquakes. The tremors were so bad that the shaking kept moving the chariots, which they tried to stabilize with stones against the wheels on the level ground. They observed frequent flashes of light in the dark, ash-laden cloud that was sweeping toward them. The sea became very turbulent and receded so much that sea creatures were stranded on the beaches; then, minutes later, the sea would crash forcefully back over the beach.

Two victims at Pompeii were immortalized in plaster almost two thousand years after being covered by volcanic ash from the eruption of Vesuvius in 79. (Library of Congress)

Pliny the Younger and his mother moved farther into the open country as the black sky seemed to reach down and envelop the sea. The island of Capri and the promontory of Misenum were no longer visible. Frightened for her son's safety and knowing that he could move faster without her, Pliny the Younger's mother urged him to go ahead without her. Pliny refused to leave her, and they traveled on slowly in the thick darkness. As visibility became worse, they heard the panicked screams of men, women, and children who had lost sight of their loved ones; other people were praying or crying in fear. The ash began to snow upon the people so thickly that they had to stand up and shake it off in order to not be buried by it.

Many hours later, daylight began to show though the ash clouds. As the air began to clear and Pliny could once again see across the bay to Vesuvius, he noticed that the smooth cone had become merely a stump. Fields that had been formerly lush with green trees and farmlands were now a gray sea of ash.

Scientific Analysis and Pliny's Narrative. Pliny the Younger's account of the eruption of Mount Vesuvius proved to be so clear and concise that all similar eruptions are now classified as "Plinian" in honor of him and his uncle. The normal sequence of events in a Plinian (violently explosive) eruption are now well understood and correlate well with aspects of Pliny's narrative.

Plinian eruptions are preceded by a slightly less violent explosion that clears the vent and allows the Plinian eruption to proceed. The eruption of Vesuvius began when the rising magma encountered water and exploded early in the morning of August 24. It was this initial explosion that frightened Pliny's friend at Resina. She sent word to Pliny some 5 miles away via a messenger, who arrived shortly after Pliny the Younger's mother saw the eruption cloud for the Plinian eruption, which began at 1:00 in the afternoon.

A Plinian eruption typically produces three types of deposits, which can be expelled multiple times. The first to form is usually an air-fall deposit that rains down from the initial explosion column. The individual particles fall independently of the other particles around them. The deposit produced, surprisingly, has the smaller particles on the bottom with larger particles occurring higher in the deposit. The larger fragments of pumice and accidental rock are often blown higher in the initial blast. The thickness of an air-fall deposit is largely controlled by the local winds.

After three days, the Vesuvius eruption of 79 C.E. produced nine different air-fall layers.

The second type of deposit in a Plinian eruption is ash flow. An ash flow begins with an initial blast called a base surge. This base surge moves at hurricane velocities (usually greater than 108 feet per second) and often will defoliate trees without charring the branches. The deposit left by this surge is surprisingly thin, usually only an inch thick. Although thin, this material is distinct because it displays ripple marks and dune structures. The Vesuvius eruption produced seven surge layers. When one of the later surges reached Pompeii the buildings that were not already buried were knocked flat.

Overlying the surge layer are the main deposits of the ash flow, which can be tens of feet thick. Ash flows can result from either avalanching of near-vent material because of explosion tremors or gravitational collapse of the eruptive ash column above the vent. An ash flow usually follows an initial air-fall eruption, when the radius of the vent has been enlarged or some of the pent-up gas has been released. Pliny's description corresponds to ash flows formed by both avalanches and cloud collapse. Six ash-flow layers were generated during the three days of the eruption of Vesuvius.

Ash flows can move incredibly fast, at speeds of 197 feet (60 meters) per second or 124 miles (200 kilometers) per hour. They can reach distances of 1,242 miles (100 kilometers) from the vent. They have sufficient momentum that they can cross ridges that are 2,297 feet (700 meters) high at a distance of 181 miles (50 kilometers) from the volcano. The great distance of travel is due to the particles still dissolving gas. Although the explosion at the vent releases the pent-up gas, the droplets of liquid take longer to release their dissolved gases.

Once moving, the flows trap and heat surrounding air as they glide down the slope. The high gas content in the flow makes the mixture behave like a fluid, and it flows with virtually no internal friction and, often, little, if any, ground friction—it flows on its own carpet of gas. It can reach speeds that approximate the velocity of free-falling objects, when the slope is taken into consideration. An ash flow that contains larger blocks of incandescent volcanic fragments (often with a diameter of a few feet or more) is called a glowing avalanche, or nuée ardente.

A cloud of ash and steam usually rises and expands above the glowing avalanche. The flow itself closely follows canyons and valleys as it moves downslope, similar in behavior to a snow avalanche. The cloud, however, is not deflected by topography, and it rolls onward over ridges and valleys, following a considerable distance behind the flow. The description that Pliny the Younger gives of the cloud overtaking the chariots near Misenum is a classic description of the ash-steam cloud of a glowing avalanche. An ash flow must have moved out across the water in the Gulf of Naples; because they ride on their own carpet of gas they do not need to have a solid surface beneath them.

Volcanic tremors (earthquakes) that displace the seafloor can cause tidal waves, or tsunamis. When ground displacement occurs a considerable distance off the coast, the water at the shoreline will recede entirely from the beach before coming back on the land as an enormous wave. Pliny's description of the Misenum sequence of an earthquake, followed by a tsunami, followed by the engulfing cloud of ash, corresponds to the normal sequence of explosive base surge and ash flow with an accompanying ash-steam cloud.

Accounts vary as to the destructive nature of the ash-steam cloud that hovers over the ash flow. In one historical case, the cloud was so hot and violent that the cloud alone destroyed an entire town and killed all the residents, while the ash flow followed a nearby stream valley and entirely missed the town. In another well-documented account, a geologist on a high ridge reported watching an ash flow sweep down the valley below him before the cloud enveloped him. He reported that there was an enormous thickness of ash in the swirling air and a very strong, almost overpowering odor of sulfur. This corresponds well to the events that are associated with the death of Pliny the Elder.

Most of the ash flows in the Vesuvius eruption were probably generated by the repeated thrusting and collapsing of the eruption column. Pliny's mother described the form of an eruption column that is classic in a Plinian eruption. The lower part is a straight vertical column, while the upper part branches out horizontally in gradually increasing distances with increasing height. The upper portion of the cloud has the appearance of an inverted cone. The lower column is propelled by gas thrusts as the gases are released from the volcanic vent. The upper cloud is propelled by convective thrusts due to the heating and rising of the air above the volcano.

A cloud's height can be calculated easily after the eruption by looking at the deposits of the ash flows. A sloping energy line exists that starts at the boundary between the upper and lower clouds and descends at a 30-degree angle to the ground. The energy line touches the ground at the distant end of the longest ash flow. Calculations based upon the ash flows from Vesuvius indicate that the eruption column was about 18.6 miles (30 kilometers) high.

Another interesting aspect of a Plinian eruption is the gradual change of color in pumice (a volcanic glass) erupting from the vent; starting out white, the pumice gradually grows darker in color as the eruption goes on. Prior to the eruption the magma in a chamber will change its composition slowly, over long periods of time. The upper regions of the chamber become very low in the element iron; the higher the content of iron, the darker the magma's color. When an eruption occurs the first lava erupted is from the upper regions of the chamber and is white in color, whereas after the eruption has gone on for some time the magma comes from lower in the chamber and is gray from the higher iron content.

At Mount Vesuvius white pumice erupted from the vent at a rate of 5,000 to 80,000 tons every second. The white pumice eruption is thought to have lasted seven hours. The white pumice, which erupted first, came from magma at the top of the chamber. It was followed by gray pumice, which originated further down in the chamber. Some scientists feel that the gray pumice, which fell on the evening of August 24, erupted from the volcano at 150,000 tons per second.

Last, it is common for a Plinian eruption to conclude with the collapse of the summit region. When sufficient magma is expelled from the chamber a large void will exist below ground, and the overlying rocks of the volcano are not sufficiently strong to support the weight of the summit area. The collapse can invert the topography around the top of the volcano. The eruption of Vesuvius expelled 247,202 cubic feet (7 cubic kilometers) of magma, and after the eruption had concluded, Pliny reported that the mountain was merely a "stump" of its former shape.

Geological and Archaeological Analyses. Quarries and construction in the region of Mount Vesuvius have exposed more than a dozen areas where the deposits of the eruption can be studied in detail. Geological and archaeological research have allowed the history of the region to be determined to a minute-by-minute level of accuracy.

The city hit hardest by the eruption was Pompeii, which was founded in 600 B.C.E. Distribution patterns of the air-fall deposits show that northwesterly winds prevailed during the eruption. These winds blew ash and pumice directly onto the city of Pompeii for almost eighteen hours, burying it under 9.8 feet (3 meters) of volcanic fragments. Some of the townspeople began to leave their homes when the heavy weight of the ash, cinders, and bombs from the eruption caused the collapse of numerous roofs and killed some of the inhabitants. Making matters worse, an ash flow spewing clouds of pumice and dust collapsed downward from the eruption column and flowed into the town at about 7:30 A.M. on August 25 (almost twenty-four hours after the eruption began). The surge flattened most of the second stories of the taller buildings (the air-fall deposits already covered the ground to a depth that covered the first floor).

Survival in the violent surge was impossible; all the residents perished in the hot blast of gas and dust. It is estimated that 2,000 people were still alive in the town when the surge hit. They were all killed within a minute. This was the fourth of six surge deposits that came from the volcano. Another surge deposit swept over the town only five minutes later. This fifth surge and ash flow carried all the way to the outskirts of Stabiae.

The sixth and last surge and ash flow was released at 8 A.M. on August 25. It was the largest and was caused by widening of the vent at the summit of the volcano. As the vent increased its diameter the eruption lost some of it force, and the existing cloud collapsed down toward the volcano. This ash flow reached Stabiae and was probably responsible for the death of Pliny the Elder. Another branch of the same ash flow swept across the waters of the Gulf toward Misenum, 20 miles away, and was recorded by Pliny the Younger.

After the eruption, the town of Pompeii and the surrounding region was a wasteland of ash. It was so devastated that there seemed to be no option but to abandon the area. The tephra, or volcanic debris, from the eruption covered hundreds of square miles, and it buried several small settlements near Pompeii, which remain buried today.

It was not until 1595 that some of the remains of Pompeii were found during construction of an aqueduct. Some coins and pieces of a marble tablet, which contained some writings about Pompeii, were found at that time. This led to the rediscovery of the forgotten city. In the seventeenth and eighteenth centuries many wealthy post-Renaissance families in Europe became interested in ancient objects of art, and Pompeii became a favorite site for uncovering statues, jewelry, and other ancient treasures. The diggings took place haphazardly, without any thought to the preservation of the city or its culture. Ravaging and pillaging took place all through the excavated areas. In the nineteenth century people realized the historical and cultural significance of Pompeii, and more coordinated and scientific methods were used in excavating the abandoned city. Many acres of the town have been excavated and are open to the public.

The archaeological excavation found uneaten food laid out on tables in some of the Pompeiian homes, leading scientists to believe that normal life continued in Pompeii until the very last second. The bodies of people killed in the disaster are quite unique, as they were quickly buried in the accumulating ash and cinders from the eruption; when rain fell on the ash, the substance formed a cement around the bodies, making molds. Some of these molds perfectly preserved facial expressions and the patterns and textures of the clothing. Nineteenth century excavators poured plaster of Paris into the molds and were able to produce three-dimensional casts of the people and animals killed. Almost 2,000 skeletons were found with their hands or cloths over their mouths, trying to protect themselves from searing, lethal gases of the surge or from breathing the ash and dust particles of the air-fall deposits.

The city of Herculaneum was located closer to Vesuvius on its western flank and had a population of about 5,000. Unlike Pompeii, which was destroyed mostly by the accumulation of air-fall tephra over a two-day period, Herculaneum was obliterated in minutes by a surge and ash flow at 1:00 in the morning of the 25th. The town had been spared from the thick fallout of the white pumice because the wind had blown the air-fall deposits to the south, toward Pompeii. However, the very first of Mount Vesuvius's six ash flows hit the town and buried it under more than 65.6 feet (20 meters) of volcanic material. Some buildings were demolished by the force of the surge; others were simply buried in ash and pumice from the ash flow.

In addition, an avalanche of mud passed over

Herculaneum, filling every crack and crevice in the buildings and sealing the city so completely that it became a lost city. When this material became impacted and hardened it became a true volcanic rock, making it very difficult to excavate. Excavation of Herculaneum has uncovered approximately eight city blocks. At first it appeared that many of the townspeople had escaped because very few bodies were uncovered. However, further exploration in what was an area of the beach during Roman times has yielded hundreds of skeletons, found huddled in buildings supported by arched chambers, which were opened to the beach and housed boats and fishing tackle. It appears that the townspeople fled to the beach, thinking that the arched chamber would protect them from the volcano.

In summary, the 79 C.E. eruption of Vesuvius was the first volcanic eruption ever to be described in detail. The eruption lasted about twenty-five hours, the last nineteen of these hours being a sustained highly explosive eruption. About 141,258 cubic feet of volcanic material was erupted and blanketed 116 square miles around the volcano. Vesuvius lost 2,297 feet of its summit area to the final collapse. More than 13,000 people were killed, and most of the farms, villages, towns, and cities in the vicinity vanished. Modern archaeological excavation of the towns of Pompeii and Herculaneum continue to reveal details of the last few minutes of life for the residents of this region.

Dion C. Stewart and Toby R. Stewart

FOR FURTHER INFORMATION:

Frances, Peter. *Volcanoes: A Planetary Perspective.* New York: Oxford University Press, 1993. A book written for general readers who have little background in geology. Gives detailed accounts of both the eruption and the volcanic deposits made by the eruption.

Scarth, Alwyn. *Volcanoes: An Introduction.* London: University College of London Press, 1994. Gives excellent descriptions of many eruptions, including Vesuvius; contains translations of Pliny the Younger.

Sigurdsson, H., S. Carey, W. Cornell, and T. Pescatore. "The Eruption of Vesuvius in A.D. 79." *National Geographic Research* 1, no. 3 (1985): 332-387. The article that unraveled the minute-by-minute sequence of events associated with the eruption.

c. 186: Taupo

DATE: c. 186
PLACE: New Zealand
VOLCANIC EXPLOSIVITY INDEX: 6+
RESULT: Created caldera

Located in the center of North Island, New Zealand, a caldera is evidence that a volcano erupted on this site; the attractive lake disguises its violent origins. Scientists investigated fossilized insects and used radiocarbon dating of ash layers to determine when Taupo erupted before the Maoris settled the island. Using such data, experts believe that most eruptions occurred approximately twenty-five times between 9850 B.C.E. and 180 C.E.

One of these eruptions resulted in the island being covered with ash in what volcanologists have hypothesized may have been the most tremendous volcanic eruption in the past two thousand years. Before the eruption, scientists estimate that Taupo was 300 feet high and expelled 1 million cubic yards of detritus per second. Experts state that debris from the eruption remains on the island and in the stratosphere in the form of ash and gas. The expulsion of such an immense amount of matter so rapidly and with great force transformed the island into a dead zone. The absence of human inhabitants limited casualties to native fauna. Lake Taupo was formed when the volcano cone exploded and water pooled inside the cavity. After the Maoris arrived on North Island, they named the volcano Taupo, meaning "cloak."

Elizabeth D. Schafer

FOR FURTHER INFORMATION:

Lentz, Harris M., III. *The Volcano Registry: Names, Locations, Descriptions, and Histories for over 1500 Sites.* Jefferson, N.C.: McFarland, 1999.

Simkin, Tom, and Lee Siebert. *Volcanoes of the World.* 2d ed. Tucson, Ariz.: Geoscience Press, 1994.

Smith, Roger. *Catastrophes and Disasters.* Edinburgh, Scotland: Chambers, 1992.

1169: Etna

DATE: 1169
PLACE: Sicily, Italy

An etching of Etna viewed from the ruins of Taormina, Italy. (Library of Congress)

VOLCANIC EXPLOSIVITY INDEX: 2
RESULT: More than 15,000 dead

Positioned above the site where the African and European Plates collide, Etna has been active for centuries. With a height of almost 11,000 feet, Etna, the tallest volcano in Europe, is considered one of the oldest-known volcanoes, and its frequent eruptions have been well documented throughout history. Biblical stories, myths, and legends mention Etna, a name that was derived from the Phoenician word *attuna*, which means "furnace." Ancient peoples believed the god Vulcan's forge was located in Etna.

When Etna erupted in 1169, more than 15,000 people were killed in Catania, located 18 miles from the volcano's base. Alarmed by the loud explosion, peasants rushed to the local cathedral, where monks attempted to use St. Agatha's veil to halt the lava flow because tradition said such a miracle happened during an eruption in the year 251. One side of the volcano's cone exploded, and lava spewed from fissures,

covering Catania and its residents. Some structures were flattened by the weight of the lava, while others burned after being ignited by ash. During the eruption, an earthquake shook Messina in Sicily. People ran to the beach, hoping to escape from both the lava and the tremors, but were inundated by a tsunami, which flooded the town.

Survivors rebuilt along the fertile land surrounding Etna. Some volcanologists believe that the 1169 damage was actually caused by a tectonic earthquake and that accounts confused other periods of volcanic activity with this event.

Elizabeth D. Schafer

FOR FURTHER INFORMATION:

Chester, D. K., A. M. Duncan, J. E. Guest, and C. R. J. Kilburn. *Mount Etna: The Anatomy of a Volcano.* London: Chapman and Hall, 1985.

Romano, R., and C. Sturiale. "The Historical Eruptions of Mt. Etna." *Memorie Società Geologica Italiana* 23 (1982): 75-97.

1362: Öræfajökull

DATE: 1362
PLACE: Iceland
VOLCANIC EXPLOSIVITY INDEX: 5
RESULT: 200 dead

Records indicate that Öræfajökull has erupted twice. The first eruption occurred in 1362 in southeastern Iceland, where geological conditions are conducive to volcanic activity. Standing 6,950 feet tall, Öræfajökull is considered Iceland's highest summit, with an apex at the northwestern rim known as Hvannadalshnúkur. With a 3-mile-wide crater, it is also that country's largest volcano. Vatnajökull, the country's biggest glacier, is located north of the volcano. Volcanologists have designated Öræfajökull a postglacial stratovolcano. It was originally known as Knappafell, or "knobby mountain."

The 1362 eruption was tremendous, devastating the Litlahérad coastal district surrounding the volcano. The catastrophic explosion spewed massive amounts of tephra, suggested to be the most ash emitted from an Icelandic volcano, and triggered flooding of adjacent territory when the ice cap in the volcano's crater melted. Approximately 200 people died, as did livestock grazing in fields. Buildings were buried in debris drifts, and pumice thrown into the ocean impeded ships. The eruption darkened the skies for several days. During the next century, settlers erected communities near Öræfajökull, which had been renamed using Icelandic terms meaning "wasteland" and "glacier." Monastery accounts and folklore narrated the volcano's history. A less powerful eruption occurred in 1727.

Elizabeth D. Schafer

FOR FURTHER INFORMATION:
Scarth, Alwyn. *Vulcan's Fury: Man Against the Volcano.* New Haven, Conn.: Yale University Press, 1999.
Thorarinsson, Sigurdur. "The Öræfajökull Eruption of 1362." *Acta Naturalia Islandica* 2 (1958): 1-98.

1586: Kelut

DATE: 1586
PLACE: Java, Indonesia
VOLCANIC EXPLOSIVITY INDEX: 5
RESULT: 10,000 dead

A stratovolcano with an elevation of 5,679 feet above sea level, Kelut is located in eastern Java. That island is the site of many volcanoes because seismic conditions and plate movement underneath Indonesia produce both earthquake and volcanic activity. Not much is known about Kelut's earliest eruptions. Chinese records indicate that the volcano first erupted in the year 1000. European traders gained access to some of the islands in the sixteenth century, including Portuguese and Dutch merchants who controlled the region's spice trade. These entrepreneurs and ship crews noted that they had observed volcanic eruptions, seen evidence of ash and lava afterwards, or heard native accounts of volcanic activity.

According to such reports, the 1586 eruption resulted in the deaths of 10,000 residents in nearby settlements. The volcano forcefully expelled huge stones and gushing waves of sulfur, which eyewitnesses said appeared to be on fire. Ash expelled into the atmosphere blocked out sunshine for three days. Mudflows may have inundated farms and leveled dwellings within miles of the volcano.

During the past two hundred years, Kelut has erupted fifteen times. Volcanologists designated Kelut's twentieth century eruptions some of its most destructive explosions and warned of future dangers from the active volcano.

Elizabeth D. Schafer

FOR FURTHER INFORMATION:
Simkin, Tom, and Lee Siebert. *Volcanoes of the World.* 2d ed. Tucson, Ariz.: Geoscience Press, 1994.
Smith, Roger. *Catastrophes and Disasters.* Edinburgh, Scotland: Chambers, 1992.

1591: Taal

DATE: 1591
PLACE: Luzon, Philippines
VOLCANIC EXPLOSIVITY INDEX: 3
RESULT: Thousands dead

The earliest history of Taal is enigmatic. Located in Lake Taal in the southern part of Luzon, the main island of the Philippines, this volcano stands 1,312 feet above sea level and has been labeled a stratovolcano. Records state that the volcano's first known eruption occurred in 1572, and at least thirty-four eruptions have been documented since then. The 1572 Taal eruption was also the first volcanic explosion chronicled in the history of the Philippines, happening eight years after the Spanish assumed control of those islands.

Volcanic activity in the Philippines is often caused by movement of the Philippine Sea Plate and the Eurasian Plate. Few facts were preserved regarding the 1591 eruption. Thousands of residents—indigenous farmers and laborers and Spanish traders and officials—probably died when mudflows covered their villages. Accompanied by an earthquake triggered by the explosive volcano, the eruption also caused a tsunami, which washed over coastal communities, and people and structures were dragged into the sea. Volcanologists describe Taal as a Peléan type of volcano because its crater and sides explode during eruptions, nearby ground fractures, the volcano produces more ash and steam than lava, and occasionally hurricane-strength winds accompany eruptions. Taal's 1911 eruption is considered to be its most destructive, and descriptions of damage and casualties during that explosion as well as characteristics of Peléan volcanoes can be used to reconstruct possible events and results of the 1591 eruption.

Elizabeth D. Schafer

FOR FURTHER INFORMATION:

Davis, Lee. *Natural Disasters: From the Black Plague to the Eruption of Mt. Pinatubo.* New York: Facts on File, 1992.

Simkin, Tom, and Lee Siebert. *Volcanoes of the World.* 2d ed. Tucson, Ariz.: Geoscience Press, 1994.

1631: Vesuvius

DATE: December 16, 1631
PLACE: Italy
VOLCANIC EXPLOSIVITY INDEX: 4
RESULT: 4,000 dead

Described as Italy's most lethal volcano, Vesuvius stands 4,200 feet above the Bay of Naples and is activated by the northward movement of the African Plate beneath the Eurasian Plate. The first documented eruption occurred in 79 C.E., when nearby Herculaneum and Pompeii were obliterated by steaming ash. More than forty eruptions happened after that, and the 1631 eruption was notable because it was the first time lava spewed by Vesuvius caused massive deaths.

Because five hundred years had passed since Vesuvius had produced a significant eruption, southern

An artist's rendering of Vesuvius and the Bay of Naples, with lava flowing down the volcano. (Library of Congress)

Italy had developed into a prosperous agricultural region by 1631. The mineral-rich volcanic ash fertilized crops, and Vesuvius's slopes were covered with vegetation and vineyards. Farmers grazed their herds in fields around the volcano. Few residents remembered the volcano ever posing a threat. When the eruption began, explosions reverberated in the valley, and a pink cloud loomed over Vesuvius, darkening the sky. Burning ashes and cinders pummeled people living in villages built on the volcano's sides. Residents were incinerated as they rushed downhill, seeking safety.

The next morning, fissures opened and lava poured from the volcano's cone and coated numerous towns. When it reached the shore, the lava boiled the water and produced steam. Later that night, mud poured on Naples and flooded towns around Vesuvius, including Resina, which stood over the ruins of Herculaneum. The mudflow was so thick and swift that it created a 1-mile strip of land into the bay. Vesuvius continued to expel lava and explode throughout the night, shaking the land. Ash and pumice drifts 6 feet deep coated Naples. Incessant rain showers during the next month exacerbated already-miserable conditions as Vesuvius continued to erupt. Vesuvius's cone decreased by 51 feet, and its crater doubled in size during the 1631 eruption. At least 4,000 people were killed, and some estimates suggested that as many as 18,000 people might have perished. Thousands of livestock died. Volcanologists believe that the 1631 eruption began a cycle of volcanic activity that concluded in 1944.

Elizabeth D. Schafer

FOR FURTHER INFORMATION:

Davis, Lee. *Natural Disasters: From the Black Plague to the Eruption of Mt. Pinatubo.* New York: Facts on File, 1992.

Scarth, Alwyn. *Vulcan's Fury: Man Against the Volcano.* New Haven, Conn.: Yale University Press, 1999.

1669: Etna

DATE: March 11, 1669
PLACE: Sicily, Italy
RESULT: More than 20,000 dead, 14 villages destroyed, 27,000 homeless

For three days in March of 1669, earthquakes shook Sicily's Mount Etna. Such seismic activity was not unusual. People who lived on the slopes of Sicily's highest mountain had experienced them frequently before, but they were aware that such tremors often preceded what they most feared: a devastating and catastrophic eruption of the smoldering volcano, whose frequent eruptions date to prehistoric times.

On March 11, 1669, the worst fears of the peasants who lived near the towering mountain became realities. Etna exploded in a series of eruptions stronger than anyone then alive could remember. The sky blackened as ash from the explosions rose toward the stratosphere. Debris fell over the eastern half of Sicily, even making its way well up into the southern Italian province of Calabria, across the Strait of Messina.

The eruptions were not confined to a single day. Two weeks after the first series, on March 25, the sky was still ominously dark and ash was falling everywhere. A wide river of molten lava was flowing relentlessly down Etna's south side, glowing orange in the subdued atmosphere. It hungrily devoured everything in its path, wiping out 14 villages in its course. Directly in the volcano's path lay the seaside town of Catania, whose population of about 20,000 people made it one of Sicily's largest cities. It lay just over 18 miles (29 kilometers) from Mount Etna's summit, and its sole protection against the oncoming lava flow were the city's defensive walls that dated back to the feudal era and surrounded the city.

These walls would prove useless against an adversary as enormous as the river of fire now lumbering toward the ill-fated town. By the time Etna returned to a quiescent state, it had reduced Catania's population from 20,000 to about 3,000. Another 3,000 people who lived in villages on Etna's slope died, mostly from suffocation, as the noxious fumes from the hot lava engulfed them.

A Towering Giant. On a clear day, nearly everyone in eastern Sicily can see Mount Etna, rising almost 11,000 feet above sea level and towering over the plain below. The highest active volcano in Europe, it dominates the eastern half of Sicily, which is Italy's largest island. Sicily is situated to the east and slightly to the south of Italy's toe. A mere 2 miles across the Strait of Messina directly across from the town of Reggio in Calabria, Sicily was in prehistoric times a part of Italy's land mass. As the oceans rose, however, it came to be separated from what is now the lower part of the Italian mainland.

ing to human life as the one that occurred in 1669.

Mount Etna covers a substantial geographical area, a total of some 460 square miles. The Catania plain that lies below it is the largest lowland in Sicily. Around Etna's base runs a railway. Small villages and terraced fields in which vegetables are grown still dot its slopes. From the cone of the volcano, the area around which is usually covered with snow, rise thin ribbons of smoke. Travelers ascending the mountain first pass through cultivated areas, where produce grows well in the rich, volcanic soil available on the mountain's lower two-thirds. At higher levels, pine forests extend almost to the top of the mountain, where the landscape becomes more bleak and where strong winds usually blow and snow often falls.

The Looming Threat. Rumblings that occurred on Etna on March 8, 1669, alerted those who lived on its slopes to a possible eruption. Those who lived in villages below the volanco's summit had frequently experienced such rumblings in the past. They

Mount Etna, named *Aitne* by the ancient Greeks and *Aetna* by the ancient Romans, is classified as a greenhouse type of volcano. Such volcanoes constantly belch gases out into the atmosphere, Etna sending more than 25 million tons of carbon dioxide into the air above it every year. These emissions contribute significantly to the phenomenon that has been termed "global warming." The typical products of the greenhouse type of volcano, besides carbon dioxide, are methane, ozone, nitrous oxides, chlorofluorocarbons, and water vapor.

The first recorded eruptions of Etna occurred in 475 B.C.E. They were noted and described in some detail by both the poet Pindar and dramatist Aeschylus. Since then, over two hundred eruptions have been documented, but none so great or so devastat-

were concerned by them but generally were not unduly alarmed. They had survived such seismic activity before and had continued to grow their produce in the fertile soil that Etna's previous eruptions, dating to prehistoric times, provided for them.

It was three days before Etna finally erupted, with a force that had hitherto not been equaled by any of the previous recorded eruptions. Lava flows began to course down the mountain, hot rivers of molten lava that obliterated everything in their paths. Pine forests were quickly leveled. Small settlements disappeared, often with most of their inhabitants. Suddenly, the south side of the huge mountain turned into a cauldron of intensely hot molten rock that slid down its sides and seemingly could be stopped only by the Ionian Sea, which stretched out to the east of

Catania. The flow continued for over two weeks, resisting every effort to thwart it.

Trying to Divert the Lava Flow. Desperate peasants whose dwellings were in villages that lay in the path of the great river of fire now advancing down the mountain had no defenses against the fiery onslaught. The air they breathed was poisoned by the fumes that rose from the volcano. Most fell helpless upon the ground, unable to breathe. They generally were dead before the molten lava reached their prostrate bodies.

The city of Catania, which from ancient times had endured Mount Etna's eruptions, was now threatened as it seldom had been before. Although some of the city's populace took the few possessions they could carry and tried to flee before the lava reached the city walls, a stalwart group of 50 men, led by Diego de Pappalardo, sought to divert the course of the flow. These men donned cowhides soaked in water to protect them from the incredible heat that the flow produced.

Carrying long iron rods, picks, and shovels, they ascended the mountain toward the slowly moving flow, which by now had created a well-defined central channel down the mountainside. High walls of cooling lava lined the channel through which the molten material was flowing. Working under extremely adverse conditions in air that was almost too polluted and fetid to sustain life, this stalwart band of brave men hacked an opening in one of the high lava walls, thereby diverting the flow of material down the central channel through which the molten lava was heading relentlessly toward Catania.

This heroic act of civil engineering appeared to be working. The flow in the central channel diminished considerably as a new channel formed outside the break in the lava wall. Keeping that break open, however, became a major problem. The Catanians were jubilant at the seeming success of their prodigious efforts, but their jubilation was short-lived.

Almost immediately, a group of 500 desperate citizens from the village of Paterno, noticing that the newly created flow was aimed directly at their village, assaulted the Catanians, forcing them away from the breaches in the lava walls that they had created with such great difficulty. Soon these breaches filled in, and the molten lava resumed its inexorable course down the central channel.

A consequence of the assault of the infuriated people from Paterno on the Catanians was the issuance of a royal decree stating that in the future no one was to interfere with the natural flow of molten lava from a volcano. Anyone doing so was to be held responsible for any damage that ensued from such efforts. This decree, in effect since 1669, was officially ratified in the nineteenth century by the Bourbon monarchy then in command. It was in force until 1983, when another eruption caused advanced engineering efforts to be employed in order to minimize the damage. The law was suspended so that these efforts could be carried out.

Actually, opening vents in the lava wall was not a viable long-term solution to controlling the lava flow during the 1669 eruption. At an elevation of about 2,600 feet, vents had been opened by the Catanians near the village of Nicolosi, but within less than twenty-four hours, the lava had flowed on and destroyed another village in its path about 2 miles farther downhill.

A century after the 1669 eruption, the devastating event was still prominently discussed by scientists. Sir William Hamilton, who published what is considered the first modern work on volcanology, *Campi Phlegraei*, in 1776, visited Mount Etna before he wrote his book, drawn there by what he had heard about the devastation in 1669.

The Destruction of Catania. Thirty-three days elapsed between the eruption of Etna on March 11, 1669, and the arrival of its lava flow at the feudal gates of Catania. Remarkably few of the city's citizens had fled as the oncoming lava approached the venerable walls, which accounts for the loss of some 17,000 Catanians in the disaster that followed.

Typically, as a lava flow proceeds on its downward journey, it builds up lava walls on both sides but also creates a lava roof, resulting in a tube through which the molten material passes. The result is that the lava stays blisteringly hot because it is not exposed to the outside air, which would reduce its temperature. This is what happened as the lava from the 1669 eruption flowed toward Catania and the sea.

This eruption was not the first to devastate Catania. In 1169, an estimated 15,000 Catanians were lost when an eruption of Mount Etna coincided with a huge tectonic earthquake shortly before the eruption that leveled most of the buildings in Catania and left many people dead in the rubble long before the lava flows reached the city. This disaster was on a scale comparable to that of the 1669 eruption.

R. Baird Shuman

FOR FURTHER INFORMATION:
Chester, D. K., A. M. Duncan, J. E. Guest, and C. R. J. Kilburn. *Mt. Etna: The Anatomy of a Volcano.* Stanford, Calif.: Stanford University Press, 1985. The most comprehensive study of Etna available, this carefully researched volume presents a panoramic view of seismic activity and eruptions on Mount Etna from the earliest times to the date of publication. An invaluable resource.
Planet Earth: Volcano. Alexandria, Va.: Time-Life Books, 1982. This volume is aimed specifically at the general reader. Its coverage of the 1669 eruption of Mount Etna is cursory, but the book provides an excellent background and is enhanced by excellent pictures.
Scarth, Alwyn. *Volcanoes: An Introduction.* College Station: Texas A&M University Press, 1994. This introduction to volcanology is thorough and generally useful, although Scarth does not specifically mention the 1669 eruption of Mount Etna. As background for the field, this volume represents an excellent starting point.
Sparks, R. S. J. *Volcanic Plumes.* New York: John Wiley & Sons, 1997. In order to understand the kinds of cones that characterize the volcano atop Mount Etna, it is helpful to read parts of this rather specialized book. Despite its specific focus, it can be read meaningfully by nonspecialists.
Sutherland, Lin. *The Volcanic Earth: Volcanoes and Plate Tectonics, Past, Present, and Future.* Sydney: University of New South Wales Press, 1995. Sutherland offers considerable detailed information about volcanoes generally and presents several useful pages of information specifically about the 1669 eruption of Mount Etna.
Wohletz, Kenneth. *Volcanology and Geothermal Energy.* Berkeley: University of California Press, 1992. It is difficult to understand the force of a volcanic eruption without realizing the kinds of geothermal energy that build up in the cones prior to an eruption. This book, although quite specialized, explains well and in detail the dynamics of volcanic activity.

1683: Timor

DATE: 1683
PLACE: Indonesia
RESULT: Hundreds dead

Because it is situated in an isolated region of southeastern Indonesia, few facts have been recorded about Timor's early volcanic history. The remote island has endured periods of political strife and civil war almost as violent as the volcanoes and earthquakes that devastate the region. Volcanologists have collected statistics about Indonesian eruptions and have determined that a 1683 volcanic explosion near Serua, off the coast of the main island of Timor in the Banda Sea, occurred. This stratovolcano expelled waves of fiery stones, which caused several hundred human casualties. More information is known about other Indonesian volcanoes such as Mount Tambora, which erupted in 1815, enabling historians and scientists to speculate what might have happened during the 1683 eruption and how it impacted the global climate.

Elizabeth D. Schafer

FOR FURTHER INFORMATION:
Lentz, Harris M., III. *The Volcano Registry: Names, Locations, Descriptions, and Histories for over 1,500 Sites,* Jefferson, N.C.: McFarland, 1999.
Simkin, Tom, and Lee Siebert. *Volcanoes of the World.* 2d ed. Tucson, Ariz.: Geoscience Press, 1994.

1741: Cotopaxi

DATE: 1741
PLACE: Ecuador
VOLCANIC EXPLOSIVITY INDEX: 2
RESULT: 1,000 dead

Rivaling Argentina's Cerro Ojos del Salado as the tallest active volcano, Cotopaxi stands more than 19,000 feet above sea level. The volcano's name is derived from native terms that mean "shining mountain." Designated a stratovolcano, Cotopaxi's first documented eruption occurred in 1534, and volcanologists hypothesize from ash-layer evidence that the volcano has experienced at least fifty explosions since then. Records provide few details about the 1741 eruption. Later eruptions suggest what may have occurred in that year: The eruption probably melted the ice cap on Cotopaxi's summit, feeding mudflows that accumulated snow as they moved down the volcano's slopes. Lava and debris were detected at far as

60 miles away from the volcano's base. An earthquake might have accompanied the eruption.

Elizabeth D. Schafer

FOR FURTHER INFORMATION:
Dyott, G. M. "The Volcanoes of Ecuador, Guideposts in Crossing South America." *National Geographic,* January, 1929, 49-93.
Lentz, Harris M., III. *The Volcano Registry: Names, Locations, Descriptions, and Histories for over 1,500 Sites.* Jefferson, N.C.: McFarland, 1999.

1759: Jorullo

DATE: September 29, 1759
PLACE: Mexico
VOLCANIC EXPLOSIVITY INDEX: 3
RESULT: Hundreds dead

Attaining an elevation of 10,397 feet, Jorullo emerged from a ravine on a hacienda in what later was named the Michoacán-Guanajuato volcanic field. A cinder-cone volcano, Jorullo is located with about one thousand similar volcanoes in a 77-square-mile area of southwestern Mexico. Before Jorullo erupted, tremors rocked the region. Eyewitnesses smelled sulfur and heard noises from the earth that sounded like cannon shots. When the volcano began erupting, it quickly enlarged, rising to a height of 820 feet within six weeks. Initially, mud, sand, and water flowed down Jorullo's slopes, and the volcano spewed ash. Then the volcano emitted only lava and ash. The first lava was mostly composed of basalt, with silica becoming more frequent in other flows.

Jorullo continued erupting for a period of fifteen years, then ceased being active. The volcano set a record for the longest duration of a cinder-cone eruption. During these eruptions, four minor cinder cones were produced by the volcano, and lava hardened on land within 3.5 square miles of Jorullo. The crater was widened to 1,640 feet at its widest dimension.

Elizabeth D. Schafer

FOR FURTHER INFORMATION:
Gadow, H. *Jorullo: The History of the Volcano of Jorullo and the Reclamation of the Devastated District of Animals and Plants.* London: Cambridge University Press, 1930.
Luhr, James F., and Tom Simkin. *Paricutin: The Volcano Born in a Mexican Cornfield.* Phoenix: Geoscience Press, 1993.

1766: Mayon

DATE: October 23-28, 1766
PLACE: Luzon, Philippines
VOLCANIC EXPLOSIVITY INDEX: 3
RESULT: 2,000 dead

A view of Mayon erupting in 1968. (National Oceanic and Atmospheric Administration)

The most active volcano in the Philippines, Mayon has been featured in that country's mythology, traditions, and oral history. Many superstitious peoples believed the volcano was possessed by evil spirits and made sacrifices in attempts to appease them. Standing approximately 8,000 feet high near Albay Gulf on Luzon Island, Mayon is considered by volcanologists to exemplify prototypal characteristics of a conically shaped stratovolcano. The volcano's first recorded eruption occurred in 1616, and it has erupted more than forty times since then. The 1766 eruption was especially catastrophic because a typhoon hit Luzon soon after Mayon stopped spewing debris. As a result, rain inundated the volcanic detritus, and mudflows raged through villages.

During what has been declared Mayon's second-worst eruption, more than 2,000 people died. Preliminary lava oozing from the cone warned residents that the volcano was about to erupt. After the initial explosion, Mayon spewed lava for four days, creating flows as wide as 200 feet within a 20-mile area. Rivers of mud hindered survivors' efforts to locate victims and dispose of their bodies. The villages of Camalig, Daraga, and Tobaco were obliterated. For two months, Mayon continued to emit ash and, occasionally, lava.

Elizabeth D. Schafer

FOR FURTHER INFORMATION:

Davis, Lee. *Natural Disasters: From the Black Plague to the Eruption of Mt. Pinatubo.* New York: Facts on File, 1992.
Simkin, Tom, and Lee Siebert. *Volcanoes of the World.* 2d ed. Tucson, Ariz.: Geoscience Press, 1994.

1772: Papandayan

DATE: August 11-12, 1772
PLACE: Java, Indonesia
VOLCANIC EXPLOSIVITY INDEX: 3
RESULT: 3,000 dead

During Papandayan's first recorded eruption, the northwestern side of the cone collapsed, triggering an avalanche of debris. The 8,700-foot-tall stratovolcano exploded, spewing scalding lava on nearby settlements. The volcano disintegrated into a lake of sulphurous lava. Approximately 3,000 people died in 40 villages located on the volcano's sides. Most victims disappeared when ash and lava inundated the area; causes of death included severe burns, suffocation, and drowning. Buildings and livestock also vanished in a region 15 miles long by 6 miles wide.

Prior to the eruption, residents had prospered, building towns near plantations on Papandayan's fertile slopes. Although people occasionally saw steam and sulfur deposits from the volcano, they were unaware of Papandayan's explosive potential and were unprepared for the eruption.

Elizabeth D. Schafer

FOR FURTHER INFORMATION:

Blong, Russell. *Volcanic Hazards: A Sourcebook on the Effects of Eruptions.* San Diego: Academic Press, 1984.
Davis, Lee. *Natural Disasters: From the Black Plague to the Eruption of Mt. Pinatubo.* New York: Facts on File, 1992.
Ritchie, David. *Encyclopedia of Earthquakes and Volcanoes.* New York: Facts on File, 1994.
Simkin, Tom, and Lee Siebert. *Volcanoes of the World.* 2d ed. Tucson, Ariz.: Geoscience Press, 1994.

1779: Sakurajima

DATE: December, 1779-January, 1780
PLACE: Japan
VOLCANIC EXPLOSIVITY INDEX: 4
RESULT: 300 dead

Rising 3,663 feet above sea level in Kagoshima Bay on Kyūshū Island, this stratovolcano's first chronicled eruption occurred in the year 708. That explosion began a cycle of frequent eruptive activity. The volcano mostly produced minor spurts of lava from its summit, creating the Aira Caldera. Powerful eruptions, however, have proven deadly. Beginning in the winter of 1779, Sakurajima erupted heavy flows of lava, which inundated nearby towns. The volcano triggered a tsunami that flooded coastal villages, drowning inhabitants who could not flee from the giant waves. Sakurajima ejected large amounts of pumice during its month-long eruption in 1779. So much debris was erupted into the sea that reports told how people could walk 23 miles from shore on the accumulated pumice that formed a rocky landmass. This volcano experiences hundreds of eruptions annually, mostly showering ash on adjacent areas but occasionally resembling conditions similar to those of the 1779 and 1780 explosions.

Elizabeth D. Schafer

FOR FURTHER INFORMATION:

Davis, Lee. *Natural Disasters: From the Black Plague to the Eruption of Mt. Pinatubo.* New York: Facts on File, 1992.

Simkin, Tom, and Lee Siebert. *Volcanoes of the World.* 2d ed. Tucson, Ariz.: Geoscience Press, 1994.

1783: Asama

DATE: 1783
PLACE: Honshū, Japan
VOLCANIC EXPLOSIVITY INDEX: 4
RESULT: 1,377 dead

Rising as high as 8,364 feet in Honshū, this complex volcano is composed of three connected parts named Asama-yama, Kurohu-yama, and Jama-yama. A newer stratovolcano that has two craters rests on a shield volcano that balances on another stratovolcano, which formed first. Records indicate Asama first erupted in the year 685 and has produced explosions of varying degrees of intensity since then. Some religious penitents identified the volcano's rim as a place for prayer, and they died during sudden eruptions.

In 1783, at least 1,377 people were killed because of a violent eruption. Asama expelled mudflows that covered villages at the base of the volcano. Lava rivers as long as 425 miles were formed. Mud accumulated in the Agatsuma River, damming the water that surged into settlements.

Approximately 1,300 houses were washed away, and over 1,000 inhabitants vanished in the floodwater. A small group climbed into a temple to escape drowning. The volcano forcefully ejected huge chunks of stone, as sizeable as 42 feet in diameter, which crushed dwellings and people. Asama also erupted so much ash and dust that the debris remained in the sky and obstructed sunlight from reaching the ground. Cold, rainy weather worsened conditions, and a prolonged famine occurred as a result of the volcano's damage to agricultural resources.

Elizabeth D. Schafer

FOR FURTHER INFORMATION:

Kuno, Hisashi. *Catalogue of the Active Volcanoes of the World Including Solfatara Fields: Part XI, Japan, Taiwan, and Marianas.* Rome: International Association of Volcanology, 1962.

1783: Laki

DATE: June, 1783-February, 1784
PLACE: Southern Iceland
RESULT: Gaseous volcanic haze and its effects killed over two-thirds of the nation's livestock and caused a year of famine, resulting in 10,000 dead

Iceland is an island nation that sits astride the Mid-Atlantic Ridge in the north Atlantic Ocean. As the ridge and seafloor spread apart here at the rate of 0.8 inch (2 centimeters) per year—at the rift where the North American Plate is drifting westward and the Eurasian Plate is drifting eastward—Iceland is also on top of a hot spot of magma (molten rock) in the mantle below. It is thus one of the world's most volcanically active locations, on an island plateau formed primarily of basaltic lava rock. It is a land of volcanic fire and glacial ice, which is regularly reminded of the power and challenge of natural events—volcanoes, earthquakes, glacial flooding, and severe weather.

There are over 150 volcanoes in Iceland that have been active since the last ice age—ending about ten thousand years ago—and about 30 of them have erupted since settlement of the island, primarily by Vikings of northern Europe, eleven hundred years ago. Iceland has an eruption, on the average, every five years or so.

The 1783 Eruption. It was here in 1783 that the largest lava eruption and flow of humankind's recorded history occurred. This geologic event devastated the agricultural environment, resulted in an ensuing famine in which over one-fifth of the nation's people died, and even altered the climate of the Northern Hemisphere for a couple of years. That latter consequence—the effect of volcanism on climate change—was speculated on for the first time then in 1784 by Benjamin Franklin, then was seriously studied and explained after the 1980's, two hundred years later.

In early June of 1783, there were a number of small earthquakes in the region of the volcano Laki in southern Iceland. Its crater peak was undistinguished, rising only about 656 feet (200 meters) above its surroundings. Trending up to the northeast was a volcanic zone of fractured earth's crust where the plate-tectonic spreading of Iceland was inexorably occurring. About 30 miles (50 kilometers) to the northeast, now under the large Vatnajökull ("Vatna glacier"), was the occasionally active volcanic region called Grimsvotn.

On June 8, fissures from Laki and extending to the southwest began erupting lava, which flowed down the Skafta River Valley. There was little explosive venting of ash. In the area, fairly remote and sparsely settled, the event was termed the Skaftareldar ("Skafta fires"). Then fissuring and erupting lava appeared from Laki toward the northeast, with the lava flowing down the Hverfisfljot River Valley. Lava flowed southward as far away as 37 miles (60 kilometers) before cooling enough to congeal and then solidify to rock. The zone of fissures and the 110 to 115 erupting volcanic craters and vents extended 15 miles (25 kilometers) in total, with Mount Laki about in the middle.

By the time of the cessation of lava flows, eight months later in February, 1784, the Lakagigar ("Laki craters") eruption had produced a volume of basaltic lava of 434,368 cubic feet (12.3 cubic kilometers), mostly erupted in June and July, plus 10,594 cubic feet (0.3 cubic kilometers) of ashfall. The latter is solid-rock equivalent; the actual volume was about 30,017 cubic feet (0.85 cubic kilometers). That volume of lava is the largest of any eruption in recorded history. The volume of ashfall, while only a small part of this event, is itself about the same as the ashfall from the Mount St. Helens eruption in Washington State in 1980.

The lava flow covered 217 square miles (565 square kilometers), to an average depth of 72 feet (22 meters). That volume of lava would fill Yosemite Valley, California, to a depth of 984 feet (300 meters), or cover Washington, D.C. (61 square miles), to a depth of 256 feet (78 meters), or the state of Delaware (2,000 square miles) to a depth of 21 feet (6.3 meters). The Icelandic lava field from Lakagigar is now a jagged, jumbled plain of lava. It is mostly covered by a growth of lichens and moss, the only vegetation that can establish itself even after a couple of centuries because of the northern-latitude climate and slowness of rock weathering to soil there.

Aftereffects. The massive eruption itself caused no deaths and little damage. However, it did produce the most severe environmental effects, and threat to health and life, that Iceland has experienced in its one thousand years of documented human history.

The huge lava outpouring of the summer of 1783 was accompanied by some ashfall, which could be carried farther afield to affect crops and grasslands for grazing. More significant was the enormous amount of gas vented. The gases included carbon dioxide and water vapor, as well as unusually large quantities of the toxic gases sulphur dioxide, hydrogen sulfide, chlorine, and fluorine. It is estimated from chemical analysis of the volcanic products that 130 million to 490 million tons of sulphur dioxide and 5 million tons of fluorine were released into the atmosphere. Sulphur dioxide reacts with water vapor to produce sulphuric acid, a prime component of acid rain. Ejected high in the atmosphere, the result can be a sulphuric acid aerosol of tiny droplets.

As a result of the gas-rich eruption, a bluish haze or "dry fog" enveloped Iceland and drifted eastward over northern Europe for the winter months. In Iceland, the combination of volcanic ash and gases stunting grass and ruining pastures and fluorine contaminating the grass caused grazing livestock to be both starved and slowly poisoned. Half the nation's cattle and three-quarters of the horses (used for transportation) and sheep (used for wool and meat) perished. The loss of livestock, the damage to croplands, the short growing season in this northerly climate, and a severe winter combined to produce a devastating famine in the country. In the next couple of years, 10,000 people died—over one-fifth of the total population of 49,000—from starvation and disease, as well as the effects of the haze.

As a postscript to the great "haze famine" of 1783-1784, it might be noted that almost a century later, in 1875, Mount Askja—northeast of Laki in central Iceland—had an explosive eruption. Its 6.2-mile-diameter crater showered 70,629 cubic feet of ash over much of eastern Iceland. The resulting near-famine prompted many Icelanders to immigrate to the United States and Canada.

Long-Term and Global Effects. There was to be a more widespread, and unexpected, consequence of the massive 1783 eruption; it was a precursor to modern discussions of atmospheric conditions and global climate change. The sulfur-dioxide-produced acidic aerosol "dry fog" that reached Europe was more annoying than poisonous there, but it was present for much of the summer and fall of 1783. While it and some ash were carried over Europe by the prevailing winds—giving Scotland the "Year of the Ashie" and dropping ash dust in Italy, 2,000 miles (3,200 kilometers) from Iceland—haze was spread as far as central Russia.

Benjamin Franklin was American representative to France and the court of King Louis XVI from 1778 to 1785. An author, printer, statesman, diplomat, philosopher, scientist, and contributor to the cause of the recent American Revolution and its subsequent government, he noted the prevalent blue haze and the abnormally cold and severe winter in Europe in 1783-1784. He speculated on a possible link between the "smoke" (fine ash and haze), perhaps being from the Iceland eruption the preceding year, and the cooling effect it might have on weather. He wrote a paper, "Meteorological Imaginations and Conjectures," which was subsequently delivered for him at a learned conference in Manchester, England, in December, 1784. It included the following:

During several of the summer months of the year 1783, when the effect of the sun's rays to heat the Earth in these northern regions should have been greater, there existed a constant fog over all Europe, and a great part of North America. The fog was of a permanent nature; it was dry . . . [The rays of the sun] were indeed rendered so faint in passing through it, that when collected in a burning glass [lens] they would scarce kindle brown paper. . . . The cause of this unusual fog is not yet ascertained . . . whether it was the vast quantity of smoke, long continuing to issue during the summer from Hecla in Iceland [Mount Hekla, a well-known volcano not erupting at the time, is just to the west of the Laki area], and that other volcano which arose out of the sea near that island [there had been a new volcano erupt and emerge from the sea off southwest Iceland in the spring of 1783], which smoke might be spread by various winds over the northern part of the world is yet uncertain.

The scenario now understood is that some major volcanic eruptions can eject enough sulphur dioxide to produce a sulphate (sulphuric acid) aerosol layer into the stratosphere, where it can reside for months or even a few years. This acts to absorb, or backscatter, the warming radiation from the sun, so there is less heating of the underlying troposphere—our zone of weather. This can result in global climate cooling in at least a belt of latitudes by a couple of degrees for many months, and thus in cooler local weather. Volcanic ash can also help to screen out incoming solar radiation, but except for an extraordinary explosion (such as dust from a large meteorite impact on Earth) it usually does not rise high enough or last in the stratosphere long enough to have a significant climate effect.

The Lakagigar eruption may be the most dramatic example in historical time of this connection between volcanically induced atmospheric change and the resulting climate cooling. In addition to the pronounced cooler winter in Iceland and much of Europe, the winter temperature during 1783-1784 in the eastern United States was 7 degrees Fahrenheit below the 225-year average there.

Similar detectable, but more modest, climate-cooling effects—by a degree or two for a couple of years, from ash and gas producing a high-altitude "mist"—were noticed for the eruptions of Krakatau in Indonesia in 1883, El Chichón in southern Mexico in 1982, and Mount Pinatubo in the Philippines in 1991.

It is believed that the magma for the Laki eruption had migrated and flowed laterally through crustal cracks opened by the ongoing tectonic rifting as Iceland spread apart astride the Mid-Atlantic Ridge. The origin was probably the large active hot spot under the volcano Grimsvotn, under the Vatnajökull glacier. If the great 1783 Laki eruption had been localized under the glacier, the eruption would have been much more explosive—producing more ash as well as the gas—and would have created great ice melting and massive flooding.

In early October, 1996, there was a modest subglacial eruption near Grimsvotn, not far from the Laki eruption site. This one lasted for two weeks, caused subsidence of the overlying glacier over a fissure zone about 4.4 miles (7 kilometers) long, and produced a glacier burst of subglacial meltwater that flooded out and caused $15 million in damage to bridges, roads, and utility systems. The previous similar event there occurred in 1938.

Robert S. Carmichael

FOR FURTHER INFORMATION:
Ballard, R. D. *Exploring Our Living Planet.* Washington, D.C.: National Geographic Society, 1983.
Decker, R., and B. Decker. *Volcanoes.* New York: W. H. Freeman, 1981.
Sigurdsson, H. "Volcanic Pollution and Climate—the 1783 Laki Eruption." *EOS/Transactions of the American Geophysical Union*, August 10, 1982, 601-602.
Thorarinsson, S. "The Lakagigar Eruption of 1783." *Bulletin Volcanologique* 33 (1969): 910-927.

1790: Kilauea

DATE: 1790
PLACE: Hawaii
VOLCANIC EXPLOSIVITY INDEX: 4
RESULT: 100 dead

The Hawaiian name of Kilauea symbolizes that the volcano continues to spread, describing its extensive lava flows. Located on the southeastern portion of the Hawaiian chain of volcanoes, Kilauea, a shield volcano, attained a height of 4,009 feet on the main island of Hawaii. A significant portion of the volcano is underneath the ocean. Although radiocarbon dating suggests that Kilauea has existed since prehistoric

times, the first eruption records are from 1750. Forty years later, Kilauea violently exploded, creating a caldera that remains visible two hundred years later. The caldera holds a pit crater known as Halemaumau.

At least 100 people, mostly soldiers and their families who were traveling to new farmland, died in 1790 when flowing streams of pumice and lava poured onto land adjacent to the volcano. One of the world's most active volcanoes, Kilauea is constantly emitting lava, spewing approximately 16 feet (5 meters) of lava into the ocean every three seconds from one of its vents since the 1980's. The volcano is coated by solidified lava that it has erupted during the past one thousand years.

Elizabeth D. Schafer

FOR FURTHER INFORMATION:
Lentz, Harris M., III. *The Volcano Registry: Names, Locations, Descriptions, and Histories for over 1,500 Sites.* Jefferson, N.C.: McFarland, 1999.
Simkin, Tom, and Lee Siebert. *Volcanoes of the World.* 2d ed. Tucson, Ariz.: Geoscience Press, 1994.

1792: Unzen

DATE: February 10, 1792
PLACE: Japan
VOLCANIC EXPLOSIVITY INDEX: 2
RESULT: 14,500 dead

An immense complex volcano composed of several linked lava domes sprawling over the Shimabara Peninsula in Kyūshū, Unzen has an elevation of 4,457 feet. The volcano is located east of Nagasaki, historically a densely populated area of Japan, and its first recorded eruption occurred in 1663. Approximately 14,500 died in 1792 when Unzen's Mayuyama lava dome exploded and the volcano collapsed, triggering both a tsunami and an avalanche. The powerful sea waves inundated communities in Higo and Amakusa Provinces, pulling people to sea, where they drowned. The volcano was accompanied by an earthquake, shattering structures that withstood the floodwater, landslides, and lava flows. Some of the land sunk into the bay, while volcanic debris also produced new islands and ridges in the East China Sea. Unzen was dormant for almost two hundred years after the 1792 eruption.

Elizabeth D. Schafer

FOR FURTHER INFORMATION:

Davis, Lee. *Natural Disasters: From the Black Plague to the Eruption of Mt. Pinatubo.* New York: Facts on File, 1992.

Kuno, Hisashi. *Catalogue of the Active Volcanoes of the World Including Solfatara Fields: Part XI, Japan, Taiwan, and Marianas.* Rome: International Association of Volcanology, 1962.

1794: Tunquraohua

DATE: 1794
PLACE: Riobamba, Ecuador
VOLCANIC EXPLOSIVITY INDEX: 2
RESULT: 40,000 dead

Known as the "Black Giant," Tunquraohua rises 16,475 feet above the Ecuadorian landscape. The volcano's name means "throat of fire" in the native Quechua Indian language. A stratovolcano, Tunquraohua's slopes are usually coated with snow because of its high elevation. The volcano's crater measures approximately 600 feet wide. Records indicate that Tunquraohua first erupted in 1641 and produced seventeen explosions in the following centuries.

Few details of the 1794 eruption have been preserved. Accounts of more recent volcanoes suggest what may have occurred in 1794. Tunquraohua's eruptions are often accompanied by earthquakes, which shake the nearby city of Baños, where thermal springs exist. Spewing basaltic lava, Tunquraohua also produces large clouds of steam, ash, and sulphurous gas, which stagnate over the area and interfere with weather patterns and agricultural production. Showers of glowing debris and mudflows threaten local populations, which are evacuated when possible in modern times to prevent massive casualties like the estimated 40,000 people who were killed by the 1794 eruption. Tunquraohua's proximity to Ecuador's biggest volcano, Chimborazo, as well as Cotopaxi, sometimes results in its eruptions being overshadowed by the activity of those volcanoes.

Elizabeth D. Schafer

FOR FURTHER INFORMATION:

Dyott, G. M. "The Volcanoes of Ecuador, Guideposts in Crossing South America." *National Geographic,* January, 1929, 49-93.

Simkin, Tom, and Lee Siebert. *Volcanoes of the World.* 2d ed. Tucson, Ariz.: Geoscience Press, 1994.

1812: La Soufrière

DATE: April 27, 1812
PLACE: St. Vincent Island, Lesser Antilles
VOLCANIC EXPLOSIVITY INDEX: 4
RESULT: More than 1,000 dead

Named for the French term for a sulfur mine, La Soufrière stratovolcano rises slightly more than 4,000 feet on the northern part of St. Vincent Island in the West Indies. Another volcano with the same name is located on Guadeloupe, 180 miles north of St. Vincent. The St. Vincent La Soufrière volcano has caused more damage than its counterpart. Although radiocarbon evidence suggests that La Soufrière has existed since 2380 B.C.E., volcanologists considered it to be one of the newest volcanoes on St. Vincent. Records indicate that indigenous peoples told explorer Christopher Columbus about the volcano's existence in 1498.

The first documented eruption in 1718 caused extensive destruction and death. The 1812 eruption resembled the devastation of the earlier explosion, and more than 1,000 were killed when their dwellings collapsed or they were struck by debris. This eruption was significant because it created a lake inside the volcano's crater. Filled with sparkling blue water, the lake was formed with 800-feet-tall walls that retained the lake's contents. Survivors of the 1812 eruption worried they might starve because they thought that their fields had been ruined. The volcanic ash, however, fertilized the soil. Abundant crops were grown, and the bountiful land supported its residents for many years. The 1812 volcanic lake became a popular tourist attraction in the West Indies.

Elizabeth D. Schafer

FOR FURTHER INFORMATION:

Fiske, R. S., and H. Sigurdsson. "Soufrière Volcano, St. Vincent: Observations of Its 1979 Eruption from the Ground, Aircraft, and Satellites." *Science* 216 (1982): 1105-1126.

Simkin, Tom, and Lee Siebert. *Volcanoes of the World.* 2d ed. Tucson, Ariz.: Geoscience Press, 1994.

1814: Mayon

DATE: February 1, 1814
PLACE: Luzon, Philippines
VOLCANIC EXPLOSIVITY INDEX: 4
RESULT: More than 2,200 dead

Mayon, known as the Philippines's most frequently erupting volcano, has been incorporated into that country's culture. Natives personified Mayon as a malevolent being and offered sacrifices in an effort to mitigate damage from eruptions. Volcanologists have declared Mayon one of the most structurally perfect volcanoes on Earth. With an elevation nearing 8,000 feet, the attractive cone of Mayon is located near Albay Gulf on the island of Luzon. Two of the volcano's earliest known eruptions in 1616 and 1766 were disastrous because of mudflows and typhoon conditions. The 1814 eruption has been labeled the worst.

Approximately 2,200 people died during the 1814 eruption, in which pumice and lava caused most of the fatalities. Earthquakes rocked the region before the island erupted. An ashen cloud covered most of the island, blocking out light. Less lava poured from the crater than in the 1766 eruption; the volcano expelled great quantities of hot sand and stones, which were thrust as high as the stratosphere before raining down on the Philippines. Damage included buildings crushed by debris and floods that occurred because rivers were dammed by mudflows. Fiery ash ignited trees, and some palm trees were completely buried by ash, which accumulated as deep as 30 feet. The villages of Badiao and Cagsauga were leveled.

Elizabeth D. Schafer

FOR FURTHER INFORMATION:

Davis, Lee. *Natural Disasters: From the Black Plague to the Eruption of Mt. Pinatubo.* New York: Facts on File, 1992.

Simkin, Tom, and Lee Siebert. *Volcanoes of the World.* 2d ed. Tucson, Ariz.: Geoscience Press, 1994.

1815: Tambora

DATE: April 5-11, 1815
PLACE: Sumbawa, Indonesia
VOLCANIC EXPLOSIVITY INDEX: 7
RESULT: 92,000 dead

Tambora is located on Sumbawa Island near the eastern end of the Indonesian archipelago. For at least five thousand years prior to its great 1815 eruption, the volcano had exhibited only minor activity. This prolonged dormant period, however, set the stage for what is, to date, the world's largest known historic eruption and also its most deadly. Tambora, even today, is relatively remote and was much more so when the eruption took place. Nevertheless, a chronology of the events of that time have been pieced together by correlating the volcanic layers deposited during the eruption with eyewitness observations as reported by Sir Thomas Raffles, who in 1815 was the Dutch East Indies' temporary lieutenant governor.

Tambora began showing signs of life in the form of minor rumblings and earthquakes several years prior to the 1815 eruption, but the events that quickly led to the cataclysmic eruption began with an

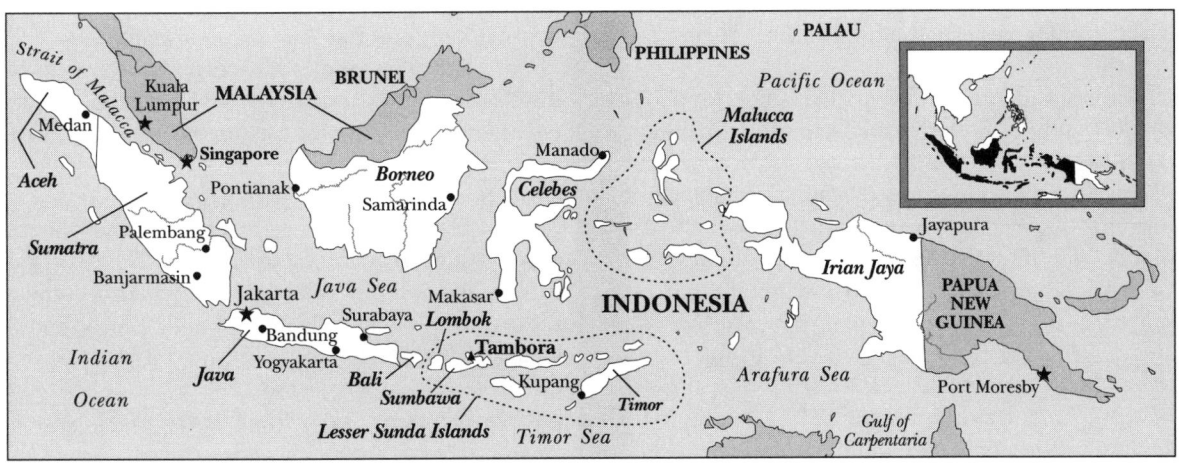

enormous explosion on the evening of April 5, 1815. The eruption produced a column of ash that raced upward 20.5 miles (33 kilometers) into the atmosphere. Although this was only a preliminary stage to the main eruption and it lasted just two hours, more ash was produced than during the entire Vesuvius eruption of 79 C.E., which buried Pompeii and Herculaneum.

Following this brief, violent outburst Tambora fell relatively silent until the evening of April 10, 1815, when, at about 7 P.M., an extremely violent explosion sent a plume of ash to an altitude of about 27 miles (44 kilometers). Observers reported columns of flame rising to a very great height from the crater and a rain of ash and pumice. As the violent eruption continued, the throat of the volcano became increasingly cleared of debris and grew wider, allowing it to eject ever-increasing amounts of ash, pumice, and rock.

By about 10 P.M., three hours into the climactic event, the volcanic plume became so loaded that its density exceeded that of the surrounding atmosphere. At this point parts of the volcanic cloud began collapsing under their own weight to produce an incandescent cloud known as an ignimbrite flow. Survivors of the eruption reported this phase of the eruption as appearing like a flowing mass of liquid fire, and high winds attending the ignimbrite flows destroyed building and uprooted trees. The ignimbrite plunged down the volcanic slopes in all directions and out across the sea, where it interacted with water to produce steam explosions. These detonations hurled fine ash upward, dispersing it widely and plunging the region into two to three days of darkness. Ignimbrite flows entering the sea are also believed to be responsible for the mild tsunamis of from 3.3 to 13 feet (1 to 4 meters) in height that were recorded in the eastern Indonesian area during the eruption.

Tambora continued in violent eruption for about twenty-four hours with repeated explosions that were heard up to 1,616 miles (2,600 kilometers) away. About 1.8 million cubic feet (50 cubic kilometers) of magma was expelled from beneath Tambora and exploded into the atmosphere as some 5.3 million (150 cubic kilometers) of porous ash and pumice. As a result, the unsupported central part of the volcano collapsed, reducing the volcano's height from an estimated 14,107 feet (4,300 meters) to 9,383 feet (2,860 meters), and forming a caldera 3.7 by 4.4 miles (6 by 7 kilometers) in diameter and more than 3,609 feet

(1,100 meters) deep. Tambora's caldera is similar in size to Crater Lake, Oregon, but it contains only a small lake that comes and goes with the seasons and vents that still send vapors up along the caldera walls.

About 92,000 people, the greatest loss of any volcanic eruption to date, are estimated to have died on Sumbawa and the nearby island of Lombok. At least 10,000 people are believed to have perished directly from the volcanic blast and from the tsunamis it generated. Most of these fatalities occurred on the island of Sumbawa, where ignimbrite flows covered all but the western coast of the island. An estimated additional 38,000 people on Sumbawa and 44,000 on nearby Lombok died as a result of starvation and disease following the eruption. Moreover, the lingering effects of Tambora's fine ash and sulfur dioxide are believed to have had an affect on global weather patterns during the following year or two.

As with the caldera-forming eruption of Krakatau sixty-eight years later, spectacular sunsets and prolonged twilights were noted as far as England in the months following the Tambora eruption. The stars appeared less bright, and sunlight was dimmed to such an extent that sunspots were visible to the naked eye, even when the sun was well above the horizon. The geographic location of Tambora, only slightly south of the equator, allowed its eruption cloud to be dispersed in the stratosphere above both the Southern and Northern Hemispheres. Although an examination of temperature records and sunlight reduction suggests that the eruption of Tambora reduced global average temperatures in 1816 by less than 34 degrees Fahrenheit (1 degree Celsius), much colder weather was experienced in eastern Canada and New England. The summer of 1816, in fact, brought such misery to parts of North America and Europe that it became known as the Year Without a Summer.

Snow fell as far south as western Massachusetts in June of 1816, and northern New England experienced frost in July and again in August. Warm-weather birds were killed, and crops, particularly corn, were lost to the freezing weather. Cold, wet weather also affected Western Europe, where there were crop failures and famine. Ireland's famine led to a typhus outbreak, which by 1819 had become a European epidemic afflicting 1.5 million people and killing 65,000. The European wine harvest was unusually late, food was in short supply, and there was public violence related to food shortages. Those who could pursued indoor activities during the dank, dark, and stormy summer of 1816, but they too were affected. In Geneva, Switzerland, for example, Lord Byron produced a gloomy poem entitled "Darkness," while his acquaintance Mary Wollstonecraft Shelley worked on the famous gothic horror novel *Frankenstein* (1818).

Eric R. Swanson

FOR FURTHER INFORMATION:
Francis, Peter. *Volcanoes: A Planetary Perspective.* New York: Oxford University Press 1993.
Stommel, Henry, and Elizabeth Stommel. *Volcano Weather: The Story of 1816, the Year Without a Summer.* Newport, R.I.: Seven Seas Press, 1983.
Stothers, Richard B. "The Great Tambora Eruption of 1815 and Its Aftermath." *Science,* June, 1984, 1191-1198.

1822: Galung Gung

DATE: October 8 and 12, 1822
PLACE: Java, Indonesia
VOLCANIC EXPLOSIVITY INDEX: 5
RESULT: 4,000 dead

A stratovolcano 7,111 feet tall, Galung Gung is located on the western end of the island of Java in Indonesia's belt of volcanoes. The volcano's name is derived from indigenous terms referring to the glowing clouds of ash produced by eruptions. The 1822 eruption was the first documented explosion of Galung Gung. Because the volcano had not been active, natives were unprepared for the ensuing disaster. Two eruptions occurred. At first, the volcano spewed boiling mud down its slopes into the surrounding villages.

The nuées ardentes covered at least 6.2 miles (10 kilometers). Four days after these lethal mudflows covered the area around Galung Gung, the volcano's cone burst because it could not withstand internal pressure caused by expanding gases and molten magma. During these eruptions, at least 4,000 people were killed in approximately 144 settlements, which were obliterated. Ash rose into the sky as high as several miles. Later eruptions further fragmented the volcano, and a caldera formed at the site of the disintegrated cone.

Elizabeth D. Schafer

FOR FURTHER INFORMATION:
Lentz, Harris M., III. *The Volcano Registry: Names, Locations, Descriptions, and Histories for over 1,500 Sites,* Jefferson, N.C.: McFarland, 1999.
Simkin, Tom, and Lee Siebert. *Volcanoes of the World.* 2d ed. Tucson, Ariz.: Geoscience Press, 1994.

1835: Cosigüina

DATE: January 22, 1835
PLACE: Nicaragua
VOLCANIC EXPLOSIVITY INDEX: 5
RESULT: Hundreds dead

A shield volcano in northwestern Nicaragua, Cosigüina stands 1,598 feet high. Located on a peninsula along the Pacific coast near other active volcanoes, this immense volcano's oval-shaped crater is more than 1 mile in diameter and 1,640 feet in depth. Cosigüina's crater was created during the 1835 eruption, when the volcano's cone collapsed. Considered historically to have been the most intense eruption in the Western Hemisphere, the explosion spewed ash, pumice, and debris over Central America and even dusted Mexico City and Jamaica, hundreds of miles to the north and east. The volcanic cloud prevented sunshine from penetrating within a 100-mile area surrounding the volcano.

Because records did not document previous eruptions, people believed that Cosigüina was extinct and did not prepare for such disaster. Two days before it erupted, the volcano emitted a cloud of white steam. Eyewitnesses in El Salvador reported seeing the volcanic plume, which became yellow and crimson in color, before strong tremors shook the ground. Ash and pumice the size of eggs showered from the volcano and obscured the sky. The atmosphere became so dark that people used lanterns during the daytime.

Occurring during a civil war, when the volcano erupted it sounded like artillery, and troops in the British Honduras and Guatemala City prepared for military action, thinking they were being attacked. Upset by the strange noises the volcano produced and seven unceasing hours of falling pumice, residents thought Judgment Day had arrived. Most of the casualties were cattle farmers who dwelled near the volcano's base. Superstitious survivors decided that sacrifices offered every quarter century would appease Cosigüina.

Elizabeth D. Schafer

FOR FURTHER INFORMATION:
Galindo, J. "On the Eruption of the Volcano Cosigüina in Nicaragua, 17th January, 1835." *Journal of the Royal Geographic Society* 1 (1835): 387-392.
Scarth, Alwyn. *Vulcan's Fury: Man Against the Volcano.* New Haven, Conn.: Yale University Press, 1999.

1845: Nevado del Ruiz

DATE: 1845
PLACE: Colombia
VOLCANIC EXPLOSIVITY INDEX: 3
RESULT: 700 dead

A stratovolcano 17,453 feet tall, Nevado del Ruiz is located west of the Colombian capital of Bogotá. Spanish maps included the volcano as early as 1570 after people witnessed its first-known eruption. Located in the Andes mountain chain, Nevado del Ruiz has a cap of snow and ice. Seismic activity occurs because the Nazca Plate moves underneath the American Plate to create the Peru-Chile Trench on the ocean floor and lift the Andes.

Farmers settled near the volcano because its ash enriched soil. Coffee, cotton, and rice grew exceptionally well in the valley. Nevado del Ruiz occasionally emitted puffs of steam for months before the eruption occurred, and mud and sulfur leaked into the Lagunilla River. Despite these warnings, people ignored the possibility of sudden catastrophe. In 1845 Nevado del Ruiz released millions of tons of mud, which melted the snowcap. At least 700 people died (some records estimate 1,000 deaths) because of the mudflows that covered the Lagunilla Valley. Ironically, the volcanic mud proved to be fertile topsoil, and new settlers built plantations around Armero and prospered economically. The 1845 eruption was considered the worst until a 1985 explosion blanketed nearby towns, killing many residents.

Elizabeth D. Schafer

FOR FURTHER INFORMATION:
Scarth, Alwyn. *Vulcan's Fury: Man Against the Volcano.* New Haven, Conn.: Yale University Press, 1999.

Simkin, Tom, and Lee Siebert. *Volcanoes of the World.* 2d ed. Tucson, Ariz.: Geoscience Press, 1994.

1853: Niuafo'ou

DATE: June 24, 1853
PLACE: Tonga Islands
RESULT: 70 dead, village mostly destroyed

Niuafo'ou is a low, circular island that is 5 miles (8 kilometers) in diameter; it is located in the south Pacific Ocean. The island is the top of a mostly submerged volcano that is exposed above the ocean surface; the inner portion of the island is a lake that fills the central cone of the volcano. Most eruptions have occurred as lava flowed from fissures along the outer edge of the island. One of these lava flows occurred in 1853 in the village of Ahau. Relatively few people have been killed by lava flows, as there is usually plenty of time to get out of the way of the flow. This was not the case in this village, however, as the lava suddenly erupted into the village at night, so few people had time to escape.

The crack from which the lava extruded stretched gradually down the street of the village, and the lava flowed to the sea. Various reports give estimates of half to two-thirds of the population of the village being killed by the unexpected eruption. Legend often springs up after events like this to explain the natural disaster: Reportedly Ahau was founded by a couple who rebelled against strict marriage, so a high chief across the island called upon the gods to destroy the couple.

Robert L. Cullers

FOR FURTHER INFORMATION:
Coleman, S. N. *Volcanoes, New and Old.* New York: John Day Press, 1946.
Tonga Chronicle, September 9, 1983, p. 10.

1872: Vesuvius

DATE: April 24-26, 1872
PLACE: Italy
RESULT: 22 dead

Mount Vesuvius is one of the world's most famous volcanoes because of its explosive eruptions into well-populated areas in southwestern Italy in 79 and 1872, which caused much death and destruction. Eruptions between 1631 and 1944 have been well documented. In a given eruption cycle (including the 1872 eruption), the initial eruptions consist of the ejection of hot, solid material to hundreds of feet into the air that are later followed by lava flows. The crater then usually collapses to depths of hundreds of feet at the end of this phase, and strong earthquakes occur. Later, this cycle is often followed by a more explosive 3- to 9-mile-high eruption column.

During the 1872 eruption, a group of 22 young people, which included 8 medical students, traveled to the Valle dell' Inferno to see the lava flows up close. Unfortunately, two tongues of lava trapped them so that they could not escape, and the lava killed them. Another lava flow traveled 2.5 to 3 miles (4 to 5 kilometers) in ten hours and destroyed buildings in several towns. Several days later, volcanic ash was erupted from the main crater up to 4,265 feet (1,300 meters) into the air and covered a large portion of the area. The explosions during the ash eruption were heard in Naples.

Robert L. Cullers

FOR FURTHER INFORMATION:

Palmieri, L. *The Eruption of Vesuvius in 1872.* London: Asher, 1873.

Rittman, A. *Volcanoes and Their Activity.* New York: Interscience, 1962.

1877: Cotopaxi

DATE: June 26, 1877
PLACE: Ecuador
RESULT: 1,000 dead, thousands of animals dead, buildings and bridges destroyed

Cotopaxi is located in north-central Ecuador. It is composed of alternating lava flows and airborne debris from the volcano, so it has fairly steep slopes. The volcano has a high enough elevation (19,393 feet) that it is covered with snow and ice. There have been thirty eruptions of the volcano since 1532; some of the eruptions are explosive, and they produce hot, airborne material that melts the snow and ice at the summit. The abundant water mixes with the volcanic material from the eruption to produce volcanic mudflows, or lahars, which move rapidly down the valleys, often to great distances.

The most destructive lahars from Cotopaxi occurred on June 26, 1877, moving at speeds up to 62 miles per hour down three main drainages and destroying many towns, bridges, and factories. Eyewitnesses report that the countryside was turned into deserts of stones and sand. Travelers filled the road in one area, and an eyewitness described the mud flowing over everyone, including galloping horses. The lahar that flowed down the north side of the volcano reached the town of Esmeralda, which was 168 miles from the volcano. Here the lahar was diluted enough with the river water that it only rose 3 feet and did not cause much destruction. The flowing water did contain cadavers, furniture, and pieces of buildings.

Robert L. Cullers

FOR FURTHER INFORMATION:

Coleman, S. N. *Volcanoes, New and Old.* New York: John Day, 1946.

Whymper, E. *Travels Amongst the Great Andes of the Equator.* Salt Lake City, Utah: Peregrine Smith Books, 1892.

1883: Krakatau

DATE: August 26-27, 1883
PLACE: Indonesia
RESULT: 36,417 dead, 165 villages and towns destroyed, 132 towns and villages damaged, two-thirds of island destroyed

The Preliminary Eruption. In 1883, Krakatau (or Krakatoa) was a small, uninhabited island covered in lush vegetation. Lying in the Sunda Strait between Java and Sumatra, then part of the Dutch East Indies (now Indonesia), it was known to be volcanic but was thought to be extinct or at least insignificant. Native legends existed about an eruption there in 416 C.E., as well as a secondhand report from a Dutch official about another eruption in 1680, but the 1680 eruption was not widely reported and had been virtually forgotten by 1883.

Thus on May 20, 1883, when windows rattled and a noise like cannon fire was heard in the capital city of

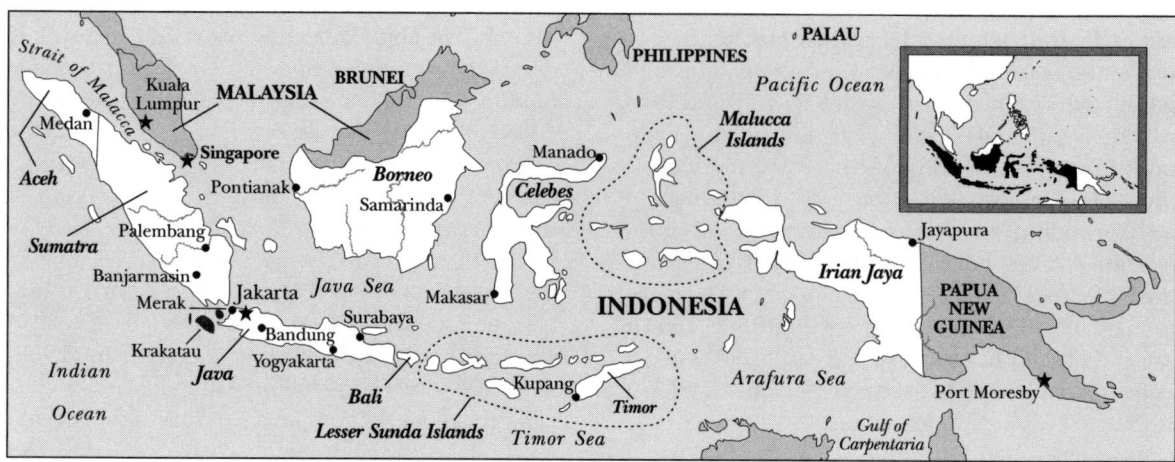

Batavia (now Jakarta) on Java, almost 100 miles away, no one's first thought was that the source was Krakatau. Some people thought they were experiencing an earthquake, but the noise was not coming from the ground. A volcanic eruption was then suspected, but still no one thought the source was Krakatau; when it was discovered that the volcano Karang, a much larger volcano than Krakatau in western Java, was not erupting, the thought was that perhaps one of the volcanoes across the strait in Sumatra was the source.

When some native fishermen reported to Dutch officials that they had been on Krakatau gathering wood and that while they were there an eruption had started beneath their feet, they were not believed at first. Reports soon came in to confirm their story: Krakatau was in eruption, producing clouds of steam, smoke, fire, and ash rising 6 or 7 miles high, along with lightning flashes, sulfurous fumes, and deposits of pumice on the surface of the sea.

The eruption cloud looked like "a giant cauliflower head," according to one eyewitness, the chaplain aboard the German warship *Elisabeth*, which was sailing through the Sunda Strait at the time. This witness also provided a striking account of the effect of ashfall; by May 21 it had turned a newly cleaned ship into something that looked "like a floating cement factory." All surfaces were covered with a gray, sticky dust more than 0.5 inch thick, which was aggravating to the eyes and lungs.

Ash continued to fall on the *Elisabeth* until it was more than 300 miles away. Ash also fell on other ships in the area and on the neighboring island of Verlaten (now Sertung), destroying the vegetation there. Veg-

etation on Krakatau itself was also destroyed. Ash fell as well on the two other islands in the Krakatau group, Lang (now Panjang) and Polish Hat but did not destroy the vegetation there.

On May 22, the ship *Sunda* reported a heavy fall of ash when it was 7 miles from Krakatau; at a distance of 10 miles from the island it reported pieces of pumice floating in the sea, and at a distance of 30 miles the pumice was so thick that a bucket lowered into the sea came up filled almost entirely with pumice and hardly any water.

The May eruption caused no casualties and stimulated more interest than alarm. In fact, on May 27 a group of sightseers took a pleasure trip to the island and looked into the smoking crater of Perboewatan, one of Krakatau's three volcanic cones (the other two being Danan and Rakata). With steam billowing around them and explosions sounding periodically, some of the sightseers even clambered into the crater to pick up pieces of pumice and lava as souvenirs. One of them took photographs, the only ones that exist of Krakatau in eruption in 1883.

Volcanic activity decreased at the end of May but picked up again after mid-June. Explosions were heard on Java and Sumatra. One witness described a thick cloud of smoke and ash hanging over the volcano for five days in late June; when this cleared away, two dense columns of rising smoke could be seen. In mid-August, ships passing by Krakatau reported heavy ashfalls that turned the sky black, along with columns of smoke, rumbling noises, and flashes of lightning.

The First August Eruption. The eruption that Krakatau is famous for began early in the afternoon of Sunday, August 26, 1883. R. D. M. Verbeek, a Dutch geologist who later wrote the first full-length study of the eruption, reported that at 1:00 P.M. he heard a rumbling sound at his home in Buitenzorg (now Bogor), a town on Java about 100 miles from Krakatau. The director of the Batavia Observatory noted that the sound was first heard there at 1:06 P.M. At first it was mistaken for thunder and, as in May, even after residents realized that they were hearing a volcanic eruption, they assumed that some volcano other than Krakatau was producing the increasingly violent explosions.

Closer to Krakatau, there was no mistaking the sounds. The ship the *Charles Bal*, which passed within 10 miles of Krakatau, reported hearing explosions from the volcano that sounded like heavy artillery. The ship later reported "chains of fire" and white balls of fire at the volcano, along with continued explosive roars, choking sulfurous fumes, and a hail of pumice stone and ash which covered the decks to a thickness of 3 or 4 inches.

The captain of the *Medea*, 76 miles away, recorded two explosions from Krakatau at 2 P.M. that shook his ship, and he noted a black eruption cloud above the volcano, calculated to be 17 miles high. Later estimates put the height of the cloud at between 15 and 50 miles.

Reports from the Javanese port of Anjer, about 30 miles from the volcano across the Sunda Strait, noted that by 2 P.M. Krakatau was enveloped in smoke, and it had become so dark that people could not see their own hands. One witness said a column of steam rose above Krakatau, looking like thousands of large white balloons, and added that the sea looked agitated. Another witness said the eruption cloud kept shifting color between black and white; he, too, noticed the agitation of the sea, which he said was turning an inky black color. A third witness reported a fiery glare above the volcano and said that the explosions grew louder after nightfall. Houses shook, and panic set in. Residents of Anjer and other towns and villages gathered their belongings and prepared to flee.

There was panic even in Batavia. Even that far from Krakatau, the noise was so loud that the sound of the regular evening gun was almost inaudible. Doors and windows rattled, walls shook, and at 2 A.M. a powerful explosion knocked out the city's gas lighting system. Residents woke and rushed into the streets. However, there were very few casualties in Batavia. Most of the deaths occurred in coastal towns and villages closer to the volcano, and most were caused not directly by the eruption or the fall of ash and stone but from the massive tsunamis that ensued on Monday morning.

The Second August Eruption. Overnight, ash continued to fall, and unusual electrical phenomena were reported on ships in the strait. The *Berbice*, about 50 miles to the west, reported hot ash falling, which burned holes in the sailors' clothes and the sails, and which was soon piled 3 feet deep on the deck. The ship was also struck by fireballs and flashes of lightning, and several members of the crew received electric shocks. On the *Gouverneur General Loudon*, 40 or 50 miles to the northwest, a mud rain fell, and lightning struck several times, creating phosphorescent effects (Saint Elmo's fire) on the masts and rigging. Saint Elmo's fire was also reported on the *Charles Bal*; its captain said "a peculiar pink flame came from fleecy clouds which seemed to touch the mast-heads and yard-arms." He also reported that the sky alternated between being pitch black one moment and ablaze with light the next.

It was not until after dawn on Monday, August 27 that the full force of Krakatau was felt. There had been numerous explosions before this, including a large one just after 5:00 P.M. on the 26th, but between dawn and 11:00 A.M. on the 27th there were four mammoth explosions (at 5:30, 6:44, 10:02, and 10:52) that dwarfed the earlier ones. The first three of these, especially the one at 10:02, were followed by tidal waves that caused most of the destruction associated with Krakatau.

Sometime between 6:00 and 6:30 A.M. a wave 33 feet high struck Anjer. The town was destroyed. All who did not flee died. The next day, a messenger sent to investigate returned from Anjer with the report that "there was no longer any such place." The houses and other buildings were gone, except for ruined remnants of the town fort; the trees were all uprooted, except for a few leafless ones covered in ash; the Anjer lighthouse had vanished; and all the monuments in the town's cemetery had been washed away. The situation was summed up by one witness in a few brief words: "All gone," he wrote. "Plenty lives lost."

An even bigger wave struck at about 10:30 A.M. and destroyed the town of Merak, about 7 miles north of Anjer along the Java coast. All but 2 or 3 of the approximately 2,700 inhabitants died, even though many of them had taken shelter on a hill behind the town, where they had survived earlier waves. The

10:30 wave seems to have been higher at Merak than anywhere else, perhaps because of the funnel-shaped strait there formed by a tiny island just offshore. Estimates put the wave height at 135 feet; elsewhere the wave attained heights estimated at between 50 and 100 feet.

In Merak, as at Anjer, all the buildings vanished, except for the floor of the house of the resident engineer on top of the hill. The railroad line leading to the Merak quarry was torn up and twisted, and locomotives and railcars were battered and tossed aside. One locomotive was carried out to sea and lay 50 yards from the beach, a battered wreck with the waves breaking over it.

The area around Merak was similarly devastated. It was a "scene of desolation," according to one witness, who added: "For miles there was not a tree standing, and where formerly stood numerous campongs (native villages), surrounded by paddy fields and cocoanut groves, there was nothing but a wilderness, more resembling the bottom of the sea than anywhere else." He saw rocks of coral that the wave had deposited several miles inland, some of them weighing as much as 100 tons. Closer to Merak he noted remnants of bedding and furniture, along with shreds of clothing.

All together, in the Merak-Anjer area the death toll was set at 7,610. In the neighboring district of Tjiringin, another 12,022 perished, 1,880 of them in the town of Tjiringin, which was swept away by the 10:30 wave. Corpses lay on the ground in Tjiringin for days, and there was much looting.

Sumatra. Parts of Sumatra, to the north of Krakatau, are closer to the volcano than Java and were directly in line with its blasts. In these areas, unlike the situation elsewhere, there were deaths from the volcano's hot ash and pumice in addition to deaths from the tidal waves. About 1,000 residents in the area north of Katimbang, on the southeast point of Sumatra 25 miles from Krakatau, died of burns; another 2,000 were burned but survived. The ash here struck not only from above but also, according to one witness, from below: spurting up like a fountain through cracks in the floor of the hut in which she had taken shelter on the slopes of Mount Radjah Bassa, north of Katimbang. Besides causing human casualties, the ash killed vegetation and, through its weight on roofs, destroyed many houses.

A drawing of Krakatau in eruption. (National Oceanic and Atmospheric Administration)

Even in Sumatra, however, most deaths were caused by the waves. Waves struck Katimbang as early as Sunday night, throwing small boats up on the shore. The whole town was washed away by the same wave that destroyed Anjer at 6:30 A.M. Monday.

Waves also struck further west, at Teluk Betong on Lampong Bay, about 50 miles from Krakatau, beginning at 6:00 P.M. on Sunday, August 26. These early waves damaged a bridge and a pier and cast some boats on the shore. The real damage came the next day, primarily from the wave that struck at 10:30 A.M. Half an hour earlier the largest of Krakatau's eruptions had been heard in Teluk Betong; then ash and mud began to fall on the town, and it became dark as night, so dark that the effects of the wave that followed were not seen until the next day. Those who went to inspect then found only ruins, corpses, and iron government cash boxes. One witness described the scene by saying "there was no destruction. There was simply . . . nothing."

One of the most remarkable episodes in this area involved a Dutch gunboat, the *Berouw*, which had been anchored in Teluk Betong harbor. Early Monday morning one of the big waves tore the *Berouw* from its moorings and carried it into the Chinese quarter of the town. The big wave at 10:30 A.M. lifted the *Berouw* again and deposited it almost 2 miles inland amid some palm trees. All 28 of its crew members died.

Altogether 2,260 people died in the Teluk Betong area, and it was difficult to send relief to the survivors because pumice in Lampong Bay made it impossible to reach the area by sea for weeks. However, amid all the devastation and suffering, one witness did note a positive result: All the mosquitoes in the area had been destroyed, by ash or mud.

Survivors' Tales. In the midst of death and destruction, some people made miraculous escapes. The telegraph master at Anjer managed to outrun the tidal wave. "Never have I run so fast in my life," he said later, "for, in the most literal sense of the word, death was at my heels." An elderly Dutch pilot in Anjer told an even more remarkable tale. He was unable to outrun the wave but found himself swept by it into a palm tree. He stayed in the tree watching corpses float by him and later made his way to safety. One resident survived by riding on the back of an alligator. A Dutch auctioneer in a small village near Batavia survived by climbing on a dead cow that floated by, on which he stayed until encountering a

tree onto which he climbed. A Dutch official in Beneawang on Semangka Bay in Sumatra floated for hours, first on a shelf, then on a tree trunk, after his house collapsed around him.

Aftermath. In addition to the deaths and damage caused on Java and Sumatra, Krakatau caused much damage to itself. After the eruption, it was discovered that the northern two-thirds of the island had disappeared, apparently sunk beneath the sea. All that remained was a sheared-off part of one of the three volcanic cones, Rakata, and one tiny rock 10 yards square sometimes called by the name Bootsmanrots. The neighboring islet of Polish Hat also disappeared. On the other hand, the nearby island of Verlaten tripled in size due to rock landing on it from the volcano, and two new islands formed: Steers and Calmeyer. However, the latter two, being composed entirely of pumice, were washed away by the sea within months.

All plant and animal life on Krakatau seems to have perished in the eruption, although some scientists have argued that seeds, insect larvae, and earthworms may have survived below ground. In any case, life did return to Krakatau fairly quickly: By 1889 plant life, bugs, and lizards were reported on the island.

Volcanic activity returned as well, in 1927, with the appearance of a new volcanic island where the northern two-thirds of the old island used to be. Anak Krakatau ("child of Krakatau"), occupying a small but growing portion of what used to be the northern part of Krakatau, has erupted periodically since its first appearance.

Causes of the Waves. Besides the dispute over the survival of life after the eruption, there has been disagreement among scientists over the process that caused the massive tidal waves, or tsunamis, at Krakatau. Several theories have been put forward: that the pumice and other ejected materials landing on the water caused the waves, that some underwater explosion caused them, that they were caused by a "lateral blast" from the side of the volcano, that a pyroclastic flow of ash and heated volcanic gases was responsible, and that the collapse of two-thirds of the island into the sea produced the effect. The last view, which posits that by ejecting masses of material into the atmosphere Krakatau created a void beneath itself into which it eventually collapsed, seems to have the most support, but scientists remain divided because the evidence is inconclusive. One scientist, in discussing this issue, has remarked that Krakatau, though one of the best-known, is also one of the least-understood volcanic eruptions.

Long-Term and Long-Range Effects. Even after the end of the eruptions, late at night on Monday, August 27, effects of Krakatau's blast continued to be felt. Darkness lingered for fifty-seven hours within 50 miles of the volcano and for twenty-two hours up to 125 miles away. Pumice choked the bays of Java and Sumatra until December and floated as far away as South Africa, nearly 5,000 miles distant, over the next two years. In the middle of the Indian Ocean, in December, 1883, the steamer *Bothwell Castle* encountered a vast field of pumice that stretched for 1,250 miles and was so thick upon the sea that the sailors were able climb onto it in some places and walk about.

The sounds of Krakatau also traveled to distant parts. In Singapore, over 500 miles from the volcano, vessels were sent out to investigate what sounded like the firing of a ship's guns. The explosion was also heard in Saigon (1,164 miles away), Borneo (1,235 miles away), Bangkok (1,413 miles away), Manila (1,800 miles away), and Ceylon (now Sri Lanka) and western Australia (up to 2,000 miles away). The most distant report came from Rodriguez Island in the Indian Ocean, 2,968 miles from the source of the blast. The waves produced by Krakatau also traveled long distances. High waves struck the coast of India on August 27, about 2,000 miles from the volcano. Tidal disturbances were also reported in New Zealand and even as far away as the English Channel.

The atmospheric effects of the eruption were among the most startling and long-lasting. Dust thrown up by Krakatau circled the globe and remained suspended in the atmosphere for two or three years. As a result, much of the globe was treated to spectacular, blood-red sunsets and a very odd-looking sun, which sometimes appeared blue or green. At times the sun also appeared with a pinkish halo around it; this halo, described at the time by the Reverend Sereno Bishop, has since been seen after other volcanic eruptions and is referred to as Bishop's ring.

Blue suns were reported in September in the Virgin Islands, Peru, and points in between. A green sun was reported in Hawaii, Panama, and Venezuela. In November the fire departments of Poughkeepsie, New York, and New Haven, Connecticut, were called out because a red glare in the sky convinced onlookers that a great fire was underway. There were so many fiery sunsets and brilliant after-sunset glows, especially in the winter of 1883-1884, that letters poured into the magazine *Nature*, which began a special department in its pages called "The Remarkable Sunsets."

Another probable consequence of the dust in the atmosphere was a cooling in the world's climate. There has been some scientific debate over this, but it is generally agreed that the volcanic dust reduced solar radiation reaching the earth by as much as 10 percent and that as a result world temperatures over the next three years dropped by 32.5 to 33 degrees Fahrenheit (0.25 to 0.5 degrees Celsius). Cooler temperatures were especially noticeable in the Northern Hemisphere.

Reputation and Misconceptions. The 1883 eruption of Krakatau was one of the largest, loudest, and most devastating in recorded history. Perhaps as a result it captured the popular imagination, giving rise to numerous legends and erroneous reports. The very earliest newspaper stories contained wild statements about millions dying and sixteen volcanoes being in eruption. Years later, in 1969, Hollywood was equally inaccurate in producing a motion picture called *Krakatoa, East of Java* (Krakatau is west of Java).

It is also not true, at least according to the scientific consensus, that Krakatau blew its top off or decapitated itself and completely disappeared. Rather than blowing itself up into the air, Krakatau, as most scientists see it, collapsed into the sea. Moreover, not all of it disappeared; one-third of the original island survived.

The fact that Krakatau was uninhabited is also not widely known. It is true that Krakatau had been inhabited at earlier times in its history. Captain James Cook's ships landed at the island in the 1770's and discovered a village and cultivation; a village was also reported on the island in 1809, and there are reports of a penal settlement there. However, by the time of the eruption the island was completely deserted, except for local fishermen who occasionally visited it.

The popular view of volcanic destruction through ash and rock and fast-flowing lava also does not apply to Krakatau, which produced most of its deaths indirectly by tidal waves. On the other hand, the tidal waves resulted from volcanic processes; there was no simultaneous earthquake.

Finally, Krakatau was not located in some obscure, out-of-the-way region. On the contrary, it was right in the middle of a major shipping route, the Sunda

Strait, not far from heavily populated coastal regions with access to the rest of the world by telegraph. It may be, in fact, that it is precisely because Krakatau was well connected to the rest of the world that its eruption has become world-famous.

Sheldon Goldfarb

FOR FURTHER INFORMATION:

Bullard, Fred M. *Volcanoes of the Earth.* 2d rev. ed. Austin: University of Texas Press, 1984.

Francis, Peter. "Four Classic Eruptions" and "The Golden Glow of Volcanic Winter." In *Volcanoes: A Planetary Perspective.* Oxford, England: Clarendon Press, 1993.

Francis, Peter, and Stephen Self. "The Eruption of Krakatoa." *Scientific American* 249, no. 5 (November, 1983): 172-187.

Furneaux, Rupert. *Krakatoa.* Engelwood Cliffs, N.J.: Prentice Hall, 1964.

Simkin, Tom, and Richard S. Fiske, eds. *Krakatau 1883: The Volcanic Eruption and Its Effects.* Washington, D.C.: Smithsonian Institution Press, 1983.

Thornton, Ian. *Krakatau: The Destruction and Reassembly of an Island Ecosystem.* Cambridge, Mass.: Harvard University Press, 1996.

Woolley, Alan, and Clive Bishop. "Krakatoa: The Decapitation of a Volcano." In *The Making of the Earth,* edited by Richard Fifield. Oxford, England: Basil Blackwell, 1985.

1888: Bandai

DATE: July 15, 1888
PLACE: Honshū, Japan
RESULT: 461 dead, 70 burned and scarred, several villages buried

Bandai is located in northern Honshū, Japan. It is composed of alternating lavas and airborne eruptive material from explosive eruptions, so it is fairly steep. The volcano erupted four times between 806 and 1888 with moderate to large eruptions. The largest was the July 15, 1888, eruption. At 7:00 A.M. on that day rumblings were heard from the volcano. At 7:30 A.M. a moderately strong explosion occurred on the north side of the volcano, and the ground trembled continuously. Another strong explosion occurred at 7:45,

and twenty more explosions were heard over the next several hours.

Coarse fragments of volcanic material were thrown upward to a height of 4,265 feet, and a black cloud composed of volcanic ash and steam billowed upward to over 21,653 feet. The rain produced from the hot updrafts from the volcano produced scalding mud. About 0.25 cubic mile of material was blown off the volcano, producing a crater with vertical sides that was 8,202 feet by 8,858 feet in size. The debris on the north side of the mountain avalanched into the stream valley and turned into mud and rock flows upon mixing with the water produced by the torrential rains. This material buried several villages along the rivers, killing at least 461 people.

The Kawakami spa near Bandai was covered by more than 131 feet of deposits. Only 117 bodies were recovered. Falling stones and a rush of exceedingly hot ash scarred and burned 70 people. The *London Daily News* described the terrible condition of some of the wounded and dead, with fractured skulls, broken limbs, and terrible burns. Some of the dead had been thrown into the air and were dangling from trees. In some places flesh dangled from branches like paper. The solar radiation that reached the earth after this eruption also markedly decreased because of the volcanic ash added to the atmosphere after this and several other volcanic eruptions that occurred within a two-year period.

Robert L. Cullers

FOR FURTHER INFORMATION:

Simkin, Tom, and Lee Siebert. *Volcanoes of the World.* 2d ed. Tucson, Ariz.: Geoscience Press, 1994.

Wilcoxson, K. *Volcanoes.* Tucson, Ariz.: Geoscience Press, 1994.

1897: Mayon

DATE: June 23, 1897
PLACE: Luzon, Philippines
RESULT: 400 dead, villages and animals destroyed

Mayon, located 202 miles southeast of Manila, Philippines, is 8,071 feet high. It has a symmetrical cone composed of alternating lava flows and volcanic ejecta thrown out of the volcano into the air. The crater at the summit is only about 656 feet across. Mayon is the most active volcano in the Philippines; it has erupted 47 times since the first recorded eruption in 1616, and 12 of these eruptions have caused deaths (1,500 total lives lost).

The eruption of June, 1897, was particularly intense. Without warning, the volcano began to erupt on June 23, and it continued until June 30. Great amounts of lava, ash, and pyroclastic flow were extruded during this time. A pyroclastic flow is particularly dangerous to life, as it is composed of very hot volcanic particles and gas that flow rapidly on a cushion of air down the volcano. This pyroclastic flow left 400 people and numerous cows, pigs, water buffalo, and horses burnt to death. Lava flows extended more than 6.8 miles to the east, and they destroyed several villages, damaging others. Large quantities of volcanic ash fell up to 106 miles away from the volcano. People from Legaspi prayed to their patron saint, Rafael, to protect them from the eruption.

Robert L. Cullers

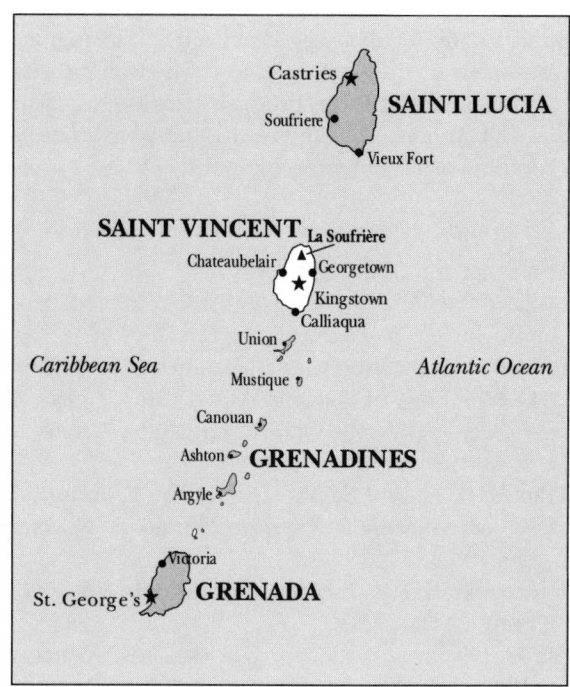

FOR FURTHER INFORMATION:

News About the Mayan Volcano in Albay in June, 1897. Nueva Caceres, Philippines: La Sagrada Familia, 1897.

1902: La Soufrière

DATE: May 7, 1902
PLACE: St. Vincent Island, Lesser Antilles
RESULT: 1,500-1,700 dead, loss of livestock and crops

At the eastern end of the Caribbean Sea, part of the Atlantic crustal plate is moving under the Caribbean Plate, producing a north-south chain of volcanic islands that is part of the Lesser Antilles. St. Vincent Island is near the southern end of the chain. St. Vincent, like all islands of the chain, is slender, extending 17.5 miles north to south by 10 miles east to west. La Soufrière, or Soufrière, an active volcano, is about 3 miles south of the north end of the island. Georgetown, capital of St. Vincent in 1902, lies on the east coast, 5.5 miles southeast of La Soufrière.

In 1902 La Soufrière rose to about 4,000 feet in elevation. The summit was capped by two craters—the old crater, dating from eruptions prior to 1812, and

the 1812 crater. The old crater held a lake in the years prior to 1902.

In April, 1902, earthquakes began to occur in the northern part of the island, and by May 1 they had so alarmed inhabitants of the western side of the island near the volcano that most of them left the area, presumably to the much safer south end. This action undoubtedly saved many lives.

During the morning of May 5 local people noted that the old-crater lake had become agitated and discolored, and steam was observed venting from the lake later in the day. This activity increased in intensity, and around 9 A.M. May 7, ash began to fall near the east coast. By noon of May 7 the eruption had become very violent, with a column of steam and ash ascending to about 30,000 feet. Large rocks could be observed in the ash column at 1 P.M.

People living in coastal villages north of Georgetown began trying to move south in the early afternoon but found the route blocked by steaming mud flowing down the valley of the Rabaka Dry River, an ephemeral stream originating on the east side of the volcano. The hot mud flow, or lahar, was apparently the result of a breach in the old crater and drainage of the crater lake with attendant volcanic ash and pumice down the southeast side of the volcano. The flow may have been enhanced by rain accompanying the eruption. Charles Alexander who was working in a field about 3 miles east of the volcano in the late morning of May 7, reported a drizzle of rain accompanied by falling ash before noon of the 7th. By early afternoon Alexander was among a group of about 90 people who had sought shelter from falling hot ash and rocks in Victor Sutherland's store in the coastal village of Overland, north of Georgetown. The building had a galvanized steel roof and wooden shutters. While the people were there, some rocks penetrated the roof.

At about 2 P.M. there was a massive explosion at the volcano. A great mass of incandescent ash and gas blasted down the slope. One witness described the phenomenon as a "terrific, huge, reddish-purplish cloud." This was clearly a nuée ardente, or ignimbrite, a high-velocity, incandescent cloud of superheated steam and volcanic ash that would have burned to death or asphyxiated anyone caught in its path. Although the shutters were closed and the building did not catch fire, only 6 of the approximately 90 people crowded into Sutherland's store survived. Alexander reported that, as the cloud passed, it became very hot in the store; choking, fine, hot ash seeped through crevices in the roof and around the shutters, and he smelled sulfur. Alexander survived but was badly burned on the exposed parts of his body.

Most of the deaths associated with the nuée ardente phase of the eruption probably can be attributed to inhalation of superheated steam mixed with poisonous gases and volcanic ash. The nuée ardente flattened trees, scorching them on the volcano side; destroyed crops, pasture, and livestock; and knocked down, or set afire, houses and other buildings. Although Georgetown apparently was not directly affected by the nuée ardente, incandescent stones up to 6 inches in diameter and large quantities of volcanic ash fell on the city. Almost all vegetation in the northern third of the island was destroyed, either by the nuée ardente or by heavy falls of hot volcanic ash that preceded and followed it.

After the onrush of the nuée ardente around 2 P.M. on May 7, almost continuous violent volcanic explosions continued through the early morning hours of May 9. Eruptions similar to the violent outburst of May 7 occurred May 18, September 1, and September 3. No loss of life was reported in connection with the later violent eruptions, but they probably contributed to the total damage reported.

The very similar, but much more destructive, explosion and nuée ardente of Mount Pelée on the island of Martinique, 90 miles north of St. Vincent, occurred at 7:50 A.M. May 8, 1902, about eighteen hours after the initial event at St. Vincent. On May 14, a United States cruiser, the *Dixie*, was sent with relief supplies from New York to Martinique and then to St. Vincent. Five prominent American volcanologists and several journalists were on the *Dixie*, and they were followed to the islands by several scientists from Great Britain and Europe. Nearly all of these scientists and journalists wrote descriptions of the two cataclysmic eruptions, some of these in *National Geographic*, and both public and scientific interest in volcanoes was greatly stimulated.

Robert E. Carver

FOR FURTHER INFORMATION:
Blong, Russell. *Volcanic Hazards.* Orlando, Fla.: Academic Press, 1984.
Bullard, Fred M. *Volcanoes of the Earth.* 2d rev. ed. Austin: University of Texas Press, 1984.

1902: Pelée

DATE: May 8, 1902
PLACE: Martinique
RESULT: Estimated 30,000 dead, city of St. Pierre destroyed

Pelée rises 4,583 feet above sea level. It is located at 14.8 degrees north latitude and 61.1 degrees west longitude. The name *pele*, meaning "bald," implies that the volcano was so named because its summit was, as it is now, an unvegetated dacitic lava dome. A lava dome was built during the eruption of the volcano in 1902, only to be destroyed by a subsequent eruption, then built up again. A stratovolcano composed mainly of pyroclastic rocks, Pelée is at the north end of the island of Martinique. It stands high over the coastal city of St. Pierre. The island is part of the Lesser Antilles volcanic arc formed by the subduction of the North American Plate under the Caribbean Plate.

Pelée is best known for the May 8, 1902, eruption, which destroyed Martinique's major city of St. Pierre, killing over 30,000 people. No other twentieth cen-

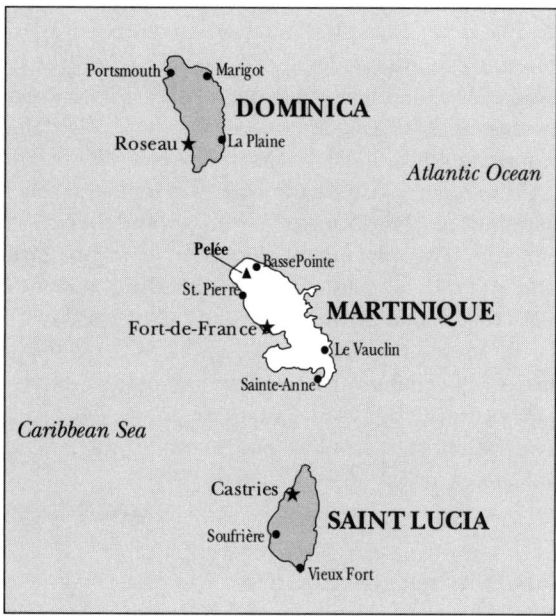

tury eruption caused as large a number of casualties, causing the Pelée eruption to be called the greatest killer volcano of the century. A nuée ardente, or "glowing cloud," type of pyroclastic flow and ash-cloud surge caused the destruction on the island. This nuée ardente detached from the lava dome and, pulled by gravity, flowed down the sides of the volcano. Pyroclastic flows, also known as volcanic hurricanes, are made up of hot incandescent solid particles; the term "pyroclastic" comes from *pyro* (fire) and *clastic* (broken).

Of six volcanic eruption styles identified by volcanologists, the most violent and extremely destructive type is the fourth, Peléan volcanism. It is identified by glowing avalanches that spread down the mountain and over the ground, heavy with ash and pumice, at up to 62 miles (100 kilometers) an hour. Peléan volcanoes can flow over water as well as land. Sometimes described us a hot cloud traveling at tremendous speed, the volcanic hurricane can carry particles the size of boulders. It may move silently and more swiftly than any atmospheric hurricane, reaching intensely hot temperatures. In fact, the heat is so intense that pyroclastic fragments can remain warm for over a year after the eruption.

This fifth type of volcano was named for the 1902 Pelée eruption, which was the culmination of an eruption cycle that had been building for a few years. This cycle involved small eruptions that sent ash up

from the volcano in a cloud to around 10,000 feet but that did not threaten to overflow the city. It can be assumed that the repeated activity had created an atmosphere of complacency that meant, in this case, that the population of 1902 assumed that the new volcanic activity was more of the same they had experienced over the past few years.

Pelée Erupts. The first hint that there was activity in the volcano occurred on April 2, 1902, when new, steaming vent holes were seen in the upper part of a ravine called La Rivière Blanche. The ravine is on the south side of the mountain, facing St. Pierre, and leads from a secondary crater named L'Étang Sec to the coast. Then, three weeks following the discovery of the holes, there were some tremors, ash clouds arose from the mountain's summit, and volcanic ash fell onto St. Pierre, the city at its base. The smell of sulfur filled the air as the volcano rumbled and shook.

Known as the Paris of the Caribbean, St. Pierre was a city of rows of well-built stone houses and downtown buildings, including an opera house, and served as the main port city for Martinique. The city rests on a large, open bay on the west coast of the island. St. Pierre was involved in an election campaign and ill prepared for the disaster about to befall it. Some people left as the ash began to fall, but most stayed so they could support the candidate of their choice in the election about to be held. Others came into the city from surrounding towns and villages to see the phenomenon of an active volcano.

By May the ash had thickened to the point that it blocked roads. Businesses were forced to close, and birds and small animals began to die from the ash and poisonous gases. On May 3 the newspaper *Les Colonies* wrote that the raining-down of ashes on the city "never stops." It reported that the ash was so thick that the wheels of moving carriages were silent as they passed through it, and the wind blew the ash from roofs and awnings into any open window.

The volcanologists of the time possessed only a primitive knowledge of the volcanic process and thus did not predict the disaster that was to occur. They were not aware of the existence of volcanic hurricanes and so did not urge people to leave the area. In fact, Gaston Landes, a professor at the St. Pierre high school, had said that the city could expect very little damage from the ash and the smell of sulfur. Even if there were lava flows, he told the city, they would be stopped by the ridges and valleys that lay between

Pelée and the city. He assured them that even if the volcano should erupt, little damage would ensue. He was correct in that there was no lava in the flow that spewed out of Pelée. However, with the limited knowledge of volcanoes of that time, he was not aware of pyroclastic flows and of the heat they contained.

Early on May 8, ash clouds were still rising from Pelée. It seemed to the residents of St. Pierre to be just another day of ash falling on their roofs and streets. Suddenly, however, at 7:50 A.M. the volcano erupted with four blasts, sending a black cloud, which lit up with sharp lightning flashes, into the sky. The cloud of steaming hot gases reached temperatures of between 2,370 and 3,270 degrees Fahrenheit (1,300 and 1,800 degrees Celsius). Within five minutes a fifth blast sent an avalanche of boiling ash and gases down the mountainside. Glowing at 1,472 degrees Fahrenheit (800 degrees Celsius), the avalanche flowed so rapidly that in a few minutes the buildings and people of St. Pierre were buried and burned, covered by searing ash and gases.

Roughly 30,000 people were killed almost instantaneously, some perhaps surviving the initial avalanche until the fires claimed them. Others who survived the force of the flow died from inhaling the ash and gases that seared their respiratory systems. It is said that 2 people survived. One was a prisoner named Auguste Siparis, who was confined in an underground jail cell; the other was a shoemaker who managed to escape the fires. The story continues that the former prisoner became a performer in a circus sideshow as a survivor of the Pelée disaster.

All that remained of the city was rubble and some partially standing walls. The heat had been enough to soften glass and windows, but copper remained unmelted. No clear volcanic deposit was found on the rubble because of the speed and violence of the flow and its makeup of ash and gases. On the volcano itself, the vegetation was stripped off, and any animals in the path of the flow were killed.

The hot ash had continued its flow to the sea, and 15 ships moored in the harbor capsized. The British steamer *Roddam* was torn free of its anchor and managed to flee to St. Lucia. It arrived with 12 dead crewmen and 10 suffering severe burns. One survivor from the *Roraima* stated that he watched red flames leap up from the top of the mountain, comparing it to the biggest oil refinery in the world burning on the mountaintop. It seemed to him that the mountain had blown apart without warning, its side ripped open, and he saw what seemed to be a solid wall of flame coming at those on the ships.

Subsequent Activity and Effects. Two months after the May 8 volcanic eruption, a second occurred. At that time two British scientists from the Royal Society were sailing past St. Pierre, studying the ruins of the city. They watched as a red glow surrounded the summit of Pelée, followed by an avalanche of heat

In May, 1902, Pelée erupted in Martinique, causing 30,000 deaths—the most caused by a volcano in the twentieth century. (Library of Congress)

and stones that poured down the mountain and across the ruins of St. Pierre. It took only a minute for the avalanche to reach the sea. They saw the black cloud, which seemed to consist of lighter particles of volcanic matter rising as heavier pieces fell to earth. The scientists described the cloud as globular, with a surface that bulged out. In fact, they said, it was covered with rounded bulging masses that swelled and multiplied, containing and moving with tremendous energy. It rushed forward toward them, over the waters, continually boiling up and changing its form. They saw it sweep over the sea, surging and moving while giving off brilliant flashes of lightning.

The scientists reported that the black cloud slowed its movement and faded, ash settling onto the surface of the sea. It then rose from the surface and passed over their heads, dropping stones and pellets of ash back down onto the sea. They smelled sulfuric acid and watched as the cloud moved out to sea, where it appeared to cover the sky—except for the horizon, which remained clear.

The major treatise on the eruption of Pelée, written by Alfred Lacroix of the French Academy of Sciences, named the phenomenon that destroyed St. Pierre a "nuée ardente," or glowing cloud. Other terms are now used: glowing avalanche, ash flow, ignimbrite, fluidized flow, and base surge. Lacroix wrote that the pyroclastic eruption clouds move along the ground as hot, dense hurricanes, or "glowing clouds." It is suspected that a pyroclastic flow travels on a cushion of air, which allows it to rise from the surface of the land or water, and in some instances can even leave portions of the surface untouched by its destructive effects. This is why the scientists in a boat on the sea could escape unscathed by the avalanche that flowed over the water.

There had been two prior recorded eruptions of Pelée: one in 1792 and another in 1851. However, the 1902 eruption was unique in its destructiveness. The violence of the 1902 eruption drew attention to pyroclastic flows and opened a new area of research for volcanologists, in which they are still engaged. Recalling the serious effects of Pelée's eruption, in 1976 the French government evacuated the entire population of the island of Guadeloupe, fearing a similar eruption might occur from the volcanic mountain La Soufrière. It did not happen, but the memory of the destruction of St. Pierre in evidence on the island of Martinique, also French-owned, is strong in the French West Indies.

On Martinique, evidence of the killer volcanic eruption of 1902 still remains. Where volcanic ash was deposited, the land is a wasteland. The sand on that side of the island is black as a result of the black cloud of ash and gases that struck with such fury. The summit of Pelée was forever changed, with a large crater that formed from the explosion. It is now filled in by lava domes that, in an explosive volcanic eruption, form near the hole where the eruption occurred. The summit is a large garden of flowers and ferns surrounded by a heavy mist.

The city of St. Pierre never completely recovered from the explosion, and a small, quiet town exists where once there had been a bustling seaport. There is a volcanological museum with pictures and artifacts from the 1902 eruption of the volcano. The ruins of the opera house and other buildings are still visible.

Colleen M. Driscoll

FOR FURTHER INFORMATION:

Fisher, Richard V., Grant Heiken, and Jeffrey B. Hulen. *Volcanoes: Crucibles of Change.* Princeton, N.J.: Princeton University Press, 1997.

1902: Santa María

DATE: October 24, 1902
PLACE: Guatemala
RESULT: 6,000 dead, animals and crops destroyed, buildings collapsed

Santa María is located in western Guatemala, and it rises 12,375 feet (3,772 meters) above sea level. This volcano was not active in historic times, but it produced one of the largest eruptions of the twentieth century, in 1902. Steam began to rise along the southwest side of the volcano on the afternoon of October 24. A large rumbling was heard at 5 P.M., and by 8 P.M., a large cloud of ash was visible over the volcano. The biggest eruption began at 1 A.M. on October 25 as strong explosions occurred, and they were heard up to 528 miles (850 kilometers) away. Ash and larger volcanic fragments rained down from 3 to 6 A.M. as strong earthquakes occurred.

By dawn on October 25, a column of ash and steam was estimated to have risen at least 15.5 miles (25 kilometers) above the volcano. Much of that day was dark over a widespread area. Steam and ash eruptions alternated with gradually diminishing activity for a few weeks after the initial eruption. The volcanic ash covered the area west of the volcano to thicknesses of tens of feet. Nearly half of the thousands of dead resulted from the collapse of buildings from the weight of the volcanic material.

Volcanic mudflows traveled up to 62 miles (100 kilometers) from the volcano, and they killed many people. Also, most of the birds over hundreds of miles were killed, so that flies, mosquitoes, and rats temporarily multiplied, making conditions even more difficult. The coffee crop was completely destroyed, causing millions of dollars in economic loss. A malaria epidemic after the eruption was estimated to have killed many more people than the eruption. After the eruption, much of the side of the volcano was found to have been blown away, forming a vertical cliff over 7,546 feet (2,300 meters) high.

Robert L. Cullers

FOR FURTHER INFORMATION:

The New York Times, October 31 and November 20, 1902.

Rose, W. I. "Notes on the 1902 Eruption of Santa María Volcano, Guatemala." *Bulletin of Volcanology* 36 (1972): 29-45.

Williams, S. N., and S. Self. "The October 1902 Plinian Eruption of Santa María Volcano, Guatemala." *Journal of Volcanology and Geothermal Research* 16 (1982): 33-56.

1905: Vesuvius

DATE: 1905-1906
PLACE: Italy
RESULT: Dozens dead, buildings destroyed

Mount Vesuvius is located near Naples, Italy, in a populated area. It erupted eighteen times between 79 and 1906. One moderate eruption began with lava flows on May 27, 1905, and lava continued to erupt through early April, 1906. Violent explosions began on April 5, 1906, as an ash cloud rose above the crater, with the explosions continuing until April 7. Lava was extruded in several places from the side of the volcano; it flowed as several streams toward populated areas, but people had plenty of time to get away from the slow-moving lava. On April 8, the biggest

lava flow moved through the town of Boscotrecase. Pictures of the event show only the highest buildings projecting above the lava flow. Some houses in the town were destroyed, and some were filled with lava. Smaller plants were incinerated, but larger trees did not appear to burn as the lava engulfed them.

The violent explosions spewed fragments of rocks and ash high into the air. Much of this material initially settled east-northeast of the volcano, up to several feet thick. Much of the loss of life was due to the collapse of the weakest buildings from the weight of the volcanic material. For instance, in San Guiseppe Vesuviano, many people crowded into a church even though a priest tried to keep them out, as he knew the roof was unsafe. An estimated 105 persons were killed, and 90 were injured as the roof collapsed. Another 100 to 200 persons were killed in Ottaiano from collapsing roofs.

On April 11, winds shifted and carried dense ash clouds to Naples. Business in the city was paralyzed as tens of thousands of people evacuated the city. A few buildings also collapsed here, killing many people. In Ottaiano and San Guiseppe, volcanic projectiles did not break windows in buildings on the sides facing the volcano but, rather, on the sides of the buildings facing away from it. This was attributed to the rush of cool air at the surface toward the volcano to replace the hot, rising air above the volcano.

Robert L. Cullers

FOR FURTHER INFORMATION:

Mastrolorenzo, G., R. Munno, and G. Rolandi. "Vesuvius 1906: A Case Study of a Paroxysmal Eruption and Its Relation to Eruption Cycles." *Journal of Volcanology and Geothermal Research* 58 (1993): 217-237.

Perret, F. A. *The Vesuvius Eruption of 1906.* Carnegie Institution Publication No. 339. Washington, D.C.: Carnegie Institution, 1993.

_____. *Volcanological Observations.* Carnegie Institution Publication No. 549. Washington, D.C.: Carnegie Institution, 1950.

1906: Masaya

DATE: January 4, 1906
PLACE: Nicaragua
RESULT: Thousands dead

Masaya is located in western Nicaragua in a populated region about 12.4 miles (20 kilometers) south of Managua. This volcano has erupted at least nineteen times since the Spanish first observed it in 1524. It is unusual in that it is one of the few explosive volcanoes that has low silica content of the lavas. This explosive character may be due partially to the buildup of gases to the point where the molten rock material explodes out of the volcanic edifice. Fences, wires, metal, and plants around the volcano have been corroded due to the continual emission of sulfur dioxide gas. In 1906, Masaya had one such explosive eruption from the central vent and the flanks, which produced moderate damage from volcanic material thrown into the air and left thousands dead.

Robert L. Cullers

FOR FURTHER INFORMATION:

Sapper, K. T. "Explosion of Masaya, Nicaragua." *Zentralblatt für Mineralogie, Geologie und Paleontologie* 1 (1906): 257-259.

Simkin, Tom, and Lee Siebert. *Volcanoes of the World.* 2d ed. Tucson, Ariz.: Geoscience Press, 1994.

1911: Taal

DATE: January 30, 1911
PLACE: Philippines
RESULT: 1,335 dead, 200 injured

Taal is located in the middle of a lake about 31 miles (50 kilometers) south of Manila, Philippines. There have been at least 11 major recorded eruptions since 1572 with mostly gas and ash emissions and little or no lava. Prior to the eruption of 1911, the central cone of the volcano rose only about 394 feet (120 meters) above the level of the lake. The crater had nearly perpendicular sides, and it contained three small lakes. Two of the lakes often boiled vigorously.

On January 27, 1911, earthquakes began under the volcano. Twenty-six earthquakes were recorded in Manila on that day, and 217 separate quakes were recorded the next day. A huge column of black ash and gases was observed coming out of the volcano on the morning of January 28. A photographer made it to the rim of the crater the next morning: The previous lakes within the crater had disappeared. For example, at the site of one lake, a tower of vapor and ash was rising and was being blown to the west. Mud was also being ejected upward.

At 1:05 A.M. on January 30, a very loud explosion awakened many people some distance from the volcano as a black, muddy cloud rose from the crater with electrical displays that were observed at least 261 miles (420 kilometers) away. A town about 12.4 miles (20 kilometers) to the northeast experienced a rain of mud just a few minutes later.

At 2:20 A.M., two major explosions in rapid succession occurred and were heard up to 621 miles (1,000 kilometers) away. These explosions blew out most of

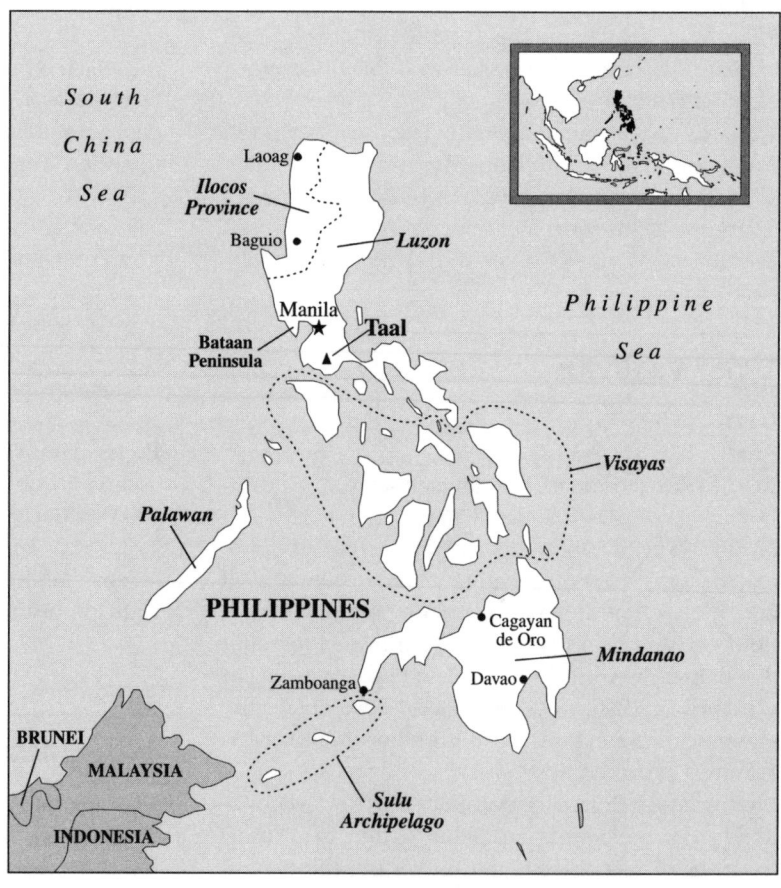

the floor of the volcano. The black cloud that formed rose at least 2.5 to 3 miles (4 to 5 kilometers) high, displaying chain lightning that was nearly continuous. A muddy rain then commenced as the cloud blew to the northeast.

As a result of the explosive eruption at 2:20 A.M., at least 1,335 persons were killed and all property was destroyed in the zone of total devastation that extended up to 7.5 miles (12 kilometers) away from the volcano. Only 732 bodies were actually found, but the actual number killed could have been much higher than the estimate because entire villages disappeared. Only a few persons were found injured but alive in the zone of total devastation. At least 700 domestic animals were also killed by this initial blast.

Much of the destruction in the zone of total devastation was likely caused by fairly hot gas-solid dispersions that flowed downward. Additional damage was produced around the lake by large waves or tsunamis that washed ashore and carried off most of the debris in thirteen villages. Villages not affected by the tsunamis had much debris thrown around, which fell to the ground in chaotic fashion.

A U.S. Army Corps of Engineers worker camped at a distance of about 4 miles (7 kilometers) from the volcano and about 0.3 mile (0.5 kilometer) from the lake gave an interesting written account of the effects at that location after the major explosions. First, a heavy wind began to blow, which broke the tent ropes and threw the tent and the worker 16.4 feet (5 meters). Then there was an ashfall, and the man had to gasp for breath for about twenty seconds. This was followed by more ash and a cold rain that lasted for about fifteen minutes. During this period the large waves from the lake rushed on shore and reached his camp; he had to run to higher ground to avoid being swept away.

The worst destruction was not at this location, but rather to the west of the volcano. A schoolmaster was the first to arrive in this area and found that villages were totally destroyed. People had lacerated flesh and fractured bones from rocks thrown out of the volcano or from falling homes. Unprotected flesh was described as being burned, although sandblasting or acidic waters rather than hot ash or gases may have been the cause. Some victims also showed signs of having suffocated. The few survivors in this zone were located in protected areas or covered themselves with mats.

All crops and grass were destroyed over much of the area. Trees up to 9.5 inches (24 centimeters) in diameter were fractured at about 1 to 1.6 feet (0.3 to 0.5 meter) in height with the ends of the stumps so shredded that they resembled brooms. Because of the lack of food for domestic animals, many of them eventually starved to death. Mud and volcanic ash were spread over an area of 1,200 square miles, with dust falling over an even larger area. The mud was fluid and ran into ravines, collecting up to a depth of 6.5 feet (2 meters) in ravines with little accumulation on ridges.

The full extent of the disaster was not known for several days because the mud, broken and tangled vegetation, and destroyed boats within the lake surrounding the volcano impeded travel into the area. Eventually, help arrived from Manila. Launches and motorboats were sent with physicians who set up dressing and receiving stations for the wounded near the lake. From these areas, the wounded were sent to nearby hospitals. The Red Cross and other relief funds were used to obtain food and housing for the homeless. Roads were also repaired from some of the relief funds, which provided temporary income for some people.

Robert L. Cullers

FOR FURTHER INFORMATION:

Blong, R. J. *Volcanic Hazards.* Orlando, Fla.: Academic Press, 1984.

Martin, C. "Observations on the Recent Eruption of Taal Volcano." *Philippine Journal of Science* 6A (1911): 87-90.

Maso, M. S. *The Eruption of Taal Volcano, January 30, 1911.* Manila, Philippines: Department of the Interior, Weather Bureau, 1911.

Noble, F. H. *Taal Volcano: Album of Views of 1911 Eruption.* Manila: Author, 1911.

Pratt, W. E. "The Eruption of Taal Volcano, January 30, 1911." *Philippine Journal of Science* 6A (1911): 63-83.

Worchester, D. C. "Taal Volcano and Its Recent Destructive Eruption." *National Geographic,* April, 1912, 313-367.

1912: Katmai

DATE: June 6, 1912
PLACE: Alaska
VOLCANIC EXPLOSIVITY INDEX: 6

RESULT: Ash covered Valley of Ten Thousand Smokes

Katmai, named for an Eskimo word meaning "uncertain," has only erupted one time, but that explosion was considered the most intense twentieth century volcanic eruption at that time. Rising 6,714 feet above sea level, Katmai belonged to a group of stratovolcanoes. Katmai and neighboring Novarupta erupted simultaneously in June of 1912. The Katmai eruption resulted in 7 cubic miles of ash being expelled during a sixty-hour period and coating 46,000 square miles of Alaska. Drifts 2 feet deep accumulated in streets at Kodiak. In the Ukak River Valley northwest of Katmai, piles of incandescent sand amassed from the eruption's lava flows, which stretched more than 15 miles from the volcano.

The National Geographic Society sponsored an expedition to the volcano in 1916, and, when explorers found the region around Katmai filled with steaming jets, they dubbed it the Valley of Ten Thousand Smokes. Because the area was uninhabited, no humans died when Katmai erupted. A caldera was created and filled with sufficient water to become a lake. The valley had been lush with vegetation before the volcano erupted; afterward, an area of 50 square miles resembled the moon's barren surface so much that the National Aeronautics and Space Administration (NASA) trained Apollo astronauts for lunar missions in the valley.

Elizabeth D. Schafer

FOR FURTHER INFORMATION:

Fierstein, J., and W. Hildreth. "The Plinian Eruptions of 1912 at Novarupta, Katmai National Park, Alaska." *Bulletin of Volcanology* 54 (1992): 646-684.

Griggs, R. F. "The Valley of Ten Thousand Smokes: National Geographic Society Explorations in the Katmai District of Alaska." *National Geographic Magazine* 81 (1917): 13-68.

Hildreth, W. "New Perspectives on the Eruption of 1912 in the Valley of Ten Thousand Smokes, Katmai National Park, Alaska." *Bulletin of Volcanology* 49 (1987): 680-693.

1917: Boquerón

DATE: June 6, 1917

PLACE: El Salvador
RESULT: 450 dead, 100,000 homeless

Boquerón is a gently sloping volcano with an elevation of 4,265 feet (1,300 meters). San Salvador, the capital of El Salvador, is located at the base òf the volcano, which has been destroyed a number of times by eruptions, including that of June 6, 1917. Initially, a series of large earthquakes occurred, and fissures to the north of the volcano began to extrude lava. The earthquakes reduced San Salvador and the surrounding area to ruins. Most of the deaths and injuries were a result of the earthquakes.

An eyewitness described the volcano as exploding into a huge sheet of flame. Then a burning rain of hot volcanic material began to fall on the dazed inhabitants. The crater contained a beautiful lake that was 2,625 feet (800 meters) deep, but on June 10, the lake began to glow as lava was extruded onto the lake bottom. The water began to evaporate, and lava was seen to periodically rise above the lake surface. The lake had completely evaporated by June 28, and the lava could easily be seen. Finally, a small fissure expanded in the bottom of the lake, and a large explosion blasted a column of steam and volcanic fragments into the air.

Robert L. Cullers

FOR FURTHER INFORMATION:

Powers, S. "Letter Concerning the San Salvador Eruption." *Vulkanologie* 4 (1918): 201.

Roy, S. K. "A Restudy of the 1917 Eruption of Volcán Boquerón, El Salvador, Central America." *Fieldiana Geology*, n.s. 10 (1957): 363-382.

1919: Kelut

DATE: May 20, 1919
PLACE: Java, Indonesia
RESULT: 5,500 dead, many villages destroyed

Kelut, on eastern Java, is rather low (5,678 feet) and has very irregular slopes. The irregularities are caused by lava plugs at the top and by the violent erosion processes that are a result of the sudden emptying of the lake in the crater during a volcanic eruption.

The crater lake typically fills between eruptions (every eight to eighteen years). Prior to the 1875 eruption, the volume of water in the lake was 102 million cubic yards (78 million cubic meters), and it was 52 million cubic yards (40 million cubic meters) after that eruption. Water in the lake is ejected during an eruption. Much of this water is mixed with the volcanic debris from the eruption, forming mudflows (lahars) that run rapidly down the slopes along gullies and stream channels to the Brantas River. The lahars are usually cold during the first part of the eruption, but they become hot later as the mud is mixed with hot volcanic debris. Some lahars form as a result of intense rains combined with volcanic ash. One such series of lahars occurred during the 1919 eruption, and they swept over an area of more than 50 square miles (130 square kilometers), destroying 104 villages and killing about 5,500 people.

After the 1919 eruption, the government tried to build controls to reduce the hazards posed by lahars. A series of tunnels were built into the side of the volcano to reduce the water level in the lake and hopefully reduce the formation of lahars. However, the work on these tunnels was hampered by high temperatures and by an accident in which the lake waters suddenly broke through a tunnel, killing 5 workers. Eventually the series of tunnels were drilled, and the volume of the lake was reduced to less than 2.6 million cubic yards (2 million cubic meters). Apparently as a result of this effort, the eruptions of 1951, 1966, and 1990 resulted in no lahars and little damage.

Robert L. Cullers

FOR FURTHER INFORMATION:

Francis, P. *Volcanoes.* Harmondsworth, Middlesex, England: Penguin Books, 1976.

Neumann van Padang, M. *Catalogue of the Active Volcanoes of Indonesia.* Naples, Italy: International Association of Volcanology, 1951.

Verstappen, H. T. "Volcanic Hazards in Columbia and Indonesia: Lahars and Related Phenomena." In *Geohazards,* edited by G. J. H. Mc-

Call, D. J. C. Lanning, and S. C. Scott. London: Chapman and Hall, 1992.

1926: Mauna Loa

DATE: April 17, 1926
PLACE: Hawaii
RESULT: Dozens dead, town of Hoopuloa destroyed

Mauna Loa is located on the island of Hawaii, which is located farthest to the southeast in the Hawaiian island chain. The volcano is located in the central to

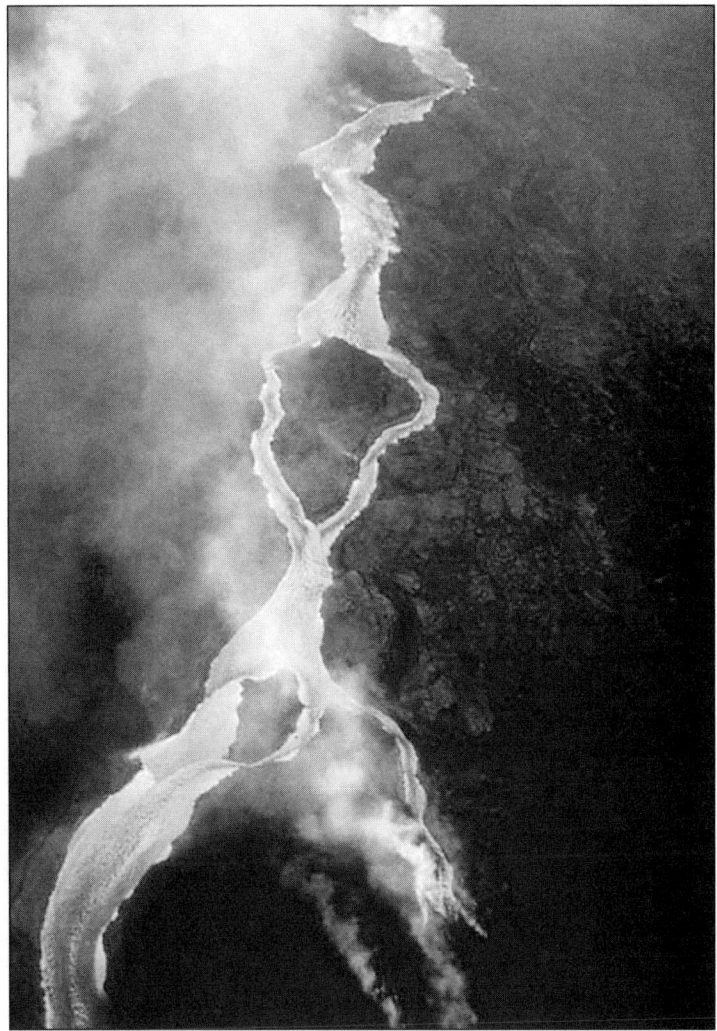

Lava streams down Mauna Loa in an undated photo. (National Oceanic and Atmospheric Administration)

southwestern portion of the island, and it rises to a height of 13,678 feet above sea level. It is one of the most active volcanoes on Earth, erupting 15 times in the twentieth century. Its eruptions are not very explosive as they extrude mostly low-silica-content lavas to build up the island.

The eruption of April 10, 1926, began at about 3:00 A.M. from lava flowing from a rift about 3 miles below the summit. Three lava tongues flowed down to the southeast for about 0.6 mile, 1.9 miles, and 5 miles, respectively, but these flows stopped before doing any damage. Another series of lava flows began erupting to the southwest on April 13. One lava tongue flowed across the belt road at 12:22 P.M. on April 16, reaching a shore platform near the village of Hoopuloa on April 17. The flow had a 1,640-foot-wide front and averaged 33 feet in height. By 4:00 A.M. on April 18, the outhouses of the village began burning; the village was completely destroyed by 8:30 A.M. There was not one building left after the flow moved through the village. As the flow hit the wharf and the seawater in the harbor, there were roars and explosions, and thousands of fish were killed. In all, dozens of people were estimated to have been killed.

Robert L. Cullers

FOR FURTHER INFORMATION:
Keating, Barbara, comp. *Hawaiian Eruptions: The Eruptions of Kilauea and Mauna Loa Volcanoes.* Honolulu: University of Hawaii Foundation, 1987.
Lockwood, John P., and P. W. Lipman. "Holocene Eruptive History of Mauna Loa Volcano." In *Volcanism in Hawaii*, edited by Robert W. Decker, Thomas L. Wright, and Peter H. Stauffer. 2 vols. Washington, D.C.: U.S. Government Printing Office, 1987.

1928: Rokatenda

DATE: August 4-5, 1928
PLACE: Paluweh, Indonesia
RESULT: 226 dead, villages and boats destroyed

Rokatenda is located in the western Pacific near Paluweh, Indonesia. This is an area of explosive volcanic activity, as Indonesia has 130 active volcanoes. Not much information exists about this eruption, most probably because of its remote location.

According to *The New York Times*, a violent eruption occurred in which half the island and six villages were destroyed. Those people driven into the ocean were swamped and killed in boats by a 16.4-foot-high seismic sea wave produced by an earthquake. An estimated 1,200 persons were killed, and 400 were injured.

Robert L. Cullers

FOR FURTHER INFORMATION:
The New York Times, August 10 and 16, 1928.

1931: Merapi

DATE: December 13-28, 1931
PLACE: Java, Indonesia
RESULT: More than 1,300 dead

Lava flows incinerated the village of Balong, Indonesia, after a Merapi eruption. (AP/ Wide World Photos)

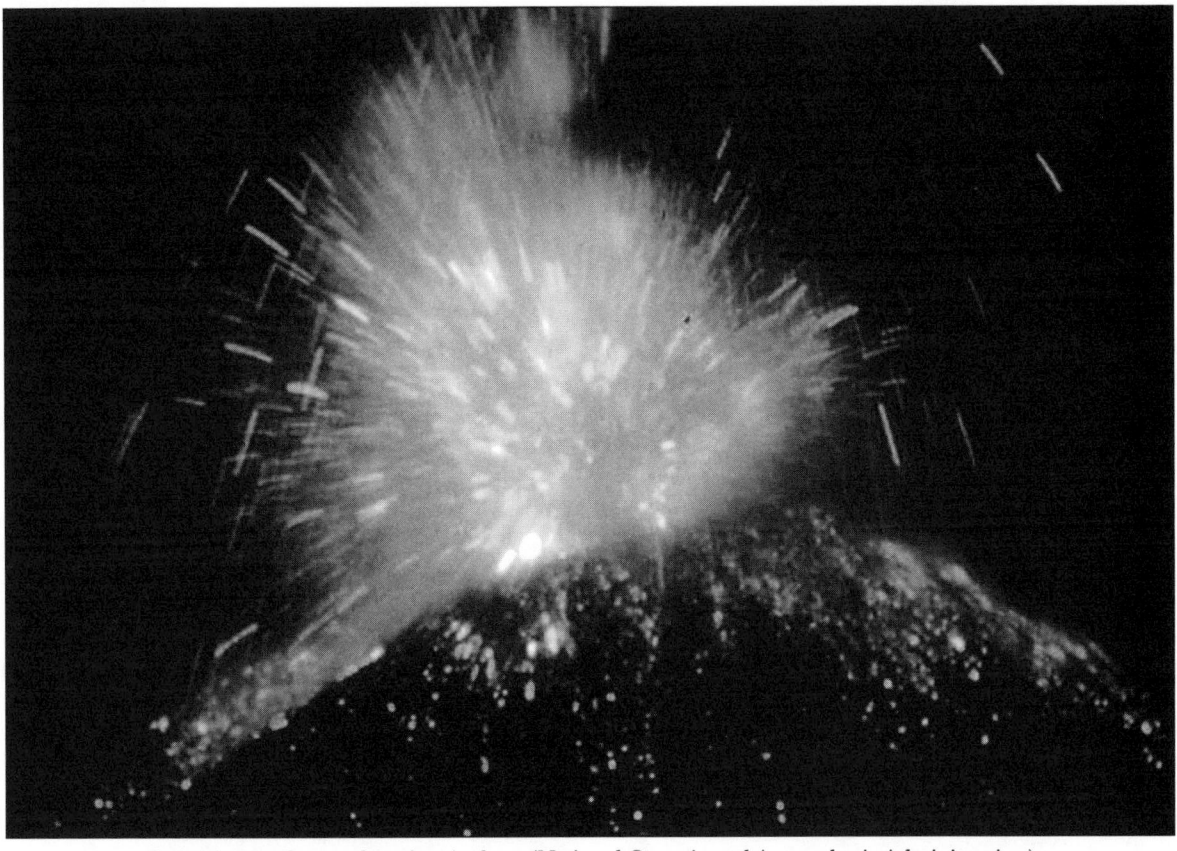

Paricutín spews lava and gas from its dome. (National Oceanic and Atmospheric Administration)

Merapi is one of the most active of the 130 explosive volcanoes in Indonesia, and it is located in a populated region. It experienced sixty-eight eruptions from 1548 to 1999, producing nuées ardentes in thirty-two of these eruptions. Nuées ardentes are the type of violent eruption in which hot gases and ash flow on a cushion of air rapidly down the slopes of volcanoes such that most life is destroyed in their path. Merapi also often extrudes large volumes of lavas and forms volcanic mudflows, as occurred in the 1931 eruption. During that eruption, copious amounts of volcanic ash periodically blew out of the volcano and descended down the slope as a nuée ardente to distances of over 12.4 miles (20 kilometers). The nuée ardente covered an area of over 7.7 square miles (20 square kilometers). A lava flow from the central crater extended over 4.4 miles (7 kilometers) and was 656 feet (200 meters) wide and 82 feet (25 meters) tall. One of the nuées ardentes killed most of the 1,300 victims.

Robert L. Cullers

FOR FURTHER INFORMATION:

Kusumadimata, K. *Data on Dasar Gunungapi, Indonesia.* Jakarta, Indonesia: Catalogue of References on Indonesian Volcanoes, Republic of Indonesia, 1979.

Neumann van Padang, M. *Catalogue of the Active Volcanoes of Indonesia.* Naples, Italy: Catalogue of the Active Volcanoes of the World, 1951.

1943: Paricutín

DATE: February 20, 1943
PLACE: Mexico
VOLCANIC EXPLOSIVITY INDEX: 3
RESULT: Growth of new volcano

Named for the village it consumed, Paricutín provided volcanologists with a unique opportunity to witness the birth of a volcano. Rising in the Michoacán-

Guanajuato volcanic region of Central Mexico, Paricutín emerged in a cornfield. Tarascan Indians who farmed that region saw the cone when it first appeared. For years, children playing near the field had reported seeing a hole in the earth, feeling unusually warm soil, and hearing strange noises in the ground. As Paricutín appeared, earthquakes shook the area around the hole, and fissures opened. Eyewitnesses smelled sulfur and saw flaming sparks shoot out of the hole. The cone rose several feet per hour.

By June, Paricutín was erupting ash and lava, which buried two villages and hundreds of houses in a 10-square-mile area. The Tarascan Indians were relocated to the village of Caltzontzin, abandoning the homeland where previous generations had lived for centuries. A local church was half covered by the debris and was opened as a tourist site. Scientists and journalists rushed to the site to watch the volcano's growth. The cone continued to rise, reaching 1,390 feet by the time it became inactive in 1952. The explosions before it became dormant were exceptionally violent. Although no casualties resulted from volcanic debris, 3 deaths were attributed to lightning related to Paricutín's eruption.

Elizabeth D. Schafer

FOR FURTHER INFORMATION:

Foshag, W. F., and J. Gonzalez-Reyna. "Birth and Development of Paricutín Volcano." *U.S. Geological Survey Bulletin* 965-D (1956): 355-489.
Luhr, James F., and Tom Simkin. *Paricutín: The Volcano Born in a Mexican Cornfield*. Phoenix: Geoscience Press, 1993.

1951: Lamington

DATE: January 17-21, 1951
PLACE: New Guinea
RESULT: Estimated 3,000 dead

Lamington, in eastern New Guinea, had not erupted in historical times until 1951. Volcanic activity was noted in the crater six days prior to the climactic eruption on January 21, but the warning signs went largely unheeded. On January 15, landslides from the crater walls were noted. From January 15 to 17, vapor rose from the crater, and earthquakes were felt

in settlements near the volcano. Electric displays of blue flashes or sheet and chain lightning were visible on January 19 as ash rose from the crater. An ash cloud rose to over 26,246 feet (8,000 meters) on January 20, but it blew over unpopulated areas so few people evacuated the area.

At 10:40 A.M. on January 21, loud explosions were heard up to 205 miles (330 kilometers) away, and an ash cloud rose to over 52,493 feet (16,000 meters) within twenty minutes. The base expanded as a nuée ardente at 62 miles per hour, and it produced complete devastation in a 24-square-mile area surrounding the volcano. The forest was flattened, and, in some places, not even the tree stumps remained. Buildings disappeared, leaving only the floors behind.

The temperature of the nuée ardente varied in places, but it was hot enough to kill 2,942 people and injure many others. People in buildings in the zone of total devastation were found with varying degrees of burns, piled on floors of houses that had disappeared. Survivors described pain in the eyes, mouth, and throat; a burning sensation in the chest; and a feeling of suffocation that was a result of inhalation of the hot air and ash mixture. Few people were killed or injured by flying debris or crushed by falling trees or buildings. The explosive eruptions continued with varying activity for the next two months.

Robert L. Cullers

FOR FURTHER INFORMATION:

Bullard, Fred M. *Volcanoes of the Earth*. 2d rev. ed. Austin: University of Texas Press, 1976.
Taylor, G. A. M. *The 1951 Eruption of Mount Lamington, Papua*. 2d ed. Canberra: Australian Government Publishing Service, 1983.

1951: Hibok-Hibok

DATE: December 2-8, 1951
PLACE: Philippines
RESULT: 500 dead

Hibok-Hibok is located 12.4 miles (20 kilometers) north of Mindanao, Philippines, on a small, populated island. It erupted in 1827, 1862, 1871 to 1875, and 1948 to 1953.

The activity of 1948 to 1953 started in August, 1948, with earth tremors and some resulting landslides. On December 4, 1951, hot blasts of glowing ash and gas rushed down the mountain (called a nuée ardente) with relatively little warning, so people had not evacuated. The nuées ardentes were so hot that houses burst into flame, animals were roasted to death, and plants were charred. A *Time* magazine reporter observed a standing water buffalo that was covered in ash, but it was dead. An estimated 500 people were killed, but only 266 bodies were found.

As a result of this eruption, the Philippines opened the Philippine Institute of Volcanology and Seismology, which monitors the active volcanoes in the country. This will hopefully give residents near the volcanoes enough time to evacuate the region if an eruption appears imminent.

Robert L. Cullers

FOR FURTHER INFORMATION:

Simkin, Tom, and Lee Siebert. *Volcanoes of the World.* 2d ed. Tucson, Ariz.: Geoscience Press, 1994.

Time, December 17, 1951, 36.

1963: Agung

DATE: March 20, 1963
PLACE: Bali, Indonesia
RESULT: More than 1,200 dead, 200,000 homeless, agricultural land destroyed

Agung is the highest mountain on Bali, Indonesia, and it is located in a populated area. The volcano had been quiet since 1843, but on March 20, 1963, it erupted hot ash and gases, lava, and volcanic

Smoke bellows from the volcano Agung behind the Besakih Temple in northeastern Bali. (AP/Wide World Photos)

mudflows over a period of several days. The glowing hot mix of gas and volcanic debris called nuées ardentes flowed down the volcano at high speed, and they were responsible for killing most of the victims. Some were killed by the volcanic mudflows called lahars that formed by mixing of the rain and hot ash and flowed rapidly down stream valleys. Others were killed by the collapse of buildings from the weight of the volcanic materials that settled on top of them.

The town of Subagen had a population of 5,000 with many substantial buildings before the eruption, but it was buried in volcanic debris that ranged in size from fine ash to boulders the size of buildings. One lahar swept away 200 people worshiping in a temple. About 25,000 acres of farmland was completely destroyed, and another 100,000 acres became unproductive for years. This disaster resulted in many tens of thousands of refugees being evacuated and fed by relief agencies for some time.

The town of Sanga was covered by a nuée ardente that killed many people instantly, but it also set a temple on fire. The temple collapsed, killing everyone inside. The survivor who described this devastation protected himself with a sarong over his head as he ran away, escaping with burns on his legs and arms.

The worst devastation occurred in the villages east of Besakih. Combinations of nuées ardentes and hot lahars completely destroyed these towns. Even two weeks after the eruption, these areas were too hot to enter. Bodies were buried or eaten by dogs where they lay.

Robert L. Cullers

FOR FURTHER INFORMATION:
Booth, W. T. "Disaster in Paradise." *National Geographic* 124 (1963): 436-458.
Zen, M. T., and D. Hodikusumo. "Preliminary Report on the 1963 Eruption of Mount Agung in Bali." *Bulletin of Volcanology* 27 (1964): 269-299.

1963: Surtsey Island

DATE: November 8, 1963-June 5, 1967
PLACE: Iceland

Surtsey Island billowing smoke. (Courtesy of R. Carmichael)

VOLCANIC EXPLOSIVITY INDEX: 3
RESULT: Island created

In 1963 the international media's attention was focused on the formation of an island 17 miles off Iceland's south coast. Created when a volcano on the ocean floor erupted, Surtsey Island was named for an Icelandic mythological character representing fire. Surtsey was produced by the Vestmannaeyjar volcanic system, which spawned Heimaey, another prominent volcanic island. A series of eruptions occurred over a three-and-a-half-year period to establish Surtsey. Eruptions released magma from an underwater vent, and the volcano extended from the seafloor 426.5 feet (130 meters) below sea level to the surface within one week.

Some explosions shot ash and steam as high as 6.2 miles (10 kilometers) above the volcano. The expelled tephra that surged to the surface or fell from the atmosphere collected into an unsteady ring of tuff (rock made of volcanic debris fused together by heat). Suddenly, on January 31, 1964, eruptions transferred to another vent 1,312 feet (400 meters) northwest of the original site, and a second tuff ring grew, which sheltered that vent from water erosion, resulting in lava flowing freely and enlarging Surtsey. In May, 1965, the volcano began a yearlong dormancy.

In August, 1966, the volcano began emitting lava through new vents, thickening the island's surface. Ten months later the volcano ceased erupting. Volcanologists estimated that the volcano had yielded 1,308 cubic yards (1 cubic kilometer) of lava and ash, with less than 10 percent remaining above the surface. Considered a scientific sanctuary, Surtsey Island is carefully observed to chronicle the history of an island and its plant and animal inhabitants from the beginning of its existence. The volcano has decreased slightly in size because of compaction.

Elizabeth D. Schafer

FOR FURTHER INFORMATION:
Moore, J. G., S. Jakobsson, and J. Holmjarn. "Subsidence of Surtsey Volcano, 1967-1991." *Bulletin of Volcanology* 55 (1992): 17-24.

Scherman, Katharine. *Daughter of Fire.* Boston: Little, Brown, 1976.

Thorarinsson, S. *Surtsey, the New Island in the North Atlantic.* New York: Viking Press, 1964.

1965: Taal

DATE: September 28, 1965
PLACE: Philippines
RESULT: 200 dead

Taal is located on an island in Lake Taal in southern Luzon, Philippines. Before September 28, 1965, there was little indication of an imminent eruption except for a gradual increase in the temperature of the lake from 86 to 113 degrees Fahrenheit (30 to 45 degrees Celsius). At 2:00 A.M. on September 28 residents of the island were awakened by load roars and hissing. Some people observed glowing material being ejected into the air. From 3:25 to 9:20 A.M., eruption clouds of gas and solid material rose 9.3 miles (15 to 20 kilometers) high, accompanied by explosions and lightning. In the lower part of this cloud, a flat, turbulent cloud spread out horizontally in all directions with hurricane speeds. Explosions of ash and hot gases continued until 3:50 P.M. on September 30. The lake temperature had risen to 170.6 degrees Fahrenheit (77 degrees Celsius).

The debris ejected from the crater consisted of both new and old ruptured volcanic material, but most of it was not very hot. Within 0.5 mile of the blasts, blocks of debris up to 20 inches (50 centimeters) across were thrown out of the volcano by the horizontal blasts, and no trees were left standing. Ejected material was much finer from 0.6 to 1.6 miles (1 to 2.5 kilometers) from the volcano. In this zone, trees remained standing, but they were sandblasted so that all the bark and much of the wood were removed in the direction facing the volcano. Farther out than 1.6 miles (2.5 kilometers), the sandblasted trees were later coated with mud up to 15.7 inches (40 centimeters) thick.

Cattle protected from the blast survived, but those in the direct line of the debris-laden cloud lost their hair and skin on one side, and some were blinded. No charring or burning of the vegetation occurred, but outside the blast area, a thick layer of ash covered houses and vegetation. Most of the deaths were caused by 15-foot-high waves in the lake, which swamped boats as the residents of the island were fleeing the blasts. The waves were apparently caused by air blasts from the explosions during the eruption.

Robert L. Cullers

Lake Taal with its volcano in eruption in 1965. (National Oceanic and Atmospheric Administration)

FOR FURTHER INFORMATION:

Moore, J. G. "Base Surge in Recent Volcanic Eruptions." *Bulletin Volcanologique* 30 (1967): 337-363.

Moore, J. G., K. Nakamura, and A. Alcaraz. "The 1965 Eruption of Taal Volcano." *Science* 151 (1966): 955-960.

1968: Arenal

DATE: July, 1968
PLACE: Costa Rica
VOLCANIC EXPLOSIVITY INDEX: 3
RESULT: 80 dead

Arenal stands 5,435 feet above sea level. A stratovolcano, Mount Arenal was mostly dormant, except for one reported explosion in the year 1500, until its eruption in 1968. Although volcanologists using radiocarbon-dating methods estimated that the volcano has existed since 3190 B.C.E., Arenal did not pose serious threats to nearby populations until the twentieth century, when it began erupting regularly. Arenal suddenly became active in July, 1968, when it violently expelled large chunks of rock and triggered avalanches of boiling lava down its west slope. Some projectiles landed 3 miles (5 kilometers) from the volcano. The eruption continued for three days. Approximately 80 people died from injuries when they were struck by debris, including pumice and rocks, or were killed by lava. Falling boulders created craters in the village of Tabacon.

After the summer of 1968, Arenal often experienced minor eruptions, spewing lava that crept down its slopes, primarily on the west and north sides. These lava flows ignited forest fires and burned crops in fields. Each eruption was erratic, sometimes occurring only minutes apart and at other times several hours apart. Arenal thrust plumes of ash as high as 0.5 foot into the atmosphere and propelled massive rocks into the air, like ammunition fired from artillery. Debris from eruption clouds fell onto adjacent communities. Mount Arenal's irregular eruption patterns represented scientists' dilemma in deciding whether a volcano that has been inactive for centuries is extinct or merely dormant.

Elizabeth D. Schafer

FOR FURTHER INFORMATION:
"Costa Rica Volcano Quiet." *The New York Times*, August 2, 1968, p. 3.
"Costa Rican Crater Continues Eruption." *The New York Times*, August 1, 1968, p. 18.
Melson, W. G., and R. Saenz. "Volume, Energy, and Cyclicity of Eruptions at Arenal Volcano, Costa Rica." *Bulletin of Volcanology* 37 (1973): 416-437.

1973: Heimaey Island

DATE: January 23, 1973
PLACE: Iceland
RESULT: More than 400 homes destroyed

Heimaey is a small island located south of Iceland. An eruption of lava and airborne volcanic material began from a fissure at 1:50 A.M. on January 23, 1973, on the east side of the island near the town of Vestmannaeyjar (5,300 residents). Within minutes of the beginning of the eruption, lava fountains up to 492 feet high were erupted from a 1,312-foot fissure that soon expanded to over 4,921 feet long. Part of the fissure was only 656 feet from the east side of town, but fortunately the lava and debris initially flowed east, away from the town. This gave the residents enough time to evacuate in fishing boats and in airplanes within four hours after the initial eruption; there were no injuries.

By the evening of January 27, the wind shifted, and volcanic debris was deposited on the town at depths that ranged from 1 foot to over 16.4 feet. Some houses collapsed from the weight of this material. Other houses caught on fire from the heat of the glowing "bombs" that entered some windows.

The residents set up more than 18.6 miles of pipe and forty-three pumps to pump seawater rapidly to

Heimaey Island erupting in 1973. The steam to the left rises over the lava flowing into the ocean. (Courtesy of R. Carmichael)

the front of the flows to cool the lava and stop its advance. This action did reduce the lava's viscosity—when it hit the piles of cool debris pushed close to the flows by bulldozers, the rubbery lava stopped. Whether the lava stopped because of this effort or because of luck will never be known.

Robert L. Cullers

FOR FURTHER INFORMATION:

Grove, N. "Volcano Overwhelms an Icelandic Village." *National Geographic* 241 (1973): 372-375.

Thorarinsson, S., S. Steinthorsson, T. H. Einarsson, H. Kristmannsdottir, and N. Oskarsson. "The Eruption on Heimaey, Iceland." *Nature* 241 (1973): 372-375.

1977: Nyiragongo

DATE: January 10, 1977
PLACE: Zaire
VOLCANIC EXPLOSIVITY INDEX: 1
RESULT: More than 1,000 dead

A stratovolcano rising 11,365 feet above sea level, Nyiragongo is located on the Virunga volcanic chain along the East African Rift. Its first documented eruption happened in 1884. Between 1928 and 1977, the volcano was often active. In the latter year, lava from Lake Kivu, positioned in the volcano's main crater, poured down the slopes at speeds of 40 miles per hour when the crater exploded and opened fissures. Within an hour, the lake had been drained of its boiling contents.

Diplomats in Zaire's capital, Kinshasa, told Belgian radio stations that 2,000 people were killed by lava flows when the volcano's rim collapsed. Zaire government officials stated that such reports were false, and some sources suggested that 50 to 100 actually died. At the city of Goma, 11 miles from Nyiragongo's summit, the regional bishop's staff told reporters that lava covered five roads, rendering them impassable, and threatened to engulf the airport's runway. At least 50,000 residents were evacuated from adjacent communities. Elephants were trapped by mudflows, forming macabre statues when they died. By the 1990's, the lake refilled to a level 500 feet lower than it was in 1977.

Elizabeth D. Schafer

FOR FURTHER INFORMATION:

"Zaire Towns Evacuated After Volcano Erupts." *The New York Times,* January 13, 1977, p. 11.

1980: Mount St. Helens

DATE: May 18, 1980
PLACE: Washington State
RESULT: 57 dead, estimated 7,000 big-game animals killed, nearly 200 homes and more than 185 miles of road damaged or destroyed, 4 billion board feet of timber blown down, detectable ashfall on 22,000 square miles

Although increased volcanic activity indicated an impending explosion, and in spite of intense efforts to anticipate its magnitude, scientists and government officials were unable to predict the catastrophic force of the 1980 eruption of Mount St. Helens. Before the eruption, the cone of the mountain had been so symmetrical that it had often been compared to Mount Fuji in Japan, but when the ash cloud cleared, only a hollowed-out, lopsided crater remained. The mountain had shrunk from the fifth highest in Washington State at 9,677 feet to the thirtieth highest at 8,364 feet, losing more than 1,314 feet of its summit.

In the first seconds of the explosion, a magnitude 5.1 earthquake on the Richter scale caused by pressure from a magma intrusion triggered the collapse of one side of the mountain. This set off an enormous "debris avalanche" of large rocks and smaller particles, all moving at speeds of 70 to 150 miles per hour—the largest avalanche in recorded history. As the weight of the north face of the mountain slipped downward, the hardened rock cap over the "cryptodome," the hot magma intrusion, was pushed aside, releasing a huge lateral explosion. Within one minute a vertical eruption column developed, and within ten minutes the ash in the column had risen more than 12 miles into a mushroom cloud 45 miles across. The successive explosions equaled the force of 27,000 atomic bombs detonated in rapid sequence, at a rate of one per second for nine hours. Lava, rock fragments, and gases stripped off nearby layers of topsoil and leveled most vegetation within a 12-mile arc to the south, west, and north of the volcano.

Fire in the Cascades. Mount St. Helens is the youngest and most active volcano in the Cascade range, the only volcanic mountains to have erupted in the contiguous United States in recorded history. These mountains form the eastern side of the Pacific "Ring of Fire" series of volcanoes. Volcanologist Stephen Harris reports 14 ash or lava eruptions from eight different Cascade peaks in the two-hundred-year span between 1780 and 1980. Only Mount Baker and Mount Rainier showed as much activity as Mount St. Helens during these years.

Legends among the indigenous cultures of the Northwest often featured Mount St. Helens, which was known as Loo-wit ("keeper of the fire"), Lawe-latla ("one from whom smoke comes"), or Tah-one-lat-clah ("fire mountain"). These names were descriptive of the volcano's continuing activity. George Vancouver became the first European to document an observation of the mountain in 1792, when he charted inlets of Puget Sound near what is now Seattle. He named the peak St. Helens after the title given a recently appointed ambassador to Spain. A major eruption occurred in 1800, between Vancouver's sighting and the Meriwether Lewis and William Clark expedition sighting in 1805. An 1847 painting by the artist Paul Kane known as *Mount St. Helens Erupting* conveys the active nature of the volcano during the middle of the nineteenth century.

Mount St. Helens has built up a symmetrical cone and then transformed it to rubble at least three times, the cone of 1980 being less than 2,000 years old. Geologists believe that the rounded summit dome formed about 330 years ago. Mount St. Helens is a stratovolcano, a volcano that repeatedly grows a composite cone made up of layers of lava, ash, and other materials. Through tree-ring dating, geologists are certain that Mount St. Helens has been dor-

mant for only two long periods since 1480, several decades between the late 1700's and the 1800 eruption and a 123-year period between 1857 and 1980. During the dormant periods the growing silica content of the magma increased its viscosity, making it resistant to flowing and more active in dome building and fragmenting. Both activities contribute to eruptions of pyroclastic materials—combinations of incandescent rock fragments and hot gases.

Using modern techniques to map old mudflows and ash deposits, geologists established the active history of Mount St. Helens in 1960, long after explora-

Earthquakes signaled the imminent eruption of Mount St. Helens in 1980. (National Oceanic and Atmospheric Administration)

tion and exploitation had begun. The first ascent of Mount St. Helens was led by Thomas J. Dryer in 1853. Timber cutting began in the Toutle River Valley in the 1880's, and mining claims were staked north of the volcano near Spirit Lake as early as 1892. Although most mining companies had ceased operations by 1929 because of declining profits, logging continued to increase and prosper. The Gifford Pinchot National Forest was established to augment logging and manage the forest.

Meanwhile, mountain-climbing enthusiasts and campers had discovered the beautiful recreation area. A Portland, Oregon, mountain-climbing group began regular ascents of Mount St. Helens shortly after 1900, and in 1909 the Portland YMCA built a summer camp on Spirit Lake, which lies at the base of the mountain on the north side. Use of the area continued to increase, so that by the 1970's as many as five hundred people might climb the summit of the volcano on a typical weekend. Spirit Lake itself offered fishing, swimming, canoeing, and other popular activities.

The mountain lies about 45 miles northeast of Vancouver, Washington, between Seattle and Portland, the two largest cities in the Northwest. Thus its symmetrical dome had been an inspiring feature of the landscape visible from many locales and observation points—including skyscrapers. After a March 20, 1980, magnitude 4.0 earthquake suggested that the sleeping volcano had awakened, officials were unable to discourage crowds of enthusiasts. Not only people who loved the mountain but also scientists, reporters, photographers, and others from all over the world wanted to witness the action. On May 18, 1980, 57 of them died.

Potential for Disaster. Native American legend discouraged travel to Mount St. Helens and the other fire-mountains. Tribes believed that the belching smoke, steam, and ashfalls were warning signals either of the Great Spirit's displeasure with human activities or evidence of wars between the gods. Male youths aspiring to become braves would climb to the tree line or slightly above and spend a tense night alone, subjecting themselves to the power of the Great Spirit. On their return to the tribe they would be accepted as men and braves. Few, if any, of the twentieth century public who visited or worked on or near the mountain, or in the surrounding area, regarded the peak as threatening to their lives or lifestyles.

After scientific confirmation of the dangerous patterns of volcanic activity in the Cascade Mountain Range in 1960, continued volcanic study focused on the volatility of Mount St. Helens. In a United States Geological Survey (USGS) pamphlet entitled *Potential Hazards from Future Eruption of Mount St. Helens,* (1978) by Dwight R. Crandell and Donald R. Mullineaux, the authors warned of future volcanic eruptions. The work mapped out regions likely to be affected by pyroclastic flows, mudflows, floods, and ashfalls. Warning signs of eruptions were described in detail. The report was carefully evaluated before potential hazard warnings were issued, then a letter was sent to Washington State informing its government of the study's findings. Awareness of the USGS report spread among officials during 1979, but their planning efforts later proved to be inadequate to the size of the event to come.

Initial Volcanic Activity. Small earthquakes began in the Mount St. Helens area on March 16, 1980. On March 20 a magnitude 4.2 earthquake signaled that the mountain's 123-year dormancy had ended. Seismic activity slowly increased, then rose dramatically on March 25. There followed a two-day series of shocks, 174 with magnitudes greater than 2.6. On March 27 came a booming explosion of steam and ash. This, the first volcanic eruption since 1857, carried pulverized ash from old rock inside the volcano and opened a small oval vent about 250 feet across. Earthquake swarms continued as a series of steam explosions shot ash 10,000 to 11,000 feet above the summit. Many of the early eruptions were single, burstlike events, some of which carried ash as far south as Bend, Oregon, 150 miles away, and as far east as Spokane, 285 miles away.

In recognition of the danger signaled by the March 20 earthquake, officials initiated a hazard watch that took effect the same day as the first steam eruption, March 27. Two hundred copies of the 1978 USGS report were distributed to key personnel. In Vancouver, Washington, the United States Forest Service (USFS) headquarters for the Gifford Pinchot National Forest quickly became the Emergency Coordination Center (ECC). Arrangements were made to monitor the volcano, prepare for a possible eruption, and dispense information to the public.

The Mount St. Helens Contingency Plan, based on forest fire models, was developed by the USFS and others, including local officials. The Washington State Department of Emergency Services (DES), the Federal Aviation Administration (FAA), and the Washington National Guard were also involved in formulating plans for their roles in the action in the case of a major eruption. Throughout the preparations, officials believed that damage would probably be confined to the area within a 50-mile radius of the mountain.

Activity at the volcano continued, with some eruptions lasting for several hours. A graben, a depression in the ground, indicated that a large fault was opening below, nearly cutting in half the remaining snow and ice within the crater. A second crater had begun to appear by March 29, and a blue flame had been observed flickering and arching from one crater to the other. Ashes rolling down the sides of the mountain generated static electricity that flashed in lightning bolts, some of which were nearly 2 miles long. On March 30 there were ninety-three eruptions recorded. On April 1 the first harmonic tremor further excited and alarmed scientists and other officials. Harmonic tremors, usually lasting from ten to thirty minutes, indicate that magma is moving or erupting underground.

These dynamic events electrified the public, and, as a result, members of the watch group in Vancouver found themselves involved in public-relations efforts as well as in monitoring the volcano activity and evaluating the current hazard. The scientists most able to predict volcanic behavior were harried and tired, often working around the clock. The first hazard map of the danger zones around the mountain was drawn up between 1 and 5 A.M. because it was the only time the ECC office was quiet enough. Public Information Officers from the USFS held numerous press conferences, but phones continued to ring constantly. Everyone wanted what proved to be impossible—stating when a major eruption would occur, who would be affected by it, and how extensive the damage would be. Meanwhile, the ashfalls blackening the snow of the mountain provided constant reminders of the activity inside.

Public interest did not deter the essential work of monitoring the activity in the mountain. Instruments

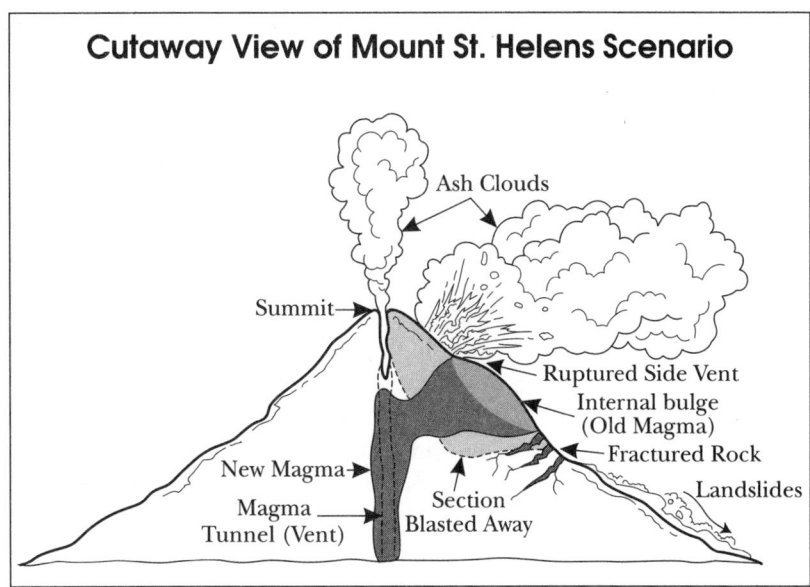

Cutaway View of Mount St. Helens Scenario

Ash Clouds

Summit

Ruptured Side Vent
Internal bulge
(Old Magma)
Fractured Rock

New Magma

Landslides

Magma
Tunnel (Vent)

Section
Blasted Away

set up by University of Washington seismologist Steve Malone, USFS geologist Don Swanson, and other scientists contributed to making the Mount St. Helens event the best-recorded volcanic eruption in history. In addition to seismometers, tiltmeters and gravity meters tracked changes in size and shifts in position of portions of the mountain. Samples of gas from the summit were collected for sulfur-dioxide testing, while surveillance planes and satellites gauged temperatures with infrared photography. In addition to geologists and photographers, volunteer ham radio operators joined in the effort to track volcanic activity and were allowed into newly restricted areas.

The USFS exercised legal control over public access to federal lands, but its jurisdiction was shared with Burlington Northern, a company that owned most the mountain itself, and Weyerhauser, owner of a large logging operation, on the nearby Toutle River. Agreements were reached, and public access to a "red zone"—all areas above timberline—was closed on March 25. A more extensive "blue zone" restricted access to an even larger area surrounding the red zone, beginning March 28. Neither zone was completely evacuated, and many individuals completely underestimated the dangers from floods, mudslides, and ash. Official warnings were discounted, and avoiding National Guard roadblocks became a game for curious or concerned spectators, especially after local residents began selling maps of the old logging roads that crisscrossed the area.

Under Siege. Mount St. Helens's normal runoff fills the tributaries of three river systems: the Kalama to the west, the Lewis to the south and east, and the Toutle with two forks on the north and northwest. The forks of the Toutle River join and flow into the Cowlitz River before it in turn enters the Columbia. Spirit Lake, north of the mountain, drains west into the North Fork of the Toutle. The road to Spirit Lake had been paved in 1946, and there were summer homes along the Toutle River road approaching the lake. Building had also taken place around the lake. After the public-access closure and evacuation, angry and persistent landowners demanded to be allowed into the area to bring out personal property. On the South Fork of the Toutle, Weyerhauser Company's 12-Road logging camp continued its operations, choosing to equip employees with ash-measuring devices as warning systems. Had the major eruption not occurred on a Sunday, 330 more workers would have been endangered.

Throughout April, monitors of the activity at the volcano observed a growing bulge caused by intrusions of magma on the north flank of the mountain. The deformation grew at a rate of about 5 feet per day. Scientists believed that it indicated a possible slope failure that could trigger a major eruption, but they had no way of knowing exactly when or even if the bulge would drop off or explode.

Geologists, worried that these observations might be in error and that instead the whole mountain could be tipping sideways, resorted to nailing yardsticks to tree stumps to verify their calculations. A bulge incident was clearly possible, perhaps likely, but without guarantees that were scientifically impossible, geologists were unable to persuade officials to enforce a complete evacuation. Debris avalanches, mudslides, and flooding increasingly threatened the Spirit Lake and Toutle River areas.

One resident who refused to leave the lake, eighty-four-year-old Harry Truman, drew national attention via the news media. He had lived at Spirit Lake for over fifty years and had buried his wife near the guest lodge he had built there. He claimed to communicate with the mountain and believed it would never hurt him, although he had stowed provisions in a nearby abandoned mine shaft, where he planned to wait out any unforeseen danger. Truman received thousands of letters expressing admiration or concern. A batch of letters from children at Clear Lake Elementary School near Salem, Oregon, did per-

suade him to take a helicopter trip to the school to explain that his place at Spirit Lake was as meaningful to him as life itself. Other local citizens, owners of vacation homes, had more pragmatic goals and continued to demand access to the restricted area.

On May 17, having persuaded then-governor and scientist Dixie Lee Ray to give them permission, twenty homeowners returned to their vacation homes near Spirit Lake to bring out their belongings. Reporters and photographers, with a Washington State Patrol airplane in the lead, accompanied them. Aware of the risks involved, the National Guard placed fifteen helicopters nearby in case rapid evacuation became necessary. A second trip was planned for the next morning.

Catastrophic Eruption. On May 18, eleven seconds after 8:32 in the morning, the eruption began. No one had been able to predict either the incredible force or the actual timing of the history-making event.

Flying just east of the summit, geologists Keith and Dorothy Stoffel observed the earliest movement within the crater of the volcano from their Cessna. In the first ten to fifteen seconds of what would turn out to be a magnitude 5.1 earthquake, the entire north side of the mountain began to ripple and churn in eerie lateral movement. Then it began sliding further north. Ash clouds plumed above and burst from the fractures in the slide itself. Starting at nearly 220 miles per hour, the ash cloud accelerated to speeds near 670 miles per hour.

The Stoffels snapped photographs until they realized how the eruption had sent a huge cloud of ash blossoming above them. Only by using a full-throttle, steep dive did they manage to outrun the mushrooming cloud of gas, rock, ash, and hunks of glacial ice. A debris avalanche, with an area of 23 square miles, went crashing down the mountainside. The material spread out and split into several lobes, one raising waves up to 600 feet above Spirit Lake, another reaching the 4.5 miles to Coldwater Creek, and a third burying 14 miles of the North Fork of the Toutle River to an average depth of 150 feet.

Within fourteen seconds of the earthquake and avalanche, a lateral blast traveling at least 300 miles per hour blew out the north side of the mountain. The blast released 24 megatons of thermal energy, leveling everything in its path and creating a 230-square-mile fan-shaped area of complete devastation. At Coldwater II, the closest observation station set by the USGS, geologist Dave Johnson had just enough time to radio in, "Vancouver, Vancouver, this is it!" before he was pushed over a ridge, along with his Jeep and travel-trailer monitoring station.

Most of the erupting blast material, known as a pyroclastic surge, consisted of gas and ash. As the surge turned into pyroclastic flow, old rock exploding from the summit and north area of the cone came to predominate. Between one-third and one-half of the cubic mile of material was fresh magma. The flows covered 6 square miles adjoining the crater and extended as far as 5 miles north of the crater.

The composites of debris from the smashed dome and gases from the blast were incredibly hot—at least 1,300 degrees Fahrenheit. Superheated air at the leading edge of the blast traveled more than 17 miles and killed millions of trees in a "scorch zone" beyond the flattened forest of the "blow-down zone." Pyroclastic flows ranged as high as 660 degrees Fahrenheit.

The heat on the mountain melted 70 percent of its snow and glaciers. Loowit and Leschi Glaciers were completely destroyed, along with parts of 7 others. When the melted snow, melted glaciers, and groundwater combined with debris from the eruption, the mixture that resulted had the consistency of wet cement, yet it was traveling at speeds from 10 to 25 miles per hour. These mudflows or lahars continued down the Toutle River to the Cowlitz, destroying homes and bridges and reducing the carrying capacity of the river at Castle Rock from 76,000 cubic feet per second to less than 15,000, a reduction of about 80 percent. Reaching farther, the flow entered the Columbia River, about 70 miles away, reducing the shipping channel depth from 40 to 14 feet. Thirty-one ships in ports above the mouth of the Cowlitz River were stranded, and another 50 were unable to travel up the river until dredging operations were completed.

Up in the Air. As if the devastation to the north and west of the volcano were not enough, the vertical eruption cloud and its contents created further havoc to the east. The volcano continued generating a plume of ash for over nine hours. Prevailing winds carried significant ashfall north and east across central and eastern Washington, northern Idaho, and western Montana. The ash reached Yakima, Washington, by 9:30 A.M., an hour after the eruption began. Residents, who had not been informed of the eruption, prepared for a thunderstorm. The magnitude of the eruption had caused so much confusion

in the staff at ECC that a public announcement of the event did not come until 10:30 A.M.

When the ash began to fall in Yakima, townspeople did not know what it was, and many feared it would be harmful to their health. Rapidly, the sky turned to a midnight gloom, earning May 18 the lasting nickname "Black Sunday." Yakima was reported to have received over 600,000 tons of ash before it stopped settling. (USGS figures were much lower, estimating the total ashfall for the entire eruption at 490 tons.)

Without doubt, the ash caused technological systems great problems. The ash was abrasive and electrically charged, affecting machinery. Air filters clogged, and carburetors failed. Across Washington, over 5,000 motorists were stranded; planes could not fly. One town, Ritzville, was inundated with talc-like ash that kept the highway closed for three days. The 1,800 residents of the town had no choice but to look after the 2,000 motorists stranded there when the highway closed. By 2:00 on the afternoon of the eruption, the ash plume hung 300 miles east over Spokane, Washington, and visibility decreased to 10 feet, closing the airport there. By 10:15 P.M. the ashfall reached West Yellowstone, Montana. On May 19 it fell visibly as far away as Denver and later in Minnesota and Oklahoma.

Aftermath. Following the catastrophic eruption May 18, Mount St. Helens experienced five more explosive incidents, but the major damage had been done. After two years of searching and study, the official death count was fixed at 57. About 200 endangered individuals escaped the volcano's impact, including 25 tree planters who were on the east face of the volcano when it erupted. Autopsies of 25 of the dead revealed that most had suffocated, dying within minutes. Some burn victims walked several miles before dying. Other victims were found still clutching cameras, and, when developed, the film from one recorded the approaching blast that killed its owner. Searchers were unable to find 27 of the presumed dead, and some people believe that there were many more casualties than the official count. Visitors may view a memorial for Harry Truman near the site of the former guest lodge; Spirit Lake Memorial Highway also commemorates the victims. The Mount St. Helens Visitor Center near Silver Lake has made information on the eruption and its effects available.

Mount St. Helens continues to be an active volcano, and the risks of damage from another major eruption increase as human activities nearby also increase. Economic recovery from the May 18, 1980, eruption was successful due to rebuilding through disaster relief funds, insurance settlements, and renewed tourist trade. Weyerhauser harvested over 850 million board feet of lumber from downed trees. However, the volcano has produced ashfalls four times greater than the 1980 eruption several times in the past and may again. Winds blowing to the west would carry ash clouds to centers of population along the coast. Mudflows may once again rush downriver, destroying rebuilt dams and roads, filling river channels, and washing out seedling trees. Nearly $1 billion has been spent on efforts to reduce flood hazards. Scientists monitoring volcanic activity can measure and warn of new activity, but they must continue working to develop methods that will predict the time and magnitude of the next eruption.

Margaret A. Dodson

FOR FURTHER INFORMATION:

Carson, Rob. *Mount St. Helens: The Eruption and Recovery of a Volcano.* Seattle: Sasquatch Books, 1990.

Findley, Rowe. "Eruption of Mount St. Helens." *National Geographic,* January, 1981, 2-65.

Harnly, Caroline D., and David A. Tyckoson. *Mount St. Helens: An Annotated Bibliography.* Metuchen, N.J.: Scarecrow Press, 1984.

Harris, Stephen L. "Mt. St. Helens: A Living 'Fire Mountain.'" In *Fire Mountains of the West: The Cascade and Mono Lake Volcanoes.* Missoula, Mont.: Mountain Press, 1988.

Pringle, Patrick T. *Roadside Geology of Mount St. Helens National Volcanic Monument and Vicinity.* Olympia: Washington Department of Natural Resources, 1993.

Saarinen, Thomas F., and James L. Sell. *Warning and Response to the Mount St. Helen's* [sic] *Eruption.* Albany: State University of New York Press, 1985.

Tilling, Robert I., Lyn Topinka, and Donald A. Swanson. *Eruptions of Mount St. Helens: Past, Present, and Future.* Washington, D.C.: Government Printing Office, 1990.

1982: El Chichón

DATE: March 28-April 4, 1982
PLACE: Mexico

VOLCANIC EXPLOSIVITY INDEX: 5
RESULT: About 2,000 dead, hundreds injured, hundreds left homeless, thousands evacuated, 9 villages destroyed, over 116 square miles of farm land ruined

An obscure and forgotten volcano erupted in 1982, becoming one of the most lethal eruptions to date. El Chichón (also known as Chinhónal) is located in the state of Chiapas in southern Mexico, about 416 miles east southeast of Mexico City. Prior to the eruptions in 1982, El Chichón was a heavily vegetated hill with an elevation of 4,429 feet and a height of about 1,640 feet. It had a shallow crater partly filled with water and a dome 1,312 feet high. After the eruption the elevation of the volcano was 3,478 feet with a height of 689 feet, making it now lower than the surrounding nonvolcanic hills.

Although aware of the hot springs and steaming fumaroles (openings from which volcanic gases escape), the people living in villages at the base of the volcano did not consider it a hazard; the volcano had been quiet for at least 130 years. The fertile volcanic soil provided the farm families their only livelihood. They would not leave their land, especially when there was no indication of danger.

History. The volcano was "discovered" in 1928 during a geological survey by Fred Mullerried. The lush vegetation cover of the volcano indicated that there had been no eruptions for years, and the memories of the local inhabitants indicated that the most recent activity was a minor air deposition of volcanic debris around 1852. In his 1932 publication, Mullerried reported on solfataras (fumaroles that emit sulfurous gases) and seismic activity in the vicinity of the volcano in 1930. Considering these observations, he concluded that the volcano was capable of renewed activity. There was increased earthquake activity in 1964 and again in 1982 prior to the eruptions.

Two geologists of the Comisión Federal de Electricidad felt earthquakes while investigating the geothermal potential of the area and correctly concluded that the volcano might be near eruption. Unfortunately, the Comisión was not responsible for safety, and their report, released only a few months prior to the explosion of El Chichón, did not allow time for appropriate agencies to be made aware of the potential danger.

Radiocarbon age dates determined since 1982 indicate that El Chichón erupts about every six hun-

dred years. Despite scientific terminology, one of the world's "extinct" volcanoes erupts about every five years, and these volcanoes, with repose intervals of hundreds of years, produce the most violent volcanic eruptions.

Destruction. It is estimated that 2,000 to 3,000 persons were killed and hundreds injured during the eruption of El Chichón. In terms of death, the 1982 eruption of El Chichón was the most destructive volcanic explosion to take place in Mexico to date. In fact, this eruption is one of the thirteen most destructive eruptions worldwide to date and one of the two most destructive volcanic eruptions from 1900 to 1999.

Early reports indicated that 153 people were killed by the collapse of house roofs and fires ignited by incandescent volcanic debris and that only 34 were killed by pyroclastic flows (flows of hot volcanic particles and gases). Ultimately, probably 90 percent of the 2,000 to 3,000 fatalities were the result directly or indirectly of pyroclastic flows. Over 116 square miles of arable land was covered by volcanic debris, leaving

it useless. As a result, the survivors lost not only their homes but also the means to sustain themselves. The land could not be farmed for years.

Eruption Size. There are several ways to describe the size of a volcanic eruption: the amount of erupted material, the energy involved in the eruption, and the volcanic hazard. The 1982 eruptions of El Chichón produced enough pyroclastic material to cover nearly six thousand American football fields to a depth of 328 feet (about 88,286 cubic feet). The energy released by the 1982 eruptions of El Chichón was about eight thousand times that liberated by a 1-kiloton atomic bomb.

The amount of energy released by a volcano is not necessarily directly correlated with the degree of volcanic hazard. For example, enormous volumes of lava have flowed quietly from Hawaiian volcanoes and have not been a major hazard despite releasing about one thousand times more energy than the eruption of El Chichón. A simple descriptive measure for volcanic hazard is provided by the Volcanic Explosivity Index (VEI). This index combines total volume of materials erupted, height of the eruption column, duration of the main eruptive phase, and several descriptive terms into a simple 0-8 scale of increasing explosivity. Most volcanoes have a VEI of 3 or greater, none has been assigned an 8, and only one has been assigned a 7 to date. In light of these observations, El Chichón's VEI of 5 is a rather high value.

Stage 1 Eruptions. In the autumn of 1981, dogs became restless, earthquakes rattled dishes in the kitchens of the local inhabitants, and breezes occasionally wafted the rotten-egg odor of hydrogen sulfide gas. Although these were items for discussion in the village plazas, the villagers continued with life as usual, not knowing that the tremors and hydrogen sulfide were precursors to an eruption. After the eruption, study of seismograph records indicated that earthquake activity had increased in early 1982 and the centers of the earthquakes had risen from a depth of 3 miles to 1 mile.

The eruptions began near midnight on March 28, 1982, but on March 29, at 5:15 A.M. local time, the morning quiet was shattered by an enormous roar and nearly continuous earthquakes. Massive explosions caused by hot gases ejected a huge ash cloud about 10,499 feet thick to a height of 59,054 to 68,241 feet, where the ash cloud was then driven northeastward by high-altitude winds. Volcanic particles deposited near the mouth of the crater were as large as 4 inches in diameter. This Plinian eruption continued for six hours, with lightning dancing in the ash cloud, accompanied by a deafening roar. (The term "Plinian" describes an explosive eruption caused by a tremendous uprushing of gas that results in a large eruption cloud.) The March 29 eruption of El Chichón removed much of the center of the volcano, converting the domed hill into a barren 0.6-mile-wide crater 984 feet deep. Rooftops were punctured by falling rocks and collapsed by layers of ash. The morning of March 31, 1982, automobiles in Austin, Texas, 994 miles away, were covered with a light coating of volcanic ash from El Chichón.

Stage 2 Eruptions. After minor explosions on March 30 and 31 and April 2, 1982, two additional major eruptions occurred on April 3 and 4 from the newly created crater. Volcanic dust from this eruption reached the height of 82,020 feet; however, the eruption column could not be maintained, and the column collapsed onto the volcano summit, dropping tons of volcanic debris from ash to block size (less than .0025 to greater than 2.5 inches in diameter, respectively). This material had great momentum and flowed downhill with hurricane speed toward the villages. Trees and buildings were ripped apart by the pyroclastic flows. What little of the villages remained was covered by ash. The flows followed the courses of stream valleys radiating from the volcano. One flow covered 38.6 square miles. The volcanic debris not only covered the land but also temporarily dammed streams. When these dams burst, the hot volcanic mud (lahars) moved down the streams, causing additional damage.

All the eruptions of El Chichón produced as much pyroclastic material (about 7 billion tons) as the 1980 eruption of Mount St. Helens in Washington State. The surge activity of April 4 resulted in the death of more than 2,000 people, and at least 9 villages within an 5-mile radius were destroyed. The villagers who had remained in their homes found some cover from the ashfall, but the homes were useless protection from the strong pyroclastic currents. Pyroclastic debris typically has a temperature between 392 and 1,472 degrees Fahrenheit (200 and 800 degrees Celsius). Two months after the eruption the pyroclastic flow deposits were still too hot to touch. Minor eruptions occurred on April 5, 6, 8, and 9.

Effect on Climate. Some especially cold years, for example 1783 and 1816, have been linked to major volcanic eruptions. Volcanic dust reflects solar radiation, resulting in cooler temperatures, but has a relatively short-lived impact on the earth's weather because these particles settle out of the atmosphere in less than two years. The dust cloud from the El Chichón eruptions circled the earth from south of the equator to as far north as Japan, producing brilliant red sunsets for months after the eruptions.

The greatest impact that volcanoes have on our weather results from the sulfur-dioxide gas they produce. In the lower atmosphere, solar energy converts the gas to sulfuric-acid aerosols, which can remain in the atmosphere for years. Sulfuric-acid aerosols reaching the stratosphere absorb infrared radiation, which cools the troposphere and scatters the solar radiation back into space, warming the stratosphere. These impacts were confirmed, in part, by data, which contained high concentrations of sulfur, collected after the eruption of El Chichón.

Compared to the Mount St. Helens 1980 eruption, the El Chichón eruptions were more gas-rich—especially regarding sulfurous compounds—resulting in more spectacular pyroclastic eruptions and producing more sulfuric-acid aerosols. Any cooling caused by the El Chichón eruptions was apparently more than compensated for by the warming from a following El Niño. Some scientists think that El Niños may be triggered by explosive volcanic eruptions such as El Chichón.

1996-1998 Observations. In 1998 fumaroles surrounded the yellow, sulfur beaches of El Chichón's shallow crater lake. Investigation of the site from 1996 to 1998 reported changes in hydrothermal activity. The surface temperature of the lake (average depth 4.3 feet) is very uniform, and even above submerged fumaroles it did not exceed 95 degrees Fahrenheit (35 degrees Celsius). This uniformity of temperature suggests that the lake water is not significantly influenced by underlying magma and is highly affected by seasonal variations in precipitation and ambient air temperature. Temperatures of water from springs on the slope of the volcano ranged from 124 to 160 degrees Fahrenheit (51 to 71 degrees Celsius), whereas water discharging from a boiling spring called Soap Pool inside the crater had a temperature of 208 degrees Fahrenheit (98 degrees Celsius). From 1997 to 1998 the flow of very saline water from Soap Pool decreased from about 44 to 13 pounds per second.

Future. Although El Chichón appears to be entering a six-hundred-year cycle of repose, this may not be the situation because of poor accuracy in the determination of the eruption cycle. Also, there is an indication that at least a minor eruption occurred as recently as 1852. Monitoring the volcano's seismic records, changes in fumaroles for release of hydrogen sulfide, and hydrothermal activity should provide a means of predicting future eruptions, regardless of the repose cycle. It is tragic that the scientific reports by Mullerried and the Comisión Federal de Electricidad were not available to the appropriate government agencies so that evacuations could have been made before the eruptions. It is difficult to say how many of the people would have responded to encouragement to evacuate since no one would have expected such a violent explosive eruption. Nonetheless, even with incomplete data and understanding, a warning could have saved hundreds of lives.

Kenneth F. Steele, Jr.

FOR FURTHER INFORMATION:
Bullard, Fred M. *Volcanoes of the Earth.* 2d rev. ed. Austin: University of Texas Press, 1984.

Chester, David. *Volcanoes and Society.* Kent, England: Edward Arnold, 1993.

Duffield, W. D., R. I. Tilling, and R. Canul. "Geology of El Chichón Volcano, Chiapas, Mexico." *Journal of Volcanology and Geothermal Research* 20 (1984).

Fisher, Richard V., Grank Heiken, and Jeffrey B. Hulen. *Volcanoes: Crucibles of Change.* Princeton, N.J.: Princeton University, 1997.

Tilling, R. I. "The 1982 Eruption of El Chichón, Southeastern Mexico." *Earthquake Information Bulletin* 14 (1982).

1985: Nevado del Ruiz

DATE: November 13, 1985
PLACE: Colombia
RESULT: 23,000 to 25,000 dead

Nevado del Ruiz is located in north-central Colombia. The volcano has year-round glacial ice and snow formed as a thin, flat cap of 8 square miles (20 square kilometers) at the summit. Ice tongues extend about 0.6 to 2 miles (1 to 3 kilometers) down valleys. The volcano has had a long history of eruptions accompanied by mudflows, or lahars, moving down stream valleys. Towns were rebuilt on the sediment deposited by the lahars.

In November and December, 1984, earthquakes were felt, and climbers reported an increase in fumaroles. This activity continued into 1985. A civic committee was formed early in that year to monitor the hazards, and several geologists recommended that a volcanic-hazards map should be made and the volcano should be seismically monitored. Little was accomplished until late August to early September, when four portable seismographs were placed around the region. Five to twenty small earthquakes were recorded daily.

On September 11, 1:30 P.M., a strong eruption of steam threw ash and volcanic blocks out of the crater at the summit. The blocks were cast for miles from the crater, and the ash blew to the northwest. By mid-afternoon enough snowmelt from the heat of the eruption caused ice and rock avalanches to the northwest of the crater, and a lahar flowed 12.4 miles (20 kilometers) down a river to the northwest of the volcano.

In mid-September, warnings were issued to inform the public of the risk along the rivers, which were being fed by ice and snowmelt from the volcano, and evacuations were recommended. Many government officials and newspapers played down the potential dangers in order to keep people calm. Meetings and discussions about the hazards continued through October, but little action was taken to prepare for an eruption. For instance, a hazard-evaluation map was criticized for causing unnecessary fear, although in retrospect more fear may have enabled authorities to set up a good warning and evacuation plan. One group estimated, for instance, that most of the people in Armero would have to travel at least 0.6 mile to escape from lahars moving down rivers to the east of the volcano.

Finally, the volcano erupted violently at 3:06 P.M. on November 13. The ash emitted drifted 31 miles (50 kilometers) to the east. Word was sent out that the volcano was erupting, but evacuations were not ordered in high-risk areas for lahars. At 9:08 P.M. another strong eruption occurred, and at least four hot volcanic flows—25 million cubic yards worth—were ejected rapidly onto and within the ice cap, melting 10 percent of the snow and ice. The melted snow and ice, rock, and alluvium cascaded rapidly down rivers to the east of the volcano, scouring out more debris along the way.

Farmers near the rivers heard the loud noise from the lahars as early as 9:15 P.M., and warnings went out. The lahars cascaded at velocities of 16.4 to 49 feet (5 to 15 meters) per second. They tended to slow down at bridges until they broke through, then pulsed even more rapidly downstream.

The town of Chinchina was hit by a lahar at 10:30 P.M. It had been partially evacuated, yet 1,100 died there. From 10:45 to 11:00 P.M., officials tried to evacuate Armero, but, because of power and communication difficulties, little evacuation was done. By then the lahar heading toward Armero was 98 to 131

Nevado del Ruiz spawned many lahars, which destroyed towns and caused many deaths in northern Colombia. (National Oceanic and Atmospheric Administration)

feet (30 to 40 meters) high within the canyon, and it was only a half hour away. Eyewitnesses near the channel reported that the noise was so loud that they could not talk to people a few feet away.

The lahar exited the canyon at 11:30 P.M. As it spread out into the plain, it divided into three branches. The biggest branch had a depth of 6.5 to 16.4 feet (2 to 5 meters), and it totally destroyed the urban part of Armero. In this short period of time, over 21,000 people died in the mud, making it the second-biggest volcanic disaster of the twentieth century.

Eyewitness accounts describe the horror of that evening. One survivor staying at a hotel in Armero said he observed ash falling at 10:50 P.M.; a geologist in his party told them to leave immediately. Radio announcers gave no warnings and told people to remain calm and stay in their homes. When the electric power went out, chaos prevailed in the darkness; mud was flowing down the streets, carrying cars, people, and beds.

Some victims ran up to the third floor of a concrete hotel, which was being approached by a wall of mud. The mud hit the hotel with a thud, and the walls began to fracture as the building disintegrated. As light dawned in the morning, the piles of bodies in the mud were overwhelming. Most were not moving, but others called for help. However, it was impossible to get into the mud to try and rescue those alive for fear of becoming trapped.

Robert L. Cullers

FOR FURTHER INFORMATION:

Lowe, Don. "Lahars Initiated by the 13 November 1985 Eruption of Nevado del Ruiz, Colombia." *Nature* 324 (1986): 51-53.

Naranjo, J. H., H. Sigurdsson, S. N. Carey, and W. Fritz. "Eruption of the Nevado del Ruiz Volcano, Colombia, on 13 November 1985: Tephra Fall and Lahars." *Science* 233 (1986): 961-963.

Pierson, Thomas C. "Perturbation and Melting of Snow and Ice by the 13 November 1985 Eruption of Nevado del Ruiz, Colombia, and Consequent Mobilization, Flow, and Deposition of Lahars." *Journal of Volcanology and Geothermal Research* 41 (1990): 17-66.

Thouret, Jean-Claude. "Effects of the November 13, 1985 Eruption on the Snow Pack and Ice Cap of Nevado del Ruiz Volcano, Colombia." *Journal of Volcanology and Geothermal Research* 41 (1990): 177-201.

Voight, Barry. "The 1985 Nevado del Ruiz Volcano Catastrophe: Anatomy and Retrospection." *Journal of Volcanology and Geothermal Research* 42 (1990): 151-188.

1986: Lake Nyos

DATE: August 21, 1986
PLACE: Cameroon
RESULT: 1,734 dead, 3,000 cattle dead, 4,000-5,000 people evacuated, 4 villages destroyed

The eruption of Lake Nyos in 1986 was the second time lethal gas released from a lake has claimed human lives. The first was on August 15, 1984, at Lake Monoun, another lake in Cameroon, when 37 people died. As the government had just put down an attempted coup at the time and was worried about the political overtones of the incident, the Monoun eruption received little public attention, but the eruption of Lake Nyos was so catastrophic that immediate international aid was needed.

History of Lake Nyos. Both lakes lie in the northwestern part of Cameroon, a tropical, West African country about the size of California. The lakes are located on the so-called Cameroon volcanic line, a zone of crustal weakness extending 1,000 miles northeast from Annobón Island in the south Atlantic through northwestern Cameroon and into northeastern Nigeria. Young cinder cones and basaltic lava flows appear along this line, as well as flat-floored explosion craters known as maars. The maars formed when rising, gas-charged magma came in explosive contact with near-surface groundwater. More than thirty of the Cameroon maars, filled by deep crater lakes, are strung out like jewels along the volcanic trend as it stretches across the nation.

The crater in which Lake Nyos lies is rimmed by vertical, bedrock fault scarps on the west, a partially collapsed volcanic cone on the east, a delta plain to the south, and an outlet spillway across the flank of an ash cone to the north. Because the ash deposits around the lake are unweathered and little eroded, geologists believe the crater in which Lake Nyos lies is only a few hundred years old. The lake itself is shaped like a lemon, with a maximum length of 1.2 miles and a maximum width of 0.7 miles. It is shallow at the

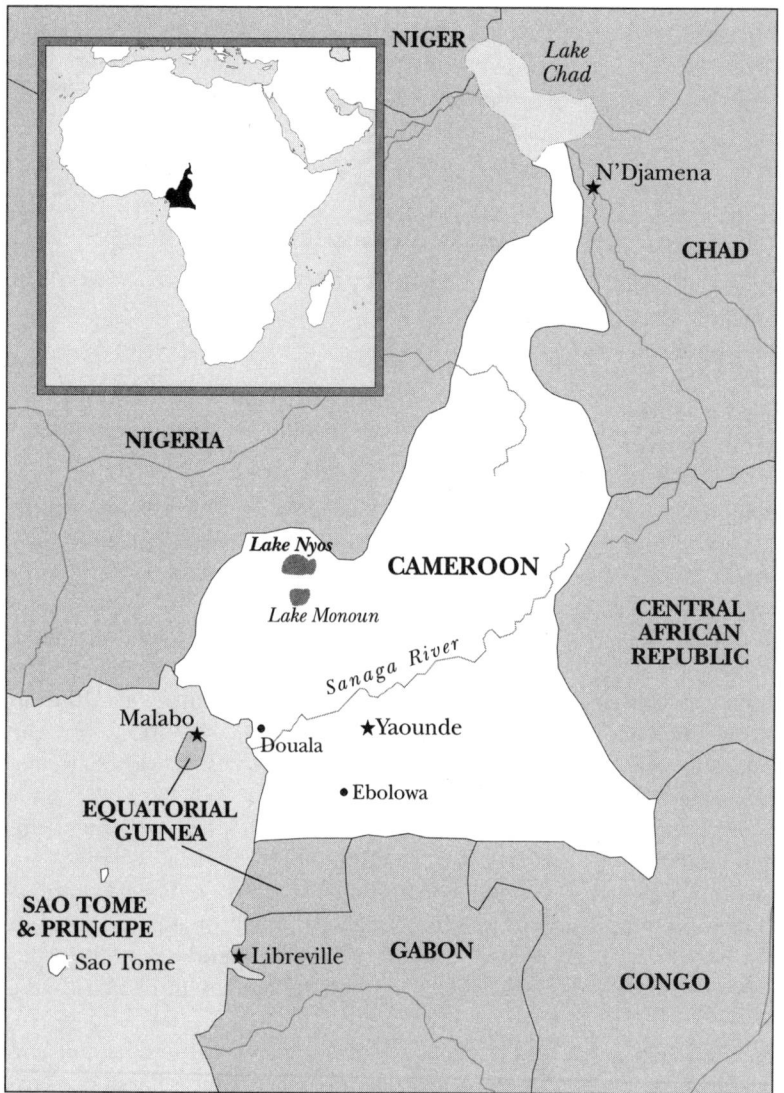

more than a row of houses strung out along the roads, people lived in thatched huts or two-room, mud-brick homes with corrugated tin roofs. Family groups lived in clusters up in the hills. None of the inhabitants had telephones or electricity.

The Eruption. The fatal eruption came without warning about 9:30 on the evening of Thursday, August 21, 1986. Although this was the rainy season, the eruption came during a lull between thunderstorms. As a result, people looked out in surprise when they heard a loud, rumbling noise, which lasted perhaps fifteen or twenty seconds, coming from the direction of the lake. One observer reported hearing a bubbling sound, and from his vantage point he saw a ghostly column of vapor rising from the lake's surface. The vapor then poured down the valley to the north, like a smoking river. He also saw a surge of water in the lake and felt a blast of air that had the odor of rotten eggs.

The people who lived in the valley north of the lake bore the brunt of the tragedy. The cloud of smoking vapor, which may have been as high as 150 feet, first struck the village of Lower Nyos, which lies about 0.3 mile beyond the lake. Thursday had been market day, and many people were still eating dinner when the cloud arrived, choking them in their homes. Those who tried to flee the cloud collapsed on the muddy roads leading out of town. Others died peacefully in their sleep. In all, some 1,200 people died in Lower Nyos that evening, with only one woman and a child known to have survived.

An additional 500 people perished in the villages of Cha, Subum, and Fang, which lay farther down valley as the toxic cloud rolled on for 5 more miles. A survivor from Subum said he had feelings of warmth and drunkenness before he lost consciousness, and

south end, near the delta plain, but drops off steeply to a flat bottom about 680 feet deep. Prior to the eruption, the inhabitants called Lake Nyos "the good lake." It shimmered like a fallen piece of blue sky amidst the jutting rock cliffs and lush, green vegetation.

The part of Cameroon in which Lake Nyos lies is a remote, mountainous region reached only by crude dirt roads. Before the eruption, some 5,000 people lived in the 4-square-mile area surrounding the lake. They were drawn here by the deeply weathered volcanic rocks that provided rich soils for their crops of cassava, maize, and yams, as well as prime grazing land for their herds of cattle. In the villages, which were little he remembered an odor like that of cooking gas. Family members acted drunk and were coughing and crying as they fell to the floor, where some lay screaming or spitting up blood. Another Subum resident awoke gasping for air but managed to drag himself into a windowless shed behind the house, where he survived.

A few victims revived six to thirty-six hours later. They described feelings of dizziness, warmth, and confusion before losing consciousness, as well as shortness of breath. Only the people living in localities more than 2 miles from the lake reported an odor of rotten eggs or of gunpowder. When morning came, survivors of the eruption found the bodies of their cattle strewn about in the fields, and the bodies of their friends and relatives where they had fallen in their homes or along the roads.

It seemed as though a neutron bomb had struck. Everyone was dead, but the buildings remained untouched. Some of the victims had even stripped off their clothes, as if in a desperate attempt to escape the feelings of heat. Others lay amid scattered pots and furniture, where they writhed as the vapors strangled them. Oil lamps were snuffed out too, although they still contained oil. The animals were dead—goats, pigs, birds, small mammals, and insects down to the smallest ant. Later that day, when the bodies of the cattle began to bloat in the hot sun, they remained untouched by flies or vultures because the scavengers were dead too. Strangely enough, plant life seemed to have been unaffected.

The survivors hurriedly began burying the dead, with attention to their relatives first, and no one made any attempt to inform the outside world of what had happened, because of the lack of telephones and the poor roads. Thus the first word people had of the tragedy was from a government worker who headed into the area from the city of Wum on his motorcycle the afternoon of Friday, August 22. As he approached Lower Nyos, he first saw a dead antelope lying beside the road. Congratulating himself upon his good luck, he stopped to strap the animal to

Lake Nyos in Cameroon a few days after deadly gas was emitted from the lake, killing over 1,700 people. (AP/Wide World Photos)

his motorcycle before continuing. Soon he encountered dead cattle and then the bodies of people. Now, beginning to feel ill himself, he turned his motorcycle around and hurried back to Wum, where he alerted the authorities. Full-scale relief efforts began on Sunday, August 24, when the president of Cameroon arrived by helicopter to inspect the scene, bringing with him doctors from Israel and a disaster team from France.

Scientific Analysis. Scientists came too, and, after the injured had been taken care of, they turned their attention to the lake. Just one glance revealed that the appearance of Lake Nyos had changed radically. Although the waters remained calm, the lake no longer looked like a fallen piece of clear blue sky, but rather an angry red eye festering in its crater socket. The water was stained a muddy, reddish brown by iron compounds that rose with the escaping gas, and mats of floating vegetation littered the lake's surface. The lake level had dropped by nearly 4 feet as well, and water had sloshed up on the south shore to a height of 80 feet and splashed over a 250-foot-high rock promontory on the southwest. The 20-foot high outlet spillway on the north had been overtopped as well, and downstream from the spillway, brush was flattened and several large fig trees lay uprooted, presumably by the blast of vapor coming from the lake.

The earliest newspaper accounts of the eruption reported that the gas expelled by the lake was hydrogen sulfide, an identification based on reports of the odor of rotten eggs. Scientists pointed out that carbon dioxide, not hydrogen sulfide, had been the culprit at Lake Monoun, and when water samples from Lake Nyos were analyzed, 98 to 99 percent of the gas still dissolved in the lake proved to be carbon dioxide. The amount of gas released by the lake during the eruption was estimated to have totaled about 1.3 billion cubic yards, based on a drop in lake level of nearly 4 feet. Because carbon dioxide weighs one and a half times as much as air, it would have hugged the ground as it moved down valley, asphyxiating its victims by forcing the breathable air aside.

Scientists considered three possible sources for this gas: volcanic, magmatic, or biogenic. If the origin were volcanic, the gas would have come from a near-surface eruption and should have had a high temperature. However, if the gas had a magmatic origin, it would have come from molten rock deep within the earth and consequently been cool by the time it reached the surface; it would also have lost its reactive constituents, such as sulfur and chlorine compounds and carbon monoxide. Temperature measurements made after the eruption indicated that the lake was still cool, so a magmatic origin was favored. Biogenic gas would have been cool too, having originated from the decomposition of organic matter on the lake's bottom, but carbon-14 tests dated the lake's gas as more than thirty-five thousand years old. This meant that the gas expelled by the lake was magmatic, for organic decomposition on the bottom of a lake only a few hundred years old could hardly account for such gas.

Springs around Lake Nyos contain high concentrations of carbon dioxide, so scientists believe the magmatic gas came into Lake Nyos with the groundwater. Once in the lake, the gas would have remained dissolved due to the weight of the overlying water. Because the lake was stratified, the gas would have concentrated in the cold, lowermost layers, gradually turning the lake into a time bomb waiting to go off. Any event that made the gas-rich water start to rise would have reduced the pressure on it and allowed carbon dioxide to bubble to the surface, just as a soda bottle fizzes when the cap is removed. Scientists could not be certain what made the water rise and initiate the eruption. Possibilities that were suggested include a rockfall into the lake, an earth tremor, a volcanic eruption, storm winds, or even seasonal cooling of the lake's upper surface, which would have caused the lake's water to overturn.

Carbon dioxide gas continued to leak into the lake after the eruption was over, and scientists predicted that in another twenty or thirty years the lake could be ready to erupt again. As a result they alerted Cameroon authorities that their crater lakes were potential hazards that would have to be monitored carefully. They also pointed out that the weak, natural dam forming the outlet spillway of Lake Nyos represented a hazard as well. Failure of this dam could cause a sudden lowering of the lake's level, triggering another explosive release of gas.

As a remedy for Cameroon's crater lakes scientists recommended reducing the gas content by controlled pumping. For an example of this, they cited an experimental project that began at Lake Monoun in 1992. Gas-rich deep water was pumped to the lake's surface, where the carbon dioxide was harmlessly released into the atmosphere, and then the degassed water was permitted to return to the lake.

Donald W. Lovejoy

FOR FURTHER INFORMATION:

Clark, Michael A., et al. *The 21 August 1986 Lake Nyos Gas Disaster, Cameroon: Final Report of the United States Scientific Team to the Office of U.S. Foreign Disaster Assistance.* Denver: U.S. Department of the Interior, U.S. Geological Survey, 1987.

Kling, George W., et al. "The 1986 Lake Nyos Gas Disaster in Cameroon, West Africa." *Science* 236, no. 4798 (April 10, 1987): 169-175.

Stager, Curt. "Silent Death from Cameroon's Killer Lake." *National Geographic* 172, no. 3 (September, 1987): 404-420.

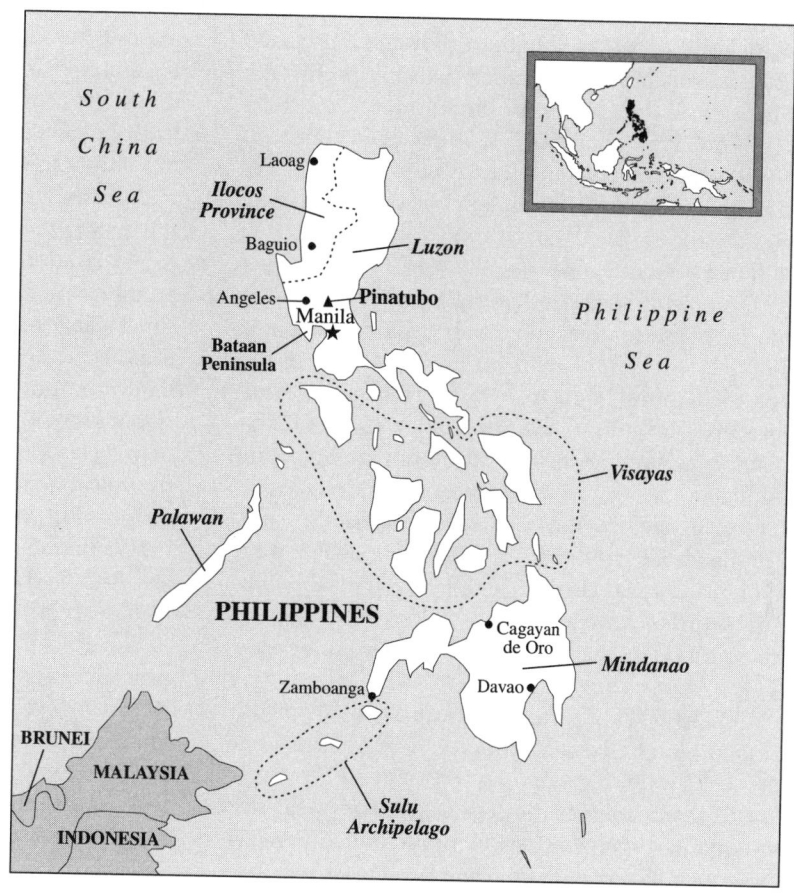

1991: Pinatubo

DATE: June 12-15, 1991
PLACE: Luzon, Philippines
RESULT: About 350 dead (mostly from collapsed roofs); extensive damage to homes, bridges, irrigation canal dikes and cropland; 20 million tons of sulfur dioxide spewed into the stratosphere up to an elevation of 15.5 miles

As early as April 2, 1991, people from a small village named Patal Pinto, on the Philippine island of Luzon, observed steam and gases smelling of rotten eggs (indicating hydrogen sulfide) emanating from near the crest of Mount Pinatubo, along with intermittent minor explosions. Within ten weeks, these early ominous activities culminated in a volcanic eruption that has come to be regarded among the largest to have occurred in the twentieth century.

Pinatubo, located about 62 miles (100 kilometers) northwest of Manila, belongs to a chain of composite volcanoes constituting a volcanic arc in the Philippines. Prior to the 1991 eruption, it had a summit elevation of 5,725 feet (1,745 meters) above sea level, believed to have been the result of a lava dome that formed about five hundred to six hundred years ago during the last-known eruption. Its lower slopes and foothills were composed primarily of pyroclastic and lahar (volcanic mudflow) deposits from voluminous eruptions that occurred in prehistoric times.

More than 30,000 people inhabited the foothills of the volcano before the 1991 eruption. Cities and villages surrounding the base of the volcano on gently sloping alluvial plains were populated by as many as 500,000 inhabitants. Located about 15.5 miles (25 kilometers) to the east of the volcano was Clark Air Base, and 25 miles (40 kilometers) to the southwest was Subic Bay Naval Station, both belonging to the United States.

Prior to the 1991 eruption, Pinatubo had the appearance of a steep, domelike spheroid that rose about 2,297 feet (700 meters) above a gently sloping apron made of pyroclastic and epiclastic materials. Such a volcano belongs to the class of stratocones, of which such well-known exemplars as Fuji and Mayon are considerably larger than Pinatubo. The extensive pyroclastic apron of Pinatubo, however, indicated that the volcano was extremely active in prehistoric times. Until the collapse of the summit in the 1991 eruption, Pinatubo rose 5,725 feet (1,745 meters) above sea level, surrounded by older volcanic centers, including an ancestral Pinatubo due south, east, and northeast.

The Onset of Eruption. Following the emission of hydrogen sulfide gas and steam together with a few minor, phreatic (steam-charged) explosions along a 1-mile-long chain of vents on the north side of the volcano around April 2, 1991, the Philippine Institute of Volcanology and Seismology (PHIVOLCS) installed seismometers near the mountain, which immediately began recording several hundred earthquakes a day. By April 5, nontelemetered seismographs installed on the northwest side of Pinatubo about 6 to 9 miles (10 to 15 kilometers) from the summit recorded between 40 and 140 seismic events (of magnitude less than 1.0 on the Richter scale) each day.

On April 23, a team of volcanologists from the United States Geological Survey (USGS) arrived at the scene following a request by PHIVOLCS to assist in the monitoring of the seismic activities near the mountain. Together, the Philippine and American experts installed a radio-telemetered seismic network and tiltmeters. These devices could locate the earthquakes and detect any new ground movement, respectively. They also measured fractures that opened during the early steam and vapor emissions from the chain of vents near the summit of the mountain.

Between May 13 and May 28, the geologists, with the help of the U.S. Air Force, measured a tenfold rise in the sulfur dioxide gas content of the steam plumes emanating from the summit. These and other measurements indicated that magma was rising within the volcano, and immediate preventive measures were necessary for the safety of people living in surrounding communities. The geologists established a set of alert levels ranging from 1 (implying low-level unrest) to 5 (indicating that eruption had started). On May 13, the alert level was set at 2, which meant that the seismic unrest probably involved magma.

Before April 2, 1991, the available geologic information on Pinatubo was quite limited. It was known to be a dacite dome complex about 2 miles (3 kilometers) in diameter, with voluminous fans of ash-flow deposits that were geologically young (less than ten thousand years old). The volcano was known to be thermally active, however, and had previously been explored as a potential geothermal energy source by the Philippine National Oil Company.

Anticipating that an eruption might be imminent, the geologists went to work designing a hazard map, in preparation for the worst-case scenario. This was an urgent matter, especially since a large number of small villages lay scattered on the northwest slope of the volcano and part of Clark Air Base and several urban communities (such as the city of Angeles, with a population of 300,000) lay within the potential range of pyroclastic and debris flows extending well beyond the volcano. Based on knowledge of the best-known distribution of each type of volcanic deposit from past eruptions, a joint USGS-PHIVOLCS team rapidly compiled a worst-case hazard map showing areas most susceptible to ash flows, mudflows, and ashfall.

Around May 23, the hazard map was distributed to officials of the Philippine civil defense organization, the local governments in neighboring communities, and the U.S. military. Based on data obtained following the actual eruption on June 15, the predictions by the hazard map vis-à-vis areas where the impact would be most severe were proven to be fairly accurate.

Near the end of May, the number of seismic events per day was fluctuating in a sufficiently random fashion, and measurements of key seismic parameters such as earthquake hypocenter locations proved quite inconclusive. The likelihood of an actual eruption, though highly plausible, could not be precisely forecast. From late May until early June, indicators such as relatively long earthquake periods interspersed with periods of tremor, as well as the location of hypocenters beneath the steam vents, were clear precursors of imminent eruption. It was also observed that the emission rate of sulfur dioxide, which had dramatically increased during the preceding two weeks, had suddenly decreased. This finding was consistent with the escape vents of the gas being sealed off by magma rising within the volcano.

The Eruption and Its Aftermath. During the second week of June, the east flank of the mountain became tilted by inflation, and a small lava dome extruded near the most vigorous steam vent. The tectonic earthquakes became progressively shallower and weaker, while the emission of low-level ash became continuous.

Residents of Botocan, Philippines, shield their faces from ash as they flee the eruption of Pinatubo in 1991. (AP/Wide World Photos)

PHIVOLCS raised the alert level to 3 on June 5, indicating that eruption was likely within two weeks. On June 7, the extrusion of a small dome on the north flank, accompanied by numerous small earthquakes, triggered a level 4 alert, signifying eruption within twenty-four hours. Residents of Zambales, Tarlac, and Pampanga Provinces, within 12.4 miles (20 kilometers) of the volcano, were evacuated. As the dome continued to grow and ash emissions increased to alarming levels, alert level 5 (signifying eruption had begun) was declared on June 9. On June 10, a total of 14,500 nonessential personnel and dependents were moved by road from Clark Air Base to Subic Bay Naval Station. Most of the aircraft had already been removed from Clark Air Base at this time.

On June 12, the first of several major explosions occurred at 8:51 A.M., spewing airborne ash to the west of the mountain and sending pyroclastic flows down its northwest slope. The ash column reached a height of 62,335 feet (19,000 meters) above sea level, according to measurements by the weather radar at Clark Air Base. Explosions continued through the night of June 12 and the morning of June 13. Part of the dome was destroyed, and a small crater was formed adjacent to it. There was intense seismic activity, with buildup periods lasting as much as several hours prior to the explosions during June 12 through 14. The long buildup periods permitted short-term notification to Philippine civil authorities and U.S. military authorities regarding impending eruptions. The city of Angeles was placed on evacuation alert.

The climactic eruptive phase began around 1:09 P.M. on June 14, following an eight-hour episode of vigorous seismic activity. Explosive eruptions continued through the night and into the morning of June 15. Around 5:55 A.M., a massive lateral blast spread north, west, southwest, and northwest from the volcano, sending a broad column of ash 39,370 feet (12,000 meters) above sea level. This climactic blast was followed by six more eruptive pulses, after which the eruption became essentially continuous, lasting between the afternoon of June 15 through the early hours of June 16.

Coincidentally, Typhoon Yunya approached Pinatubo around the same time. The extreme combination of hazards, including the explosive eruption, a complete loss of telemetry between the summit and the observatories, and uncertainty regarding the effect of Yunya on the flow of volcanic debris, made it necessary to rapidly evacuate all remaining USGS, Air Force, and PHIVOLCS personnel from Clark Air Base. This task was accomplished by around 2:30 P.M. on June 15.

The volcano continued to erupt a column of ash rising 32,808 feet (10,000 meters) above sea level for several weeks, even though the overall seismic activity started to decline by late June 15. When the weather cleared on June 16, it was observed that the top of the volcano had been replaced by a 1-mile-wide caldera, and vast areas surrounding the volcano were covered by around 6,540 or 7,847 cubic yards (5 or 6 cubic kilometers) of pyroclastic deposits.

The presence of Yunya exacerbated the volcanic mudflows and the dispersal of water-saturated ash across a large number of cities and villages. Cyclonic winds spread tephra over at least 7,722 square miles (20,000 square kilometers) surrounding the volcano. The weight of the wet, heavy ash led to the collapse of many buildings, which turned out to be the leading cause of the loss of 350 or so lives from the eruption. Mudflows triggered by the cyclone and heavy rainfall destroyed homes, bridges, and irrigation-canal dikes and buried vast areas of cropland.

The Pinatubo eruption was one of the largest in the twentieth century (being about ten times larger than the eruption of Mount St. Helens in the United States in 1980) and potentially threatened 1 million lives. Overall, it must be concluded that the evacuation and safety procedures followed jointly by the USGS, PHIVOLCS, and the various military and civil defense organizations via effective communication and timely, responsible action, helped avert disaster of a far higher magnitude. In fact, it is estimated that timely and effective intervention saved many thousands of lives (the actual casualty figure would be much lower had it not been for the presence of the typhoon), and at least $1 billion in property which might otherwise have been lost. In terms of accurate eruption prediction and highly effective response, the 1991 Pinatubo eruption provides an important model for future volcanic eruptions and other geological cataclysms.

Monish R. Chatterjee

FOR FURTHER INFORMATION:

Chouet, Bernard. "Long-Period Volcano Seismicity: Its Source and Use in Eruption Forecasting." *Nature* 380 (March 28, 1996): 309-315.

_____. *New Methods and Future Trends in Seismological Volcano Monitoring.* Berlin: Springer-Verlag, 1994.

Fiocco, Giorgio, Daniele Fuá, and Guido Visconti, eds. *The Mount Pinatubo Eruption: Effects on the Atmosphere and Climate.* New York: Springer, 1996.

Newhall, Christopher G., James W. Hendley II, and Peter H. Stauffer. *The Cataclysmic 1991 Eruption of Mount Pinatubo, Philippines.* Vancouver, Wash.: U.S. Geological Survey, 1997.

Newhall, Christopher G., and Raymundo S. Punongbayan, eds. *Fire and Mud: Eruptions and Lahars of Mount Pinatubo, Philippines.* Seattle: University of Washington Press, 1996.

Pinatubo Volcano Observatory Team. "Lessons from a Major Eruption: Mount Pinatubo, Philippines." *EOS/Transactions of the American Geophysical Union* 72 (1991): 554-555.

Wolfe, Edward. "The 1991 Eruptions of Mount Pinatubo, Philippines." *Earthquakes and Volcanoes* 23, no. 1 (1992): 5-37.

Wright, Thomas L., and Thomas C. Pierson. *Living with Volcanos: The U.S. Geological Survey's Volcano Hazards Program.* Denver: U.S. Geological Survey, 1992.

1994: Merapi

DATE: November 22, 1994
PLACE: Java, Indonesia
RESULT: At least 31 dead

Merapi is one of the most active volcanoes in Indonesia and is located in a populated region. It had 68 eruptions from 1548 to 1999. Typically, the initial eruption at Merapi causes the volcano to dome and produce unstable blocks that collapse or explode as avalanche blocks or as nuées ardentes (hot, glowing gas-ash mixtures that slide down the volcanoes slopes on a cushion of air). Then the activity can last several years. Small eruptions have occurred here every two to four years, larger ones every nine to sixteen years, and the largest eruptions about every fifty years.

The 1992-1994 eruption cycle produced glowing rockfalls, nuées ardentes, lavas, and volcanic mudflows mostly flowing down the southwest slope of the volcano as the lava dome expanded. The nuée ardente of November 22, 1994, traveled a distance of 4.7 miles (7.5 kilometers) to the south-southwest, possibly killing hundreds of people and injuring many others, although many fewer were confirmed dead. Many of the dead and injured were badly burned from the hot gas-ash mixture that may have had temperatures up to 1,472 degrees Fahrenheit (800 degrees Celsius). Trees and telephone poles were toppled and burned. Houses were buried in debris along with people and animals, so the death toll was difficult to estimate; some were too badly burned to identify. About 6,000 people were evacuated.

Robert L. Cullers

FOR FURTHER INFORMATION:

Purbawinata, M. A. *Merapi Volcano: A Guide Book.* Bandung, Indonesia: Volcanological Survey of Indonesia, 1997.

Subibyakto, A. S. H. "The Eruption of Merapi Volcano, November 22, 1994." *Indonesian Journal of Geography* 28 (1996): 1-10.

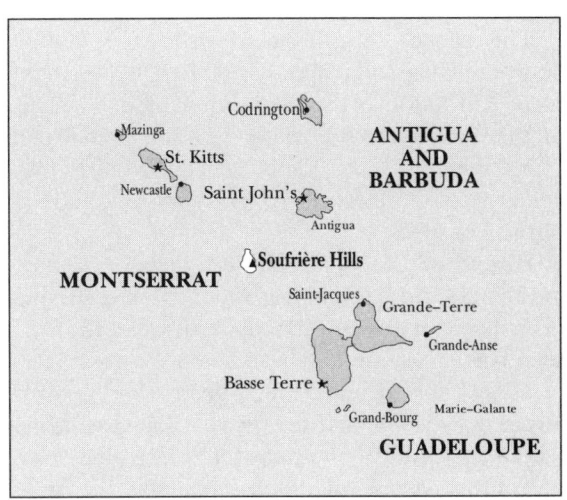

1997: Soufrière Hills

DATE: June 25, 1997
PLACE: Montserrat, Caribbean
RESULT: 19 dead, 8,000 evacuated

When explorer Christopher Columbus sighted an eastern Caribbean island and named it Montserrat in 1493, no one then knew enough geography to understand what lands he could yet discover in the region, and no one yet knew—and would not know for another four and a half centuries—about plate tectonics and the geological reason for the island's existence. After permanent settlers arrived from England and Ireland in 1632, and then indentured servants and slaves from West Africa later in that century, they would be intermittently reminded of the dramatic power of volcanic activity and the evolution of such an island—a lesson that continues to this day.

Geography. Montserrat is an island of 39 square miles (102 square kilometers). It is one of an eastern Caribbean chain of islands, the Lesser Antilles, extending in a crescent 400 miles (650 kilometers) long, which connects the Virgin Islands in the north to Trinidad near Venezuela in the south. Montserrat is a dependent island governed by Great Britain. Some of the better-known islands in the chain are St. Kitts, Antigua, Montserrat, Guadeloupe, Dominica, Martinique, St. Lucia, St. Vincent, and Grenada. They owe their existence to the collision of tectonic plates moving slowly under the earth's surface.

While the American Plate is moving westward from the spreading Mid-Atlantic Ridge, the small Caribbean Plate (from Cuba and the West Indies south to South America) is moving relatively eastward at about 0.4 inch per year. The slow collision in the eastern Caribbean causes oceanic crust to be thrust downward, causing partial melting in the mantle, and magma (molten rock) erupts periodically to form volcanic islands.

Montserrat is, like the others in the Lesser Antilles, a typical stratovolcanic or composite-type volcano, built up of successive lava flows plus layers of ejecta (ash and larger rock fragments) erupted explosively. The process creates attractive conical-shaped volcanoes with dangerous capabilities for destruction. The magma in this crustal environment tends to be viscous, and it can congeal into a domed plug in the crater at the top of the vent of the volcano. The pressure in the subterranean magma, especially from its contained gases, can build up and produce periodic plumes of ash or, occasionally, a catastrophic and massive eruption with much ash and gas. Many of these islands have experienced volcanic activity in the past few thousand years.

The active volcano on Montserrat is called Soufrière Hills, and is about 3,000 feet (915 meters) high. The bottom of the volcano, and of the island, is on the seafloor, at a subsea depth of about 4,900 feet (1,500 meters). *La soufrière* is French for "sulfur pit," and in creole French it also refers to volcanic and sulfurous hot springs.

History of Eruption. Soufrière began erupting, mostly ash and gas, on July 18, 1995, after having been dormant since the island's settlement. Unusual subterranean activity had been noted as early as 1989 by a local seismograph, which detects and records seismic wave vibrations from such behavior as magma cracking rock as it wells upward. The instrument was one of thirty-two seismographs situated in the Antilles Islands and operated by the Seismic Research Unit of the University of the West Indies, in Trinidad. With the active eruptive activity, an international team of geologists and geophysicists was gathered, from the Trinidad unit, the British Geological Survey, and the U.S. Geological Survey. They set up monitoring instruments on and around the volcano—seismographs and ground-deformation and gravity instruments—to try to monitor the pulse of the volcano to assess and possibly predict its future activity. This would be done at the Montserrat Volcano Observatory, which was recently established.

For several weeks, a series of earthquakes caused the volcano to tremble, and there were intermittent small phreatic (steam-charged) eruptions of fine gray ash and sulfurous gases. The ash showered the southern half of the island, including the main town and capital, Plymouth, on the southwest coast only 3 miles away.

The volcano crater began to fill with a viscous lava dome that plugged the vent. If this plug, like a cork in

Soufrière Hills was still emitting smoke and ash two months after its major eruption in June of 1997. (AP/Wide World Photos)

a bottle, could not contain the pressure, it and the underlying magma could explode up into a plume of ash and could generate fearsome pyroclastic flows down the volcano's slopes. Pyroclastic, from the Greek *pyro* for fire and *klastos* for broken, refers to the hot fragmental material being erupted, in this case as a flowing cloud of searing hot ash and gas, much of the latter poisonous. Such hot gaseous flows, or nuées ardentes, are one of the greatest hazards of eruptions. They are denser than air and thus hug the slopes, travel very fast—up to 70 to 120 miles per hour (110 to 190 kilometers per hour)—and kill people by scorching, roasting, and asphyxiating.

In late August, 1995, a series of eruptive ash events darkened the sky over Plymouth. The authorities recommended the evacuation of the south half of the island, either to the sparsely settled north end or to other islands or countries. Because no one could know when—if ever—the volcano might erupt massively, this was a wrenching development for the island society. There is uncertainty with a dome-building, slowly erupting volcano, because an end can come—after months or years—with a final catastrophic explosion or it can simply fizzle out.

Plymouth itself housed half the island's population of 11,000 as well as the nation's only port, only hospital, government, industries, and people's homes. Most of Plymouth had just been reconstructed from the effects of the devastating Hurricane Hugo of 1989. Tourism—the main economic activity, along with agriculture and a small but thriving music industry—would be decimated, unemployment would soar, and people would have to abandon their homes, schools, and farms for an indefinite time.

By the following April, 5,000 people had moved to the north end of the island, and 3,000 people had left the island. Of the latter, about 1,000 went to Great Britain, which was also providing funds on Montserrat for resettlement, social services, and maintenance of island life.

On September 17, 1996, the lava dome collapsed to produce a pyroclastic flow that moved quickly toward the sea to the east, as well as an ash plume over 32,000 feet (10 kilometers) high. The ashfall darkened the sky, and there was a sulfurous smell; the lava doming continued. By early June the following year, there were more earthquakes from the volcano and its subterranean magma chamber. A few farmers, disobeying the evacuation orders, still tended their crops on the fertile lower slopes of the volcano.

The Big Eruption. On June 25, 1997, there was a more persistent ash eruption, and at about 1 P.M. a major eruption began, finally, but as the volcanologists had feared. The crater's lava dome collapsed, and the pyroclastic ash and rubble cascaded down the volcanic slopes at more than 70 miles per hour and with a temperature of about 15,000 degrees Fahrenheit (8,000 degrees Celsius). Trees were flattened and scorched, and structures were devastated. Nineteen people were killed, by burning or asphyxiation, and many were entombed in the pyroclastic flow. Twenty-seven other people were rescued in time from the mountain region by helicopter.

In late August, 1997, there were more pyroclastic flows in all directions off the mountain. These covered the now-desolate and deserted southern half of the island and smothered Plymouth's structures that were still standing. More people left the island—many probably permanently—as life and the environment became progressively less hospitable and more uncertain. For two years, Soufrière Hills on Montserrat had been volcanically active and making the lands progressively more uninhabitable. However, some good things resulted from the eruptions: Once the activity subsided to dormancy again the ash would weather in the warm moist climate there to create new fertile soil. Also, the oceanic island was enlarged, in an age-old process, by the volcanic flows that reached and extended the shoreline.

Other Eruptions. There are other notable eruptions in the Lesser Antilles that also involved the hazard of pyroclastic flows. In 1979, St. Vincent's volcanic peak, La Soufrière, erupted, but a prior evacuation of the area saved many lives. This was unlike May 7, 1902, there, when an explosive eruption created an ash and steam plume that rose over 30,000 feet (9 kilometers) and a pyroclastic flow that caused about 1,600 deaths. In 1976, some eruptive activity of another volcano named La Soufrière, on Guadeloupe just to the southeast of Montserrat, prompted an evacuation of 70,000 people for several months; however, in this case there were only minor explosions. The most devastating eruption was from Mount Pelée, on the island of Martinique farther to the south. On May 8, 1902, an explosion generated a pyroclastic flow that killed 30,000 people—virtually the entire town of St. Pierre.

Robert S. Carmichael

FOR FURTHER INFORMATION:

Graham, W. "Getting to Know the Volcano." *The New Yorker,* February 17, 1997, 43-47.

Smithsonian Institution, National Museum of Natural History's Global Volcanism Project. http://www.volcano.si.edu/grp, 1999.

Williams, A. R. "Montserrat: Under the Volcano." *National Geographic,* July, 1997, 58-77.

Wind Gusts

(AP/Wide World Photos)

Wind gusts can be violent, with loss of property and life measured in millions, even billions of dollars. They can occur anywhere on earth, sometimes without warning. Wind shear, a localized wind gust, can imperil aircraft, causing collisions with terrain on takeoff and landing.

FACTORS INVOLVED: Geography, temperature, topography, weather conditions, atmospheric pressure, wind
REGIONS AFFECTED: Cities, coasts, forests, mountains, plains, towns, and valleys

SCIENCE

Wind gusts, also called wind shear, occur for a number of reasons, sometimes seemingly at random. No place on the earth's surface is immune to wind gusts, although some areas are more likely to experience them than others. Gusts may be localized differences in atmospheric pressure caused by frontal weather changes. These occur most often in the spring and fall seasons. Normally, fronts having a temperature difference at the surface of 10 degrees Fahrenheit

(5 degrees Celsius) or more and with a frontal speed of at least 30 knots are prone to creating wind gust conditions.

These so-called cold fronts contain a wedge of cold air at their leading edge. This wedge of cold air pushes warm air that is ahead of it upward very rapidly. If the warm air is rich in water vapor, as is seen in the southeastern United States, severe storms erupt ahead of the cold front and may continue until it passes. The weather proverb "If the clouds move against the wind, rain will follow" implies a cold front where clouds in the upper wind are moving in a different direction from clouds driven by lower winds. Most experienced aircraft pilots know how to fly cold frontal boundaries for fuel efficiency, in effect gaining a tailwind both ahead of and into the front

To determine the strength of wind gusts, a good reference is the Beaufort scale. Beaufort numbers vary from 0, no wind, to 12, which depicts winds in excess of 73 miles per hour. People can start to feel the wind at Beaufort 2. A Beaufort 6 means that an umbrella is hard to control and large tree branches are moving. Serious damage potential arrives with Beaufort 10, when trees are uprooted and considerable structural damage can be incurred by anything in the path of the wind gust.

Thunderstorms, whether a product of a cold front or local air mass heating, are responsible for the majority of wind gusts. Thousands of thunderstorms occur across the earth's surface every day. Typical of thunderstorms are the "first gust," the rapid shift and increase in wind velocity just before a thunderstorm hits, and the "downburst," or rapid downward movement of cooled air in and around the thunderstorm cell. A thunderstorm pulls in relatively warm air near the earth's surface, then sends it skyward at several thousand feet per minute, rapidly cooling it. The cool air, becoming more dense and heavy, then plummets back down to the earth's surface. This downward plunge of 7 to 10 miles creates tremendous inertia that can only be dissipated by outflow when the mass strikes the surface. This effect can be compared to dumping a bucket of water on a concrete surface: The "splash" is the same as the outflow from the downburst.

The gusty winds associated with mature thunderstorms are the result of these large downdrafts striking the earth's surface and spreading out horizontally. Some gusts can change direction by as much as 180 degrees very rapidly and reach velocities of 100 knots as far as 10 miles ahead of the thunderstorm. Low-level gusts, typically between the earth's surface and an altitude of 1,500 feet, may increase as much as 50 percent, with most of the increase occurring in the first 150 feet. This makes them particularly dangerous for aircraft in takeoff and landing.

The downburst is an extremely intense localized downdraft from a thunderstorm. The downdraft frequently exceeds 720 feet per minute in vertical velocity at 300 feet above the earth's surface. This velocity can exceed an aircraft's climb capability, even large commercial and military jets. This downdraft is usually much closer to the thunderstorm than the first gust. One clue is the presence of dust clouds, roll clouds, or intense rainfall.

Hurricanes and cyclones also breed large wind gusts. Although winds from these weather phenomena have predictable direction and velocity, tornadoes and whirlwinds imbedded in them can produce wind gusts capable of major damage.

Very local gusting is often referred to as wind shear, and it can be horizontal or vertical. Horizontal shear can move an aircraft off the centerline of a precision approach to an airport. While annoying, it is not usually harmful. Vertical shear, however, is potentially lethal to aircraft. The change in velocity or direction can cause serious changes in lift, indicated airspeed, and thrust requirements, often exceeding the pilot's and aircraft's ability to recover.

A decreasing head wind can cause airspeed and lift of the aircraft to decrease. The pilot reacts with application of power and nose-up attitude of the aircraft. Although overshoots of the intended approach may occur, the pilot is usually able to go around and land safely. Decreasing tailwind causes an increased lift, and the aircraft climbs above the intended approach path.

Modern commercial pilot training devotes significant time to wind-shear problems. Using computerized flight simulators, the entire array of wind-shear problems can be programmed for flight crews. This increases their awareness and application of wind shear recovery without exposing them to the hazards of ineffective recovery techniques if using actual aircraft.

GEOGRAPHY

Topographic features, both natural and human-made, can promote wind gusts. Most people have experienced this in cities with tall buildings, where the wind intensity is much greater in the gaps between large buildings and swirling winds are expected.

Conditions peculiar to the southwestern United States prompt the formation of temperature inversions. These inversions are caused by overnight cooling, where a relatively cool air mass hugs the ground and is overlain by warmer air in the low-level jetstream. High winds from the low-level jet sometimes mix with this inversion, and significant wind gusts may occur at the interface with 90-degree shifts in direction and 20- to 30-knot increases in wind velocity common.

On a much larger scale are the gusts resulting from high winds in mountain passes, on the leeward side of large mountains, and across valleys between mountain ranges. A weather phenomenon often called a "mountain rotor" results from differential heating across a valley between two mountain ranges. Air flowing down an upwind mountain during the day is heated, traverses a relatively cool air mass in the valley, then moves across the downwind mountain, causing the turbulence at the boundary of the cooled and heated air masses described above. As the air is heated in the morning, a weak rising motion of the cool air is induced and pulls the air currents attempting to climb the downwind mountain back into the valley. This back-rotation creates a rotary motion that contains both horizontal and vertical wind gusts.

At least one commercial aircraft accident has been tentatively blamed on a rotor. Rotors can be seen, unless the atmosphere is devoid of moisture, as nearly round symmetrical clouds in mountain valleys. Pilots undergoing mountain-flying training are cautioned to steer clear of these rotors. A flight into a dry rotor is usually dangerous.

The roughness of the earth's surface plays a major role in determining wind-gust intensity. This roughness can occur from obstacles or terrain contours, called orography. Orography promotes tunnel effects (mountain passes) and hill effects (lee—the side sheltered from the wind—of mountains). Pilots are very familiar with this effect. A very calm outbound flight in the morning after a cold-front passage can mean a bumpy return flight in the afternoon as the frontal wind gains intensity and flows over rough topography.

In general, the rougher the earth's surface, the more the wind will be slowed. Forests and large cities slow the wind more than lakes and prairies. Surface roughness can be classified as to its ability to slow wind. For example, landscapes with many trees and buildings have a roughness class of 3 or 4, while a large water surface has a roughness class of 0. Open terrain has a roughness class of 0.5. Roughness length is used with roughness class, and relates to the distance above ground level where the wind speed theoretically should be 0.

PREVENTION AND PREPARATIONS

The aviation industry has been particularly interested in wind gusts, or wind shear, because of their potential effect on aircraft performance in takeoff and landing. According to National Transportation Safety Board (NTSB) records, wind shears contributed to approximately 50 percent of all commercial airline fatalities between 1974 and 1985. The Federal Aviation Administration (FAA) has required some type of wind shear hazard detection systems on scheduled commercial aircraft since 1995.

Pulsed Doppler radar is the primary means of detection of wind gusts for aircraft crews and ground-based air controllers and weather prognosticators. Doppler radar senses speed and direction in the same manner as police traffic radar. A well-understood Doppler effect is a train whistle that is always higher in pitch when the train is approaching than when moving away.

Doppler weather radar bounces its pulses off raindrops in storm clouds. If the raindrops are moving toward the radar set, the reflected signal is higher in frequency than if the rain is falling vertically. Frequencies are compared, and color displays are created to depict areas of precipitation and wind shear. Some Doppler radar sets create an audible warning to aircrews if wind shear is nearby. Effective though dangerous indicators of wind shear are reports from pilots experiencing it. Air-traffic controllers solicit these reports, and many may be received in a short period of time in areas where pilots are experiencing wind-shear conditions.

Aside from aviation and its vulnerability to wind gusts, other modes of transportation are frequently disturbed by wind gusts. Mountain valleys and other gust-prone locations often experience upended tractor-trailer rigs, which are typically top-heavy and show a considerable broadside resistance to the wind. Sailing ships and relatively light watercraft are also prone to upset by wind gusts. Even with no sails in the wind, boats are difficult to steer with changing wind speeds bearing against their hulls.

RESCUE AND RELIEF EFFORTS

Wind gusts produce the same results as tornadoes but are even more localized. Building damage and injury to humans and animals can occur. Trauma-related injuries are typical, including broken bones, excessive lacerations, and imbedded debris. Police and fire officials usually handle the localized nature of wind-gust damage, although for widespread damage, the Red Cross and Salvation Army, as well as other relief organizations, may assist victims.

Local authorities also customarily oversee property damage. Clearing may be necessary to restore public utilities and roadways. Insurance adjusters are frequent visitors to damage sites so that they can assess the severity of the damage to client property and recommend compensation.

IMPACT

Like that of tornadoes, wind-gust damage is not long-lasting. It has no significant effect on local topography, but it can cause extensive damage to human-made structures. The famous "Galloping Gertie," or Tacoma Narrows Bridge, was set in motion by wind gusts and ultimately destroyed by its own harmonic frequencies. Windows and trim in large buildings can be damaged or even removed by wind gusts. Large signs and other similar displays are also frequently damaged or dislodged by gusty winds. These articles pose a risk to passersby on the streets below.

Perhaps most important, wind gusts damage aircraft quite easily. Those aircraft on the ground not secured by tie-down lines may be blown around by gusty winds and receive extensive damage. However, the most important damage to aircraft occurs when wind gusts overcome the pilot's ability to maintain flying conditions in takeoff or landing configurations. Aircraft collisions with the ground cause minor damage or extensive loss of life and totally destroy aircraft. Literally thousands of aircraft accidents can be traced to wind gusts as the primary cause of or at least a major contributor to the accident. A portion of the avionics industry is devoted exclusively to the severity of wind shear to operation of aircraft. Even local television stations proudly advertise that their weather gurus are equipped with the most modern Doppler radar for the safety and convenience of their viewers.

Charles Haynes

BIBLIOGRAPHY

Freier, George D. *Weather Proverbs: How Six Hundred Proverbs, Sayings, and Poems Accurately Explain Our Weather.* Tucson, Ariz.: Fisher Books, 1992. A very interesting book on weather phenomena, with modern explanations given to ancient weather lore.

Kimble, George H. T. *Our American Weather.* New York: McGraw Hill, 1955. This is a very readable book, unique in that it depicts U.S. weather by month. Entertaining as well as informative.

National Aeronautics and Space Administration. *Making the Skies Safe from Windshear.* www.larc.nasa .gov/org/pao/PAIS/windshear.html. A series of NASA documents that detail its research into the causes and detection of wind shear as it affects aircraft.

National Transportation Safety Board. www.nasdac .faa.gov/cgi-shl/ntsbhtml.pl. This is the NTSB's aviation accident/incident database. Although cold and cryptic details are the essence of this Web site, it nevertheless details the mounting toll of aircraft accidents resulting in part from wind gusts.

Palmen, E., and C. W. Newton. *Atmospheric Circulation Systems.* New York: Academic Press, 1969. Although some knowledge of calculus is necessary to master this book, it still has many readable pages concerning global weather at the lower altitudes that can be understood by most individuals.

Ruffner, James. *The Weather Almanac.* Detroit: Gale Research, 1974. Provides a detailed description of the Beaufort number for wind speed and contains much weather data.

Notable Events

1879: Scotland

BRIDGE COLLAPSE
DATE: December 28, 1879
PLACE: Dundee, Scotland
RESULT: 80 dead

The evening of December 28, 1879, was wet and stormy with severe gales. The wind was blowing hard at right angles as the loaded Edinburgh mail train of the North British Railway moved onto the single track of the bridge over the Firth of Tay near Dundee in Scotland at about 7:15 P.M. The train was partway across when observers on shore saw what appeared to be sparks and flame falling into the river. However, the central navigation section of the bridge, a thirteen-span high girder section, with the six-car train inside it, was being blown into the river. Not a single person on board survived. Estimates indicated that 80 people (including the train crew) died in the icy waters, making it one of the worst bridge disasters and structural engineering failures in the United Kingdom. The bridge had been in service for just eighteen months.

The bridge, built in 1878, at 2.75 miles in length was at the time of its building the longest railroad bridge in the world. Spanning a tidal estuary, it had all the forces of moving water around the foundations and supports, and it was open to wind and weather. From the beginning of construction, there were problems. Because of the lack of a solid rock base, engineers had to manage the largely soft riverbed by using caissons and building the bridge off masonry bases, using six vertical cast-iron columns for each pier. These weak columns, filled with concrete, were bolted together, providing enough sec-

tions on top of each other to reach desired track level; wrought-iron tie bars, attached to lugs, provided bracing. These piers carried the wrought-iron girders, which formed a truss that supported a single railroad track, the structure being high enough to provide clearance for shipping at 88 feet above the high-water mark.

At the inspection of the bridge prior to its opening, there were some misgivings concerning the effect strong winds might have on the 27-foot-tall "high girder" sections that the trains passed through. After a few months, defects were discovered—tie bars that became loose, requiring constant tightening of their fastenings, and defective lugs on the cast-iron columns owing to poor casting.

After the collapse, Thomas Bouch, the engineer, designer, and contractor of the bridge, said he made no special provision for wind pressure, although high winds were common in the area. Examination afterward by engineers as part of a full court of inquiry found that the bridge was badly designed, badly built, and badly maintained. A 1990 computer model suggests that the bridge was significantly underdesigned for the wind loading and that, even if the cross bracing and its fastenings had been properly constructed, there was little chance of surviving the heavy gales encountered there.

The collapse of the bridge was a reminder to engineers that the effect of wind strength has to be properly considered and calculated in bridge designs and that materials of suitable strengths must be used. The tragedy had a major influence on the design of the Firth of Forth Bridge in the 1880's, where the designer Benjamin Baker conducted extensive wind-pressure measurements.

Stephen B. Dobrow

The wreck of the dirigible USS Shenandoah *in 1925.* (AP/Wide World Photos)

FOR FURTHER INFORMATION:

Hopkins, H. J. *A Span of Bridges: An Illustrated History.* New York: Praeger, 1970.

Swinfen, D. *The Fall of the Tay Bridge.* Edinburgh, Scotland: Mercat Press, 1994.

1925: Ohio

AIRSHIP CRASH
DATE: September 3, 1925
PLACE: Over Ava, Ohio
RESULT: 14 dead

The USS *Shenandoah* was the first of four rigid airships commissioned into the U.S. Navy; its first flight was September 4, 1923. It was 680 feet long and 79 feet in diameter, and it had a volume of 2.1 million cubic feet. Its performance did not meet expectations, partially because it was designed to carry hydrogen but instead used the heavier, but safer, helium.

Basically a trainer, it flew 509 flights for 740 hours before it crashed on September 3, 1925, in Ohio as a result of unforecast violent thunderstorms, long before the development of national weather advisories.

On the afternoon of the day before, the *Shenandoah* had left Lakewood, New Jersey, under unsettled weather with forty-three people aboard for a tour of midwestern state fairs. The airship had already flown 25,000 miles in all kinds of weather. At midnight, the airship's five engines propelled it westward under partially overcast skies.

At 3 A.M., a storm began to brew in the northwest, and the airship was soon making little progress against a strong head wind. For an hour and a half, the slender airship struggled westward, drifting from side to side. The *Shenandoah* stopped responding to the controls and started rising. Rolling like a raft on the sea, it continued directly into the storm. In the squall, the airship was in the grip of two opposing forces, each wrenching it in a different direction. The *Shenandoah*'s rise stopped abruptly at 6,300 feet, and it began falling fast. The fall was stopped at 2,500 feet, but then the airship started to rise quickly again. At 3,500 feet, the airship began to turn rapidly; girders began to twist and tear, and the *Shenandoah* began breaking apart in the middle. Control wires held the pieces together; however, 2 crewmen were pitched out of the ship through the openings.

Wind and torsion broke the struts that held the big gondola to the control car. The commanding officer, Lieutenant Commander Zachary Landsdowne, and 7 others died when the control car went down. The control car and aft section fell directly to earth, while the forward section, with 7 aboard, free-ballooned for one hour before landing safely 12 miles from the crash. Eighteen survived in the 350-foot stern section; 4 of 8 passengers survived in the center section. The fragments of the airship, and its 29 survivors, were scattered across 12 miles of landscape. In all, 14 of its crew of 43 died because the airship had been torn apart by a severe squall line.

Stephen B. Dobrow

FOR FURTHER INFORMATION:

Althoff, William. *Sky Ships: A History of the Airship in the United States Navy.* Pacifica, Calif.: Pacifica Press, 1994.

Robinson, Douglas. *Giants in the Sky: History of the Rigid Airships.* Seattle: University of Washington Press, 1973.

Toland, John. "Death of a Dirigible." *American Heritage* 10, no. 2 (February, 1959): 18-22, 90-93.

1932: California

AIRSHIP UNMOORING
DATE: May 11, 1932
PLACE: Camp Kearney in San Diego, California
RESULT: 2 dead

The USS *Akron* was the first of two rigid dirigibles of 6.5 million cubic feet in volume. It was designed to allow four heavier-than-air scout planes (which could be launched or recovered by a retractable trapeze assembly) to be stowed in an internal hanger. Designed to be helium-filled, eight engines were located inside the hull with propellers driven by shafts and gearing that allowed upward, downward, or reverse thrust. The first flight of this airship, 785 feet long and 133 feet in diameter, was September 23, 1931.

The airship USS Akron *shown in flight over New York City in November, 1931, six months before the dirigible became unmoored in San Diego, killing 2.* (AP/Wide World Photos)

It was not until April, 1932, that the airship was equipped for scouting exercises. On May 8, the *Akron* was sent from its Lakehurst, New Jersey, base to the West Coast with the intention of flying a few exercises with the scouting force and the naval fleet. Rough weather along the way duplicated the stability problems encountered by earlier airships. The climax came during efforts to make an emergency mooring at Camp Kearney, California, to replenish the fuel tanks.

Several attempts to tie down the large dirigible had been made by a ground crew of three groups of thirty. On the third attempt, a cable parted after the airship had supposedly been safely moored. The remaining two groups struggled to hold the craft, but upward currents caught it. Most let the rope go before it got too high, but 3 members of the mooring crew continued to cling to the landing line. Two of them lost their grip as the rope continued to rise, falling 150 and 200 feet to their deaths, respectively, in the view of newsreel cameramen and ten thousand spectators. The third member, Bud Cowart, was carried aloft for two hours, dangling at the end of a 300-foot rope. A height of 2,000 feet was reached, but he maintained his grip. The *Akron* rocked up and down in the bumpy air with Cowart hanging on. Finally he and the rope were dragged upward by a windlass on the *Akron* until he was pulled aboard through a porthole. The airship landed successfully later in the day.

Stephen B. Dobrow

FOR FURTHER INFORMATION:

Althoff, William. *Sky Ships: A History of the Airship in the United States Navy.* Pacifica, Calif.: Pacifica Press, 1994.

The New York Times, May, 1932.

Robinson, Douglas. *Giants in the Sky: History of the Rigid Airships.* Seattle: University of Washington Press, 1973.

1940: Washington State

BRIDGE COLLAPSE
DATE: November 7, 1940
PLACE: Tacoma, Washington
RESULT: 1 dog dead

The first Tacoma Narrows Bridge, a 5,939-foot-long span costing $7 million, opened to traffic on July 1, 1940, after two years of construction, linking Tacoma and Gig Harbor, Washington. It collapsed just four months later during a 42-mile-per-hour windstorm on November 7, 1940. The only casualty was a dog stranded in a car. Professor Burt Farquharson of the University of Washington filmed the collapse, producing the classic film of structural failure. The bridge had received the nickname "Galloping Gertie" because of its rolling, undulating behavior. Motorists traversing the 2,800-foot center span could actually see the cars ahead disappearing into a wave-like trough as if they were on a giant roller coaster. The up-down motion reached the order of 3 feet.

Because the bridge was built with 8-foot-deep solid girders and not the more conventional 20- or 30-foot-deep truss work, it was extremely flexible, graceful, and streamlined. Unfortunately, rather than allowing it to pass through, the girders caught the wind. This effect would have been survivable had not catastrophic nonlinear motions been induced by wind vortexes. A structure has a critical velocity that triggers a self-excited unstable condition, a shift from one-dimensional to torsional modes of oscillation. As the wind's intensity increased, so did the rolling, corkscrew motion of the bridge, which self-excited in torsion and shook itself to pieces in a moderate wind after four short months of operation.

The bridge started this day with a 30-hertz transverse vibration, which shifted into a 14-hertz twisting motion. As the structure twisted, the roadway rocked back and forth, with the high side rising 20 feet above the opposing side. At its peak, the displacement reached 28 feet. Then a 600-foot piece of bridge completely broke away and fell into the sound below. Up until this time, suspension-bridge decks had been designed on the basis of their deflection under vertical load from self-weight and traffic. It had been assumed that long-span suspension bridges could be built simply with the minimum stiffness required to distribute the weight of traffic; aerodynamic factors were not considered.

It came as a shock to engineers to realize that the increasingly thinner decks could act as airfoils to the wind, and the disaster led to much research on aerodynamic stability of bridges. A cable-supported bridge is subject to wind-induced drag (a static component), torsional flutter (the instability that destroyed the Tacoma Narrows Bridge), and buffeting

The Tacoma Narrows Bridge shortly before it collapsed on November 7, 1940, in a windstorm. (AP/Wide World Photos)

(gusts shaking the bridge). Bridge design had to consider upward wind thrust, not just horizontal forces. As a result of the collapse, other bridges, such as the Bronx-Whitestone Bridge in New York City, were quickly modified to prevent a repeat of the Tacoma collapse. Control of aerodynamic instabilities was achieved by aerodynamically shaped decks, stiffness, mass, and active or passive damping.

Stephen B. Dobrow

For Further Information:

Petroski, Henry. *Engineers of Dreams: Great Bridge Builders and the Spanning of America.* New York: Alfred A. Knopf, 1995.

Ratigan, William. *Highways over Broad Waters: Life and Times of David B. Steinman, Bridgebuilder.* Grand Rapids, Mich.: Wm. B. Eerdmans, 1959.

1985: Texas

Plane crash

Date: August 2, 1985
Place: Dallas/Ft. Worth International Airport, Texas
Result: 135 dead, 15 seriously injured, 13 with minor injuries, aircraft destroyed

Delta Airlines flight 191 departed Fort Lauderdale, Florida, in the early afternoon on August 2, 1985, traveling nonstop to the Dallas/Ft. Worth International Airport (DFW). Because air-mass thunderstorms are possible on any summer day in the southern United States, the cockpit crew was well aware that flight path deviations were a possibility, particularly in the climb and approach phases of flight. The Lockheed L-1011 aircraft used in this flight routinely cruises above 30,000 feet, so the en-route phase of the trip was routinely spent monitoring instruments while the autopilot handled the navigation tasks. The DFW weather forecast called for possible scattered thunderstorms, the usual summertime afternoon forecast for north central Texas, so there was nothing particularly ominous for the crew to anticipate.

The en-route phase of the flight was uneventful. However, several large thunderstorm cells were de-veloping in the area of DFW at the time of arrival for flight 191. DFW flight controllers brought these cells to the attention of the flight crew, even though the pi-lots undoubtedly saw them on the color radar display in the cockpit. The flight was vectored around a large cell and was then sequenced behind another aircraft and cleared for an instrument landing system (ILS) runway 17 approach. A runway 17 approach means that the landing direction is 170 degrees magnetic, or

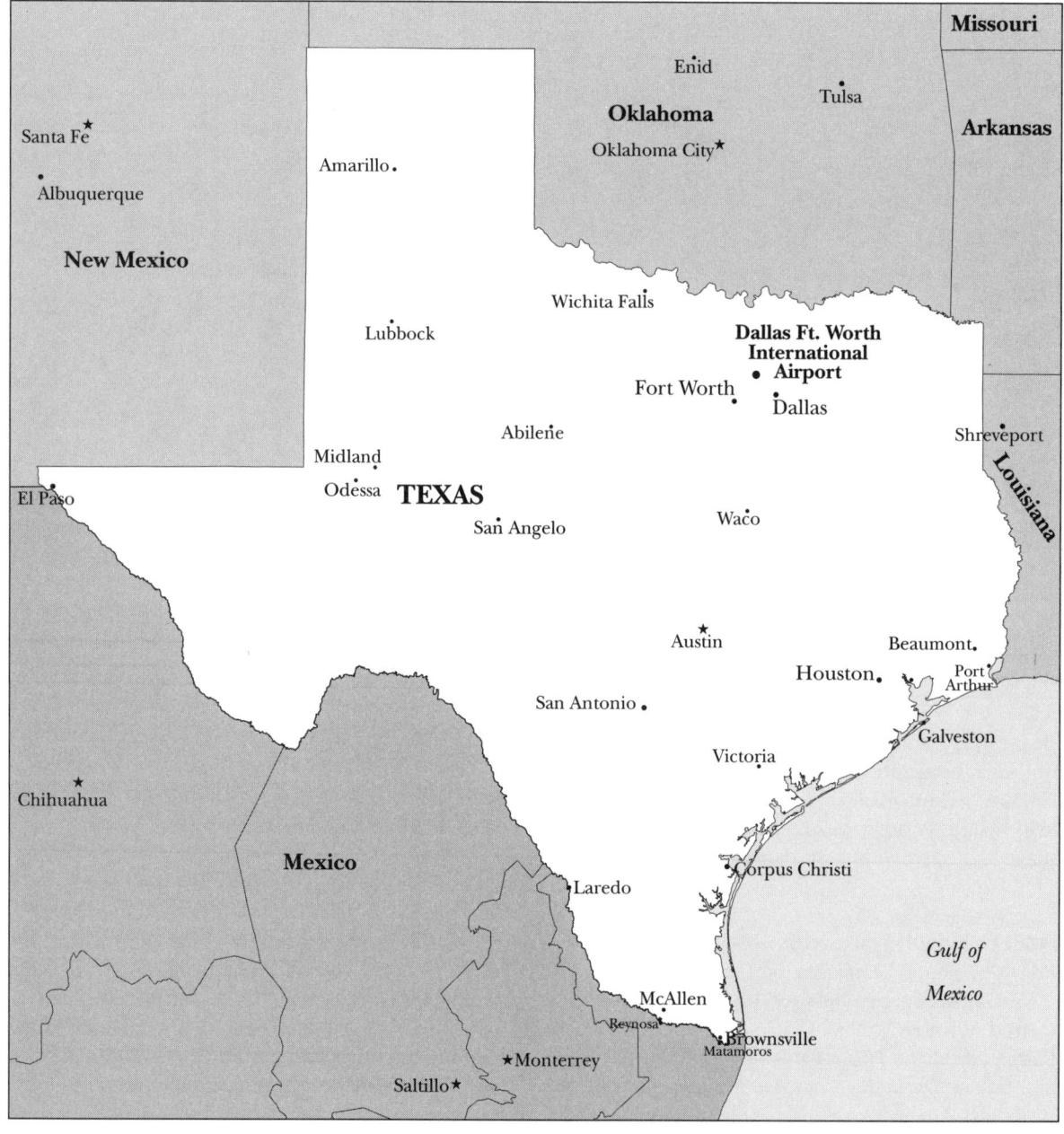

nearly due south. As such, the aircraft would have been positioned north of the airport on its initial approach. The flight crew, as well as other air crews preceding flight 191, saw lightning in a cell north of the airport but continued their approaches without reporting it. The basic weather as given by approach control was IFR, meaning instrument meteorological conditions. However, widespread IFR conditions in the summer are rare, so the report was probably confined to the immediate vicinity of the airport, where the thunderstorms had the ceiling and visibility below visual approach minimums.

The crew of flight 191 was apprehensive about the weather conditions on final approach, but the aircraft preceding it did not report difficulty. The flight 191 crew then committed themselves to the final approach. The first officer (copilot) was flying, and he encountered torrential rain and a strong headwind from the thunderstorm cell outflow. He immediately retarded the engine thrust, anticipating an updraft, in order to remain on the glide slope, but instead encountered what was believed to be a 73-knot wind shear, with up- and downdrafts, vortex flow, and a strong tailwind.

The L-1011 aircraft, with its three Rolls Royce RB-211-22B turbofan engines, is classified as "heavy," meaning that its 430,000 certified maximum gross weight places it into a special category of aircraft. Heavy aircraft produce a particularly strong vortex from their wingtips (erroneously called "propwash"), requiring following or crossing aircraft to be spaced at wider intervals to avoid the sharp turbulence associated with the vortices. An aircraft of this size, even with its enormous power, is vulnerable when near its stall speed because its inertia resists abrupt changes to the application and reduction of thrust. These thrust changes do not provide immediate responses in heavy aircraft performance, as would be expected from aircraft with lesser gross weights. Added to this vulnerability is the relatively slow reaction time for turbojet engines to "spool-up," or react to sudden application of throttle. While turbofan engines are considerably improved in spool-up time as compared to earlier turbojet engines, they still react more slowly to throttle application than propeller-driven aircraft.

Thus, the stage was set for flight stability problems if the approach weather was gusty. In other words, with retarded throttles and a slowing airspeed, the aircraft was vulnerable to a following wind that would provide the appearance of speed over the ground but would create a high sink rate. When the downdrafts struck, the aircraft could not remain on the proper glide slope, even with the application of go-around thrust. The aircraft was now very close to the ground, denying the pilots the comfort of altitude to sort out what had become a very difficult approach.

Having been overcome by the downburst, flight 191 struck the ground approximately 6,300 feet north of the runway 17L approach end, hit an automobile on the interstate highway that borders the airport, killing its occupant, and continued skidding across the northern end of the airport. At this time, small fires were breaking out where the aircraft fuel tanks were being ruptured, but the fuselage most likely remained intact at this point. There was probably cause for optimism by the flight crew as the aircraft decelerated on the ground. However, two large water tanks were located just to the left of the runway 17L centerline. The skidding aircraft, now completely out of control, veered toward these tanks, collided with them, and broke apart. This collision created an inferno with resulting widespread death among its passengers and crew. The intense rainfall obscured visual observation of the aircraft breakup from control tower personnel, although word of the accident was received by rescue personnel quickly from observers on the highway north of the airport.

The National Transportation Safety Board (NTSB) accident investigation, finding nothing defective with the aircraft, focused on the change in weather conditions during the final approach of flight 191. It was found that between 5:52 and 6:00 P.M. central daylight time, the thunderstorm cell north of the airport grew from Level 1 to Level 4, a size that no prudent flight crew would challenge. One experienced weather observer, seeing the cell development on videotape afterward, commented that it was the fastest-growing cell he had seen.

The accident investigation focused on the flight crew and weather-observation personnel responsible for alerting the flight crew to hazardous conditions in the area. In this phase of the investigation, it was found that a key weather observer was on duty but not watching his radar and the development of the thunderstorm cell at the time of its rapid growth. The captain's decision to continue the approach did not comply with Delta's weather avoidance procedures, and this was compounded by a lack of specific guidance and training for flight crews to avoid and escape low-altitude wind shear. Of minor consequence was the captain's decision to permit the first officer to continue the approach in view of the worsening weather conditions.

This accident, as well as others like it in the 1980's, formed the basis for current procedures to combat wind-shear conditions in full-motion flight simulators. Today's commercial pilots become proficient in executing extreme wind-shear maneuvers as part of their mandatory training.

Charles Haynes

FOR FURTHER INFORMATION:

"The Crash of Flight 191." *Maclean's* 98 (August 12, 1985): 20.

"Dallas/Fort Worth ATC Releases Transcript of Delta L-1011 Crash." *Aviation Week and Space Technology* 123 (August 26, 1985): 75.

Marbach, W. D. "Delta 191: Needless Tragedy?" *Newsweek* 106 (August 19, 1985): 24.

Morganthau, T. "Delta 191: Death in Dallas." *Newsweek* 106 (August 12, 1985): 30-32.

Glossary

Acid rain: Rain with higher levels of acidity than normal; the source of the high levels of acidity is polluted air.

Acquired immunodeficiency syndrome (AIDS): A progressive loss of immune function and susceptibility to secondary infections that arises from chronic infection with HIV.

African sleeping sickness: An infectious disease transmitted through the bite of a tsetse fly with symptoms of fever, lymph node swelling, fatigue, and possibly coma and death.

Aftershock: A minor shock following the main tremor of an earthquake.

AIDS. *See* Acquired immunodeficiency syndrome (AIDS)

Airship: A lighter-than-air aircraft that uses hydrogen for buoyancy.

Alluvium: Sediment deposited by flowing water.

Alpine glacier: A small, elongate, usually tongue-shaped glacier commonly occupying a preexisting valley in a mountain range.

Amplitude: Wave height.

Angle of repose: The maximum angle of steepness that a pile of loose material such as sand or rock can assume and remain stable; the angle varies with the size, shape, moisture, and angularity of the material.

Anthrax: An infectious disease caused by a bacterium, with symptoms of external nodules or lesions in the lungs.

Antibiotic: Any substance that destroys or inhibits the growth of microorganisms, especially bacteria.

Antibody: A protein substance produced by white blood cells in response to an antigen; combats bacterial, viral, chemical, or other invasive agents in the body and provides immunity against disease-causing microorganisms.

Aquifer: A water-bearing bed of rock, sand, or gravel, capable of yielding substantial quantities of water to wells or springs.

Arson: The willful or malicious burning of property.

Ash: Fine-grained pyroclastic material less than 2 millimeters in diameter, ejected from an erupting volcano.

Asteroid: A small, rocky body in orbit around the sun; a minor planet.

Asteroid belt: The region between the orbits of Mars and Jupiter, containing the majority of asteroids.

Atmosphere: The five clearly defined regions composed of layers of gases and mixtures of gases, water vapor, and solid and liquid particles, extending up to 483 kilometers above the earth.

Atoll: A tropical island on which a massive coral reef, often ringlike, generally rests on a volcanic base.

Avalanche: Any large mass of snow, ice, rock, soil, or a mixture of these materials that falls, slides, or flows rapidly downslope; velocities may reach in excess of 500 kilometers per hour.

Bacteria: Microscopic single-celled organisms that multiply by means of simple division; bacteria are found everywhere and most are beneficial, with only a few species causing disease.

Base surge: The initial volcanic blast of an ash flow.

Basin: A regionally depressed structure in which sediments accumulate.

Bathymetry: The measurement of water depth at various places in a body of water.

Beaufort scale: A scale from 0 to 12 that measures wind velocity.

Blizzard: A long, severe snowstorm.

Body wave: A seismic wave that propagates interior to a body; there are two kinds—P waves and S waves—that travel through the earth, reflecting and refracting off of the several layered boundaries within the earth.

Bore: A nearly vertical advancing wall of water that may be produced by tides, a tsunami, or a seiche.

Brisance: The shattering or crushing effect of an explosive.

Brushfire: A wildfire.

Bubo: An inflammatory swelling of a lymph gland.

Bubonic plague: A form of plague characterized by the sudden onset of fever, chills, weakness, headache, and buboes in the groin, armpits, or neck.

Caldera: A large, flat-floored volcanic depression that is formed on top of a large, shallow magma chamber during the eruption or withdrawal of magma; calderas are usually tens of kilometers across and can be a kilometer or more in depth.

Calve: To separate a piece from an ice mass.

Cannibalism: The eating of human flesh by human beings.

CD4 cell: A type of white blood cell (helper T cell) that helps other immune cells work together to fight a variety of diseases.

Cholera: A disease marked by severe gastrointestinal symptoms.

Cinder cone: A small volcano composed of cinder or lumps of lava containing many gas bubbles, or vesicles; often the early stage of a stratovolcano.

Cirque: A steep-sided, gentle-floored, semicircular hollow produced by erosion at the head of a glacier high on a mountain peak.

Coal: Dark brown to black rock formed by heat and compression from the accumulation of plant material in swampy environments.

Cold front: The contact between two air masses when a bulge of cold, polar air surges southward into regions of warmer air.

Combustion: An exothermic, self-sustaining, chemical reaction usually involving the oxidation of a fuel by oxygen in the atmosphere and the emission of heat, light, and mechanical energy, such as sound.

Comet: A solar system body, usually in an elongated and randomly oriented orbit, composed of rocky and icy materials that form a flowing head and extended tail when the body nears the sun.

Comet nucleus: The central core of a comet, composed of frozen gases and dust; the source of all cometary activity.

Conduction: Heat transfer between two bodies in direct contact with each other.

Cone: The hill or mountain, more or less conical, surrounding a volcanic vent and created by its ejecta; it is normally surmounted by a crater.

Conflagration: A fire that spreads from building to building through flame spread over some distance, often a portion of a city or a town.

Continental glacier or ice sheet: A glacier of considerable thickness that completely covers a large part of a continent, obscuring the relief of the underlying surface.

Convection: Heat transfer within a fluid.

Cordillera: A long, elevated mountain chain marked by a valley-and-ridge structure.

Core: The spherical, mostly liquid mass located 2,900 kilometers below the earth's surface; a central, solid part is known as the inner core.

Couloir: A mountain-side gorge.

Crater: The circular depression atop a volcanic cone or formed by meteoritic impact.

Creep: The slow, more or less continuous downslope movement of earth material.

Crust: The outermost layer of the earth; the continental crust, composed of dominantly silicon-rich igneous rocks, metamorphic rocks, and sedimentary rocks, is between 30 and 40 kilometers thick, while the oceanic crust, composed of magnesium- and iron-rich rocks such as basalt, is merely 5 kilometers thick.

Cwm: A cirque.

Cyclone: A major tropical storm that originates in the Indian Ocean.

Debris flow: A flowing mass consisting of water and a high concentration of sediment with a wide range of size, from fine muds to coarse gravels.

Deflagration: An explosive reaction that spreads outward as burning materials ignite the materials next to them at a rate slower than the speed of sound.

Deforestation: The process of clearing forests.

Delta: A deposit of sediment, often triangular, formed at a river mouth where the wave action of the sea is low.

Deoxyribonucleic acid (DNA): A protein found in the nucleus of a cell comprising chromosomes that contain the genetic instructions of an organism.

Detonation: An explosive reaction in which a shock wave progressively combusts materials by compressing them when the rate is faster than the speed of sound.

Dew point: The temperature at which a vapor begins to condense.

Dike: A tabular igneous rock body that cuts across the fabric of the solid rocks.

Dilatancy: An increase in volume as a result of rock forming cracks by expansion, pressure, or agitation.

Diphtheria: A highly contagious bacterial infection that usually affects the respiratory system.

DNA. *See* Deoxyribonucleic acid (DNA)

Doppler radar: A radar system that measures velocity (as of wind).

Downburst: A downward outflowing of air and the associated wind shear from a thunderstorm that is especially hazardous to aircraft.

Downdraft: A downward current of air or gas.

Drainage basin: The land area that contributes water to a particular stream; the edge of such a basin is a drainage divide.

Drought: An extended period of below-normal precipitation that is sufficiently long and severe that crops fail and normal water demand cannot be met.

Dust Bowl: The period from 1932 to 1938 in the U.S. Midwest and Southeast during which drought conditions caused much dust to form and drift.

Dust devil: A rotating column of rising air, made visible by the dust it contains; smaller and less destructive than a tornado, it has winds of less than 60 kilometers per hour.

Dust storm: The result of wind erosion, desertification, and physical deterioration of the soil caused by persistent or temporary lack of rainfall and wind gusts.

Earthquake: A sudden release of strain energy in a fault zone as a result of violent motion of a part of the earth along the fault.

Ebola virus: A disease in which the patient experiences fever, muscle pain, blood clots in vital organs, hemorrhaging, shock, kidney failure, and often death.

Ejecta: The material ejected from the crater made by a meteoric impact; also, material thrown out of a volcano during eruption.

El Niño: Part of a gigantic meteorological system called the Southern Oscillation that links the ocean and atmosphere in the Pacific, causing periodic changes in climate.

Elastic waves: Waves that travel through a material because of its ability to recover from an instantaneous elastic deformation.

Encephalitis: Inflammation of the brain.

Enzootic: An infection that is present in an animal community at all times but manifests itself only in a small fraction of instances.

Ephemeral stream: A river or stream that flows briefly in response to nearby rainfall; such streams are common in arid and semiarid regions.

Epicenter: The point on the earth's surface directly above the focus of an earthquake.

Epidemic: A disease that affects a large human population.

Epidemiology: The medical field that studies the distribution of disease among human populations, as well as the factors responsible for this distribution.

Epizootic: An outbreak of disease in which many animals become infected at the same time.

Ergotism: A disease of the central nervous system caused by ingesting the alkaloids (one of which is LSD) of the ergot fungus, *Claviceps purpurea*, which infects rye grain; symptoms include numbness of the extremities, vomiting and diarrhea, dizziness, and delusions and convulsions usually ending in a painful death.

Erosion: The removal of weathered rock and mineral fragments and grains from an area by the action of wind, ice, gravity, or running water.

Eruption: Volcanic activity of such force as to propel significant amounts of magmatic products over the rim of the crater.

Evaporite: A rock largely composed of minerals that have precipitated upon evaporation of seawater or lake water.

Evapotranspiration: The movement of water from the soil to the atmosphere in response to heat, combining transpiration in plants and evaporation.

Exothermic reaction: A reaction in which the new substances produced have less energy than the original substances.

Explosion: Combustion that expands so quickly that the fuel volume cannot shed energy rapidly enough to remain stable.

Extinction: The disappearance of a species or large group of animals or plants.

Extrusion: The emission of magma or lava and the rock so formed onto the earth's surface.

Extrusive rock: Igneous rock that has been erupted onto the surface of the earth.

Eye: The calm central region of a hurricane, composed of a tunnel with strong sides.

Eyewall: The area surrounding the eye, or center, of a hurricane.

Famine: A lack of access to food, the cause of which can be a natural disaster, such as a drought, or a situation created by humans, such as a civil war.

Fault: A fracture or system of fractures across which relative movement of rock bodies has occurred.

Fault drag: The bending of rocks adjacent to a fault.

Fault slip: The direction and amount of relative movement between the two blocks of rock separated by a fault.

Fifty-year-flood: A hypothetical flood whose severity is such that it would occur on average only once in a period of fifty years, which equates to a 2 percent probability each year.

Fire: The process of combustion.

Fireball: A very large and bright meteor that often explodes with fragments falling to the ground as meteorites; sometimes called a bolide.

Firebrand: A piece of burning material from a building that is carried by convective forces, such as wind, to a nearby building.

Firestorm: A large, usually stationary fire characterized by very high temperatures, in which the central column of rising, heated air induces strong inward winds that supply oxygen to the fire.

Flash floods: Floods that begin very quickly and last only a short time.

Flash point: The minimum temperature at which vapors above a volatile substance ignite in air when exposed to flame.

Flood: The result of a river overflowing its banks and spreading out over the bordering floodplain; defined in terms of the volume of water moving past a given point in the stream channel per unit of time (cubic feet per second).

Floodplain: The relatively flat valley floor on either side of a river which may be partly or wholly occupied by water during a flood.

Flow rate: The amount of water that passes a reference point in a specific amount of time, measured in liters per second.

Flu. *See* Influenza

Fluvial: Of or related to streams and their actions.

Focus: The region within the earth from which earthquake waves emanate; also called the hypocenter.

Foehn: A warm, dry wind blowing in the valleys of a mountain.

Fog: Dense water vapor, reducing visibility to less than 0.6 mile (1 kilometer), that occurs when the temperature of any surface falls below the dew point of the air directly above it.

Freeze: The occurrence of abnormally low temperatures for an extended period of time over a region.

Fresh water: Water with less than 0.2 percent dissolved salts, such as is found in most streams, rivers, and lakes.

Front: The boundary between two dissimilar air masses.

Fuel: A material that will burn.

Fujita scale: A rating scale that examines structural damage to assess the wind speed of a tornado.

Fumarole: A vent that emits only gases.

Glacier: An accumulation of ice that flows viscously as a result of its own weight; a glacier forms when snowfall accumulates and recrystallizes into a granular snow (firn, or névé), which becomes compacted and converted into solid, interlocking glacial ice.

Graben: A roughly symmetrical crustal depression formed by the lowering of a crustal block between two normal faults that slope toward each other.

Graupel: Soft hail.

Groundwater: Water that is located beneath the surface of the earth in interconnected pores.

Hail: Precipitation consisting of layers of ice and snow in the form of small balls.

Harmonic tremor: A movement or shaking of the ground accompanying volcanic eruptions.

Hawaiian eruption: A low-intensity volcanic eruption (VEI values of 0 or 1) characterized by a calm outpouring of low-viscosity, low-silicon lava.

Headwater: The source of a stream.

Heat Index: A scale that measures how hot it feels when the relative humidity is factored into the actual air temperature.

Heat wave: The occurrence of abnormally high air temperatures for an extended period of time over a region, destroying crops, damaging infrastructures, and sometimes causing both animal and human deaths.

HIV. *See* Human immunodeficiency virus (HIV)

Host: A living animal or plant giving lodgment to a parasite.

Hot spot: A zone of hot, upwelling rock that is rooted in the earth's upper mantle; as plates of the earth's crust and lithosphere glide over a mantle plume, a trail of hot spot volcanoes is formed and the earth's surface bulges upward in a dome several hundred kilometers wide by 1 kilometer high. Also called a mantle plume.

Human immunodeficiency virus (HIV): A retrovirus that makes the immune system weak by destroying CD4 cells, causing the body to be susceptible to infection; the virus that causes AIDS.

Hundred-year-flood: A hypothetical flood whose severity is such that it would occur on average only once in a period of one hundred years, which equates to a 1 percent probability each year.

Hurricane: A severe tropical storm with winds exceeding 119 kilometers per hour that originates in tropical regions; the term "hurricane" is sometimes used only for storms originating in the Atlantic Ocean, with "typhoon" used for those originating in the Pacific Ocean and "cyclone" used for those originating in the Indian Ocean.

Hydrocarbon: An organic compound composed of carbon and hydrogen often occurring in petroleum, natural gas, coal, and bitumens.

Hyperthermia: Excessively high body temperature.

Hypocenter: The central underground location of an earth tremor; also called the focus.

Hypothermia: The decrease in the body core temperature of an organism.

Ice storm: Rain falling from an above-freezing layer of upper air to a layer of below-freezing air on or near the earth's surface, coating everything with a layer of ice called glaze.

Iceberg: An ice mass, originating from a glacier, that typically floats in an ocean.

Ignimbrite: An igneous rock deposited from a hot, mobile, groundhugging cloud of ash and pumice.

Immune system: The body system that is responsible for fighting off infectious disease.

Impact basin: A large cavity produced by a meteorite impact.

Impact crater: A depression, usually circular, in a planetary surface, caused by the high-speed impact of rocky debris or comet nuclei.

Influenza: Any one of a group of serious respiratory disease caused by viruses.

Intensity: An arbitrary measure of an earthquake's effect on people and buildings, based on the modified Mercalli scale.

Island arc: A curved chain of volcanic islands, generally located a few hundred kilometers from a trench where active subduction of one oceanic plate under another is occurring.

Jet stream: A narrow current of high-speed winds in the upper atmosphere.

K/T boundary: The thin clay layer that lies between the rocks of the Cretaceous geological period and the rocks of the following Tertiary period.

La Niña: The part of the Southern Oscillation that brings cold water to the South American coasts, which makes easterly trade winds stronger, the waters of the Pacific off South America colder, and ocean temperatures in the western equatorial Pacific warmer than normal.

Lahar: A mudflow composed chiefly of volcanic debris on the flanks of a volcano.

Landslide: A general term that applies to any downslope movement of materials; landslides include avalanches, earthflows, mudflows, rockfalls, and slumps.

Lava: The fluid rock issued from a volcano or fissure and the solidified rock it forms when it cools.

Lava tube: A cavern structure formed by the draining out of liquid lava in a pahoehoe flow.

Legionnaires' disease: An acute bacterial pneumonia caused by a bacterial infection, with symptoms of fever, chills, and muscle pain; also called legionellosis.

Levee: A dikelike structure, usually made of compacted earth and reinforced with other materials, that is designed to contain the stream flow in its natural channel.

Lightning: A high-voltage electrical spark which occurs most often when a cloud attempts to balance the differences between positive and negative charges within itself.

Limestone: A common sedimentary rock containing the mineral calcite; the calcite originated from fossil shells of marine plants and animals or by precipitation directly from seawater.

Liquefaction: The loss in cohesiveness of water-saturated soil as a result of ground shaking caused by an earthquake.

Low: An area of low barometric pressure.

Lymphocyte: A white blood cell that produces antibodies.

Macrophage: A tissue cell that protects the body from infection.

Magma: Molten silicate liquid plus any crystals, rock inclusions, or gases trapped therein.

Magnitude: A measure of the amount of energy released by an earthquake, based on the relation between the logarithm of ground motion at the detecting instrument and its distance from the epicenter.

Mantle: The portion of the earth's interior extending from about 60 kilometers in depth to 2,900 kilometers; it is composed of relatively high-density minerals that consist primarily of silicates.

Mantle plume: Hot spot.

Marine: Referring to a seawater, ocean environment.

Meteor: A bright streak of light in the sky, sometimes called a shooting star, produced by a meteoroid entering the earth's atmosphere at high speed and heating to incandescence.

Meteor shower: A meteor display caused by comet dust particles burning up in the upper atmosphere during the annual passage of earth through a cometary wake or debris field.

Meteoric water: Surface water that infiltrates porous and fractured crustal rocks; the same as groundwater.

Meteorite: The remnant of an interplanetary body that survives a fall through the earth's atmosphere and reaches the ground.

Meteoroid: A natural, solid object traveling through interplanetary space.

Meteorology: The study of weather.

Modified Mercalli scale: A means of calculating the intensity of shaking at the surface of the earth.

Monsoon: A seasonal pattern of wind at boundaries between warm ocean bodies and landmasses.

Mudflow: Both the process and the landform characterized by very fluid movement of fine-grained material with a high (sometimes more than 50 percent) water content.

Nuée ardente: A hot cloud of rock fragments, ash, and gases that suddenly and explosively erupt from some volcanoes and flow rapidly down their slopes.

Orography: A branch of physical geography that deals with mountains.

Oxidant: A substance that combines another substance with oxygen.

Oxidation: A chemical reaction in which an oxidizing agent and a reducing agent combine to form a product with less energy than the original materials.

Ozone: A gas containing three atoms of oxygen; it is highly concentrated in a zone of the stratosphere.

P wave: A type of seismic wave generated at the focus of an earthquake, traveling 6-8 kilometers per second, with a push-pull vibratory motion parallel to the direction of propagation; P stands for "primary," as P waves are the fastest and first to arrive at a seismic station.

Palmer Drought Index (PDI): Defines drought as the period of time, generally measured in months or years, when the actual moisture supply at a specified location is always below the climatically anticipated or appropriate supply of moisture.

Pandemic: A disease occurring over a wide geographic area.

PDI. *See* Palmer Drought Index (PDI)

Peléan eruption: A volcanic eruption often considered a subclass of Vulcanian eruption, in which nuées ardentes often cause the collapse or explosion of a volcanic dome sitting over the vent.

Photochemical smog: Smog caused by the action of solar ultraviolet radiation on an atmosphere polluted with hydrocarbons and nitrogen oxides from automobile exhaust.

Phreatic eruption: An eruption in which water plays a major role; also called hydrovolcanic.

Plague: An infection transmitted by fleas, which may prove fatal if left untreated.

Plate tectonics: The theory that the outer surface of the earth consists of large moving plates that interact to produce seismic, volcanic, and orogenic activity.

Plinian eruption: The most explosive and rare of the volcanic eruptions of historic record, having VEI values of 4 to 6; they spew an abundance of ash into the stratosphere.

Pneumonic plague: A form of plague, limited to humans, which directly transmits the infection via infected aerosol droplets from a person with a lung infection.

Point-release avalanche: A loose-snow avalanche caused by a cohesionless snow layer resting on a slope steeper than its angle of repose.

Poliomyelitis: A viral illness that may cause meningitis and permanent paralysis; it can be prevented through immunization.

Pollution: A condition in which air, soil, or water contains substances that make it hazardous for human use.

Precipice: A steep or overhanging area of earth or rock.

Primary explosives: Fuels that explode when ignited by a nonexplosive source.

Pumice: A vesicular glassy rock commonly having the composition of rhyolite; a common constituent of silica-rich explosive volcanic eruptions.

Pyroclastic fall: The settling of debris under the influence of gravity from an explosively generated plume of material.

Pyroclastic flow: A highly heated mixture of volcanic gases and ash that travels down the flanks of a volcano.

Pyroclastic rocks: Rocks formed in the process of volcanic ejection and composed of fragments of ash, rock, and glass.

Pyrolysis: The process of breaking a substance down through the application of heat into its constituent elements before it can be oxidized.

Quarantine: A state of enforced isolation designed to prevent the spread of disease.

Radiant heat transfer: Heat transfer by electromagnetic waves across distances.

Recurrence interval: The average time interval, expressed in number of years, between occurrences of a flood of a given or greater magnitude than others in a measured series of floods.

Ribonucleic acid (RNA): The material contained in the core of many viruses that is responsible for directing the replication of the virus inside the host cell.

Richter scale: The scale, devised by Charles F. Richter, used for measuring the magnitude of earthquakes.

Rift valley: A region of extensional deformation in which the central block has dropped down in relation to the two adjacent blocks.

Right-lateral strike-slip: Sideways motion along a steep fault in which the block of the earth's crust across the fault from the observer appears to be displaced to the right; left-slip faults are displaced to the left.

Ring of Fire: The ring of earthquake zones and volcanoes in the Pacific Ocean.

RNA. *See* Ribonucleic acid

Rock: A naturally occurring, consolidated material of one or more minerals.

Rockfall: A relatively free-falling movement of rock material from a cliff or steep slope.

Runoff: The total amount of water flowing in a stream, including overland flow, return flow, interflow, and base flow.

S wave: The secondary seismic wave, traveling more slowly than the P wave and consisting of elastic vibrations transverse to the direction of travel; S waves cannot propagate in a liquid medium.

Saltation: The process of small particles being lifted off the surface, traveling 10 to 15 times the height to which they are lifted, then spinning downward with sufficient force to dislodge other soil particles and break down earth clods.

Sandstorm: A dust storm that results from dislodging larger, heavier particles of soil and rock; sandstorms tend to occur in conjunction with desert cyclones.

Scarp: A steep cliff or slope created by rapid movement along a fault.

Seiche: An oscillation in a partially enclosed body of water such as a bay or estuary.

Seismic: Pertaining to an earthquake.

Seismic belt: A region of relatively high seismicity, globally distributed; seismic belts mark regions of plate interactions.

Seismic waves: Elastic oscillatory disturbances spreading outward from an earthquake or human-made explosion; they provide the most important data about the earth's interior.

Seismicity: The occurrence of earthquakes, which is expressed as a function of location and time.

Seismogram: An image of earthquake wave vibrations recorded on paper, photographic film, or a video screen.

Seismograph: An instrument used for recording the motions of the earth's surface, caused by seismic waves, as a function of time.

Seismology: The application of the physics of elastic wave transmission and reflection to subsurface rock geometry.

Shallow-focus earthquake: An earthquake having a focus less than 60 kilometers below the surface.

Shear: A stress that forces two contiguous parts of an object apart in a direction parallel to their plane of contact, as opposed to a stretching, compressing, or twisting force; also called shear stress.

Shield volcano: A volcano in the shape of a flattened dome, broad and low, built by flows of very fluid basaltic lava.

Shock wave: A compressional wave formed when a body undergoes a hypervelocity impact; it produces abrupt changes in pressure, temperature, density, and velocity in the target material as it passes through.

Sinkhole: A hole or depression in the landscape, produced by dissolving bedrock; sinkholes can range in size from a few meters across and deep to kilometers wide and hundreds of meters deep.

Slab avalanche: An avalanche in which a large slab of the snow layer is released.

Sleet: Frozen or partly frozen rain.

Slump: A term that applies to the rotational slippage of material and the mass of material actually moved; the mass has component parts called scarp, failure plane, head, foot, toe, and blocks; the toe may grade downslope in a flow.

Smallpox: A highly contagious viral disease with symptoms of fever, cough, and a rash; it has been eradicated worldwide.

Smog: Air pollution in the form of haze, which can be sulfurous or photochemical in origin.

Solfatara: A volcanic vent that emits hot vapors and sulfurous gases.

Spillway: A broad reinforced channel near the top of the dam, designed to allow rising waters to escape the reservoir without overtopping the dam.

Squall line: A line of vigorous thunderstorms created by a cold downdraft with rain, which spreads out ahead of a fast-moving cold front.

Storm surge: A general rise above normal water level, resulting from a hurricane or other severe coastal storm.

Stratovolcano: A volcano constructed of layers of lava and pyroclastic rock; also called a composite volcano.

Stress: The force per unit area acting at any point within a solid body such as rock, calculated from a knowledge of force and area.

Strike-slip fault: A fault across which the relative movement is mainly lateral.

Strombolian eruption: A weakly explosive volcanic eruption (VEI values of 1 or 2) that usually begins with the volcano tossing out molten debris to form cinders and clots of liquid that solidify in the air to fall as bombs.

Subduction zone: A region where a plate, generally oceanic lithosphere, sinks beneath another plate into the mantle.

Sulfurous smog: Smog caused by the mixture of particulate matter and sulfurous compounds in the atmosphere when coal is burned.

Syncline: A folded structure created when rocks are bent downward; the limbs of the fold dip toward one another, and the youngest rocks are exposed in the middle of the fold.

Syncytium: A multinucleate mass of protoplasm resulting from fusion of cells.

Syphilis: An often sexually transmitted disease that causes widespread tissue destruction and, potentially, death if left untreated by penicillin.

T lymphocytes: Small white blood cells that kill host cells infected by bacteria or viruses or that produce a chemical compound which mediates the destruction of the host cells.

T-test: A statistical test used especially in testing hypotheses about means of normal distributions when the standard deviations are unknown.

Tectonic plates: Segments that comprise the crust (either oceanic or continental crust) and a portion of the earth's mantle beneath it

Tectonics: The study of the processes that formed the structural features of the earth's crust; it usually addresses the creation and movement of immense crustal plates.

Teleseism: An earthquake recorded at great epicentral distances.

Tephra: All pyroclastic materials blown out of a volcanic vent, from dust to large chunks.

Thermocline: A layer within a water body, characterized by a rapid change in temperature.

Thunder: A loud sound resulting from the heating of air surrounding a lightning bolt, which causes a very rapid expansion of air that moves at supersonic speeds and forms shock waves.

Tidal wave: The popular but inaccurate term for a tsunami.

Torino Impact Hazard Scale: A scale dealing with the perceived probability of an asteroid or comet hitting Earth.

Tornado: A violent rotating column of air extending downward from a thunderhead cloud and having the appearance of a funnel, rope, or column.

Tornado Alley: An area of the United States where tornadoes are common, extending from Texas northward to Nebraska.

Trade winds: Winds in the tropics that blow from the subtropical highs to the equatorial low.

Transform fault: A fault connecting offset segments of an ocean ridge along which two plates slide past each other.

Trench: A long and narrow deep trough on the sea floor that forms where the ocean floor is pulled downward because of plate subduction.

Triage: Quick evaluation of victims before administering emergency assistance; victims are grouped according to those likely to survive without immediate treatment, those likely to survive only with immediate treatment, and those unlikely to survive even with emergency treatment.

Tropical storm: A severe storm with winds ranging from 45 to 120 kilometers.

Tsunami: A seismic sea wave created by an undersea earthquake, a violent volcanic eruption, or a landslide at sea.

Tuff: A general term for all consolidated pyroclastic rocks.

Twenty-year-flood: A hypothetical flood whose severity is such that it would occur on average only once in a period of twenty years, which equates to a 5 percent probability each year.

Typhoid fever: A particular disease syndrome most often associated with infection by *Salmonella typhi* but occasionally caused by other types of salmonella bacteria.

Typhoon: A major tropical storm that originates in the Pacific Ocean.

Typhus: An acute infectious disease caused by rickettsiae, microorganisms that are smaller than bacteria but larger than viruses.

Ultra-Plinian eruption: A highly explosive volcanic eruption (VEI values of 7 and 8); none has occurred in recorded history.

Vaccine: A preparation of killed microorganisms or living organisms that is administered to produce or artificially increase immunity to a particular disease.

VEI. *See* Volcanic Explosivity Index (VEI)

Vent: A break or tear on the side of a mountain through which magma and pressure can escape.

Vesiculation: The process of water being released from magma and boiling to form bubbles.

Vigra: Precipitation that falls from clouds and evaporates before reaching the ground.

Viscosity: A substance's ability to flow; the lower the viscosity, the greater the ability to flow.

Volcanic earthquakes: Small-magnitude earthquakes that occur at relatively shallow depths beneath active or potentially active volcanoes.

Volcanic Explosivity Index (VEI): A scale from 0 to 8 that classifies the intensity of volcanic eruptions.

Volcanic rocks: Igneous rocks formed at the surface of the earth.

Volcanic tremor: A long, continuous vibration, detected only at active volcanoes.

Volcano: A vent at the earth's surface in which gases, rocks, and magma erupt at the surface and build a more or less cone-shaped mountain.

Vulcanian eruption: An explosive volcanic eruption (VEI values ranging from 2 to 4) in which the magma is viscous, there are few lava flows, and thick liquid clots are shot far into the air.

Watershed: A region bounded by a divide and draining to a particular body of water.

Waterspout: A tornado occurring over water.

Whiteout: A blizzard that severely reduces visibility.

Wildfire: An outdoor fire, occurring in forests, grasslands, or farms, that is caused either by an act of nature, such as a lightning strike, or by human actions; also called a brushfire.

Wind gust: A localized difference in atmospheric pressure caused by frontal weather changes.

Wind shear: Radical shift in wind speed and direction.

Yellow fever: An acute viral infection of the liver, kidneys, and heart muscle with such symptoms as fever, muscle pain, vomiting of blood, and jaundiced (yellow) skin.

Zoonosis: An animal disease that can also be transferred to humans.

General Bibliography

AVALANCHES

Armstrong, Betsy R. *Avalanche Hazard in Ouray County, Colorado, 1877-1976*. Boulder: Institute of Arctic and Alpine Research, University of Colorado, 1977.

Armstrong, Betsy R., and K. Williams. *The Avalanche Book*. Golden, Colo.: Fulcrum Press, 1986.

Facklam, Howard, and Margary Facklam. *Avalanche!* Columbus, Ohio: Silver Burdett, 1991.

Floods, Avalanches, and Tidal Waves. http://www.info please.lycos.com/ipa/a0001440.html.

Graydon, E. *Mountaineering: The Freedom of the Hill*. Seattle: Mountaineers Books, 1992.

La Chapelle, R. R. *The ABC of Avalanche Safety*. Seattle: Mountaineers Books, 1985.

Logan, Nick, and Dale Atkins. *The Snowy Torrents: Avalanche Accidents in the United States, 1980-86*. Denver: Colorado Geological Survey, Department of Natural Resources, 1996.

Mears, Arthur I. *Avalanche Forecasting Methods, Highway 550*. Denver: Colorado Department of Transportation, 1996.

National Research Council Panel on Snow Avalanches. *Snow Avalanche Hazards and Mitigation in the United States*. Washington, D.C.: National Academy Press, 1990.

Parfit, M. "Living with Natural Hazards." *National Geographic* 194 (July, 1998): 2-39.

Rosen, Michael J. *Avalanche*. Cambridge, Mass.: Candlewick Press, 1998.

Sound-Producing Sand Avalanches. http://www.per sonal.engin.umich.edu/ nori/booming_sand .html.

USDA Forest Service. *Snow Avalanche: General Rules for Avoiding and Surviving Snow Avalanches*. Portland, Oreg.: USDA Forest Service, Pacific North West Region, 1982.

Vortex Avalanches. http://www.personal.umich.edu/ ~colson/aval_index.html.

BLIZZARDS, FREEZES, ICE STORMS, AND HAIL

Allaby, Michael. *Blizzards*. New York: Facts on File, 1997.

Annual Frequency of Hailstorms in the United States. http://www.nhoem.state.nh.ua/mitigation/fig percent203-17.htm.

Battan, Louis J. *Weather in Your Life*. New York: W. H. Freeman, 1983.

Christian, Spencer, and Tom Biracree. *Spencer Christian's Weather Book*. New York: Prentice-Hall, 1993.

Eagleman, Joe R. *Severe and Unusual Weather*. New York: Van Nostrand, 1983.

Erikson, Jon. *Violent Storms*. Blue Ridge Summit, Pa.: Tab, 1988.

Gokhale, Narayan. *Hailstorms and Hailstone Growth*. Albany: State University of New York Press, 1975.

Hailstorms and Their Environment. http://www.hail .ersa.fvg.it/morgan/hail/forty.htm.

Hailstorms: Do They Look Different from Other Storms? http://www.chaseday.com/hailstorms.htm.

Ludlum, David M. *National Audubon Society Field Guide to North American Weather*. New York: Alfred A. Knopf, 1997.

_____. *The Weather Factor*. Boston: Houghton Mifflin, 1984.

Lyons, Walter A. *The Handy Weather Answer Book*. Detroit: Visible Ink Press, 1997.

Riehl, Herbert. *Introduction to the Atmosphere*. New York: McGraw-Hill, 1978.

DISASTER RELIEF

Comerio, Mary C. *Disaster Hits Home: New Policy for Urban Housing Recovery*. Berkeley: University of California Press, 1998.

Godwin, Barry K. *The Economics of Crop Insurance and Disaster Aid*. Washington, D.C.: AEI Press, 1995.

Haas, J. Eugene, et al., eds. *Reconstruction Following Disaster*. Cambridge: Massachusetts Institute of Technology Press, 1977.

Meyer, Larry I. *California Quake*. Nashville: Sherbourne Press, 1977.

Sorenson, John, ed. *Disaster and Development in the Horn of Africa*. New York: St. Martin's Press, 1995.

Verluise, Pierre. *Armenia in Crisis: The 1988 Earthquake*. Translated by Levon Chorbajian. Detroit: Wayne State University Press, 1995.

DROUGHTS

Andryszewski, Tricia. *The Dust Bowl: Disaster on the Plains.* Brookfield, Conn.: Milbrook Press, 1994.

Benson, Charlotte, and Edward Clay. *The Impact of Drought on Sub-Saharan African Economies: A Preliminary Examination.* Washington, D.C.: World Bank, 1998.

Berk, Richard A., et al. *Water Shortage: Lessons in Conservation from the Great California Drought, 1976-1977.* Cambridge, Mass.: Abt Books, 1981.

Bryson, Reid A., and Thomas J. Murray. *Climates of Hunger.* Madison: University of Wisconsin, 1977.

Carr, John T. *Texas Droughts: Causes, Classification, and Prediction.* Austin: Texas Water Development Board, 1966.

Dixon, Lloyd S., Nancy Y. Moore, and Ellen M. Pint. *Drought Management Policies and Economic Effects in Urban Areas of California, 1987-92.* Santa Monica, Calif.: Rand, 1996.

Dolan, Edward F. *Drought: The Past, Present, and Future Enemy.* New York: Franklin Watts, 1990.

Frederiksen, Harald D. *Drought Planning and Water Resources: Implications in Water Resources Management.* Washington, D.C.: World Bank, 1992.

Ganzel, Bill. *Dust Bowl Descent.* Lincoln: University of Nebraska Press, 1984.

Garcia, Rolando V., and Pierre Spitz. *Drought and Man: The Roots of Catastrophe.* Vol. 3. New York: Pergamon Press, 1986.

Gonzalez, Nancie L., ed. *Social and Technological Management in Dry Lands: Past and Present, Indigenous and Imposed.* Boulder, Colo.: Westview Press, 1978.

King, Clyde Richard. *Wagons East: The Great Drought of 1886, an Episode in Natural Disaster, Human Relations, and Press Leadership.* Austin: School of Journalism Development Program, University of Texas, 1965.

Mather, John R. *Drought Indices for Water Managers.* Vol. 38. Newark: University of Delaware, Center of Climatic Research, Publications in Climatology, 1985.

Riggio, Robert P., George W. Bomar, and Thomas I. Larkin. *Texas Drought: Its Recent History, 1931-1985.* Austin: Texas Water Commission, 1987.

Riney-Kehrberg, Pamela. *Rooted in Dust: Surviving Drought and Depression in Southwestern Kansas.* Lawrence: University Press of Kansas, 1993.

Rosenberg, Norman J., ed. *North American Droughts.* Boulder, Colo.: Westview Press, 1978.

Russell, Clifford S., David G. Arey, and Robert W. Kates. *Drought and Water Supply.* Baltimore: The Johns Hopkins University Press, 1970.

Shindo, Charles J. *Dust Bowl Migrants in the American Imagination.* Lawrence: University Press of Kansas, 1997.

Wilhite, Donald A., and William E. Easterling, eds., with Deborah A. Wood. *Planning for Drought: Toward a Reduction of Societal Vulnerability.* Boulder, Colo.: Westview Press, 1987.

Woodruff, Ann Elizabeth. *As Rare as Rain: Federal Relief in the Great Southern Drought of 1930-31.* Urbana: University of Illinois Press, 1985.

DUST STORMS AND SANDSTORMS

Morales, Chister, ed. *Saharan Dust: Mobilization, Transport, Deposition.* Chichester, England: John Wiley & Sons, 1979.

Pewe, Troy L., ed. *Desert Dust: Origin, Characteristics, and Effect on Man.* Boulder, Colo.: Geological Society of America, 1981.

Shindo, Charles J. *Dust Bowl Migrants in the American Imagination.* Lawrence: University Press of Kansas, 1997.

Sundar, Christopher A., et al. *Radiative Effects of Aerosols Generated from Biomass Burning, Dust Storms, and Forest Fires.* Washington, D.C.: National Aeronautics and Space Administration, 1996.

Tannehill, Ivan Ray. *Drought: Its Causes and Effects.* Princeton, N.J.: Princeton University Press, 1947.

Worster, Donald. *Dust Bowl: The Southern Plains in the 1930's.* New York: Oxford University Press, 1941.

EARTHQUAKES

Ambrose, James E. *Simplified Building Design for Wind and Earthquake Forces.* New York: John Wiley & Sons, 1980.

American Society of Civil Engineers. *Earthquake Damage Evaluation and Design Considerations for Underground Structures.* Los Angeles: American Society of Civil Engineers, 1974.

Bath, Markus. *Introduction to Seismology.* Boston: Birkhauser, 1979.

Berg, Glen Virgil. *Anchorage and the Alaska Earthquake of March 27, 1964.* New York: American Iron and Steel Institute, 1964.

_____. *The Skopje, Yugoslavia Earthquake, July 26, 1963.* New York: American Iron and Steel Institute, 1964.

Bolt, Bruce A. *Earthquakes.* New York: W. H. Freeman, 1993.

_____. *Earthquakes and Geological Discovery.* New York: Scientific American Library, 1993.

Briggs, Peter. *Will California Fall into the Sea?* New York: D. McKay, 1972.

Brumbaugh, David S. *Earthquakes, Science, and Society.* Upper Saddle River, N.J.: Prentice-Hall, 1999.

Coburn, Andrew. *Earthquake Protection.* New York: John Wiley & Sons, 1992.

Coch, Nicholas K. "Earthquake Hazards." In *Geohazards.* Englewood Cliffs, N.J.: Prentice-Hall, 1995.

Comerio, Mary C. *Disaster Hits Home: New Policy for Urban Housing Recovery.* Berkeley: University of California Press, 1998.

Daly, Reginald Aldworth. *Our Mobile Earth.* New York: Charles Scribner's Sons, 1926.

Earthquake Engineering Research Institute. *Learning from Earthquakes: 1977 Planning and Field Guides.* Oakland, Calif.: Author, 1977.

Eiby, G. A. *About Earthquakes.* New York: Harper, 1957.

Englekirk, Robert E. *Earthquake Design of Concrete Masonry Buildings.* Englewood Cliffs, N.J.: Prentice-Hall, 1982.

Farley, John E. *Earthquake Fears, Predictions, and Preparations in Mid-America.* Carbondale: Southern Illinois University Press, 1998.

Fried, John J. *Life Along the San Andreas Fault.* New York: Saturday Review Press, 1973.

Gere, James M. *Terra Non Firma: Understanding and Preparing for Earthquakes.* New York: W. H. Freeman, 1984.

Golden, Frederic. *The Trembling Earth: Probing and Predicting Quakes.* New York: Charles Scribner's Sons, 1983.

Green, Norman B. *Earthquake Resistant Building Design and Construction.* New York: Van Nostrand Reinhold, 1978.

Gribbin, John R. *The Jupiter Effect.* New York: Walker, 1974.

_____. *This Shaking Earth.* New York: Putnam, 1978.

Gutenberg, Beno, and C. F. Richter. *Seismicity of the Earth and Associated Phenomena.* Princeton, N.J.: Princeton University Press, 1954.

Halacy, Daniel Stephen. *Earthquakes: A Natural History.* Indianapolis: Bobbs-Merrill, 1974.

Hanson, Robert D. *The Venezuela Earthquake, July 29, 1967.* New York: American Iron and Steel Institute, 1969.

Heppenheimer, T. A. *The Coming Quake: Science and Trembling on the California Earthquake Frontier.* New York: Random House, 1988.

Hodgson, John H. *Earthquakes and Earth Structure.* Englewood Cliffs, N.J.: Prentice-Hall, 1964.

Hook, Robert. *Lectures and Discourses of Earthquakes and Subterraneous Eruptions.* New York: Arno Press, 1978.

Iacopi, Robert. *Earthquake Country.* Menlo Park, Calif.: Lane, 1964.

Jacob, Klaus H., and Carl J. Turkstra. *Earthquake Hazards and the Design of Constructed Facilities in the Eastern United States.* New York: New York Academy of Sciences, 1989.

Kasahara, Keichi. *Earthquake Mechanics.* New York: Cambridge University Press, 1981.

Keller, Edward A., and Nicholas Pinter. *Active Tectonics: Earthquakes, Uplift, and Landscape.* Upper Saddle River, N.J.: Prentice-Hall, 1996.

Key, David. *Earthquake Design Practice for Buildings.* London: Telford, 1988.

Kimball, Virginia. *Earthquake Ready.* Culver City, Calif.: Peace Press, 1981.

Koyama, Junji. *The Complex Faulting Process of Earthquakes.* Boston: Kluwer, 1997.

Leet, Lewis Don. *Causes of Catastrophe: Earthquakes, Volcanoes, Tidal Waves, and Hurricanes.* New York: Whittlesey House, 1948.

Levy, Matthys, and Mario Salvadori. *Why the Earth Quakes: The Story of Earthuakes and Volcanoes.* New York: W. W. Norton, 1995.

Lomnitz, Cinna. *Fundamentals of Earthquake Prediction.* New York: John Wiley & Sons, 1994.

_____. *Global Tectonics and Earthquake Risk.* New York: Elsevier Scientific, 1974.

Lundgren, Lawrence W. "Earthquake Hazards." In *Environmental Geology.* 2d ed. Upper Saddle River, N.J.: Prentice-Hall, 1999.

Macelwane, James Bernard. *When the Earth Quakes.* Milwaukee: Bruce, 1947.

Meyer, Larry L. *California Quake.* Nashville: Sherbourne Press, 1977.

Mogi, Kiyoo. *Earthquake Prediction.* Orlando, Fla.: Academic Press, 1985.

Moran, Douglas E., ed. *Geology, Seismicity, and Environmental Impact.* Los Angeles: University, 1973.

Neumann, Frank. *Earthquake Intensity and Related Ground Motion.* Seattle: University of Washington Press, 1954.

Oakeshott, Gordon B. *Volcanoes and Earthquakes, Geologic Violence.* New York: McGraw-Hill, 1976.

Okamoto, Shunzo. *Introduction to Earthquake Engineering.* New York: John Wiley & Sons, 1973.

Recent Earthquakes in California: Index Map. http://www.quake.wr.usgs.gov/recenteqs.

Rikitake, Tsunej. *Earthquake Prediction.* New York: Elsevier Scientific, 1976.

Robinson, Andrew. *Earth Shock: Hurricanes, Volcanoes, Earthquakes, Tornadoes, and Other Forces of Nature.* New York: Thames and Hudson, 1993.

Shedlock, Kaye M. *Earthquakes.* Washington, D.C.: U.S. Department of the Interior, U.S. Geological Survey, 1999.

Simon, Seymour. *Danger from Below: Earthquakes, Past, Present, and Future.* New York: Four Winds Press, 1979.

Stover, Carl W. *Seismicity of the United States, 1568-1989.* Rev. ed. Washington, D.C.: U.S. Government Printing Office, 1993.

Tributsch, Helmut. *When the Snakes Awake: Animals and Earthquake Prediction.* Cambridge, Mass.: MIT Press, 1982.

Understanding Earthquakes. http://www.quake.crustal.ucsb.edu/ics/understanding.

Van Cleave, Janice Pratt. *Earthquakes.* New York: John Wiley & Sons, 1993.

Van Rose, Susanna. *Earthquakes.* New Rochelle, Mass.: Cambridge University Press, 1986.

Verney, Peter. *The Earthquake Handbook.* New York: Paddington Press, 1979.

Wyss, Max, ed. *Earthquake Prediction and Seismicity Patterns.* Boston: Birkhauser, 1979.

EL NIÑO

Allan, Rob, Janette Lindesay, and David Parker. *El Niño Southern Oscillation and Climatic Variability.* Collingwood, Australia: CSIRO, 1997.

Arnold, Caroline. *El Niño: Stormy Weather for People and Wildlife.* New York: Clarion, 1998.

Diaz, Henry F., and Vera Markgraf, eds. *El Niño: Historical and Paleoclimatic Aspects of the Southern Oscillation.* New York: Cambridge University Press, 1992.

El Niño Scenario. http://www.crseo.ucsb.edu/geos/el-nono.html.

Fagan, Brian. *Floods, Famines, and Emperors: El Niño and the Fate of Civilization.* New York: Basic Books, 1999.

Glantz, Michael H. *Currents of Change: El Niño's Impact on Climate and Society.* New York: Cambridge University Press, 1996.

Lyons, Walter A. *The Handy Weather Answer Book.* Detroit: Visible Ink Press, 1997.

Philander, S. George. *Is the Temperature Rising? The Uncertain Science of Global Warming.* Princeton, N.J.: Princeton University Press, 1998.

EPIDEMICS

Bailey, Norman T. J. *The Mathematical Theory of Epidemics.* New York: Hafner, 1957.

Cartwright, Frederick Fox. *Disease and History.* New York: Crowell, 1972.

Case Studies of Historic Epidemics. http://www.hokinsbiodefense.org/pages/cases.html.

Cloudsley-Thompson, J. L. *Insects and History.* New York: St. Martin's Press, 1976.

Cook, Noble David. *Born to Die: Disease and New World Conquest, 1492-1650.* Cambridge, England: Cambridge University Press, 1998.

Crosby, Alfred W. *Germs, Seeds, and Animals: Studies in Ecological History.* Armonk, N.Y.: M. E. Sharpe, 1994.

Dudley, William, ed. *Epidemics: Opposing Viewpoints.* San Diego: Greenhaven Press, 1999.

Epidemics and Military Battles. http://www.everest.ento.vt.edu/IHS/militaryEpidemics.html.

Ernester, Virginia L. "Epidemiology." In *McGraw-Hill Encyclopedia of Science and Technology.* 8th ed. New York: McGraw-Hill, 1997.

Ghayourmanesh, Soraya. "Ebola Virus." In *Magill's Medical Guide.* Rev. ed. Pasadena, Calif.: Salem Press, 1998.

_____. "Typhoid Fever and Typhus." In *Magill's Medical Guide.* Rev. ed. Pasadena, Calif.: Salem Press, 1998.

Hill, Justina Hamilton. *Silent Enemies: The Story of the Diseases of War and Their Control.* Freeport: Books for Libraries Press, 1942.

Hoppensteadt, F. C. *Mathematical Theories of Populations: Demographics, Genetics and Epidemics.* Philadelphia: Society for Industrial and Applied Mathematics, 1997.

Karlen, Arno. *Man and Microbes: Disease and Plagues in History and Modern Times.* New York: Putnam, 1995.

Lampton, Christopher F. *Epidemic.* Brookfield, Mass.: Milbrook Press, 1992.

Mack, Arien, ed. *In Time of Plague: The History and Social Consequences of Lethal Epidemic Disease.* New York: New York University Press, 1991.

McNeill, William Hardy. *Plagues and Peoples.* Garden City, N.Y.: Doubleday, 1998.

Marks, Geoffrey. *Epidemics.* New York: Charles Scribner's Sons, 1976.

Nardo, Don, ed. *The Black Death.* San Diego: Greenhaven Press, 1999.

The Plague and Other Epidemics Related to Plumbing Sanitation. http://www.plumbingworld.com/history plague.html.

Post, John Dexter. *The Last Great Subsistence Crisis in the Western World.* Baltimore: The Johns Hopkins University Press, 1977.

Ranger, Terence, and Paul Slack, eds. *Epidemics and Ideas: Essays in the Historical Perception of Pestilence.* New York: Cambridge University Press, 1997.

Smith, Geddes. *Plague on Us.* London: Oxford University Press, 1941.

Thomas, Gordon. *Anatomy of an Epidemic.* Garden City, N.Y.: Doubleday, 1982.

Turkington, Carol. *Hepatitis C: The Silent Killer.* Lincolnwood, Ill.: Contemporary Books, 1998.

Watts, Sheldon J. *Epidemics and History: Disease, Power, and Imperialism.* New Haven, Conn.: Yale University Press, 1998.

FAMINES

Aaseng, Nathan. *Ending World Hunger.* New York: Franklin Watts, 1991.

Appleby, Andrew B. *Famine in Tudor and Stuart England.* Stanford, Calif.: Stanford University Press, 1978.

Aptekar, Lewis. *Environmental Disasters in Global Perspective.* New York: G. K. Hall, 1994.

Are Famines So Difficult to Predict? http://www.dir .ucar.edu/esig/ijas/ijas.html.

Aykroyd, Wallace Ruddell. *The Conquest of Famine.* New York: Reader's Digest Press, 1974.

Clay, Jason W. *Politics and the Ethiopian Famine, 1984-1985.* Cambridge, Mass: Survival Books, 1986.

———. *The Spoils of Famine: Ethiopian Famine Policy and Peasant Agriculture.* Cambridge, Mass.: Cultural Survival, 1988.

Conquest, Robert. *The Harvest of Sorrow: Soviet Collectivization and the Terror-Famine.* New York: Oxford University Press, 1986.

Curtis, Donald, Michael Hubbard, and Andrew Shepherd. *Preventing Famine: Policies and Prospects for Africa.* London: Routledge, 1988.

Dando, William A. *The Geography of Famine.* New York: John Wiley & Sons, 1980.

DeRose, Laurie Fields. *Who's Hungry? And How Do We Know? Food Shortage, Poverty, and Deprivation.* New York: United Nations University Press, 1998.

Droughts and Famines. http://www.kids.infoplease .lycos.com/ipka/AO768999.html.

Famines and the Environment: The Case of the Great Irish Famine. http://www.infohwy.com/gfewer/ envfam.htm.

Field, John Osgood, ed. *The Challenge of Famine: Recent Experience, Lessons Learned.* West Hartford, Conn.: Kumarian Press, 1993.

Golkin, Arline T. *Famine, A Heritage of Hunger: A Guide to Issues and References.* Claremont, Calif.: Regina Books, 1987.

Harley, Richard M. *Breakthroughs on Hunger: A Journalist's Encounter with Global Change.* Washington, D.C.: Smithsonian Institution Press, 1990.

Jordan, William C. *The Great Famine: Northern Europe in the Early Fourteenth Century.* Princeton, N.J.: Princeton University Press, 1996.

Kaplan, Robert D. *Surrender or Starve: The Wars Behind the Famine.* Boulder, Colo.: Westview Press, 1988.

Kutzner, Patricia L. *World Hunger: A Reference Handbook.* Santa Barbara, Calif.: ABC-Clio, 1991.

Lucas, George R., Jr. and Thomas W. Ogletree. *Lifeboat Ethics: The Moral Dilemmas of World Hunger.* New York: Harper & Row, 1976.

Maharatna, Arup. *The Demography of Famines: An Indian Historical Perspective.* Delhi, India: Oxford University Press, 1996.

Ó'Gráda, Cormac. *The Great Irish Famine.* Cambridge, England: Cambridge University Press, 1995.

Percival, John. *The Great Famine: Ireland's Potato Famine, 1845-51.* London: BBC Books, 1995.

Ravallion, Martin. *Markets and Famines.* Oxford, England: Clarendon Press, 1987.

Sen, Amartya Kumar. *Poverty and Famines: An Essay on Entitlement and Deprivation.* Oxford, England: Clarendon Press, 1981.

Sorokin, Pitirim Aleksandrovich. *Hunger as a Factor in Human Affairs.* Gainesville: University Presses of Florida, 1975.

Varnis, Stephen. *Reluctant Aid or Aiding the Reluctant: U.S. Food Aid Policy and Ethiopian Famine Relief.* New Brunswick, N.J.: Transaction, 1990.

Vegfam. http://www.veganvillage.co.uk/vegfam/feed.htm.

Vicker, Ray. *This Hungry World.* New York: Charles Scribner's Sons, 1975.

Watts, Michael. *Silent Violence: Food, Famine, and Peasantry in Northern Nigeria.* Berkeley: University of California Press, 1983.

FIRES

Agee, James K., ed. *Fire and Fuel Management in Mediterranean-Climate Ecosystems: Research Priorities and Programmes.* Paris: Unesco, 1979.

Beaty, Jeanne Kellar. *Lookout Wife.* New York: Random House, 1953.

Branigan, Francis. *Building Construction for the Fire Service.* Quincy, Mass.: National Fire Protection Association, 1995.

Brown, Arthur Allen. *Forest Fire: Control and Use.* New York: McGraw-Hill, 1973.

Cote, Arthur, ed. *Fire Protection Handbook.* 18th ed. Quincy, Mass.: National Fire Protection Association, 1995.

Fire Safe Building Design. Emmitsburg, Md.: United States Fire Administration National Fire Academy, 1997.

Holbrook, Stewart Hall. *Burning an Empire: The Story of American Forest Fires.* New York: Macmillan, 1943.

Keltner, N. R., N. J. Alvares, and S. J. Grayson, eds. *Very Large-Scale Fires.* West Conshohocken, Pa.: ASTM, 1998.

Lathrop, James K., ed. *Life Safety Code Handbook.* 5th ed. Quincy, Mass.: National Fire Protection Association, 1991.

Lyons, Paul Robert. *Fire in America.* Quincy, Mass.: National Fire Protection Association, 1976.

Milne, Lorus Johnson. *The Pheonix Forest.* New York: Atheneum, 1968.

National Fire Protection Association. Forest Committee. *Air Operations for Forest, Brush and Grass Fires: A Report of the NFPA Forest Committee.* Boston: Author, 1965.

————. *Chemicals for Forest Fire Fighting: A Report.* Boston: Author, 1967.

1999 Florida Wildfires. http://www.arl.noaa.gov/ready/floridafire.html.

Owen, Howard R. *Fire and You.* Garden City, N.Y.: Doubleday, 1977.

Pringle, Laurence P. *Natural Fire: Its Ecology in Forests.* New York: William Morrow, 1979.

Pyne, Stephen J. *Fire in America: A Cultural History of Wildland and Rural Fire.* Princeton, N.J.: Princeton University Press, 1982.

Wildfires. http://www.mcema.net/wildfire.html.

FLOODS

Beyer, Jacqueline L. "Human Response to Floods." In *Perspectives on Water,* edited by David H. Spiedel, Lon C. Ruedisili, and Allen F. Agnew. New York: Oxford University Press, 1988.

Comerio, Mary C. *Disaster Hits Home: New Policy for Urban Housing Recovery.* Berkeley: University of California Press, 1998.

Coping with Floods: Information for Dealing with Floods. http://www.ag.ndsu.nodak.edu/flood.

Dunne, Thomas, and Luna B. Leopold. *Water in Environmental Planning.* New York: W. H. Freeman, 1978.

Dzurik, Andrew A. *Water Resources Planning.* 2d ed. New York: Rowman & Littlefield, 1996.

Hornberger, George M., Jeffrey P. Raffensberger, Patricia L. Wilberg, and Keith N. Eshleman. *Elements of Physical Hydrology.* Baltimore: The John Hopkins University Press, 1998.

Huggett, Richard J. *Cataclysms and Earth History: The Develoment of Diluvialism.* Oxford, England: Clarendon Press, 1989.

Jones, J. A. A. *Global Hydrology.* Essex, England: Longman, 1997.

Myers, Mary Fran, and Gilbert F. White. "The Challenge of the Mississippi Floods." In *Environmental Management,* edited by Lewis Owen and Tim Unwin. Malden, Mass.: Blackwell, 1997.

Paulson, Richard W., Edith B. Chase, Robert S. Roberts, and David W. Moody, comps. *National Water Summary 1988-89.* U.S. Geological Survey Water-Supply Paper 2375. Denver: Books and Open-File Reports Section, 1991.

Phillipi, Nancy S. *Floodplain Management: Ecologic and Economic Perspectives.* San Diego: Academic Press, 1996.

Strahler, Alan H., and Arthur N. Strahler. *Modern Physical Geography.* 4th ed. New York: John Wiley & Sons, 1992.

Tai, Kon Chin. *Analysis and Synthesis of Flood Control Measures.* Fort Collins: Colorado State University, 1975.

Ward, R. C. *Floods: A Geographical Perspective.* New York: John Wiley & Sons, 1978.

White, Gilbert F. *Choice of Adjustment to Floods.* Department of Geography Research 93. Chicago: University of Chicago, 1964.

HURRICANES

Allaby, Michael. *Hurricanes.* New York: Facts on File, 1997.

Allen, Everett S. *A Wind to Shake the World: The Story of the 1938 Hurricane.* Boston: Little, Brown, 1976.

Bush, David M. *Living by the Rules of the Sea.* Durham, N.C.: Duke University Press, 1996.

Carr, John T. *Hurricanes Affecting the Texas Gulf Coast.* Austin: Texas Water Development Board, 1967.

Dunn, Gordon E. *Atlantic Hurricanes.* Baton Rouge: Louisiana State University Press, 1964.

53rd WRS Hurricane Hunters. http://www.hurricane hunters.com/.

Fisher, David E. *The Scariest Place on Earth: Eye to Eye with Hurricanes.* New York: Random House, 1994.

Grozier, R. U., et al. *Floods from Hurricane Beulah in South Texas and Northeastern Mexico, September-October, 1967.* Austin: Texas Water Development Board, 1968.

Hayes, Miles O. *Hurricanes as Geological Agents: Case Studies of Hurricanes Carla, 1961, and Cindy, 1963.* Austin, Tex.: n.p., 1967.

Helm, Thomas. *Hurricanes: Weather at Its Worst.* New York: Dodd, Mead, 1967.

Hogan, Warren L., ed. *Hurricane Carla: A Tribute to the New Media: Newspaper, Radio, Television.* Houston: Leaman-Hogan, 1961.

Hurricanes, Typhoons, and Tropical Cyclones. http://www.solar.ifa.hawaii.edu/Tropical

Lauber, Patricia. *Hurricanes: Earth's Mightiest Storms.* New York: Scholastic Press, 1996.

Lester, Paul. *The Great Galveston Disaster.* Gretna, La.: Pelican, 2000.

Longshore, David. *Encyclopedia of Hurricanes, Typhoons, and Cyclones.* New York: Facts on File, 1998.

McCarthy, Joe. *Hurricane!* New York: American Heritage Press, 1969.

McGowen, J. H., et. al. *Effects of Hurricane Celia: A Focus on Environmental Geologic Problems of the Texas Coastal Zone.* Austin: University of Texas at Austin, 1970.

The Memphis Hurricanes. http://www.advantageweb.net/hurricanes.

Moore, Harry Estill. *Before the Wind: A Study of the Response to Hurricane Carla.* Washington, D.C.: National Academy of Sciences-National Research Council, 1963.

Pielke, Roger A. *The Hurricane.* London: Routledge, 1990.

_____. *Hurricanes: Their Nature and Impacts on Society.* New York: John Wiley & Sons, 1997.

Robinson, Andrew. *Earth Shock: Hurricanes, Volcanoes, Earthquakes, Tornadoes, and Other Forces of Nature.* New York: Thames and Hudson, 1993.

Simpson, Robert H. *The Hurricane and Its Impact.* Baton Rouge: Louisiana State University Press, 1981.

Tannehill, Ivan Ray. *Hurricanes: Their Nature and History, Particularly Those of the West Indies and the Southern Coasts of the United States.* Princeton, N.J.: Princeton University Press, 1952.

LANDSLIDES, MUDSLIDES, AND ROCKSLIDES

Bloom, Arthur. *Geomorphology: A Systematic Analysis of Late Cenozoic Landforms.* 3d ed. Upper Saddle River, N.J.: Prentice-Hall, 1998.

Bryant, Edward A. *Natural Hazards.* New York: Cambridge University Press, 1991.

Cooke, R. U., and J. C. Doornkamp. *Geomorphology in Environmental Management.* Oxford, England: Clarendon Press, 1990.

Easterbrook, Don J. *Surface Processes and Landforms.* 2d ed. Upper Saddle River, N.J.: Prentice-Hall, 1999.

Erickson, Jon. *Quakes, Eruptions, and Other Geological Cataclysms.* New York: Facts on File, 1994.

Fleming, Robert W. *Landslides in Colluvium: The Behavior of Colluvial Landslides Is Strongly Affected by Differences in Thickness.* Washington, D.C.: U.S. Government Printing Office, 1994.

Landslides: Effects of El Niño Geologic Hazards Information. http://www.usgs.gov/themes/landslid.html.

Landslides . . . Unsafe at Any Speed. http://www.anaheim-landslide.com/unsafe.htm.

Larson, Robert A., and James E. Slosson. *Storm-Induced Geologic Hazards: Case Histories from the 1992-1993 Winter in Southern California and Arizona.* Boulder, Colo.: Geological Society of America, 1997.

Lee, Fitzhugh T., Jack K. Odum, and John D. Lee. *Rockfalls and Debris Avalanches in the Smugglers Notch Area, Vermont.* Washington, D.C.: U.S. Government Printing Office, 1994.

Mears, Arthur I. *Debris-Flow Hazard Analysis and Mitigation: An Example from Glenwood Springs, Colorado.* Denver: Colorado Geological Survey, Department of Natural Resources, 1977.

Plummer, Charles C., David McGeary, and Diane H. Carlson. *Physical Geology.* 8th ed. New York: McGraw-Hill/Wm. C. Brown, 1999.

Ritter, Dale F., R. Craig Kochel, and Jerry R. Miller. *Process Geomorphology.* 3d ed. Dubuque, Iowa: Wm. C. Brown, 1995.

Russell, Richard Joel. *Landslide Lakes of the Northwestern Great Basin.* New York: Johnson Reprint, 1968.

Schultz, Arthur P., and Randall W. Jibson. *Landslide Processes of the Eastern United States and Puerto Rico.* Boulder, Colo.: Geological Society of America, 1989.

Shreve, Ronald L. *The Blackhawk Landslide.* Boulder, Colo.: Geological Society of America, 1968.

Voight, Barry, ed. *Rockslides and Avalanches.* New York: Elsevier Scientific, 1978-1979.

LIGHTNING STRIKES

Dennins, J., and G. Wolf. *It's Raining Frogs and Fishes: Four Seasons of Natural Phenomena and Oddities of the Sky.* New York: HarperCollins, 1992.

Salanave, L. E. *Lightning and Its Spectrum.* Tuscon: University of Arizona Press, 1980.

Uman, M. A. *The Lightning Discharge.* New York: Academic Press, 1987.

Williams, J. *The Weather Book.* New York: Vintage Books, 1992.

METEORITES AND COMETS

Barnes-Svarney, Patricia L. *Asteroid: Earth Destroyer or New Frontier?* New York: Plenum Press, 1996.

Burke, John G. *Cosmic Debris: Meteorites in History.* Berkeley: University of California Press, 1986.

Chapman, Clark R., and David Morrison. *Cosmic Catastrophes.* New York: Plenum Press, 1989.

Cox, Donald W., and James H. Chestek. *Doomsday Asteroid.* Amherst, N.Y.: Prometheus Books, 1996.

Lewis, John S. *Rain of Iron and Ice: The Very Real Threat of Comet and Asteroid Bombardment.* Reading, Mass.: Addison-Wesley, 1996.

Sagan, Carl, and Ann Druyan. *Comet.* New York: Random House, 1985.

Steel, Duncan. *Rogue Asteroids and Doomsday Comets: The Search for the Million Megaton Menace That Threatens Life on Earth.* New York: John Wiley & Sons, 1995.

Verschuur, Gerit L. *Impact! The Threat of Comets and Asteroids.* New York: Oxford University Press, 1996.

NATURAL DISASTERS—VARIOUS

Frank, Beryl. *Great Disasters of the World.* New York: Galahad Books, 1981.

Nash, Jay Robert. *Darkest Hours.* Chicago: Nelson-Hall, 1976.

Robinson, Andrew. *Earth Shock: Hurricanes, Volcanoes, Earthquakes, Tornadoes, and Other Forces of Nature.* New York: Thames and Hudson, 1993.

SAFETY GUIDES

Adams, Christopher R. *Building Better Warning Partnerships: National Weather Service Emergency Management Forum.* Upland, Pa.: Diane, 1997.

American Red Cross: Glossary of Disaster Safety Information. http://www.redcross.org/disastersafety/gloss.html.

Daffern, Tony. *Avalanche Safety: For Skiers and Climbers.* Seattle: Mountaineers Books, 1999.

Leonard, Barry, ed. *Automated Local Flood Warning Systems Handbook.* Upland, Pa.: Diane, 1998.

Palm, Risa, and John Carroll. *Illusions of Safety: Culture and Earthquake Hazard Response in California and Japan.* Boulder, Colo.: Westview Press, 1997.

Stringfield, William H. *Emergency Planning and Management: Ensuring Your Company's Survival in the Event of a Disaster.* Rockville, Md.: Government Institutes, 1999.

SMOG

Benarde, Melvin A. *Our Precarious Habitat.* New York: John Wiley & Sons, 1989.

Elsom, Derek M. *Atmospheric Pollution: A Global Problem.* Oxford, England: Blackwell Scientific, 1992.

Graedel, T. E., and Paul J. Crutzen. *Atmospheric Change.* New York: W. H. Freeman, 1993.

Group Against Smog and Pollution—GASP. http://www
.gasp-pgh.org/.

Hidy, George M., ed. *The Character and Origins of Smog Aerosols: A Digest of Results from the California Aerosol Characterization Experiment (ACHEX).* New York: John Wiley & Sons, 1980.

Keller, Edward A. *Environmental Geology.* New York: Macmillan, 1992.

Latest Smog Watch Information. http://www.psclean air.org/smoginfo.htm.

Smog Laws in California. http://www.smogcheck .com/smoglaws.htm.

Smog—Who Does It Hurt? What You Need to Know About Ozone and Your Health. Washington, D.C.: U.S. Environmental Protection Agency, Air and Radiation, 1999. See also http://www.purl.access .gpo.gov/GPO/LPS3707.

Sooros, Marvin S. *The Endangered Atmosphere.* Columbia: University of South Carolina Press, 1997.

TORNADOES

Bluestein, Howard. *Tornado Alley: Monster Storms of the Great Plains.* New York: Oxford University Press, 1999.

Church, Christopher, Donald Burgess, Charles Doswell, and Robert Davies-Jones, eds. *The Tornado: Its Structure, Dynamics, Prediction, and Hazards.* Washington, D.C.: American Geophysical Union, 1993.

Eagleman, Joe R. "The Strongest Storm on Earth." In *Severe and Unusual Weather.* Lenexa, Kans.: Trimedia, 1990.

Flora, Snowden D. *Tornadoes of the United States.* Norman: University of Oklahoma Press, 1953.

Grazulis, Thomas. *Siginificant Tornadoes: 1680-1991.* St. Johnsbury, Vt.: Environmental Films, 1993.

Lane, Frank. *The Violent Earth.* Topsfield, Mass.: Salem House, 1986.

Ludlum, David. *Early American Tornadoes: 1586-1870.* Boston: American Meterological Society, 1970.

Thunderstorms and Tornados. http://www.ssi-pci.net/ rbrown/thunder/thunder.html.

Tornado Book. http://www.moberlymo.com/mlh/ tornado.htm.

Whipple, A. B. "Thunderstorms and Their Progeny." In *Storm.* Alexandria, Va.: Time-Life Books, 1982.

TSUNAMIS

Cornell, James. "Tsunami." In *The Great International Disaster Book.* New York: Charles Scribner's Sons, 1976.

Lander, James F., and Patricia A. Lockridge. *United States Tsunamis, 1690-1988.* Boulder, Colo.: National Geophysical Data Center, 1989.

Lockridge, Patricia A., and Ronald H. Smith. *Tsunamis in the Pacific Basin, 1900-1983.* Boulder, Colo.: National Geohysical Data Center and World Data Center A for Solid Earth Geophysics, 1984.

Myles, Douglas. *The Great Waves.* New York: McGraw-Hill, 1985.

Petak, William J., and Arthur A. Atkisson. *Natural Hazard Risk Assessment and Public Policy: Anticipating the Unexpected.* New York: Springer-Verlag, 1982.

Robinson, Andrew. "Floods, Dambursts, and Tsunamis." In *Earth Shock: Hurricanes, Volcanoes, Earthquakes, Tornadoes, and Other Forces of Nature.* London: Thames and Hudson, 1993.

Solovev, Sergei, and Chan Nalm Go. *Catalogue of Tsunamis on the Eastern Shore of the Pacific Ocean.* Sidney, British Columbia: Institute of Ocean Sciences, Department of Fisheries and Oceans, 1984.

_____. *Catalogue of Tsunamis on the Western Shore of the Pacific Ocean.* Sidney, British Columbia: Institute of Ocean Sciences, Department of Fisheries and Oceans, 1984.

Survey of Great Tsunamis. http://www.geophys.wash ington.edu/tsunami/general/historic/historic .html.

Welcome to Tsunami! http://www.geophys.washington .edu/tsunami/welcome.html.

Whittow, John. *Disasters: An Anatomy of Environmental Hazards.* Athens: University of Georgia Press, 1979.

VOLCANIC ERUPTIONS

Bullard, Fred M. *Volcanoes of the Earth.* Austin: University of Texas Press, 1976.

Decker, Robert, and Barbara Decker. *Volcanoes.* 3d ed. New York: W. H. Freeman, 1997.

Fisher, Richard V. *Out of the Crater: Chronicles of a Volcanologist.* Princeton, N.J.: Princeton University Press, 1999.

Francis, Peter. *Volcanoes: A Planetary Perspective.* Oxford, England: Oxford University Press, 1993.

Macdonald, Gordon A. *Volcanoes.* Englewood Cliffs, N.J.: Prentice-Hall, 1972.

Scarth, Alwyn. *Volcanoes: An Introduction.* College Station: Texas A&M University Press, 1994.

Williams, Howel, and Alexander R. McBirney. *Volcanology.* San Francisco: W. H. Freeman, 1979.

WIND GUSTS

Cape Blanco High Wind Gusts. http://www.light keeper.com/wind.html.

Kimble, George H. T. *Our American Weather.* New York: McGraw-Hill, 1955.

National Aeronautics and Space Administration. *Making the Skies Safe from Windshear.* http://www .larc.nasa.gov/org/pao/PAIS/windshear.html.

National Transportation and Safety Bureau. "Aviation Accident/Incident Database." http://www .nasdac.faa.gov/cgi-shl/ntsbhtml.pl.

Palmen, E., and C. W. Newton. *Atmospheric Circulation Systems.* New York: Academic Press, 1969.

Ruffner, James. *The Weather Almanac.* Detroit: Gale Research, 1974.

Taylor, Richard L. *Fair-Weather Flying.* New York: Macmillan, 1974.

Victoria Price

Organizations and Agencies

America Oxford Committee for Famine Relief (Oxfam)
Information: Oxfam America
26 West Street
Boston, MA 02111
Ph.: (800) 77-OXFAM, (617) 482-1211
Fax: (617) 728-2594
E-mail: info@oxfamamerica.org
Web site: http://www.oxfamamerica.org/
Donations: Oxfam America
P.O. Box 1745
Boston, MA 02105-1745
Ph.: (800) OXFAM-US
Creates solutions to hunger, poverty, and social injustice around the world. Provides emergency aid when disaster strikes, assisting refugees and survivors of natural disasters.

American Friends Service Committee (AFSC)
1501 Cherry Street
Philadelphia, PA 19102
Ph.: (215) 241-7000, (888) 588-2372 (donations)
Fax: (215) 241-7275
E-mail: afscinfo@afsc.org
Web site: http://www.afsc.org/
A Quaker organization that focuses on issues related to economic and social justice in the United States, Africa, Asia, Latin America, and the Middle East.

American Jewish Joint Distribution Committee
E-mail: admin@jdc.org
Web site: http://www.jdc.org/
Sponsors programs of relief, rescue, and reconstruction to Jews affected by natural and human-made disasters around the world.

American Red Cross Disaster Relief Fund
P.O. Box 37243
Washington, DC 20013
Ph.: (800) HELP-NOW
Web site: http://www.redcross.org/
Provides relief to victims of disasters and helps people prevent, prepare for, and respond to emergencies.

Americares Foundation
E-mail: info@americares.org
Web site: http://www.americares.org/
Dispenses emergency medicines, medical supplies, and nutritional items to victims of disasters, famine, and war to over 130 countries worldwide. Supports long-term health care programs.

Baptist World Alliance
6733 Curran St.
McLean, VA 22101
Ph.: (703) 790-8980
Fax: (703) 893-5160
E-mail: bwa@bwanet.org
Web site: http://www.bwanet.org/bwaid/
Supports refugees and victims of famine and natural disasters. Feeds the starving and malnourished, especially in countries suffering from drought and food shortages.

Brother's Brother Foundation
1501 Reedsdale Street, Suite 3005
Pittsburgh, PA 15233-2341
Ph.: (412) 321-3160
Fax: (412) 321-3325
E-mail: BBFound@aol.com
Web site: http://www.brothersbrother.com/
Links America's vast medical resources to global health care needs. Provides immunizations and donates medical supplies and equipment, seed, other agricultural inputs, and educational materials to needy countries across the globe.

Caribbean Disaster Emergency Response Agency (CDERA)
The Garrison, St. Micheal
Barbados
Ph.: (246) 436-9651
Fax: (246) 437-7649
E-mail: CDERA@Caribsurf.com
Web site: http://www.cdera.org/
Coordinates regional disaster management activities within 16 states. Mobilizes and arranges disaster relief from governmental and nongovernmental

organizations for affected participating states. Aims for response to, recovery from, rebuilding from, and prevention of natural disasters.

Catholic Relief Services

Information: 209 West Fayette Street
Baltimore, MD 21201-3443
Ph.: (410) 625-2220, (800) 235-2772,
Fax: (410) 685-1635
E-mail: webmaster@catholicrelief.org
Web site: http://www.catholicrelief.org/
Donations: P.O. Box 17090
Baltimore, Maryland 21203-7090
Ph.: (800) 736-3467
Gives assistance based on need to people affected by natural disasters in more than 80 countries around the world.

Christian Relief Services

8815 Telegraph Road
Lorton, VA 22079
Ph.: (703) 550-2472
E-mail: info@christianrelief.org
Web site: http://www.christianrelief.org/
Collaborates with grass-roots charitable groups, churches, and human service agencies to help those in need in their own communities. Enables people to help themselves.

Cooperative for American Relief to Everywhere (CARE)

151 Ellis Street NE
Atlanta, GA 30303-2439
Ph.: (800) 521-CARE, ext. 999
E-mail: info@care.org
Web site: http://www.care.org/
Reaches tens of millions of people whose lives are devastated by humanitarian emergencies each year in more than 60 countries. Provides food, water, shelter, and health care to survivors of natural disasters and armed conflicts.

Direct Relief International

27 S. La Patera Lane
Santa Barbara, CA 93117
Ph.: (805) 964-4767, (800) 676-1638 (donations)
Fax: (805) 681-4838
Web site: http://www.directrelief.org/
A nonprofit, nonsectarian medical relief organization that provides medical support with new and used medical equipment, pharmaceuticals, and supplies to over three thousand charitable health facilities worldwide. Distributes product contributions from manufacturers, hospitals, and health clinics.

Disaster Preparedness and Emergency Response Association International (DERA)

P.O. Box 280795
Denver, CO 80228
Ph.: (303) 809-441
E-mail: dera@disasters.org
Web site: http://www.disasters.org/
Assists communities worldwide in disaster preparedness, response, and recovery. Serves as a professional association linking professionals, volunteers, and organizations in all phases of emergency preparedness and management.

DisasterRelief.org

Web site: http://www.DisasterRelief.org/
A cooperative effort between the American Red Cross, CNN Interactive, and IBM, which helps disaster victims and the disaster relief community worldwide by facilitating the exchange of information on the Internet. Informs victims where and how to find support and recovery assistance, supplies relief updates and advisories, and accepts donations for relief.

Do Unto Others (DUO)

21 Tamal Vista Blvd.
Corte Madera Plaza, Suite 209
Corte Madera, CA 94925
Ph.: (800) 934-9755
Fax: (415) 924-1379
Web site: http://www.duo.org/
Responds to human-made and natural disasters wherever they occur in the world. Works to ease the suffering of people affected by war, natural disaster, famine, and epidemics.

Doctors Without Borders

Information: 6 East 39th Street, 8th floor
New York, NY 10016
Ph.: (212) 679-6800
Fax: (212) 679-7016
E-mail: doctors@newyork.msf.org
Web site: http://www.dwb.org/
Donations: Doctors Without Borders USA, Inc.

P.O. Box 2247
New York, NY 10116-2247
Ph.: (888) 392-0392
The world's largest independent international medical relief agency, aiding victims of armed conflict, epidemics, and natural and human-made disasters in over 80 countries. Provides primary health care, performs surgery, vaccinates children, operates emergency nutrition and sanitation programs, and trains local medical staff. Also known as Médecins Sans Frontières (MSF).

Farm Service Agency (FSA)
Web site: http://www.fsa.usda.gov/edso/
An agency of the United States Department of Agriculture (USDA). Offers assistance to farmers and ranchers suffering from droughts, floods, freezes, tornadoes, or other natural disasters. Shares the cost of rehabilitating eligible farmlands damaged by natural disaster and provides emergency water assistance. Programs include the Noninsured Crop Disaster Assistance Program (NAP), Emergency Loan (EM) Assistance, and Emergency Haying and Grazing Assistance.

Federal Emergency Management Agency (FEMA)
Federal Center Plaza
500 C. Street SW
Washington, DC 20472
Ph.: (800) 462-9029 to apply for disaster assistance
Web site: http://www.fema.gov/
An independent agency of the federal government founded in 1979. Helps millions of Americans face disaster and its terrifying consequences. Aims to reduce loss of life and property and protect the U.S. infrastructure from all types of hazards through a comprehensive, risk-based, emergency management program of mitigation, preparedness, response, and recovery.

Global Development Center
1250 24th Street, NW, Suite 300
Washington, DC 20037
Ph.: (202) 467-8366
Fax: (202) 467-2793
E-mail: center@globaldevelopment.org
Web site: http://www.globaldevelopment.org/
Provides disaster relief around the world.

International Aid
17011 W. Hickory Street
Spring Lake, MI 49456
Ph.: (800) 251-2502
E-mail: iai@internationalaid.org
Web site: http://www.internationalaid.org/
Provides medicines, medical supplies, food, blankets, and other tangible resources to local groups caring for people in over 170 countries affected by natural disasters. Partners with local and national churches and agencies that provide distribution, logistical support, and on-site administration for overseas relief efforts.

International Federation of Red Cross and Red Crescent Societies
P.O. Box 372
CH-1211 Geneva 19
Switzerland
Ph.: (+41 22) 730 42 22
Fax: (+41 22) 733 03 95
E-mail: secretariat@ifrc.org
Web site: http://www.ifrc.org/
The Red Crescent is used in place of the Red Cross in many Islamic countries. Provides humanitarian relief to people affected by disasters or other emergencies and development assistance to empower vulnerable people to become more self-sufficient in 176 countries.

International Medical Corps (IMC)
11500 West Olympic Blvd., Suite 506
Los Angeles, CA 90064
Ph.: (310) 826-7800, (800) 481-4IMC (24-hour donor hotline)
Fax: (310) 442-6622
E-mail: imc@imc-la.org
Web site: http://www.imc-la.com/
Responds rapidly to emerging epidemics, purchases vaccines and emergency medical supplies to vaccinate children against disease and prevent thousands of needless deaths. Rehabilitates health posts in remote areas in 16 countries.

International Service Agencies (ISA)
66 Canal Center Plaza, Suite 310
Alexandria, VA 22314
Ph.: (800) 638-8079
Web site: http://www.charity.org/

A coalition of America's leading international relief and development organizations. Helps people who suffer from hunger, poverty, disease, or natural disasters.

Lutheran World Relief
Information: 700 Light Street
Baltimore, MD 21230
Ph.: (410) 230-2700
Fax: (410) 230-2882
Web site: http://www.lwr.org/
Donations: P.O. Box 17061
Baltimore, MD 21298-9832
Ph.: (800) LWR-LWR2
Offers health care, food, water, and other relief supplies around the world. Works to improve harvests, health, and education in some 50 countries.

Medical Assistance Programs International (MAP)
P.O. Box 215000
Brunswick, GA 31521-5000
Ph.: (912) 265-6010, (800) 225-8550
Fax: (912) 265-6170
E-mail: mapus@map.org
Web site: http://www.map.org/
Provides essential medicines, works for the prevention and eradication of disease, and promotes community health development worldwide.

Mercy Corps International
3030 SW First Avenue
Portland, OR 97201
Ph.: (800) 292-3355, ext. 250
E-mail: info@mercycorps.org
Web site: http://www.mercycorps.org/
Works to alleviate suffering, poverty, and oppression caused by drought and famine. Provides food, shelter, health care, and economic opportunity to more than 3 million people in 68 countries, sending emergency goods and material aid.

National Relief Network
P.O. Box 150023
Grand Rapids, MI 49515
Ph.: (616) 222-4444
E-mail: info@nrn.org
Web site: http://www.nrn.org/
Brings large numbers of volunteers to areas struck by natural disasters for as long as it takes to bring help to each and every family in need.

Nazarene Disaster Response USA
P.O. Box 585186
Orlando, FL 32858-5186
Ph.: (888) 256-5886
Fax: (407) 294-2275
E-mail: jvmor@aol.com
Web site: http://www.ndr.nazarene.org/cg/ndr/
Provides disaster relief to victims in the United States.

Unitarian Universalist Service Committee (UUSC)
130 Prospect Street
Cambridge, MA 02139-1845
Ph.: (800) 766-5236
Fax: (617) 868-7102
Web site: http://www.uusc.org/
A nonsectarian organization that promotes human rights and social justice in the United States, South and Southeast Asia, Central Africa, Latin America, and the Caribbean. Provides financial and technical support when disasters strike impoverished areas.

United Nations Office for the Coordination of Humanitarian Affairs (OCHA)
New York, NY 10017
Ph.: (212) 963-1234
Fax: (212) 963-1312
E-mail: ochany@un.org
Web site: http://www.reliefweb.int/ocha_ol/index.html
Provides information on emergencies and natural disasters collected from over 170 sources. Coordinates emergency response primarily through the Inter-Agency Standing Committee (IASC), with the participation of humanitarian partners such as the Red Cross.

U.S. Agency for International Development (USAID)
Ronald Reagan Building
Washington, DC 20523-0016
Ph.: (202) 712-4810
Fax: (202) 216-3524
Web site: http://www.info.usaid.gov/
A federal government agency that implements America's foreign economic and humanitarian assistance programs. The principal U.S. agency to extend assistance to countries recovering from disaster.

U.S. Committee for UNICEF
333 East 38th Street
New York, NY 10016
Ph.: (800) FOR-KIDS
E-mail: webmaster@unicefusa.org/
Web site: http://www.unicefusa.org/
Raises money for UNICEF, which works in more than 160 countries and territories providing health care, clean water, improved nutrition, and education to millions of children in Africa, Asia, Central and Eastern Europe, Latin America, and the Middle East. Promotes the survival, protection, and development of children worldwide.

World Association for Disaster and Emergency Medicine (WADEM)
Safar Center for Resuscitation Research
University of Pittsburgh
3434 Fifth Ave., Suite 201
Pittsburgh, PA 15260
Ph.: (412) 383-1900
Fax: (412) 624-0943
Web site: http://www.pitt.edu/HOME/GHNet/wadem/wadem.html
Promotes the worldwide development and improvement of emergency and disaster medicine. Gives help to patients involved in medical emergencies, major accidents, and national and international disasters.

World Concern
International Headquarters
19303 Fremont Avenue North
Seattle, Washington 98133
Ph.: (800) 755-5022
Fax: (206) 546-7569
E-mail: wconcern@crista.org
Web site: http://www.worldconcern.org
Provides food relief and life skill enrichment to impoverished families worldwide. Offers emergency relief, rehabilitation, and long-term development.

World Food Program (WFP)
WFP Headquarters
Via C.G.Viola 68, Parco dé Medici
00148 Rome, Italy
Ph.: +39-06-6513 2628
Fax: +39-06-6513 2840
E-mail: wfpinfo@wfp.org

Web site: http://www.wfp.org/index.htm
WFP Liaison Offices
Room DC2-2500
Two United Nations Plaza, New York, NY 10017
Ph.: (212) 963-8364
Fax: (212) 963-8019
Donations: U.S. Friends of the World Food Programme
P.O. Box 11856
Washington, DC 20008
Provides food aid to areas experiencing food deficits caused by human-made and natural disasters. Works for more than 86 million people in 82 countries.

World Health Organization (WHO)
Avenue Appia 20
1211 Geneva 27
Switzerland
Ph: (+00 41 22) 791 21 11
Fax: (+00 41 22) 791 3111
E-mail: info@who.int
Web site: http://www.who.int/
Promotes technical cooperation for health among nations, carries out programs to control and eradicate disease, and cooperates with governments in strengthening national health programs. Develops and transfers appropriate health technology, information, and standards and strives to improve the quality of human life. A specialized agency of the United Nations with 191 member countries.

World Relief Corporation
International Office: P.O. Box WRC
Wheaton, IL 60189-8004
Ph.: (630) 665-0235, (800) 535-LIFE
Fax: (630) 665-4473
E-mail: worldrelief@wr.org
Web site: http://www.wr.org/
National Office: 201 Route 9W North
Congers, NY 10920
Ph.: (914) 268-4135
Fax: (914) 268-2271
E-mail: USMinistries@wr.org
Provides quick, effective assistance to the most vulnerable victims of earthquakes, hurricanes, drought, or war. Combats poverty and disease to keep children healthy. Part of the World Evangelical Fellowship.

World Vision
34834 Weyerhaeuser Way South
Federal Way, WA 98001
Ph.: (888) 511-6598, (253) 815-1000
Web site: http://www.worldvision.org/

Serves the world's poor and displaced by providing programs that help save lives, bring hope, and restore dignity.

Lauren Mitchell

Natural Disasters

Time Line

1799:	Spain and North Africa yellow fever epidemic
1806:	Guadeloupe hurricane
1807:	Luxembourg lightning strike
1811:	New Madrid earthquakes, Missouri
1812:	Venezuela earthquake
1812:	La Soufrière eruption, St. Vincent
1814:	Mayon eruption, Philippines
1815:	Tambora eruption, Indonesia
1815:	Year Without a Summer famine, United States and Europe
1819:	Gulf Coast hurricane
1822:	Galung Gung eruption, Indonesia
1822:	Chile earthquake
1824:	Neva River flood, Russia
1825:	Puerto Rico hurricane
1825:	Canada fire
1829:	Europe cholera or Asiatic cholera epidemic
1831:	Caribbean and Gulf Coast hurricane
1832:	New York City cholera epidemic
1832:	New Orleans cholera epidemic
1833:	India famine
1835:	Cosigüina eruption, Nicaragua
1835:	Chile earthquake
1835:	Florida hurricane
1837:	West Indies hurricane
1840:	Worldwide cholera epidemic
1840:	Mississippi tornado
1841:	The October Gale, Massachusetts (hurricane)
1842:	Germany fire
1844:	Mexico hurricane
1845:	Nevado del Ruiz eruption, Colombia
1845:	The Great Irish Famine
1846:	Florida hurricane
1846:	The Donner Party famine, California
1848:	New York City cholera epidemic
1848:	Turkey fire
1851:	San Francisco fire
1853:	India hailstorm
1853:	Niuafo'ou eruption, Tonga
1853:	New Orleans yellow fever epidemic
1856:	Greece lightning strike
1856:	Louisiana hurricane
1857:	Fort Tejon earthquake, California
1859:	Ecuador earthquake
1860:	Iowa tornado
1862:	Massachusetts hurricane
1862:	China typhoon

1863:	Philippines earthquake
1866:	Georgia hurricane
1866:	Canada fire
1867:	New Orleans yellow fever epidemic
1867:	San Narciso Hurricane, Puerto Rico and Virgin Islands
1868:	South America earthquake
1868:	California earthquake
1869:	Sexby's Gale, Massachusetts (hurricane)
1870:	Turkey fire
1871:	Wisconsin fire
1871:	The Great Chicago Fire
1872:	Owens Valley earthquake, California
1872:	Zanzibar hurricane
1872:	Vesuvius eruption, Italy
1872:	The Great Boston Fire
1873:	The Great Nova Scotia Hurricane
1876:	India famine
1876:	China famine
1877:	Cotopaxi eruption, Ecuador
1878:	Mississippi Valley yellow fever epidemic
1879:	Scotland bridge collapse (wind gusts)
1880:	Missouri tornado
1880:	England mine explosion
1881:	Turkey earthquake
1882:	Iowa tornado
1883:	North Sea ship collision (fog)
1883:	Krakatau eruption, Indonesia
1883:	North Atlantic ship collision (fog)
1884:	U.S. South tornadoes
1884:	Colorado mine explosion
1884:	Virginia mine explosion
1885:	India earthquake
1886:	U.S. Midwest blizzard
1886:	Minnesota tornado
1886:	Texas hurricane
1886:	Charleston earthquake, South Carolina
1887:	Riviera earthquakes
1887:	Switzerland flood
1887:	Yellow River flood, China
1887:	English Channel ship collision (fog)
1888:	The Great Blizzard of 1888, U.S. Northeast
1888:	India hailstorm
1888:	Bandai eruption, Japan
1889:	The Johnstown Flood, Pennsylvania
1890:	Mississippi River flood
1890:	Kentucky tornado
1890:	English Channel shipwreck (fog)
1891:	U.S. Midwest blizzard

1891:	Japan earthquake		1907:	Jamaica earthquake
1892:	Worldwide cholera epidemic		1907:	West Virginia mine explosion
1892:	Worldwide bubonic plague epidemic		1907:	Pennsylvania mine explosion
1892:	Oklahoma mine explosion		1908:	Massachusetts fire
1892:	Switzerland avalanche		1908:	U.S. South tornadoes
1893:	The Sea Islands Hurricane, Georgia and the Carolinas		1908:	Siberia comet or meteorite
			1908:	Pennsylvania mine explosion
1893:	U.S. South hurricane		1908:	Italy earthquake
1894:	Minnesota fire		1909:	Caribbean and Mexico hurricane
1896:	Texas tornado		1909:	U.S. South hurricane
1896:	St. Louis tornado		1909:	Illinois fire
1896:	Japan tsunami		1910:	Washington State avalanche
1897:	India earthquake		1911:	Taal eruption, Philippines
1897:	Mayon eruption, Philippines		1911:	New York and Pennsylvania heat wave
1898:	U.S. Northeast blizzard		1911:	Yangtze River flood, China
1899:	Wisconsin tornado		1912:	Mississippi River flood
1899:	San Ciriaco Hurricane, Puerto Rico		1912:	The Sinking of *Titanic* (iceberg)
1899:	Alaska earthquake		1912:	Katmai eruption, Alaska
1900:	Galveston Hurricane, Texas		1912:	The Black River Hurricane, Jamaica
1900:	Uganda African sleeping sickness epidemic		1913:	Nebraska tornadoes
			1913:	Ohio, Indiana, and Illinois flood
1900:	New York State typhoid epidemic		1913:	New Mexico mine explosion
1900:	New Jersey fire		1914:	West Virginia mine explosion
1902:	Russia earthquake		1914:	Canada ship collision (fog)
1902:	Guatemala earthquake		1915:	Italy earthquake
1902:	La Soufrière eruption, St. Vincent		1915:	British Columbia avalanche
1902:	Pelée eruption, Martinique		1915:	Zhu River flood, China
1902:	Texas tornado		1915:	Texas and Louisiana hurricane
1902:	Pennsylvania mine explosion		1915:	Louisiana hurricane
1902:	Santa María eruption, Guatemala		1916:	Netherlands flood
1902:	Turkestan earthquake		1916:	Southern California flood
1903:	South Pacific tsunami		1916:	Chicago heat wave
1903:	Canada rockslide		1916:	United States polio epidemic
1903:	Armenia earthquake		1916:	Alps avalanche, Italy
1903:	Kansas and Missouri Rivers flood		1917:	English Channel ship collision (fog)
1903:	Georgia tornado		1917:	Colorado mine explosion
1903:	Willow Creek flood, Oregon		1917:	Illinois tornadoes
1903:	Wyoming mine explosion		1917:	Boquerón eruption, El Salvador
1904:	Maryland fire		1917:	New York City heat wave
1904:	Arkansas River flood, Colorado		1917:	Nova Scotia ship explosion
1905:	India earthquake		1918:	Worldwide influenza epidemic
1905:	Oklahoma tornado		1918:	Minnesota fire
1905:	Vesuvius eruption, Italy		1919:	Kelut eruption, Indonesia
1905:	Italy earthquake		1919:	Minnesota tornado
1906:	Masaya eruption, Nicaragua		1919:	Florida and Texas hurricane
1906:	Colombia and Ecuador earthquakes		1920:	Chicago tornado
1906:	Taiwan earthquake		1920:	U.S. South tornado
1906:	San Francisco earthquake		1920:	The Great Russian Famine
1906:	Chile earthquake		1920:	China earthquake
1906:	Florida hurricane		1921:	Arkansas River flood, Colorado

1921:	San Antonio River flood, Texas
1922:	U.S. East Coast blizzard
1923:	Wyoming mine explosion
1923:	The Great Kwanto Earthquake, Japan
1923:	Northern California fire
1924:	West Virginia mine explosion
1924:	U.S. South tornado
1924:	Ohio tornado
1925:	The Great Tri-State Tornado, Missouri, Illinois, and Indiana
1925:	Ohio airship crash (wind gusts)
1926:	Mauna Loa eruption, Hawaii
1926:	New Jersey lightning strike
1926:	The Great Miami Hurricane
1926:	Cuba hurricane
1926:	Colombia landslide
1927:	Texas tornado
1927:	Mississippi River flood
1927:	U.S. Midwest tornado
1927:	China earthquake
1927:	Kentucky River flood
1927:	St. Louis tornado
1927:	New England flood
1927:	Pittsburgh factory explosion
1928:	St. Francis Dam Collapse, Southern California (flood)
1928:	Pennsylvania mine explosion
1928:	Rokatenda eruption, Indonesia
1928:	San Felipe Hurricane, Florida and Caribbean
1929:	Pennsylvania mine explosion
1930:	Dominican Republic hurricane
1931:	Ecuador landslide
1931:	Italy avalanche
1931:	New Zealand earthquake
1931:	China mine explosion
1931:	United States heat wave
1931:	Yangtze River flood, China
1931:	The Great Belize Hurricane
1931:	Merapi eruption, Indonesia
1932:	U.S. South tornadoes
1932:	Dust Bowl, Great Plains (dust storms)
1932:	France mudslides
1932:	California airship unmooring (wind gusts)
1932:	San Ciprian Hurricane, Puerto Rico
1932:	Cuba hurricane
1933:	Japan tsunami
1933:	Long Beach earthquake
1933:	Mexico hurricane
1933:	France train collision (fog)
1934:	India earthquake
1934:	Japan fire
1935:	Florida hurricane
1935:	The Hairpin Hurricane, Caribbean and Central America
1936:	U.S. South tornadoes
1937:	Ohio River flood, U.S. Midwest
1937:	Texas school explosion
1937:	The *Hindenburg* Disaster, New Jersey (explosion)
1938:	Custer Creek flood, Montana
1938:	The Great New England Hurricane of 1938
1939:	Chile earthquake
1939:	Yellow River flood, China
1939:	Japan blizzard
1939:	Turkey earthquake
1940:	Washington State bridge collapse (wind gusts)
1940:	U.S. Midwest blizzard
1941:	China freeze
1941:	U.S. Midwest blizzard
1941:	Peru mudslide
1942:	Mississippi tornadoes
1943:	Paricutín eruption, Mexico
1943:	Montana mine explosion
1943:	Black Wednesday smog, Los Angeles
1944:	India ship explosion
1944:	West Virginia, Pennsylvania, and Maryland tornado
1944:	Cleveland gas tanks explosion
1944:	Typhoon Cobra, Philippines
1945:	U.S. Midwest tornadoes
1945:	New York City plane crash (fog)
1946:	Hawaii tsunami
1946:	Japan tsunami
1947:	Western Europe freeze
1947:	Texas, Oklahoma, and Kansas tornadoes
1947:	Texas ship explosion
1947:	Florida and Gulf Coast hurricane
1948:	U.S. South freeze
1948:	U.S. Midwest and East freeze
1948:	Columbia River flood, U.S. Northwest
1948:	Japan earthquake
1948:	New York City heat wave
1948:	Pennsylvania smog
1949:	Missouri tornado
1949:	Ecuador earthquake

1949:	China fire
1950:	India earthquake
1950:	Nebraska flood
1950:	Huai and Yangtze Rivers flood, China
1951:	Lamington eruption, New Guinea
1951:	Alps avalanche
1951:	Kansas and Missouri Rivers flood
1951:	Texas heat wave
1951:	Hurricane Charlie, Jamaica and Mexico
1951:	Po River flood, Italy
1951:	Hibok-Hibok eruption, Philippines
1951:	Illinois mine explosion
1952:	Sierra Nevada blizzard
1952:	Austria avalanches
1952:	U.S. South tornadoes
1952:	Kern County earthquake, California
1952:	The Great London Fog (smog)
1952:	Austria avalanche
1953:	North Sea flood, Netherlands, Great Britain, and Belgium
1953:	Texas tornado
1953:	The Flint-Beecher Tornado, Michigan and Ohio
1953:	Massachusetts tornado
1954:	Alps avalanche, Austria, Italy, Germany, Switzerland
1954:	Rio Grande flood, Texas and Mexico
1954:	Tibet flood
1954:	Iran flood
1954:	Hurricane Carol, U.S. East Coast
1954:	Algeria earthquake
1954:	Hurricane Hazel, Caribbean, U.S. East Coast, Canada
1954:	Haiti landslide
1955:	Kansas and Oklahoma tornadoes
1955:	Hurricanes Connie and Diane, U.S. East Coast
1955:	Typhoon Iris, China
1955:	California heat wave
1955:	Hurricane Hilda, Mexico
1955:	Hurricane Janet, Windward Islands, Belize, and Mexico
1955:	Mexico landslide
1955:	Northern California flood
1956:	Europe blizzard
1956:	New England ice storm
1956:	North Atlantic ship collision (fog)
1956:	Hurricane Flossy, southeastern United States
1956:	Cleveland National Forest fire

1957:	Virginia mine explosion
1957:	Missouri tornado
1957:	Hurricane Audrey, Louisiana and Texas
1957:	Western Europe heat wave
1957:	Iran earthquake
1957:	Finland lightning strike
1957:	Iraq hailstorm
1957:	England train collision (fog)
1958:	U.S. East Coast and Midwest blizzard
1958:	Saudi Arabia heat wave
1958:	Nova Scotia rockslide
1959:	The Great Leap Forward Famine, China
1959:	North Sea ship collision (iceberg)
1959:	St. Louis tornado
1959:	Malpasset Dam Collapse, France (flood)
1960:	South Africa rockslide
1960:	Philippines rockslide
1960:	Morocco earthquakes
1960:	Chile earthquake
1960:	Hawaii tsunami
1960:	India heat wave
1960:	Hurricane Donna, Caribbean, U.S. East Coast
1960:	New York City plane collision (fog)
1961:	Ukraine mudslide
1961:	Japan landslides and mudslides
1961:	Hurricane Carla, Texas
1961:	Hurricane Hattie, Belize
1962:	Peru avalanche
1962:	Germany mine explosion
1962:	Germany flood
1962:	Peru mudslide
1962:	Iran earthquake
1962:	Spain flood
1962:	London smog
1962:	Pennsylvania mine explosion
1963:	Agung eruption, Indonesia
1963:	Yugoslavia earthquake
1963:	Hurricane Flora, Haiti and Cuba
1963:	The Vaiont Dam Disaster, Italy (rockslide)
1963:	Surtsey Island eruption, Iceland
1963:	Japan mine explosion
1963:	Maryland lightning strike
1964:	The Great Alaska Earthquake
1964:	Hurricane Cleo, Caribbean and Florida
1965:	British Columbia avalanche
1965:	Chile earthquake
1965:	U.S. Midwest tornadoes
1965:	India mine explosion

1965:	Japan mine explosion	1972:	Rhodesia mine explosion
1965:	India heat wave	1972:	Rapid Creek flood, South Dakota
1965:	Arkansas and South Platte Rivers flood, Great Plains	1972:	Hong Kong landslides
		1972:	Hurricane Agnes, U.S. East Coast
1965:	Hurricane Betsy, Florida and Louisiana	1972:	Philippines flood
1965:	Taal eruption, Philippines	1972:	Africa, Asia famine
1965:	Brazil heat wave	1972:	Nicaragua earthquakes
1966:	Brazil flood	1973:	Heimaey Island eruption, Iceland
1966:	Rio de Janeiro landslides, mudslides, and rockslides	1973:	Mississippi River flood
		1973:	Mexico earthquake
1966:	India heat wave	1974:	Australia flood
1966:	New York City heat wave	1974:	Tubarão River flood, Brazil
1966:	Turkey earthquake	1974:	The Jumbo Tornado Outbreak, U.S. South, Midwest, and Canada
1966:	Hurricane Inez, Caribbean, Florida, and Mexico		
		1974:	Bangladesh flood
1966:	The Aberfan Disaster, Wales (landslide)	1974:	Hurricane Fifi, Mexico, Central America
1966:	Italy flood		
1967:	Brazil flood	1974:	Cyclone Tracy, Australia
1967:	Rio de Janeiro landslides, mudslides, and rockslides	1974:	Pakistan earthquake
		1975:	China earthquake
1967:	Mexico heat wave	1975:	Turkey earthquake
1967:	Portugal flood	1975:	Rhodesia lightning strike
1967:	U.S. Southwest blizzard	1975:	India mine explosion
1968:	Democratic Republic of Congo mudslide	1976:	Guatemala earthquake
		1976:	Italy earthquake
1968:	Mexico heat wave	1976:	Teton Dam Collapse, Idaho (flood)
1968:	Arenal eruption, Costa Rica	1976:	Zaire, Sudan Ebola virus epidemic
1968:	India flood	1976:	Philadelphia Legionnaires' disease epidemic
1968:	Japan heat wave		
1968:	North Africa drought	1976:	China earthquake
1968:	Iran earthquake	1976:	Big Thompson River flood, Colorado
1969:	Southern California mudslides	1976:	Hurricane Belle, U.S. East Coast
1969:	Hurricane Camille, U.S. South	1976:	Philippines earthquake
1969:	Tunisia flood	1976:	Turkey earthquake
1969:	Rio de Janeiro heat wave	1977:	Nyiragongo eruption, Zaire
1970:	France avalanche	1977:	Romania earthquake
1970:	Texas tornado	1977:	Tenerife plane collision, Canary Islands (fog)
1970:	Peru earthquake		
1970:	East Pakistan cyclone	1978:	Scotland blizzard
1971:	Sylmar earthquake, Southern California	1978:	Yamuna and Ganges Rivers flood, India
		1978:	Iran earthquake
1971:	Mississippi Delta tornadoes	1979:	Soviet Union anthrax epidemic
1971:	Peru avalanche	1979:	Texas and Oklahoma tornadoes
1971:	Afghanistan landslide	1979:	Hurricane David, Dominican Republic, Puerto Rico, and the U.S. South
1972:	Argentina heat wave		
1972:	Iran blizzard	1979:	Hurricane Frederic, Alabama and Mississippi
1972:	Buffalo Creek flood, West Virginia		
1972:	Bangladesh tornado	1980:	Worldwide AIDS epidemic
1972:	Iran earthquake	1980:	Mount St. Helens eruption, Washington
1972:	India heat wave		

1980:	United States heat wave		1991:	The Oakland Hills Fire, Northern California
1980:	Hurricane Allen, Caribbean, Mexico, and Texas		1991:	Tropical Storm Thelma, Philippines
1980:	Algeria earthquake		1991:	California dust storm
1980:	Italy earthquake		1992:	Turkey earthquakes
1981:	Africa drought		1992:	Mexico sewer explosion
1981:	Yellow River flood, China		1992:	Landers and Big Bear earthquakes, Southern California
1982:	San Francisco landslides and mudslides		1992:	Hurricane Andrew, Florida, Louisiana, and the Bahamas
1982:	Austria avalanche		1992:	Indonesia earthquake
1982:	Alps avalanches, France		1993:	U.S. East Coast blizzard
1982:	El Chichón eruption, Mexico		1993:	The Great Mississippi River Flood of 1993
1982:	Nicaragua and Honduras flood			
1982:	Pacific Ocean El Niño		1993:	India earthquakes
1982:	Ganges River flood, India		1993:	Southern California fire
1982:	North Yemen earthquake		1994:	Northridge earthquake, Southern California
1983:	Australia fire			
1983:	Ganges and Brahmaputra Rivers flood, Bangladesh		1994:	U.S. South tornado
			1994:	Bolivia earthquake
1984:	Africa famine		1994:	Tropical Storm Gordon, Caribbean and Florida
1984:	The Carolinas tornadoes			
1985:	Canada, Ohio, and Pennsylvania tornadoes		1994:	Merapi eruption, Indonesia
			1995:	California flood
1985:	Italy flood		1995:	Northern Europe flood
1985:	Texas plane crash (wind gusts)		1995:	Kobe earthquake, Japan
1985:	Mexico City earthquake		1995:	India avalanche
1985:	Nevado del Ruiz eruption, Colombia		1995:	Zaire Ebola virus epidemic
1986:	Lake Nyos eruption, Cameroon		1995:	Arizona dust storm
1986:	California drought		1995:	Texas hailstorm
1987:	Ecuador earthquake		1995:	Russia earthquake
1987:	China fire		1995:	Honduras lightning strike
1987:	Texas tornado		1995:	India heat wave
1987:	Whittier earthquake, Southern California		1995:	U.S. Midwest and Northwest heat wave
			1995:	Hurricane Luis, Caribbean
1988:	Bangladesh flood		1995:	Hurricane Marilyn, U.S. Virgin Islands
1988:	Yellowstone National Park fire		1995:	Hurricane Opal, U.S. South
1988:	Hurricane Gilbert, Jamaica and Mexico		1995:	Iceland avalanche
1988:	Armenia earthquakes		1996:	The Blizzard of '96, U.S. East Coast
1989:	Soviet Union pipeline explosion		1996:	India avalanches
1989:	Hurricane Hugo, Caribbean and the Carolinas		1996:	Sudan sandstorm
			1996:	Nepal blizzard
1989:	Loma Prieta earthquake, Northern California		1996:	Pakistan heat wave
			1996:	Oklahoma and Texas heat wave
1989:	Alabama tornado		1996:	Hurricane Bertha, Puerto Rico, Virgin Islands, U.S. East Coast
1990:	Iran earthquake			
1990:	Philippines earthquake		1996:	Yosemite National Park rockslide
1991:	Italy ship collision (fog)		1996:	Spain flood
1991:	Kansas tornado		1996:	India blizzard
1991:	Bangladesh cyclone		1996:	Hurricane Fran, U.S. East Coast
1991:	Pinatubo eruption, Philippines			
1991:	Yangtze River flood, China			

1996: Hurricane Hortense, Dominican Republic and Puerto Rico
1996: Iceland flooding (glacier)
1996: Hurricane Lili, Central America, Cuba, and Great Britain
1996: Oregon mudslides
1996: Europe freeze
1996: U.S. West Coast flood
1997: Pacific Ocean El Niño
1997: Iran earthquakes (northwest)
1997: Pakistan earthquake
1997: Red River flood, North Dakota and Minnesota
1997: Egypt sandstorm
1997: Iran earthquake (northeast)
1997: Hong Kong avian influenza epidemic
1997: Texas tornado
1997: Soufrière Hills eruption, Montserrat
1997: Rhine and Oder Rivers flood, Central Europe
1997: Michigan tornado
1997: Australia landslide
1997: Colorado River flood, Arizona
1997: Hurricane Nora, Mexico, California, and Arizona
1997: Indonesia fire
1997: Italy earthquakes
1997: Hurricane Pauline, Mexico
1998: Canada ice storm
1998: U.S. Northeast ice storm
1998: Afghanistan earthquake
1998: Mississippi, Alabama, and Georgia tornado

1998: U.S. South heat wave
1998: U.S. East Coast and Midwest drought
1998: Papua New Guinea tsunami
1998: Yangtze River flood, China
1998: Hurricane Georges, Caribbean and U.S. South
1998: Texas flood
1998: Nigeria pipeline explosion
1998: Democratic Republic of Congo lightning strike
1998: Hurricane Mitch, Central America
1999: The Blizzard of '99, U.S. Midwest and East Coast
1999: Colombia earthquake
1999: France avalanche
1999: Washington State avalanche
1999: Switzerland avalanche
1999: Austria avalanches
1999: Alaska avalanche
1999: Oklahoma and Kansas tornado
1999: U.S. Midwest and East Coast heat wave
1999: New York encephalitis epidemic
1999: Utah tornado
1999: Turkey earthquake
1999: Mexico flood
1999: Hurricane Floyd, Bahamas, U.S. East Coast
1999: Taiwan earthquake
1999: Venezuela flood
2000: Georgia tornadoes
2000: Mozambique flood
2000: New Mexico fire

Geographical List

AFGHANISTAN
1971: Afghanistan landslide
1998: Afghanistan earthquake

AFRICA. *See also individual countries*
217 B.C.E.: North Africa earthquake
1799: Spain and North Africa yellow fever
    epidemic
1968: North Africa drought
1972: Africa, Asia famine
1981: Africa drought
1984: Africa famine

ALABAMA
1979: Hurricane Frederic, Alabama and Mississippi
1989: Alabama tornado
1995: Hurricane Opal, U.S. South

ALASKA
1899: Alaska earthquake
1912: Katmai eruption, Alaska
1964: The Great Alaska Earthquake
1999: Alaska avalanche

ALGERIA
1954: Algeria earthquake
1980: Algeria earthquake

ALPS
218 B.C.E.: Alps avalanche, Italy
1916: Alps avalanche, Italy
1951: Alps avalanche
1954: Alps avalanche, Austria, Italy, Germany,
    Switzerland
1982: Alps avalanches, France

ARGENTINA
1972: Argentina heat wave

ARIZONA
c. 48,000-13,000 B.C.E.: Arizona meteorite
1995: Arizona dust storm
1997: Colorado River flood, Arizona
1997: Hurricane Nora, Mexico, California, and
    Arizona

ARMENIA
1903: Armenia earthquake
1988: Armenia earthquakes

ASIA. *See also individual countries*
1972: Africa, Asia famine

ATLANTIC OCEAN
c. 65,000,000 B.C.E.: Atlantic Ocean meteorite
1883: North Sea ship collision (fog)
1883: North Atlantic ship collision (fog)
1887: English Channel ship collision (fog)
1890: English Channel shipwreck (fog)
1912: The Sinking of *Titanic* (iceberg)
1917: English Channel ship collision (fog)
1953: North Sea flood, Netherlands, Great Britain,
    and Belgium
1956: North Atlantic ship collision (fog)
1959: North Sea ship collision (iceberg)
1977: Tenerife plane collision, Canary Islands (fog)

AUSTRALIA
1974: Australia flood
1974: Cyclone Tracy, Australia
1983: Australia fire
1997: Australia landslide

AUSTRIA
1952: Austria avalanches
1952: Austria avalanche
1954: Alps avalanche, Austria, Italy, Germany,
    Switzerland
1982: Austria avalanche
1999: Austria avalanches

BAHAMAS
1992: Hurricane Andrew, Florida, Louisiana, and
    the Bahamas
1999: Hurricane Floyd, Bahamas, U.S. East Coast

BANGLADESH. *See also* EAST PAKISTAN
1972: Bangladesh tornado
1974: Bangladesh flood
1983: Ganges and Brahmaputra Rivers flood,
    Bangladesh

1988: Bangladesh flood
1991: Bangladesh cyclone

BELGIUM
1953: North Sea flood, Netherlands, Great Britain, and Belgium

BELIZE
1931: The Great Belize Hurricane
1955: Hurricane Janet, Windward Islands, Belize, and Mexico
1961: Hurricane Hattie, Belize
1974: Hurricane Fifi, Mexico, Central America

BOLIVIA
1994: Bolivia earthquake

BRAZIL
1965: Brazil heat wave
1966: Rio de Janeiro landslides, mudslides, and rockslides
1966: Brazil flood
1967: Brazil flood
1967: Rio de Janeiro landslides, mudslides, and rockslides
1969: Rio de Janeiro heat wave
1974: Tubarão River flood, Brazil

BRITISH COLUMBIA
1915: British Columbia avalanche
1965: British Columbia avalanche

CALIFORNIA
1846: The Donner Party famine, California
1851: San Francisco fire
1857: Fort Tejon earthquake, California
1868: California earthquake
1872: Owens Valley earthquake, California
1906: San Francisco earthquake
1916: Southern California flood
1923: Northern California fire
1928: St. Francis Dam Collapse, Southern California (flood)
1932: California airship unmooring (wind gusts)
1933: Long Beach earthquake
1943: Black Wednesday smog, Los Angeles
1952: Sierra Nevada blizzard
1952: Kern County earthquake, California
1955: California heat wave

1955: Northern California flood
1956: Cleveland National Forest fire
1969: Southern California mudslides
1971: Sylmar earthquake, Southern California
1982: San Francisco landslides and mudslides
1986: California drought
1987: Whittier earthquake, Southern California
1989: Loma Prieta earthquake, Northern California
1991: The Oakland Hills Fire, Northern California
1991: California dust storm
1992: Landers and Big Bear earthquakes, Southern California
1993: Southern California fire
1994: Northridge earthquake, Southern California
1995: California flood
1996: Yosemite National Park rockslide
1997: Hurricane Nora, Mexico, California, and Arizona

CAMEROON
1986: Lake Nyos eruption, Cameroon

CANADA
1825: Canada fire
1866: Canada fire
1873: The Great Nova Scotia Hurricane
1903: Canada rockslide
1914: Canada ship collision (fog)
1915: British Columbia avalanche
1917: Nova Scotia ship explosion
1954: Hurricane Hazel, Caribbean, U.S. East Coast, Canada
1958: Nova Scotia rockslide
1965: British Columbia avalanche
1985: Canada, Ohio, and Pennsylvania tornadoes
1998: Canada ice storm

CANARY ISLANDS
1977: Tenerife plane collision, Canary Islands (fog)

CARIBBEAN
1502: Dominican Republic hurricane
1622: Cuba hurricane
1666: West Indies hurricane
1692: Jamaica earthquakes
1722: Jamaica hurricane
1780: The Great Hurricane of 1780, Caribbean
1788: Jamaica famine
1806: Guadeloupe hurricane

1812: La Soufrière eruption, St. Vincent
1825: Puerto Rico hurricane
1831: Caribbean and Gulf Coast hurricane
1837: West Indies hurricane
1867: San Narciso Hurricane, Puerto Rico and
  Virgin Islands
1899: San Ciriaco Hurricane, Puerto Rico
1902: La Soufrière eruption, St. Vincent
1902: Pelée eruption, Martinique
1907: Jamaica earthquake
1909: Caribbean and Mexico hurricane
1912: The Black River Hurricane, Jamaica
1926: Cuba hurricane
1928: San Felipe Hurricane, Florida and Caribbean
1930: Dominican Republic hurricane
1932: San Ciprian Hurricane, Puerto Rico
1932: Cuba hurricane
1935: The Hairpin Hurricane, Caribbean and
  Central America
1951: Hurricane Charlie, Jamaica and Mexico
1954: Hurricane Hazel, Caribbean, U.S. East Coast,
  Canada
1954: Haiti landslide
1955: Hurricane Janet, Windward Islands, Belize,
  and Mexico
1960: Hurricane Donna, Caribbean, U.S. East
  Coast
1963: Hurricane Flora, Haiti and Cuba
1964: Hurricane Cleo, Caribbean and Florida
1966: Hurricane Inez, Caribbean, Florida, and
  Mexico
1979: Hurricane David, Dominican Republic,
  Puerto Rico, and the U.S. South
1980: Hurricane Allen, Caribbean, Mexico, and
  Texas
1988: Hurricane Gilbert, Jamaica and Mexico
1989: Hurricane Hugo, Caribbean and the
  Carolinas
1992: Hurricane Andrew, Florida, Louisiana, and
  the Bahamas
1994: Tropical Storm Gordon, Caribbean and
  Florida
1995: Hurricane Luis, Caribbean
1995: Hurricane Marilyn, U.S. Virgin Islands and
  Puerto Rico
1996: Hurricane Bertha, Puerto Rico, Virgin
  Islands, U.S. East Coast
1996: Hurricane Hortense, Dominican Republic
  and Puerto Rico

1996: Hurricane Lili, Central America, Cuba, and
  Great Britain
1997: Soufrière Hills eruption, Montserrat
1998: Hurricane Georges, Caribbean and U.S.
  South
1999: Hurricane Floyd, Bahamas, U.S. East Coast

CENTRAL AMERICA. *See also individual countries*
1935: The Hairpin Hurricane, Caribbean and
  Central America
1998: Hurricane Mitch, Central America

CHILE
1822: Chile earthquake
1835: Chile earthquake
1906: Chile earthquake
1939: Chile earthquake
1960: Chile earthquake
1965: Chile earthquake

CHINA
1290: China earthquake
1556: China earthquake
1642: China flood
1862: China typhoon
1876: China famine
1887: Yellow River flood, China
1911: Yangtze River flood, China
1915: Zhu River flood, China
1920: China earthquake
1927: China earthquake
1931: China mine explosion
1931: Yangtze River flood, China
1939: Yellow River flood, China
1941: China freeze
1949: China fire
1950: Huai and Yangtze Rivers flood, China
1955: Typhoon Iris, China
1959: The Great Leap Forward Famine, China
1975: China earthquake
1976: China earthquake
1981: Yellow River flood, China
1987: China fire
1991: Yangtze River flood, China
1998: Yangtze River flood, China

COLOMBIA
1845: Nevado del Ruiz eruption, Colombia
1906: Colombia and Ecuador earthquakes

HAWAII
1790: Kilauea eruption, Hawaii
1926: Mauna Loa eruption, Hawaii
1946: Hawaii tsunami
1960: Hawaii tsunami

HONDURAS
1974: Hurricane Fifi, Mexico, Central America
1995: Honduras lightning strike
1996: Hurricane Lili, Central America, Cuba, and
    Great Britain

HONG KONG
1972: Hong Kong landslides
1997: Hong Kong avian influenza epidemic

ICELAND
1362: Öræfajökull eruption, Iceland
1783: Laki eruption, Iceland
1963: Surtsey Island eruption, Iceland
1973: Heimaey Island eruption, Iceland
1995: Iceland avalanche
1996: Iceland flooding (glacier)

IDAHO
1976: Teton Dam Collapse, Idaho (flood)
1988: Yellowstone National Park fire

ILLINOIS
1871: The Great Chicago Fire
1909: Illinois fire
1916: Chicago heat wave
1917: Illinois tornadoes
1920: Chicago tornado
1925: The Great Tri-State Tornado, Missouri,
    Illinois, and Indiana
1951: Illinois mine explosion

INDIA
1737: Bay of Bengal cyclone
1769: India famine
1790: Skull Famine, India
1833: India famine
1853: India hailstorm
1876: India famine
1885: India earthquake
1888: India hailstorm
1897: India earthquake
1905: India earthquake

1934: India earthquake
1944: India ship explosion
1950: India earthquake
1960: India heat wave
1965: India mine explosion
1965: India heat wave
1966: India heat wave
1968: India flood
1972: India heat wave
1975: India mine explosion
1978: Yamuna and Ganges Rivers flood, India
1982: Ganges River flood, India
1993: India earthquakes
1995: India avalanche
1995: India heat wave
1996: India avalanches
1996: India blizzard

INDIANA
1925: The Great Tri-State Tornado, Missouri,
    Illinois, and Indiana

INDONESIA
1586: Kelut eruption, Indonesia
1683: Timor eruption, Indonesia
1772: Papandayan eruption, Indonesia
1815: Tambora eruption, Indonesia
1822: Galung Gung eruption, Indonesia
1883: Krakatau eruption, Indonesia
1919: Kelut eruption, Indonesia
1928: Rokatenda eruption, Indonesia
1931: Merapi eruption, Indonesia
1963: Agung eruption, Indonesia
1992: Indonesia earthquake
1994: Merapi eruption, Indonesia
1997: Indonesia fire

IOWA
1860: Iowa tornado
1882: Iowa tornado

IRAN
1954: Iran flood
1957: Iran earthquake
1962: Iran earthquake
1968: Iran earthquake
1972: Iran blizzard
1972: Iran earthquake
1978: Iran earthquake

1990: Iran earthquake
1997: Iran earthquakes (northwest)
1997: Iran earthquake (northeast)

IRAQ
1957: Iraq hailstorm

IRELAND
1740: Ireland famine
1845: The Great Irish Famine

ITALY
218 B.C.E.: Alps avalanche, Italy
64 C.E.: The Great Fire of Rome
79: Vesuvius eruption, Italy
1169: Etna eruption, Sicily
1631: Vesuvius eruption, Italy
1669: Etna eruption, Sicily
1769: Italy lightning strike
1783: Italy earthquake
1872: Vesuvius eruption, Italy
1887: Riviera earthquakes
1905: Vesuvius eruption, Italy
1905: Italy earthquake
1908: Italy earthquake
1915: Italy earthquake
1916: Alps avalanche, Italy
1931: Italy avalanche
1951: Po River flood, Italy
1954: Alps avalanche, Austria, Italy, Germany,
    Switzerland
1963: The Vaiont Dam Disaster, Italy
    (rockslide)
1966: Italy flood
1976: Italy earthquake
1980: Italy earthquake
1985: Italy flood
1991: Italy ship collision (fog)
1997: Italy earthquakes

JAMAICA
1692: Jamaica earthquakes
1722: Jamaica hurricane
1788: Jamaica famine
1907: Jamaica earthquake
1912: The Black River Hurricane, Jamaica
1951: Hurricane Charlie, Jamaica and Mexico
1988: Hurricane Gilbert, Jamaica and Mexico

JAPAN
1281: Japan typhoon
1596: Japan tsunami
1640: Japan tsunami
1657: The Meireki Fire, Japan
1703: Japan earthquake
1741: Japan tsunami
1779: Sakurajima eruption, Japan
1783: Asama eruption, Japan
1792: Unzen eruption, Japan
1888: Bandai eruption, Japan
1891: Japan earthquake
1896: Japan tsunami
1923: The Great Kwanto Earthquake, Japan
1933: Japan tsunami
1934: Japan fire
1939: Japan blizzard
1946: Japan tsunami
1948: Japan earthquake
1961: Japan landslides and mudslides
1963: Japan mine explosion
1965: Japan mine explosion
1968: Japan heat wave
1995: Kobe earthquake, Japan

KANSAS
1903: Kansas and Missouri Rivers flood
1947: Texas, Oklahoma, and Kansas tornadoes
1951: Kansas and Missouri Rivers flood
1955: Kansas and Oklahoma tornadoes
1991: Kansas tornado

KENTUCKY
1890: Kentucky tornado
1927: Kentucky River flood

LOUISIANA
1832: New Orleans cholera epidemic
1853: New Orleans yellow fever epidemic
1856: Louisiana hurricane
1867: New Orleans yellow fever epidemic
1915: Texas and Louisiana hurricane
1915: Louisiana hurricane
1957: Hurricane Audrey, Louisiana and Texas
1965: Hurricane Betsy, Florida and Louisiana
1971: Mississippi Delta tornadoes
1992: Hurricane Andrew, Florida, Louisiana, and
    the Bahamas

MISSISSIPPI RIVER
1890: Mississippi River flood
1912: Mississippi River flood
1927: Mississippi River flood
1973: Mississippi River flood
1993: The Great Mississippi River Flood of 1993

MISSOURI
1811: New Madrid earthquakes, Missouri
1880: Missouri tornado
1896: St. Louis tornado
1903: Kansas and Missouri Rivers flood
1925: The Great Tri-State Tornado, Missouri,
    Illinois, and Indiana
1927: St. Louis tornado
1949: Missouri tornado
1951: Kansas and Missouri Rivers flood
1957: Missouri tornado
1959: St. Louis tornado

MONTANA
1938: Custer Creek flood, Montana
1943: Montana mine explosion
1988: Yellowstone National Park fire

MONTSERRAT
1997: Soufrière Hills eruption, Montserrat

MOROCCO
1960: Morocco earthquakes

MOZAMBIQUE
2000: Mozambique flood

NEBRASKA
1913: Nebraska tornadoes
1950: Nebraska flood

NEPAL
1996: Nepal blizzard

NETHERLANDS
1228: Netherlands flood
1421: Netherlands flood
1570: Netherlands flood
1574: The Flood of Leiden, Netherlands
1916: Netherlands flood
1953: North Sea flood, Netherlands, Great Britain,
    and Belgium

NEW ENGLAND
1735: New England diphtheria epidemic
1798: New England blizzard
1927: New England flood
1938: The Great New England Hurricane of 1938
1954: Hurricane Carol, U.S. East Coast
1956: New England ice storm
1960: Hurricane Donna, Caribbean, U.S. East
    Coast

NEW GUINEA
1951: Lamington eruption, New Guinea

NEW JERSEY
1900: New Jersey fire
1926: New Jersey lightning strike
1937: The *Hindenburg* Disaster, New Jersey
    (explosion)

NEW MEXICO
1913: New Mexico mine explosion
2000: New Mexico fire

NEW YORK
1832: New York City cholera epidemic
1848: New York City cholera epidemic
1900: New York State typhoid epidemic
1911: New York and Pennsylvania heat wave
1917: New York City heat wave
1945: New York City plane crash (fog)
1948: New York City heat wave
1960: New York City plane collision (fog)
1966: New York City heat wave
1999: New York encephalitis epidemic

NEW ZEALAND
c. 186: Taupo eruption, New Zealand
1931: New Zealand earthquake

NICARAGUA
1835: Cosigüina eruption, Nicaragua
1906: Masaya eruption, Nicaragua
1972: Nicaragua earthquakes
1982: Nicaragua and Honduras flood
1996: Hurricane Lili, Central America, Cuba, and
    Great Britain

NIGERIA
1998: Nigeria pipeline explosion

NORTH CAROLINA
1713: North Carolina hurricane
1893: The Sea Islands Hurricane, Georgia and the Carolinas
1954: Hurricane Carol, U.S. East Coast
1984: The Carolinas tornadoes
1989: Hurricane Hugo, Caribbean and the Carolinas
1995: Hurricane Opal, U.S. South
1996: Hurricane Fran, U.S. East Coast
1999: Hurricane Floyd, Bahamas, U.S. East Coast

NORTH DAKOTA
1997: Red River flood, North Dakota and Minnesota

NORTH SEA
1883: North Sea ship collision (fog)
1953: North Sea flood, Netherlands, Great Britain, and Belgium
1959: North Sea ship collision (iceberg)

NORTH YEMEN
1982: North Yemen earthquake

NOVA SCOTIA
1873: The Great Nova Scotia Hurricane
1917: Nova Scotia ship explosion
1958: Nova Scotia rockslide

OHIO
1913: Ohio, Indiana, and Illinois flood
1924: Ohio tornado
1925: Ohio airship crash (wind gusts)
1944: Cleveland gas tanks explosion
1953: The Flint-Beecher Tornado, Michigan and Ohio

OKLAHOMA
1892: Oklahoma mine explosion
1905: Oklahoma tornado
1947: Texas, Oklahoma, and Kansas tornadoes
1979: Texas and Oklahoma tornadoes
1996: Oklahoma and Texas heat wave
1999: Oklahoma and Kansas tornado

OREGON
c. 5000 B.C.E.: Mazama eruption, Oregon
1903: Willow Creek flood, Oregon
1996: Oregon mudslides

PACIFIC OCEAN
1853: Niuafo'ou eruption, Tonga
1903: South Pacific tsunami
1951: Lamington eruption, New Guinea
1982: Pacific Ocean El Niño
1997: Pacific Ocean El Niño

PAKISTAN
1974: Pakistan earthquake
1996: Pakistan heat wave
1997: Pakistan earthquake

PAPUA NEW GUINEA
1951: Lamington eruption, New Guinea
1998: Papua New Guinea tsunami

PENNSYLVANIA
1793: Philadelphia yellow fever epidemic
1889: The Johnstown Flood, Pennsylvania
1902: Pennsylvania mine explosion
1907: Pennsylvania mine explosion
1908: Pennsylvania mine explosion
1927: Pittsburgh factory explosion
1928: Pennsylvania mine explosion
1929: Pennsylvania mine explosion
1944: West Virginia, Pennsylvania, and Maryland tornado
1948: Pennsylvania smog
1962: Pennsylvania mine explosion
1976: Philadelphia Legionnaires' disease epidemic

PERU
1941: Peru mudslide
1962: Peru avalanche
1962: Peru mudslide
1970: Peru earthquake
1971: Peru avalanche

PHILIPPINES
1591: Taal eruption, Philippines
1766: Mayon eruption, Philippines
1814: Mayon eruption, Philippines
1863: Philippines earthquake
1897: Mayon eruption, Philippines
1911: Taal eruption, Philippines
1944: Typhoon Cobra, Philippines
1951: Hibok-Hibok eruption, Philippines
1960: Philippines rockslide

1977: Tenerife plane collision, Canary Islands (fog)
1996: Spain flood

SUDAN
1976: Zaire, Sudan Ebola virus epidemic
1996: Sudan sandstorm

SWITZERLAND
1718: Switzerland avalanche
1887: Switzerland flood
1892: Switzerland avalanche
1954: Alps avalanche, Austria, Italy, Germany,
     Switzerland
1999: Switzerland avalanche

SYRIA
526: Syria earthquake

TAIWAN
1906: Taiwan earthquake
1999: Taiwan earthquake

TENERIFE
1977: Tenerife plane collision, Canary Islands (fog)

TENNESSEE
1971: Mississippi Delta tornadoes

TEXAS
1886: Texas hurricane
1896: Texas tornado
1900: Galveston Hurricane, Texas
1902: Texas tornado
1915: Texas and Louisiana hurricane
1919: Florida and Texas hurricane
1921: San Antonio River flood, Texas
1927: Texas tornado
1937: Texas school explosion
1947: Texas, Oklahoma, and Kansas tornadoes
1947: Texas ship explosion
1951: Texas heat wave
1953: Texas tornado
1954: Rio Grande flood, Texas and Mexico
1957: Hurricane Audrey, Louisiana and Texas
1961: Hurricane Carla, Texas
1970: Texas tornado
1979: Texas and Oklahoma tornadoes
1980: Hurricane Allen, Caribbean, Mexico, and
     Texas

1985: Texas plane crash (wind gusts)
1987: Texas tornado
1995: Texas hailstorm
1997: Texas tornado
1998: Texas flood

TIBET
1954: Tibet flood

TONGA
1853: Niuafo'ou eruption, Tonga

TUNISIA
1969: Tunisia flood

TURKESTAN
1902: Turkestan earthquake

TURKEY
541: The Plague of Justinian, Constantinople and
     the Mediterranean
1848: Turkey fire
1870: Turkey fire
1881: Turkey earthquake
1939: Turkey earthquake
1966: Turkey earthquake
1975: Turkey earthquake
1976: Turkey earthquake
1992: Turkey earthquakes
1999: Turkey earthquake

UGANDA
1900: Uganda African sleeping sickness epidemic

UKRAINE
1961: Ukraine mudslide

UNITED STATES. *See also individual states and
     regions*
1735: New England diphtheria epidemic
1775: The Hurricane of Independence, East Coast
1798: New England blizzard
1815: Year Without a Summer, United States and
     Europe
1884: South tornadoes
1886: Midwest blizzard
1888: The Great Blizzard of 1888, Northeast
1891: Midwest blizzard
1893: South hurricane

1898: Northeast blizzard
1908: South tornadoes
1909: South hurricane
1916: United States polio epidemic
1920: South tornado
1922: East Coast blizzard
1924: South tornado
1927: New England flood
1927: Midwest tornado
1931: United States heat wave
1932: South tornadoes
1932: Dust Bowl, Great Plains
1936: South tornadoes
1937: Ohio River flood, Midwest
1938: The Great New England Hurricane of 1938
1940: Midwest blizzard
1941: Midwest blizzard
1945: Midwest tornadoes
1948: South freeze
1948: Midwest and East freeze
1948: Columbia River flood, Northwest
1952: South tornadoes
1954: Hurricane Carol, U.S. East Coast
1954: Hurricane Hazel, Caribbean, U.S. East Coast, Canada
1955: Hurricanes Connie and Diane, U.S. East Coast
1956: New England ice storm
1956: Hurricane Flossy, U.S. Southeast
1958: East Coast and Midwest blizzard
1960: Hurricane Donna, Caribbean, U.S. East Coast
1965: Midwest tornadoes
1965: Arkansas and South Platte Rivers flood, Great Plains
1967: Southwest blizzard
1969: Hurricane Camille, U.S. South
1972: Hurricane Agnes, U.S. East Coast
1974: The Jumbo Tornado Outbreak, South, Midwest, and Canada
1976: Hurricane Belle, East Coast
1979: Hurricane David, Dominican Republic, Puerto Rico, and the South
1980: United States heat wave
1993: East Coast blizzard
1994: South tornado
1995: Midwest and Northwest heat wave
1996: The Blizzard of '96, East Coast

1996: Hurricane Bertha, Puerto Rico, Virgin Islands, U.S. East Coast
1996: West Coast flood
1998: Northeast ice storm
1998: South heat wave
1998: East Coast and Midwest drought
1998: Hurricane Georges, Caribbean and South
1999: The Blizzard of '99, Midwest and East Coast
1999: Midwest and East Coast heat wave
1999: New England encephalitis epidemic
1999: Hurricane Floyd, Bahamas, U.S. East Coast

UTAH
1999: Utah tornado

VENEZUELA
1812: Venezuela earthquake
1999: Venezuela flood

VIRGIN ISLANDS
1867: San Narciso Hurricane, Puerto Rico and Virgin Islands
1995: Hurricane Marilyn, U.S. Virgin Islands and Puerto Rico
1996: Hurricane Bertha, Puerto Rico, Virgin Islands, U.S. East Coast

VIRGINIA
1884: Virginia mine explosion
1957: Virginia mine explosion
1996: Hurricane Fran, U.S. East Coast

WALES
1966: The Aberfan Disaster, Wales (landslide)

WASHINGTON STATE
1910: Washington State avalanche
1940: Washington State bridge collapse (wind gusts)
1980: Mount St. Helens eruption, Washington
1999: Washington State avalanche

WEST INDIES
1666: West Indies hurricane
1806: Guadeloupe hurricane
1837: West Indies hurricane
1867: San Narciso Hurricane, Puerto Rico and Virgin Islands

Index

A page range in **boldface** type indicates a full chapter devoted to that topic.